Equity

CFA® PROGRAM CURRICULUM • VOLUME 4

LEVEL II
2012

PEARSON

Please visit our website at *www.pearsoned.com*

ISBN 10: 0-558-92509-X
ISBN 13: 978-0-558-92509-3

CONTENTS

HOW TO USE THE CFA PROGRAM CURRICULUM

Congratulations on passing Level I of the Chartered Financial Analyst (CFA®) Program. This exciting and rewarding program of study reflects your desire to become a serious investment professional. You are embarking on a program noted for its high ethical standards and the breadth of knowledge, skills, and abilities it develops. Your commitment to the CFA Program should be educationally and professionally rewarding.

The credential you seek is respected around the world as a mark of accomplishment and dedication. Each level of the program represents a distinct achievement in professional development. Successful completion of the program is rewarded with membership in a prestigious global community of investment professionals. CFA charterholders are dedicated to life-long learning and maintaining currency with the ever-changing dynamics of a challenging profession. The CFA Program represents the first step towards a career-long commitment to professional education.

The CFA examination measures your degree of mastery of the assigned CFA Program curriculum. Therefore, the key to your success on the examination is to master the Candidate Body of Knowledge (CBOK™), which can be accomplished by reading and studying the CFA Program curriculum. The CBOK contains the core knowledge, skills, and abilities (competencies) that are generally accepted and applied by investment professionals. These competencies are used in practice in a generalist context and are expected to be demonstrated by a recently qualified CFA charterholder. The remaining sections provide background on the CBOK, the organization of the curriculum, and tips for developing an effective study program.

Curriculum Development

The CFA Program curriculum is grounded in the practice of the investment profession. Utilizing the Global Body of Investment Knowledge (GBIK) collaborative website, CFA Institute performs a continuous practice analysis with investment professionals around the world to determine the knowledge, skills, and abilities that are relevant to the profession. Regional expert panels and targeted surveys are conducted annually to verify and reinforce the continuous feedback from the GBIK collaborative website. The practice analysis process ultimately defines the CBOK. The CBOK consists of four components:

▶ A broad topic outline that lists the major top-level topic areas (CBOK Topic Outline)

▶ Topic area weights that indicate the relative exam weightings of the top-level topic areas

▶ Learning Outcome Statements (LOS) that advise candidates about the specific knowledge, skills, and abilities they should acquire from readings covering a topic area (LOS are provided in online study sessions and at the beginning of each reading)

▶ The curriculum of material (readings and end-of-reading questions) that candidates receive upon exam registration and are expected to master

A committee consisting of practicing charterholders, in conjunction with CFA Institute staff, designs the CFA Program curriculum to deliver the CBOK to candidates. The examinations, also written by practicing charterholders, are designed to allow you to demonstrate your mastery of the CBOK as set forth in the CFA Program curriculum. As you structure your personal study program, you should emphasize mastery of the CBOK and the practical application of that knowledge. For more information on the practice analysis, CBOK, and development of the CFA Program curriculum, please visit www.cfainstitute.org.

Organization of the Curriculum

The Level II CFA Program curriculum is organized into 10 topic areas. Each topic area begins with a brief statement of the material and the depth of knowledge expected.

Each topic area is then divided into one or more study sessions. These study sessions—18 sessions in the Level II curriculum—should form the basic structure of your reading and preparation.

Each study session includes a statement of its structure and objective, and is further divided into specific reading assignments. The outline on the inside front cover of each volume illustrates the organization of these 18 study sessions.

The reading assignments are the basis for all examination questions, and are selected or developed specifically to teach the knowledge, skills, and abilities reflected in the CBOK. These readings are drawn from CFA Program-commissioned content, textbook chapters, professional journal articles, research analyst reports, and cases. All readings include problems and solutions as well as appendices to help you understand and master the topic areas.

Reading-specific Learning Outcome Statements (LOS) are listed at the beginning of each reading. These LOS indicate what you should be able to accomplish after studying the reading. The LOS, the reading, and the end-of-reading questions are dependent on each other, with the reading and questions providing context for understanding the scope of the LOS.

You should use the LOS to guide and focus your study, as each examination question is based on an assigned reading and one or more LOS. The readings provide context for the LOS and enable you to apply a principle or concept in a variety of scenarios. The candidate is responsible for the entirety of all of the required material in a study session, the assigned readings as well as the end-of-reading questions and problems.

We encourage you to review the material on LOS, including the descriptions of LOS "command words," at www.cfainstitute.org.

Features of the Curriculum

► **Required vs. Optional Segments** - You should read all of an assigned reading. In some cases, however, we have reprinted an entire chapter or article and marked certain parts as "optional." The CFA examination is based only on the required segments, and the optional segments are included only when they might help you to better understand the required segments (by seeing the required material in its full context). When an optional segment begins, you will see an icon and a solid vertical bar in the outside margin that will continue until the optional segment ends, accompanied by another icon. *Unless the material is specifically marked as optional, you should assume it is required.* You should rely on the required segments and the reading-specific LOS in preparing for the examination.

► **Problems/Solutions** - *All questions and problems in the readings as well as their solutions (which are provided directly following the problems) are part of the curriculum and required material for the exam.* When appropriate, we have included problems within and after the readings to demonstrate practical application and reinforce your understanding of the concepts presented.

The questions and problems are designed to help you learn these concepts and may serve as a basis for exam questions. Many of these questions are adapted from past CFA examinations.

▶ **Margins** - The wide margins in each volume provide space for your note-taking.

▶ **Six-volume Structure** - For portability of the curriculum, the material is spread over six volumes.

▶ **Glossary and Index** - For your convenience, we have printed a comprehensive glossary and volume-specific index in each volume. Throughout the curriculum, a **bolded blue** word in a reading denotes a term defined in the glossary.

▶ **Source Material** - The authorship, publisher, and copyright owners are given for each reading for your reference. We recommend that you use this CFA Institute curriculum rather than the original source materials because the curriculum may include only selected pages from outside readings, updated sections within the readings, and contains problems and solutions tailored to the CFA Program.

▶ **LOS Self-check** - We have inserted checkboxes next to each LOS that you can use to track your progress in mastering the concepts in each reading.

Designing Your Personal Study Program

Create a Schedule - An orderly, systematic approach to examination preparation is critical. You should dedicate a consistent block of time every week to reading and studying. Complete all reading assignments and the associated problems and solutions in each study session. Review the LOS both before and after you study each reading to ensure that you have mastered the applicable content and can demonstrate the knowledge, skill, or ability described by the LOS and the assigned reading. Use the LOS self-check to track your progress and highlight areas of weakness for later review.

You will receive periodic e-mail communications that contain important study tips and preparation strategies. Be sure to read these carefully. Curriculum errata are periodically updated and posted on the study session page at www.cfainstitute.org. You may also sign up for an RSS feed to alert you to the latest errata update.

Successful candidates report an average of 300 hours preparing for each exam. Your preparation time will vary based on your prior education and experience. For each level of the curriculum, there are 18 study sessions, so a good plan is to devote 15–20 hours per week, for 18 weeks, to studying the material. Use the final four to six weeks before the exam to review what you've learned and practice with sample and mock exams. This recommendation, however, may substantially underestimate the hours needed for appropriate examination preparation depending on your individual circumstances, relevant experience, and academic background. You will undoubtedly adjust your study time to conform to your own strengths and weaknesses, and your educational and professional background.

You will probably spend more time on some study sessions than on others, but on average you should plan on devoting 15 hours per study session. You should allow ample time for both in-depth study of all topic areas and additional concentration on those topic areas for which you feel least prepared.

Online Sample Examinations - CFA Institute online sample examinations are intended to assess your exam preparation as you progress toward the end of your study. After each question, you will receive immediate feedback noting the correct response and indicating the relevant assigned reading, so you'll be able to identify areas of weakness for further study. The 120-minute sample examinations reflect the question formats, topics, and level of difficulty of the actual CFA examinations. Aggregate data indicate that the CFA examination pass rate was higher among candidates who took one or more online sample examinations than among candidates who did not take the online sample examinations. For more information on the online sample examinations, please visit www.cfainstitute.org.

Online Mock Examinations - In response to candidate requests, CFA Institute has developed mock examinations that mimic the actual CFA examinations not only in question format and level of difficulty, but also in length. The three-hour online mock exams simulate the morning and afternoon sessions of the actual CFA exam, and are intended to be taken after you complete your study of the full curriculum, so you can test your understanding of the CBOK and your readiness for the exam. To further differentiate, the mock exams are available in a printable PDF format with feedback provided at the end of the exam, rather than after each question as with the sample exams. CFA Institute recommends that you take these mock exams at the final stage of your preparation toward the actual CFA examination. For more information on the online mock examinations, please visit www.cfainstitute.org.

Preparatory Providers - After you enroll in the CFA Program, you may receive numerous solicitations for preparatory courses and review materials. When considering a prep course, make sure the provider is in compliance with the CFA Institute Prep Provider Guidelines Program (www.cfainstitute .org/partners/examprep/pages/cfa_prep_provider_prog_participants.aspx). Just remember, there are no shortcuts to success on the CFA examinations; reading and studying the CFA curriculum is the key to success on the examination. The CFA examinations reference only the CFA Institute assigned curriculum—no preparatory course or review course materials are consulted or referenced.

SUMMARY

Every question on the CFA examination is based on specific pages in the required readings and on one or more LOS. Frequently, an examination question is also tied to a specific example highlighted within a reading or to a specific end-of-reading question and/or problem and its solution. To make effective use of the curriculum, please remember these key points:

1. All pages printed in the Custom Curriculum are required reading for the examination except for occasional sections marked as optional. You may read optional pages as background, but you will not be tested on them.

2. All questions, problems, and their solutions - printed at the end of readings - are part of the curriculum and required study material for the examination.

3. You should make appropriate use of the online sample/mock examinations and other resources available at www.cfainstitute.org.

4. You should schedule and commit sufficient study time to cover the 18 study sessions, review the materials, and take sample/mock examinations.

5. **Note:** Some of the concepts in the study sessions may be superseded by updated rulings and/or pronouncements issued after a reading was published. Candidates are expected to be familiar with the overall analytical framework contained in the assigned readings. Candidates are not responsible for changes that occur after the material was written.

Feedback

At CFA Institute, we are committed to delivering a comprehensive and rigorous curriculum for the development of competent, ethically grounded investment professionals. We rely on candidate and member feedback as we work to incorporate content, design, and packaging improvements. You can be assured that we will continue to listen to your suggestions. Please send any comments or feedback to curriculum@cfainstitute.org. Ongoing improvements in the curriculum will help you prepare for success on the upcoming examinations, and for a lifetime of learning as a serious investment professional.

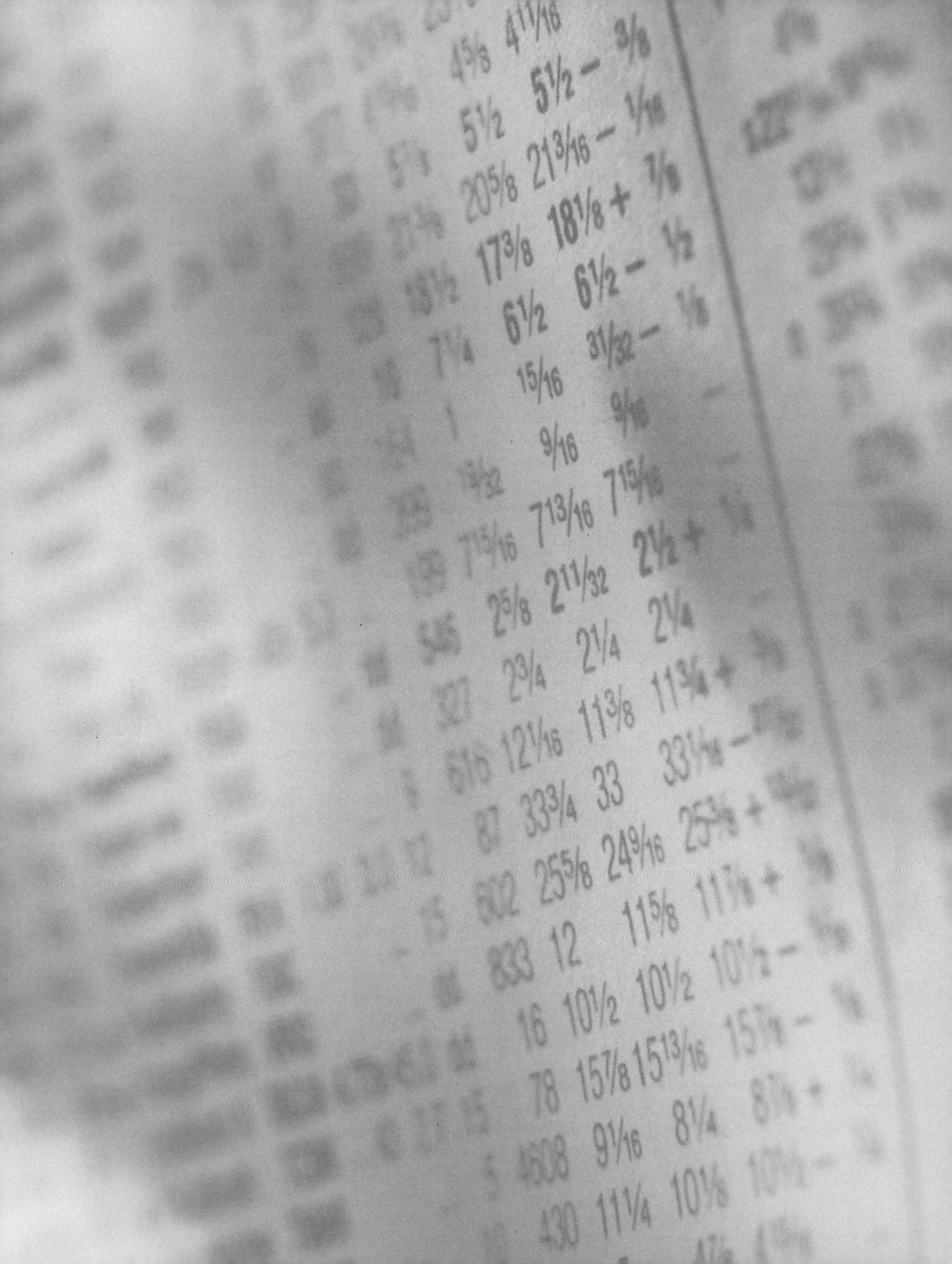

4⅝ 4¹¹⁄₁₆ — ⅜

5½ 5½ —

5½ 21³⁄₁₆ — ¹⁄₁₆

20⅝ 18⅛ + ⅞

17⅜ 6½ — ½

6½ 31⁄32 — ⅛

7¼ 15⁄16

9⁄16 ⁵⁄₁₆

7¹⁵⁄₁₆ 7¹³⁄₁₆ 7¹⁵⁄₁₆

2⅝ 2¹¹⁄₃₂ 2½ +

2¾ 2¼ 2¼

12¹⁄₁₆ 11⅜ 11¾ +

33¾ 33 33⅛ —

25⅝ 24⁹⁄₁₆ 25⅜ +

12 11⅝ 11⅛ +

10½ 10½ 10½ —

15⅝ 15¹³⁄₁₆ 15⅛ —

9⁹⁄₁₆ 8¼ 8⅛ +

11¼ 10⅛

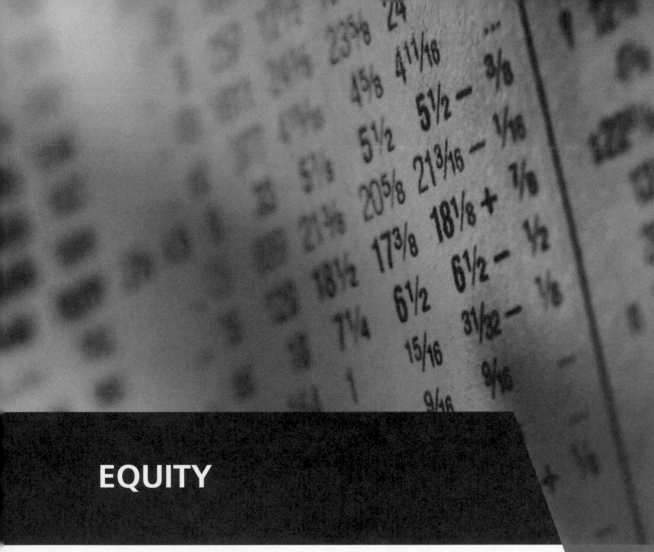

EQUITY

TOPIC LEVEL LEARNING OUTCOME

The candidate should be able to analyze and evaluate equity securities using appropriate valuation concepts and techniques. The candidate should be able to estimate risk and expected return of equities in global contexts.

$4\frac{5}{8}$ $4\frac{11}{16}$ $\frac{3}{8}$

$5\frac{1}{2}$ $-$ $\frac{3}{8}$

$5\frac{1}{2}$

$20\frac{5}{8}$ $21\frac{3}{16}$ $-$ $\frac{1}{16}$

$17\frac{3}{8}$ $18\frac{1}{8}$ $+$ $\frac{7}{8}$

$6\frac{1}{2}$ $6\frac{1}{2}$ $-$ $\frac{1}{2}$

$7\frac{1}{4}$ $6\frac{1}{2}$

$\frac{15}{16}$ $\frac{31}{32}$ $-$ $\frac{1}{8}$

$9\frac{1}{16}$ $\frac{9}{16}$

$7\frac{15}{16}$ $7\frac{13}{16}$ $7\frac{15}{16}$

$2\frac{5}{8}$ $2\frac{11}{32}$ $2\frac{1}{2}$ $+$

$2\frac{3}{4}$ $2\frac{1}{4}$ $2\frac{1}{4}$

$12\frac{1}{16}$ $11\frac{3}{8}$ $11\frac{3}{4}$ $+$

87   $33\frac{3}{4}$ 33 $33\frac{1}{8}$ $-$

602   $25\frac{5}{8}$ $24\frac{9}{16}$ $25\frac{5}{8}$ $+$

833   12 $11\frac{5}{8}$ $11\frac{7}{8}$ $+$

16   $10\frac{1}{2}$ $10\frac{1}{2}$ $10\frac{1}{2}$ $-$

78   $15\frac{7}{8}$ $15\frac{13}{16}$ $15\frac{7}{8}$ $-$

308   $9\frac{1}{16}$ $8\frac{1}{4}$ $8\frac{1}{8}$ $+$

430   $11\frac{1}{4}$ $10\frac{7}{8}$

STUDY SESSION 10
EQUITY VALUATION:
Valuation Concepts

This study session examines the well-established methodologies of security analysis, the process an analyst uses in applying these models, and the limitations of each methodology. The readings contrast the characteristics of equity markets around the world. The session ends with a presentation of alternative return concepts, theories, and calculations.

READING ASSIGNMENTS

Reading 33   A Note on Asset Valuation
                   by George H. Troughton, CFA

Reading 34   Equity Valuation: Applications and Processes
                   Equity Asset Valuation, Second Edition, by Jerald Pinto, CFA,
                   Elaine Henry, CFA, Thomas Robinson, CFA, and John Stowe, CFA

Reading 35   Return Concepts
                   Equity Asset Valuation, Second Edition, by Jerald Pinto, CFA,
                   Elaine Henry, CFA, Thomas Robinson, CFA, and John Stowe, CFA

A NOTE ON ASSET VALUATION

by George H. Troughton, CFA

LEARNING OUTCOME

The candidate should be able to explain how the classic works on asset valuation by Graham and Dodd and John Burr Williams are reflected in modern techniques of equity valuation.	Mastery ☐

In the 1940s, Benjamin Graham, often called the dean of security analysis, began championing the idea of a professional rating for security analysts. In the premier issue of the *Analysts Journal* (now the *Financial Analysts Journal*) in January 1945, Graham summarized the issue as follows: "The crux of the question is whether security analysis as a calling has enough of the professional attribute to justify the requirement that its practitioners present to the public evidence of fitness for their work."[1] It took almost two decades to decide that question in the affirmative, but in June of 1963, some 300 security analysts sat for the examination that would earn them the designation of Chartered Financial Analyst.

In the first decade of the CFA Study Program, the primary valuation text for Level II candidates was the fourth edition of the (by then) classic *Security Analysis*, co-authored by Benjamin Graham and his Columbia Business School colleague David Dodd. That epic work stressed a philosophy of investing centered on the concept of "intrinsic value."

In their early readings, Graham and Dodd discussed the common elements of analysis that applied to various asset classes. The following discussions present some of Graham and Dodd's philosophy to today's candidate. In their view, distinguishing investment from speculation is essential:

> . . . investment is grounded on the past whereas speculation looks primarily to the future. But this statement is far from complete. Both investment and speculation

---

[1] Nancy Regan, *The Institute of Chartered Financial Analysts: A Twenty-Five Year History* (Charlottesville, VA: The Institute of Chartered Financial Analysts, 1987), p. 5.

must meet the test of the future; they are subject to its vicissitudes and are judged by its verdict. But what we have said about the analyst and the future applies equally well to the concept of investment. For investment, the future is something to be guarded against rather than to be profited from. If the future brings improvement, so much the better; but investment as such cannot be founded in any important degree upon the expectation of improvement. Speculation, on the other hand, may always properly—and often soundly—derive its basis and its justification from prospective developments that differ from past performance.[2]

Graham and Dodd stipulated that investing, as opposed to speculating, requires the purchase of leading issues, such as growth stocks, at prices within a range of their intrinsic value or the purchase of secondary issues, such as cyclical stocks and medium quality bonds, at bargain prices. Intrinsic value is to be determined independently of market price. The most important factor in determining a security's intrinsic value is a forecast of "earning power."

An additional criterion that distinguished investment from speculation was that the investment asset's earning power should provide a margin of safety. When analyzing bonds and preferred stock, the analyst was to determine whether the securities had a sufficient earning power in excess of interest and preferred stock dividend requirements. When analyzing common stocks, the analyst was to forecast earning power and multiply that prediction by an appropriate capitalization factor. Earning power was the *unifying* factor in determining the attractiveness of all securities from the highest-grade bond down to the secondary common stocks that were considered investment opportunities because their prices were well below indicated minimum intrinsic values. In investing, diversification was counted on to offset the recognized risk of individual securities.

Graham and Dodd applied their philosophy to the leading asset classes at that time—common stocks, preferred stocks, high-grade fixed-income securities, senior securities of questionable quality, and warrants. In the decades that followed the publication of the last revision of Graham and Dodd's *Security Analysis* in 1962, asset classes expanded rapidly and the Level II CFA curriculum changed to reflect a wide array of assets. The asset valuation curriculum now includes readings from several sources rather than one primary text. Equity analysis, which traditionally centered on common stocks, now includes such securities as real estate, venture capital, and closely held securities. In addition, whereas the analysis of fixed-income securities once centered on credit analysis, much of the fixed-income curriculum now focuses on structured securities such as asset-backed securities. Derivative securities—options, futures, forwards, and swaps—are used for both speculation and to modify the risk and return characteristics of both debt and equity securities.

In the twenty-first century, candidates naturally tend to regard the investment valuation process as segmented, with peculiar terminology and techniques associated with particular assets. In the study sessions that follow, the candidate should realize that certain general principles underlie the valuation process regardless of asset class. The readings in corporate finance, for example, take an "inside the company" look at corporate financial performance, with emphasis on capital budgeting, leverage, cost of capital, dividend policy, and mergers and restructurings. The Porter and Hooke readings focus on industry and company factors. All of these methodologies are related to Graham and Dodd's estimate of earning power.

---

[2] Benjamin Graham, David L. Dodd, and Sidney Cottle, *Security Analysis*, 4th edition (New York: McGraw-Hill, 1962), p. 52.

The Fabozzi fixed income valuation readings supplement Graham and Dodd's emphasis on credit analysis with a valuation framework that includes term structure, interest rate volatility, and embedded options.

The Stowe, Robinson, Pinto, and McLeavey readings on equity valuation and the Fabozzi readings on fixed income valuation reinforce Graham and Dodd's philosophy by emphasizing the common elements in determining the value of various asset classes. These readings emphasize that valuation models are universal, not country specific, and as such they are also applicable to markets outside the United States. Although Stowe, et al. sometimes use different terminology (such as free cash flow to firm and free cash flow to equity) in the valuation process, their methodology is consistent with Graham and Dodd's approach of determining whether earning power is sufficient to provide a margin of safety. In their reading on price multiples, Stowe et al. revive Graham and Dodd's justifiable multiple approach.

Another work, John Burr Williams' *The Theory of Investment Value*,[3] used a financial technique called discounting that was incorporated in the CFA Program within its first decade. Williams proposed that a share of common stock had an intrinsic value that could be estimated by calculating the present value of all future dividends per share. Candidates will find that Stowe et al. refine the discounted cash flow technique.

Taken together, Graham and Dodd, and John Burr Williams provided the core of the equity valuation study sessions in the early CFA Candidate Program. This work, sometimes called "blocking and tackling" is continued and updated in the readings currently assigned in the Program.

To some extent, then, as the CFA candidate curriculum approaches its sixth decade, things have come full circle.

---

[3] John Burr Williams, *The Theory of Investment Value* (Cambridge: Harvard University Press, c1938).

4⅝ 4¹¹/₁₆
5½ 5½ — ³/₈
5½ 21³/₁₆ — ⅛
20⅝ 18⅛ + ⅞
17⅜
6½ 6½ — ½
6½ 31/₃₂ — ⅛
7¼
15/₁₆
9/₁₆ 9/₁₆
9/₃₂ 7¹⁵/₁₆
7¹³/₁₆
7⁵/₁₆
2½ +
2⅝ 2¹¹/₃₂
2¾ 2¼ 2¼
6⅛ 12¹/₁₆ 11⅜ 11¾ +
87 33¾ 33 33¹/₁₆ —
602 25⅝ 24⁹/₁₆ 25⅝ +
833 12 11⅝ 11⅞ +
16 10½ 10½ 10½ —
78 15⅞ 15¹³/₁₆ 15¾ —
9¹/₁₆ 8¼ 8⅞ +
430 11¼ 10⅛

EQUITY VALUATION: APPLICATIONS AND PROCESSES

by Jerald Pinto, CFA, Elaine Henry, CFA, Thomas Robinson, CFA, and John Stowe, CFA

LEARNING OUTCOMES

The candidate should be able to:	Mastery
a. define valuation and intrinsic value, and explain possible sources of perceived mispricing;	☐
b. explain the going concern assumption, contrast a going concern value to a liquidation value, and identify the definition of value most relevant to public company valuation;	☐
c. describe applications of equity valuation;	☐
d. explain the elements of industry and competitive analysis and the importance of evaluating the quality of financial statement information;	☐
e. contrast absolute and relative valuation models, and describe examples of each type of model;	☐
f. explain broad criteria for choosing an appropriate approach for valuing a given company.	☐

INTRODUCTION 1

Every day, thousands of participants in the investment profession—investors, portfolio managers, regulators, researchers—face a common and often perplexing question: What is the value of a particular asset? The answers to this question usually determine success or failure in achieving investment objectives. For one group of those participants—equity analysts—the question and its potential answers are particularly critical, because determining the value of an ownership stake is at the heart of their professional activities and decisions.

Valuation is the estimation of an asset's value based on variables perceived to be related to future investment returns, on comparisons with similar assets, or, when relevant, on estimates of immediate liquidation proceeds. Skill in valuation is a very important element of success in investing.

Equity Asset Valuation, Second Edition, by Jerald Pinto, CFA, Elaine Henry, CFA, Thomas Robinson, CFA, and John Stowe, CFA. Copyright © 2009 by CFA Institute. Reprinted with permission.

In this introductory reading, we address some basic questions: What is value? Who uses equity valuations? What is the importance of industry knowledge? How can the analyst effectively communicate his analysis? This reading answers these and other questions and lays a foundation for the remaining valuation readings.

The balance of this reading is organized as follows: Section 2 defines value and describes the various uses of equity valuation. Section 3 examines the steps in the valuation process, including a discussion of the analyst's role and responsibilities. Section 4 discusses how valuation results are communicated and provides some guidance on the content and format of an effective research report. The final section summarizes the reading, and practice problems conclude.

2   VALUE DEFINITIONS AND VALUATION APPLICATIONS

Before summarizing the various applications of equity valuation tools, it is helpful to define what is meant by "value" and to understand that the meaning can vary in different contexts. The context of a valuation, including its objective, generally determines the appropriate definition of value and thus affects the analyst's selection of a valuation approach.

2.1 What Is Value?

Several perspectives on value serve as the foundation for the variety of valuation models available to the equity analyst. Intrinsic value is the necessary starting point, but other concepts of value—going-concern value, liquidation value, and fair value—are also important.

2.1.1 Intrinsic Value

A critical assumption in equity valuation, as applied to publicly traded securities, is that the market *price* of a security can differ from its intrinsic *value*. The **intrinsic value** of any asset is the value of the asset given a hypothetically complete understanding of the asset's investment characteristics. For any particular investor, an estimate of intrinsic value reflects his or her view of the "true" or "real" value of an asset. If one assumed that the market price of an equity security perfectly reflected its intrinsic value, "valuation" would simply require looking at the market price. Roughly, it is just such an assumption that underpins traditional efficient market theory, which suggests that an asset's market price is the best available estimate of its intrinsic value.

An important theoretical counter to the notion that market price and intrinsic value are identical can be found in the Grossman–Stiglitz paradox. If market prices, which are essentially freely obtainable, perfectly reflect a security's intrinsic value, then a rational investor would not incur the costs of obtaining and analyzing information to obtain a second estimate of the security's value. If no investor obtains and analyzes information about a security, however, then how can the market price reflect the security's intrinsic value? The **rational efficient markets formulation** (Grossman and Stiglitz, 1980) recognizes that investors will not rationally incur the expenses of gathering information unless they expect to be rewarded by higher gross returns compared with the free alternative of accepting the market price. Furthermore, modern theorists recognize that when intrinsic value is difficult to determine, as is the case for common stock, and when trading costs exist, even further room exists for price to diverge from value (Lee, Myers, and Swaminathan, 1999).

Thus, analysts often view market prices both with respect and with skepticism. They seek to identify mispricing. At the same time, they often rely on price eventually converging to intrinsic value. They also recognize distinctions among the levels of market efficiency in different markets or tiers of markets (for example, stocks heavily followed by analysts and stocks neglected by analysts). Overall, equity valuation, when applied to market-traded securities, admits the possibility of mispricing. Throughout these readings, then, we distinguish between the market price, P, and the intrinsic value ("value" for short), V.

For an active investment manager, valuation is an inherent part of the attempt to produce investment returns that exceed the returns commensurate with the investment's risk; that is, positive excess risk-adjusted return. An excess risk-adjusted return is also called an **abnormal return** or **alpha**. (Return concepts will be more fully discussed in a later reading.) The active investment manager hopes to capture a positive alpha as a result of his or her efforts to estimate intrinsic value. Any departure of market price from the manager's estimate of intrinsic value is a perceived **mispricing** (a difference between the estimated intrinsic value and the market price of an asset).

These ideas can be illuminated through the following expression that identifies two possible sources of perceived mispricing:[1]

$$V_E - P = (V - P) + (V_E - V)$$

where

V_E = estimated value
P = market price
V = intrinsic value

This expression states that the difference between a valuation estimate and the prevailing market price is, by definition, equal to the sum of two components. The first component is the true mispricing, that is, the difference between the true but unobservable intrinsic value V and the observed market price P (this difference contributes to the abnormal return). The second component is the difference between the valuation estimate and the true but unobservable intrinsic value, that is, the error in the estimate of the intrinsic value.

To obtain a useful estimate of intrinsic value, an analyst must combine accurate forecasts with an appropriate valuation model. The quality of the analyst's forecasts, in particular the expectational inputs used in valuation models, is a key element in determining investment success. For an active security selection to be consistently successful, the manager's expectations must differ from consensus expectations and be, on average, correct as well.

Uncertainty is constantly present in equity valuation. Confidence in one's expectations is always realistically partial. In applying any valuation approach, analysts can never be sure that they have accounted for all the sources of risk reflected in an asset's price. Because competing equity risk models will always

---

[1] Derived as $V_E - P = V_E - P + V - V = (V - P) + (V_E - V)$.

exist, there is no obvious final resolution to this dilemma. Even if an analyst makes adequate risk adjustments, develops accurate forecasts, and employs appropriate valuation models, success is not assured. Temporal market conditions may prevent the investor from capturing the benefits of any perceived mispricing. Convergence of the market price to perceived intrinsic value may not happen within the investor's investment horizon, if at all. So, besides evidence of mispricing, some active investors look for the presence of a particular market or corporate event (**catalyst**) that will cause the marketplace to re-evaluate a company's prospects.

2.1.2 Going-Concern Value and Liquidation Value

A company generally has one value if it is to be immediately dissolved and another value if it will continue in operation. In estimating value, a **going-concern assumption** is the assumption that the company will continue its business activities into the foreseeable future. In other words, the company will continue to produce and sell its goods and services, use its assets in a value-maximizing way for a relevant economic time frame, and access its optimal sources of financing. The **going-concern value** of a company is its value under a going-concern assumption. Models of going-concern value are the focus of these readings.

Nevertheless, a going-concern assumption may not be appropriate for a company in financial distress. An alternative to a company's going-concern value is its value if it were dissolved and its assets sold individually, known as its **liquidation value**. For many companies, the value added by assets working together and by human capital applied to managing those assets makes estimated going-concern value greater than liquidation value (although a persistently unprofitable business may be worth more "dead" than "alive"). Beyond the value added by assets working together or by applying managerial skill to those assets, the value of a company's assets would likely differ depending on the time frame available for liquidating them. For example, the value of nonperishable inventory that had to be immediately liquidated would typically be lower than the value of inventory that could be sold during a longer period of time, i.e., in an "orderly" fashion. Thus, concepts such as **orderly liquidation value** are sometimes distinguished.

2.1.3 Fair Market Value and Investment Value

For an analyst valuing public equities, intrinsic value is typically the relevant concept of value. In other contexts, however, other definitions of value are relevant. For example, a buy–sell agreement among the owners of a private business—specifying how and when the owners (e.g., shareholders or partners) can sell their ownership interest and at what price—might be primarily concerned with equitable treatment of both sellers and buyers. In that context, the relevant definition of value would likely be fair market value. **Fair market value** is the price at which an asset (or liability) would change hands between a willing buyer and a willing seller when the former is not under any compulsion to buy and the latter is not under any compulsion to sell. Furthermore, the concept of fair market value generally includes an assumption that both buyer and seller are informed of all material aspects of the underlying investment. Fair market value has often been used in valuation related to assessing taxes. In a financial reporting context—for example, in valuing an asset for the purpose of impairment testing—financial reporting standards reference **fair value**, a related (but not identical) concept.[2]

Assuming the marketplace has confidence that the company's management is acting in the owners' best interests, market prices should tend, in the long run, to reflect fair market value. In some situations, however, an asset is worth more to a particular buyer (e.g., because of potential operating synergies). The concept of value to a specific buyer taking account of potential synergies and based on the investor's requirements and expectations is called **investment value**.

2.1.4 Definitions of Value: Summary

Analysts valuing an asset need to be aware of the definition or definitions of value relevant to the assignment. For the valuation of public equities, an intrinsic value definition of values is generally relevant. Intrinsic value, estimated under a going-concern assumption, is the focus of these equity valuation readings.

2.2 Applications of Equity Valuation

Investment analysts work in a wide variety of organizations and positions; as a result, they apply the tools of equity valuation to address a range of practical problems. In particular, analysts use valuation concepts and models to accomplish the following:

- ▶ *Selecting stocks.* Stock selection is the primary use of the tools presented in these readings. Equity analysts continually address the same question for every common stock that is either a current or prospective portfolio holding, or for every stock that he or she is responsible for covering: Is this security fairly priced, overpriced, or underpriced relative to its current estimated intrinsic value and relative to the prices of comparable securities?

- ▶ *Inferring* (*extracting*) *market expectations.* Market prices reflect the expectations of investors about the future performance of companies. Analysts may ask: What expectations about a company's future performance are consistent with the current market price for that company's stock? What assumptions about the company's fundamentals would justify the current price? (**Fundamentals** are characteristics of a company related to profitability, financial strength, or risk.) These questions may be relevant to the analyst for several reasons:
    - ▶ The analyst can evaluate the reasonableness of the expectations implied by the market price by comparing the market's implied expectations to his own expectations.
    - ▶ The market's expectations for a fundamental characteristic of one company may be useful as a benchmark or comparison value of the same characteristic for another company.

---

[2] Accounting standards provide specific definitions of fair value. Fair value is the amount for which an asset could be exchanged, a liability settled, or an equity instrument granted could be exchanged between knowledgeable, willing parties in an arm's length transaction.

To extract or reverse-engineer a market expectation, the analyst selects a valuation model that relates value to expectations about fundamentals and is appropriate given the characteristics of the stock. Next, the analyst estimates values for all fundamentals in the model except the fundamental of interest. The analyst then solves for that value of the fundamental of interest that results in a model value equal to the current market price.

▶ *Evaluating corporate events.* Investment bankers, corporate analysts, and investment analysts use valuation tools to assess the impact of such corporate events as mergers, acquisitions, divestitures, spin-offs, and going private transactions. (A **merger** is the general term for the combination of two companies. An **acquisition** is also a combination of two companies, with one of the companies identified as the acquirer, the other the acquired. In a **divestiture**, a company sells some major component of its business. In a **spin-off**, the company separates one of its component businesses and transfers the ownership of the separated business to its shareholders. A **leveraged buyout** is an acquisition involving significant leverage [i.e., debt], which is often collateralized by the assets of the company being acquired.) Each of these events affects a company's future cash flows and thus the value of its equity. Furthermore, in mergers and acquisitions, the company's own common stock is often used as currency for the purchase; investors then want to know whether the stock is fairly valued.

▶ *Rendering fairness opinions.* The parties to a merger may be required to seek a fairness opinion on the terms of the merger from a third party, such as an investment bank. Valuation is central to such opinions.

▶ *Evaluating business strategies and models.* Companies concerned with maximizing shareholder value evaluate the effect of alternative strategies on share value.

▶ *Communicating with analysts and shareholders.* Valuation concepts facilitate communication and discussion among company management, shareholders, and analysts on a range of corporate issues affecting company value.

▶ *Appraising private businesses.* Valuation of the equity of private businesses is important for transactional purposes (e.g., acquisitions of such companies or buy–sell agreements for the transfer of equity interests among owners when one of them dies or retires) and tax reporting purposes (e.g., for the taxation of estates) among others. The absence of a market price imparts distinctive characteristics to such valuations, although the fundamental models are shared with public equity valuation. An analyst encounters these characteristics when evaluating initial public offerings, for example. An **initial public offering** (IPO) is the initial issuance of common stock registered for public trading by a company whose shares were not formerly publicly traded, either because it was formerly privately owned or government-owned, or because it is a newly formed entity.

▶ *Share-based payment (compensation).* Share-based payments (e.g., restricted stock grants) are sometimes part of executive compensation. Estimation of their value frequently depends on using equity valuation tools.

EXAMPLE 1

Inferring Market Expectations

On 21 September 2000, Intel Corporation (NASDAQ-GS: INTC)[3] issued a press release containing information about its expected revenue growth for the third quarter of 2000. The announced growth fell short of the company's own prior prediction by 2 to 4 percentage points and short of analysts' projections by 3 to 7 percentage points. In response to the announcement, Intel's stock price fell nearly 30 percent during the following five days—from $61.50 just prior to the press release to only $43.31 five days later.

To assess whether the information in Intel's announcement was sufficient to explain such a large loss of value, Cornell (2001) estimated the value of a company's equity as the present value of expected future cash flows from operations minus the expenditures needed to maintain the company's growth. (We will discuss such *free cash flow models* in detail in a later reading.)

Using a conservatively low discount rate, Cornell estimated that Intel's price before the announcement, $61.50, was consistent with a forecasted growth rate of 20 percent a year for the subsequent 10 years and then 6 percent per year thereafter. Intel's price after the announcement, $43.31, was consistent with a decline of the 10-year growth rate to well under 15 percent per year. In the final year of the forecast horizon (2009), projected revenues with the lower growth rate would be $50 billion below the projected revenues based on the pre-announcement price. Because the press release did not obviously point to any changes in Intel's fundamental long-run business conditions (Intel attributed the quarterly revenue growth shortfall to a cyclical slowing of demand in Europe), Cornell's detailed analysis left him skeptical that the stock market's reaction could be explained in terms of fundamentals.

Assuming Cornell's methodology was sound, one interpretation is that investors' reaction to the press release was irrational. An alternative interpretation is that Intel's stock was overvalued prior to the press release, and the press release was "a kind of catalyst that caused movement toward a more rational price, even though the release itself did not contain sufficient long-run valuation information to justify that movement" (Cornell 2001, p. 134). How could one evaluate these two possible interpretations?

Solution: To evaluate whether the market reaction to Intel's announcement was an irrational reaction or a rational reduction of a previously overvalued price, one could compare the expected 20 percent growth implicit in the pre-announcement stock price to some benchmark—for example, the company's actual recent revenue growth, the industry's recent growth, and/or forecasts for the growth of the industry or the economy. Finding the growth rate implied in the

---

[3] In these readings, the shares of real companies are identified by an abbreviation for the stock exchange or electronic marketplace where the shares of the company are traded, followed by a ticker symbol or formal acronym for the shares. For example, NASDAQ-GS stands for "NASDAQ Global Select Market," and INTC is the ticker symbol for Intel Corporation on the NASDAQ-GS. (Many stocks are traded on a number of exchanges worldwide, and some stocks may have more than one formal acronym; we usually state just one marketplace and one ticker symbol.)

company's stock price is an example of using a valuation model and a company's actual stock price to infer market expectations.

Note: Cornell (2001) observed that the 20 percent revenue growth rate implied by the pre-announcement stock price was much higher than Intel's average growth rate during the previous five years, which occurred when the company was much smaller. He concluded that Intel's stock was overvalued prior to the press release.

The example above describes the market reaction to an earnings release by Intel in 2000. A retrospective on Intel eight years later (in September 2008, the company's share price was around $20) illustrates the difficulty of equity valuation and the risk to growth stocks from disappointing results as compared to optimistic previous expectations. This example also illustrates that differences between market price and intrinsic value sometimes persist, offering opportunities for the astute investment manager to generate alpha.

3   THE VALUATION PROCESS

In general, the valuation process involves the following five steps:

1. *Understanding the business.* Industry and competitive analysis, together with an analysis of financial statements and other company disclosures, provides a basis for forecasting company performance.

2. *Forecasting company performance.* Forecasts of sales, earnings, dividends, and financial position (pro forma analysis) provide the inputs for most valuation models.

3. *Selecting the appropriate valuation model.* Depending on the characteristics of the company and the context of valuation, some valuation models will be more appropriate than others.

4. *Converting forecasts to a valuation.* Beyond mechanically obtaining the "output" of valuation models, estimating value involves judgment.

5. *Applying the valuation conclusions.* Depending on the purpose, an analyst may use the valuation conclusions to make an investment recommendation about a particular stock, provide an opinion about the price of a transaction, or evaluate the economic merits of a potential strategic investment.

Most of these steps are addressed in detail in the succeeding valuation readings; here, we provide an overview of each.

3.1 Understanding the Business

To forecast a company's financial performance that will, in turn, determine the value of an investment in the company or its securities, it is helpful to understand the economic and industry context in which the company operates, the company's strategy, and the company's previous financial performance. Industry and competitive analysis, together with an analysis of the company's financial reports, provides a basis for forecasting performance.

3.1.1 Industry and Competitive Analysis

Because similar economic and technological factors typically affect all companies in an industry, industry knowledge helps analysts understand the basic characteristics of the markets served by a company and the economics of the company. An airline industry analyst will know that labor costs and jet fuel costs are the two largest expenses of airlines, and that in many markets airlines have difficulty passing through higher fuel prices by raising ticket prices. Using this knowledge, the analyst may inquire about the degree to which different airlines hedge the commodity price risk inherent in jet fuel costs. With such information in hand, the analyst is better able to evaluate risk and forecast future cash flows. In addition, the analyst would run sensitivity analyses to determine how different levels of fuel prices would affect valuation.

Various frameworks exist for industry and competitive analysis. The primary usefulness of such frameworks is that they can help ensure that an analysis gives appropriate attention to the most important economic drivers of a business. In other words, the objective is *not* to prepare some formal framework representing industry structure or corporate strategy, but rather to use a framework to organize thoughts about an industry and to better understand a company's prospects for success in competition with other companies in that industry. Further, although frameworks can provide a template, obviously the informational content added by an analyst makes the framework relevant to valuation. Ultimately, an industry and competitive analysis should highlight which aspects of a company's business present the greatest challenges and opportunities and should thus be the subject of further investigation, and/or more extensive **sensitivity analysis** (an analysis to determine how changes in an assumed input would affect the outcome of an analysis). Frameworks may be useful as analysts focus on questions relevant to understanding a business.

▶ *How attractive are the industries in which the company operates, in terms of offering prospects for sustained profitability?*

Inherent industry profitability is one important factor in determining a company's profitability. Analysts should try to understand **industry structure**—the industry's underlying economic and technical characteristics—and the trends affecting that structure. Basic economic factors—supply and demand—provide a fundamental framework for understanding an industry.

Porter's (1985, 1998, 2008) five forces characterizing industry structure are summarized below with an explanation of how that force could positively affect inherent industry profitability. For each force, the opposite situation would negatively affect inherent industry profitability.

i. *Intra-industry rivalry.* Lower rivalry among industry participants—for example, in a faster growing industry with relatively few competitors and/or good brand identification—enhances inherent industry profitability.

ii. *New entrants.* Relatively high costs to enter an industry (or other entry barriers, such as government policies) result in fewer new participants and less competition, thus enhancing inherent industry profitability.

iii. *Substitutes.* When few potential substitutes exist and/or the cost to switch to a substitute is high, industry participants are less constrained in raising prices, thus enhancing inherent industry profitability.

iv. *Supplier power.* When many suppliers of the inputs needed by industry participants exist, suppliers have limited power to raise prices and thus would not represent inherent downward pressure on industry profitability.

v. *Buyer power.* When many customers for an industry's product exist, customers have limited power to negotiate lower prices and thus would not represent inherent downward pressure on industry profitability.

Analysts must also stay current on facts and news concerning all the industries in which the company operates, including recent developments (e.g., management, technological, or financial). Particularly important to valuation are any factors likely to affect the industry's longer term profitability and growth prospects such as demographic trends.

▶ *What is the company's relative competitive position within its industry, and what is its competitive strategy?*

The level and trend of the company's market share indicate its relative competitive position within an industry. In general, a company's value is higher to the extent that it can create and sustain an advantage relative to its competition. Porter identifies three generic corporate strategies for achieving above-average performance:

i. Cost leadership: being the lowest cost producer while offering products comparable to those of other companies, so that products can be priced at or near the industry average;

ii. Differentiation: offering unique products or services along some dimensions that are widely valued by buyers so that the company can command premium prices; and

iii. Focus: seeking a competitive advantage within a target segment or segments of the industry, based on either cost leadership (cost focus) or differentiation (differentiation focus).

The term "business model" refers generally to how a company makes money: which customers it targets, what products or services it will sell to those customers, and how it delivers those products or services (including how it finances its activities). The term is broadly used and sometimes encompasses aspects of the generic strategies described above. For example, an airline with a generic cost leadership strategy might have a business model characterized as a low-cost carrier. Low-cost carriers offer a single class of service and use a single type of aircraft to minimize training costs and maintenance charges.

▶ *How well has the company executed its strategy and what are its prospects for future execution?*

Competitive success requires both appropriate strategic choices and competent execution. Analyzing the company's financial reports provides a basis for evaluating a company's performance against its strategic objectives and for developing expectations about a company's likely future performance. A historical analysis means more than just reviewing, say, the 10-year historical record in the most recent annual report. It very often means looking at the annual reports from 10 years prior, 5 years prior, and the most recent two years. Why? Because looking at annual reports from prior years often provides useful insights into how management has historically foreseen challenges and has adapted to changes in business conditions through time. (In general, the investor relations sections of most publicly traded companies' websites provide electronic copies of their annual reports from at least the most recent years.)

In examining financial and operational strategic execution, two caveats merit mention. First, the importance of qualitative, that is, non-numeric factors, must be considered. Such non-numeric factors include, for example, the company's ownership structure, its intellectual and physical property, the terms of its intangible assets such as licenses and franchise agreements, and the potential consequences of legal disputes or other contingent liabilities. Second, it is important to avoid simply extrapolating past operating results when forecasting future performance. In general, economic and technological forces can often contribute to the phenomenon of "regression toward the mean." Specifically, successful companies tend to draw more competitors into their industries and find that their ability to generate above average profits comes under pressure. Conversely, poorly performing companies are often restructured in such a manner as to improve their long-term profitability. Thus, in many cases, analysts making long-term horizon growth forecasts for a company's earnings and profits (e.g., forecasts beyond the next 10 years) plausibly assume company convergence toward the forecasted average growth rate for the underlying economy.

3.1.2 Analysis of Financial Reports

The aspects of a financial report that are most relevant for evaluating a company's success in implementing strategic choices vary across companies and industries. For established companies, financial ratio analysis is useful. Individual drivers of profitability for merchandising and manufacturing companies can be evaluated against the company's stated strategic objectives. For example, a manufacturing company aiming to create a sustainable competitive advantage by building strong brand recognition could be expected to have substantial expenditures for advertising but relatively higher prices. Compared with a company aiming to compete on cost, the branded company would be expected to have higher gross margins but also higher selling expenses as a percent of sales.

EXAMPLE 2

Competitive Analysis

According to Standard & Poor's Corporation (S&P), the five largest providers of oilfield services (based on January 2008 market capitalization) are Schlumberger Ltd. (NYSE: SLB), Halliburton Co. (NYSE: HAL), National Oilwell Varco (NYSE: NOV), Baker Hughes Inc. (NYSE: BHI), and Weatherford International Ltd. (NYSE: WFT). These companies provide tools and services—often of a very technical nature—to expedite the drilling activities of oil and gas producers and drilling companies.

1. Discuss the economic factors that may affect demand for the services provided by oilfield services companies, and explain a logical framework for analyzing and forecasting revenue for these companies.
2. Explain how comparing the level and trend in profit margin (net income/sales) and revenue per employee for the above companies may help in evaluating whether one of these companies is the cost leader in the peer group.

Solution to 1: Because the products and services of these companies relate to oil and gas exploration and production, the levels of exploration and production activities by oil and gas producers are probably the major factors that determine the demand for their services. In turn, the prices of natural gas and crude oil are important in determining the level of exploration and production activities. Therefore, among other economic factors, an analyst should research those relating to supply and demand for natural gas and crude oil.

► Supply factors in natural gas, such as natural gas inventory levels.

► Demand factors in natural gas, including household and commercial use of natural gas and the amount of new power generation equipment being fired by natural gas.

► Supply factors in crude oil, including capacity constraints and production levels in OPEC and other oil producing countries, as well as new discoveries of off-shore, and land-based oil reserves.

► Demand factors in crude oil, such as household and commercial use of oil and the amount of new power generation equipment using oil products as its primary fuel.

► For both crude oil and natural gas, projected economic growth rates could be examined as a demand factor and depletion rates as a supply side factor.

Note: Energy analysts should be familiar with sources for researching supply and demand information, such as the International Energy Agency (IEA), the European Petroleum Industry Association (EUROPIA), the Energy Information Administration (EIA), the American Gas Association (AGA), and the American Petroleum Institute (API).

Solution to 2: Profit margin reflects cost structure; in interpreting profit margin, however, analysts should evaluate any differences in companies' abilities to affect profit margin through power over price. A successfully executed cost leadership strategy will lower costs and raise profit margins. All else equal, we would also expect a cost leader to have relatively high sales per employee, reflecting efficient use of human resources.

With newer companies, or companies involved in creating new products or markets, nonfinancial measures may be critical to obtaining an accurate picture of corporate prospects. For example, a biotechnology company's clinical trial results or an internet company's unique visitors per day may provide information helpful for evaluating future revenue.

3.1.3 Sources of Information

An important perspective on industry and competition is sometimes provided by companies themselves in regulator-mandated disclosures, regulatory filings, company press releases, investor relations materials, and contacts with analysts. Analysts can compare the information provided directly by companies to their own independent research.

Regulatory requirements concerning disclosures and filings vary internationally. In some markets, such as Canada and the United States, some mandatory filings require management to provide industry and competitive information and access to those filings is freely available on the internet (e.g., www.sedar.com for Canadian filings and at www.sec.gov for U.S. filings). To take the case of the United States, in annual filings with the Securities and Exchange Commission made on Form 10-K for U.S. companies and Form 20-F for non-U.S. companies, companies provide industry and competitive information in the business description section and in the management discussion and analysis (MD&A). Interim filings (e.g., the quarterly SEC Form 10-Q for U.S. companies and Form 6-K for non-U.S. companies) provide interim financial statements but typically less detailed coverage of industry and competition.

So far as analyst–management contacts are concerned, analysts must be aware when regulations (e.g., Regulation FD in the United States) prohibit companies from disclosing material nonpublic information to analysts without also disseminating that information to the public.[4] General management insights based on public information, however, can still be useful to analysts, and many analysts consider in-person meetings with a company's management to be essential to understanding a company.

The CFA Institute Code of Ethics and Standards of Professional Conduct prohibit use of material inside information, and Regulation FD (and similar regulations in other countries) is designed to prohibit companies from selectively offering such information. These ethical and legal requirements assist analysts by clarifying their main role and purpose.

Company-provided sources of information in addition to regulatory filings include press releases and investor relations materials. The press releases of most relevance to analysts are the press releases that companies issue to announce their periodic earnings. Companies typically issue these earnings press releases several weeks after the end of an accounting period and several weeks before they file their interim financial statements. Earnings press releases summarize the company's performance for the period, usually include explanations for the performance, and usually include financial statements (often abbreviated versions). Following their earnings press releases, many companies host conference calls in which they further elaborate on their reported performance and typically allocate some time to answer questions posed by analysts. On their corporate websites, many companies post audio downloads and transcripts of conference calls and of presentations made in analyst conferences. The audio files and transcripts of conference calls and conference presentations provide access not only to the company's reports but also to analysts' questions and the company's answers to those questions.

Apart from company-provided sources of information, analysts also obtain information from third party sources such as industry organizations, regulatory agencies, and commercial providers of market intelligence.

3.1.4 Considerations in Using Accounting Information

In evaluating a company's historical performance and developing forecasts of future performance, analysts typically rely heavily on companies' accounting information and financial disclosures. Companies' reported results vary in their persistence, i.e., sustainability. In addition, the information that companies disclose can vary substantially with respect to the *accuracy* of reported accounting

---

[4] There may be special filings, for example Form 8-K in the United States, associated with public disclosure of material corporate events.

results as reflections of economic performance and the detail in which results are disclosed.

The term **quality of earnings analysis** broadly includes the scrutiny of *all* financial statements, including the balance sheet, to evaluate both the sustainability of the companies' performance and how accurately the reported information reflects economic reality. Equity analysts will generally develop better insights into a company and improve forecast accuracy by developing an ability to assess a company's quality of earnings. With regard to sustainability of performance, an analyst aims to identify aspects of reported performance that are less likely to recur. For example, earnings with significant components of nonrecurring events such as positive litigation settlements, nonpermanent tax reductions, or gains on sales of nonoperating assets are considered to be of lower quality than earnings derived mainly from the company's core business operations.

In addition to identifying nonrecurring events, an analyst aims to identify reporting decisions that may result in a level of reported earnings that are unlikely to continue. A good starting point for this type of quality of earnings analysis is a comparison of a company's net income with its operating cash flow. As a simple hypothetical example, consider a company that generates revenues and net income but no operating cash flow because it makes all sales on account and never collects its receivables. One systematic way to make the comparison is to decompose net income into a cash component (combining operating and investing cash flows) and an accrual component (defined as net income minus the cash component). Capital markets research shows that the cash component is more persistent than the accrual component of earnings, with the result that a company with a relatively higher amount of current accruals will have a relatively lower ROA in the future (Sloan 1996). Here, greater persistency means that, compared to accruals in the current period, the cash component in the current period is more predictive of future net income. A relatively higher proportion of accruals can be interpreted as lower earnings quality.

A quality of earnings analysis for a particular company requires careful scrutiny of accounting statements, footnotes, and other relevant disclosures. Sources for studying quality of earnings analysis and accounting risk factors include Richardson and Tuna (2008), Mulford and Comiskey (2005), and Schilit (2002), as well as American Institute of Certified Public Accountants *Consideration of Fraud in a Financial Statement Audit* (28 February 2002) and International Federation of Accountants, International Standards on Auditing 240, *The Auditor's Responsibility to Consider Fraud and Error in an Audit of Financial Statements* (March 2001). Examples of a few of the many available indicators of possible problems with a company's quality of earnings are provided in Exhibit 1.

EXHIBIT 1	Selected Quality of Earnings Indicators	
Category	**Observation**	**Potential Interpretation**
Revenues and gains	Recognizing revenue early, for example: ▶ bill-and-hold sales, and ▶ recording sales of equipment or software prior to installation and acceptance by customer.	Acceleration in the recognition of revenue boosts reported income, masking a decline in operating performance.
	Classification of nonoperating income or gains as part of operations.	Income or gains may be nonrecurring and may not relate to true operating performance, possibly masking declines in operating performance.
Expenses and losses	Recognizing too much or too little reserves in the current year, such as: ▶ restructuring reserves; ▶ loan-loss or bad-debt reserves; and ▶ valuation allowances against deferred tax assets.	May boost current income at the expense of future income, or alternatively may decrease current year's earnings to boost future years' performance.
	Deferral of expenses by capitalizing expenditures as an asset, for example: ▶ customer acquisition costs, and ▶ product development costs.	May boost current income at the expense of future income. May mask problems with underlying business performance.
	Use of aggressive estimates and assumptions, such as: ▶ asset impairments; ▶ long depreciable lives; ▶ long periods of amortization; ▶ high assumed discount rate for pension liabilities; ▶ low assumed rate of compensation growth for pension liabilities; and ▶ high expected return on assets for pension.	Aggressive estimates may indicate actions taken to boost current reported income. Changes in assumptions may indicate an attempt to mask problems with underlying performance in the current period.
Balance sheet issues (may also affect earnings)	Use of **off-balance sheet financing** (financing that does not appear on the balance sheet), such as leasing assets or securitizing receivables.	Assets and/or liabilities may not be properly reflected on the balance sheet.
Operating cash flow	Characterization of an increase in a bank overdraft as operating cash flow.	Operating cash flow may be artificially inflated.

The following example illustrates the importance of accounting practices in influencing reported financial results and the need for analysts to exercise judgment when using those results in any valuation model.

EXAMPLE 3

Quality of Earnings Warning Signs: Aggressive Estimates

In the section of his 2007 letter to the shareholders of Berkshire Hathaway titled "Fanciful Figures—How Public Companies Juice Earnings," Warren Buffett referred to the investment return assumption (the anticipated return on a defined-benefit pension plan's current and future assets):

> "Decades of option-accounting nonsense have now been put to rest, but other accounting choices remain—important among these [is] the investment-return assumption a company uses in calculating pension expense. It will come as no surprise that many companies continue to choose an assumption that allows them to report less-than-solid 'earnings.' For the 363 companies in the S&P that have pension plans, this assumption in 2006 averaged 8%." (www.berkshirehathaway.com/letters/2007ltr.pdf. See pp.18–19.)

In his explanation, Buffet assumes a 5 percent return on cash and bonds, which average 28 percent of pension fund assets. Therefore, this implies that the remaining 72 percent of pension fund assets—predominately invested in equities—must earn a return of 9.2 percent, after all fees, to achieve the 8 percent overall return on the pension fund assets. To illustrate one perspective on an average pension fund achieving that 9.2 percent return, he estimates that the Dow Jones Industrial Index would need to close at about 2,000,000 on 31 December 2099 (compared to a level under 13,000 at the time of his writing) for this century's returns on that U.S. stock index to match just the 5.3 percent average annual compound return achieved in the 20th century.

1. How do aggressively optimistic estimates for returns on pension assets affect pension expense?
2. Where can information about a company's assumed returns on its pension assets be found?

Solution to 1: The amount of "expected return on plan assets" associated with the return assumption is a deduction in calculating pension expense. An aggressively optimistic estimate for the rate of return that pension assets will earn means a larger-than-warranted deduction in calculating pension expense, and subtraction will lead to understating pension expense and overstating net income. In fact, pension expense could become pension income depending on the numbers involved.

Solution to 2: Information about a company's assumed return on its pension assets can be found in the footnotes to the company's financial statements.

The next example of poor earnings quality, in which management made choices going beyond making an aggressive estimate, is reminiscent of a humorous vignette from Benjamin Graham in which the chairman of a company outlines plans for return to profitability, as follows: "Contrary to expectations, no changes will be made in the company's manufacturing or selling policies. Instead, the bookkeeping system is to be entirely revamped. By adopting and further improving a number of modern accounting and financial devices, the corporation's earning power will be amazingly transformed."[5]

EXAMPLE 4

Quality of Earnings Warning Signs: An Extreme Case

Livent, Inc. was a publicly traded theatrical production company that staged a number of smash hits such as Tony-award winning productions of *Showboat* and *Fosse*. Livent capitalized preproduction costs including expenses for pre-opening advertising, publicity and promotion, set construction, props, costumes, and salaries and fees paid to the cast, crew, and musicians during rehearsals. The company then amortized these capitalized costs over the expected life of the theatrical production based on anticipated revenues.[6]

1. State the effect of Livent's accounting for preproduction costs on its reported earnings per share.

2. State the effect of Livent's accounting for preproduction costs on its balance sheet.

3. If an analyst calculated EBITDA/interest expense and debt/EBITDA based on Livent's accounting for preproduction costs without adjustment, how might the analyst be misled in assessing Livent's financial strength? (Recall that EBITDA is defined as earnings before interest, taxes, depreciation, and amortization. Ratios such as EBITDA/interest expense and debt/EBITDA indicate one aspect of a company's financial strength, debt-paying ability.)

Solution to 1: Livent's accounting for preproduction costs immediately increased reported earnings per share because it deferred expenses.

Solution to 2: Instead of immediately expensing costs, Livent reported the amounts on its balance sheet as an asset. The warning signal—the deferral of expenses—can indicate aggressive accounting; preproduction costs should have been expensed immediately because of the tremendous uncertainty about revenues from theatrical productions. There was no assurance that there would be revenues against which expenses could be matched.

Solution to 3: Livent did not deduct preproduction costs from earnings as expenses. If the amortization of capitalized preproduction costs were then added back to earnings, the EBITDA/interest and debt/EBITDA ratios would not reflect in any way the cash outflows associated with items such as paying pre-opening salaries; but cash

---

[5] Graham 1936.

[6] The discussion in this example is indebted to Moody's Investor Services (2000).

outflows reduce funds available to meet debt obligations. The analyst who mechanically added back amortization of preproduction costs to calculate EBITDA would be misled into overestimating Livent's financial strength. Based on a closer look at the company's accounting, the analyst would properly not add back amortization of preproduction expenses in computing EBITDA. If preproduction expenses are not added back, a very different picture of Livent's financial health would emerge. In 1996, Livent's reported debt/EBITDA ratio was 1.7, but the ratio without adding back amortization for preproduction costs was 5.5. In 1997, debt/EBITDA was 3.7 based on positive EBITDA of $58.3 million, but EBITDA without the add-back was *negative* $52.6 million.

Note: In November 1998, Livent declared bankruptcy and is now defunct. The criminal trial, in Canada, began in May 2008.

In general, growth in an asset account (such as deferred costs in the Livent example) at a much faster rate than the growth rate of sales may indicate aggressive accounting. Analysts recognize a variety of risk factors that may signal possible future negative surprises. A working selection of these risk factors would include the following (AICPA 2002):

▶ Poor quality of accounting disclosures, such as segment information, acquisitions, accounting policies and assumptions, and a lack of discussion of negative factors.

▶ Existence of related-party transactions.

▶ Existence of excessive officer, employee, or director loans.

▶ High management or director turnover.

▶ Excessive pressure on company personnel to make revenue or earnings targets, particularly when combined with a dominant, aggressive management team or individual.

▶ Material nonaudit services performed by audit firm.

▶ Reported (through regulatory filings) disputes with and/or changes in auditors.

▶ Management and/or directors' compensation tied to profitability or stock price (through ownership or compensation plans). Although such arrangements are usually desirable, they can be a risk factor for aggressive financial reporting.

▶ Economic, industry, or company-specific pressures on profitability, such as loss of market share or declining margins.

▶ Management pressure to meet debt covenants or earnings expectations.

▶ A history of securities law violations, reporting violations, or persistent late filings.

3.2 Forecasting Company Performance

The second step in the valuation process—forecasting company performance—can be viewed from two perspectives: the economic environment in which the company operates and the company's own operating and financial characteristics.

Companies do business within larger contexts of particular industries, national economies, and world trade. Viewing a company within those larger contexts, a **top-down forecasting approach** moves from international and national macroeconomic forecasts to industry forecasts and then to individual company and asset forecasts.[7] For example, a revenue forecast for a major home appliance manufacturer could start with industry unit sales forecasts that are in turn based on GDP forecasts. Forecasted company unit sales would equal forecasted industry unit sales multiplied by the appliance manufacturer's forecasted market share. A revenue projection would be based on forecasted company unit sales and sales prices.

Alternatively, a **bottom-up forecasting approach** aggregates forecasts at a micro level to larger scale forecasts, under specific assumptions. For example, a clothing retailer may have several stores in operation with two new stores about to open. Using information based on the sales per square meter of the existing stores (perhaps during their initial period of operation), the analyst could forecast sales per square meter of the new stores that, added to forecasts of a similar type for existing stores, would give a sales forecast for the company as a whole. In making such a bottom-up sales forecast, the analyst would be making assumptions about selling prices and merchandise costs. Forecasts for individual retailers could be aggregated into forecasts for the group, continuing in a bottom-up fashion.

In general, analysts integrate insights from industry and competitive analysis with financial statement analysis to formulate specific forecasts of such items as a company's sales, earnings, and cash flow. Analysts generally consider qualitative as well as quantitative factors in financial forecasting and valuation. For example, an analyst might modify his or her forecasts and valuation judgments based on qualitative factors, such as the analyst's opinion about the business acumen and integrity of management, and/or the transparency and quality of a company's accounting practices. Such qualitative factors are necessarily subjective.

3.3 Selecting the Appropriate Valuation Model

This section discusses the third step in the valuation process—selecting the appropriate model for the valuation task at hand. Detailed descriptions of the valuation models are presented in later readings. Absolute valuation models and relative valuation models are the two broad types of valuation models that incorporate a going-concern assumption. Here, we describe absolute and relative valuation models in general terms and discuss a number of issues in model selection. In practice, an analyst may use a variety of models to estimate the value of a company or its common stock.

3.3.1 Absolute Valuation Models

An **absolute valuation model** is a model that specifies an asset's intrinsic value. Such models are used to produce an estimate of value that can be compared with the asset's market price. The most important type of absolute equity valuation models are present value models. In finance theory, present value models are

---

[7] A related but distinct concept is **top-down investing** versus **bottom-up investing** as one broad description of types of active investment styles. For example, a top-down investor uses macroeconomic forecasts to identify sectors of the economy representing potentially attractive investment opportunities. In contrast, an investor following a bottom-up investing approach might decide that a security is undervalued based on some valuation indicator, for example, without making an explicit judgment on the overall economy or the relative value of different sectors.

considered the fundamental approach to equity valuation. The logic of such models is that the value of an asset to an investor must be related to the returns that investor expects to receive from holding that asset. Generally speaking, those returns can be referred to as the asset's cash flows, and present value models are also referred to as discounted cash flow models.

A **present value model** or **discounted cash flow model** applied to equity valuation derives the value of common stock as the present or discounted value of its expected future cash flows.[8] For common stock, one familiar type of cash flow is dividends, which are discretionary distributions to shareholders authorized by a corporation's board of directors. Dividends represent cash flows at the shareholder level in the sense that they are paid directly to shareholders. Present value models based on dividends are called **dividend discount models**. Rather than defining cash flows as dividends, analysts frequently define cash flows at the company level. Common shareholders in principle have an equity ownership claim on the balance of the cash flows generated by a company after payments have been made to claimants senior to common equity, such as bondholders and preferred stockholders (and the government as well, which takes taxes), whether such flows are distributed in the form of dividends.

The two main company-level definitions of cash flow in current use are free cash flow and residual income. Free cash flow is based on cash flow from operations but takes into account the reinvestment in fixed assets and working capital necessary for a going concern. The **free cash flow to equity model** defines cash flow net of payments to providers of debt, whereas the **free cash flow to the firm model** defines cash flows before those payments. We will define free cash flow and each model with more precision in later readings. **Residual income models** are based on accrual accounting earnings in excess of the opportunity cost of generating those earnings.

Because the present value approach is the familiar technique for valuing bonds,[9] it is helpful to contrast the application of present value models to equity valuation with present value models as applied to bond valuation. The application of present value models to common stock typically involves greater uncertainty than is the case with bonds; that uncertainty centers on two critical inputs for present value models—the cash flows and the discount rate(s). Bond valuation discounts a stream of cash payments specified in a legal contract (the **bond indenture**). In contrast, in equity valuation an analyst must define the specific cash flow stream to be valued—dividends or free cash flow—and then forecast the amounts of those cash flows. Unlike bond valuation, no cash flow stream is contractually owed to common stockholders. Clearly, a company's total cash flows, and therefore the cash flows potentially available to common stockholders, will be affected by business, financial, technological, and other factors and are subject to greater variation than the contractual cash flow of a bond. Furthermore, the forecasts for common stock cash flows extend indefinitely into the future because common stock has no maturity date. In addition to the greater uncertainty involved in forecasting cash flows for equity valuation, significant uncertainty exists in estimating an appropriate rate at which to discount those cash flows. In contrast with bond valuation, in which a discount rate can usually be based on market interest rates and bond ratings, equity valuation typically involves a more subjective and uncertain assessment of the appropriate discount

---

[8] In private business appraisal, such models are known as income models of valuation.

[9] The word "bond" throughout this section is used in the general sense and refers to all debt securities and loans.

rate.[10] Finally, in addition to the uncertainty associated with cash flows and discount rates, the equity analyst may need to address other issues, such as the value of corporate control or the value of unused assets.

The present value approach applied to stock valuation, therefore, presents a high order of complexity. Present value models are ambitious in what they attempt—an estimate of intrinsic value—and offer many challenges in application. Graham and Dodd (1934) suggested that the analyst consider stating a range of intrinsic values, and that suggestion remains a valid one. To that end, **sensitivity analysis** is an essential tool in applying discounted cash flow valuation. We discuss sensitivity analysis in more detail below.

Another type of absolute valuation is **asset-based valuation** that values a company on the basis of the market value of the assets or resources it controls. For appropriate companies, asset-based valuation can provide an independent estimate of value, and an analyst typically finds alternative, independent estimates of value to be useful. The following example describes instances in which this approach to absolute valuation could be appropriate.

EXAMPLE 5

Asset-Based Valuation

Analysts often apply asset-based valuation to natural resource companies. For example, a crude oil producer such as Petrobras (NYSE: PBR) might be valued on the basis of the market value of its current proven reserves in barrels of oil, minus a discount for estimated extraction costs. A forest industry company such as Weyerhaeuser (NYSE: WY) might be valued on the basis of the board meters (or board feet) of timber it controls. Today, however, fewer companies than in the past are involved only in natural resources extraction or production. For example, Occidental Petroleum (NYSE: OXY) features petroleum in its name but also has substantial chemical manufacturing operations. For such cases, the total company might be valued as the sum of its divisions, with the natural resource division valued on the basis of its proven resources.

3.3.2 Relative Valuation Models

Relative valuation models constitute the second broad type of going-concern valuation models. **Relative valuation models** estimate an asset's value relative to that of another asset. The idea underlying relative valuation is that similar assets should sell at similar prices, and relative valuation is typically implemented using price multiples (ratios of stock price to a fundamental such as cash flow per share) or enterprise multiples (ratios of the total value of common stock and debt net of cash and short-term investments to certain of a company's operating assets to a fundamental such as operating earnings).

Perhaps the most familiar price multiple is the price-to-earnings ratio (P/E), which is the ratio of a stock's market price to the company's earnings per share. A stock selling at a P/E that is low relative to the P/E of another closely comparable

---

[10] For some bond market instruments such as mortgage-backed securities and structured notes the estimation of cash flows and an appropriate discount rate can pose challenges comparable to equity investment.

stock (in terms of anticipated earnings growth rates and risk, for example) is *relatively undervalued* (a good buy) relative to the comparison stock. For brevity, an analyst might state simply *undervalued*, but the analyst must realize that if the comparison stock is overvalued (in an absolute sense, in relation to intrinsic value), so might be the stock being called undervalued. Therefore, it is useful to maintain the distinction between *undervalued* and *relatively undervalued*. Investing to exploit perceived mispricing in either case (absolute or relative mispricing) relies on a basis of differential expectations, that is, investor expectations that differ from and are more accurate than those reflected in market prices, as discussed earlier.

The more conservative investing strategies based on relative valuation involve overweighting (underweighting) relatively undervalued (overvalued) assets, with reference to benchmark weights. The more aggressive strategies allow short selling of perceived overvalued assets. Such aggressive approaches are known as relative value investing (or relative spread investing, if using implied discount factors). A classic example is **pairs trading** that utilizes pairs of closely related stocks (e.g., two automotive stocks), buying the relatively undervalued stock and selling short the relatively overvalued stock. Regardless of which direction the overall stock market goes, the investor will be better off to the extent that the relatively undervalued stock ultimately rises more (falls less) than the relatively overvalued stock.

Frequently, relative valuation involves a group of comparison assets, such as an industry group, rather than a single comparison asset. The application of relative valuation to equity is often called the method of comparables (or just comparables) and is the subject of a later reading.

EXAMPLE 6

Relative Valuation Models

While researching Smithson Genomics, Inc., a (fictitious) healthcare information services company, you encounter a difference of opinions. One analyst's report claims that Smithson is at least 15 percent *overvalued*, based on a comparison of its P/E with the median P/E of peer companies in the healthcare information services industry and taking account of company and peer group fundamentals. A second analyst asserts that Smithson is *undervalued* by 10 percent, based on a comparison of Smithson's P/E with the median P/E of the Russell 3000 Index, a broad-based U.S. equity index. Both analyses appear to be carefully executed and reported. Can both analysts be right?

Solution: Yes. The assertions of both analysts concern *relative* valuations, and their benchmarks for comparisons differ. The first analyst compared Smithson to its peers in the healthcare information services industry and considers the company to be *relatively overvalued* compared to that group. The second analyst compared Smithson to the overall market as represented by the Russell 3000 and considers the company to be *relatively undervalued* compared to that group. If the entire healthcare information services industry is undervalued in relation to the Russell 3000, both analysts can be right because they are making relative valuations.

The investment implications of each analyst's valuation generally would depend on additional considerations including whether the market price of the Russell 3000 fairly represents that index's intrinsic value and whether the market liquidity of an otherwise attractive investment would accommodate the intended position size. The analyst in many cases may want to supplement relative valuation with estimates of intrinsic value.

The method of comparables is characterized by a wide range of possible implementation choices; a later reading discusses various alternative price and enterprise multiples. Practitioners will often examine a number of price and enterprise multiples for the complementary information they can provide. In summary, the method of comparables does not specify intrinsic value without making the further assumption that the comparison asset is fairly valued. The method of comparables has the advantages of being simple, related to market prices, and grounded in a sound economic principle (that similar assets should sell at similar prices). Price and enterprise multiples are widely recognized by investors, so analysts can communicate the results of an absolute valuation in terms of a price or enterprise multiple.

3.3.3 *Valuation of the Total Entity and Its Components*

A variation to valuing a company as a single entity is to estimate its value as the sum of the estimated values of its various businesses considered as independent, going-concern entities. A valuation that sums the estimated values of each of the company's businesses as if each business were an independent going concern is known as a **sum-of-the-parts valuation**. The value derived using a sum-of-the-parts valuation is sometimes called the **breakup value** or **private market value**; however, such a valuation approach need not imply an expectation about restructuring.

Each of these valuation methods could potentially be applied either to the total entity or to one or more of its component parts. Example 7, showing a case in which a sum-of-the-parts valuation approach would be appropriate, refers to in-process research and development. **In-process research and development (IPRD)** are R&D costs relating to projects that are not yet completed, such as have been incurred by a company that is being acquired.

EXAMPLE 7

Sum-of-the-Parts Valuation

Schering-Plough Corporation's (NYSE:SGP) 10-K for 2007 indicates that the company has three reportable segments: Human Prescription Pharmaceuticals, Animal Health, and Consumer Health Care. The first segment, the company's pharmaceutical business, discovers and manufactures pharmaceutical products for humans. The company's animal health segment discovers and markets products for animals, such as vaccines. The consumer segment manufactures and markets OTC (over-the-counter) products, i.e., medications that can be sold without prescriptions, such as the company's non-sedating antihistamines and nasal decongestants. The consumer business also manufactures foot care products under the Dr. Scholl's brand and sun care products, such as Coppertone sun care products. The following two tables show the company's net sales by segment and operating profit by segment.

Net Sales by Segment (Dollars in Millions)

Year Ended 31 December	2007	2006	2005
Human Prescription	$10,173	$8,561	$7,564
Animal Health	1,251	910	851
Consumer Health Care	1,266	1,123	1,093
Consolidated net sales	$12,690	$10,594	$9,508

(Loss)/Profit by Segment (Dollars in Millions)

Year Ended 31 December	2007[1]	2006	2005
Human Prescription Pharmaceuticals	$(1,206)	$1,394	$733
Animal Health	(582)	120	120
Consumer Health Care	275	228	235
Corporate and other (including net interest income of $150 million, $125 million, and $13 million in 2007, 2006, and 2005, respectively)	298	(259)	(591)
Consolidated (loss)/profit before tax and cumulative effect of a change in accounting principle	$(1,215)	$1,483	$497

[1] In 2007, the Human Prescription Pharmaceuticals segment's loss includes $3.4 billion of purchase accounting items, including acquired in-process research and development of $3.2 billion. In 2007, the Animal Health segment's loss includes $721 million of purchase accounting items, including acquired in-process research and development of $600 million.

1. Why might an analyst use the sum-of-the-parts approach to value Schering Plough?

2. Footnote 1 to the operating profits table indicates that the two segments reporting losses had substantial "acquired in-process research and development." When these financial statements were prepared, U.S. accounting standards required companies to separately identify any portion of acquisition costs associated with acquiring in-process research and development (IPRD) and then to immediately expense those amounts. After the U.S. standard was

changed in December 2007 to converge with international accounting standards, immediate write-off is no longer required. With this background in mind, what operating profits would the segments have shown if the company had been permitted to capitalize rather than expense the in-process research and development? How would these IPRD charges and the nonrecurring nature of acquisition charges affect valuation generally?

3. How might an analyst use the above information in an analysis and valuation?

Solution to 1: An analyst might use the sum-of-the-parts approach to value Schering Plough because its three operating segments have very different economic profiles. For example, pharmaceutical companies rely on successful research efforts, and valuation requires an understanding of the company's specific products (including patent protection) and its pipeline of drugs undergoing requisite approvals prior to sale, whereas consumer products businesses rely on strong brands and efficient distribution channels. Analysis and valuation typically involve identifying competitors of the company of interest. The relevant group of competitors would differ for each of Schering Plough's businesses.

Solution to 2: If Schering Plough had been permitted to capitalize rather than expense the entire IPRD charges, its human pharmaceutical products segment would have reported operating profits of $1,994 million (the loss of $1,206 million adjusted for $3,200 million IPRD that would not have been expensed). The company's animal health segment would have reported operating profits of $18 million (the loss of $582 million adjusted for $600 million IPRD). In general, the IPRD charges and nonrecurring acquisition charges could adversely affect valuation, unless the analyst made the indicated adjustments.

Solution to 3: An analyst might use the above information to develop separate valuations for each of the segments, based on each segment's reported sales and profitability. The value of the company in total would be the sum of the value of each of the segments, adjusted for corporate items such as taxes, overhead expenses, and assets/liabilities not directly attributable to the separate operating segments.

The concept of a conglomerate discount often arises in connection with situations warranting a sum-of-the-parts valuation. **Conglomerate discount** refers to the concept that the market applies a discount to the stock of company operating in multiple, unrelated businesses compared to the stock of companies with narrower focuses. Alternative explanations for the conglomerate discount include 1) inefficiency of internal capital markets (i.e., companies' allocation of investment capital among divisions does not maximize overall shareholder value), 2) endogenous factors (i.e., poorly performing companies tend to expand by making acquisitions in unrelated businesses), and 3) research measurement errors (i.e., conglomerate discounts do not actually exist, and evidence suggesting that they do is a result of flawed measurement).[11] Examples in which conglomerate discounts appear most observable occur when companies divest parts of the company that have limited synergies with their core businesses.

Note that a break-up value in excess of a company's unadjusted going-concern value may prompt strategic actions such as a divestiture or spin-off.

3.3.4 Issues in Model Selection and Interpretation

How does one select a valuation model? The broad criteria for model selection are that the valuation model be:

► consistent with the characteristics of the company being valued;

► appropriate given the availability and quality of data; and

► consistent with the purpose of valuation, including the analyst's perspective.

Note that using more than one model can yield incremental insights.

Selection of a model consistent with the characteristics of the company being valued is facilitated by having a good understanding of the business, which is the first step in the valuation process. Part of understanding a company is understanding the nature of its assets and how it uses those assets to create value. For example, a bank is composed largely of marketable or potentially marketable assets and securities, and thus for a bank, a relative valuation based on assets (as recognized in accounting) has more relevance than a similar exercise for a service company with few marketable assets.

In selecting a model, data availability and quality can be limiting factors. For example, a dividend discount model is the simplest discounted cash flow model; but if a company has never paid dividends and no other information exists to assess a company's future dividend policy, an analyst may have more confidence applying an apparently more complex present value model. Similar considerations also apply in selecting a specific relative valuation approach. For example, meaningful comparisons using P/Es may be hard to make for a company with highly volatile or persistently negative earnings.

Model selection can also be influenced by the purpose of the valuation or the perspective of the analyst. For example, an investor seeking a controlling equity position in a company may elect to value the company based on forecasted free cash flows rather than forecasted dividends because such flows might potentially be redirected by such an acquirer without affecting the value of the acquisition (this valuation approach will be discussed in detail in another reading). When an analyst reads valuations and research reports prepared by others, the analyst should consider how the writer's perspective (and potential biases) may have affected the choice of a particular valuation approach and/or valuation inputs. Later readings, discussing present value models and price multiples, offer specific guidance on model selection.

As a final note to this introduction of model selection, it is important to recognize that professionals frequently use multiple valuation models or factors in common stock selection. According to the *Merrill Lynch Institutional Factor Survey* (2006), respondent institutional investors report using an average of approximately nine valuation factors in selecting stocks.[12] There are a variety of ways in

---

[11] See, for example, Lamont and Polk (2002) and Burch and Nanda (2003).

[12] In the report, the term *factors* covers valuation models as well as variables such as return on equity.

which multiple factors can be used in stock selection. One prominent way, stock screens, will be discussed in a later reading. As another example, analysts can rank each security in a given investment universe by relative attractiveness according to a particular valuation factor. The rankings for individual securities could be combined into a single composite ranking by assigning weights to the individual factors. Analysts may use a quantitative model to assign those weights.

3.4 Converting Forecasts to a Valuation

Converting forecasts to valuation involves more than inputting the forecast amounts to a model to obtain an estimate of the value of a company or its securities. Two important aspects of converting forecasts to valuation are sensitivity analysis and situational adjustments.

Sensitivity analysis is an analysis to determine how changes in an assumed input would affect the outcome. Some sensitivity analyses are common to most valuations. For example, a sensitivity analysis can be used to assess how a change in assumptions about a company's future growth—for example, decomposed by sales growth forecasts and margin forecasts—and/or a change in discount rates would affect the estimated value. Other sensitivity analyses depend on the context. For example, assume an analyst is aware that a competitor to the target company plans to introduce a competing product. Given uncertainty about the target company's competitive response—will the company lower prices to retain market share, offer discounts to its distributors, increase advertising, or change a product feature—the analyst could create a baseline forecast and then analyze how different competitive responses would affect the forecasted financials and in turn the estimated valuation.

Situational adjustments may be required to incorporate the valuation impact of specific issues. Three such issues that could affect value estimates are control premiums, lack of marketability discounts, and illiquidity discounts. A controlling ownership position in a company (e.g., more than 50 percent of outstanding shares, although a far smaller percentage often affords an investor the ability to significantly influence a company) carries with it control of the board of directors and the valuable options of redeploying the company's assets or changing the company's capital structure. The value of a stock investment that would give an investor a controlling position will generally reflect a **control premium**; that is, it will be higher than a valuation produced by a generic quantitative valuation expression that did not explicitly model such a premium. A second issue generally not explicitly modeled is that investors require an extra return to compensate for lack of a public market or lack of marketability. The value of non-publicly traded stocks generally reflects a **lack of marketability discount**. Among publicly traded (i.e., marketable) stocks, the prices of shares with less depth to their markets (less liquidity) often reflect an **illiquidity discount**. An illiquidity discount would also apply if an investor wishes to sell an amount of stock that is large relative to that stock's trading volume (assuming it is not large enough to constitute a controlling ownership). The price that could be realized for that block of shares would generally be lower than the market price for a smaller amount of stock, a so-called **blockage factor**.[13]

---

[13] Note, however, that the U.S. fair value accounting standard (SFAS No. 157) does not permit a blockage factor adjustment for actively traded shares. The value of a position is the product of the quoted price times the quantity held.

3.5 Applying the Valuation Conclusion: The Analyst's Role and Responsibilities

As noted earlier, the purposes of valuation and the intended consumer of the valuation vary:

▶ Analysts associated with investment firms' brokerage operations are perhaps the most visible group of analysts offering valuation judgments—their research reports are widely distributed to current and prospective retail and institutional brokerage clients. Analysts who work at brokerage firms are known as **sell-side analysts** (because brokerage firms sell investments and services to institutions such as investment management firms).[14]

▶ In investment management firms, trusts and bank trust departments, and similar institutions, an analyst may report valuation judgments to a portfolio manager or to an investment committee as input to an investment decision. Such analysts are widely known as **buy-side analysts**. The analyst's valuation expertise is important not only in investment disciplines involving security selection based on detailed company analysis, but also in highly quantitative investment disciplines; quantitative analysts work in developing, testing, and updating security selection methodologies.[15]

▶ Analysts at corporations may perform some valuation tasks similar to those of analysts at money management firms (e.g., when the corporation manages in-house a sponsored pension plan). Both corporate analysts and investment bank analysts may also identify and value companies that could become acquisition targets.

▶ Analysts at independent vendors of financial information usually offer valuation information and opinions in publicly distributed research reports, although some focus solely on organizing and analyzing corporate information.

In conducting their valuation activities, investment analysts play a critical role in collecting, organizing, analyzing, and communicating corporate information, and in some contexts, recommending appropriate investment actions based on sound analysis. When they do those tasks well, analysts help their clients, the capital markets, and the suppliers of capital:

▶ Analysts help their clients achieve their investment objectives by enabling those clients to make better buy and sell decisions.

▶ Analysts contribute to the efficient functioning of capital markets by providing analysis that leads to informed buy and sell decisions, and thus to asset prices that better reflect underlying values. When asset prices accurately reflect underlying values, capital flows more easily to its highest-value uses.

▶ Analysts benefit the suppliers of capital, including shareholders, when they are effective monitors of management's performance. This monitoring can serve to keep managers' actions more closely aligned with shareholders' best interests.[16]

---

[14] **Brokerage** is the business of acting as agents for buyers or sellers, usually in return for commissions.

[15] Ranking stocks by some measure(s) of relative attractiveness (subject to a risk control discipline), as we will discuss in more detail later, forms one key part of quantitative equity investment disciplines.

[16] See Jensen and Meckling (1976) for a classic analysis of the costs of stockholder–manager conflicts.

EXAMPLE 8

What Are Analysts Expected to Do?

When analysts at brokerage firms recommend a stock to the public that later performs very poorly, or when they fail to uncover negative corporate activities, they can sometimes come under public scrutiny. Industry leaders may then be asked to respond to such criticism and to comment on expectations about the role and responsibilities of analysts. One such instance occurred in the United States as a consequence of the late 2001 collapse of Enron Corporation, an energy, utility, trading, and telecommunication company. In testimony before the U.S. Senate (excerpted below), the President and CEO of AIMR (predecessor organization of CFA Institute) offered a summary of the working conditions and responsibilities of brokerage analysts. In the following passage, **due diligence** refers to investigation and analysis in support of a recommendation; the failure to exercise due diligence may sometimes result in liability according to various securities laws. "Wall Street analysts" refers to analysts working in the U.S. brokerage industry (sell-side analysts).

> What are Wall Street analysts expected to do? These analysts are assigned companies and industries to follow, are expected to research fully these companies and the industries in which they operate, and to forecast their future prospects. Based on this analysis, and using appropriate valuation models, they must then determine an appropriate fair price for the company's securities. After comparing this fair price to the current market price, the analyst is able to make a recommendation. If the analyst's "fair price" is significantly above the current market price, it would be expected that the stock be rated a "buy" or "market outperform."

> How do Wall Street analysts get their information? Through hard work and due diligence. They must study and try to comprehend the information in numerous public disclosure documents, such as the annual report to shareholders and regulatory filings . . . and gather the necessary quantitative and qualitative inputs to their valuation models.

> This due diligence isn't simply reading and analyzing annual reports. It also involves talking to company management, other company employees, competitors, and others, to get answers to questions that arise from their review of public documents. Talking to management must go beyond participation in regular conference calls. Not all questions can be voiced in those calls because of time constraints, for example, and because analysts, like journalists, rightly might not wish to "show their cards," and reveal the insights they have gotten through their hard work, by asking a particularly probing question in the presence of their competitors.

> Wall Street analysts are also expected to understand the dynamics of the industry and general economic conditions before finalizing a research report and making a recommendation. Therefore, in order for their firm to justify their continued employment, Wall Street analysts must issue research reports on their assigned companies and must make recommendations based on their reports to clients who purchase their firm's research.[17]

---

[17] Thomas A. Bowman, CFA. Testimony to the Committee on Governmental Affairs (excerpted) U. S. Senate, 27 February 2002.

From the beginnings of the movement to organize financial analysis as a profession rather than as a commercial trade, one guiding principle has been that the analyst must hold himself accountable to both standards of competence and standards of conduct. Competence in investment analysis requires a high degree of training, experience, and discipline.[18] Additionally, the investment professional is in a position of trust, requiring ethical conduct toward the public, clients, prospects, employers, employees, and fellow analysts. For CFA Institute members, this position of trust is reflected in the Code of Ethics and Standards of Professional Conduct, as well as in the Professional Conduct Statement that they submit annually. The Code and Standards, which guide the analyst to independent, well-researched, and well-documented analysis, are described in the following sections.

4   COMMUNICATING VALUATION RESULTS

Writing is an important part of an analyst's job. Whether a research report is for review by an investment committee or a portfolio manager in an investment management firm, or for distribution to the retail or institutional clients of a brokerage firm, research reports share several common elements. In this section we discuss the content of an effective research report, one adaptable format for writing such a report, and the analyst's responsibilities in preparing a research report. In many cases, institutional norms will guide the format and content of the written report.

4.1 Contents of a Research Report

A primary determinant of a research report's contents is what the intended readers seek to gain from reading the report. From a sell-side analyst's report, an intended reader would be interested in the investment recommendation. In evaluating how much attention and weight to give to a recommendation, the reader will look for persuasive supporting arguments. A key element supporting any recommendation is the intrinsic value of the security.

Given the importance of the estimated intrinsic value of the security, most research reports provide the reader with information about the key assumptions and expectations underlying that estimated intrinsic value. The information typically includes an update on the company's financial and operating results, a description of relevant aspects of the current macroeconomic and industry context, and an analysis and forecast for the industry and company. Because some readers of research reports are interested in background information, some reports contain detailed historical descriptive statistics about the industry and company.

A report can include specific forecasts, key valuation inputs (e.g., the estimated cost of capital), a description of the valuation model, and a discussion of qualitative factors and other considerations that affect valuation. Superior research reports also objectively address the uncertainty associated with investing in the security, and/or the valuation inputs involving the greatest amount of uncertainty. By converting forecasts into estimated intrinsic value, a comparison

---

[18] Competence in this sense is reflected in the examination and work experience requirements that are prerequisites for obtaining the CFA designation.

between intrinsic value and market price provides the basis for an investment recommendation. When a research report states a target price for a stock (based on its intrinsic value) in its investment recommendation, the report should clarify the basis for computing the target, a time frame for reaching the target, and information on the uncertainty of reaching the target. An investment recommendation may be accompanied by an explanation of the underlying rationale, i.e., investment thesis, which summarizes why a particular investment offer would provide a way to profit from the analyst's outlook.

Although a well-written report cannot compensate for a poor analysis, a poorly written report can detract from the credibility of an excellent analysis. Writing an effective research report is a challenging task. In summary, an effective research report:

► contains timely information;

► is written in clear, incisive language;

► is objective and well researched, with key assumptions clearly identified;

► distinguishes clearly between facts and opinions;

► contains analysis, forecasts, valuation, and a recommendation that are internally consistent;

► presents sufficient information to allow a reader to critique the valuation;

► states the key risk factors involved in an investment in the company; and

► discloses any potential conflicts of interests faced by the analyst.

Although these general characteristics are all desirable attributes of a useful and respected report, in some situations the requirements are more specific. For example, regulations governing disclosures of conflicts and potential conflicts of interest vary across countries, so an analyst must remain up-to-date on relevant disclosure requirements. As another example, in some situations, investment recommendations are affected by policies of the firm employing an analyst; for example, a policy might require that a security's price must be X percent below its estimated intrinsic value to be considered a "buy." Even in the absence of such a policy, an analyst needs to maintain a conceptual distinction between a "good company" and a "good investment" because returns on a common stock investment always depend on the price paid for the stock, whether the business prospects of the issuing company are good, bad, or indifferent.

EXAMPLE 9

Research Reports

The following two passages are closely based on the valuation discussions of actual companies in two actual short research notes. The dates and company names used in the passages, however, are fictional.

A. At a recent multiple of 6.5, our earnings per share multiple for 2007, the shares were at a discount to our projection of 14 percent growth for the period . . . MXI has two operating segments . . . In valuing the segments separately, employing relative acquisition multiples and peer mean values, we found fair value to be above recent market value. In addition, the shares trade at a discount to book value (0.76). Based on the value indicated by these two valuation metrics, we view the shares as worth holding. However, in light of a weaker economy over the near term, dampening demand for MXI's services, our enthusiasm is tempered. [*Elsewhere in the report, MXI is evaluated as being in the firm's top category of investment attractiveness.*]

B. Although TXI outperformed the overall stock market by 20 percent since the start of the year, it definitely looks undervalued as shown by its low multiples . . . [*the values of the P/E and another multiple are stated*]. According to our dividend discount model valuation, we get to a valuation of €3.08 implying an upside potential of 36.8 percent based on current prices. The market outperform recommendation is reiterated. [*In a parenthetical expression, the current dividend, assumed dividend growth rates, and their time horizons are given. The analyst also briefly explains and calculates the discount rate. Elsewhere in the report the current price of TXI is given as €2.25.*]

Although some of the concepts mentioned in the two passages may not yet be familiar, you can begin to assess the two reporting efforts.

Passage A communicates the analysis awkwardly. The meaning of "the shares were at a discount to our projection of 14 percent growth for the period" is not completely clear. Presumably the analyst is projecting the earnings growth rate for 2007 and stating that the P/E is low in relation to that expected growth rate. The analyst next discusses valuing MXI as the sum of its divisions. In describing the method as "employing relative acquisition multiples and peer mean values," the analyst does not convey a clear picture of what was done. It is probable that companies similar to each of MXI's divisions were identified; then the mean or average value of some unidentified multiple for those comparison companies was calculated and used as the basis for valuing MXI. The writer is vague, however, on the extent of MXI's undervaluation. The analyst states that MXI's price is below its book value (an accounting measure of shareholders' investment) but draws no comparison with the average price-to-book value ratio for stocks similar to MXI, for example. (The price-to-book ratio is discussed in a later reading.) Finally, the verbal summation is feeble and hedged. Although filled with technical verbiage, Passage A does not communicate a coherent valuation of MXI.

In the second sentence of Passage B, by contrast, the analyst gives an explicit valuation of TXI and the information needed to critique it. The reader can also see that €3.08, which is elsewhere stated in the research note as the target price for TXI, implies the stated price appreciation potential for TXI [(€3.08/€2.25) − 1, approximately 37 percent]. In the first sentence in Passage B, the analyst gives information that might support the conclusion that TXI is undervalued, although the statement lacks strength because the analyst does not explain why the P/E is "low." The verbal summary is clear. Using less space than the analyst in Passage A, the analyst in Passage B has done a better job of communicating the results of his valuation.

4.2 Format of a Research Report

Equity research reports may be logically presented in several ways. The firm in which the analyst works sometimes specifies a fixed format for consistency and quality control purposes. Without claiming superiority to other ways to organize a report, we offer Exhibit 2 as an adaptable format by which the analyst can communicate research and valuation findings in detail. (Shorter research reports and research notes obviously may employ a more compact format.)

EXHIBIT 2	A Format for Research Reports		
Section	**Purpose**	**Content**	**Comments**
Table of Contents	▶ Show report's organization	▶ Consistent with narrative in sequence and language	This is typically used in very long research reports only.
Summary and Investment Conclusion	▶ Communicate the large picture ▶ Communicate major specific conclusions of the analysis ▶ Recommend an investment course of action	▶ Capsule description of the company ▶ Major recent developments ▶ Earnings projections ▶ Other major conclusions ▶ Valuation summary ▶ Investment action	An executive summary; may be called simply "Summary."
Business Summary	▶ Present the company in more detail ▶ Communicate a detailed understanding of the company's economics and current situation ▶ Provide and explain specific forecasts[a]	▶ Company description to the divisional level ▶ Industry analysis ▶ Competitive analysis ▶ Historical performance ▶ Financial forecasts	Reflects the first and second steps of the valuation process. Financial forecasts should be explained adequately and reflect quality of earnings analysis.
Risks	▶ Alert readers to the risk factors in investing in the security	▶ Possible negative industry developments ▶ Possible negative regulatory and legal developments ▶ Possible negative company developments ▶ Risks in the forecasts ▶ Other risks	Readers should have enough information to determine how the analyst is defining and assessing the risks specific to investing in the security.
Valuation	▶ Communicate a clear and careful valuation	▶ Description of model(s) used ▶ Recapitulation of inputs ▶ Statement of conclusions	Readers should have enough information to critique the analysis.

(Exhibit continued on next page . . .)

EXHIBIT 2	(continued)		
Section	**Purpose**	**Content**	**Comments**
Historical and Pro Forma Tables	▶ Organize and present data to support the analysis in the Business Summary		This is generally a separate section in longer research reports only. Many reports fold all or some of this information into the Business Summary section.

ᵃ Actual outcomes can and generally will differ from forecasts. A discussion of key random factors and an examination of the sensitivity of outcomes to the outcomes of those factors are useful.

4.3 Research Reporting Responsibilities

All analysts have an obligation to provide substantive and meaningful content in a clear and comprehensive report format. Analysts who are CFA Institute members, however, have an additional and overriding responsibility to adhere to the Code of Ethics and the Standards of Professional Conduct in all activities pertaining to their research reports. The CFA Institute Code of Ethics states:

> Members of CFA Institute must . . . use reasonable care and exercise independent professional judgment when conducting investment analysis, making investment recommendations, taking investment actions, and engaging in other professional activities.

Going beyond this general statement of responsibility, some specific Standards of Professional Conduct particularly relevant to an analyst writing a research report are shown in Exhibit 3.

EXHIBIT 3	Selected CFA Institute Standards of Professional Conduct Pertaining to Research Reports*
Standard of Professional Conduct	**Responsibility**
I(B)	Members and Candidates must use reasonable care and judgment to achieve and maintain independence and objectivity in their professional activities. Members and Candidates must not offer, solicit, or accept any gift, benefit, compensation, or consideration that reasonably could be expected to compromise their own or another's independence and objectivity.
I(C)	Members and Candidates must not knowingly make any misrepresentations relating to investment analysis, recommendations, actions, or other professional activities.

(Exhibit continued on next page . . .)

EXHIBIT 3   (continued)

Standard of Professional Conduct	Responsibility
V(A)1	Members and Candidates must exercise diligence, independence, and thoroughness in analyzing investments, making investment recommendations, and taking investment actions.
V(A)2	Members and Candidates must have a reasonable and adequate basis, supported by appropriate research and investigation, for any investment analysis, recommendation, or action.
V(B)1	Members and Candidates must disclose to clients and prospective clients the basic format and general principles of the investment processes used to analyze investments, select securities, and construct portfolios and must promptly disclose any changes that might materially affect those processes.
V(B)2	Members and Candidates must use reasonable judgment in identifying which factors are important to their investment analyses, recommendations, or actions and include those factors in communications with clients and prospective clients.
V(B)3	Members and Candidates must distinguish between fact and opinion in the presentation of investment analysis and recommendations.
V(C)	Members and Candidates must develop and maintain appropriate records to support their investment analysis, recommendations, actions, and other investment-related communications with clients and prospective clients.

* See the most recent edition of the CFA Institute *Standards of Practice Handbook* (www.cfainstitute.org).

SUMMARY

In this reading, we have discussed the scope of equity valuation, outlined the valuation process, introduced valuation concepts and models, discussed the analyst's role and responsibilities in conducting valuation, and described the elements of an effective research report in which analysts communicate their valuation analysis.

▶ Valuation is the estimation of an asset's value based on variables perceived to be related to future investment returns, or based on comparisons with closely similar assets.

▶ The intrinsic value of an asset is its value given a hypothetically complete understanding of the asset's investment characteristics.

▶ The assumption that the market price of a security can diverge from its intrinsic value—as suggested by the rational efficient markets formulation of efficient market theory—underpins active investing.

▶ Intrinsic value incorporates the going-concern assumption, that is, the assumption that a company will continue operating for the foreseeable future. In contrast, liquidation value is the company's value if it were dissolved and its assets sold individually.

▶ Fair value is the price at which an asset (or liability) would change hands if neither buyer nor seller were under compulsion to buy/sell and both were informed about material underlying facts.

▶ In addition to stock selection by active traders, valuation is also used for:
  ▶ inferring (extracting) market expectations;
  ▶ evaluating corporate events;
  ▶ issuing fairness opinions;
  ▶ evaluating business strategies and models; and
  ▶ appraising private businesses.

▶ The valuation process has five steps:
  1. Understanding the business.
  2. Forecasting company performance.
  3. Selecting the appropriate valuation model.
  4. Converting forecasts to a valuation.
  5. Applying the analytical results in the form of recommendations and conclusions.

▶ Understanding the business includes evaluating industry prospects, competitive position, and corporate strategies, all of which contribute to making more accurate forecasts. Understanding the business also involves analysis of financial reports, including evaluating the quality of a company's earnings.

▶ In forecasting company performance, a top-down forecasting approach moves from macroeconomic forecasts to industry forecasts and then to individual company and asset forecasts. A bottom-up forecasting approach aggregates individual company forecasts to industry forecasts, which in turn may be aggregated to macroeconomic forecasts.

► Selecting the appropriate valuation approach means choosing an approach that is:

  ► consistent with the characteristics of the company being valued;

  ► appropriate given the availability and quality of the data; and

  ► consistent with the analyst's valuation purpose and perspective.

► Two broad categories of valuation models are absolute valuation models and relative valuation models.

  ► Absolute valuation models specify an asset's intrinsic value, supplying a point estimate of value that can be compared with market price. Present value models of common stock (also called discounted cash flow models) are the most important type of absolute valuation model.

  ► Relative valuation models specify an asset's value relative to the value of another asset. As applied to equity valuation, relative valuation is also known as the method of comparables, which involves comparison of a stock's price multiple to a benchmark price multiple. The benchmark price multiple can be based on a similar stock or on the average price multiple of some group of stocks.

► Two important aspects of converting forecasts to valuation are sensitivity analysis and situational adjustments.

  ► Sensitivity analysis is an analysis to determine how changes in an assumed input would affect the outcome of an analysis.

  ► Situational adjustments include control premiums (premiums for a controlling interest in the company), discounts for lack of marketability (discounts reflecting the lack of a public market for the company's shares), and illiquidity discounts (discounts reflecting the lack of a liquid market for the company's shares).

► Applying valuation conclusions depends on the purpose of the valuation.

► In performing valuations, analysts must hold themselves accountable to both standards of competence and standards of conduct.

► An effective research report:

  ► contains timely information;

  ► is written in clear, incisive language;

  ► is objective and well researched, with key assumptions clearly identified;

  ► distinguishes clearly between facts and opinions;

  ► contains analysis, forecasts, valuation, and a recommendation that are internally consistent;

  ► presents sufficient information that the reader can critique the valuation;

  ► states the risk factors for an investment in the company; and

  ► discloses any potential conflicts of interests faced by the analyst.

► Analysts have an obligation to provide substantive and meaningful content. CFA Institute members have an additional overriding responsibility to adhere to the CFA Institute Code of Ethics and relevant specific Standards of Professional Conduct.

PRACTICE PROBLEMS FOR READING 34

1. Critique the statement: "No equity investor needs to understand valuation models because real-time market prices for equities are easy to obtain online."

2. The reading defined intrinsic value as "the value of an asset given a hypothetically complete understanding of the asset's investment characteristics." Discuss why "hypothetically" is included in the definition and the practical implication(s).

3. **A.** Explain why liquidation value is generally not relevant to estimating intrinsic value for profitable companies.

   B. Explain whether making a going-concern assumption would affect the value placed on a company's inventory.

4. Explain how the procedure for using a valuation model to infer market expectations about a company's future growth differs from using the same model to obtain an independent estimate of value.

5. Example 1, based on a study of Intel Corporation that used a present value model (Cornell 2001), examined what future revenue growth rates were consistent with Intel's stock price of $61.50 just prior to its earnings announcement, and $43.31 only five days later. The example states, "Using a conservatively low discount rate, Cornell estimated that Intel's price before the announcement, $61.50, was consistent with a forecasted growth rate of 20 percent a year for the subsequent 10 years and then 6 percent per year thereafter." Discuss the implications of using a higher discount rate than Cornell did.

6. Discuss how understanding a company's business (the first step in equity valuation) might be useful in performing a sensitivity analysis related to a valuation of the company.

7. In a research note on the ordinary shares of the Milan Fashion Group (MFG) dated early July 2007 when a recent price was €7.73 and projected annual dividends were €0.05, an analyst stated a target price of €9.20. The research note did not discuss how the target price was obtained or how it should be interpreted. Assume the target price represents the expected price of MFG. What further specific pieces of information would you need to form an opinion on whether MFG was fairly valued, overvalued, or undervalued?

Practice Problems and Solutions: *Equity Asset Valuation*, Second Edition, by Jerald Pinto, CFA, Elaine Henry, CFA, Thomas Robinson, CFA, and John Stowe, CFA. Copyright © 2009 by CFA Institute. Reprinted with permission.

8. You are researching XMI Corporation (XMI). XMI has shown steady earnings per share growth (18 percent a year during the last seven years) and trades at a very high multiple to earnings (its P/E is currently 40 percent above the average P/E for a group of the most comparable stocks). XMI has generally grown through acquisition, by using XMI stock to purchase other companies whose stock traded at lower P/Es. In investigating the financial disclosures of these acquired companies and talking to industry contacts, you conclude that XMI has been forcing the companies it acquires to accelerate the payment of expenses before the acquisition deals are closed. As one example, XMI asks acquired companies to immediately pay all pending accounts payable, whether or not they are due. Subsequent to the acquisition, XMI reinstitutes normal expense payment patterns.

   A. What are the effects of XMI's pre-acquisition expensing policies?

   B. The statement is made that XMI's "P/E is currently 40 percent above the average P/E for a group of the most comparable stocks." What type of valuation model is implicit in that statement?

SOLUTIONS FOR READING 34

1. The statement is flawed in at least two ways. First, active investors believe that stock prices do not always accurately reflect all relevant information on the security; for such investors, knowledge of equity valuation models is important for identifying investment opportunities because they represent a way to translate the investor's forecasts into value estimates for comparison with market prices. Thus, the "all" in "all investors" is misleading. Second, not all equities are publicly traded and have market prices, and the most recent market price can be stale for the many public equities that trade only infrequently.

2. No matter how diligent the analyst, some uncertainty always exists concerning 1) the accuracy of the analyst's forecasts and 2) whether an intrinsic value estimate accounts for all sources of risk reflected in market price. Thus, knowledge of a stock's investment characteristics is always incomplete. The practical consequences are that an investor can only estimate intrinsic value and active security selection carries the risk of making mistakes in estimating value.

3. A. Liquidation value is typically not relevant to estimating intrinsic value for profitable companies because, in general, value would be destroyed by selling such a company's assets individually. Stated another way, the value added by being a going concern is a relevant investment characteristic that an intrinsic value estimate would recognize.

   B. A going-concern assumption generally increases the value placed on a company's inventory relative to not making that assumption. Usually, inventory that can be sold in the company's regular distribution channels would realize higher amounts than inventory that must be sold immediately because a company is being liquidated.

4. The key difference is that for inferring investor expectations the market price is used as the model input for value whereas for obtaining an independent estimate of value, value is left as the unknown in the model. In the latter case, value is estimated based on the analyst's estimates for the variables that determine value.

5. Consider the present value of a single cash flow. If one increased the discount rate, one would also need to increase the cash flow if a constant present value were to be maintained. By a similar argument, if Cornell had used a higher discount rate, he would have needed to project a higher level of assumed future cash flows than he did for their present value to have been consistent with the given pre-announcement price of $61.50. Thus, the implied growth rate consistent with a price of $61.50 would have been higher than the 20 percent growth rate estimated by Cornell.

6. An understanding of the company's business facilitates a focus on the key business aspects that affect value, and from a practical perspective, highlights the critical inputs to a forecast that should be tested using sensitivity analysis.

7. You need to know 1) the time horizon for the price target and 2) the required rate of return on MFG. The price target of €9.20 represents a potential 20 percent return from investing in the stock if the time horizon

is one year, calculated as $(€9.20 + €0.05)/€7.73 - 1.0 = 0.197$; without a time frame, however, you cannot evaluate the attractiveness of that return. Given that the time frame for the return is established, you need to have an estimate of the required rate of return over the same time horizon.

If the expected return of 19.7 percent exceeds the security's required return for the same horizon—in other words, if the share's expected alpha is positive—then MFG would appear to be undervalued.

8. A. Accelerating the payment of expenses reduces the acquired companies' last reported pre-acquisition cash flow. Accelerating expense recognition reduces the acquired companies' last reported pre-acquisition earnings. XMI's cash flow and earnings growth rates following the acquisitions would be expected to be biased upwards because of the depressed levels for the acquirees.

B. That is an example of a relative valuation model (or the method of comparables), which compares a company's market multiple to the multiples of similar companies.

45/8 41 1/16
5 1/2   5 1/2   − 3/8
5 1/2   5 1/2   − 1/16
20 5/8   21 3/16
17 3/8   **18 1/8** +   7/8
16 1/2   6 1/2   −   1/2
7 1/4   6 1/2   6 1/2 −
15/16   31/32   − 1/8
9/16
9/16   9/16
1 9/32
7 15/16   7 13/16   7 15/16
2 5/8   2 11/32   **2 1/2** +
2 3/4   2 1/4   2 1/4
6 1/8   12 1/16   11 3/8   11 3/8 +
87   33 3/4   33   33 1/8 −
502   25 5/8   24 9/16   25 5/8 +
833   12   11 5/8   11 7/8 +
16   10 1/2   10 1/2   10 1/2 −
78   15 5/8   15 13/16   15 5/8 −
4508   9 1/16   8 1/4   8 1/8 +
430   11 1/4   10 1/8

RETURN CONCEPTS

by John Stowe, CFA, Thomas Robinson, CFA, Jerald Pinto, CFA, and Dennis McLeavey, CFA

LEARNING OUTCOMES

The candidate should be able to:	Mastery
a. distinguish among expected holding period return, realized holding period return, required return, return from convergence of price to intrinsic value, discount rate, and internal rate of return;	☐
b. calculate and interpret an equity risk premium using historical and forward-looking estimation approaches;	☐
c. estimate the required return on an equity investment using the capital asset pricing model (CAPM), the Fama–French model (FFM), the Pastor–Stambaugh model (PSM), macroeconomic multifactor models, and the build-up method (e.g., bond yield plus risk premium);	☐
d. explain beta estimation for public companies, thinly traded public companies, and nonpublic companies;	☐
e. describe strengths and weaknesses of methods used to estimate the required return on an equity investment;	☐
f. explain international considerations in required return estimation;	☐
g. explain and calculate the weighted average cost of capital for a company;	☐
h. evaluate the appropriateness of using a particular rate of return as a discount rate, given a description of the cash flow to be discounted and other relevant facts.	☐

Equity Asset Valuation, Second Edition, by Jerald Pinto, CFA, Elaine Henry, CFA, Thomas Robinson, CFA, and John Stowe, CFA. Copyright © 2009 by CFA Institute. Reprinted with permission.

1   INTRODUCTION

The return on an investment is a fundamental element in evaluating an investment:

▶ Investors evaluate an investment in terms of the return they expect to earn on it compared to a level of return viewed as fair given everything they know about the investment, including its risk.

▶ Analysts need to specify the appropriate rate or rates with which to discount expected future cash flows when using present value models of stock value.

This reading presents and illustrates key return measures relevant to valuation and is organized as follows. Section 2 provides an overview of return concepts. Section 3 presents the chief approaches to estimating the equity risk premium, a key input in determining the required rate of return on equity in several important models. With a means to estimate the equity risk premium in hand, Section 4 discusses and illustrates the major models for estimating the required return on equity. Section 5 presents the weighted average cost of capital, a discount rate used when finding the present value of cash flows to all providers of capital. Section 6 presents certain facts concerning discount rate selection. A summary and practice problems conclude the reading.

2   RETURN CONCEPTS

A sound investment decision depends critically on the correct use and evaluation of rate of return measures. The following sections explain the major return concepts most relevant to valuation.[1]

2.1 Holding Period Return

The holding period rate of return (for short, the **holding period return**)[2] is the return earned from investing in an asset over a specified time period. The specified time period is the holding period under examination, whether it is one day, two weeks, four years, or any other length of time. To use a hypothetical return figure of 0.8 percent for a one-day holding period, we would say that "the one-day holding period return is 0.8 percent" (or equivalently, "the one-day return is 0.8 percent" or "the return is 0.8 percent over one day"). Such returns can be separated into investment income and price appreciation components. If the asset is a share purchased now (at $t = 0$, with t denoting time) and sold at $t = H$, the holding period is $t = 0$ to $t = H$ and the holding period return is

---

[1] This is by no means an exhaustive list of return concepts. In particular, other areas of finance such as performance evaluation make use of return concepts not covered here (e.g., time-weighted rate of return).

[2] References to *return* in this reading refer to *rate of return*, not a money amount of return.

$$r = \frac{D_H + P_H}{P_0} - 1 = \frac{D_H}{P_0} + \frac{P_H - P_0}{P_0} = \text{Dividend yield} + \text{Price appreciation return}$$ (1)

where D_t and P_t are per-share dividends and share price at time t. Equation 1 shows that the holding period return is the sum of two components: dividend yield (D_H/P_0) and price appreciation return $([P_H - P_0]/P_0)$, also known as the capital gains yield.

Equation 1 assumes, for simplicity, that any dividend is received at the end of the holding period. More generally, the holding period return would be calculated based on reinvesting any dividend received between $t = 0$ and $t = H$ in additional shares on the date the dividend was received at the price then available. Holding period returns are sometimes annualized—e.g., the return for a specific holding period may be converted to an annualized return, usually based on compounding at the holding period rate. For example, $(1.008)^{365} - 1 = 17.3271$ or 1,732.71 percent, is one way to annualize a one-day 0.80 percent return. As the example shows, however, annualizing holding period returns, when the holding period is a fraction of a year, is unrealistic when the reinvestment rate is not an actual, available reinvestment rate.

2.2 Realized and Expected (Holding Period) Return

In the expression for the holding period return, the selling price, P_H, and in general, the dividend, D_H, are not known as of $t = 0$. For a holding period in the past, the selling price and the dividend are known, and the return is called a realized holding period return, or more simply, a realized return. For example, with a beginning price of €50.00, an ending or selling price of €52.00 six months later, and a dividend equal to €1.00 (all amounts referring to the past), the realized return is €1.00/€50.00 + (€52.00 − €50.00)/€50.00 = 0.02 + 0.04 = 0.06 or 6 percent over 6 months. In forward-looking contexts, holding-period returns are random variables because future selling prices and dividends may both take on a range of values. Nevertheless, an investor can form an expectation concerning the dividend and selling price and thereby have an **expected holding-period return**, or simply expected return, for the stock that consists of the expected dividend yield and the expected price appreciation return.

Although professional investors often formulate expected returns based on explicit valuation models, a return expectation does not have to be based on a model or on specific valuation knowledge. Any investor can have a personal viewpoint on the future returns on an asset. In fact, because investors formulate expectations in varying ways and on the basis of different information, different investors generally have different expected returns for an asset. The comparison point for interpreting the investment implication of the expected return for an asset is its required return, the subject of the next section.

2.3 Required Return

A **required rate of return** (for short, required return) is the minimum level of expected return that an investor requires in order to invest in the asset over a specified time period, given the asset's riskiness. It represents the opportunity cost for investing in the asset—the highest level of expected return available elsewhere from investments of similar risk. As the opportunity cost for investing in the asset, the required return represents a threshold value for being fairly compensated for the risk of the asset. If the investor's expected return exceeds the required return, the asset will appear to be undervalued because it is expected to return more-than-fair compensation for the asset's risk. By contrast, if the expected return on the asset falls short of the required rate of return, the asset will appear to be overvalued.

The valuation examples presented in these readings will illustrate the use of required return estimates grounded in market data (such as observed asset returns) and explicit models for required return. We will refer to any such estimate of the required return used in an example as *the* required return on the asset for the sake of simplicity, although other estimates are usually defensible. For example, using the capital asset pricing model (discussed in more detail later), the required return for an asset is equal to the risk-free rate of return plus a premium (or discount) related to the asset's sensitivity to market returns. That sensitivity can be estimated based on returns for an observed market portfolio and the asset. That is one example of a required return estimate grounded in a formal model based on marketplace variables (rather than a single investor's return requirements). Market variables should contain information about investors' asset risk perceptions and their level of risk aversion, both of which are important in determining fair compensation for risk.

In this reading, we use the notation r for the required rate of return on the asset being discussed. The required rate of return on common stock and debt are also known as the **cost of equity** and **cost of debt**, respectively, taking the perspective of the issuer. To raise new capital, the issuer would have to price the security to offer a level of expected return that is competitive with the expected returns being offered by similarly risky securities. The required return on a security is therefore the issuer's marginal cost for raising additional capital of the same type.

The difference between the expected return and the required rate of return on an asset is the asset's expected alpha (or *ex ante* alpha) or expected abnormal return:

$$\text{Expected alpha} = \text{Expected return} - \text{Required return} \qquad \textbf{(2a)}$$

When an asset is efficiently priced (its price equals its intrinsic value), expected return should equal required return and the expected alpha is zero. In investment decision-making and valuation, the focus is on expected alpha. However, to evaluate the actual results of an investment discipline, the analyst would examine realized alpha. Realized alpha (or *ex post* alpha) over a given holding period is

$$\begin{aligned}\text{Realized alpha} = \ &\text{Actual holding-period return} \\ &- \text{Contemporaneous required return}\end{aligned} \qquad \textbf{(2b)}$$

Estimates of required returns are essential for using present value models of value. Present value models require the analyst to establish appropriate discount rates for determining the present values of expected future cash flows.

Expected return and *required rate of return* are sometimes used interchangeably in conversation and writing.[3] As discussed, that is not necessarily correct. When

---

[3] Some financial models—such as the standard capital asset pricing model discussed later—assume that investors have the same expectations about the parameters of assets' return distributions and derive the level of required return for risky assets that clears the market for those assets. In the context of such a model with homogenous expectations, the required return is also *the* expected return for the asset. In discussions of such models, therefore, *expected return* and *required return* are used interchangeably.

current price equals perceived value, expected return should be the same as the required rate of return. However, when price is below (above) the perceived value, expected return will exceed (be less than) the required return as long as the investor expects price to converge to value over his or her time horizon.

Given an investor's expected holding-period return, we defined expected alpha in relation to a required return estimate. In the next section, we show the conversion of a value estimate into an estimate of expected-holding period return.

2.4 Expected Return Estimates from Intrinsic Value Estimates

When an asset is mispriced, one of several outcomes is possible. Take the case of an asset that an investor believes is 25 percent undervalued in the marketplace. Over the investment time horizon, the mispricing may:

► increase (the asset may become more undervalued);

► stay the same (the asset may remain 25 percent undervalued);

► be partially corrected (e.g., the asset may become undervalued by 15 percent);

► be corrected (price changes to exactly reflect value); or

► reverse, or be overcorrected (the asset may become overvalued).

Generally, convergence of price to value is the equilibrium and anticipated outcome when the investor's value estimate is more accurate than the market's, as reflected in the market price. In that case, the investor's expected rate of return has two components: the required return (earned on the asset's current market price) and a return from convergence of price to value.

We can illustrate how expected return may be estimated when an investor's value estimate, V_0, is different from the market price. Suppose the investor expects price to fully converge to value over τ years. $(V_0 - P_0)/P_0$ is an estimate of the return from convergence over the period of that length, essentially the expected alpha for the asset stated on a per-period basis. With r_τ being the required return on a periodic (not annualized) basis and $E(R_\tau)$ the expected holding-period return on the same basis, then:

$$E(R_\tau) \approx r_\tau + \frac{V_0 - P_0}{P_0}$$

Although only an approximation, the expression does illustrate that an expected return can be viewed as the sum of two returns: the required return and a return from convergence of price to intrinsic value.[4]

To illustrate, as of the end of the first quarter of 2007, one estimate of the required return for Proctor & Gamble (NYSE: PG) shares was 7.6 percent. At a time when PG's market price was $63.16, a research report estimated PG's

---

[4] The expression assumes that the required rate of return and intrinsic value are static over the holding period and that convergence happens smoothly over the holding period (or all at once at its end). We conduct the analysis on a periodic (holding period) basis because one cannot assume reinvestment at a rate incorporating a return from convergence is feasible. For example, a 12.4 percent return from convergence earned over a month would be over 300 percent annualized, which is not meaningful as a performance expectation.

intrinsic value at $71.00 share. Thus, in the report author's view, PG was under-valued by $V_0 - P_0 = \$71 - \$63.16 = \$7.84$, or 12.4 percent as a fraction of the market price ($7.84/$63.16). If price were expected to converge to value in exactly one year, an investor would earn 7.6% + 12.4% = 20%. The expected alpha of Proctor & Gamble is 12.4 percent per annum. But if the investor expected the undervaluation to disappear by the end of nine months, then the investor might anticipate achieving a return of about 18 percent over the 9-month period. The required return on a nine-month basis ($\tau = 9/12 = 0.75$) is $(1.076)^{0.75} - 1 = 0.0565$ or 5.65 percent, so the total expected return is

$$E(R_\tau) \approx r_\tau + \frac{V_0 - P_0}{P_0}$$

$$= 5.65\% + 12.4\%$$

$$= 18.05 \text{ percent}$$

In this case, expected alpha is 12.4 percent on a nine-month basis which, when added to the required return of 5.65 percent on a nine-month basis, gives an estimate of the nine-month holding period return of 18.05 percent. Another possibility is that price converges to value in two years. The expected two-year expected holding period return would be 15.78% + 12.4% = 28.18%, in which the required return component is calculated as $(1.076)^2 - 1 = 0.1578$. This expected return based on two-year convergence could be compared to the expected return based on one-year convergence of 20 percent by annualizing it: $(1.2818)^{1/2} - 1 = 0.1322$ or 13.22 percent per year.

Active investors essentially "second-guess" the market price. The risks of that activity include the risks that 1) their value estimates are not more accurate than the market price, and that, 2) even if they are more accurate, the value discrepancy may not narrow over the investors' time horizon. Clearly, the convergence component of expected return can be quite risky.

EXAMPLE 1

An Analyst Case Study (1): The Required Return on Microsoft Shares

Thomas Weeramantry and Françoise Delacour are co-managers of a U.S.-based diversified global equity portfolio. They are researching Microsoft Corporation (NASDAQ-GS: MSFT),[5] the largest U.S.-headquartered technology sector company. Weeramantry gathered a number of research reports on MSFT and began his analysis of the company in late August 2007, when the current price for MSFT was $28.27. In one research report, the analyst offered the following facts, opinions, and estimates concerning MSFT:

▶ The most recent quarterly dividend was $0.10 per share. Over the coming year, two more quarterly dividends of $0.10 are expected, followed by two quarterly dividends of $0.11 per share.

▶ MSFT's required return on equity is 9.5 percent.

▶ A one-year target price for MSFT is $32.00.

[5] NASDAQ-GS: The Global Select Market tier of NASDAQ.

An analyst's target price is the price at which the analyst believes the security should sell at a stated future point in time. Based only on the information given, answer the following questions concerning MSFT. For both questions, ignore returns from reinvesting the quarterly dividends.

1. What is the analyst's one-year expected return?

2. What is a target price that is *most* consistent with MSFT being fairly valued?

Solution to 1: Over one year, the analyst expects MSFT to pay $0.10 + $0.10 + $0.11 + $0.11 = $0.42 in dividends. Using the target price of $32.00 and dividends of $0.42, the analyst's expected return is ($0.42/$28.27) + ($32.00 − $28.27)/$28.27 = 0.015 + 0.132 = 0.147 or 14.7 percent.

Solution to 2: If MSFT is fairly valued, it should return its cost of equity (required return), which is 9.5 percent. Under that assumption, Target price = Current price × (1 + Required return) − Dividend = $28.27(1.095) − $0.42 = $30.54; the dividend is subtracted to isolate the return from price appreciation. Another solution approach involves subtracting the dividend yield from the required return to isolate the anticipated price appreciation return: 9.5% − 1.5% = 8%. Thus, (1.08)($28.27) = $30.53 (the one cent difference from this approach's answer comes from rounding the dividend yield to 1.5 percent).

2.5 Discount Rate

Discount rate is a general term for any rate used in finding the present value of a future cash flow. A discount rate reflects the compensation required by investors for delaying consumption—generally assumed to equal the risk-free rate—and their required compensation for the risk of the cash flow. Generally, the discount rate used to determine intrinsic value depends on the characteristics of the investment rather than on the characteristics of the purchaser. That is, *for the purposes of estimating intrinsic value*, a required return based on marketplace variables is used rather than a personal required return influenced by such factors as whether the investor is diversified in his or her personal portfolio. On the other hand, some investors will make judgmental adjustments to such required return estimates, knowing the limitations of the finance models used to estimate such returns.

In principle, because of varying expected future inflation rates and the possibly varying risk of expected future cash flows, a distinct discount rate could be applicable to each distinct expected future cash flow. In practice, a single required return is generally used to discount all expected future cash flows.[6]

Sometimes an internal rate of return is used as a required return estimate, as discussed in the next section.

---

[6] When analysts sort expected future cash flows into multiple groups and each group has a different assumed growth rate, analysts sometimes apply different required returns to the different groups in discounting expected cash flows.

2.6 Internal Rate of Return

The **internal rate of return** (IRR) on an investment is the discount rate that equates the present value of the asset's expected future cash flows to the asset's price—i.e., the amount of money needed today to purchase a right to those cash flows.

In a model that views the intrinsic value of a common equity share as the present value of expected future cash flows, if price is equal to current intrinsic value—the condition of market informational efficiency—then, generally, a discount rate can be found, usually by iteration, which equates that present value to the market price. An IRR computed under the assumption of market efficiency has been used to estimate the required return on equity. An example is the historical practice of many U.S. state regulators of estimating the cost of equity for regulated utilities using the model illustrated in Equation 3b below.[7] (The issue of cost of equity arises because regulators set prices sufficient for utilities to earn their cost of capital.)[8]

To illustrate, the simplest version of a present value model results from defining cash flows as dividends and assuming a stable dividend growth rate for the indefinite future. The stable growth rate assumption reduces the sum of results in a very simple expression for intrinsic value:[9]

$$\text{Intrinsic value} = \frac{\text{Year-ahead dividend}}{\text{Required return} - \text{Expected dividend growth rate}}$$

(3a)

If the asset is correctly valued now (Market price = Intrinsic value), given consensus estimates of the year-ahead dividend and future dividend growth rate (which are estimates of the dividend expectations built into the price), we can solve for a required return—an IRR implied by the market price:

$$\text{Required return estimate} = \frac{\text{Year-ahead dividend}}{\text{Market price}}$$
$$+ \text{Expected dividend growth rate} \quad \textbf{(3b)}$$

The use of such an IRR as a required return estimate assumes not only market efficiency, but also the correctness of the particular present value model (in the above example, the stable growth rate assumption is critical) and the estimated inputs to the selected model. In Equation 3b and similar cases, although the asset's risk is incorporated indirectly into the required return estimate via the market price, the adjustment for risk is not explicit as it is in many competing models that will be presented.

Finally, obtaining an IRR from a present value model should not be confused with the somewhat similar-looking exercise that involves inferring what the market price implies about future growth rates of cash flows, given an independent estimate of required return: that exercise has the purpose of assessing the reasonableness of the market price.

---

[7] See Cornell (1999), p. 103, or Brealey, Myers, and Allen (2006) for an introduction to this use.

[8] To avoid circularity, analysts must avoid using such an estimate as the discount rate in the same or closely similar present value model solved for intrinsic value.

[9] This will be discussed in more detail in the reading on discounted dividend valuation.

THE EQUITY RISK PREMIUM

The equity risk premium is the incremental return (*premium*) that investors require for holding equities rather than a risk-free asset. Thus, it is the difference between the required return on equities and a specified expected risk-free rate of return. The equity risk premium, like the required return, depends strictly on expectations for the future because the investor's returns depend only on the investment's future cash flows. Possibly confusingly, *equity risk premium* is also commonly used to refer to the realized excess return of stocks over a risk-free asset over a given past time period. The realized excess return could be very different from the premium that, based on available information, was contemporaneously being expected by investors.[10]

Using the equity risk premium, the required return on the broad equity market or an average-systematic-risk equity security is

Required return on equity = Current expected risk-free return
+ Equity risk premium

where, for consistency, the definition of risk-free asset (e.g., government bills or government bonds) used in estimating the equity risk premium should correspond to the one used in specifying the current expected risk-free return.

The importance of the equity risk premium in valuation is that, in perhaps a majority of cases in practice, analysts estimate the required return on a common equity issue as either

Required return on share i = Current expected risk-free return
$+ \beta_i$(Equity risk premium)   **(4)**

or

Required return on share i = Current expected risk-free return + Equity
risk premium

$\pm$ Other risk premia/discounts
appropriate for i **(5)**

► Equation 4 adjusts the equity risk premium for the share's particular level of systematic risk as measured by beta (β_i)—an average systematic risk security has a beta of 1, whereas beta values above and below 1 indicate greater-than-average and smaller-than-average systematic risk. Equation 4 will be explained in Section 4.1 as the capital asset pricing model (CAPM).

► Equation 5 does not make a beta adjustment to the equity risk premium but adds premia/discounts required to develop an overall equity risk adjustment. Equation 5 will be explained in Section 4.3 as the build-up method for estimating the required return. It is primarily used in the valuation of private businesses.

Typically, analysts estimate the equity risk premium for the national equity market of the issues being analyzed (but if a global CAPM is being used, a world equity premium is estimated that takes into account the totality of equity markets).

---

[10] Bernstein and Arnott (2002) underscore and discuss this topic at length.

Even for the longest established developed markets, the magnitude of the equity risk premium is difficult to estimate and can be a reason for differing investment conclusions among analysts. Therefore, we will introduce the topic of estimation in some detail. Whatever estimates analysts decide to use, when an equity risk premium estimate enters into a valuation, analysts should be sensitive to how their value conclusions could be affected by estimation error.

Two broad approaches are available for estimating the equity risk premium. One is based on historical average differences between equity market returns and government debt returns, and the other is based on current expectational data. These are presented in the following sections.

3.1 Historical Estimates

A historical equity risk premium estimate is usually calculated as the mean value of the differences between broad-based equity-market-index returns and government debt returns over some selected sample period. When reliable long-term records of equity returns are available, historical estimates have been a familiar and popular choice of estimation. If investors do not make systematic errors in forming expectations, then, over the long term, average returns should be an unbiased estimate of what investors expected. The fact that historical estimates are based on data also gives them an objective quality.

In using a historical estimate to represent the equity risk premium going forward, the analyst is assuming that returns are stationary—that is, the parameters that describe the return-generating process are constant over the past and into the future.

The analyst's major decisions in developing a historical equity risk premium estimate include the selection of:

▶ the equity index to represent equity market returns;

▶ the time period for computing the estimate;

▶ the type of mean calculated; and

▶ the proxy for the risk-free return.

Analysts try to select an equity index that accurately represents the average returns earned by equity investors in the market being examined. Broad-based, market-value weighted indices are typically selected.

Specifying the length of the sample period typically involves trade-offs. Dividing a data period of a given length into smaller subperiods does not increase precision in estimating the mean—only extending the length of the data set can increase precision.[11] Thus, a common choice is to use the longest reliable returns series available. However, the assumption of stationarity is usually more difficult to maintain as the series starting point is extended to the distant past. The specifics of the type of nonstationarity are also important. For a number of equity markets, research has brought forth abundant evidence of nonconstant underlying return volatility. Nonstationarity—in which the equity risk premium has fluctuated in the short term, but around a central value—is a less serious impediment to using a long data series than the case in which the risk premium has shifted to a permanently different level.[12] Empirically, the expected equity risk premium is countercyclical in the United States—that is, the expected premium is high dur-

---

[11] See Merton (1980). This result contrasts with the estimation of variance and covariance in which higher frequency of estimation for a given time span does increase the precision in estimating variance and covariance.

[12] See Cornell (1999).

ing bad times but low during good times.[13] This property leads to some interesting challenges: For example, when a series of strong market returns has increased enthusiasm for equities and raised historical-mean equity risk premium estimates, the forward-looking equity risk premium may have actually declined.

Practitioners taking a historical approach to equity premium estimation often focus on the type of mean calculated and the proxy for the risk-free return. There are two choices for computing the mean and two broad choices for the proxy for the risk-free return.

The mean return of a historical set of annual return differences between equities and government debt securities can be calculated using a geometric mean or an arithmetic mean:

▶ A geometric mean equity risk premium estimate equal to the compound annual excess return of equities over the risk-free return, or

▶ An arithmetic mean equity risk premium estimate equal to the sum of the annual return differences divided by the number of observations in the sample.

The risk-free rate can also be represented in two ways:

▶ as a long-term government bond return, or

▶ as a short-term government debt instrument (Treasury bill) return.

Dimson, Marsh, and Staunton (2008) presented authoritative evidence on realized excess returns of stocks over government debt ("historical equity risk premia") using survivorship-bias free return datasets for 17 developed markets for the 108 years extending from 1900 through 2007.[14] Exhibit 1 excerpts their findings, showing results for the four combinations of mean computation and risk-free return representation (two mean return choices × two risk-free return choices). In the table, *standard deviation* is the standard deviation of the annual excess return series and *minimum value* and *maximum value* are, respectively, the smallest and largest observed values of that series.

EXHIBIT 1	Historical Equity Risk Premia: Seventeen Major Markets, 1900–2007

Panel A: Historical Equity Risk Premia Relative to Bonds, 1900–2007

Country	Geometric Mean	Arithmetic Mean	Standard Deviation	Minimum Value	Maximum Value
Australia	6.4%	8.0%	18.7%	−30.6%	66.3%
Belgium	2.7	4.5	20.0	−36.2	79.8
Canada	4.2	5.7	17.9	−36.8	56.6
Denmark	2.3	3.5	16.1	−29.8	74.9
France	4.1	6.2	22.2	−37.7	84.3
Germany*	5.6	8.6	27.2	−46.3	116.6
Ireland	3.5	5.1	18.6	−36.5	83.2

(Exhibit continued on next page . . .)

---

[13] Fama and French (1989) and Ferson and Harvey (1991).

[14] In a given year, the excess return of stocks over government debt is calculated as $[(1 + \text{Equity market return})/(1 + \text{Risk-free rate of return})] - 1 \approx \text{Equity market return} - \text{Risk-free rate of return}$, where a specified government debt instrument return represents the risk-free rate of return.

EXHIBIT 1   (continued)

Panel A: Historical Equity Risk Premia Relative to Bonds, 1900–2007

Country	Geometric Mean	Arithmetic Mean	Standard Deviation	Minimum Value	Maximum Value
Italy	4.4	7.7	29.5	−39.6	152.2
Japan	5.7	9.7	32.8	−43.3	193.0
Netherlands	4.1	6.1	21.5	−43.9	107.6
Norway	2.9	5.6	27.3	−45.1	192.1
South Africa	5.7	7.4	19.3	−29.2	70.9
Spain	2.7	4.6	20.3	−34.0	69.1
Sweden	5.3	7.6	22.2	−42.0	88.1
Switzerland	1.9	3.4	17.5	−35.2	52.2
United Kingdom	4.1	5.4	16.5	−38.1	80.8
United States	4.5	6.5	20.0	−40.8	57.4
World	4.0	5.1	14.9	−33.2	38.4

Panel B: Historical Equity Risk Premia Relative to Bills, 1900–2007

Country	Geometric Mean	Arithmetic Mean	Standard Deviation	Minimum Value	Maximum Value
Australia	7.2%	8.6%	16.9%	−30.2%	49.2%
Belgium	2.9	5.1	22.9	−35.6	120.6
Canada	4.6	5.9	16.6	−34.7	49.1
Denmark	3.0	4.6	19.7	−32.0	95.3
France	6.8	9.3	24.0	−34.3	85.7
Germany*	4.1	9.2	33.2	−88.6	131.4
Ireland	3.9	5.9	20.5	−49.8	72.0
Italy	6.5	10.4	31.9	−48.6	150.3
Japan	6.5	9.6	27.6	−48.3	108.6
Netherlands	4.6	6.7	22.2	−35.0	126.7
Norway	3.3	6.0	25.8	−49.7	157.1
South Africa	6.4	8.5	22.0	−33.9	106.2
Spain	3.7	5.7	21.5	−38.6	98.1
Sweden	5.8	8.0	22.0	−38.6	85.1
Switzerland	3.7	5.3	18.7	−37.0	54.8
United Kingdom	4.4	6.1	19.7	−54.6	121.8
United States	5.5	7.4	19.5	−44.5	56.8
World	4.8	6.1	16.5	−41.5	70.2

* German data based on 106 years, excluding 1922–1923.

Note: "World" represents a market-capitalization-weighted (in early decades, GDP-weighted) average of country results in USD terms.

Source: Dimson, Marsh, and Staunton (2008), Tables 10, 11.

The excerpt from Exhibit 1 presented below presents a comparison of historical equity risk premium estimates for the United States and Japan. This comparison highlights some of the issues that can arise in using historical estimates. As background to the discussion, note that as a mathematical fact, the geometric mean is always less than (or equal to) the arithmetic mean; furthermore, the yield curve is typically upward sloping (long-term bond yields are typically higher than short-term yields).

EXHIBIT 1	Historical Equity Risk Premia: 1900–2007 (excerpted)			
	United States		**Japan**	
	Geometric Mean	**Arithmetic Mean**	**Geometric Mean**	**Arithmetic Mean**
Premium relative to bills	5.5%	7.4%	6.5%	9.6%
Premium relative to bonds	4.5	6.5	5.7	9.7

For the United States, estimates of the equity risk premium relative to long-term government bonds runs from 4.5 percent (geometric mean relative to bonds) to 7.4 percent (arithmetic mean relative to bills). The United States illustrates the typical case in which realized values relative to bills, for any definition of mean, are higher than those relative to bonds.

The premium estimates for Japan are notably higher than for the United States. Because the promised yield on long-term bonds is usually higher than that on short-term bills, the higher arithmetic mean premium relative to bonds compared to bills in the case of Japan is atypical. The analyst would need to investigate the reasons for it and believe they applied to the future before using the estimate as a forecast for the future. In virtually all markets, the geometric mean premium relative to long-term bonds gives the smallest risk premium estimate (the exception is Germany). Note the following:

▶ For each market, the variation in year-to-year results is very large as shown by standard deviations and ranges (maximum – minimum values). As a result, the sample mean estimates the true mean with potentially substantial error. To explain, the standard deviation of the sample mean in estimating the underlying mean (the standard error) is given by sample standard deviation ÷ square root of the number of observations: For example, 20.0 percent ÷ $\sqrt{108} \approx 1.9$ percent for the United States relative to bonds.[15] So a two standard deviation interval for the underlying mean (an interval within which the underlying mean is expected to lie with a 0.95 probability) is a wide 2.7 percent to 10.3 percent (i.e., 6.5% ± 3.8%) even with 108 years of data. This problem of sampling error becomes more acute, the shorter the series on which the mean estimate is based.

---

[15] The statement can be made by appealing to the central limit theorem which states, informally, that the sample mean is approximately normally distributed for large samples. The calculation shown assumes that returns are serially uncorrelated and provides a lower limit for the standard error of the mean. In the case where returns are serially correlated, the standard error is larger.

EXHIBIT 2	Distribution of Geometric Mean Realized Premium Relative to Bonds					

Interval for Realized Premium *x* (in percent):

		$1 \leqslant x < 2$	$2 \leqslant x < 3$	$3 \leqslant x < 4$	$4 \leqslant x < 5$	$5 \leqslant x < 6$	$6 \leqslant x \leqslant 7$
No. of Markets	7						
	6				Canada		
	5				France		
	4		Belgium		Italy	Germany	
	3		Denmark		Netherlands	Japan	
	2		Norway		U.K.	So. Africa	
	1	Switzerland	Spain	Ireland	U.S.	Sweden	Australia

▶ The variation in the historical equity risk premium estimates across countries is substantial. Referring to Panel A of Exhibit 1, the histogram in Exhibit 2, focusing on the geometric mean, shows that roughly 88 percent of values fall in one-percentage-point intervals from 2 percent to 6 percent. The modal interval is 4–5 percent and, as Exhibit 1, Panel A shows, the mean ("World") value is 4 percent. However, approximately 12 percent of values fall in the two extreme intervals.

The next two sections discuss choices related to the calculation of a historical equity risk premium estimate.

3.1.1 Arithmetic Mean or Geometric Mean

A decision with an important impact on the risk premium estimate is the choice between an arithmetic mean and a geometric mean: the geometric mean is smaller by an amount equal to about one half the variance of returns, so it is always smaller than the arithmetic mean given any variability in returns (the geometric mean is equal to the arithmetic mean when the returns for all periods are equal).

In actual professional practice, both means have been used in equity risk premium estimation.

The arithmetic mean return as the average one-period return best represents the mean return in a single period. There are two traditional arguments in favor of using the arithmetic mean in equity risk premium estimation, one relating to the type of model in which the estimates are used and the second relating to a statistical property. The major finance models for estimating required return—in particular the CAPM and multifactor models—are single-period models; so the arithmetic mean, with its focus on single-period returns, appears to be a model-consistent choice. A statistical argument has also been made for the arithmetic mean: With serially uncorrelated returns and a *known* underlying arithmetic mean, the unbiased estimate of the expected terminal value of an investment is found by compounding forward at the arithmetic mean. For example, if the arithmetic mean is 8 percent, an unbiased estimate of the expected terminal value of a €1 million investment in 5 years is €1(1.08)^5 = €1.47 million. In practice, however, the underlying mean is not known. It has been established that compounding forward using the *sample* arithmetic mean, whether or not returns are serially uncorrelated, overestimates the expected terminal value of wealth.[16] In the example, if 8 percent is merely the sample arithmetic mean (used as an estimate of the unknown underlying mean), we would expect terminal wealth to be less than €1.47 million. Practically, only the first traditional argument still has force.

The geometric mean return of a sample represents the compound rate of growth that equates the beginning value to the ending value of one unit of money initially invested in an asset. Present value models involve the discounting over multiple time periods. Discounting is just the reverse side of compounding in terms of finding amounts of equivalent worth at different points in time; because the geometric mean is a compound growth rate, it appears to be a logical choice for estimating a required return in a multiperiod context, even when using a single-period required return model. In contrast to the sample arithmetic mean, using the sample geometric mean does not introduce bias in the calculated expected terminal value of an investment.[17] Equity risk premium estimates based on the geometric mean have tended to be closer to supply-side and demand-side estimates from economic theory than arithmetic mean estimates.[18] For the above reasons, the geometric mean is increasingly preferred for use in historical estimates of the equity risk premium.

3.1.2 Long-Term Government Bonds or Short-Term Government Bills

The choices for the risk-free rate are a short-term government debt rate, such as a 30-day T-bill rate, or a long-term government bond yield to maturity (YTM). Government bonds are preferred to even the highest rated corporate bonds as they typically have less (near zero) default and equity market risk.

A bond-based equity risk premium estimate in almost all cases is smaller than a bill-based estimate (see Exhibit 1). But a normal upward-sloping yield curve tends to offset the effect of the risk-free rate choice on a required return estimate, because the current expected risk-free rate based on a bond will be larger than the expectation based on a bill. However, with an inverted yield curve, the short-term yields exceed long-term yields and the required return estimate based on using a risk-free rate based on a bill can be much higher.

Industry practice has tended to favor use of a long-term government bond rate in premium estimates despite the fact that such estimates are often used in one-period models such as the CAPM. A risk premium based on a bill rate may produce a better estimate of the required rate of return for discounting a one-year-ahead cash flow, but a premium relative to bonds should produce a more plausible required return/discount rate in a multiperiod context of valuation.[19]

To illustrate a reason for the preference, take the case of bill-relative and bond-relative premia estimates of 5.5 percent and 4.5 percent, respectively, for a given market. Assume the yield curve is inverted: The current bill rate is 9 percent and the bond rate is 6 percent, respectively. The required return on average-risk equity based on bills is 14.5 percent (9% + 5.5%) compared with

---

[16] See Hughson, Stutzer, and Yung (2006) for a proof. Even when returns are not serially uncorrelated, using the arithmetic mean (even a known value) tends to overestimate the expected value of terminal wealth. Returns that revert to the mean are one example of serial correlation of practical concern.

[17] See Hughson, Stutzer, and Yung (2006).

[18] The relatively large size of the historical U.S. equity premium relative to that predicted by demand-side theory is known as the "equity premium puzzle" (Mehra and Prescott 1985). Cornell (1999) provides an accessible summary of the research.

[19] The argument is also made by Arzac (2005).

10.5 percent based on bonds (6% + 4.5%). That 14.5 percent rate may be appropriate for discounting a one-year-ahead cash flow in a current high interest and inflation environment. The inverted yield curve, however, predicts a downward path for short-rates and inflation. Most of the cash flows lie in the future and the premium for expected average inflation rates built into the long-bond rate is more plausible. A practical principle is that for the purpose of valuation, the analyst should try to match the duration of the risk-free-rate measure to the duration of the asset being valued.[20] If the analyst has adopted a short-term risk-free rate definition, nevertheless, a practical approach to dealing with the situation just presented would be to use an expected average short-term bill rate rather than the current 9 percent rate. Advocates of using short-term rates point out that long-term government bonds are subject to risks, such as interest rate risk, that complicate their interpretation.

In practice, many analysts use the current YTM on a long-term government bond as an approximation for the expected return on it. The analyst needs to be clear that he or she is using a current yield observation, reflecting current inflation expectations. The yield on a recently issued ("on the run") bond mitigates distortions related to liquidity and discounts/premiums relative to face value. The available maturities of liquid government bonds change over time and differ among national markets. If a 20-year maturity is available and trades in a liquid market, however, its yield is a reasonable choice as an estimate of the risk-free rate for equity valuation.[21] In many international markets, only bonds of shorter maturity are available or have a liquid market. A 10-year government bond yield is another common choice.

Valuation requires definite estimates of required returns. The data in Exhibit 1 provide one practical starting point for an estimate of equity risk premium for the markets given. As discussed, one mainstream choice among alternative estimates of the historical equity risk premium is the geometric mean historical equity risk premium relative to government bonds.

3.1.3 Adjusted Historical Estimates

A historical risk premium estimate may be adjusted in several ways to neutralize the effect of biases that may be present in the underlying equity market return series. One type of adjustment is made to offset the effect of biases in the data series being used to estimate the equity risk premium. A second type of adjustment is made to take account of an independent estimate of the equity risk premium. In both cases the adjustment could be upward or downward.

One issue is **survivorship bias** in equity market data series. The bias arises when poorly performing or defunct companies are removed from membership in an index, so that only relative winners remain. Survivorship bias tends to inflate historical estimates of the equity risk premium. For many developed markets, equity returns series are now available that are free or nearly free of survivorship bias (see Exhibit 1). When using a series that has such bias, however, the historical risk premium estimate should be adjusted downward. Guidance for such adjustment based on research is sometimes available.[22]

---

[20] **Duration** is a measure of the price sensitivity of an asset (or liability) to interest-rate changes. See Fabozzi (2004) for details.

[21] The Ibbotson U.S. long-term government bond yield is based on a portfolio of 20-year average maturity T-bonds. We use that series in the suggested historical estimate of the U.S. equity risk premium.

[22] Copeland, Koller, and Murrin (2000) recommend a downward adjustment of 1.5 percent to 2.0 percent for survivorship bias in the S&P 500 Index, using arithmetic mean estimates. Dimson et al. (2006), the source for Exhibit 1, took care to correct for survivorship bias. See also Dimson, Marsh, and Staunton (2002), which explains survivorship bias in greater detail.

A conceptually related issue with historical estimates can arise when a market has experienced a string of unexpectedly positive or negative events and the surprises do not balance out over the period of sampled data. For example, a string of positive inflation and productivity surprises may result in a series of high returns that increase the historical mean estimate of the equity risk premium. In such cases, a forward-looking model estimate may suggest a much lower value of the equity risk premium. To mitigate that concern, the analyst may adjust the historical estimate downward based on an independent forward-looking estimate (or upward, in the case of a string of negative surprises). Many experts believe that the historical record for various major world markets has benefited from a majority of favorable circumstances that cannot be expected to be duplicated in the future; their recommended adjustments to historical mean estimates is downward. Dimson, Marsh, and Staunton (2002) have argued that historical returns have been advantaged by re-pricings as increasing scope for diversification has led to a lower level of market risk. In the case of the United States, Ibbotson and Chen (2001) recommended a 1.25 percentage point downward adjustment to the Morningstar (Ibbotson) historical mean U.S. equity risk premium estimate based on a lower estimate from a supply-side analysis of the equity risk premium.

Example 2 illustrates difficulties in historical data that could lead to a preference for an adjusted historical or forward-looking estimate.

EXAMPLE 2

The Indian Equity Risk Premium: Historical Estimates of the Equity Risk Premium in a Developing Market[23]

Historical estimates of the equity risk premium in developing markets are often attended by a range of concerns. The case of India can serve as an example. A number of equity indexes are available and each has possible limitations. Although not as broad-based as the alternatives, the Bombay Stock Exchange Sensex 30, a market-capitalization weighted index of the shares of 30 leading companies, has the longest available record: Compiled since 1986, returns go back to 1979. Note the following facts concerning this index and other issues relevant to estimating the equity risk premium:

▶ The backfilled returns from 1979 to 1985 are based on the initial 30 issues selected in 1986, which were among the largest market-cap as of 1986.

▶ The Sensex is a price index; a total return version of the index incorporating dividends is available from 1997 forward.

▶ Interest rates were suppressed by regulation prior to 1991 and moved higher thereafter. The post-regulation period appears to be associated with higher stock market volatility.

▶ Objective estimates of the extent of any bias can be developed.

---

[23] Jayanth R. Varma and Samir K. Barua, "A First Cut Estimate of the Equity Risk Premium in India," Indian Institute of Management Ahmedabad, Working Paper No. 2006-06-04, June 2006, is the source for most of the institutional background used in this example.

Based only on the information given, address the following.

1. What factors could bias an unadjusted historical risk premium estimate upward?
2. What factors could bias an unadjusted historical risk premium estimate downward?
3. State and explain two indications that the historical time series is nonstationary.
4. Recommend and justify a preference for a historical or an adjusted historical equity risk premium estimate.

Solution to 1: The backfilling of returns from 1979 to 1985 based on companies selected in 1986 could upward bias the estimate because of survivorship bias. The companies that were selected in 1986 are likely to have been among the most successful of the companies on the exchange as of 1979. Another but less clear factor is the suppression of interest rates prior to 1991. An artificially low risk-free rate would bias the equity risk premium estimate upward unless the required return on equity was smaller by an equal amount.

Solution to 2: The failure to incorporate the return from dividends biases the equity risk premium estimate downward.

Solution to 3: The different levels of interest rates before and after the lifting of regulation in 1991 is one indication that the equity risk premium pre- and post-1991 could be different and that the overall series is nonstationary. A second is the higher level of stock market volatility pre- and postregulation.

Solution to 4: Given that objective estimates of the extent of biases can be developed, an adjusted historical estimate would be preferred because such an estimate is more likely to be unbiased and accurate.

In Example 2, one criticism that could be raised relative to any historical estimate is the shortness of the period in the data set—the post-1991 reform period—that is definitely relevant to the present. Sampling error in any mean estimate—even one based on clean data—would be a major concern for this data set. The analyst might address specific concerns through an adjusted historical estimate. The analyst may also decide to investigate one or more forward-looking estimates. Forward-looking estimates are the subject of the next section. A later section on international issues will have more information on equity risk premium estimation for emerging markets such as India.

3.2 Forward-Looking Estimates

Because the equity risk premium is based only on expectations for economic and financial variables from the present going forward, it is logical to estimate the premium directly based on current information and expectations concerning such variables. Such estimates are often called forward-looking or *ex ante* estimates. In principle, such estimates may agree with, be higher, or be lower than historical equity risk premium estimates.[24] *Ex ante* estimates are likely to be less subject to an issue such as nonstationarity or data biases than historical estimates. However, such estimates are often subject to other potential errors related to financial and economic models and potential behavioral biases in forecasting.

3.2.1 Gordon Growth Model Estimates

Probably the most frequently encountered forward-looking estimate of the equity risk premium is based on a very simple form of a present value model called the constant growth dividend discount model or Gordon growth model, already shown as Equation 3a. For mature developed equity markets such as Eurozone, the United Kingdom, and North American markets, the assumptions of this model are often met, at least approximately. Broad-based equity indices are nearly always associated with a dividend yield, and year-ahead dividend payment may be fairly predictable. The expected dividend growth rate may be inferred based on published analyst or economic expectations, such as consensus analyst expectations of the earnings growth rate for an equity market index (which may be based on forecasts for the constituent companies or a top-down forecast). Specifically, the Gordon growth model (GGM) equity risk premium estimate is:[25]

GGM equity risk premium estimate
= Dividend yield on the index based on year-ahead aggregate forecasted
   dividends and aggregate market value
   + Consensus long-term earnings growth rate
   − Current long-term government bond yield   **(6)**

We can illustrate with the case of the United States. As of September 2007, the dividend yield on the S&P 500 as defined in Equation 6 was approximately 1.9 percent based on a price level of the S&P 500 of 1,471. The consensus analyst view was that earnings on the S&P 500 would grow from a trailing amount of $86.38 to $95.18 over the next year, a 10.2 percent growth rate. However, at a five-year horizon (the longest analyst forecast horizon commonly available), a consensus growth estimate was close to the 7 percent long-term average growth rate.[26] We will use the 7 percent long-term average growth rate as the long-term earnings growth forecast. Dividend growth should track earnings growth over the long term. The 20-year U.S. government bond yield was 5.0 percent. Therefore, according to Equation 6, the Gordon growth model estimate of the U.S. equity risk premium was 1.9% + 7.0% − 5% or 3.9%. Like historical estimates, Gordon growth model estimates generally change through time. For example, the risk premium estimate of 3.9 percent just given compares with a GGM estimate of 2.4 percent (computed as 1.2% + 7% − 5.8%) made in the last edition of this reading, as of the end of 2001.

[24] Fama and French (2001) found that prior to 1950, the historical and Gordon growth model estimates for the U.S. equity risk premium agree, but from 1950–99, the Gordon growth model estimate averages less than half the historical estimate. They attribute the difference to the effect of positive earnings surprises relative to expectations on realized returns.

[25] Recent examples of the application of this model (to U.S. markets) are Jagannathan, McGrattan, and Scherbina (2000) and Fama and French (2001). The GGM estimate has also been used in institutional research for international markets (Stux 1994). Most analysts forecast the earnings growth rate rather than the dividend growth rate, which is technically specified in theory, so we use the earnings growth rate in the expression. Given a constant dividend payout ratio, a reasonable approximation for broad equity indexes, the two growth rates should be equal.

[26] www.standardandpoors.com.

Equation 6 is based on an assumption of earnings growth at a stable rate. An assumption of multiple earnings growth stages is more appropriate for very rapidly growing economies. Taking an equity index in such an economy, the analyst may forecast a fast growth stage for the aggregate of companies included in the index, followed by a transition stage in which growth rates decline and a mature growth stage characterized by growth at a moderate, sustainable rate. The discount rate r that equates the sum of the present values of the expected cash flows of the three stages to the current market price of the equity index defines an IRR. Letting PVFastGrowthStage(r) stand for the present value of the cash flows of the fast earnings growth stage with the present value shown as a function of the discount rate r, and using a self-explanatory notation for the present values of the other phases, the equation for IRR is as follows:

$$\text{Equity index price} = \text{PVFastGrowthStage}(r) + \text{PVTransition}(r) + \text{PVMatureGrowthStage}(r)$$

The IRR is computable using a spreadsheet's IRR function. Using the IRR as an estimate of the required return on equities (as described in Section 2.6), subtracting a government bond yield gives an equity risk premium estimate.

A consequence of the model underlying Equation 6, making assumptions of a constant dividend payout ratio and efficient markets, is that earnings, dividends, and prices are expected to grow at dividend growth rate, so that the P/E ratio is constant. The analyst may believe, however, that the P/E ratio will expand or contract. Some analysts make an adjustment to the estimate in Equation 6 to reflect P/E multiple expansion or contraction. From a given starting market level associated with a given level of earnings and a given P/E ratio, the return from capital appreciation cannot be greater than the earnings growth rate unless the P/E multiple expands. P/E multiple expansion can result from an increase in the earnings growth rate and/or a decrease in risk.

3.2.2 Macroeconomic Model Estimates

Using relationships between macroeconomic variables and the financial variables that figure in equity valuation models, analysts can develop equity risk premium estimates. Such models may be more reliable when public equities represent a relatively large share of the economy, as in many developed markets. Many such analyses focus on the supply-side variables that fuel gross domestic product (GDP) growth (and are thus known as supply-side estimates). The Gordon growth model estimate, when based on a top-down economic analysis rather than using consensus analyst estimates, can be viewed as a supply-side estimate.[27]

To illustrate a supply-side analysis, the total return to equity can be analyzed into four components as explained by Ibbotson and Chen:[28]

▶ expected inflation: EINFL;

▶ expected growth rate in real earnings per share: EGREPS;

▶ expected growth rate in the P/E ratio (the ratio of share price to earnings per share): EGPE; and

▶ expected income component (including return from reinvestment of income): EINC.

---

[27] Demand-side models estimate the equity risk premium based on estimates of investors' average risk aversion and the correlation of asset returns with changes in consumption. Such models are rarely encountered in professional practice, however.

[28] This is based on Ibbotson and Chen's (2003) method 3, the earnings method.

The growth in P/E arises as a factor from a decomposition of the capital appreciation portion of returns.[29] So,

$$\text{Equity risk premium} = \{[(1 + \text{EINFL})(1 + \text{EGREPS})(1 + \text{EGPE}) - 1.0] + \text{EINC}\} - \text{Expected risk-free return} \qquad (7)$$

In the following we illustrate this type of analysis using data for U.S. equity markets as represented by the S&P 500.

▶ *Expected inflation.* A market forecast is available from the U.S. treasury and U.S. treasury inflation protected securities (TIPS) yield curve:

$$\text{Implicit inflation forecast} \approx \frac{1 + \text{YTM of 20-year maturity T-bonds}}{1 + \text{YTM of 20-year maturity TIPS}} - 1$$

$$= \frac{1.05}{1.026} - 1$$

$$= 0.023 \text{ or } 2.3 \text{ percent.}$$

We will use an estimate of 2.5 percent per year, consistent with the TIPS analysis and other long-term forecasts. So, $1 + \text{EINFL} = 1.025$.

▶ *Expected growth in real earnings per share.* This quantity should approximately track the real GDP growth rate. An adjustment upward or downward to the real GDP growth rate can be made for any expected differential growth between the companies represented in the equity index being used to represent the stock market and the overall economy.

According to economic theory, the real GDP growth rate should equal the sum of labor productivity growth and the labor supply growth rate (which can be estimated as the sum of the population growth rate and the increase in the labor force participation rate). A forecasted 2 percent per year U.S. labor productivity growth rate and 1 percent per year labor supply growth rate produces a 3 percent overall real GDP growth rate estimate of 3 percent. So, $1 + \text{EGREPS} = 1.03$.

▶ *Expected growth in the P/E ratio.* The baseline value for this factor is zero, reflecting an efficient markets view. When the analyst views a current P/E level as reflecting overvaluation or undervaluation, however, a negative or positive value, respectively, can be used, reflecting the analyst's investment time horizon. So, without presenting a case for misevaluation, $1 + \text{EGPE} = 1$.

▶ *Expected income component.* Historically, for U.S. markets the long-term value has been close to 4.5 percent (including reinvestment return of 20 bps).[30] However, the current S&P 500 dividend yield is below the long-term average. A forward looking estimate based on the forward expected dividend yield of 2.1 percent and 10 bps reinvestment return is 2.2 percent. So, $\text{EINC} = 0.022$.

Using the Ibbotson–Chen format and a risk-free rate of 5 percent, an estimate of the U.S. equity risk premium estimate is

$$\{[(1.025)(1.03)(1) - 1.0] + 0.022\} - 0.05 = 0.078 - 0.05 = 2.8\%$$

---

[29] That is, $(P_t/P_{t-1}) - 1.0 = [(P_t/E_t)/(P_{t-1}/E_{t-1})](E_t/E_{t-1}) - 1.0 = (1 + \text{EGPE})(1 + \text{EGREPS}) - 1.0$.

[30] See Ibbotson and Chen (2003), p. 90.

The supply side estimate of 2.8 percent is smaller than the historical geometric mean estimate of 4.5 percent, although the difference is within one standard error (2 percentage points) of the latter forecast.[31]

3.2.3 Survey Estimates

One way to gauge expectations is to ask people what they expect. Survey estimates of the equity risk premium involve asking a sample of people—frequently, experts—about their expectations for it, or for capital market expectations from which the premium can be inferred.

For example, a 2002 survey of global bond investors by Schroder Salomon Smith Barney found an average equity risk premium in the range of 2–2.5 percent, while a Goldman Sachs survey of global clients recorded a mean long-run equity risk premium of 3.9 percent.[32]

4   THE REQUIRED RETURN ON EQUITY

With means to estimate the equity risk premium in hand, the analyst can estimate the required return on the equity of a particular issuer. The choices include the following:

► the CAPM;

► a multifactor model such as the Fama–French or related models; and

► a build-up method, such as the bond yield plus risk premium method.

4.1 The Capital Asset Pricing Model

The CAPM is an equation for required return that should hold in **equilibrium** (the condition in which supply equals demand) if the model's assumptions are met; among the key assumptions are that investors are risk averse and that they make investment decisions based on the mean return and variance of returns of their total portfolio. The chief insight of the model is that investors evaluate the risk of an asset in terms of the asset's contribution to the systematic risk of their total portfolio (systematic risk is risk that cannot be shed by portfolio diversification). Because the CAPM provides an economically grounded and relatively objective procedure for required return estimation, it has been widely used in valuation.

The expression for the CAPM that is used in practice was given earlier as Equation 4:[33]

Required return on share i = Current expected risk-free return
+ β_i (Equity risk premium)

---

[31] Strictly speaking, standard errors apply only to the arithmetic mean; but as an approximate guide to "closeness," they have also been applied to the geometric mean. See Dimson, Marsh, and Staunton (2002), p. 168.

[32] See Ilmanen, Byrne, Gunasekera, and Minikin (2002) and O'Neill, Wilson, and Masih (2002).

[33] Formally, the CAPM is $E(R_i) = R_F + \beta_i[E(R_M) - R_F]$ where $E(R_i)$ is asset i's expected return in equilibrium given its beta, equal to its required return, R_F is the risk-free rate of return, and $E(R_M)$ is the expected return on the market portfolio. In theory, the market portfolio is defined to include all risky assets held according to their market value weights. In typical practice when applying the CAPM to value equities, a broad equity index is used to represent the market portfolio and an estimate of the equity risk premium is used for $E(R_M) - R_F$.

For example, if the current expected risk-free return is 5 percent, the asset's beta is 1.20, and the equity risk premium is 4.5 percent, then the asset's required return is

$$\text{Required return on share } i = 0.05 + 1.20(0.045) = 0.104 \text{ or } 10.4 \text{ percent}$$

The asset's beta measures its market or systematic risk, which in theory is the sensitivity of its returns to the returns on the "market portfolio" of risky assets. Concretely, beta equals the covariance of returns with the returns on the market portfolio divided by the market portfolio's variance of returns. In typical practice for equity valuation, the market portfolio is represented by a broad value-weighted equity market index. The asset's beta is estimated by a least squares regression of the asset's returns on the index's returns and is available also from many vendors. In effect, in Equation 4 the analyst is adjusting the equity risk premium up or down for the asset's level of systematic risk by multiplying it by the asset's beta, adding that asset-specific risk premium to the current expected risk-free return to obtain a required return estimate.

In the typical case in which the equity risk premium is based on a national equity market index and estimated beta is based on sensitivity to that index, the assumption is being made implicitly that equity prices are largely determined by *local* investors. When equities markets are *segmented* in that sense (i.e., local market prices are largely determined by local investors rather than by investors worldwide), two issues with the same risk characteristics can have different required returns if they trade in different markets.

The opposite assumption is that all investors worldwide participate equally in setting prices (perfectly integrated markets). That assumption results in the international CAPM (or world CAPM) in which the risk premium is relative to a world market portfolio. Taking an equity view of the market portfolio, the world equity risk premium can be estimated historically based on the MSCI World index (returns available from 1970), for example, or indirectly as the (U.S. equity risk premium estimate)/(beta of U.S. stocks relative to MSCI World) = 4.5%/0.9218 = 4.9%. Computing beta relative to MSCI World and using a national risk-free interest rate, the analyst can obtain international CAPM estimates of required return. In practice, the international CAPM is not commonly relied on for required return on equity estimation.[34]

4.1.1 Beta Estimation for a Public Company

The simplest estimate of beta results from an ordinary least squares regression of the return on the stock on the return on the market. The result is often called an unadjusted or "raw" historical beta. The actual values of beta estimates are influenced by several choices:

▶ *The choice of the index used to represent the market portfolio.* For a number of markets there are traditional choices. For U.S. equities, the S&P 500 (vendors include Morningstar/Ibbotson, Merrill Lynch, Compustat) and NYSE Composite (vendors include Value Line) have been traditional choices.

▶ *The length of data period and the frequency of observations.* The most common choice is five years of monthly data, yielding 60 observations

---

[34] Other methods appear to give more plausible estimates in practice. See Morningstar (2007), pp. 177–179, 184. One variation on the international CAPM, called the Singer–Terhaar method, that does find use in professional practice, particularly for asset classes, is discussed in Calverley, Meder, Singer, and Staub (2007); this approach involves taking a weighted average of domestic and international CAPM estimates.

(Morningstar/Ibbotson, Merrill Lynch, Compustat make that choice). Value Line uses five years of weekly observations. The Bloomberg default is two years of weekly observations, which can be changed at the user's option. One study of U.S. stocks found support for five years of monthly data over alternatives.[35] An argument can be made that the Bloomberg default can be especially appropriate in fast growing markets.

The beta value in a future period has been found to be on average closer to the mean value of 1.0, the beta of an average-systematic-risk security, than to the value of the raw beta. Because valuation is forward looking, it is logical to adjust the raw beta so it more accurately predicts a future beta. The most commonly used adjustment was introduced by Blume (1971):

$$\text{Adjusted beta} = (2/3)(\text{Unadjusted beta}) + (1/3)(1.0) \qquad \textbf{(8)}$$

For example, if the beta from a regression of an asset's returns on the market return is 1.30, adjusted beta is $(2/3)(1.30) + (1/3)(1.0) = 1.20$. Vendors of financial information often report raw and adjusted beta estimates together. Although most vendors use the Blume adjustment, some do not. For example, Morningstar (Ibbotson) adjusts raw beta toward the peer mean value (rather than toward the overall mean value of 1.0). The analyst of course needs to understand the basis behind the presentation of any data that he or she uses.

The following examples apply the CAPM to estimate the required return on equity.

EXAMPLE 3

An Analyst Case Study (2): The Required Return on Larsen & Toubro Shares

While Weeramantry has been researching Microsoft, his colleague Delacour has been investigating the required return on Larsen & Toubro Ltd shares (BSE: 500510, NSE: LT).[36] Larsen & Toubro Ltd. is the largest India-based engineering and construction company. Calling up the beta function for LT on her Bloomberg terminal on 5 September 2007, Delacour sees the screen shown in Exhibit 3.

Delacour notes that Bloomberg has chosen the BSE Sensex 30 as the equity index for estimating beta. Delacour changes the Bloomberg default for time period/frequency to the specification shown in the exhibit for consistency with her other estimation work; in doing so, she notes approvingly that the beta estimate is approximately the same at both horizons.

Raw beta, 1.157, is the slope of the regression line running through the scatterplot of 60 points denoting the return on LT (*y*-axis) for different returns on the Sensex (*x*-axis); a bar graph of the distribution of returns in local currency terms is superimposed over the *x*-axis.

Noting from R^2 that beta explains more than 56 percent of variation in LT returns—an exceptionally good fit—Delacour also decides to use the

---

[35] Bartholdy and Peare (2004).

[36] BSE: Bombay Stock Exchange; NSE: National Stock Exchange. The Bloomberg reference for the company is LT IN whereas the Reuters reference is LART.BO.

EXHIBIT 3	A Bloomberg Screen for Beta Larsen & Toubro Ltd.

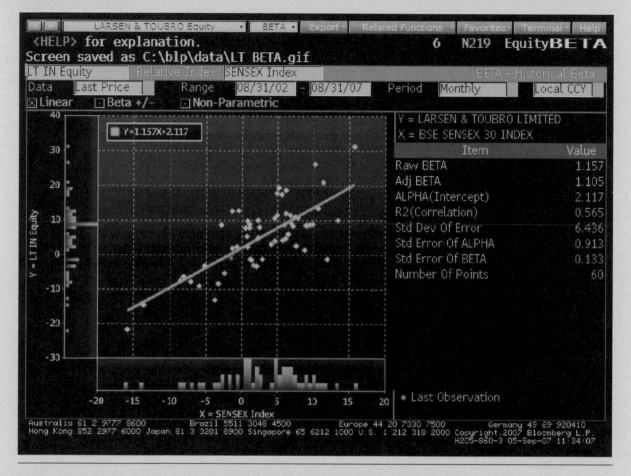

CAPM to estimate LT stock's required return.[37] Delacour has decided to use her own adjusted historical estimate of 7 percent for the Indian equity risk premium and the 10-year Indian government bond yield of 7.9 percent as the risk-free rate.[38] Delacour notes that a 7.9 percent yield is shown on the Bloomberg cost of capital screen for LT (as the "bond rate") and that the same screen shows an estimate of the Indian equity risk premium ("country premium") of 7.46 percent—close to her own estimate of 7 percent.

Based only on the information given, address the following:

1. Demonstrate the calculation of adjusted beta using the Blume method.
2. Estimate the required return on LT using the CAPM with an adjusted beta.
3. Explain one fact from the Bloomberg screen as evidence that beta has been estimated with accuracy.

---

[37] The Bloomberg screen interprets R^2 as "correlation." More precisely, in a univariate regression as here, it is equivalent to the squared correlation between the dependent (stock return) and independent (market return) variables. It is interpreted as the fraction of the variation in the dependent variable explained by the independent variable.

[38] Varma and Barua (2006) estimated a historical geometric mean equity risk premium of 8.75 percent for Indian equities using their own database. This was adjusted downward by 1.7 percentage points based on a supply-side analysis. Some estimates of the Indian equity risk premium, e.g., country risk rating estimates, are much higher.

Solution to 1: The calculation for adjusted beta is $(2/3)(1.157) + (1/3)(1.0) = 1.105$.

Solution to 2: $r = 7.9\% + 1.105(7\%) = 15.6$ percent.

Solution to 3: The standard error of beta at 0.133 is relatively small in relation to the magnitude of the raw estimate, 1.157.

EXAMPLE 4

Calculating the Required Return on Equity Using the CAPM (1)

Exxon Mobil Corporation, BP p.l.c., and Total S.A. are three "super major" integrated oil and gas companies headquartered, respectively, in the United States, the United Kingdom, and France. An analyst estimates that the equity risk premium in the United States, the United Kingdom, and the Eurozone are, respectively, 4.5 percent, 4.1 percent, and 4.0 percent. Other information is summarized in Exhibit 4.

EXHIBIT 4		Exxon Mobile, BP, and Total	
Company	Beta	Estimated Equity Risk Premium	Risk-Free Rate
Exxon Mobil Corp (NYSE: XOM)	0.74	4.5%	4.9%
BP p.l.c. (LSE SETS: BP, NYSE: BP)	1.00	4.1	5.0
Total S.A. (Euronext: FR0000120271, NYSE: TOT)	1.07	4.0	4.75

Sources: Standard & Poor's, Reuters.

Using the capital asset pricing model, calculate the required return on equity for

1. Exxon Mobil.
2. BP p.l.c.
3. Total.

Solution to 1: The required return on Exxon Mobil according to the CAPM is $4.9\% + 0.74(4.5\%) = 8.23$ percent.

Solution to 2: The required return on BP according to the CAPM is $5.0\% + 1.00(4.1\%) = 9.10$ percent.

Solution to 3: The required return on Total stock according to the CAPM is $4.75 + 1.07(4.0) = 9.03$ percent.

EXAMPLE 5

Calculating the Required Return on Equity Using the CAPM (2): Non-Traded Asset Case

Jill Adams is an analyst at a hedge fund that has been offered an equity stake in a privately held U.S. property and liability insurer. Adams identifies Alleghany Corporation (NYSE: Y) as a publicly traded comparable company, and intends to use information about Alleghany in evaluating the offer. One sell-side analyst that Adams contacts puts Alleghany's required return on equity at 10.0 percent. Researching the required return herself, Adams determines that Alleghany has the historical betas shown in Exhibit 5 as of late August 2007:

EXHIBIT 5	Alleghany Corporation: Historical Betas
5-Year Beta	**10-Year Beta**
0.30	0.21

Source: Bloomberg LLC.

The estimated U.S. equity risk premium (relative to bonds) is 4.5 percent. The YTM for:

▶ 30-day U.S. Treasury bills is 3.9 percent.

▶ 20-year U.S. government bonds is 4.9 percent.

Adams follows the most common industry practices concerning time period for estimating beta and adjustments to beta.

1. Estimate Alleghany Corporation's adjusted beta and required return based on the CAPM.

2. Is the sell-side analyst's estimate of 10 percent for Alleghany's cost of equity *most* consistent with Alleghany shares having above-average or below-average systematic risk?

Solution to 1: Adjusted beta = $(2/3)(0.30) + (1/3) = 0.533$ or 0.53. Using a five-year horizon for calculating beta is the most common practice. Consistent with the definition of the equity risk premium, a long-bond yield is used in the CAPM: $4.9\% + 0.53(4.5) = 7.29\%$ or 7.3 percent, approximately.

Solution to 2: The analyst's estimate implies above-average systematic risk. A beta of 1 by definition represents the beta of the market and so shares of average systematic risk. A beta of 1 implies a required return of $4.9\% + 1.0(4.5\%) = 9.4\%$.

When a share issue trades infrequently, the most recent transaction price may be stale and not reflect underlying changes in value. If beta is estimated based on, for example, a monthly data series in which missing values are filled with the most recent transaction price, the estimated beta will be too small and the required return on equity will be underestimated. There are several econometric techniques that can be used to estimate the beta of infrequently traded securities.[39] A practical alternative is to base the beta estimate on the beta of a comparable security.

4.1.2 Beta Estimation for Thinly Traded Stocks and Nonpublic Companies

Analysts do not have access to a series of market price observations for nonpublic companies with which to calculate a regression estimate of beta. However, using an industry classification system such as the MSCI/Standard & Poor's Global Industry Classification Standard (GICS) or the Dow Jones/FTSE Industry Classification Benchmark (ICB) to identify publicly traded peer companies, the analyst can estimate indirectly the beta of the nonpublic company on the basis of the public peer's beta.

The procedure must take into account the effect on beta of differences in financial leverage between the nonpublic company and the benchmark. First, the benchmark beta is unlevered to estimate the beta of the benchmark's assets—reflecting just the systematic risk arising from the economics of the industry. Then, the asset beta is re-levered to reflect the financial leverage of the nonpublic company.

Let β_E be the equity beta before removing the effects of leverage, if any. This is the benchmark beta. If the debt of the benchmark is high quality (so an assumption that the debt's beta is zero should be approximately true), analysts can use the following expression for unleveraging the beta:[40]

$$\beta_U \approx \left[\frac{1}{1 + (D/E)} \right] \beta_E. \tag{9a}$$

Then, if the subject company has debt and equity levels D' and E', respectively, and assuming the subject company's debt is high grade, the subject company's equity beta, β'_E, is estimated as follows:

$$\beta'_E \approx [1 + (D'/E')]\beta_U \tag{9b}$$

Expressions 9a and 9b hold under the assumption that the level of debt adjusts to the target capital structure weight as total firm value changes, consistent with the definition for the weighted average cost of capital that will be presented later.[41] Exhibit 6 summarizes the steps.

---

[39] See Elton, Gruber, Brown, and Goetzmann (2005) for a summary of the methods of Scholes and Williams (1977) and Dimson (1979).

[40] Equation 9a comes from the expression $\beta_U \approx [1 + (D/E)]^{-1}[\beta_E + (D/E) \beta_D]$, making the assumption that $\beta_D = 0$. The expression in this footnote can be used when the debt's beta is known to be definitely non-zero.

[41] See Miles and Ezzell (1985). Another expression (the one usually presented by textbooks) is appropriate under the typically less plausible assumption that the level of debt is constant from period to period: Still assuming the beta of debt is zero, the correct expression to unlever is then $\beta_U = [1 + (1 - t)(D/E)]^{-1} \beta_E$ and re-leveraging is done using $\beta_E = [1 + (1 - t)(D'/E')] \beta_U$ as shown by Hamada (1972). See Arzac (2005) for a more detailed presentation.

| EXHIBIT 6 | Estimating a Beta for a Non-Traded Company |

Step 1
Select the benchmark (comparable)

Step 2
Estimate benchmark's beta

Step 3
Unlever the benchmark's beta

Step 4
Lever the beta to reflect the
subject company's financial leverage

To illustrate, suppose that a benchmark company is identified (Step 1) that is 40 percent funded by debt. By contrast, the weight of debt in the subject company's capital structure is only 20 percent. The benchmark's beta is estimated at 1.2 (Step 2). The 40 percent weight of debt in the benchmark implies that the weight of equity is $100\% - 40\% = 60$ percent. Unlevering the benchmark beta (Step 3):

$$\beta_U \approx \left[\frac{1}{1 + (D/E)}\right]\beta_E = \left[\frac{1}{1 + (40/60)}\right]1.2 = 0.6 \times 1.2 = 0.72$$

Next, the unlevered beta of 0.72 is re-levered according to the financial leverage of the subject company, which uses 20 percent debt and 80 percent equity:

$$\beta_E' \approx [1 + (D'/E')]\beta_U = [1 + (20/80)]0.72 = 1.25 \times 0.72 = 0.90$$

Sometimes, instead of using an individual company as a benchmark, the required return will be benchmarked on a median or average industry beta. A process of unlevering and re-levering can be applied to such a beta based on the median or average industry capital structure.

| EXAMPLE 6 |

Calculating the Required Return on Equity Using the CAPM (3)

Adams turns to determining a beta for use in evaluating the offer of an equity stake in a private insurer and rounds her beta estimate of Alleghany, the public comparable, to 0.5. As of the valuation date, Alleghany Corporation has no debt in its capital structure. The private insurer is 20 percent funded by debt.

If a beta of 0.50 is assumed for the comparable, what is the estimated beta of the private insurer?

Solution: Because Alleghany does not use debt, its beta does not have to be unlevered. For the private insurer, if debt is 20 percent of capital then equity is 80 percent of capital and $D'/E' = 20/80 = 0.25$. Therefore, the estimate of the private insurer's equity beta is $(1.25)(0.50) = 0.625$ or 0.63.

The CAPM is a simple, widely accepted, theory-based method of estimating the cost of equity. Beta, its measure of risk, is readily obtainable for a wide range of securities from a variety of sources and can be estimated easily when not available from a vendor. In portfolios, the idiosyncratic risk of individual securities tends to offset against each other leaving largely beta (market) risk. For individual securities, idiosyncratic risk can overwhelm market risk and, in that case, beta may be a poor predictor of future average return. Thus the analyst needs to have multiple tools available.

4.2 Multifactor Models

A substantial amount of evidence has accumulated that the CAPM beta describes risk incompletely. In practice, coefficients of determination (R-squared) for individual stocks' beta regressions may range from 2 percent to 40 percent, with many under 10 percent. For many markets, evidence suggests that multiple factors drive returns. At the cost of greater complexity and expense, the analyst can consider a model for required return based on multiple factors. Greater complexity does not ensure greater explanatory power, however, and any selected multifactor model should be examined for the value it is adding.

Whereas the CAPM adds a single risk premium to the risk-free rate, arbitrage pricing theory (APT) models add a set of risk premia. APT models are based on a multifactor representation of the drivers of return. Formally, APT models express the required return on an asset as follows:

$$r = R_F + (\text{Risk premium})_1 + (\text{Risk premium})_2 + ...$$
$$+ (\text{Risk premium})_K \qquad \textbf{(10)}$$

where $(\text{Risk premium})_i = (\text{Factor sensitivity})_i \times (\text{Factor risk premium})_i$. **Factor sensitivity** or **factor beta** is the asset's sensitivity to a particular factor (holding all other factors constant). In general, the **factor risk premium** for factor i is the expected return in excess of the risk-free rate accruing to an asset with unit sensitivity to factor i and zero sensitivity to all other factors.[42]

One of the best known models based on multiple factors expands upon the CAPM with two additional factors. That model, the Fama–French model, is discussed next.

4.2.1 The Fama–French Model

By the end of the 1980s, empirical evidence had accumulated that, at least over certain long time periods, in the U.S. and several other equity markets, investment strategies biased toward small-market capitalization securities and/or value might generate higher returns over the long-run than the CAPM predicts.[43]

In 1993, researchers Eugene Fama and Kenneth French addressed these perceived weaknesses of the CAPM in a model with three factors, known as the Fama–French model (FFM). The FFM is among the most widely known nonproprietary multifactor models. The factors are:

---

[42] In the case of the Fama–French model, however, the premiums of two factors are not stated as quantities in excess of the risk-free rate.

[43] For example, Fama and French (1993) and Strong and Xu (1997) documented size and book-to-market premiums for the United States and the United Kingdom, respectively. Capaul, Rowley, and Sharpe (1993) and Chen and Zhang (1998) documented a value premium in developed markets internationally.

► RMRF, standing for $R_M - R_F$, the return on a market value-weighted equity index in excess of the one-month T-bill rate—this is one way the equity risk premium can be represented and is the factor shared with the CAPM.

► SMB (small minus big), a size (market capitalization) factor. SMB is the average return on three small-cap portfolios minus the average return on three large-cap portfolios. Thus SMB represents a small-cap return premium.

► HML (high minus low), the average return on two high book-to-market portfolios minus the average return on two low book-to-market portfolios.[44] With high book-to-market (equivalently, low price-to-book) shares representing a value bias and low book-to-market representing a growth bias, in general, HML represents a value return premium.

Each of the factors can be viewed as the mean return to a zero-net investment, long–short portfolio. SMB represents the mean return to shorting large-cap shares and investing the proceeds in small-cap shares; HML is the mean return from shorting low book-to-market (high P/B) shares and investing the proceeds in high book-to-market shares. The FFM estimate of the required return is:

$$r_i = R_F + \beta_i^{\text{mkt}}\text{RMRF} + \beta_i^{\text{size}}\text{SMB} + \beta_i^{\text{value}}\text{HML}. \tag{11}$$

Historical data on the factors are publicly available for at least 24 countries.[45] The historical approach is frequently used in estimating the risk premia of this model. The definitions of RMRF, SMB, and HML have a specificity that lends itself to such estimation. Nevertheless, the range of estimation approaches discussed earlier could also be applied to estimating the FFM factors. Note the definition of RMRF in terms of a short-term rate; available historical series are in terms of a premium over a short-term government debt rate. In using Equation 11, we would take a current short-term risk-free rate. Note as well that because other factors besides the market factor are included in Equation 11, the beta on the market in Equation 11 is generally not exactly the same value as the CAPM beta for a given stock.

We can illustrate the FFM using the case of the U.S. equity market. A current short-term interest rate is 4.1 percent. We take RMRF to be 5.5 percent based on Panel B of Exhibit 1. The historical size premium is 2.7 percent based on Fama–French data from 1926. However, over the last quarter century approximately (1980 to 2006) the realized SML premium has averaged about one-half of that. Therefore, the historical estimate is adjusted downward to 2.0 percent. The realized value premium has had wide swings, but absent the case for a secular decline as for the size premium, we take the historical value of 4.3 percent based on Fama–French data. Thus, one estimate of the FFM for the U.S. market as of 2007 is:

$$r_i = 0.041 + \beta_i^{\text{mkt}}0.055 + \beta_i^{\text{size}}0.02 + \beta_i^{\text{value}}0.043$$

[44] See http://mba.tuck.dartmouth.edu/pages/faculty/ken.french/ for more information on the Fama–French model and factor data information.

[45] The countries include Australia, Austria, Belgium, Canada, Denmark, Finland, France, Germany, Hong Kong, Ireland, Italy, Japan, Malaysia, Netherlands, New Zealand, Norway, Singapore, Spain, Sweden, Switzerland, the United Kingdom, and the United States. See http://mba.tuck.dartmouth.edu/pages/faculty/ken.french/ for more information on the Fama–French model and factor data information.

Consider the case of a small-cap issue with value characteristics and above-average market risk—assume the FFM market beta is 1.20. If the issue's market capitalization is small, we expect it to have a positive size beta; for example, $\beta_i^{size} = 0.5$. If the shares sell cheaply in relation to book equity (i.e., they have a high book-to-market ratio), the value beta is also expected to be positive; for example, $\beta_i^{value} = 0.8$. For both the size and value betas, zero is the neutral value, in contrast with the market beta, where the neutral value is 1. Thus, according to the FFM, the shares' required return is slightly over 15 percent:

$$r_i = 0.041 + 1.20(0.055) + 0.5(0.02) + 0.8(0.043) = 0.151$$

The FFM market beta of 1.2 could be above or below the CAPM beta, but for this comparison, suppose it is 1.20. The CAPM estimate would be $0.041 + 1.20(0.055) = 0.107$ or less by about $15.1 - 10.7$ or 4.4 percentage points. In this case, positive size and value exposures help account for the different estimates in the two models.

Returning to the specification of the FFM to discuss its interpretation, note that the FFM factors are of two types:

▶ an equity market factor, which is identified with systematic risk as in the CAPM; and

▶ two factors related to company characteristics and valuation, size (SMB) and value (HML).

The FFM views the size and value factors as representing ("proxying for") a set of underlying risk factors. For example, small market-cap companies may be subject to risk factors such as less ready access to private and public credit markets and competitive disadvantages. High book-to-market may represent shares with depressed prices because of exposure to financial distress. The FFM views the return premiums to small size and value as compensation for bearing types of systematic risk. Many practitioners and researchers believe, however, that those return premiums arise from market inefficiencies rather than compensation for systematic risk.[46]

EXAMPLE 7

An Analyst Case Study (3): The Required Return on Microsoft Shares

Weeramantry's next task in researching Microsoft shares is to estimate a required return on equity (which is also a required return on total capital because Microsoft has no long-term debt). Weeramantry uses an equally weighted average of the CAPM and FFM estimates unless one method appears to be superior as judged by more than a five point difference in adjusted R^2; in that case, only the estimate with superior explanatory power is used. Exhibit 7 shows the cost of equity information for Microsoft Corporation. All the beta estimates in Exhibit 7 are significant at the 5 percent level.

---

[46] Lakonishok, Shleifer, and Vishny (1994) and La Porta, Lakonishok, Shleifer, and Vishny (1997).

	Model A	Model B
EXHIBIT 7 — CAPM and FFM Required Return Estimates, Microsoft Corporation		
1) Current risk-free rate	4.7%	4.7%
2) Beta	1.04	1.14
3) Market (equity) risk premium	5.5%	5.5%
Premium for stock: (2) × (3) =	*5.72%*	*6.27%*
4) Size beta	—	–0.222
5) Size Premium (SMB)	—	2.7%
Premium for stock: (4) × (5) =	—	*–0.60%*
6) Value beta	—	–0.328
7) Value Premium	—	4.3%
Premium for stock: (6) × (7) =	—	*–1.41%*
R^2	0.34	0.35
Adjusted R^2	0.33	0.32

Sources: http://mba.tuck.dartmouth.edu/pages/faculty/ken.french/data_library.html for size and value historical premia data (1926–2006) and Morningstar Ibbotson, The Cost of Capital Resources (March 2007 report for Microsoft) for CAPM and FFM betas and R^2.

Weeramantry's and Delacour's fund holds positions for 4 years on average. Weeramantry and his colleague Delacour are apprised that their firm's economic unit expects that the marketplace will favor growth-oriented equities over the coming year. Reviewing all the information, Delacour makes the following statements:

▶ "Microsoft's cost of equity benefits from the company's above average market capitalization, which offsets the stock's above average premium for market risk."

▶ "If our economic unit's analysis is correct, growth-oriented portfolios are expected to outperform value-oriented portfolios over the next year. As a consequence, we should favor the CAPM required return estimate over the Fama–French estimate."

Using only the above information, address the following.

1. Estimate Microsoft's cost of equity using the:
   A. CAPM.
   B. Fama–French model.
2. Judge whether Delacour's first statement, concerning Microsoft's cost of equity, is accurate.

> **3.** Judge whether Delacour's second statement, concerning the expected relative performance of growth-oriented portfolios and the use of the CAPM and FFM required return estimates, is correct.
>
> **Solution to 1:**
> **A.** The required return according to the CAPM is 4.7% + 1.04(5.5%) = 4.7% + 5.72% = 10.42%.
> **B.** The required return according to the FFM is 4.7% + 1.14(5.5%) + (−0.222)(2.7%) + (−0.328)(4.3%) = 4.7% + 6.27% + (−0.60%) + (−1.41%) = 8.96 percent.
>
> **Solution to 2:** The statement is accurate. Because the SMB premium is positive and Microsoft has negative exposure to it (size beta is −0.222), the effect of size on Microsoft's required return is to reduce it, offsetting the opposite effect on the required return of Microsoft's above average market risk (Microsoft's market beta is above 1.0).
>
> **Solution to 3:** The statement is incorrect. It suggests that computing a required return using a positive value premium is questionable when the investor short-term forecast is for growth to outperform value. Required return estimates should reflect the expected or long-run compensation for risk. The positive value of the value premium in the FFM reflects expected compensation for bearing risk over the long run, consistent with the company's cash flows extending out to the indefinite future. The economic unit's prediction for a short-term time horizon does not invalidate the use of a positive value premium for the Fama–French model.

The regression fit statistics for both the CAPM and FFM in Example 7 were high. There is more to learn about the relative merits of the CAPM and FFM in practice, but the FFM appears to have the potential for being a practical addition to the analyst's toolkit. One study contrasting the CAPM and FFM for U.S. markets found that whereas differences in the CAPM beta explained on average 3 percent of the cross-sectional differences in returns of the stocks over the next year, the FFM betas explained on average 5 percent of the differences.[47] Neither performance appears to be impressive, but keep in mind that equity returns are subject to a very high degree of randomness over short horizons.

4.2.2 Extensions to the Fama–French Model

The thought process behind the FFM of extending the CAPM to capture observed patterns in equity returns that differences in the CAPM beta appear not to explain has been extended by other researchers. One well-established relationship is that investors demand a return premium for assets that are relatively illiquid—assets that cannot be quickly sold in quantity without high explicit or implicit transaction costs. Pastor and Stambaugh (2003) extended the FFM to encompass compensation for the degree of liquidity of an equity investment.

---

[47] Bartholdy and Peare (2004).

This model has been applied to public security investment as well as certain private security investments.[48] The Pastor–Stambaugh model (PSM) adds to the FFM a fourth factor, LIQ, representing the excess returns to a portfolio that invests the proceeds from shorting high-liquidity stocks in a portfolio of low-liquidity stocks:

$$r_i = R_F + \beta_i^{mkt}RMRF + \beta_i^{size}SMB + \beta_i^{value}HML + \beta_i^{liq}LIQ \qquad \textbf{(12)}$$

An estimate of the liquidity premium for U.S. equity markets is 4.5 percent.[49] An estimate of the PSM model for U.S. markets is:

$$r_i = 0.041 + \beta_i^{mkt}\,0.055 + \beta_i^{size}\,0.02 + \beta_i^{value}\,0.043 + \beta_i^{liq}\,0.045$$

An average-liquidity equity should have a liquidity beta of 0, with no impact on required return. But below-average liquidity (positive liquidity beta) and above-average liquidity (negative liquidity beta) will tend to increase and decrease required return, respectively.

EXAMPLE 8

The Required Return for a Common Stock Investment

A common stock has the following characteristics:

Market beta	1.50
Size beta	0.15
Value beta	−0.52
Liquidity beta	0.20

Based only on the information given, infer the style characteristics of the above common stock issue.

Solution: The issue appears to be small-cap and have a growth orientation. The positive size beta indicates sensitivity to small-cap returns as would characterize small-cap stocks. (A positive liquidity beta, as shown, would also be typical for small-cap stocks because they usually trade in less liquid markets than do large-cap stocks.) The negative value beta indicates a growth orientation.

The concept of liquidity may be distinguished from marketability. With reference to equities, liquidity relates to the ease and potential price impact of the sale of an equity interest into the market. Liquidity is a function of several factors including the size of the interest and the depth and breadth of the market and its ability to absorb a block (i.e., a large position) without an adverse price impact. In the strictest sense, marketability relates to the right to sell an asset.

---

[48] See Metrick (2007).

[49] Metrick (2007), pp. 77–78, applied the PSM to venture capital fund investment.

Barring securities law or other contractual restrictions, all equity interests are potentially marketable, i.e., they can be potentially marketed for sale in the sense of the existence of a market into which the security can be sold. However, in private business valuation, the two terms are often used interchangeably.[50] The typical treatment in that context is to take a discount for lack of marketability (liquidity) from the value estimate, where justified,[51] rather than incorporate the effect in the discount rate, as in the PSM.

4.2.3 Macroeconomic and Statistical Multifactor Models

The FFM and PSM are examples of one type of a range of models for required return that are based on multiple fundamental factors (factors that are attributes of the stocks or companies themselves, e.g., the price-to-earnings ratio for a share or the company's financial leverage); the group includes several proprietary models as well. Models for required return have also been based on macroeconomic and statistical factors.

▶ In macroeconomic factor models the factors are economic variables that affect the expected future cash flows of companies and/or the discount rate that is appropriate to determining their present values.

▶ In statistical factor models, statistical methods are applied to historical returns to determine portfolios of securities (serving as factors) that explain those returns in various senses.

A specific example of macroeconomic factor models is the five-factor BIRR model, presented in Burmeister, Roll, and Ross (1994), with factor definitions as follows:

1. Confidence risk: the unanticipated change in the return difference between risky corporate bonds and government bonds, both with maturities of 20 years. To explain the factor's name, when their confidence is high, investors are willing to accept a smaller reward for bearing the added risk of corporate bonds.

2. Time horizon risk: the unanticipated change in the return difference between 20-year government bonds and 30-day Treasury bills. This factor reflects investors' willingness to invest for the long term.

3. Inflation risk: the unexpected change in the inflation rate. Nearly all stocks have negative exposure to this factor, as their returns decline with positive surprises in inflation.

4. Business cycle risk: the unexpected change in the level of real business activity. A positive surprise or unanticipated change indicates that the expected growth rate of the economy, measured in constant dollars, has increased.

5. Market timing risk: The portion of the total return of an equity market proxy (e.g., the S&P 500 for the United States) that remains unexplained by the first four risk factors. Almost all stocks have positive sensitivity to this factor.

---

[50] Hitchner (2006), p. 390.

[51] See Hitchner (2006), pp. 390–391.

The fifth factor acknowledges the uncertainty surrounding the correct set of underlying variables for asset pricing; this factor captures influences on the returns to the market proxy not explained by the first four factors. For example, using such a model, the required return for a security could have the form

$$r_i = \text{T-bill rate} + (\text{Sensitivity to confidence risk} \times 2.59\%) - (\text{Sensitivity to time horizon risk} \times 0.66\%) - (\text{Sensitivity to inflation risk} \times 4.32\%) + (\text{Sensitivity to business-cycle risk} \times 1.49\%) + (\text{Sensitivity to market-timing risk} \times 3.61\%)$$

where the risk premia estimates are developed using econometric techniques referenced in Burmeister, et al. (1994). Similar to models based on fundamental factors, models based on macroeconomic and statistical factors have various proprietary implementations.

4.3 Build-Up Method Estimates of the Required Return on Equity

Widely used by valuators of closely held businesses, the build-up method estimates the required return on an equity investment as the sum of the risk-free rate and a set of risk premia:

$$r_i = \text{Risk-free rate} + \text{Equity risk premium} \pm \text{One or more premia (discounts)}$$

The build-up method parallels the risk premium approach embodied in multifactor models with the difference that specific beta adjustments are not applied to factor risk premiums.

4.3.1 Build-Up Approaches for Private Business Valuation

The need for estimates of the required return on the equity of a private business arises when present value models—known in such contexts as income models—are used in the process of valuing business interests. Because the valuation of such interests takes place not only for completely private investment purposes but where courts and tax authorities may play a role—e.g., in the valuation of a business included in an estate or the valuation of an equity interest for a legal dispute—the valuator may need to research which methods such authorities have found to be acceptable.

Standard approaches to estimating the required return on equity for publicly traded companies, such as the CAPM and the FFM, are adaptable for estimating the required rate of return for non-publicly traded companies. However, valuators often use an approach to valuation that relies on building up the required rate of return as a set of premia added to the risk-free rate. The premia include the equity risk premium and one or more additional premia, often based on factors such as size and perceived company-specific risk, depending on the facts of the exercise and the valuator's analysis of them. An expression for the build-up approach was presented in Equation 5. A traditional specific implementation is as follows:[52]

r_i = Risk-free rate + Equity risk premium + Size premium$_i$
    + Specific-company premium$_i$

Exhibit 8 explains the logic for a typical case. The equity risk premium is often estimated with reference to equity indices of publicly traded companies. The market's largest market-capitalization companies typically constitute a large fraction of such indices' value. With a beta of 1.0 implicitly multiplying the equity risk premium, the sum of the risk-free rate and equity risk premium is effectively the required return on an average-systematic-risk large-cap public equity issue. In the great majority of cases, private business valuation concerns companies much smaller in size than public large-cap issues. Valuators often add a premium related to the excess returns of small stocks over large stocks reflecting an incremental return for small size. (The premium is typically after adjustment for the differences in the betas of small- and large-cap stocks to isolate the effect of size—a beta-adjusted size premium.) The level of the size premium is typically assumed to be inversely related to the size of the company being valued. When the size premium estimate is appropriately based on the lowest market-cap decile—frequently the case because many private businesses are small relative to publicly traded companies—the result corresponds to the return on an average-systematic-risk micro-cap public equity issue. An analysis of risk factors that are incremental to those captured by the previously included premia may lead the valuator to add a specific company premium. This risk premium sometimes includes a premium for unsystematic risk of the subject company under the premise that such risk related to a privately-held company may be less easily diversified away.

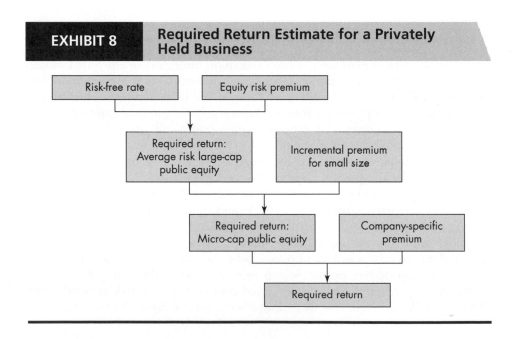

EXHIBIT 8   Required Return Estimate for a Privately Held Business

---

[52] See Hitchner (2006), p. 173.

Two additional issues related to required return estimation for private companies include 1) consideration of the relative values of controlling versus minority interests in share value and 2) the effect on share value of the lack of ready marketability for a small equity interest in a private company. Lack of marketability is the inability to immediately sell shares due to lack of access to public equity markets because the shares are not registered for public trading. (Marketability may also be restricted by contractual or other reasons.)

With respect to the potential adjustment for the relative control associated with an equity interest in a private company, any adjustments related to the type of interest (controlling or minority) are traditionally not made in the required return but, if appropriate, directly to the preliminary value estimate. The issues involved in such adjustments are complex with some diversity of viewpoints among practitioners. Given these considerations, a detailed discussion is outside the scope of this reading.[53] Similarly, adjustments for lack of marketability are traditionally taken as an adjustment to the estimated value for an equity interest after any adjustment for the degree of control of the equity interest.

To illustrate, suppose an analyst is valuing a private integrated document management solutions company. The risk-free rate is 5 percent, the analyst's estimate of the equity risk premium is 4.5 percent, and based on assets and revenues the company appears to correspond to the top half of the 10th decile of U.S. public companies, which is decile 10a in Exhibit 9 with market capitalizations of equity ranging from about $174 million to about $314 million.

EXHIBIT 9	Estimates of U.S. Beta Adjusted Size Premia	
Market Cap Decile	**Market Cap Range (Millions)**	**Size Premium**
6	$1,379.267 to $1,946.588	1.67%
7	$977.912 to $1,378.476	1.62
8	$627.017 to $976.624	2.28
9	$314.912 to $626.955	2.70
10	$2.247 to $314.433	6.27
	Breakdown of the 10th Decile	
10a	$173.664 to $314.433	4.35%
10b	$2.247 to $173.439	9.68

Source: Ibbotson (2007), p. 262.

Thus, ignoring any appropriate specific-company premium, an estimate of the required return on equity is 5% + 4.5% + 4.35% = 13.85%. A caution is that the size premium for the smallest decile (and especially the 10b component) may reflect not only the premium for healthy small-cap companies, but former large-cap companies that are in financial distress. If that is the case, the historical estimate may not be applicable without a downward adjustment for estimating the required return for a small but financially healthy private company.

---

[53] For more information on adjustments for relative control, see Hitchner (2006), ch. 8, and Bruner (2004), ch.15.

A so-called modified CAPM formulation would seek to capture departures from average systematic risk. For example, if the analyst estimated that the company would have a beta of 1.2 if publicly traded, based on its publicly traded peer group, the required return estimate would be

Risk-free rate + Beta × Equity risk premium + Size premium

or 5% + 1.2 × 4.5% + 4.35% = 14.75%. This result could be reconciled to a simple build-up estimate by including a differential return of (1.2 − 1.0)(4.5%) = 0.9% in the specific-company premium.

4.3.2 Bond Yield Plus Risk Premium

For companies with publicly traded debt, the **bond yield plus risk premium method** provides a quick estimate of the cost of equity.[54] The estimate is

$$\text{BYPRP cost of equity} = \text{YTM on the company's long-term debt} + \text{Risk premium} \tag{13}$$

The YTM on the company's long-term debt includes:

▶ a real interest rate and a premium for expected inflation, which are also factors embodied in a government bond yield; and

▶ a default risk premium.

The default risk premium captures factors such as profitability, the sensitivity of profitability to the business cycle, and leverage (operating and financial) that also affect the returns to equity. The risk premium in Equation 13 is the premium that compensates for the additional risk of the equity issue compared with the debt issue (recognizing that debt has a prior claim on the cash flows of the company). In U.S. markets, the typical risk premium added is 3–4 percent, based on experience.

In the first edition of the book from which this reading was taken, IBM's required return was estimated as 12.9 percent using the CAPM; the inputs used were an equity risk premium estimate of 5.7 percent, a beta of 1.24, and a risk-free rate of 5.8. Based on the YTM of 6.238 percent for the IBM 8.375s of 2019, a bond yield plus risk premium estimate was 9.2 percent.

EXAMPLE 9

The Cost of Equity of IBM from Two Perspectives

You are valuing the stock of International Business Machines Corporation (NYSE: IBM) as of early September 2007, and you have gathered the following information:

20-year T-bond YTM:	5.0%
IBM 8.375s of 2019 YTM:	5.632%

---

[54] Although simple, the method has been used in serious contexts. For example, the Board of Regents of the University of California in a retirement plan asset/liability study (July 2000) used the 20-year T-bond rate plus 3.3 percent as the single estimate of the equity risk premium.

The IBM bonds, you note, are investment grade (rated A1 by Standard & Poor's, A+ by Moody's Investors Service, and A by Fitch). The beta on IBM stock is 1.72. In prior valuations you have used a risk premium of 3 percent in the bond yield plus risk premium approach. However, the estimated beta of IBM has increased by more than one-third over the past five years. As a matter of judgment, you have decided as a consequence to use a risk premium of 3.5 percent in the bond yield plus risk premium approach.

1. Calculate the cost of equity using the CAPM. Assume that the equity risk premium is 4.5 percent.

2. Calculate the cost of equity using the bond yield plus risk premium approach, with a risk premium of 3.5 percent.

3. Suppose you found that IBM stock, which closed at 117.43 on 4 September 2007, was slightly undervalued based on a DCF valuation using the CAPM cost of equity from Question 1. Does the alternative estimate of the cost of equity from Question 2 support the conclusion based on Question 1?

Solution to 1: $5\% + 1.72(4.5\%) = 12.7\%$.

Solution to 2: Add 3.5 percent to the IBM bond YTM: $5.632\% + 3.5\% = 9.132\%$, or 9.1 percent. Note that the difference between the IBM bond YTM and T-bond YTM is 0.632 percent, or 63 basis points. This amount plus 3.5 percent is the total estimated risk premium versus Treasury debt.

Solution to 3: *Undervalued* means that the value of a security is greater than market price. All else equal, the lower the discount rate, the higher the estimate of value. The inverse relationship between discount rate and value, holding all else constant, is a basic relationship in valuation. If IBM appears to be undervalued using the CAPM cost of equity estimate of 12.7 percent, it will appear to be even more undervalued using a 9.1 percent cost of equity based on the bond yield plus risk premium method.

Thus, updating Example 9 to 2007 shows that a lower equity risk premium estimate is offset by IBM's higher current beta, leaving the required return on equity almost unchanged according to the CAPM. With IBM's credit rating unchanged, the lower level of interest rates in 2007 would have lowered the bond yield plus risk premium estimate, all else equal. Because a lower level of interest rates is consistent with lower opportunity costs for investors, that result would have been logical. Because IBM's systematic risk had increased, a risk premium increase was justified and the cost of equity estimate was essentially unchanged.

The bond yield plus risk premium method can be viewed as a build-up method applying to companies with publicly traded debt. The estimate provided can be a useful check when the explanatory power of more rigorous models is low. Given that a company's shares have positive systematic risk, the yield on its long-term debt is revealing as a check on cost of equity estimate. For example, Abitibi-Consolidated Inc.'s 7.5 debentures (rated by Moody's and Standard &

Poor's as B3 and B, respectively) mature in 2028 and were priced to yield approximately 11 percent as of mid August 2007, so required return estimates for its stock (NYSE: ABY) not greater than 11 percent would be suspect.

4.4 The Required Return on Equity: International Issues

Among the issues that concern analysts estimating the required return of equities in a global context are:

▶ exchange rates, and

▶ data and model issues in emerging markets.

An investor is ultimately concerned with returns and volatility stated in terms of his or her own currency. Historical returns are often available or can be constructed in local currency and home currency terms. Equity risk premium estimates in home currency terms can be higher or lower than estimates in local currency terms because exchange rate gains and losses from the equity component are generally not exactly offset by gains and losses from the government security component of the equity risk premium. For example, the arithmetic mean U.K. premium over 1970 to 2005 was 6.58 percent in pound sterling terms but for a U.S. investor it was 5.54 percent.[55] The U.S. dollar estimate more accurately reflects a U.S. investor's historical experience. A sound approach for any investor is to focus on the local currency record, incorporating any exchange rate forecasts.

The difficulty of required return and risk premium estimation in emerging markets has been previously mentioned. Of the numerous approaches that have been proposed to supplement or replace traditional historical and forward looking methods, we can mention two.

▶ The country spread model for the equity risk premium. For an emerging equity market, this states that:

$$\text{Equity risk premium estimate} = \text{Equity risk premium for a developed market} + \text{Country premium}$$

The country premium represents a premium associated with the expected greater risk of the emerging market compared to the benchmark developed market. Typically, analysts hope that a sovereign bond yield spread is adequate for approximating this premium. Thus, the country premium is often estimated as the yield on emerging market bonds (denominated in the currency of the developed market) minus the yield on developed market government bonds.

To illustrate, taking the approximate 13 percent yield differential between U.S. dollar denominated government of Russia bonds ("Brady bonds") and U.S. Treasury bonds as the Russian country premium and using an estimate of 4.5 percent for the U.S. equity risk premium, the Russian equity risk premium equals 4.5% + 13% = 17.5%.

▶ The country risk rating model[56] provides a regression-based estimate of the equity risk premium based on the empirical relationship between

---

[55] Morningstar (2007), p. 176.

[56] Erb, Claude, Campbell R. Harvey, and Tadas Viskanta, "Country Credit Risk and Global Portfolio Selection," *Journal of Portfolio Management*, Winter 1995: 74–83.

developed equity market returns and Institutional Investor's semi-annual risk ratings for those markets. The estimated regression equation is then used with the risk ratings for less developed markets to predict the required return for those markets. This model has been recommended by Morningstar (Ibbotson).

THE WEIGHTED AVERAGE COST OF CAPITAL 5

The overall required rate of return of a company's suppliers of capital is usually referred to as the company's cost of capital. The cost of capital is most commonly estimated using the company's after-tax weighted average cost of capital, or weighted average cost of capital (WACC) for short: a weighted average of required rates of return for the component sources of capital.

The cost of capital is relevant to equity valuation when an analyst takes an indirect, total firm value approach using a present value model. Using the cost of capital to discount expected future cash flows available to debt and equity, the total value of these claims is estimated. The balance of this value after subtracting off the market value of debt is the estimate of the value of equity.

In many jurisdictions, corporations may deduct net interest expense from income in calculating taxes owed, but they cannot deduct payments to shareholders, such as dividends. The following discussion reflects that base case.

If the suppliers of capital are creditors and common stockholders, the expression for WACC is

$$\text{WACC} = \frac{\text{MVD}}{\text{MVD} + \text{MVCE}} r_d (1 - \text{Tax rate}) + \frac{\text{MVCE}}{\text{MVD} + \text{MVCE}} r \qquad \textbf{(14)}$$

where MVD and MVCE are the current market values of debt and (common) equity, not their book or accounting values. Dividing MVD or MVCE by the total market value of the firm, which is MVD + MVCE, gives the proportions of the company's total capital from debt or equity, respectively. These weights will sum to 1.0. The expression for WACC multiplies the weights of debt and equity in the company's financing by, respectively, the after-tax required rates of return for the company's debt and equity under current market conditions. "After-tax," it is important to note, refers to just corporate taxes in this discussion. Multiplying the before-tax required return on debt (r_d) by 1 minus the marginal corporate tax rate (1 − Tax rate) adjusts the pretax rate r_d downward to reflect the tax deductibility of corporate interest payments that is being assumed. Because distributions to equity are assumed not to be deductible by the corporations, a corporation's before and after-tax costs of equity are the same; no adjustment to r involving the corporate tax rate is appropriate. Generally speaking, it is appropriate to use a company's marginal tax rate rather than its current effective tax rate (reported taxes divided by pretax income) because the effective tax rate can reflect nonrecurring items. A cost of capital based on the marginal tax rate usually better reflects a company's future costs in raising funds.

Because the company's capital structure (the proportions of debt and equity financing) can change over time, WACC may also change over time. In addition, the company's current capital structure may also differ substantially from what it will be in future years. For these reasons, analysts often use *target* weights instead of the current market-value weights when calculating WACC. These target weights incorporate both the analyst's and investors' expectations about the target capital structure that the company will tend to use over time. Target weights provide a good approximation of the WACC for cases in which the current weights misrepresent the company's normal capital structure.[57]

The before-tax required return on debt is typically estimated using the expected YTM of the company's debt based on current market values. Analysts can choose from any of the methods presented in this reading for estimating the required return on equity, r. No tax adjustment is appropriate for the cost of equity assuming payments to shareholders such as dividends are not tax deductible by companies.

EXAMPLE 10

The Weighted Average Cost of Capital for IBM

Taking an indirect, total firm value approach to valuing equity, suppose you have the inputs for estimating the cost of capital shown in Exhibit 10. Based only on the information given, estimate IBM's WACC.

EXHIBIT 10   Cost of Capital Data: IBM

Panel A: Capital Structure	Value
Long-term debt as a percent of total capital, at market value	35%
Tax rate	29%

Panel B: Component Costs of Capital	
Cost of equity: CAPM estimate	12.7%
YTM of IBM long bond	5.6%

Source: Estimates based on company reports; Standard & Poor's.

Solution: Long-term debt as a percent of total capital stated at market value is the weight to be applied to IBM's after-tax cost of debt in the WACC calculation. Therefore, IBM's WACC is approximately 9.65 percent, calculated as follows:

$$\text{WACC} = 0.35(5.6\%)(1 - 0.29) + 0.65(12.7\%)$$
$$= 1.392\% + 8.255\% = 9.647 \text{ percent}$$

---

[57] See a modern corporate finance textbook, such as Brealey, Myers, and Allen (2006), for a review of capital structure theory.

DISCOUNT RATE SELECTION IN RELATION TO CASH FLOWS

When used as discount rates in valuation, required returns need to be defined appropriately relative to the cash flows to be discounted.

A cash flow after more senior claims (e.g., promised payments on debt and taxes) have been fulfilled is a cash flow to equity. When a cash flow to equity is discounted, the required return on equity is an appropriate discount rate. When a cash flow is available to meet the claims of all of a company's capital providers—usually called a cash flow to the firm—the firm's cost of capital is the appropriate discount rate.

Cash flows may be stated in nominal or real terms. When cash flows are stated in real terms, amounts reflect offsets made for actual or anticipated changes in the purchasing power of money. Nominal discount rates must be used with nominal cash flows and real discount rates must be used with real cash flows. In valuing equity, we will use only nominal cash flows and therefore we will make use of nominal discount rates. Because the tax rates applying to corporate earnings are generally stated in nominal money terms—such and such tax rates applying at stated levels of nominal pretax earnings—using nominal quantities is an exact approach because it reflects taxes accurately.

Equation 14 presents an after-tax weighted average cost of capital using the after-tax cost of debt. In later readings, we will present cash flow to the firm definitions for which it is appropriate to use that definition of the cost of capital as the discount rate (i.e., rather than a pretax cost of capital reflecting a pretax cost of debt). The exploration of the topic is outside the scope of this reading because the definitions of cash flows have not been introduced and explained.[58]

In short, in later readings we will be able to illustrate present value models of stock value using only two discount rates: the nominal required return on equity when the cash flows are those available to common shareholders, and the nominal after-tax weighted average cost of capital when the cash flows are those available to all the company's capital providers.

---

[58] Technically, in discounting a cash flow to the company, the definitions of the cash flow and cost of capital should be coordinated so the value of the tax saving associated with the deductibility of interest expense is not counted twice (i.e., in the cash flow and the discount rate).

SUMMARY

In this reading we introduced several important return concepts. Required returns are important because they are used as discount rates in determining the present value of expected future cash flows. When an investor's intrinsic value estimate for an asset differs from its market price, the investor generally expects to earn the required return plus a return from the convergence of price to value. When an asset's intrinsic value equals price, however, the investor only expects to earn the required return.

For two important approaches to estimating a company's required return, the CAPM and the build-up model, the analyst needs an estimate of the equity risk premium. This reading examined realized equity risk premia for a group of major world equity markets and also explained forward-looking estimation methods. For determining the required return on equity, the analyst may choose from the CAPM and various multifactor models such as the Fama–French model and its extensions, examining regression fit statistics to assess the reliability of these methods. For private companies, the analyst can adapt public equity valuation models for required return using public company comparables, or use a build-up model, which starts with the risk-free rate and the estimated equity risk premium and adds additional appropriate risk premia.

When the analyst approaches the valuation of equity indirectly, by first valuing the total firm as the present value of expected future cash flows to all sources of capital, the appropriate discount rate is a weighted average cost of capital based on all sources of capital. Discount rates must be on a nominal (real) basis if cash flows are on a nominal (real) basis.

Among the reading's major points are the following:

► The return from investing in an asset over a specified time period is called the *holding period return*. *Realized return* refers to a return achieved in the past, and *expected return* refers to an anticipated return over a future time period. A *required return* is the minimum level of expected return that an investor requires to invest in the asset over a specified time period, given the asset's riskiness. The (*market*) *required return*, a required rate of return on an asset that is inferred using market prices or returns, is typically used as the *discount rate* in finding the present values of expected future cash flows. If an asset is perceived (is not perceived) as fairly priced in the marketplace, the required return should (should not) equal the investor's expected return. When an asset is believed to be mispriced, investors should earn a *return from convergence of price to intrinsic value*.

► An estimate of the equity risk premium—the incremental return that investors require for holding equities rather than a risk-free asset—is used in the CAPM and in the build-up approach to required return estimation.

► Approaches to equity risk premium estimation include historical, adjusted historical, and forward-looking approaches.

► In historical estimation, the analyst must decide whether to use a short-term or a long-term government bond rate to represent the risk-free rate and whether to calculate a geometric or arithmetic mean for the equity risk premium estimate. Forward-looking estimates include Gordon growth model estimates, supply-side models, and survey estimates. Adjusted historical estimates can involve an adjustment for biases in data series and an adjustment to incorporate an independent estimate of the equity risk premium.

▶ The CAPM is a widely used model for required return estimation that uses beta relative to a market portfolio proxy to adjust for risk. The Fama–French model (FFM) is a three factor model that incorporates the market factor, a size factor, and a value factor. The Pastor-Stambaugh extension to the FFM adds a liquidity factor. The bond yield plus risk premium approach finds a required return estimate as the sum of the YTM of the subject company's debt plus a subjective risk premium (often 3 percent to 4 percent).

▶ When a stock is thinly traded or not publicly traded, its beta may be estimated on the basis of a peer company's beta. The procedure involves unlevering the peer company's beta and then re-levering it to reflect the subject company's use of financial leverage. The procedure adjusts for the effect of differences of financial leverage between the peer and subject company.

▶ Emerging markets pose special challenges to required return estimation. The country spread model estimates the equity risk premium as the equity risk premium for a developed market plus a country premium. The country risk rating model approach uses risk ratings for developed markets to infer risk ratings and equity risk premiums for emerging markets.

▶ The weighted average cost of capital is used when valuing the total firm and is generally understood as the nominal after-tax weighted average cost of capital, which is used in discounting nominal cash flows to the firm in later readings. The nominal required return on equity is used in discounting cash flows to equity.

PRACTICE PROBLEMS FOR READING 35

1. A Canada-based investor buys shares of Toronto-Dominion Bank (Toronto: TD.TO) for C$72.08 on 15 October 2007 with the intent of holding them for a year. The dividend rate was C$2.11 per year. The investor actually sells the shares on 5 November 2007 for C$69.52. The investor notes the following additional facts:

   ▶ No dividends were paid between 15 October and 5 November.

   ▶ The required return on TD.TO equity was 8.7 percent on an annual basis and 0.161 percent on a weekly basis.

   A. State the lengths of the expected and actual holding-periods.

   B. Given that TD.TO was fairly priced, calculate the price appreciation return (capital gains yield) anticipated by the investor given his initial expectations and initial expected holding period.

   C. Calculate the investor's realized return.

   D. Calculate the realized alpha.

2. The estimated betas for AOL Time Warner (NYSE: AOL), J.P. Morgan Chase & Company (NYSE: JPM), and The Boeing Company (NYSE: BA) are 2.50, 1.50, and 0.80, respectively. The risk-free rate of return is 4.35 percent and the equity risk premium is 8.04 percent. Calculate the required rates of return for these three stocks using the CAPM.

3. The estimated factor sensitivities of TerraNova Energy to Fama–French factors and the risk premia associated with those factors are given in the table below:

	Factor Sensitivity	Risk Premium (%)
Market factor	1.20	4.5
Size factor	−0.50	2.7
Value factor	−0.15	4.3

   A. Based on the Fama–French model, calculate the required return for TerraNova Energy using these estimates. Assume that the Treasury bill rate is 4.7 percent.

   B. Describe the expected style characteristics of TerraNova based on its factor sensitivities.

4. Newmont Mining (NYSE: NEM) has an estimated beta of −0.2. The risk-free rate of return is 4.5 percent, and the equity risk premium is estimated to be 7.5 percent. Using the CAPM, calculate the required rate of return for investors in NEM.

5. An analyst wants to account for financial distress and market-capitalization as well as market risk in his cost of equity estimate for a particular traded company. Which of the following models is *most appropriate* for achieving that objective?

   A. The capital asset pricing model (CAPM).

   B. The Fama–French model.

   C. A macroeconomic factor model.

6. The following facts describe Larsen & Toubro Ltd's component costs of capital and capital structure. Based on the information given, calculate Larsen & Toubro's WACC.

Component Costs of Capital	(%)
Cost of equity based on the CAPM:	15.6
Pretax cost of debt:	8.28
Tax rate:	30
Target weight in capital structure:	Equity 80, Debt 20

The following information relates to Questions 7–12

An equity index is established in 2001 for a country that has relatively recently established a market economy. The index vendor constructed returns for the five years prior to 2001 based on the initial group of companies constituting the index in 2001. Over 2004 to 2006 a series of military confrontations concerning a disputed border disrupted the economy and financial markets. The dispute is conclusively arbitrated at the end of 2006. In total, ten years of equity market return history is available as of the beginning of 2007. The geometric mean return relative to 10-year government bond returns over 10 years is 2 percent per year. The forward dividend yield on the index is 1 percent. Stock returns over 2004 to 2006 reflect the setbacks but economists predict the country will be on a path of a 4 percent real GDP growth rate by 2009. Earnings in the public corporate sector are expected to grow at a 5 percent per year real growth rate. Consistent with that, the market P/E ratio is expected to grow at 1 percent per year. Although inflation is currently high at 6 percent per year, the long-term forecast is for an inflation rate of 4 percent per year. Although the yield curve has usually been upward sloping, currently the government yield curve is inverted; at the short-end, yields are 9 percent and at 10-year maturities, yields are 7 percent.

7. The inclusion of index returns prior to 2001 would be expected to:
  A. bias the historical equity risk premium estimate upwards.
  B. bias the historical equity risk premium estimate downwards.
  C. have no effect on the historical equity risk premium estimate.

8. The events of 2004 to 2006 would be expected to:
  A. bias the historical equity risk premium estimate upwards.
  B. bias the historical equity risk premium estimate downwards.
  C. have no effect on the historical equity risk premium estimate.

9. In the current interest rate environment, using a required return estimate based on the short-term government bond rate and a historical equity risk premium defined in terms of a short-term government bond rate would be expected to:
  A. bias long-term required return on equity estimates upwards.
  B. bias long-term required return on equity estimates downwards.
  C. have no effect on long-term required return on equity estimates.

10. A supply side estimate of the equity risk premium as presented by the Ibbotson–Chen earnings model is *closest* to:

   A. 3.2 percent.

   B. 4.0 percent.

   C. 4.3 percent.

11. Common stock issues in the above market with average systematic risk are *most likely* to have required rates of return:

   A. between 2 percent and 7 percent.

   B. between 7 and 9 percent.

   C. 9 percent or greater.

12. Which of the following statements is *most accurate?* If two equity issues have the same market risk but the first issue has higher leverage, greater liquidity, and a higher required return, the higher required return *is most likely* the result of the first issue's:

   A. greater liquidity.

   B. higher leverage.

   C. higher leverage and greater liquidity.

SOLUTIONS FOR READING 35

1. A. The expected holding was one year. The actual holding period was from 15 October 2007 to 5 November 2007, which is three weeks.

B. Given fair pricing, the expected return equals the required return, 8.7 percent. The expected price appreciation return over the initial anticipated one-year holding period must be equal to the required return minus the dividend yield, $2.11/72.08 = 0.0293$ or 2.93 percent. Thus expected price appreciation return was $8.7\% - 2.93\% = 5.77$ percent.

C. The realized return was $(\$69.52 - \$72.08)/\$72.08 = -0.03552$ or negative 3.55 percent over three weeks. There was no dividend yield return over the actual holding period.

D. The required return over a three-week holding period was $(1.00161)^3 - 1 = 0.484$ percent. Using the answer to C, the realized alpha was $-3.552 - 0.484 = -4.036$ percent or -4.04 percent.

2. For AOL Time Warner, the required return is

$$r = R_F + \beta[E(R_M) - R_F] = 4.35\% + 2.50(8.04\%) = 4.35\% + 20.10\% = 24.45\%$$

For J.P. Morgan Chase, the required return is

$$r = R_F + \beta[E(R_M) - R_F] = 4.35\% + 1.50(8.04\%) = 4.35\% + 12.06\% = 16.41\%$$

For Boeing, the required return is

$$r = R_F + \beta[E(R_M) - R_F] = 4.35\% + 0.80(8.04\%) = 4.35\% + 6.43\% = 10.78\%$$

3. A. The Fama–French model gives the required return as

= T-bill rate + (Sensitivity to equity market factor × Equity risk premium) + (Sensitivity to size factor × Size risk premium) + (Sensitivity to value factor × Value risk premium)

For TerraNova Energy, the required return is

$r = 4.7\% + (1.20 \times 4.5\%) + (-0.50 \times 2.7\%) + (-0.15 \times 4.3\%)$

$= 4.7\% + 5.4\% - 1.35\% - 0.645\%$

$= 8.1\%$

B. TerraNova Energy appears to be a large-cap, growth-oriented, high market risk stock as indicated by its negative size beta, negative value beta, and market beta above 1.0.

4. The required return is given by

$r = 0.045 + (-0.2)(0.075) = 4.5\% - 1.5\% = 3.0\%$

This example indicates that Newmont Mining has a required return of 3 percent. When beta is negative, an asset has a CAPM required rate of return that is below the risk-free rate. Cases of equities with negative betas are relatively rare.

5. B is correct. The Fama–French model incorporates market, size, and value risk factors. One possible interpretation of the value risk factor is that it relates to financial distress.

6. Larsen & Toubro Ltd's WACC is 13.64 percent calculated as follows:

	Equity	**Debt**	**WACC**
Weight	0.80	0.20	
After-Tax Cost	15.6%	$(1 - 0.30)8.28\%$	
Weight × Cost	12.48% +	1.16%	= 13.64%

7. A is correct. The backfilling of index returns using companies that have survived to the index construction date is expected to introduce a positive survivorship bias into returns.

8. B is correct. The events of 2004 to 2006 depressed share returns but 1) are not a persistent feature of the stock market environment, 2) were not offset by other positive events within the historical record, and 3) have led to relatively low valuation levels, which are expected to rebound.

9. A is correct. The required return reflects the magnitude of the historical equity risk premium, which is generally higher when based on a short-term interest rate (as a result of the normal upward sloping yield curve), and the current value of the rate being used to represent the risk-free rate. The short-term rate is currently higher than the long-term rate, which will also increase the required return estimate. The short-term interest rate, however, overstates the long-term expected inflation rate. Using the short-term interest rate, estimates of the long-term required return on equity will be biased upwards.

10. C is correct. According to this model, the equity risk premium is

$$\text{Equity risk premium} = \{[(1 + EINFL)(1 + EGREPS)(1 + EGPE) - 1.0] + EINC\} - \text{Expected risk-free return}$$

Here:

EINFL	= 4 percent per year (long-term forecast of inflation)
EGREPS	= 5 percent per year (growth in real earnings)
EGPE	= 1 percent per year (growth in market P/E ratio)
EINC	= 1 percent per year (dividend yield or the income portion)

Risk-free return = 7 percent per year (for 10-year maturities)

By substitution, we get:

$$\{[(1.04)(1.05)(1.01) - 1.0] + 0.01\} - 0.07$$
$$= 0.113 - 0.07 = 0.043 \text{ or } 4.3 \text{ percent.}$$

11. C is correct. Based on a long-term government bond yield of 7 percent, a beta of 1, and any of the risk premium estimates that can be calculated from the givens (e.g., a 2 percent historical risk premium estimate or 4.3 percent supply side equity risk premium estimate), the required rate of return would be at least 9 percent. Based on using a short-term rate of 9 percent, C is the correct choice.

12. B is correct. All else equal, the first issue's greater liquidity would tend to make its required return lower than the second issue's. However, the required return on equity increases as leverage increases. The first issue's higher required return must result from its higher leverage, more than offsetting the effect of its greater liquidity, given that both issues have the same market risk.

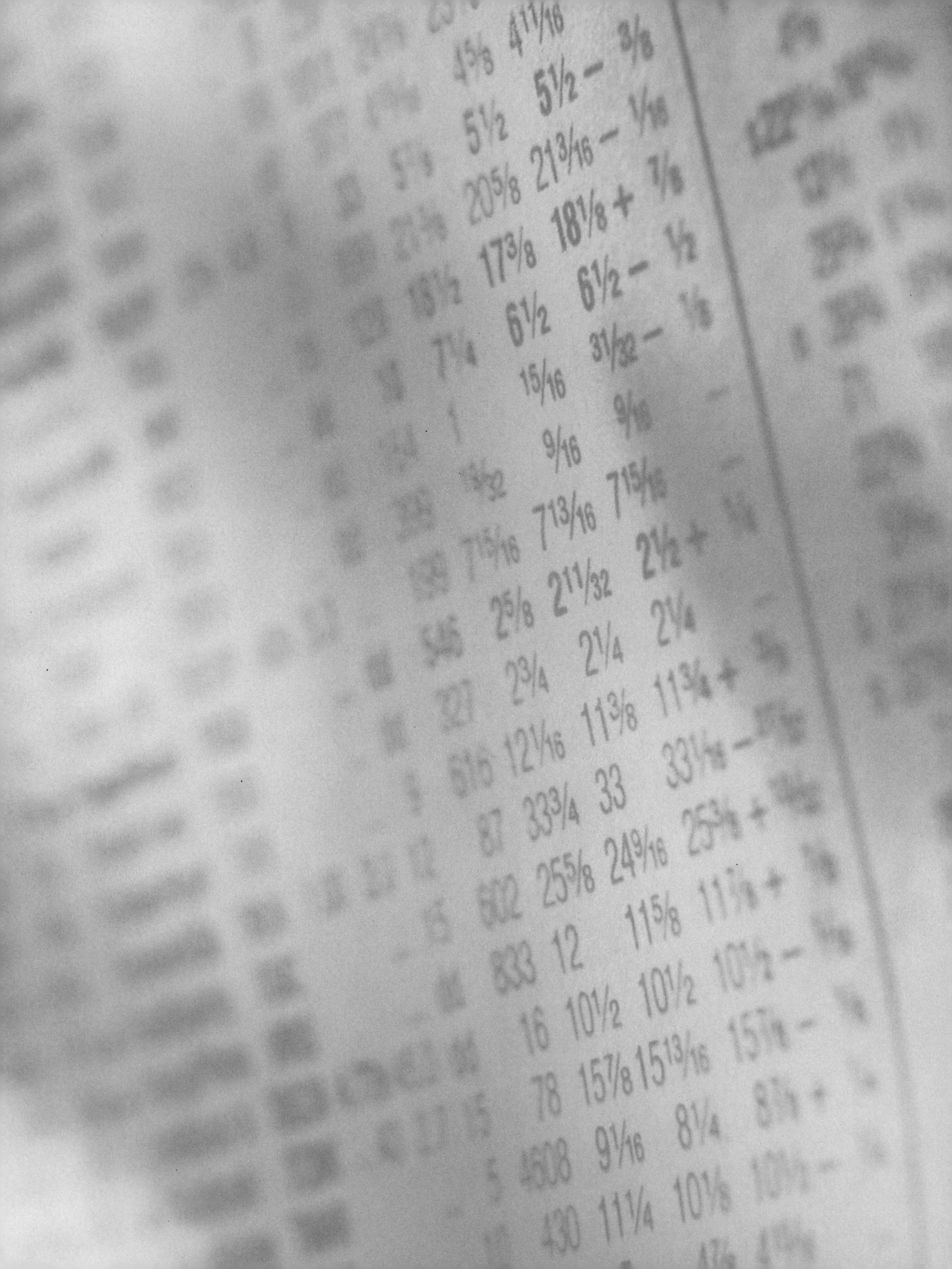

4⅝ 4¹¹/₁₆ — ⅜
5½ 5½ — ⅜
5½ 21¹³/₁₆ — ¼₁₆
20⅝ 21¹³/₁₆ — ¼₁₆
17⅜ 18⅛ + ⅞
18½ 18⅛ +
6½ 6½ — ½
7¼ 6½ — ⅛
15/₁₆ 31/₃₂ —
1 9/₁₆ 9/₁₆
1/₃₂ 9/₁₆
7¹⁵/₁₆ 7¹³/₁₆ 7¹⁵/₁₆
2⅝ 2¹¹/₃₂ 2½ +
2¾ 2¼ 2¼
12¹/₁₆ 11⅜ 11¼ +
87 33¾ 33 33¼ —
802 25⅝ 24⁹/₁₆ 25⅝ +
833 12 11⅝ 11⅝ +
16 10½ 10½ 10½ —
78 15⅞ 15¹³/₁₆ 15⅞ —
508 9/₁₆ 8¼ 8¼ +
430 11¼ 10⅝ 10⅝ —

STUDY SESSION 11
EQUITY VALUATION:
Industry and Company Analysis in a Global Context

This study session provides insights on issues that affect security valuation internationally. Analyzing industries in a global context and evaluating competitive forces that will affect returns provide a foundation for security valuation decisions. Discounted dividend models are examined in detail.

READING ASSIGNMENTS

Reading 36   The Five Competitive Forces That Shape Strategy
Harvard Business Review

Reading 37   Industry Analysis
Security Analysis on Wall Street: A Comprehensive Guide to Today's Valuation Methods, by Jeffrey C. Hooke

Reading 38   Valuation in Emerging Markets
Valuation: Measuring and Managing the Value of Companies, Fourth Edition, by Tim Koller, Marc Goedhart, and David Wessels

Reading 39   Discounted Dividend Valuation
Equity Asset Valuation, Second Edition, by Jerald Pinto, CFA, Elaine Henry, CFA, Thomas Robinson, CFA, and John Stowe, CFA

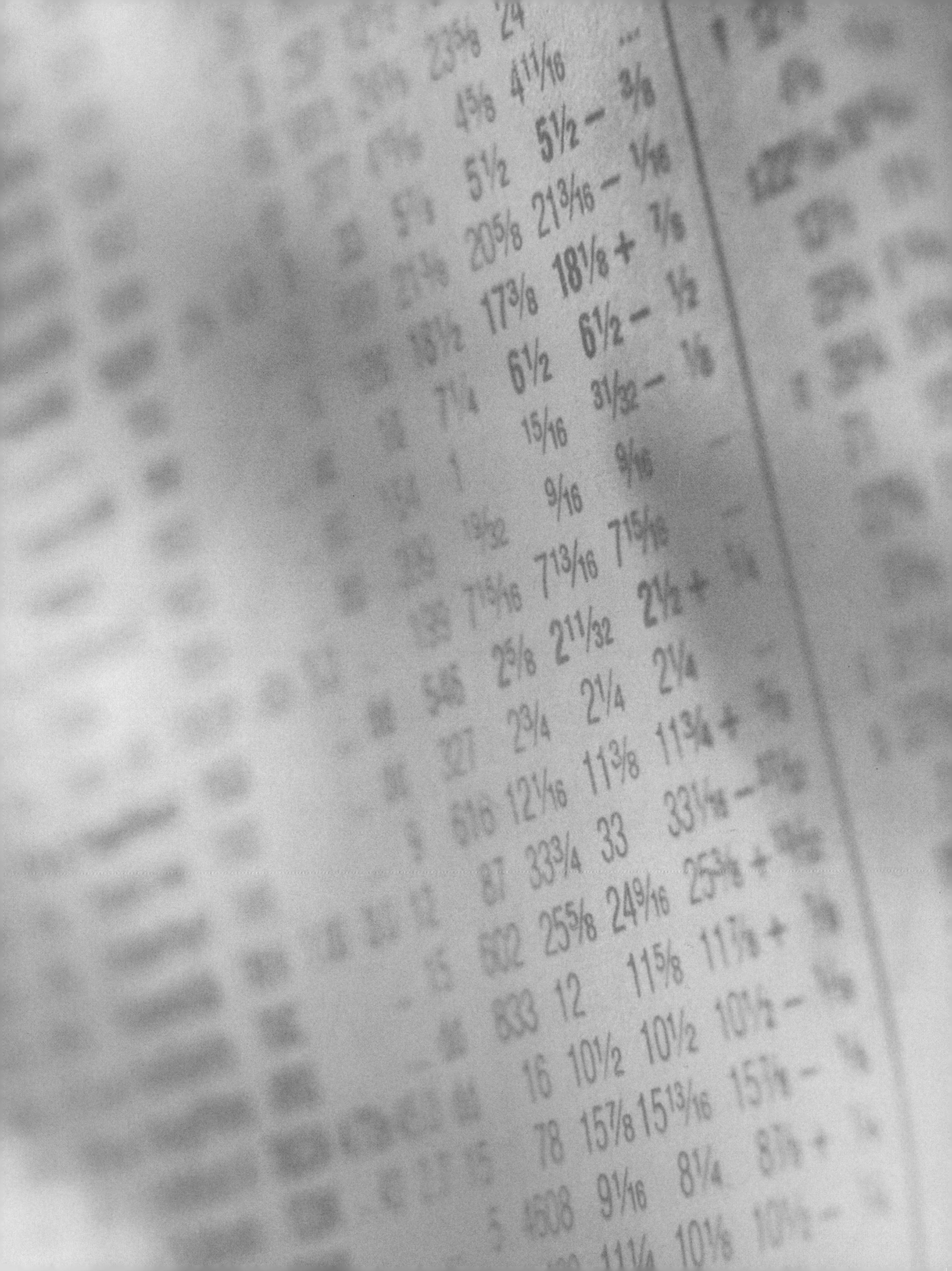

23⅝ 24

4⅝ 4¹¹⁄₁₆ ... ...

5½ 5½ − ⅜ − ⅜

5½ 5½ − ⅛

20⅝ 21¹³⁄₁₆ − ⅛

17⅜ 18⅛ + ⅞

15½ 6½ 6½ −

7¼ 6½ 31⁄32 − ½

15⁄16 − ⅛

1 9⁄16 9⁄16

19⁄32 9⁄16

7⁵⁄₁₆ 7¹³⁄₁₆ 7¹⁵⁄₁₆

2⅝ 2¹¹⁄32 2½ +

327 2¾ 2¼ 2¼

5⅛ 12¹⁄₁₆ 11⅜ 11¾ +

87 33¾ 33 33¼ −

502 25⅝ 24⁹⁄₁₆ 25⅝ +

833 12 11⅝ 11⅝ +

16 10½ 10½ 10⅛ −

78 15⅝ 15¹³⁄₁₆ 15⅝ −

4508 9¹⁄₁₆ 8¼ 8⅝ +

11¼ 10⅛ 10⅛

THE FIVE COMPETITIVE FORCES
THAT SHAPE STRATEGY
by Michael E. Porter

LEARNING OUTCOMES

The candidate should be able to:	Mastery
a. distinguish among the five competitive forces that drive industry profitability in the medium and long run;	☐
b. explain how competitive forces drive industry profitability;	☐
c. describe why industry growth rate, technology and innovation, government, and complementary products and services are fleeting factors rather than forces shaping industry structure;	☐
d. identify changes in industry structure, and forecast their effects on the industry's profit potential;	☐
e. explain how positioning a company, exploiting industry change, and shaping industry structure may be used to achieve a competitive advantage.	☐

Awareness of the five forces can help a company understand the structure of its industry and stake out a position that is more profitable and less vulnerable to attack.

Michael E. Porter is the Bishop William Lawrence University Professor at Harvard University, based at Harvard Business School in Boston. He is a six-time McKinsey Award winner, including for his most recent HBR article, "Strategy and Society," coauthored with Mark R. Kramer (December 2006).

Editor's Note: In 1979, *Harvard Business Review* published "How Competitive Forces Shape Strategy" by a young economist and associate professor, Michael E. Porter. It was his first HBR article, and it started a revolution in the strategy field. In subsequent decades, Porter has brought his signature economic rigor to the study of competitive strategy for corporations, regions, nations, and, more recently, health care and philanthropy. "Porter's five forces" have shaped a generation of academic research and business practice. With prodding and assistance from Harvard Business School Professor Jan Rivkin and longtime colleague Joan Magretta, Porter here reaffirms, updates, and extends the classic work. He also addresses common misunderstandings, provides practical guidance for users of the framework, and offers a deeper view of implications for strategy today.

THE FIVE COMPETITIVE FORCES THAT SHAPE STRATEGY

The Idea in Brief

You know that to sustain long-term profitability you must respond strategically to competition. And you naturally keep tabs on your **established rivals**. But as you scan the competitive arena, are you also looking *beyond* your direct competitors? As Porter explains in this update of his revolutionary 1979 HBR article, four additional competitive forces can hurt your prospective profits:

► Savvy **customers** can force down prices by playing you and your rivals against one another.

► Powerful **suppliers** may constrain your profits if they charge higher prices.

► Aspiring **entrants**, armed with new capacity and hungry for market share, can ratchet up the investment required for you to stay in the game.

► **Substitute offerings** can lure customers away.

Consider commercial aviation: It's one of the least profitable industries because all five forces are strong. **Established rivals** compete intensely on price. **Customers** are fickle, searching for the best deal regardless of carrier. **Suppliers**—plane and engine manufacturers, along with unionized labor forces—bargain away the lion's share of airlines' profits. **New players** enter the industry in a constant stream. And **substitutes** are readily available—such as train or car travel.

By analyzing all five competitive forces, you gain a complete picture of what's influencing profitability in your industry. You identify game-changing trends early, so you can swiftly exploit them. And you spot ways to work around constraints on profitability—or even reshape the forces in your favor.

The Idea in Practice

By understanding how the five competitive forces influence profitability in your industry, you can develop a strategy for enhancing your company's long-term profits. Porter suggests the following:

Position Your Company Where the Forces Are Weakest

► Example:
In the heavy-truck industry, many buyers operate large fleets and are highly motivated to drive down truck prices. Trucks are built to regulated standards and offer similar features, so price competition is stiff; unions exercise considerable supplier power; and buyers can use substitutes such as cargo delivery by rail.

To create and sustain long-term profitability within this industry, heavy-truck maker Paccar chose to focus on one customer group where competitive forces are weakest: individual drivers who own their trucks and contract directly with suppliers. These operators have limited clout as buyers and are less price sensitive because of their emotional ties to and economic dependence on their own trucks.

For these customers, Paccar has developed such features as luxurious sleeper cabins, plush leather seats, and sleek exterior styling. Buyers can select from thousands of options to put their personal signature on these built-to-order trucks.

Customers pay Paccar a 10% premium, and the company has been profitable for 68 straight years and earned a long-run return on equity above 20%.

Exploit Changes in the Forces

► Example:
With the advent of the Internet and digital distribution of music, unauthorized downloading created an illegal but potent substitute for record companies' services. The record companies tried to develop technical platforms for digital distribution themselves, but major labels didn't want to sell their music through a platform owned by a rival.

Into this vacuum stepped Apple, with its iTunes music store supporting its iPod music player. The birth of this powerful new gatekeeper has whittled down the number of major labels from six in 1997 to four today.

Reshape the Forces in Your Favor

Use tactics designed specifically to reduce the share of profits leaking to other players. For example:

► To neutralize **supplier power**, standardize specifications for parts so your company can switch more easily among vendors.
► To counter **customer power**, expand your services so it's harder for customers to leave you for a rival.
► To temper price wars initiated by **established rivals**, invest more heavily in products that differ significantly from competitors' offerings.
► To scare off **new entrants**, elevate the fixed costs of competing; for instance, by escalating your R&D expenditures.
► To limit the threat of **substitutes**, offer better value through wider product accessibility. Soft-drink producers did this by introducing vending machines and convenience store channels, which dramatically improved the availability of soft drinks relative to other beverages.

1   INTRODUCTION

In essence, the job of the strategist is to understand and cope with competition. Often, however, managers define competition too narrowly, as if it occurred only among today's direct competitors. Yet competition for profits goes beyond established industry rivals to include four other competitive forces as well: customers, suppliers, potential entrants, and substitute products. The extended rivalry that results from all five forces defines an industry's structure and shapes the nature of competitive interaction within an industry.

As different from one another as industries might appear on the surface, the underlying drivers of profitability are the same. The global auto industry, for instance, appears to have nothing in common with the worldwide market for art masterpieces or the heavily regulated health-care delivery industry in Europe. But to understand industry competition and profitability in each of those three cases, one must analyze the industry's underlying structure in terms of the five forces. (See Exhibit 1, "The Five Forces that Shape Industry Competition.")

If the forces are intense, as they are in such industries as airlines, textiles, and hotels, almost no company earns attractive returns on investment. If the forces are benign, as they are in industries such as software, soft drinks, and toiletries, many companies are profitable. Industry structure drives competition and profitability, not whether an industry produces a product or service, is emerging or mature, high tech or low tech, regulated or unregulated. While a myriad of factors can affect industry profitability in the short run—including the weather and the

EXHIBIT 1   **The Five Forces That Shape Industry Competition**

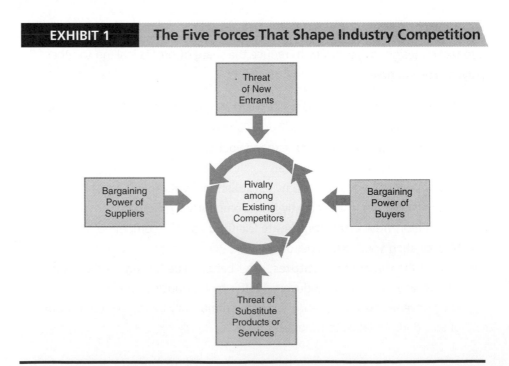

EXHIBIT 2	Differences in Industry Profitability

The average return on invested capital varies markedly from industry to industry. Between 1992 and 2006, for example, average return on invested capital in U.S. industries ranged as low as zero or even negative to more than 50%. At the high end are industries like soft drinks and prepackaged software, which have been almost six times more profitable than the airline industry over the period.

FIGURE 1 Average Return on Invested Capital in U.S. Industries, 1992–2006

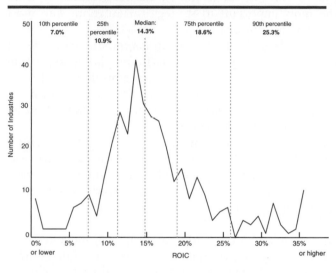

Return on invested capital (ROIC) is the appropriate measure of profitability for strategy formulation, not to mention for equity investors. Return on sales or the growth rate of profits fail to account for the capital required to compete in the industry. Here, we utilize earnings before interest and taxes divided by average invested capital less excess cash as the measure of ROIC. This measure controls for idiosyncratic differences in capital structure and tax rates across companies and industries.

FIGURE 2 Profitability of Selected U.S. Industries
Average ROIC, 1992–2006

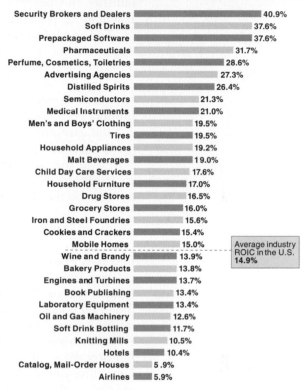

Industry	Average ROIC
Security Brokers and Dealers	40.9%
Soft Drinks	37.6%
Prepackaged Software	37.6%
Pharmaceuticals	31.7%
Perfume, Cosmetics, Toiletries	28.6%
Advertising Agencies	27.3%
Distilled Spirits	26.4%
Semiconductors	21.3%
Medical Instruments	21.0%
Men's and Boys' Clothing	19.5%
Tires	19.5%
Household Appliances	19.2%
Malt Beverages	19.0%
Child Day Care Services	17.6%
Household Furniture	17.0%
Drug Stores	16.5%
Grocery Stores	16.0%
Iron and Steel Foundries	15.6%
Cookies and Crackers	15.4%
Mobile Homes	15.0%
Wine and Brandy	13.9%
Bakery Products	13.8%
Engines and Turbines	13.7%
Book Publishing	13.4%
Laboratory Equipment	13.4%
Oil and Gas Machinery	12.6%
Soft Drink Bottling	11.7%
Knitting Mills	10.5%
Hotels	10.4%
Catalog, Mail-Order Houses	5.9%
Airlines	5.9%

Average industry ROIC in the U.S. 14.9%

Sources: Standard & Poor's, Compustat, and author's calculations.

business cycle—industry structure, manifested in the competitive forces, sets industry profitability in the medium and long run. (See Exhibit 2, "Differences in Industry Profitability.")

Understanding the competitive forces, and their underlying causes, reveals the roots of an industry's current profitability while providing a framework for anticipating and influencing competition (and profitability) over time. A healthy industry structure should be as much a competitive concern to strategists as their company's own position. Understanding industry structure is also essential to effective strategic positioning. As we will see, defending against the competitive forces and shaping them in a company's favor are crucial to strategy.

2   FORCES THAT SHAPE COMPETITION

The configuration of the five forces differs by industry. In the market for commercial aircraft, fierce rivalry between dominant producers Airbus and Boeing and the bargaining power of the airlines that place huge orders for aircraft are strong, while the threat of entry, the threat of substitutes, and the power of suppliers are more benign. In the movie theater industry, the proliferation of substitute forms of entertainment and the power of the movie producers and distributors who supply movies, the critical input, are important.

The strongest competitive force or forces determine the profitability of an industry and become the most important to strategy formulation. The most salient force, however, is not always obvious.

For example, even though rivalry is often fierce in commodity industries, it may not be the factor limiting profitability. Low returns in the photographic film industry, for instance, are the result of a superior substitute product—as Kodak and Fuji, the world's leading producers of photographic film, learned with the advent of digital photography. In such a situation, coping with the substitute product becomes the number one strategic priority.

Industry structure grows out of a set of economic and technical characteristics that determine the strength of each competitive force. We will examine these drivers in the pages that follow, taking the perspective of an incumbent, or a company already present in the industry. The analysis can be readily extended to understand the challenges facing a potential entrant.

Threat of Entry   New entrants to an industry bring new capacity and a desire to gain market share that puts pressure on prices, costs, and the rate of investment necessary to compete. Particularly when new entrants are diversifying from other markets, they can leverage existing capabilities and cash flows to shake up competition, as Pepsi did when it entered the bottled water industry, Microsoft did when it began to offer internet browsers, and Apple did when it entered the music distribution business.

The threat of entry, therefore, puts a cap on the profit potential of an industry. When the threat is high, incumbents must hold down their prices or boost investment to deter new competitors. In specialty coffee retailing, for example, relatively low entry barriers mean that Starbucks must invest aggressively in modernizing stores and menus.

The threat of entry in an industry depends on the height of entry barriers that are present and on the reaction entrants can expect from incumbents. If entry barriers are low and newcomers expect little retaliation from the entrenched competitors, the threat of entry is high and industry profitability is moderated. It is the *threat* of entry, not whether entry actually occurs, that holds down profitability.

Barriers to entry. Entry barriers are advantages that incumbents have relative to new entrants. There are seven major sources:

1. *Supply-side economies of scale.* These economies arise when firms that produce at larger volumes enjoy lower costs per unit because they can spread fixed costs over more units, employ more efficient technology, or command better terms from suppliers. Supply-side scale economies deter entry by forcing the aspiring entrant either to come into the industry on a large scale, which requires dislodging entrenched competitors, or to accept a cost disadvantage.

Scale economies can be found in virtually every activity in the value chain; which ones are most important varies by industry.[1] In microprocessors, incumbents such as Intel are protected by scale economies in research, chip fabrication, and consumer marketing. For lawn care companies like Scotts Miracle-Gro, the most important scale economies are found in the supply chain and media advertising. In small-package delivery, economies of scale arise in national logistical systems and information technology.

2. *Demand-side benefits of scale.* These benefits, also known as network effects, arise in industries where a buyer's willingness to pay for a company's product increases with the number of other buyers who also patronize the company. Buyers may trust larger companies more for a crucial product: Recall the old adage that no one ever got fired for buying from IBM (when it was the dominant computer maker). Buyers may also value being in a "network" with a larger number of fellow customers. For instance, online auction participants are attracted to eBay because it offers the most potential trading partners. Demand-side benefits of scale discourage entry by limiting the willingness of customers to buy from a newcomer and by reducing the price the newcomer can command until it builds up a large base of customers.

3. *Customer switching costs.* Switching costs are fixed costs that buyers face when they change suppliers. Such costs may arise because a buyer who switches vendors must, for example, alter product specifications, retrain employees to use a new product, or modify processes or information systems. The larger the switching costs, the harder it will be for an entrant to gain customers. Enterprise resource planning (ERP) software is an example of a product with very high switching costs. Once a company has installed SAP's ERP system, for example, the costs of moving to a new vendor are astronomical because of embedded data, the fact that internal processes have been adapted to SAP, major retraining needs, and the mission-critical nature of the applications.

4. *Capital requirements.* The need to invest large financial resources in order to compete can deter new entrants. Capital may be necessary not only for fixed facilities but also to extend customer credit, build inventories, and fund start-up losses. The barrier is particularly great if the capital is required for unrecoverable and therefore harder-to-finance expenditures, such as up-front advertising or research and development. While major corporations have the financial resources to invade almost any industry, the huge capital requirements in certain fields limit the pool of likely entrants. Conversely, in such fields as tax preparation services or short-haul trucking, capital requirements are minimal and potential entrants plentiful.

It is important not to overstate the degree to which capital requirements alone deter entry. If industry returns are attractive and are expected to remain so, and if capital markets are efficient, investors will provide entrants with the funds they need. For aspiring air carriers, for instance, financing is available to purchase expensive aircraft because of their high resale value, one reason why there have been numerous new airlines in almost every region.

---

[1] For a discussion of the value chain framework, see Michael E. Porter, *Competitive Advantage: Creating and Sustaining Superior Performance* (The Free Press, 1998).

5. *Incumbency advantages independent of size.* No matter what their size, incumbents may have cost or quality advantages not available to potential rivals. These advantages can stem from such sources as proprietary technology, preferential access to the best raw material sources, preemption of the most favorable geographic locations, established brand identities, or cumulative experience that has allowed incumbents to learn how to produce more efficiently. Entrants try to bypass such advantages. Upstart discounters such as Target and Wal-Mart, for example, have located stores in free-standing sites rather than regional shopping centers where established department stores were well entrenched.

6. *Unequal access to distribution channels.* The new entrant must, of course, secure distribution of its product or service. A new food item, for example, must displace others from the supermarket shelf via price breaks, promotions, intense selling efforts, or some other means. The more limited the wholesale or retail channels are and the more that existing competitors have tied them up, the tougher entry into an industry will be. Sometimes access to distribution is so high a barrier that new entrants must bypass distribution channels altogether or create their own. Thus, upstart low-cost airlines have avoided distribution through travel agents (who tend to favor established higher-fare carriers) and have encouraged passengers to book their own flights on the internet.

7. *Restrictive government policy.* Government policy can hinder or aid new entry directly, as well as amplify (or nullify) the other entry barriers. Government directly limits or even forecloses entry into industries through, for instance, licensing requirements and restrictions on foreign investment. Regulated industries like liquor retailing, taxi services, and airlines are visible examples. Government policy can heighten other entry barriers through such means as expansive patenting rules that protect proprietary technology from imitation or environmental or safety regulations that raise scale economies facing newcomers. Of course, government policies may also make entry easier—directly through subsidies, for instance, or indirectly by funding basic research and making it available to all firms, new and old, reducing scale economies.

Entry barriers should be assessed relative to the capabilities of potential entrants, which may be start-ups, foreign firms, or companies in related industries. And, as some of our examples illustrate, the strategist must be mindful of the creative ways newcomers might find to circumvent apparent barriers.

Expected retaliation. How potential entrants believe incumbents may react will also influence their decision to enter or stay out of an industry. If reaction is vigorous and protracted enough, the profit potential of participating in the industry can fall below the cost of capital. Incumbents often use public statements and responses to one entrant to send a message to other prospective entrants about their commitment to defending market share.

Newcomers are likely to fear expected retaliation if:

▶ Incumbents have previously responded vigorously to new entrants.

▶ Incumbents possess substantial resources to fight back, including excess cash and unused borrowing power, available productive capacity, or clout with distribution channels and customers.

▶ Incumbents seem likely to cut prices because they are committed to retaining market share at all costs or because the industry has high fixed costs, which create a strong motivation to drop prices to fill excess capacity.

BOX 1 INDUSTRY ANALYSIS IN PRACTICE

Good industry analysis looks rigorously at the structural underpinnings of profitability. A first step is to understand the appropriate time horizon. One of the essential tasks in industry analysis is to distinguish temporary or cyclical changes from structural changes. A good guideline for the appropriate time horizon is the full business cycle for the particular industry. For most industries, a three-to-five-year horizon is appropriate, although in some industries with long lead times, such as mining, the appropriate horizon might be a decade or more. It is average profitability over this period, not profitability in any particular year, that should be the focus of analysis.

The point of industry analysis is not to declare the industry attractive or unattractive but to understand the underpinnings of competition and the root causes of profitability. As much as possible, analysts should look at industry structure quantitatively, rather than be satisfied with lists of qualitative factors. Many elements of the five forces can be quantified: the percentage of the buyer's total cost accounted for by the industry's product (to understand buyer price sensitivity); the percentage of industry sales required to fill a plant or operate a logistical network of efficient scale (to help assess barriers to entry); the buyer's switching cost (determining the inducement an entrant or rival must offer customers).

The strength of the competitive forces affects prices, costs, and the investment required to compete; thus the forces are directly tied to the income statements and balance sheets of industry participants. Industry structure defines the gap between revenues and costs. For example, intense rivalry drives down prices or elevates the costs of marketing, R&D, or customer service, reducing margins. How much? Strong suppliers drive up input costs. How much? Buyer power lowers prices or elevates the costs of meeting buyers' demands, such as the requirement to hold more inventory or provide financing. How much? Low barriers to entry or close substitutes limit the level of sustainable prices. How much? It is these economic relationships that sharpen the strategist's understanding of industry competition.

Finally, good industry analysis does not just list pluses and minuses but sees an industry in overall, systemic terms. Which forces are underpinning (or constraining) today's profitability? How might shifts in one competitive force trigger reactions in others? Answering such questions is often the source of true strategic insights.

▶ Industry growth is slow so newcomers can gain volume only by taking it from incumbents.

An analysis of barriers to entry and expected retaliation is obviously crucial for any company contemplating entry into a new industry. The challenge is to find ways to surmount the entry barriers without nullifying, through heavy investment, the profitability of participating in the industry.

The Power of Suppliers   Powerful suppliers capture more of the value for themselves by charging higher prices, limiting quality or services, or shifting costs to industry participants. Powerful suppliers, including suppliers of labor, can squeeze profitability out of an industry that is unable to pass on cost increases in its own prices. Microsoft, for instance, has contributed to the erosion of profitability among personal computer makers by raising prices on operating systems. PC makers, competing fiercely for customers who can easily switch among them, have limited freedom to raise their prices accordingly.

Companies depend on a wide range of different supplier groups for inputs. A supplier group is powerful if:

► It is more concentrated than the industry it sells to. Microsoft's near monopoly in operating systems, coupled with the fragmentation of PC assemblers, exemplifies this situation.

► The supplier group does not depend heavily on the industry for its revenues. Suppliers serving many industries will not hesitate to extract maximum profits from each one. If a particular industry accounts for a large portion of a supplier group's volume or profit, however, suppliers will want to protect the industry through reasonable pricing and assist in activities such as R&D and lobbying.

► Industry participants face switching costs in changing suppliers. For example, shifting suppliers is difficult if companies have invested heavily in specialized ancillary equipment or in learning how to operate a supplier's equipment (as with Bloomberg terminals used by financial professionals). Or firms may have located their production lines adjacent to a supplier's manufacturing facilities (as in the case of some beverage companies and container manufacturers). When switching costs are high, industry participants find it hard to play suppliers off against one another. (Note that suppliers may have switching costs as well. This limits their power.)

► Suppliers offer products that are differentiated. Pharmaceutical companies that offer patented drugs with distinctive medical benefits have more power over hospitals, health maintenance organizations, and other drug buyers, for example, than drug companies offering me-too or generic products.

► There is no substitute for what the supplier group provides. Pilots' unions, for example, exercise considerable supplier power over airlines partly because there is no good alternative to a well-trained pilot in the cockpit.

► The supplier group can credibly threaten to integrate forward into the industry. In that case, if industry participants make too much money relative to suppliers, they will induce suppliers to enter the market.

The Power of Buyers Powerful customers—the flip side of powerful suppliers—can capture more value by forcing down prices, demanding better quality or more service (thereby driving up costs), and generally playing industry participants off against one another, all at the expense of industry profitability. Buyers are powerful if they have negotiating leverage relative to industry participants, especially if they are price sensitive, using their clout primarily to pressure price reductions.

As with suppliers, there may be distinct groups of customers who differ in bargaining power. A customer group has negotiating leverage if:

► There are few buyers, or each one purchases in volumes that are large relative to the size of a single vendor. Large-volume buyers are particularly powerful in industries with high fixed costs, such as telecommunications equipment, offshore drilling, and bulk chemicals. High fixed costs and low marginal costs amplify the pressure on rivals to keep capacity filled through discounting.

► The industry's products are standardized or undifferentiated. If buyers believe they can always find an equivalent product, they tend to play one vendor against another.

► Buyers face few switching costs in changing vendors.

► Buyers can credibly threaten to integrate backward and produce the industry's product themselves if vendors are too profitable. Producers of soft drinks and beer have long controlled the power of packaging manufacturers by threatening to make, and at times actually making, packaging materials themselves.

A buyer group is price sensitive if:

► The product it purchases from the industry represents a significant fraction of its cost structure or procurement budget. Here buyers are likely to shop around and bargain hard, as consumers do for home mortgages. Where the product sold by an industry is a small fraction of buyers' costs or expenditures, buyers are usually less price sensitive.

► The buyer group earns low profits, is strapped for cash, or is otherwise under pressure to trim its purchasing costs. Highly profitable or cash-rich customers, in contrast, are generally less price sensitive (that is, of course, if the item does not represent a large fraction of their costs).

► The quality of buyers' products or services is little affected by the industry's product. Where quality is very much affected by the industry's product, buyers are generally less price sensitive. When purchasing or renting production quality cameras, for instance, makers of major motion pictures opt for highly reliable equipment with the latest features. They pay limited attention to price.

► The industry's product has little effect on the buyer's other costs. Here, buyers focus on price. Conversely, where an industry's product or service can pay for itself many times over by improving performance or reducing labor, material, or other costs, buyers are usually more interested in quality than in price. Examples include products and services like tax accounting or well logging (which measures below-ground conditions of oil wells) that can save or even make the buyer money. Similarly, buyers tend not to be price sensitive in services such as investment banking, where poor performance can be costly and embarrassing.

Most sources of buyer power apply equally to consumers and to business-to-business customers. Like industrial customers, consumers tend to be more price sensitive if they are purchasing products that are undifferentiated, expensive relative to their incomes, and of a sort where product performance has limited consequences. The major difference with consumers is that their needs can be more intangible and harder to quantify.

Intermediate customers, or customers who purchase the product but are not the end user (such as assemblers or distribution channels), can be analyzed the same way as other buyers, with one important addition. Intermediate customers gain significant bargaining power when they can influence the purchasing decisions of customers downstream. Consumer electronics retailers, jewelry retailers, and agricultural-equipment distributors are examples of distribution channels that exert a strong influence on end customers.

Producers often attempt to diminish channel clout through exclusive arrangements with particular distributors or retailers or by marketing directly to end users. Component manufacturers seek to develop power over assemblers by creating preferences for their components with downstream customers. Such is the case with bicycle parts and with sweeteners. DuPont has created enormous clout by advertising its Stainmaster brand of carpet fibers not only to the carpet manufacturers that actually buy them but also to downstream consumers. Many consumers request Stainmaster carpet even though DuPont is not a carpet manufacturer.

The Threat of Substitutes   A substitute performs the same or a similar function as an industry's product by a different means. Video-conferencing is a substitute for travel. Plastic is a substitute for aluminum. E-mail is a substitute for express mail. Sometimes, the threat of substitution is downstream or indirect, when a substitute replaces a buyer industry's product. For example, lawn-care products and services are threatened when multifamily homes in urban areas substitute for single-family homes in the suburbs. Software sold to agents is threatened when airline and travel websites substitute for travel agents.

Substitutes are always present, but they are easy to overlook because they may appear to be very different from the industry's product: To someone searching for a Father's Day gift, neckties and power tools may be substitutes. It is a substitute to do without, to purchase a used product rather than a new one, or to do it yourself (bring the service or product in-house).

When the threat of substitutes is high, industry profitability suffers. Substitute products or services limit an industry's profit potential by placing a ceiling on prices. If an industry does not distance itself from substitutes through product performance, marketing, or other means, it will suffer in terms of profitability—and often growth potential.

Substitutes not only limit profits in normal times, they also reduce the bonanza an industry can reap in good times. In emerging economies, for example, the surge in demand for wired telephone lines has been capped as many consumers opt to make a mobile telephone their first and only phone line.

The threat of a substitute is high if:

▶ It offers an attractive price-performance trade-off to the industry's product. The better the relative value of the substitute, the tighter is the lid on an industry's profit potential. For example, conventional providers of long-distance telephone service have suffered from the advent of inexpensive internet-based phone services such as Vonage and Skype. Similarly, video rental outlets are struggling with the emergence of cable and satellite video-on-demand services, online video rental services such as Netflix, and the rise of internet video sites like Google's YouTube.

▶ The buyer's cost of switching to the substitute is low. Switching from a proprietary, branded drug to a generic drug usually involves minimal costs, for example, which is why the shift to generics (and the fall in prices) is so substantial and rapid.

Strategists should be particularly alert to changes in other industries that may make them attractive substitutes when they were not before. Improvements in plastic materials, for example, allowed them to substitute for steel in many automobile components. In this way, technological changes or competitive discontinuities in seemingly unrelated businesses can have major impacts on industry profitability. Of course the substitution threat can also shift in favor of an industry, which bodes well for its future profitability and growth potential.

Rivalry among Existing Competitors   Rivalry among existing competitors takes many familiar forms, including price discounting, new product introductions, advertising campaigns, and service improvements. High rivalry limits the profitability of an industry. The degree to which rivalry drives down an industry's profit potential depends, first, on the *intensity* with which companies compete and, second, on the *basis* on which they compete.

The intensity of rivalry is greatest if:

► Competitors are numerous or are roughly equal in size and power. In such situations, rivals find it hard to avoid poaching business. Without an industry leader, practices desirable for the industry as a whole go unenforced.

► Industry growth is slow. Slow growth precipitates fights for market share.

► Exit barriers are high. Exit barriers, the flip side of entry barriers, arise because of such things as highly specialized assets or management's devotion to a particular business. These barriers keep companies in the market even though they may be earning low or negative returns. Excess capacity remains in use, and the profitability of healthy competitors suffers as the sick ones hang on.

► Rivals are highly committed to the business and have aspirations for leadership, especially if they have goals that go beyond economic performance in the particular industry. High commitment to a business arises for a variety of reasons. For example, state-owned competitors may have goals that include employment or prestige. Units of larger companies may participate in an industry for image reasons or to offer a full line. Clashes of personality and ego have sometimes exaggerated rivalry to the detriment of profitability in fields such as the media and high technology.

► Firms cannot read each other's signals well because of lack of familiarity with one another, diverse approaches to competing, or differing goals.

The strength of rivalry reflects not just the intensity of competition but also the basis of competition. The *dimensions* on which competition takes place, and whether rivals converge to compete on the *same dimensions,* have a major influence on profitability.

Rivalry is especially destructive to profitability if it gravitates solely to price because price competition transfers profits directly from an industry to its customers. Price cuts are usually easy for competitors to see and match, making successive rounds of retaliation likely. Sustained price competition also trains customers to pay less attention to product features and service.

Price competition is most liable to occur if:

► Products or services of rivals are nearly identical and there are few switching costs for buyers. This encourages competitors to cut prices to win new customers. Years of airline price wars reflect these circumstances in that industry.

► Fixed costs are high and marginal costs are low. This creates intense pressure for competitors to cut prices below their average costs, even close to their marginal costs, to steal incremental customers while still making some contribution to covering fixed costs. Many basic-materials businesses, such as paper and aluminum, suffer from this problem, especially if demand is not growing. So do delivery companies with fixed networks of routes that must be served regardless of volume.

► Capacity must be expanded in large increments to be efficient. The need for large capacity expansions, as in the polyvinyl chloride business, disrupts the industry's supply-demand balance and often leads to long and recurring periods of overcapacity and price cutting.

► The product is perishable. Perishability creates a strong temptation to cut prices and sell a product while it still has value. More products and services are perishable than is commonly thought. Just as tomatoes are perishable because they rot, models of computers are perishable because they soon become obsolete, and information may be perishable if it diffuses rapidly or becomes outdated, thereby losing its value. Services such as hotel accommodations are perishable in the sense that unused capacity can never be recovered.

Competition on dimensions other than price—on product features, support services, delivery time, or brand image, for instance—is less likely to erode profitability because it improves customer value and can support higher prices. Also, rivalry focused on such dimensions can improve value relative to substitutes or raise the barriers facing new entrants. While nonprice rivalry sometimes escalates to levels that undermine industry profitability, this is less likely to occur than it is with price rivalry.

As important as the dimensions of rivalry is whether rivals compete on the *same* dimensions. When all or many competitors aim to meet the same needs or compete on the same attributes, the result is zero-sum competition. Here, one firm's gain is often another's loss, driving down profitability. While price competition runs a stronger risk than nonprice competition of becoming zero sum, this may not happen if companies take care to segment their markets, targeting their low-price offerings to different customers.

Rivalry can be positive sum, or actually increase the average profitability of an industry, when each competitor aims to serve the needs of different customer segments, with different mixes of price, products, services, features, or brand identities. Such competition can not only support higher average profitability but also expand the industry, as the needs of more customer groups are better met. The opportunity for positive-sum competition will be greater in industries serving diverse customer groups. With a clear understanding of the structural underpinnings of rivalry, strategists can sometimes take steps to shift the nature of competition in a more positive direction.

3 FACTORS, NOT FORCES

Industry structure, as manifested in the strength of the five competitive forces, determines the industry's long-run profit potential because it determines how the economic value created by the industry is divided—how much is retained by companies in the industry versus bargained away by customers and suppliers, limited by substitutes, or constrained by potential new entrants. By considering all five forces, a strategist keeps overall structure in mind instead of gravitating to any one element. In addition, the strategist's attention remains focused on structural conditions rather than on fleeting factors.

It is especially important to avoid the common pitfall of mistaking certain visible attributes of an industry for its underlying structure. Consider the following:

Industry Growth Rate A common mistake is to assume that fast-growing industries are always attractive. Growth does tend to mute rivalry, because an expanding pie offers opportunities for all competitors. But fast growth can put suppliers in a powerful position, and high growth with low entry barriers will draw in entrants. Even without new entrants, a high growth rate will not guarantee profitability if customers are powerful or substitutes are attractive. Indeed, some fast-growth businesses, such as personal computers, have been among the least profitable industries in recent years. A narrow focus on growth is one of the major causes of bad strategy decisions.

Technology and Innovation   Advanced technology or innovations are not by themselves enough to make an industry structurally attractive (or unattractive). Mundane, low-technology industries with price-insensitive buyers, high switching costs, or high entry barriers arising from scale economies are often far more profitable than sexy industries, such as software and internet technologies, that attract competitors.[2]

Government   Government is not best understood as a sixth force because government involvement is neither inherently good nor bad for industry profitability. The best way to understand the influence of government on competition is to analyze how specific government policies affect the five competitive forces. For instance, patents raise barriers to entry, boosting industry profit potential. Conversely, government policies favoring unions may raise supplier power and diminish profit potential. Bankruptcy rules that allow failing companies to reorganize rather than exit can lead to excess capacity and intense rivalry. Government operates at multiple levels and through many different policies, each of which will affect structure in different ways.

Complementary Products and Services   Complements are products or services used together with an industry's product. Complements arise when the customer benefit of two products combined is greater than the sum of each product's value in isolation. Computer hardware and software, for instance, are valuable together and worthless when separated.

In recent years, strategy researchers have highlighted the role of complements, especially in high-technology industries where they are most obvious.[3] By no means, however, do complements appear only there. The value of a car, for example, is greater when the driver also has access to gasoline stations, roadside assistance, and auto insurance.

Complements can be important when they affect the overall demand for an industry's product. However, like government policy, complements are not a sixth force determining industry profitability since the presence of strong complements is not necessarily bad (or good) for industry profitability. Complements affect profitability through the way they influence the five forces.

The strategist must trace the positive or negative influence of complements on all five forces to ascertain their impact on profitability. The presence of complements can raise or lower barriers to entry. In application software, for example, barriers to entry were lowered when producers of complementary operating system software, notably Microsoft, provided tool sets making it easier to write applications. Conversely, the need to attract producers of complements can raise barriers to entry, as it does in video game hardware.

The presence of complements can also affect the threat of substitutes. For instance, the need for appropriate fueling stations makes it difficult for cars using alternative fuels to substitute for conventional vehicles. But complements can also make substitution easier. For example, Apple's iTunes hastened the substitution from CDs to digital music.

---

[2] For a discussion of how internet technology improves the attractiveness of some industries while eroding the profitability of others, see Michael E. Porter, "Strategy and the Internet" (HBR, March 2001).

[3] See, for instance, Adam M. Brandenburger and Barry J. Nalebuff, *Co-opetition* (Currency Doubleday, 1996).

Complements can factor into industry rivalry either positively (as when they raise switching costs) or negatively (as when they neutralize product differentiation). Similar analyses can be done for buyer and supplier power. Sometimes companies compete by altering conditions in complementary industries in their favor, such as when videocassette-recorder producer JVC persuaded movie studios to favor its standard in issuing prerecorded tapes even though rival Sony's standard was probably superior from a technical standpoint.

Identifying complements is part of the analyst's work. As with government policies or important technologies, the strategic significance of complements will be best understood through the lens of the five forces.

4   CHANGES IN INDUSTRY STRUCTURE

So far, we have discussed the competitive forces at a single point in time. Industry structure proves to be relatively stable, and industry profitability differences are remarkably persistent over time in practice. However, industry structure is constantly undergoing modest adjustment—and occasionally it can change abruptly.

Shifts in structure may emanate from outside an industry or from within. They can boost the industry's profit potential or reduce it. They may be caused by changes in technology, changes in customer needs, or other events. The five competitive forces provide a framework for identifying the most important industry developments and for anticipating their impact on industry attractiveness.

Shifting Threat of New Entry   Changes to any of the seven barriers described above can raise or lower the threat of new entry. The expiration of a patent, for instance, may unleash new entrants. On the day that Merck's patents for the cholesterol reducer Zocor expired, three pharmaceutical makers entered the market for the drug. Conversely, the proliferation of products in the ice cream industry has gradually filled up the limited freezer space in grocery stores, making it harder for new ice cream makers to gain access to distribution in North America and Europe.

Strategic decisions of leading competitors often have a major impact on the threat of entry. Starting in the 1970s, for example, retailers such as Wal-Mart, Kmart, and Toys "R" Us began to adopt new procurement, distribution, and inventory control technologies with large fixed costs, including automated distribution centers, bar coding, and point-of-sale terminals. These investments increased the economies of scale and made it more difficult for small retailers to enter the business (and for existing small players to survive).

Changing Supplier or Buyer Power   As the factors underlying the power of suppliers and buyers change with time, their clout rises or declines. In the global appliance industry, for instance, competitors including Electrolux, General Electric, and Whirlpool have been squeezed by the consolidation of retail channels (the decline of appliance specialty stores, for instance, and the rise of big-box retailers like Best Buy and Home Depot in the United States). Another example is travel agents, who depend on airlines as a key supplier. When the internet allowed airlines to sell tickets directly to customers, this significantly increased their power to bargain down agents' commissions.

Shifting Threat of Substitution   The most common reason substitutes become more or less threatening over time is that advances in technology create new substitutes or shift price-performance comparisons in one direction or the other. The earliest microwave ovens, for example, were large and priced above $2,000, making them poor substitutes for conventional ovens. With technological advances, they became serious substitutes. Flash computer memory has improved enough recently to become a meaningful substitute for low-capacity hard-disk drives. Trends in the availability or performance of complementary producers also shift the threat of substitutes.

New Bases of Rivalry Rivalry often intensifies naturally over time. As an industry matures, growth slows. Competitors become more alike as industry conventions emerge, technology diffuses, and consumer tastes converge. Industry profitability falls, and weaker competitors are driven from the business. This story has played out in industry after industry; televisions, snowmobiles, and telecommunications equipment are just a few examples.

A trend toward intensifying price competition and other forms of rivalry, however, is by no means inevitable. For example, there has been enormous competitive activity in the U.S. casino industry in recent decades, but most of it has been positive-sum competition directed toward new niches and geographic segments (such as riverboats, trophy properties, Native American reservations, international expansion, and novel customer groups like families). Head-to-head rivalry that lowers prices or boosts the payouts to winners has been limited.

The nature of rivalry in an industry is altered by mergers and acquisitions that introduce new capabilities and ways of competing. Or, technological innovation can reshape rivalry. In the retail brokerage industry, the advent of the internet lowered marginal costs and reduced differentiation, triggering far more intense competition on commissions and fees than in the past.

In some industries, companies turn to mergers and consolidation not to improve cost and quality but to attempt to stop intense competition. Eliminating rivals is a risky strategy, however. The five competitive forces tell us that a profit windfall from removing today's competitors often attracts new competitors and backlash from customers and suppliers. In New York banking, for example, the 1980s and 1990s saw escalating consolidations of commercial and savings banks, including Manufacturers Hanover, Chemical, Chase, and Dime Savings. But today the retail-banking landscape of Manhattan is as diverse as ever, as new entrants such as Wachovia, Bank of America, and Washington Mutual have entered the market.

IMPLICATIONS FOR STRATEGY   5

Understanding the forces that shape industry competition is the starting point for developing strategy. Every company should already know what the average profitability of its industry is and how that has been changing over time. The five forces reveal *why* industry profitability is what it is. Only then can a company incorporate industry conditions into strategy.

The forces reveal the most significant aspects of the competitive environment. They also provide a baseline for sizing up a company's strengths and weaknesses: Where does the company stand versus buyers, suppliers, entrants, rivals, and substitutes? Most importantly, an understanding of industry structure guides managers toward fruitful possibilities for strategic action, which may include any or all of the following: positioning the company to better cope with the current competitive forces; anticipating and exploiting shifts in the forces; and shaping the balance of forces to create a new industry structure that is more favorable to the company. The best strategies exploit more than one of these possibilities.

Positioning the Company Strategy can be viewed as building defenses against the competitive forces or finding a position in the industry where the forces are weakest. Consider, for instance, the position of Paccar in the market for heavy trucks. The heavy-truck industry is structurally challenging. Many buyers operate large fleets or are large leasing companies, with both the leverage and the motivation to drive down the price of one of their largest purchases. Most trucks are built to regulated standards and offer similar features, so price competition is rampant. Capital intensity causes rivalry to be fierce, especially during the recurring cyclical downturns. Unions exercise considerable supplier power. Though there are few direct substitutes for an 18-wheeler, truck buyers face important substitutes for their services, such as cargo delivery by rail.

In this setting, Paccar, a Bellevue, Washington–based company with about 20% of the North American heavy-truck market, has chosen to focus on one group of customers: owner-operators—drivers who own their trucks and contract directly with shippers or serve as subcontractors to larger trucking companies. Such small operators have limited clout as truck buyers. They are also less price sensitive because of their strong emotional ties to and economic dependence on the product. They take great pride in their trucks, in which they spend most of their time.

Paccar has invested heavily to develop an array of features with owner-operators in mind: luxurious sleeper cabins, plush leather seats, noise-insulated cabins, sleek exterior styling, and so on. At the company's extensive network of dealers, prospective buyers use software to select among thousands of options to put their personal signature on their trucks. These customized trucks are built to order, not to stock, and delivered in six to eight weeks. Paccar's trucks also have aerodynamic designs that reduce fuel consumption, and they maintain their resale value better than other trucks. Paccar's roadside assistance program and IT-supported system for distributing spare parts reduce the time a truck is out of service. All these are crucial considerations for an owner-operator. Customers pay Paccar a 10% premium, and its Kenworth and Peterbilt brands are considered status symbols at truck stops.

Paccar illustrates the principles of positioning a company within a given industry structure. The firm has found a portion of its industry where the competitive forces are weaker—where it can avoid buyer power and price-based rivalry. And it has tailored every single part of the value chain to cope well with the forces in its segment. As a result, Paccar has been profitable for 68 years straight and has earned a long-run return on equity above 20%.

In addition to revealing positioning opportunities within an existing industry, the five forces framework allows companies to rigorously analyze entry and exit. Both depend on answering the difficult question: "What is the potential of this business?" Exit is indicated when industry structure is poor or declining and the company has no prospect of a superior positioning. In considering entry into a new industry, creative strategists can use the framework to spot an industry with a good future before this good future is reflected in the prices of acquisition candidates. Five forces analysis may also reveal industries that are not necessarily attractive for the average entrant but in which a company has good reason to believe it can surmount entry barriers at lower cost than most firms or has a unique ability to cope with the industry's competitive forces.

Exploiting Industry Change Industry changes bring the opportunity to spot and claim promising new strategic positions if the strategist has a sophisticated understanding of the competitive forces and their underpinnings. Consider, for instance, the evolution of the music industry during the past decade. With the advent of the internet and the digital distribution of music, some analysts predicted the birth of thousands of music labels (that is, record companies that develop artists and bring their music to market). This, the analysts argued, would break a pattern that had held since Edison invented the phonograph: Between three and six major record companies had always dominated the industry. The internet would, they predicted, remove distribution as a barrier to entry, unleashing a flood of new players into the music industry.

A careful analysis, however, would have revealed that physical distribution was not the crucial barrier to entry. Rather, entry was barred by other benefits that large music labels enjoyed. Large labels could pool the risks of developing new artists over many bets, cushioning the impact of inevitable failures. Even more important, they had advantages in breaking through the clutter and getting their new artists heard. To do so, they could promise radio stations and record stores access to well-known artists in exchange for promotion of new artists. New labels would find this nearly impossible to match. The major labels stayed the course, and new music labels have been rare.

This is not to say that the music industry is structurally unchanged by digital distribution. Unauthorized downloading created an illegal but potent substitute. The labels tried for years to develop technical platforms for digital distribution themselves, but major companies hesitated to sell their music through a platform owned by a rival. Into this vacuum stepped Apple with its iTunes music store, launched in 2003 to support its iPod music player. By permitting the creation of a powerful new gatekeeper, the major labels allowed industry structure to shift against them. The number of major record companies has actually declined—from six in 1997 to four today—as companies struggled to cope with the digital phenomenon.

When industry structure is in flux, new and promising competitive positions may appear. Structural changes open up new needs and new ways to serve existing needs. Established leaders may overlook these or be constrained by past strategies from pursuing them. Smaller competitors in the industry can capitalize on such changes, or the void may well be filled by new entrants.

Shaping Industry Structure   When a company exploits structural change, it is recognizing, and reacting to, the inevitable. However, companies also have the ability to shape industry structure. A firm can lead its industry toward new ways of competing that alter the five forces for the better. In reshaping structure, a company wants its competitors to follow so that the entire industry will be transformed. While many industry participants may benefit in the process, the innovator can benefit most if it can shift competition in directions where it can excel.

An industry's structure can be reshaped in two ways: by redividing profitability in favor of incumbents or by expanding the overall profit pool. Redividing the industry pie aims to increase the share of profits to industry competitors instead of to suppliers, buyers, substitutes, and keeping out potential entrants. Expanding the profit pool involves increasing the overall pool of economic value generated by the industry in which rivals, buyers, and suppliers can all share.

Redividing profitability. To capture more profits for industry rivals, the starting point is to determine which force or forces are currently constraining industry profitability and address them. A company can potentially influence all of the competitive forces. The strategist's goal here is to reduce the share of profits that leak to suppliers, buyers, and substitutes or are sacrificed to deter entrants.

To neutralize supplier power, for example, a firm can standardize specifications for parts to make it easier to switch among suppliers. It can cultivate additional vendors, or alter technology to avoid a powerful supplier group altogether. To counter customer power, companies may expand services that raise buyers' switching costs or find alternative means of reaching customers to neutralize powerful channels. To temper profit-eroding price rivalry, companies can invest more heavily in unique products, as pharmaceutical firms have done, or expand support services to customers. To scare off entrants, incumbents can elevate the fixed cost of competing—for instance, by escalating their R&D or marketing expenditures. To limit the threat of substitutes, companies can offer better value through new features or wider product accessibility. When soft-drink producers introduced vending machines and convenience store channels, for example, they dramatically improved the availability of soft drinks relative to other beverages.

Sysco, the largest food-service distributor in North America, offers a revealing example of how an industry leader can change the structure of an industry for the better. Food-service distributors purchase food and related items from farmers and food processors. They then warehouse and deliver these items to restaurants, hospitals, employer cafeterias, schools, and other food-service institutions. Given low barriers to entry, the food-service distribution industry has historically been highly fragmented, with numerous local competitors. While rivals try to cultivate customer relationships, buyers are price sensitive because food represents a large share of their costs. Buyers can also choose the substitute approaches of purchasing directly from manufacturers or using retail sources, avoiding distributors altogether. Suppliers wield bargaining power: They are often large companies with strong brand names that food preparers and consumers recognize. Average profitability in the industry has been modest.

Sysco recognized that, given its size and national reach, it might change this state of affairs. It led the move to introduce private-label distributor brands with specifications tailored to the food-service market, moderating supplier power. Sysco emphasized value-added services to buyers such as credit, menu planning, and inventory management to shift the basis of competition away from just price. These moves, together with stepped-up investments in information technology and regional distribution centers, substantially raised the bar for new entrants while making the substitutes less attractive. Not surprisingly, the industry has been consolidating, and industry profitability appears to be rising.

Industry leaders have a special responsibility for improving industry structure. Doing so often requires resources that only large players possess. Moreover, an improved industry structure is a public good because it benefits every firm in the industry, not just the company that initiated the improvement. Often, it is more in the interests of an industry leader than any other participant to invest for the common good because leaders will usually benefit the most. Indeed, improving the industry may be a leader's most profitable strategic opportunity, in part because attempts to gain further market share can trigger strong reactions from rivals, customers, and even suppliers.

There is a dark side to shaping industry structure that is equally important to understand. Ill-advised changes in competitive positioning and operating practices can *undermine* industry structure. Faced with pressures to gain market share or enamored with innovation for its own sake, managers may trigger new kinds of competition that no incumbent can win. When taking actions to improve their own company's competitive advantage, then, strategists should ask whether they are setting in motion dynamics that will undermine industry structure in the long run. In the early days of the personal computer industry, for instance, IBM tried to make up for its late entry by offering an open architecture that would set industry standards and attract complementary makers of application software and peripherals. In the process, it ceded ownership of the critical components of the PC—the operating system and the microprocessor—to Microsoft and Intel. By standardizing PCs, it encouraged price-based rivalry and shifted power to suppliers. Consequently, IBM became the temporarily dominant firm in an industry with an enduringly unattractive structure.

Expanding the profit pool. When overall demand grows, the industry's quality level rises, intrinsic costs are reduced, or waste is eliminated, the pie expands. The total pool of value available to competitors, suppliers, and buyers grows. The total profit pool expands, for example, when channels become more competitive or when an industry discovers latent buyers for its product that are not currently being served. When soft-drink producers rationalized their independent bottler networks to make them more efficient and effective, both the soft-drink companies and the bottlers benefited. Overall value can also expand when firms work collaboratively with suppliers to improve coordination and limit unnecessary costs incurred in the supply chain. This lowers the inherent cost structure of the industry, allowing higher profit, greater demand through lower prices, or both. Or, agreeing on quality standards can bring up industrywide quality and service levels, and hence prices, benefiting rivals, suppliers, and customers.

Expanding the overall profit pool creates win-win opportunities for multiple industry participants. It can also reduce the risk of destructive rivalry that arises when incumbents attempt to shift bargaining power or capture more market share. However, expanding the pie does not reduce the importance of industry structure. How the expanded pie is divided will ultimately be determined by the five forces. The most successful companies are those that expand the industry profit pool in ways that allow them to share disproportionately in the benefits.

Defining the Industry   The five competitive forces also hold the key to defining the relevant industry (or industries) in which a company competes. Drawing industry boundaries correctly, around the arena in which competition actually takes place, will clarify the causes of profitability and the appropriate unit for setting strategy. A company needs a separate strategy for each distinct industry. Mistakes in industry definition made by competitors present opportunities for staking out superior strategic positions. (See Box 2, "Defining the Relevant Industry.")

COMPETITION AND VALUE   6

The competitive forces reveal the drivers of industry competition. A company strategist who understands that competition extends well beyond existing rivals will detect wider competitive threats and be better equipped to address them. At the same time, thinking comprehensively about an industry's structure can uncover opportunities: differences in customers, suppliers, substitutes, potential entrants, and rivals that can become the basis for distinct strategies yielding superior performance. In a world of more open competition and relentless change, it is more important than ever to think structurally about competition.

Understanding industry structure is equally important for investors as for managers. The five competitive forces reveal whether an industry is truly attractive, and they help investors anticipate positive or negative shifts in industry structure before they are obvious. The five forces distinguish short-term blips from structural changes and allow investors to take advantage of undue pessimism or optimism. Those companies whose strategies have industry-transforming potential become far clearer. This deeper thinking about competition is a more powerful way to achieve genuine investment success than the financial projections and trend extrapolation that dominate today's investment analysis.

BOX 2   DEFINING THE RELEVANT INDUSTRY

Defining the industry in which competition actually takes place is important for good industry analysis, not to mention for developing strategy and setting business unit boundaries. Many strategy errors emanate from mistaking the relevant industry, defining it too broadly or too narrowly. Defining the industry too broadly obscures differences among products, customers, or geographic regions that are important to competition, strategic positioning, and profitability. Defining the industry too narrowly overlooks commonalities and linkages across related products or geographic markets that are crucial to competitive advantage. Also, strategists must be sensitive to the possibility that industry boundaries can shift.

The boundaries of an industry consist of two primary dimensions. First is the *scope of products or services*. For example, is motor oil used in cars part of the same industry as motor oil used in heavy trucks and stationary engines, or are these different industries? The second dimension is *geographic scope*. Most industries are present in many parts of the world. However, is competition contained within each state, or is it national? Does competition take place within regions such as Europe or North America, or is there a single global industry?

The five forces are the basic tool to resolve these questions. If industry structure for two products is the same or very similar (that is, if they have the same buyers, suppliers, barriers to entry, and so forth), then the products are best treated as being part of the same industry. If industry structure differs markedly, however, the two products may be best understood as separate industries.

In lubricants, the oil used in cars is similar or even identical to the oil used in trucks, but the similarity largely ends there. Automotive motor oil is sold to fragmented, generally unsophisticated customers through numerous and often powerful channels, using extensive advertising. Products are packaged in small containers and logistical costs are high, necessitating local production. Truck and power generation lubricants are sold to entirely different buyers in entirely different ways using a separate supply chain. Industry structure (buyer power, barriers to entry, and so forth) is substantially different. Automotive oil is thus a distinct industry from oil for truck and stationary engine uses. Industry profitability will differ in these two cases, and a lubricant company will need a separate strategy for competing in each area.

Differences in the five competitive forces also reveal the geographic scope of competition. If an industry has a similar structure in every country (rivals, buyers, and so on), the presumption is that competition is global, and the five forces analyzed from a global perspective will set average profitability. A single global strategy is needed. If an industry has quite different structures in different geographic regions, however, each region may well be a distinct industry. Otherwise, competition would have leveled the differences. The five forces analyzed for each region will set profitability there.

The extent of differences in the five forces for related products or across geographic areas is a matter of degree, making industry definition often a matter of judgment. A rule of thumb is that where the differences in any one force are large, and where the differences involve more than one force, distinct industries may well be present.

Fortunately, however, even if industry boundaries are drawn incorrectly, careful five forces analysis should reveal important competitive threats. A closely related product omitted from the industry definition will show up as a substitute, for example, or competitors overlooked as rivals will be recognized as potential entrants. At the same time, the five forces analysis should reveal major differences within overly broad industries that will indicate the need to adjust industry boundaries or strategies.

BOX 3 TYPICAL STEPS IN INDUSTRY ANALYSIS

Define the relevant industry:

► What products are in it? Which ones are part of another distinct industry?

► What is the geographic scope of competition?

Identify the participants and segment them into groups, if appropriate:
Who are

► the buyers and buyer groups?

► the suppliers and supplier groups?

► the competitors?

► the substitutes?

► the potential entrants?

Assess the underlying drivers of each competitive force to determine which forces are strong and which are weak and why.

Determine overall industry structure, and test the analysis for consistency:

► *Why* is the level of profitability what it is?

► Which are the *controlling* forces for profitability?

► Is the industry analysis consistent with actual long-run profitability?

► Are more-profitable players better positioned in relation to the five forces?

Analyze recent and likely future changes in each force, both positive and negative.

Identify aspects of industry structure that might be influenced by competitors, by new entrants, or by your company.

BOX 4 COMMON PITFALLS

In conducting the analysis avoid the following common mistakes:

► Defining the industry too broadly or too narrowly.

► Making lists instead of engaging in rigorous analysis.

► Paying equal attention to all of the forces rather than digging deeply into the most important ones.

► Confusing effect (price sensitivity) with cause (buyer economics).

► Using static analysis that ignores industry trends.

► Confusing cyclical or transient changes with true structural changes.

► Using the framework to declare an industry attractive or unattractive rather than using it to guide strategic choices.

If both executives and investors looked at competition this way, capital markets would be a far more effective force for company success and economic prosperity. Executives and investors would both be focused on the same fundamentals that drive sustained profitability. The conversation between investors and executives would focus on the structural, not the transient. Imagine the improvement in company performance—and in the economy as a whole—if all the energy expended in "pleasing the Street" were redirected toward the factors that create true economic value.

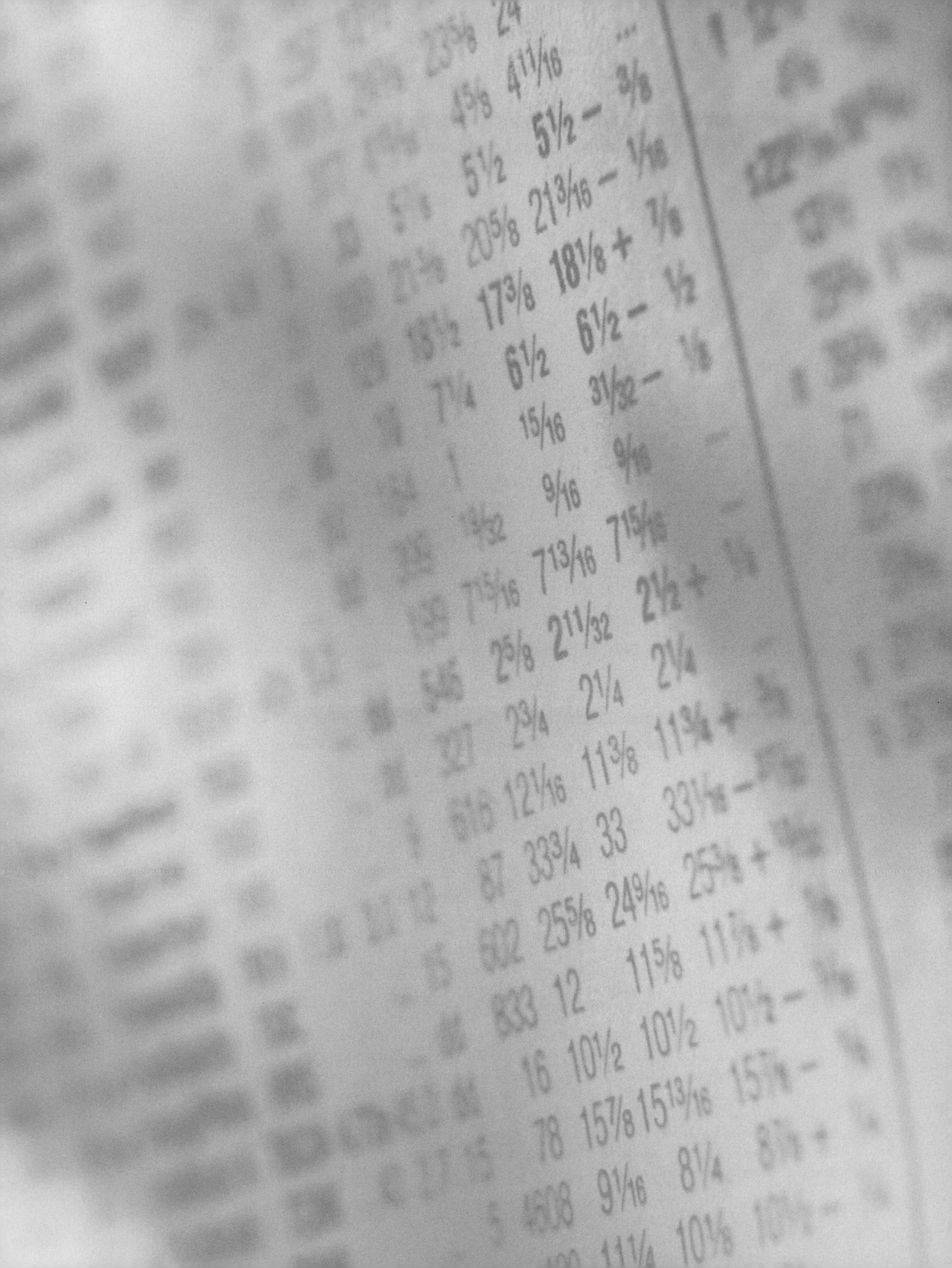

23⅜ 24
4⅝ 4¹¹⁄₁₆ — ⅜
5½ 5½ —
5½ 5½ — ⅛
20⅝ 21¹³⁄₁₆ — ⅛
17⅜ 18⅛ + ⅞
13½ 6½ 6½ — ½
7¼ 6½ 3³¹⁄₃₂ — ⅛
15⁄16 9⁄16
9⁄16
¹⁹⁄₃₂ 7¹⁵⁄₁₆ 7¹³⁄₁₆ 7¹⁵⁄₁₆
7¹⁵⁄₁₆ 2⅝ 2¹¹⁄₃₂ 2½ +
23⁄4 21⁄4 21⁄4
61⁄5 12¹⁄₁₆ 11⅜ 11⅜ +
87 33¾ 33 33¼ —
602 25⅝ 24⁹⁄₁₆ 25⅞ +
833 12 11⅝ 11⅝ +
16 10½ 10½ 10½ —
78 15⅞ 15¹³⁄₁₆ 15⅞ —
608 9¹⁄₁₆ 8¼ 8⅛
11¼ 10⅛ 10⅛

INDUSTRY ANALYSIS
by Jeffrey C. Hooke

LEARNING OUTCOMES

The candidate should be able to:	Mastery
a. explain key components that should be included in an industry analysis model;	☐
b. describe the life cycle of a typical industry;	☐
c. analyze the effects of business cycles on industry classification (i.e., growth, defensive, cyclical);	☐
d. analyze the impact of external factors (e.g., technology, government, foreign influences, demography, and social changes) on industries;	☐
e. describe inputs and methods used in preparing industry demand and supply analyses;	☐
f. explain factors that affect industry pricing practices.	☐

The industry analysis is an important part of the research report. The proper organization of this analysis, the five principal themes of such a study and the common pitfalls of an industry evaluation are discussed herein.

In developing investment recommendations, the typical analyst begins serious research at the industry level. The analyst receives "top-down" economic and capital market forecasts from others. The initial responsibility is tying these macro parameters into an industry outlook, thus laying the groundwork for judging the prospects of selected participants. The fortunes of an individual company are closely intertwined with those of the industry in which it operates. An in-depth industry study is thus a prerequisite for a proper security analysis. A thorough understanding of the industry facilitates the evaluation process, and for this reason, many practitioners limit themselves to one or two industries. This reading

Security Analysis On Wall Street: A Comprehensive Guide To Today's Valuation Methods, Jeffrey C. Hooke. Copyright © 1998 by John Wiley & Sons. All rights reserved. Used under license from John Wiley & Sons, Inc.

EXHIBIT 1 | **Model Research Report**

1. Introduction
2. Macroeconomic Review
3. Relevant Stock Market Prospects
4. Review of the Company and Its Business ✔
   Industry Analysis ✔
5. Financial Analysis
6. Financial Projections
7. Application of Valuation Methodologies
8. Recommendation

---

reviews preparing an industry analysis, which is covered under Section 4 of the model research report (Exhibit 1).

1 BACKGROUND

Whatever outlook an analyst develops for a particular industry, not all companies have prospects mirroring the broader view. Some perform better than the general expectation; others worse. Consider the waste disposal industry in December 1996. The principal companies were mired in the industry's image of operating problems, poor economics in recycling, and a glut of landfill space. As a result, their P/E ratios suffered. Meanwhile, three young enterprises carried premium P/E ratios, as the market showed interest in their strong acquisition programs (see Exhibit 2).

The dual track status of waste disposal firms is duplicated in other industries. Wal-Mart, for example, has enjoyed far higher valuation ratios than other general merchandise retailers, such as Sears, although many of these competitors make money. The big difference has been Wal-Mart's higher growth rate.

EXHIBIT 2 | **Snapshot of the Waste Disposal Industry**

Established Companies	P/E Ratio
Laidlaw	23
WMX Technologies	25
Browning-Ferris	18

New Acquisitive Players	
Allied Waste	56
USA Waste Services	26
Republic Industries	72

As a general rule, institutional investors want analysts to stick to industries with a positive outlook. Even the best buggy whip manufacturer was a poor bet at the turn of the 20th century. Similarly, the most attractive CB radio producer turned out to be a loser in the 1980s. The chosen industries don't have to be stellar performers; they just require a reasonable justification for investment.

Broad Industry Trends

While the competent analyst has a broad knowledge of the industry he covers, his research reports have a narrow focus, limiting reviews of industry trends to those that affect a specific company's future performance. Contributing to the reader's understanding of the industry requires comparisons. For example, analysts covering the early years of the VCR compared it with the introduction of the television. Original themes are important. Rehashing widely available data is of little use to the reader, unless it sets the stage for company-specific projections. These forecasts appear toward the end of the research report, after a groundwork has been laid.

As the subject company grows larger, the industry analysis becomes complicated. Major corporations today have multiple lines, many of which are not comparable. General Electric has 13 separate divisions producing products as dissimilar as gas turbines and home appliances. For those firms with disparate businesses, the industry analysis evolves into an *industries* analysis, as each distinct segment is valued separately as a part of a larger whole.

Contrary Opinions

Of particular interest to investors are contrarian opinions. Research analysts are reluctant to stick their necks out. They follow the herd, and as a result, their reports are disappointingly similar. For the most part, analysts work around the edges of the consensus view on an industry's prospects and a company's forecasts. When a practitioner reaches a strikingly different conclusion from that of everyone else, he tends to couch it in vague terms. Then, if he ends up wrong, his error is less obvious. The depressing outcome of this environment is that many analysts, particularly those on the sell side, are reduced to arguing about a company's next quarterly earnings report. Will earnings be 46 cents per share or 45 cents? When a respected analyst goes against the grain and replies that earnings will be 15 cents instead of 45 cents, institutional investors sit up and take notice.

Few analysts predict reversals of trends that have been long accepted on Wall Street, despite the frequency of such occurrences, so a fresh look at the status quo is real news. One important industry reversal happened in June 1996. After years of raising prices for their brand-name products, Kellogg Co., General Mills, and Ralcorp.—the three principal U.S. cereal makers—cut prices by 20 percent in response to declining demand for their products. In a few days, cereal prices dropped to the levels of the late 1980s. Some observers had noticed increasing consumer resistance to high cereal prices, but few analysts predicted this change, which caused cereal company share prices to decline as earnings projections fell.

ORGANIZING AN INDUSTRY ANALYSIS   2

An industry analysis can take various forms, but the outline set forth in Exhibit 3 is customary. The industry analysis begins with positioning the specific industry within its life cycle. Defining a sector in this way is important on Wall Street. Investors place

---

EXHIBIT 3   Model of an Industry Analysis

Industry classification
  Life cycle position
  Business cycle

External factors
  Technology
  Government
  Social
  Demographic
  Foreign

Demand analysis
  End users
  Real and nominal growth
  Trends and cyclical variation around trends

Supply analysis
  Degree of concentration
  Ease of entry
  Industry capacity

Profitability
  Supply/demand analysis
  Cost factors
  Pricing

International competition and markets

Source: Association for Investment Management and Research. Note how the industry analysis is broken down into its key components.

---

a premium on simple investment themes. Thus, the faster the analyst pigeonholes an industry into the "life cycle" chart, the better.

3   INDUSTRY CLASSIFICATION

Classification by Industrial Life Cycle

In general conversation, industries are described by the product they produce or the service they provide. Hospital chains, HMOs, and physician health groups are "medical service" industries. Newspaper firms, magazine publishers, and book companies fall in the "publishing" category. Sporting goods manufacturers, recorded music distributors, and toy producers are lumped into the "recreation" sector. Security analysis uses these descriptions, while further classifying industries by certain economic characteristics.

The most popular segmentation tool is the industrial life cycle, which reflects the vitality of an industry over time. A staple of business textbooks and management consulting firms, the life cycle theory outlines four phases that

EXHIBIT 4	Industry Classification: The Industrial Life Cycle

Life Cycle Phase	Description
Pioneer	Product acceptance is questionable and implementation of business strategy is unclear. There is high risk and many failures.
Growth	Product acceptance is established. Roll-out begins and growth accelerates in sales and earnings. Proper execution of strategy remains an issue.
Mature	Industry trend line corresponds to the general economy. Participants compete for share in a stable industry.
Decline	Shifting tastes or technologies have overtaken the industry, and demand for its products steadily decreases.

mark the beginning to end of an industry: the *pioneer, growth, mature,* and *decline* phases (see Exhibit 4).

As its name implies, the pioneer phase is the riskiest point of corporate life. The industry is struggling to establish a market for its products. Cash needs for working capital and fixed assets are substantial, yet the industry is losing money or is marginally profitable. Its potential for success attracts equity investors, who are prepared to take a total loss on their investment and know that. Seven out of 10 start-up businesses fail to survive. During overheated stock markets, speculative ventures often go public and become fodder for the security analyst community.

The second stage is the growth phase. Here, practitioners acknowledge the industry's product acceptance and have a brief historical framework for estimating future demand. The big questions are: How far, and how fast? So-called growth industries occupy a large amount of analysts' time, because they sometimes provide excellent returns. Of particular interest to analysts is identifying a growth industry at the ground floor, before everyone jumps on the bandwagon and boosts the stock price.

A classic growth industry spurs demand for a product that the consumer (or the industrial client) didn't know he needed. The best example is a new technology; cellular advances, for example, sparked a demand for car phones, which few people realized they needed beforehand. Another growth story is the better mousetrap. Before Office Depot, few people realized they needed an office supply superstore; most shopped at local stationers and department stores for these items. The total market for office supplies is stagnant, but office superstores represent a legitimate growth industry within the larger market. Growth companies prosper independent of the business cycle.

Besides experiencing rapidly increasing sales, growth industries frequently enjoy fat profit margins. This happy situation continues until new competitors, attracted to the high returns, enter the industry. As competition stabilizes and market penetration reaches practical limits, the industry progresses to the mature phase.

If growth industries have above-average increases in sales and earnings, mature industries produce "average" results. Unit sales gains follow economic growth. Thus, if the economy improves by 3 percent in one year, an analyst expects a mature industry's unit sales to rise by 3 percent. Adding a 5 percent inflation factor means the industry's sales increase by 8 percent annually. Mature industries usually provide a staple product or service. Examples include the food, auto, and furniture industries.

Within a mature industry may be one or more *growth companies*. Typically, such firms achieve above-average growth in one of two ways. First, they gain market share by offering an improved quality or service (i.e., the better mousetrap). American Greetings' market share in the mature greeting card industry has increased from 33 to 35 percent over the past five years. Consumers like its products better than those of the competition. Alternatively, a company grows in a mature industry by gobbling up others. Since 1991, Service Corporation International has increased its market share in the funeral business from 5 to 10 percent, by acquiring over 200 competitors. Sales in its industry advanced 8 percent annually over that time, but Service Corporation's gains averaged 31 percent each year.

The last stage in the life cycle is the decline phase. Demand for the industry's products decreases and the remaining participants fight over shares of a smaller market. With no new capacity needs and diminished profit margins, the industry attracts little capital and established firms begin to exit the sector. As demand dries up, companies fail and the remaining participants consolidate. The better-managed survivors anticipate this fate and avoid it by using cash flow to diversify into promising industries. Westinghouse's takeover of CBS exemplified such diversification.

Classification by Business Cycle Reaction

In addition to the industry life cycle, Wall Street characterizes industries by the way in which they react to the business cycle. Market economies do not grow in a straight line. They expand, go into a recession where growth slows or stops, and then enter a recovery, which leads into the next expansion (see Exhibit 5). The duration of a U.S. business cycle can be 5 to 10 years. Certain industries

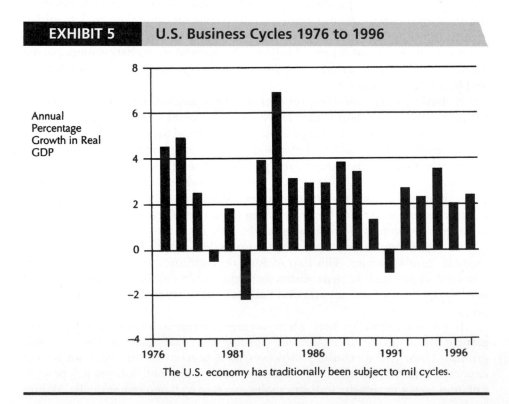

| EXHIBIT 5 | U.S. Business Cycles 1976 to 1996 |

Annual Percentage Growth in Real GDP

The U.S. economy has traditionally been subject to mil cycles.

EXHIBIT 6	Industry Classification by Business Cycle Behavior

Behavior Pattern	Description
Growth	Above-normal expansion in sales and profits occurs independent of the business cycle.
Defensive	Stable performance during both ups and downs of business cycle.
Cyclical	Profitability tracks the business cycle, often in an exaggerated manner.

prosper more than others during different phases of the business cycle. Industry's behavior places it into one of three categories: *growth, defensive,* or *cyclical* (see Exhibit 6).

A growth industry achieves an above-normal rate of expansion, independent of the business cycle. Even if the economy is in a recession, the growth industry's sales and earnings rise. New technology and products are the hallmarks of a growth industry. The computer software industry sailed through the 1990–1991 recession with higher revenues.

Defensive industries exhibit stable performance through the business cycle. Sales and earnings proceed in an upward direction. Strong growth is apparent during an economic upturn, but there is a slight dip in profitability during recession years. Defensive industries usually fall into the mature category. Examples include 1) electric and gas utilities since people require heat and light in their homes regardless of economic conditions; 2) food, cigarette, and beer companies since demand for their products remains inelastic (although consumers may shift to lower-priced brands); and 3) government contractors since governments tend to spend whether or not the economy expands.

Cyclical industries are those whose earnings track the cycle. Their profits benefit from economic upturns, but suffer in a downturn. The earnings movement is exaggerated. Boom times are followed by "bust times." Thus, when economic growth rates only move a few percentage points, cyclicals go from substantial losses to huge profits. General Motors' operating loss in 1991 was $2.8 billion; its 1996 operating profit topped $4 billion, representing a huge swing in profitability.

Classic cyclical businesses produce discretionary products, the consumption of which is dependent on economic optimism. The auto industry is cyclical, because consumers defer large purchases until they are confident of the economy's positive direction. Heavy equipment and machine tool producers are cyclical businesses. Their customers, capital-intensive concerns, defer investment during recessions and increase spending during recoveries.

Exhibits 7 and 8 provide examples of three firms and how their earnings changed over the preceding business cycle.

Certain cyclical firms experience earnings patterns that do not correlate well against the general economy, but trend against other economic variables. Brokerage firms, for example, show cyclicality based on stock prices. Agricultural firms exhibit earnings tied to the crop price cycle. These firms are lumped into the cyclical category.

The characterization of an industry through the life cycle or business cycle techniques colors the follow-up analysis. Practitioners compare those industries with similar designations and draw inferences about future revenue, earnings

EXHIBIT 7	Business Cycle Earnings Comparison Gross National Product (GNP) versus Earnings per Share (EPS)

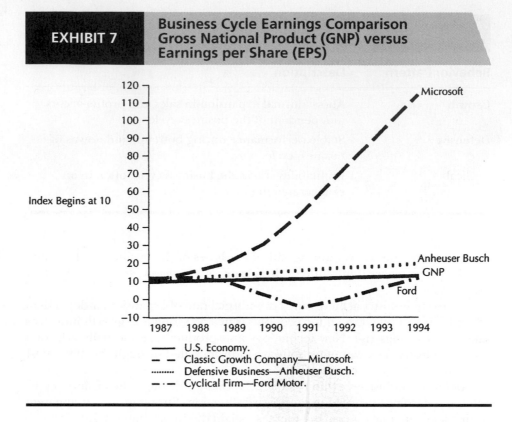

EXHIBIT 8	Business Cycle Earnings Comparison GNP Changes versus EPS Changes

		1987	1988	1989	1990	1991	1992	1993	1994
Real GDP	% Chg	2.9	3.8	3.4	1.3	−1.0	2.7	2.3	3.5
Growth company—	EPS	0.16	0.25	0.34	0.52	0.82	1.21	1.58	1.98
Microsoft	% Chg	77.8	56.3	36.0	52.9	57.7	47.6	30.6	25.3
Defensive business—	EPS	1.02	1.23	1.34	1.48	1.63	1.73	1.78	1.94
Anheuser Busch	% Chg	20.0	20.6	8.9	10.4	10.1	6.1	2.9	9.0
Cyclical firm— Ford Motor	EPS	4.53	5.48	4.57	0.93	−2.40	−0.73	2.28	4.97
	% Chg	47.1	21.0	−16.6	−79.6	Neg.	Neg.	—	218.0

Note: The recession began in 1990 and extended through 1991. The cyclical behavior of Ford Motor is evident.

performance, and valuation. In such side-by-side evaluations, industry-specific nuances are ignored in favor of the broader theme.

A second problem associated with industry classification is self-deception. Once an analyst labels an industry as a growth industry, he (and his audience) is tempted to place subsequent facts that come to light within the growth framework. Pigeonholing an industry helps in telling the investment story, but the experienced analyst doesn't let labels prejudge developments that don't fit the model.

As one illustration, consider the internet service industry in 1996. Many early investors compared this industry with cable TV in the late 1970s. Both internet and cable TV were hooked into the home by wire and both required monthly subscription charges. As analysts monitored the internet services industry more closely, however, they noticed a significant difference. Internet service was not a quasi monopoly like cable TV, and customers switched suppliers more frequently than cable TV subscribers. The internet industry fell into the growth classification, but practitioners needed a fresh look at its economics. Internet stock prices dropped accordingly in late 1996.

Likewise, the bagel chain industry attracts comparisons with the formerly fast food business. Dennis Lombardi, who heads a restaurant consulting practice, repeated a familiar premise, "There's an awful lot of room for more bagel shops. All you have to do is contrast it to the hamburger chains." With 11,000 restaurants, McDonald's has several times the total number of bagel shops, but the differences are compelling. Hamburgers are viewed as all-American lunch and dinner food. In contrast, bagels occupy the breakfast segment and have an ethnic tradition.

A common error with industry classification occurs when the analyst paints all industry participants with the same brush. Inevitably, not all companies in a *mature* industry are *mature* companies. Beer brewing is a mature industry, yet small microbrewers are considered growth companies. Steel is a cyclical industry, but Nucor's stability defies this classification.

The process of placing an industry into its life cycle and business cycle categories involves performing the work outlined in Exhibit 3. By studying the industry's external influences, demand trends, supply factors, profitability and competition, an analyst forms opinions about its prospects and suitability for investment.

EXTERNAL FACTORS   4

No industry operates in a vacuum. Each is subject to numerous outside influences that significantly impact sales and earnings. The first stage of the top-down analysis considers the economic variables that affect industry performance, and the life cycle and business cycle techniques provide direction in this regard. As the industry study unfolds, however, the practitioner examines external factors that aren't purely economic (see Exhibit 9).

External issues fall into five broad categories: technology, government, social changes, demographics, and foreign influences. For each of these categories, there are "big picture" themes that affect a particular industry, and the analyst's job is twofold. One, he avoids the temptation to fall into the role of futuristic visionary. Instead, he concentrates on trends that can demonstrably affect the industry over a three- to five-year period. Two, he addresses the impact of these trends in quantifiable form. It is not enough to say "advances in satellite technology and capacity will fuel the global pager business"; investors want to know the percentage gains in industry sales from these factors. A numerical forecast is better than a vague pronouncement.

EXHIBIT 9	Industry Analysis—External Factors Affecting Sales and Profitability
Technology	For established industries, the question is: Does the industry face obsolescence from competing technologies? (Typewriters were quickly replaced by word processors in the early 1980s). Infant industries introducing new technologies pose a different question: Will the market accept innovation?
Government	Government plays a large role in many industries. New regulations, or changes to old laws, can impact an industry's sales and earnings. In certain cases, government policies create new industries (e.g., the automobile protective safety bag industry).
Social changes	Changes in lifestyle spark many industries. The rise of two-earner families fueled growth in the convenience food and restaurant industries. Concern over animal rights hurt the fur retailing industry.
Demographics	Demographic shifts are watched by analysts. The "greying" of America supports nursing home stocks. It is also a factor in the rebound of the golf equipment industry, as baby boomers reduce strenuous activity in their later years.
Foreign influences	The United States is the largest economy, but its industries are subject to foreign influences. Overseas textile firms decimated the U.S. textile industry. Higher income levels in developing nations, meanwhile, contributed to huge overseas demand for U.S. movies and musical recordings.

In the majority of research reports, the basic assumption regarding the industry's external environment is that history will repeat itself. Past trends continue into the future, and thus, most industry sales projections are based on time series analysis. Projecting the sales of new industries is more tricky, but 99 percent of public companies are beyond the start-up stage, so analysts extrapolate brief historical results into a forecast. Unless there is a firm basis for a contrary opinion, this rearview-mirror approach is reasonable. As noted earlier, this method encourages complacency, and the analyst relying on it can miss important reversals. Nonetheless, a historical grounding in an industry is a prerequisite for an evaluation of external influences. Exhibit 10 provides an example of the effects of external factors on an industry.

Technology

The initial analysis of technology focuses on *survival*. Will the industry's product offerings fend off perceived substitutes derived from newer technology?

EXHIBIT 10	**Sample External Factors Affecting Health Care Industry Sales**

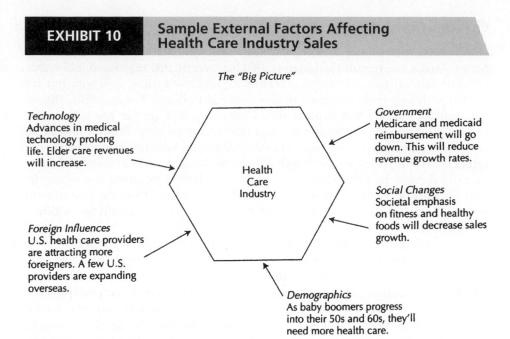

The "Big Picture"

Technology
Advances in medical technology prolong life. Elder care revenues will increase.

Foreign Influences
U.S. health care providers are attracting more foreigners. A few U.S. providers are expanding overseas.

Health Care Industry

Government
Medicare and medicaid reimbursement will go down. This will reduce revenue growth rates.

Social Changes
Societal emphasis on fitness and healthy foods will decrease sales growth.

Demographics
As baby boomers progress into their 50s and 60s, they'll need more health care.

The eyeglass industry, for example, has prospered for years against several contact lens technologies. The record player industry, in contrast, became obsolete with the introduction of the CD player.

In many cases, an outside technological idea enhances an industry. Gains in the biotechnology area were eventually transferred to the agricultural industry, where they contributed to higher crop yields. Improvements in civil aviation technology led directly to a travel boom, which lifted tourist industry revenues. VCRs represented 100 percent of electric appliance sales growth in the mid-1980s. Current pundits believe digital technology will spur growth in digital TV sales.

Sometimes, a new technology is a blessing and a curse. Nuclear power originated in the defense industry. Transferred to electric utilities, nuclear power was quickly accepted in the 1970s because its variable costs were lower than conventional technologies, such as coal and oil generation. Unforeseen problems in safety and the environment tainted nuclear power in the 1980s, and the related expenses crippled many utilities.

In the case of a new competing technology, the established industry usually has several years to prepare a defense. A common strategic response is either:

1. Copy the competition, as Wal-Mart did in the wholesale club industry with Sam's Wholesale Club (a virtual clone of Price Club).

2. Buy the competition, as IBM's software division did when it acquired Lotus Development Corporation.

Competent managements recognize technological trends and adjust their companies accordingly.

Government

Government taxes, laws, and regulations impact every industry in the United States. That's one reason Washington, DC, has over 50,000 registered lobbyists.

The federal tax code serves a legitimate revenue raising function, but it's loaded with loopholes designed to serve special interests. For example, the oil exploration industry has depreciation allowances that are far more favorable than those available to the average manufacturing industry. Federal quotas on imported goods provide certain industries with extra benefits. For example, the quota levied on Japanese auto imports protects the sales and earnings of domestic producers. A negative shift in the political fortunes of either the oil exploration industry or the auto industry could result in unfavorable government actions, leading to lower earnings. The analyst's projections would be modified accordingly.

Business organizations complain about regulation, but regulations play a valuable role in promoting worker safety, consumer protection, and fair play. Government influence cuts both ways. Some government agencies practice regulatory overkill that harms industry unnecessarily, but it is a fact that multiple businesses were founded on new government initiatives or rely on government regulation to prosper. If you're a business, what better way to avoid risk than to have the government require a minimum price for your products, set up barriers to foreign imports, or allow you to merge with the competition? Regulation "creep" has continued in Republican and Democratic administrations, and the analysts of the 1990s monitor government developments much more closely than did their 1960s' counterparts.

A recent example of a negative external influence is the government assault on the tobacco industry. By declaring tobacco a drug and placing it under FDA jurisdiction, the government clearly seeks to diminish the industry's prospects. Alternatively, the federal emphasis on environment enforcement is a boon to the environmental services sector. One relatively new industry that received a huge leg up from the government was the cellular phone industry. Rather than sell cellular monopolies to the highest bidder, the government gave the rights away via lottery in the 1980s, saving the operators billions of dollars. State deregulation is sweeping through the electric utilities, and this turning point means dramatic changes for this staid industry.

Consider Paxson Communications Corp., a network of 46 UHF stations that run half-hour informercials most of the day. Faced with limited capacity, many cable TV systems declined to carry these broadcasts, but in March 1997 the U.S. Supreme Court upheld the government's "must carry" rules, requiring cable companies to show any and all local broadcast channels, even Paxson's low-rent UHF programs. On the day of the ruling, the company's share price jumped 30 percent, illustrating the effect of government.

Federal, state, and local government spending accounts for 35 percent of gross national product. Any shifts in the spending patterns of these organizations influence the affected industries. Declines in the defense budget during the 1990s prompted a wave of consolidations among defense contractors. At the local level, the privatization of municipal waste services contributed to revenue gains among waste management firms. Imagine the shift in dollars if the government privatized just a small portion of the public education system!

External factors relating to government play a significant role in the analysis of foreign stocks. Most countries have more restrictive trade regimes than the United States, and local producers get complacent after years of protection. A dramatic liberalization in tariff policy can destroy a local industry that is uncompetitive with the global multinationals. Similarly, nations set up artificial barriers to protect favored industries (and companies) from outside threats. Japan, for example, has a maze of bizarre regulations that limit U.S. agricultural imports, thereby assisting Japanese farmers. Brazil's "local content" rules forestall the importation of cars and ensure the survival of the inefficient local auto industry. Argentina has a special tax on cola drinks, designed to punish Coke and Pepsi bottlers in favor of local fruit drink producers.

Social Changes

Social factors boil down to lifestyle and fashion changes. In either case, the analyst is ready to evaluate their impacts on the relevant industry.

Of the two social influences, fashion is the more unpredictable, and this complicates the job of researching fashion-oriented industries. The women's fashion cycle, for example, is quite short, and a hot clothing item may only have a shelf life of one, maybe two years, before it is replaced by another style. Baseline sales for the industry trend upward, but fashion changes impact short-term projections. Similar phenomena occur in the toy, recreation, and film industries.

Analysts can mistake a short-term fashion cycle for a long-term trend. In one of my financings, an analyst projected a steady upward move in leather coat sales, despite evidence that demand for such garments historically went through up and down cycles. Three years after the transaction, leather coat sales had dropped by over 20 percent.

Lifestyle changes, in contrast, take place over long periods of time. An increase in health consciousness, for example, resulted in a per capita decline in hard liquor consumption. Given fair warning, several spirits producers, such as Seagram's, responded by diversifying into the production of wine, which increased in popularity over the same time span. The gradual shift of women into the workforce, from 41 percent in 1965 to 58 percent in 1995, and the increasing suburbanization of society, acutely affected the auto industry. Besides spawning a need for two cars per family, these changes prompted the minivan boom, as suburban parents juggled responsibilities for ferrying children to after-school activities.

Demographics

Demography is the science that studies the vital statistics of population, such as distribution, age, and income. By observing trends in these statistics, analysts develop investment themes regarding various industries. In the United States for example, the age shift of the baby boomers into their 40s and 50s has sparked a strong interest in retirement planning. The result has been higher revenues for money management firms as the boomers put savings into stocks and bonds. In Malaysia, about 50 percent of the population is under the age of 21, and analysts tout local brewing stocks, in anticipation of a large increase in the beer-drinking population. In Indonesia, rising per capita incomes push a demand for electric appliances, giving analysts reason to be optimistic about the future growth of local utilities.

Demographic trends unfold over long periods of time, and they are thus easier to identify and track than other external factors. This circumstance doesn't lead to absolute certainty. Analysts frequently agree on the existence of a trend (e.g., the rising percentage of single-parent families) but disagreement occurs in sizing up its impact on relevant industries.

Foreign Influences

As global trade expands, industries become sensitive to foreign influences. For example, the U.S. economy's health is heavily dependent on imported oil. Overseas disruptions in the supply/demand dynamic of this resource ripple through several industries, including the oil, chemical, and leisure sectors. Other U.S. industries are under assault from foreign competitors: automobile parts, apparel, and electronics are three of the more popular targets. At the same time, U.S. exports have never been stronger, reflecting the economic liberalization of nations previously keeping out U.S. products.

Reflecting this liberalization theme, analysts evaluate selected industries on a global basis. Demand projections are aggregated by country, and the external influences referred to herein are considered from a global perspective. This approach is appropriate for worldwide commodity businesses such as oil, metals, and agricultural products, although it is applied at times to categories such as defense, semiconductors, and airlines.

Keeping Your Focus

Big-picture trends are interesting to study, but undisciplined research does little to advance an equity evaluation. Isolating the critical elements in an external analysis is difficult and most research reports fail in this regard. The reports often present outside factors that resemble a jumble of competing influences, and the identifiable opportunities for an industry seem canceled out by the emerging threats. The end result: analysts extrapolate the past into the future, and fail to uncover compelling changes that can move an industry's sales off historical trends. As noted earlier, this rearview-mirror method is appropriate for many industries, but an incisive effort is required either to unlock an industry's potential or to spot its incumbent weakness.

Two external reviews are set forth in the following case studies.

CASE STUDY

Cable TV Industry

The cable TV industry is a latter stage growth business. It is a defensive industry in terms of the business cycle, with growth aspects. Most U.S. homes have been wired for cable TV, but the industry is still grabbing advertising dollars away from the broadcast networks. Cable TV is fundamentally a regulated monopoly, and regulators generally allow monthly subscriber charges to track inflation.

December 1996 research reports emphasized the influence of technology and government in the industry's future, as shown in Exhibit 11.

The external factors were largely positive in 1996, and analysts concluded that the cable TV industry's above-average revenue growth rate would continue. Higher pay-TV revenues and increased channel availability would enable the industry to garner a growing share of ad revenues, while docile regulators would rubber-stamp inflation-driven subscriber rates. Direct broadcast satellite service, an obvious cable TV substitute was a minor threat. It had just a 3 percent market share in TV homes and its premium service (and rates) were acceptable to only high-end consumers.

| EXHIBIT 11 | Cable TV Industry External Factors and Related Threats |

Technology

Opportunities

Improved pay TV technology increases revenues.

More compression means more channels *and* more revenues.

New technology permits phone service over cable lines.

Threats

Improved technology enhances the direct broadcast satellite (DBS) industry's ability to attract customers.

Technology may be available for phone companies to send TV programming through telephone wires.

Government

Opportunities

There is no political will to cut the industry's monthly subscriber rates.

Liberal regulatory policies expand cable merger options to phone companies and software providers.

After new telecommunications law passed, U.S. West (5th largest telephone company) agreed to merge with Continental Cablevision (third largest cable TV company).

Threats

Regulators can change their minds on subscriber fees.

New law allows phone companies to compete in cable TV. These companies are larger and have more resources than most cable firms.

Social Changes

Opportunities

No significant opportunities were gleaned from existing social trends.

Threats

American television viewing on a per capita basis is up 5% from 1990 to 1995, but it may be reaching a saturation point at 4.3 hours per day.

Demographics

No significant opportunities or threats are apparent from underlying demographic changes.

Foreign Influences

The industry's customers and principal suppliers are located in the United States. Foreign influences are practically nil.

CASE STUDY

Trucking Industry

The trucking industry is divided into two sectors, the long-haul business, whereby a full truckload is shipped long distances over several days; and the short-haul business, which consists primarily of less than full loads shipped within a 200-mile radius. Trucking is a cyclical industry, and its volumes are directly correlated to industrial production. The industry also follows a capacity cycle. The industry over-expands during good times, and new trucks may be running half empty when the economy is prospering. Labor costs are 60 percent of sales and qualified drivers are hard to find. This capacity problem and labor issue can lead to rate cuts in good economic times and lower profits. The primary competitors are railroads in the long-haul segment and air freight companies in the short-haul business. Exhibit 12 lists external factors affecting the trucking industry.

No external factors threaten the industry's survival. Trucking is going to be with us for a long time, but serious issues involve new competition and a driver shortage, with few counterbalancing opportunities. External factors contribute to the consensus belief that trucking industry revenues will grow slower than the general economy. Future profitability will be below average.

| EXHIBIT 12 | Trucking Industry External Factors and Related Threats |

Technology

Opportunities	*Threats*
Growing use of on-board computers and satellite tracking improve delivery times for truckers.	Railroads' introduction of *Roadrailer* (a trailer equipped with highway and rail wheels) and the *Iron Highway* (a flexible train that facilitates truck trailer hauling) brings new competitive threats to the short-haul market.
Just-in-time-inventory acceptance is helping truckers vis-à-vis railroads.	

Government

Opportunities	*Threats*
No significance.	The federal government is permitting large railroad mergers, which will increase pressure on the long-haul segment.
	New safety regulations tighten the driver licensing process, acerbating a shortage of drivers.
	Government is cutting back its loan program to truck driving schools, thus contributing to the driver shortage.

(Exhibit continued on next page . . .)

EXHIBIT 12	(continued)

Social Changes

Opportunities	*Threats*
Increasing acceptance of women and minorities as truck drivers could relieve driver shortage.	Desire to spend more time at home reduces pool of applicants, as people choose alternative professions.

Demographics

Opportunities	*Threats*
No special issues.	Truck driving is a younger person's profession. The baby boom years (1946–1964) were followed by a birth decline, so there's a smaller pool of eligible drivers.

Foreign Influences

The trucking industry's customers and principal suppliers are located in the United States, except for oil, which is 50% imported. Gasoline costs account for 15% to 20% of revenues, but gas prices are reasonably stable.

DEMAND ANALYSIS   5

The ultimate purpose of preparing an economic analysis, industry life cycle placement, and external factor review is an assessment of future demand for the industry's products. Applying such study to numerical forecasts is accomplished differently, as discussed below:

1. *Top-down economic analysis.* We look for specific macroeconomic variables that affect an industry's sales. An ideal situation is when revenues correlate strongly to one economic statistic, thus reducing the need for multiple forecast inputs. Cement demand growth in Mexico, for example, is historically $1.7 \times$ GNP growth. Analysts, as a result, rely on GNP forecasts to project cement unit volume.

2. *Industry life cycle.* Categorizing the industry within its life cycle position (or its business cycle sensitivity) provides a framework for demand forecasts. The U.S. food industry is "mature," so unit sales should track GNP and population growth. The internet industry is "growing," and this characterization provides a guide to above-normal sales increases.

3. *External factors.* Many outside factors are fairly stable, and their impact on an industry are easily predictable. Others are highly variable, and thus bring an element of uncertainty into the analysis. Including these items, items into a sales forecast is a qualitative exercise, requiring judgment.

By considering the preceding three major themes, the analyst establishes a future sales line for the industry. Most times, this sales trend turns out to be an extrapolation of past history, as suggested by the trend line for the established industry in Exhibit 13, but not always. Sometimes, careful study reveals the likelihood of a turning point that affects the industry's fortunes dramatically. Even an extrapolation result provides useful insights. For example, the water service industry has shown a 7 percent growth rate. Suppose your analysis indicates a continuation of the trend, but only at 5 percent. The 2 percent difference leads you to believe the industry's prospects are overblown, and you sell your shareholdings while prices are still high. In Exhibit 13, a mild decrease in the growth rate produces 10 percent lower sales in the future.

Once a trend has been forecast, the analyst's next step is studying the industry's customers. Where does the demand originate? Who's buying and why?

Customer Study

A forecast of aggregate demand is helpful, but a full understanding of what drives an industry's revenue is achieved through learning the customers. Since a typical industry serves thousands of clients, evaluating them individually is impossible. Segmenting the customers into submarkets, on the other hand, enables the analyst to study a smaller number of factors that contribute to demand. As he sequentially studies each submarket, he builds an aggregate demand profile, submarket by submarket.

For example, the demand forecast for the Mexican cement market relied heavily on GNP trends. As a backup to this methodology, I subdivided the market into five segments and considered demand in each segment to verify the accu-

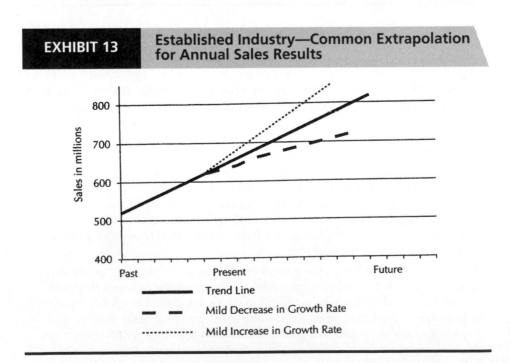

| EXHIBIT 13 | Established Industry—Common Extrapolation for Annual Sales Results |

EXHIBIT 14	Mexican Cement Market—Building Aggregate Demand by Submarket

Submarket	Estimated Demand (MM Tons)
Residential	10.5
Commercial	8.2
Infrastructure	7.3
Transformers[a]	2.2
Export	3.0
Total Submarket Demand	31.2
GNP-Based Demand	30.4

[a] Manufacturing of concrete block, concrete pipe, and so on.

racy of the GNP multiplier. Both methods revealed a likely demand around 31 million tons, including exports (see Exhibit 14).

In Exhibit 14, I categorized the submarkets by usage: homebuilding, infrastructure projects, and commercial construction. But demand segments can be classified by different definitions. David Aaker, a noted business strategist, divides segments between customer characteristics and product-related approaches. Exhibit 15 shows samples from the U.S. market.

A careful analyst studies demand on the basis of several submarket classifications. Following Dr. Aaker's advice, I examined Mexican cement forecasts on a geographic basis. I divided Mexico into five regions and looked at individual market need (see Exhibit 16). In this instance, the GNP, usage, and geographic methods delivered aggregate forecasts that were highly correlated. Utilizing multiple approaches is a good double check for any sales forecast.

Established Industries   For established industries, the analyst should contact long-time customers to figure what drives demand in each submarket. What guides the customer's buying decisions? How does it differ by submarket? What changes are occurring in the customer's motivation? What implication will they have on industry revenues? Discussions with customers and a study of buying habits indicate whether prior trends continue.

For example, VCRs captured 70 percent of the U.S. housing market after ten years. Unit growth dropped in the 1990s. Personal computers represent a newer appliance. They appear in 32 percent of U.S. homes but are concentrated in the higher income households. This low penetration (relative to VCRs) promotes a high growth rate until computer saturation occurs in all income segments (see Exhibit 17).

Growth Industries   A growth industry has yet to penetrate all its future submarkets. In addition to researching the existing customer base, the analyst considers new outlets for the industry's products. The pager business, for example, was

EXHIBIT 15	Approaches to Defining Demand Segments

Customer Characteristics	Demand Segment
Geographic	Southern region as a market for trendy clothing versus the West Coast
Type of business	Computer needs of restaurants versus manufacturing firms versus banks versus retailers
Size of firm	Large hospital versus midsize versus small
Lifestyle	Tendency of Jaguar buyers to be more adventurous, less conservative than buyers of Mercedes-Benz
Sex	The Virginia Slims cigarettes for women
Age	Cereals for children versus adults
Occupation	The paper copier needs of lawyers versus dentists

Product-Related Approaches	Demand Segment
User type	Appliance buyer—home builder, homeowner, small business
Usage	The heavy potato users—the fast-food outlets
Benefits sought	Dessert eaters—those who are calorie-conscious versus those who are more concerned with convenience
Price sensitivity	Price-sensitive Honda Civic buyer versus the luxury Mercedes-Benz buyer
Competitor	Those computer users now committed to IBM
Application	Professional users of chain saws versus the homeowner
Brand loyalty	Those committed to IBM versus others

Source: *Developing Business Strategies*, by David Aaker (New York: John Wiley & Sons, Inc., 1995).

confined to businesspeople. In recent years, it has expanded to personal use. Fast-food chains were selling to the lunch and dinner market. In the 1980s, they attracted the breakfast segment. Identifying a new use or user group is important to confirming a growth industry's upward movement.

Untested Industries   Some publicly-traded companies furnish a truly new product or service. Given a minimal level of product acceptance, these firms have little or no track record from which the analyst can build a sales forecast. Although the risk profile of these stocks is higher than most, the decision process is not entirely speculative.

EXHIBIT 16	Mexican Cement Market Building Aggregate Demand by Submarket Geographic Basis

Geographic Market	Estimated Demand (MM Tons)
Central Mexico	11.2
Northern Gulf	5.9
South Mexico	5.2
Central Pacific	3.2
North Pacific	2.2
Export	3.0
Total Geographic Market Demand	30.7
Submarket Based Demand	31.2
GNP-Based Demand	30.4

A first step is determining whether the new industry fulfills a need that 1) exists, and 2) isn't being met by another industry. The managed care industry was founded in response to the urgent need of corporations to cut employee medical costs. Assuming a need is verified, analysts typically forecast new industry sales based on the experience of a similar industry.

One illustration is the office products superstore industry, as typified by Office Depot and Staples. No sooner did these two companies go public than analysts settled into a comparison with discount warehouse clubs, such as Price Club and Costco. Market share and saturation levels for Office Depot and Staples were calculated on models similar to the warehouse club experience. For every 250,000 people in a metropolitan market, for example, analysts figured one warehouse club could succeed. After some observation, they used similar logic in quantifying 25,000 white collar workers and 100,000 people per office products superstore.

EXHIBIT 17	Comparable Household Penetration Two Electronic Products

	1980	1985	1990
VCR	2%	37%	70%

	1985	1990	1995
Personal computers	10%	23%	32%

EXHIBIT 18	Demand Analysis Model for the Hotel Furniture Market

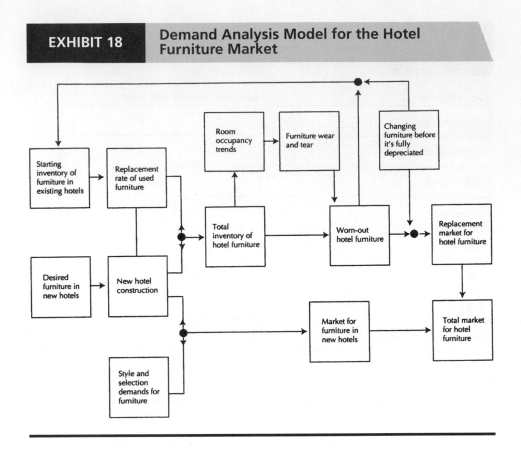

Input/Output and Industry Demand Forecasts

Input-output analysis observes the flow of goods and services through the production process, including intermediate steps as the goods proceed raw-material to finished product. A rising consumption of the finished product boosts demand for industries supplying the intermediate steps. For example, the personal computer boom elevates the demand for the semiconductor, an important PC component.

If one industry is a major customer of another, an analyst uses input-output analysis to derive partial demand for the latter's products. Alternatively, the higher consumption of one industry's offerings sparks demand for complementary products. The wide-scale introduction of the VCR boosted the video rental business. In the 1980s, analysts calculated video demand through algebraic formulas based on VCR purchases. A typical formula was that one VCR purchase meant three video rentals per month. The demand models can be complex and contain many variables. Exhibit 18 shows one rendition for the hotel furniture market.

6   SUPPLY ANALYSIS IN THE INDUSTRY STUDY

In reviewing industries, analysts spend most of their time studying *demand* trends. They usually assume the supply side of the equation takes care of itself. If industry revenues are rising, more investment pours in. If revenues are declining, existing capacity services the falling demand. This model is valid in the long term, but its applicability over the short to intermediate term varies by industry.

The temporary help industry fits the classic model well. With its emphasis on low-skilled workers, the industry can find new employees quickly, thus ramping up capacity in a short time. In contrast, supply that is dependent on capital intensive producers is a different story. Steel and packaging require three- to five-year periods to build plants that add capacity. Industries that use highly skilled workers, such as software, can face short-term capacity constraints as they wait for training programs to provide new employees.

Projecting Supply Availability

Supply is a function of unused capacity and the ability to bring on new capacity. Interpreting these variables well enough to make a reasonable forecast is complicated. That's why few analysts attempt the job. Ideally, a supply forecast dovetails with a demand forecast, and the analyst has an idea about future market equilibrium. If future supply and demand are out of balance, prices for the industry's products will be affected unless the suppliers change their behavior in time. The ideal research report has a supply/demand graph like the one shown in Exhibit 19. In this case, the graph predicts a future capacity problem.

The supply projection is easiest when the industry has only a few competitors, generating output at a discrete number of sizable facilities. It also helps if the industry's economics make imports prohibitively expensive, so the analyst can ignore foreign capacity. The cement industry is a good example of this model. First, only large plants, with long construction lead times, make cement. Second, the low value per ton makes transportation uneconomical beyond a 250-mile radius from the plant. Thus, it's a simple matter to forecast available supply: An analyst counts nearby capacity and adds expansions planned for the next three to five years.

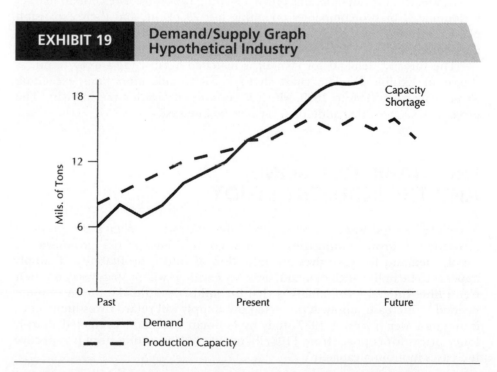

| EXHIBIT 19 | Demand/Supply Graph Hypothetical Industry |

Note: There's a capacity shortage in the future. This could mean higher product prices.

EXHIBIT 20	1996 Mexican Cement Market Availability of Supply Calculation (Millions of Tons per Year)			
	1996	**1997**	**1998**	**1999**
1996 capacity	36.0	36.0	36.0	36.0
1997 additions, net	—	1.0	1.0	1.0
1998 additions, net	—	—	3.7	3.7
1999 additions, net	—	—	—	1.3
Total estimated capacity	36.0	37.0	40.7	42.0

Note: Additions are net of closures.

EXHIBIT 21	1996 Supply/Demand Forecast Mexican Cement Industry			
	1996	**1997**	**1998**	**1999**
Available capacity	36.0	37.0	40.7	42.0
Expected demand	31.0	33.0	35.5	38.0
Capacity utilization	86%	89%	87%	90.5%

In Mexico, for example, this process is straightforward. The cement market is dominated by two companies operating just 29 plants, and their expansion plans are public knowledge. All plants have ample reserves of raw materials. An illustrative calculation for supply appears in Exhibit 20.

The forecast demand for cement is matched against the supply trend, as shown in Exhibit 21. The chart shows capacity utilization rates exceeding 88 percent from 1996 to 1999, which is considered *high* for the industry. The projection suggests that additional capacity be initiated.

7 PROFITABILITY, PRICING, AND THE INDUSTRY STUDY

A security analyst wants to select profitable industries. What's the point of investing in growth industries if sales go up, but profits go down? A supply/demand forecast gives an indication of future profitability. If supply appears to be in line with demand, industry earnings will probably stay on their trend line. Indeed, profitability is vital for industries to make the investment needed to increase supply. A projected oversupply will retard investment since it augurs lower prices. A 1997 study by Lehman Brothers* predicted sharply lower prices for copper (from 110¢/lb. to 60¢/lb.), resulting from prospective increases in mining capacity.

---

*Barclays has acquired Lehman Brothers and will maintain the family of Lehman Brothers indices and the associated index calculation, publication, and analytical infrastructure and tools.

Factors contributing to *pricing* include:

► Product segmentation.
► Degree of industry concentration.
► Ease of industry entry.
► Price changes in key supply inputs.

To begin, most industries effectively segment their product offerings by brand name, reputation, or service, even when the products are quite similar. Over-the-counter medicines are one example. The ingredients of the store brand and the name-brand are typically identical, yet the name-brand product has a 40 percent price premium.

An industry with a high degree of concentration inhibits price movements. Assuming that demand and supply are in reasonable balance, the major players have an incentive to engage in monopolistic behavior. Artificially high prices can be sustained by price signaling, confidential agreements, and other means. Outsiders have problems breaking into the inner circle to learn what's going on. In Mexico's cement market, for example, the two major producers control 85 percent of the market, and they barely hide the fact that collusion exists. In several U.S. industries, similar behavior occurs, but it's kept behind closed doors.

Monopolies promote artificial pricing, and an industry's ease of entry is a key variable in holding prices to the free market model. Semiconductor production poses an obvious problem; the entry ticket—a new plant—costs $1 billion. The specialty retailing industry, in contrast, is wide-open. An entrepreneur can rent store space, lease fixtures, and stock inventory for less than $75,000.

Certain industries rely heavily on one or two inputs. Price changes in these inputs affect products costs and profitability. Sometimes, the industry can pass through increased costs in the form of higher prices. At other times, competitive pressures stand in the way. In 1996, for example, the price of corn, a key chicken feed, reached historical highs. Poultry producers, such as Tyson Foods and WLR Corp., were unable to raise prices enough to compensate and their profitability fell.

Industry Profitability Is Important

Supply/demand analysis, cost factors, and pricing flexibility are critical elements in determining future industry profitability. Without earnings, an industry can't finance the commitment to personnel, plant, and research and development that is needed to prosper. An industry with a poor profit outlook is an unlikely investment candidate indeed.

INTERNATIONAL COMPETITION AND MARKETS   8

Competition

Competitive analysis is the topic of many books. Michael Porter of the Harvard Business School, is a leader in the field, and approaches competition from multiple directions, as set forth in Exhibit 22. Security analysis synthesizes the work of experts like Dr. Porter, and this section provides a brief treatment of the subject.

EXHIBIT 22	Five Competitive Forces That Determine Industry Profitability

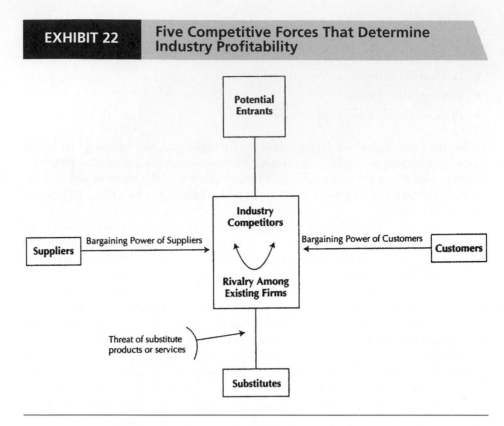

Source: *Competitive Advantage*, by Michael E. Porter (New York: The Free Press, 1985).

A first step in the competitive analysis is defining the industry. While this task was discussed earlier, it is helpful to remember that some analysts cover the chemical industry; some follow the chemical fertilizer industry; and still others research the specialty chemical industry. Industries are segmented into smaller industries. *Institutional Investor* magazine divides the computer industry into seven subindustries: computer services, data networking, the Internet, PC hardware, PC software, server and enterprise hardware, and server and enterprise software. Placing your company into its subindustry and identifying its competitors becomes the second step in your competitive analysis.

For each competitor, the analyst develops an appreciation of its business strategy and its effects on the company under study. For example, in the managed care business, Aetna pursues a national program. Physician Health Services focuses on the Southeast region. Managed Care Solutions sticks to Medicaid managed care. If Aetna shifted to Medicaid contracts, it would harm Managed Care Solutions' prospects.

Finally, the analyst is advised to outline the strengths and weaknesses of industry participants. Exhibit 23 illustrates many of the items considered in such an outline. Financial track record and balance sheet strength are priorities for analysts, but a review of other factors reveals whether better results can be achieved by the competition, perhaps at the expense of the subject company. Similarly, if the subject company's strengths dominate areas where the competition is weak, a higher degree of confidence is gained for your forecasts.

Each industry has a few dominant success factors that can be drawn from Exhibit 23. Analysts (and corporate strategists) inventory these items and the relative positions of competitors. Exhibit 24 presents this comparative analysis in tabular form.

EXHIBIT 23	Competitive Analysis: Analysis of Strengths and Weaknesses of Each Industry Participant

Innovation	Management
Technical product or service superiority	Quality of top and middle management
New product capability	Knowledge of business
Research & development	Culture
Technologies	Strategic goals and plans
Patents	Entrepreneurial thrust
	Planning/operation system
	Loyalty—turnover
	Quality of strategic decision making

Manufacturing	Marketing
Cost structure	Product quality reputation
Flexible production operations	Product characteristics/differentiation
Equipment	Brand-name recognition
Access to raw material	Breadth of product line—systems capability
Vertical integration	Customer orientation
Workforce attitude and motivation	Segmentation/focus
Capacity	Distribution
	Retailer relationship
	Advertising/promotion skills
	Sales force
	Customer service/product support

Finance—Access to Capital	Customer Base
From operations	Size and loyalty
From cash on hand	Market share
Ability to use debt and equity financing	Growth of segments served

Source: *Developing Business Strategies*, by David Aaker (New York: John Wiley & Sons, Inc., 1995).

A firm's ability to sustain its sales and earnings is highly dependent on the status of the competition. Does the subject company have the ability to be aggressive—take the offense? Or, does it have to protect market share and husband financial resources—play defense? The competitor profile facilitates game theory for the practitioner.

EXHIBIT 24	Sample Competitor Analysis for a Research Report

	Major Competitors			
Competition Indicators	**A**	**B**	**C**	**D**
Market position	Vulnerable	Prevalent	Strong	Vulnerable
Profitability	Low	Average	Average	Average
Financial strength	Low	High	Unknown	Low
Product mix	Narrow	Broad	Narrow	Narrow
Technological capability	Average	Strong	Average	Weak
Product quality	Minimum	Good	Satisfactory	Minimum

Source: *Management Policy, Strategy and Plans*, by Milton Leontiades (New York: Little, Brown & Company, 1982).

International Competition

The world is becoming a smaller place and industries increasingly reflect a globalization theme. This characterization is most advanced with commodity industries such as oil, metals, and basic foodstuffs, but it also dominates intermediate sectors such as textiles, semiconductors, and chemicals. Indeed, about 40 percent of the S&P 500's earnings are connected to international activities.

The United States is the leading economy, has the greatest number of publicly traded securities, and operates the most developed financial markets. For these reasons, the security analysis profession has made great strides here. The downside of this situation has been a nearsightedness on the part of many United States practitioners. Even though industries extend globally, Wall Street research often stops at the U.S. border, and analysts frequently give short shrift to corporate foreign operations and international trends. As institutions emphasize global research, more work will be dedicated to this important area.

SUMMARY

The industry analysis is a continuation of the top-down approach. By studying the industry, its external environment, demand and supply balance, likely profitability and competitive situation, the security analyst confirms whether the industry is appropriate for investment. The written research report only presents a limited amount of information and practitioners highlight a few key factors in reviewing an industry. Frequently, their audience prefers a one-word summary in the industry review, such as *growth, mature,* or *decline.* With a knowledge of the industry terrain, the analyst proceeds to a specific stock selection. Which of the participants are the winners? Which are the losers?

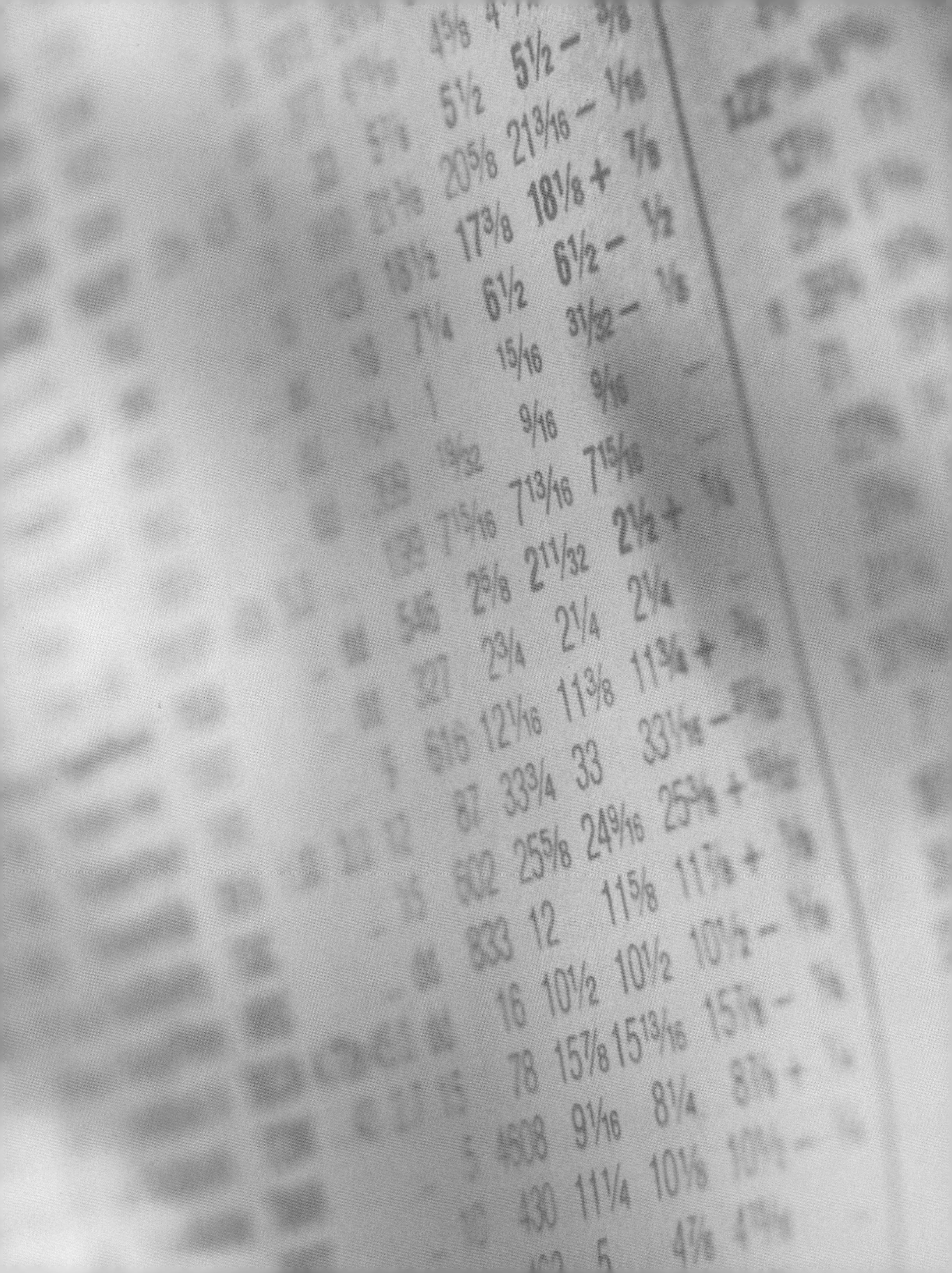

4⅝ 4
5½ 5½ − ⅜
5½ 2¹³⁄₁₆ − ⅛
20⅝ 21³⁄₁₆ − ¼
17⅜ 18⅛ + ⅞
13½ 6½ 6½ − ½
7¼ 31³⁄₃₂ − ⅛
15⁄₁₆ 9⁄₁₆
9⁄₁₆ 9⁄₁₆
¹⁹⁄₃₂
7¹⁵⁄₁₆ 7¹³⁄₁₆ 7⅝
2⅝ 2¹¹⁄₃₂ 2½ +
2¾ 2¼ 2¼
6½ 12¹⁄₁₆ 11⅜ 11¾ +
87 33¾ 33 33¹⁄₁₆ −
502 25⅝ 24⁹⁄₁₆ 25⅜ +
833 12 11⅝ 11⅞ +
16 10½ 10½ 10½ −
78 15⅞ 15¹³⁄₁₆ 15⅞ −
808 9¹⁄₁₆ 8¼ 8⅞ +
430 11¼ 10⅛ 10⅞
5 4⅞ 4⅞

VALUATION IN EMERGING MARKETS

by Tim Koller, Marc Goedhart, and David Wessels

LEARNING OUTCOMES

The candidate should be able to:	Mastery
a. describe how inflation affects the estimation of cash flows for a company domiciled in an emerging market;	☐
b. evaluate an emerging market company using a discounted cash flow model based on nominal and real financial projections;	☐
c. explain arguments for adjusting cash flows, rather than adjusting the discount rate, to account for emerging market risks (e.g., inflation, macroeconomic volatility, capital control, and political risk) in a scenario analysis;	☐
d. estimate the cost of capital for emerging market companies, and calculate and interpret a country risk premium.	☐

The emerging economies in Asia and South America will experience strong growth over the next decades; many analysts see China and India moving into the ranks of the world's largest economies.[1] This sometimes spectacular economic development will produce many situations requiring sound analysis and valuation. In the rising number of privatizations, joint ventures, mergers and acquisitions, local financial parties such as banks and capital markets will display growing sophistication. Institutional investors will also continue to diversify their portfolios, adding international holdings in emerging-market stocks.

In this reading we focus on issues that arise in financial analysis and valuation of businesses in emerging markets. Valuation is much more difficult in these

---

Special thanks to our colleagues William Jones and Gustavo Wigman, who contributed to this reading.

[1] See, for example, D. Wilson and R. Purushothaman, "Dreaming with BRICs: The Path to 2050" (Global Economics paper no. 99, Goldman Sachs & Co., October 2003).

environments because of risks and obstacles to businesses, including great macroeconomic uncertainty, illiquid capital markets, controls on the flow of capital into and out of the country, less-rigorous accounting standards and disclosure levels, and high levels of political risk. Academics, investment bankers, and industry practitioners have yet to agree on how to address these challenges. Methods vary considerably and practitioners often make arbitrary adjustments based on intuition and limited empirical evidence.

With agreement lacking and emerging-market valuations so complex, we recommend a triangulation approach—comparing estimates of the value from three methods. First, we use discounted cash flows with probability-weighted scenarios that explicitly model the risks the business faces. Then we compare the value obtained from this approach with the results of two secondary approaches: a DCF approach with a country risk premium built into the cost of capital, and a valuation based on comparable trading and transaction multiples.

The basics of estimating a DCF value are the same in emerging markets as elsewhere. Therefore, we focus on complications specific to emerging-market valuations:

▶ handling foreign exchange rates, inflation, and interest rate gaps with developed markets consistently when making financial projections
▶ factoring inflation into historical financial analysis and cash flow projections
▶ incorporating special emerging-market risks consistently in the valuation
▶ estimating the cost of capital in emerging markets
▶ using market-based references such as trading multiples and transaction multiples when interpreting and calibrating valuation results

We will apply our valuation approach in this reading to ConsuCo, a leading Brazilian manufacturer of consumer goods.[2]

1   EXCHANGE RATES, INFLATION, AND INTEREST RATE GAPS

Because exchange rates, inflation, and interest rates can fluctuate wildly from year to year in emerging markets, assumptions underlying estimates of future financial results in domestic or foreign currency and cost of capital must be consistent. Some fundamental monetary assumptions should be defined consistently to avoid any biases in the valuation results. This becomes even more important when you value companies in emerging markets.

The components of the cash flows of emerging-market companies are often denominated in several currencies. Consider an oil exporter. Its revenues are determined by the dollar price of oil, while many of its costs (labor and domestic

---

[2] This case illustration is a disguised example.

purchases) are determined by the domestic currency. If foreign-exchange rates would perfectly reflect inflation differentials—so that purchasing power parity would hold—the company's operating margins and cash flows in real terms would be unaffected. In that case, changes in exchange rates would be irrelevant for valuation purposes.

However, at least in the short run, this does not always hold, because in emerging markets, exchange rates move far and fast. For example, in Argentina at the end of 2001, the exchange rate rose from 1.0 peso per U.S. dollar to nearly 1.9 pesos per U.S. dollar in 15 days, and to 3.1 in less than 4 months. During a period of just a couple of weeks in 1999, Brazil's currency, the Real, weakened by more than 50 percent relative to the U.S. dollar.

When estimating the impact of exchange rate movements on cash flow forecasts, keep in mind that evidence shows that, over the long run, purchasing power parity does hold,[3] even between emerging and developed economies. In other words, exchange rates ultimately do adjust for differences in inflation between countries. For example, if you held $100 million of Brazilian currency in 1964, by 2004 it would have been practically worthless in U.S. dollars. Yet, if we adjust for purchasing power, the value of the currency didn't change very much, as Exhibit 1 shows. In other words, suppose that, instead of holding $100 million of Brazilian currency, you held $100 million of assets in Brazil whose value increased with inflation. In 2004, your assets would have been worth about $90 million (in real terms). Therefore, when you perform valuations, your best assumption is that purchasing power parity holds in the long term; any other approach implies taking a bet on future real exchange rate movements.

Nevertheless, as Exhibit 1 also shows, exchange rates can deviate from purchasing power parity (PPP) by as much as 20 percent to 30 percent for several years (keeping in mind that PPP-adjusted exchange rates are difficult to

| **EXHIBIT 1** | **Brazilian PPP-Adjusted Dollar Exchange Rates** |

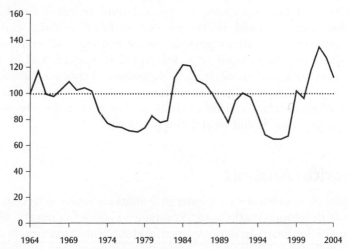

Reais per U.S. dollar index, 1964 = 100

Source: MCM Consultants, IMF International Financial Statistics.

---

[3] For a recent overview, see Alan M. Taylor and Mark Peter Taylor, "The Purchasing Power Parity Debate" (CEPR discussion paper no. 4495, 2004).

estimate). Therefore, before making financial projections, assess whether the current exchange rate is over- or undervalued on a PPP basis and, if so, by how much. Then model the convergence of currency rates to purchasing power parity, and reflect its impact on the company's profitability in your long-term financial projections. Because it is hard to predict how long the current PPP deviation will persist, you could conduct a sensitivity analysis to assess the valuation impact of the timing of the return to purchasing power parity. As you develop your forecasts, remember your overall perspective about the economics of the business. The long-term sustainable operating profit margin and ROIC should not be affected by any short-term deviations from PPP. Relying on a set of fundamental monetary assumptions keeps your projections consistent with your cost of capital whether you project in domestic, foreign, real, or nominal currency.

Regardless of any short- or long-term economic exposure to varying exchange rates, your valuation results should be independent of the currency or mix of currencies in which you forecast the company's cash flows. Use actual or synthetic forward exchange rates to convert any future cash flow into another currency. In many emerging economies, the forward-exchange market is nonexistent or illiquid, so actual forward rates provide little guidance on likely future exchange rate movements or inflation differentials. In that case, estimate a synthetic forward rate from your assumptions about future inflation and interest rates for the currencies concerned.

2 FACTORING INFLATION INTO HISTORICAL ANALYSIS AND FORECASTS

Even with consistent assumptions about inflation, interest rates, and foreign exchange rates, sound analysis and forecasting of the financial performance of emerging-market companies remains challenging. Inflation distorts the financial statements, so it is hard to make year-to-year historical comparisons, perform ratio analysis, or forecast performance.

For companies operating in high-inflation environments, historical analysis and forecasting should be carried out in both nominal and real (constant currency) terms whenever possible. As we will explain, nominal indicators are sometimes not meaningful (e.g., for capital turnover), and in other cases, real indicators are problematic (e.g., to determine corporate income taxes). Proper valuation requires insights from both nominal- and real-terms historical analyses. Financial projections can be made in real or nominal terms or both; properly done projections should yield an identical value.

Historical Analysis

Accounting conventions in emerging markets often differ substantially from those of developed markets, so a company's economics may be difficult to understand. Furthermore, in many countries, complicated tax credits and adjustments make cash taxes harder to estimate than in developed markets. For example, Brazil has made large and frequent changes to its tax code. Brazil eliminated inflation accounting and reduced the corporate tax rate to 30.5 percent in 1996, and in 1997 disallowed the deductibility of the social contribution tax, effectively increasing the tax rate to 33 percent. To make up for the loss of the tax shields that inflation accounting had generated, Brazil's government allowed companies to deduct deemed interest on equity net of a withholding tax of 15 percent.

Large accounting and tax differences are frequently eliminated when the income statement and the balance sheet are brought together in the cash flow calculation. Still, before starting a valuation, you need to understand these differences. Unfortunately, the differences across emerging markets are too complex and varied for a detailed discussion in this reading. Instead, we highlight the most common issues involving the impact of high inflation on your historical analysis.

In countries experiencing extreme inflation (more than 25 percent per year), companies often report in year-end currency. In the income statement, items such as revenues and costs that were booked throughout the year are restated at year-end purchasing power. Otherwise, the addition of these items would not be meaningful. The balance sheet usually has adjustments to fixed assets, inventory, and equity; the accounts payable and receivable are already in year-end terms.

In most countries, however, financial statements are not adjusted to reflect the effects of inflation. If inflation is high, this leads to distortions in the balance sheet and income statement. In the balance sheet, so-called nonmonetary assets, such as inventories and property, plant, and equipment, are shown at values far below current replacement value if they are long-lived assets. In the income statement, depreciation charges are too low relative to current replacement costs. Sales and costs in December and January of the same year are typically added as if they represent the same purchasing power.

As a result, many financial indicators typically used in historical analyses can be distorted when calculated directly from the financial statements. In emerging markets, companies often index their internal management accounts to overcome these issues. If they do not, or if you are doing an outside-in analysis, at least correct for the following distortions:

▶ Growth is overstated in times of inflation, so restate it in real terms by deflating with an annual inflation index if sales are evenly spread across the year. If sales are not spread evenly, use quarterly or monthly inflation indexes to deflate the sales in each corresponding interval.

▶ Capital turnover is typically overstated because operating assets are carried at historical costs. You can approximate the current costs of long-lived assets by adjusting their reported value with an inflation index for their estimated average lifetime. Or consider developing ratios of real sales relative to physical capacity indicators appropriate for the sector—for example, sales per square meter in consumer retail. Inventory levels also need restating if turnover is low and inflation is very high.

▶ Operating margins (operating profit over sales) can be overstated because of too-low depreciation and large holding gains on slow-moving inventories. Corrections for depreciation charges follow from adjustments to property, plant, and equipment. You can estimate cash operating expenses at current-cost basis by inflating the reported costs for the average time held in inventory. Alternatively, use historical EBITDA-to-sales ratios to assess the company's performance relative to peers; these ratios at least do not suffer from any depreciation-induced bias.

▶ Use caution in interpreting credit ratios and other indicators of capital structure health. Distortions are especially significant in solvency ratios such as debt to equity or total assets, because long-lived assets are understated relative to replacement costs, and floating-rate debt is at current currency units. Use coverage ratios such as EBITDA to interest expense.[4] These are

---

[4] Distortions occur in the ratio of EBITA to interest coverage if operating profit is overstated due to low depreciation charges and low costs of procured materials.

less exposed to accounting distortions because depreciation has no impact and debt financing in emerging markets is mostly at floating interest rates or in foreign currency.

Financial Projections in Real and Nominal Terms

When you make financial projections of income statements and balance sheets under high inflation for a valuation, keep in mind that accounting adjustments cannot affect free cash flow. Thus, for valuation purposes, we project financial statements without any accounting adjustments for inflation. The projections can be made in nominal or real terms. Exhibit 2 summarizes the major advantages and shortcomings of each approach.

Neither approach is perfect, so use elements of both to prepare consistent financial projections. Specifically, when projecting in real terms, it is often difficult to calculate taxes correctly, as taxes are often calculated based on nominal financial statements. Furthermore, you need to explicitly project the cash flow effects of working capital changes because these do not automatically follow from the annual change in working capital. The main downside of using nominal cash flows is that future capital expenditures are difficult to project because the typically stable relationship between revenues and fixed assets does not hold under high inflation. As a result, depreciation charges and EBITA also are difficult to project.

EXHIBIT 2	Combining Real and Nominal Approaches to Financial Modeling

Estimates	Modeling approach		Preferred application
	Real	Nominal	
Operational performance			
Sales	✓	✓	
EBITDA	✓	✓	
EBITA	✓	–	
Capital expenditures	✓	–	
Investments in working capital	✓ a	✓	
Income taxes	–	✓	
Financial statements	✓ b	✓	
Continuing value	✓ a	✓	

a If inflation impact on investments in working capital is explicitly included.
b If inflation corrections are separately modeled and included in income statement and balance sheet.

Five-Step Approach to Combined Nominal and Real-Terms Financial Projections

We illustrate below how to combine both nominal and real forecasts in a DCF valuation. In this example, the company's revenues grow at 2 percent in real terms, and the annual inflation rate is 20 percent in the first forecasted year and 10 percent thereafter (see Exhibit 3). To simplify, we assumed that all cash flows

		Forecasts				
Operations	Year 1	**2**	**3**	**4**	**5**	**25**
Real growth rate (percent)	2	2	2	2	2	
Real revenues	1,000	1,020	1,040	1,061	1,082	1,608
Real EBITDA	300	306	312	318	325	483
Net working capital/revenues (percent)	20	20	20	20	20	20
Real net PPE/real revenues (percent)	40	40	40	40	40	40
Lifetime of net PPE	5					
Other						
Inflation rate (percent)		20	10	10	10	10
Inflation index	1.00	1.20	1.32	1.45	1.60	10.75
Tax rate (percent)	35	35	35	35	35	35
Real WACC (percent)		8.0	8.0	8.0	8.0	8.0
Nominal WACC (percent)		29.6	18.8	18.8	18.8	18.8

EXHIBIT 3 **DCF under Inflation: Key Assumptions**

Note: Adjusted formula for real-terms continuing value.

occur at the end of the year. Under extreme inflation levels, this assumption could distort financial projections because the cash flows that accumulate throughout the year are subject to different inflation rates. In that case, split the year into quarterly or even monthly intervals, project cash flows for each interval, and discount the cash flows at the appropriate discount rate for that interval.

In practice, many more issues around financial projections arise in emerging-market valuations than in this simplified example. Nevertheless, it shows how to address some key issues when developing a cash flow forecast under high inflation, by means of the following step-by-step approach, leading to the real and nominal valuation results shown in Exhibit 4.

Step 1: Forecast Operating Performance in Real Terms To the extent possible, convert historical nominal balance sheets and income statements into real terms (usually at the current year's currency value). At a minimum, make a real-terms approximation of the historical development of the key value drivers: growth and return on capital and the underlying capital turnover and EBITA margin, so you can understand the true economics of the business. With these approximations, forecast the operating performance of the business in real terms:

▶ Project future revenues and cash expenses to obtain EBITDA forecasts.[5]

▶ Estimate property, plant, and equipment (PPE) and capital expenditures from your assumptions on real-terms capital turnover.

▶ Working capital follows from projected revenues and assumptions on days of working capital required.

▶ From projected net PPE and assumptions on the lifetime of the assets, derive the annual depreciation to estimate real-terms EBITA.

---

[5] This step assumes that all expenses included in EBITDA are cash costs.

EXHIBIT 4 DCF under Inflation: Real and Nominal Models

	Real projections						Nominal projections					
	Year 1	2	3	4	5	25	Year 1	2	3	4	5	25
NOPLAT												
Revenues	1,000	1,020	1,040	1,061	1,082	1,608	1,000	1,224	1,373	1,541	1,729	17,283
EBITDA	300	306	312	318	325	483	300	367	412	462	519	5,185
Depreciation	(80)	(80)	(82)	(83)	(85)	(126)	(80)	(80)	(85)	(92)	(100)	(926)
EBITA	220	226	231	235	240	356	220	287	327	370	419	4,259
Taxes	(77)	(84)	(87)	(89)	(92)	(139)	(77)	(101)	(114)	(130)	(147)	(1,491)
NOPLAT	143	142	144	146	148	218	143	187	212	241	272	2,768
Free cash flow												
NOPLAT	143	142	144	146	148	218	143	187	212	241	272	2,768
Depreciation	80	80	82	83	85	126	80	80	85	92	100	926
Capital expenditures	(80)	(88)	(90)	(92)	(93)	(139)	(80)	(106)	(118)	(133)	(149)	(1,491)
Investment in net working capital		(37)	(23)	(23)	(24)	(35)		(45)	(30)	(34)	(38)	(376)
Free cash flow		97	113	114	116	170		116	149	166	185	1,827
Invested capital												
Net PPE (beginning of year)	400	400	408	416	424	631	400	400	426	459	500	4,631
Depreciation	(80)	(80)	(82)	(83)	(85)	(126)	(80)	(80)	(85)	(92)	(100)	(926)
Capital expenditures	80	88	90	92	93	139	80	106	118	133	149	1,491
Net PPE (end of year)	400	408	416	424	433	643	400	426	459	500	549	5,196
Net working capital	200	204	208	212	216	322	200	245	275	308	346	3,457
Invested capital	600	612	624	637	649	965	600	670	734	808	895	8,653
Ratios (percent)												
Net PPE/revenues		40	40	40	40	40		35	33	32	32	30
Net working capital/revenues		20	20	20	20	20		20	20	20	20	20
ROIC		23	23	23	23	23		31	32	33	34	36
Free cash flow growth rate			17	1	1	2			28	11	12	12
DCF valuation												
Free cash flow		97	113	114	116	170		116	149	166	185	1,827
Continuing value (value driver formula)[a]						2,891						31,063
Continuing value (cash flow perpetuity formula)						2,891						31,064
Present value factor		0.93	0.86	0.79	0.74	0.16		0.77	0.65	0.55	0.46	0.01
DCF value	1,795						1,795					

[a] Adjusted formula for real-terms continuing value.

Step 2: Build Financial Statements in Nominal Terms   Nominal projections can be readily derived by converting the real operating projections into nominal terms (note that these projections do not include any monetary adjustments as under, for example, inflation accounting):

► Project nominal revenues, cash expenses, EBITDA, and capital expenditures by multiplying their real-terms equivalents by the inflation index for the year.

► Estimate net property, plant, and equipment on a year-by-year basis from the prior-year balance plus nominal capital expenditures minus nominal depreciation (which is estimated as a percentage of net PPE according to the estimated lifetime).

► Working capital follows from revenues and days of working capital required.

► Subtract the depreciation charges from EBITDA to obtain nominal EBITA.

► Calculate income taxes on nominal EBITA without inflation corrections. (Always check the local tax rules for the reasonableness of this assumption.)

In contrast to the real-terms projections, the capital turnover is now increasing over time because nominal net PPE grows slower than revenues in a high-inflation environment. In this example, we did not build a complete balance sheet and income statement. That would require the following additional steps:

► Forecast interest expense and other nonoperating income statement items in nominal terms (based on the prior year's balance sheet).

► Equity should equal last year's equity plus earnings, less dividends, plus or minus any share issues or repurchases.

► Finally, balance the balance sheet with debt or marketable securities.[6]

Step 3: Build Financial Statements in Real Terms   Most of the operating items for the real-terms income statement and balance sheet were already estimated in step 1. Now also include the real-terms taxes on EBITA by deflating the nominal taxes as estimated in step 2. For full financial statements, use the inflation index to convert debt, marketable securities, interest expense, income taxes, and nonoperating terms from the nominal statements into real terms. The real-terms equity account is a plug to balance the balance sheet. To make sure you have done this correctly, be sure the real equity account equals last year's equity plus earnings, less dividends, plus or minus share issues or repurchases, and plus or minus inflationary gains or losses on the monetary assets (such as cash, receivables, payables, and debt).

Step 4: Forecast the Future Free Cash Flows in Real and Nominal Terms from the Projected Income Statements and Balance Sheets   The real-terms investment

---

[6] As noted, these projections are made for valuation purposes and not necessarily in accordance with local or international accounting standards prescribing any inflation or monetary corrections for particular groups of assets and liabilities. Free cash flows are not affected by such adjustments.

in net working capital (NWC^R) is equal to the increase in working capital plus a monetary loss due to inflation:[7]

$$\text{Investment in NWC}_t = \text{Increase in NWC}_t^R + \text{NWC}_{t-1}^R\left[1 - \frac{IX_{t-1}}{IX_t}\right]$$

where IX_t is the inflation index for the year t.

To check for consistency, use the inflation index to convert the free cash flows from the nominal projections to real terms. These should equal the free cash flows from the real-terms projections in each year.

Step 5:   Estimate DCF Value in Real and Nominal Terms   When discounting real and nominal cash flows under high inflation, you must address three key issues:

1. Ensure that the WACC estimates in real terms ($WACC^R$) and nominal terms ($WACC^N$) are defined consistently with the inflation assumptions in each year:

$$(1 + WACC_t^N) = (1 + WACC_t^R) \times (1 + \text{Inflation}_t)$$

Later in this reading, we will discuss how to estimate WACC for companies in emerging markets.

2. The value-driver formula should be adjusted when estimating continuing value in real terms. The returns on capital in real-terms projections overestimate the economic returns in the case of positive net working capital. The free cash flow in real terms differs from the cash flow implied by the value driver formula by an amount equal to the annual monetary loss on net working capital:

$$FCF_t^R = \left(1 - \frac{g_t^R}{ROIC_t^R}\right) \times NOPLAT_t^R - NWC_{t-1}^R\left(1 - \frac{IX_{t-1}}{IX_t}\right)$$

Assuming constant real growth, the continuing value in real terms is:

$$CV^R = \frac{FCF^R}{WACC^R - g^R}$$

3. When using the continuing-value formulas, make sure the explicit forecast period is long enough for the model to reach a steady state with constant growth rates of free cash flow. Because of the way inflation affects capital expenditures and depreciation, you need a much longer horizon than for valuations with no or low inflation.

ConsuCo Case Example: Inflation Adjustments

Let's explore how to handle inflation and accounting issues in the financial analysis and valuation of ConsuCo.

---

[7] Even for assets held at constant levels in real-terms balance sheets, replacement investments are required at increasing prices in an inflationary environment. These replacement investments represent a cash outflow, also in real terms, but do not show up from real-terms balance sheet differences from year to year. In contrast, the nominal investment cash flow does follow from the nominal balance sheet differences from year to year.

Historical Analysis In analyzing ConsuCo's historical financial statements, we made adjustments in two areas. First, we rearranged the balance sheet and the income statements to get the statements for NOPLAT, invested capital, and free cash flow. The ConsuCo statements follow Brazilian GAAP, so we had to make some additional adjustments. Most of these were relatively minor. The largest involved the consolidation of a securitization vehicle, for which only the net asset position is shown under Brazilian GAAP.

Second, we estimated some key financial ratios on an approximate real-terms basis. Although annual inflation in Brazil has been moderate since 1997 at levels between 5 and 10 percent, ratios such as operating margin and capital turnover are likely to be biased when directly calculated from the financial statements. Therefore, we looked at trends in cash operating margins (EBITDA over sales). In addition, we estimated the sales revenues in real terms per unit of production capacity over time to better understand the development of real-terms capital turnover.

The results are reflected in Exhibit 5. Between 1998 and 2003, ConsuCo's sales grew significantly in real terms at around 15 percent per year, largely driven by acquisitions. But growth has slowed considerably since 2000. Cash operating margins improved significantly, from 5.7 percent in 1998 to 9.2 percent in 2003. In real terms, annual sales per unit of production capacity have been fairly stable since 2000 at around 6.0 to 6.5 million Reais, as have nominal turnover levels for invested capital (excluding goodwill).

Financial projections Based on the findings from the historical analysis and analyst consensus forecasts as of July 2004, we made the operating and financial forecasts summarized in Exhibit 6 in real and nominal terms. We assumed that no major economic crisis will materialize in Brazil.

ConsuCo is investing heavily for future growth. Real-terms sales growth is projected to peak at 8 percent in 2005 and then gradually decline over the next four years to around 3 percent, close to Brazil's long-term expected real GDP growth. Cash margins will continue to rise to 9.7 percent in 2005 and stay at that level in perpetuity. Tougher competition will create downward pressure on

---

| EXHIBIT 5 | ConsuCo: Key Historical Financial Indicators |

percent

Nominal indicators	1998	1999	2000	2001	2002	2003
Sales growth	41	32	31	6	17	14
Adjusted EBITA/sales	3.5	4.6	5.7	5.3	5.3	6.9
NOPLAT/sales	2.9	3.3	4.8	4.5	3.9	5.3
Invested capital (excluding goodwill)/sales	35.2	34.8	57.0	64.9	62.4	64.5
Invested capital (including goodwill)/sales	42.3	40.3	61.9	74.7	71.7	72.9
ROIC (excluding goodwill)	8.3	9.5	8.4	6.9	6.2	8.2
ROIC (including goodwill)	6.9	8.2	7.7	6.0	5.4	7.3
Approximate real indicators						
Sales growth (inflation-adjusted)	32	24	23	(2)	9	5
EBITDA/sales	5.7	6.7	7.2	7.6	7.5	9.2
Sales/capacity[a]	8.7	7.9	7.0	6.4	6.3	6.2

[a]In inflation-adjusted Reais million per capacity unit.

EXHIBIT 6	ConsuCo: Summary Financial Projections, Base Case

Reais million, percent

	2004	2005	2006	2007	2008	2009	2014	2019
Operating projections								
Sales growth (real, percent)	7.0	8.0	7.0	6.0	5.0	3.0	3.0	3.0
EBITDA/sales (percent)	9.5	9.7	9.7	9.7	9.7	9.7	9.7	9.7
EBITDA (real terms, percent)	2,201	2,427	2,597	2,753	2,890	2,977	3,451	4,001
Sales/capacity[a]	6.2	6.2	6.2	6.2	6.2	6.2	6.2	6.2
Capacity units	3,757	4,058	4,342	4,602	4,832	4,977	5,770	6,689
Capital expenditures (expansion)[b]	558	682	645	591	522	329	382	442
Capital expenditures (maintenance)[b]	663	709	766	819	869	912	1,057	1,226
Real projections								
Sales	23,126	24,976	26,724	28,327	29,744	30,636	35,516	41,172
Adjusted EBITA/sales (percent)	7.2	7.4	7.5	7.5	7.6	7.6	7.7	7.8
NOPLAT/sales (percent)	4.8	4.8	4.7	4.6	4.5	4.4	4.2	4.1
Invested capital (excluding goodwill)/ sales (percent)	70.2	69.3	68.6	68.0	67.6	67.2	65.9	65.0
ROIC (excluding goodwill, percent)	7.6	7.6	7.4	7.3	7.2	7.0	6.7	6.6
Nominal projections								
Sales	24,778	28,258	31,721	35,164	38,558	41,474	59,717	85,984
Adjusted EBITA/sales (percent)	6.9	7.0	7.0	7.0	6.9	6.9	6.8	6.8
NOPLAT/sales (percent)	5.0	5.2	5.2	5.2	5.2	5.1	5.1	5.1
Invested capital (excluding goodwill)/ sales (percent)	60.0	58.3	57.2	56.3	55.5	54.7	52.2	51.0
ROIC (excluding goodwill, percent)	8.4	8.9	9.0	9.2	9.3	9.3	9.8	10.1

[a] In inflation-adjusted Reais million per capacity unit.
[b] In inflation-adjusted Reais million.

margins, but the company's improvements in selling, general and administrative expenses compensate for this.

Capacity requirements are derived from sales forecasts in real terms, assuming sales productivity of 6.2 million Reais per unit of capacity. Capital expenditures for maintenance are estimated in real terms as a percentage of projected total capacity and expenditures for capacity expansion are projected at around 2.3 million Reais per unit. The future development of net PPE in real terms is derived from the capital expenditure projections.

The resulting ROIC (excluding goodwill) in real terms for ConsuCo decreases from its current value of around 7.6 percent to around 6.6 percent in the continuing value period. In contrast, the ROIC in nominal terms increases from 8.4 to around 10.1 percent because of the inflation impact on capital turnover.

3   INCORPORATING EMERGING-MARKET RISKS IN THE VALUATION

The major distinction between valuing companies in developed markets and emerging markets is the increased level of risk. Not only must you account for risks related to the company's strategy, market position, and industry dynamics, as you would in a developed market, you must also deal with the risks caused by greater volatility in the capital markets and in the macroeconomic and political environments.

There is no consensus on how to reflect this higher level of risk in a DCF valuation. The most common approach is to add a country risk premium to the discount rate. The alternative is to model risks explicitly in the cash flow projections in what we call the *scenario DCF approach*. Both methodologies, if correctly and consistently applied, lead to the same result. We show this in the following example of an investment in two identical production plants, one in Europe and the other in an emerging economy (see Exhibit 7). However, the scenario DCF approach is analytically more robust and better shows the impact of emerging-market risks on value.

Scenario DCF Approach

The scenario DCF approach simulates alternative trajectories for future cash flows. At a minimum, model two scenarios: One should assume that cash flow develops according to conditions reflecting business as usual (i.e., without major economic distress). The second should reflect cash flows assuming that any emerging-market risks materialize.

In the example, the cash flows for the European plant grow steadily at 3 percent per year into perpetuity. For the plant in the emerging market, the cash flow growth is the same under a business-as-usual scenario, but there is a 25 percent probability of economic distress resulting in a cash flow that is 55 percent lower into perpetuity. The emerging-market risk is taken into account, not in the cost of capital, but in the lower expected value of future cash flows from weighting both scenarios at the assumed probabilities. The resulting value of the emerging-market plant (€1,917) is clearly below the value of its European sister plant (€2,222), using a WACC of 7.5 percent.

We assumed for simplicity that if adverse economic conditions develop in the emerging market, they will do so in the first year of the plant's operation. In reality, of course, the investment will face a probability of domestic economic distress in each year of its lifetime. Modeling risk over time would require more complex calculations yet would not change the basic results. We also assumed that in a local crisis, the emerging-market business would face significantly lower cash flows but not wind up entirely worthless.

Country Risk Premium DCF Approach

The second approach is to add a country risk premium to the cost of capital for comparable investments in developed markets. We then apply the resulting discount rate to the cash flow projections following a business-as-usual scenario. The key drawback is that there is no objective way to establish the country risk premium. For our two-plant example, we can derive in hindsight what the premium should be to obtain the same result as under the scenario DCF approach. For us to arrive at a value of €1,917 for the emerging-market plant, the discount rate for the business-as-usual projections would have to be 8.2 percent, which translates to a country risk premium of 0.7 percent.

On occasion, practitioners make the mistake of adding the country risk premium to the cost of capital to discount the *expected* value of future cash flows rather

EXHIBIT 7   Scenario DCF versus Country Risk Premium DCF

Net present value for identical facilities in ...

... a European market

Scenario approach

Cash flows in perpetuity[a]

Probability		Year 1	2	3	4...
100%	"As usual"	100	103	106	109
0%	"Distressed"				
	Expected cash flows	100	103	106	109

Cost of capital   7.5%
Net present value   2,222

Country risk premium approach

Cash flows in perpetuity[a]

	Year 1	2	3	4...
"As usual"	100	103	106	109

Cost of capital   7.5%
Net present value   2,222

... an emerging market

Scenario approach

Cash flows in perpetuity[b]

Probability		Year 1	2	3	4...
75%	"As usual"	100	103	106	109
25%	"Distressed"	45	46	48	49
	Expected cash flows	86	89	92	94

Cost of capital   7.5%
Net present value   1,917   86% of European NPV

Country risk premium approach

Cash flows in perpetuity[b]

	Year 1	2	3	4...
"As usual"	100	103	106	109

Cost of capital   7.5%
Country risk premium   0.7%
Adjusted cost of capital 8.2%
Net present value   1,917   86% of European NPV

---

[a] Assuming perpetuity cash flow growth of 3%.
[b] Assuming perpetuity cash flow growth of 3% and recovery under distress of 45% of cash flows "as usual."

than to the "promised" cash flows of a business-as-usual scenario. The resulting value is too low because the probability of a crisis is accounted for twice.[8]

Scenario DCF as Prime Valuation Approach

Some surveys show that managers generally adjust for emerging-market risks by adding a risk premium to the discount rate.[9] Nonetheless, we recommend the scenario DCF approach. It provides a more solid analytical foundation and a more robust understanding of the value than incorporating country risks in the discount rate.

One reason is that most country risks, including expropriation, devaluation, and war, are largely diversifiable (though not entirely, as the economic crisis in 1998 demonstrated). Consider the international consumer goods player illustrated in Exhibit 8. Its returns on capital were highly volatile for individual emerging markets, but taken together, these markets were hardly more volatile than developed markets; the corporate portfolio diversified away most of the risks. Finance theory clearly indicates that the cost of capital should not reflect risk that can be diversified. This does not mean that diversifiable risk is irrelevant for a valuation: the possibility of adverse future events will affect the level of expected cash flows, as in the example in Exhibit 7. But once this has been incorporated in the forecast for cash flows, there is no need for an additional markup of the cost of capital if the risk is diversifiable.

EXHIBIT 8	Returns on Diverse Emerging Market Portfolio

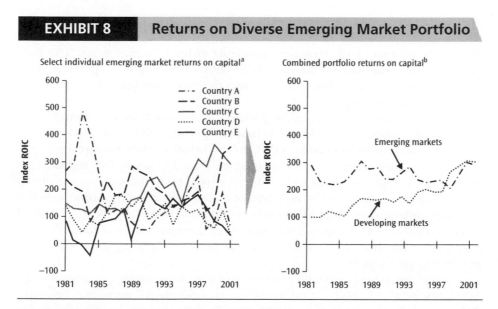

[a] In stable currency and adjusted for local accounting differences.
[b] Combined portfolio included additional countries not reflected here.

Source: Company information.

---

[8] This is analogous to the error made by discounting the expected coupon and principal payments on a corporate bond at the promised yield (i.e., the yield to maturity) instead of the expected yield (i.e., the cost of debt).

[9] T. Keck, E. Levengood, and A. Longfield, "Using Discounted Cash Flow Analysis in an International Setting: A Survey of Issues in Modeling the Cost of Capital," *Journal of Applied Corporate Finance*, 11(3) (1998).

Another argument against a country risk premium is that many country risks apply unequally to companies in a given country. For example, banks are more likely to be affected than retailers. Some companies (raw-materials exporters) might benefit from a currency devaluation, while others (raw-materials importers) will be damaged. For the consumer goods company in Exhibit 8, economic crises had only a short-term impact on sales and profit as measured in stable currency. In most cases, after a year or two, sales and profits roughly regained their original growth trajectories. Applying the same risk premium to all companies in an emerging market could overstate the risk for some businesses and understate it for others.

Furthermore, there is no systematic method to calculate a country risk premium. In our example, we could reengineer this premium because the true value of the plant was already known from the scenario approach. In practice, the country risk premium is sometimes set at the spread of the local government debt rate[10] denominated in U.S. dollars and a U.S. government bond of similar maturity. However, that is reasonable only if the returns on local government debt are highly correlated with returns on corporate investments.

Finally, when managers have to discuss emerging-market risks and their effect on cash flow in scenarios, they gain more insights than they would get from a "black box" addition to the discount rate. By identifying specific factors with a large impact on value, managers can plan to mitigate these risks. Furthermore, managers easily underestimate the impact of even a small country risk premium in the discount rate: In the example, setting a country risk premium to 3 percent would be equivalent to assuming a 70 percent probability of economic distress.

Constructing Cash Flow Scenarios and Probabilities

To use the scenario DCF approach, construct at least two scenarios. The base case, or business-as-usual scenario, describes how the business will perform if no major crises occur. The downside scenario describes the financial results if a major crisis does occur.

For both scenarios, start by projecting the macroeconomic environment because this influences industry and company performance. The major macroeconomic variables to forecast are GDP growth, inflation rates, foreign-exchange rates, and interest rates. These items must be linked in a way that reflects economic realities and should be included in the basic set of monetary assumptions underlying your valuation. For instance, when constructing a downside scenario with high inflation, make sure that the same inflation rates underlie the financial projections and cost of capital estimates for the company to be valued. Foreign exchange rates should also reflect this inflation in the long run because of purchasing power parity.

Given the assumptions for macroeconomic performance, construct the industry scenarios basically in the same way as in developed markets. The major difference is in the greater uncertainty involved in modeling outcomes under severe crises for which there may be no precedent.

While estimating probabilities for the cash flow scenarios is ultimately a matter of management judgment, there are indicators of reasonable probabilities.

---

[10] This is also a promised yield rather than an expected yield on government bonds, further underlining the point that the cost of capital based on country risk premium should not be applied to expected cash flows, but to "promised" cash flows (those following a business-as-usual scenario in which no country risk materializes).

Historical data on previous crises can give some indication of frequency and severity of country risk and the time required for recovery. Analyzing the changes in GDP of 20 emerging economies over the past 20 years, we found that these economies had experienced economic distress about once every five years (a real-terms GDP decline of more than 5 percent). This would suggest a 20 percent probability for a downside scenario.

Another source of information for estimating probabilities is prospective data from current government bond prices.[11] Recent academic research suggests that government default probabilities five years into the future in emerging markets such as Argentina, were around 30 percent in nondistress years.[12]

ConsuCo Case Example: Cash Flow Scenarios and Probabilities

Returning to the ConsuCo example, we already constructed a business-as-usual scenario in the previous section. For a downward scenario, we analyzed ConsuCo's performance under more adverse economic conditions in the past. Brazil has experienced several severe economic and monetary downturns, including an inflation rate that surpassed 2,000 percent in 1993. Judging by its key financial indicators, such as EBITDA to sales and real-terms sales growth, the impact on ConsuCo's business performance was significant. ConsuCo's cash operating margin was negative for four years, at around -10 to -5 percent, and then recovered to its normal levels. In the same period, sales in real terms declined by 10 to 15 percent per year but grew sharply after the crisis. For the downside scenario projections, we assumed similar negative cash margins and real-terms sales decline for up to five years, followed by a gradual return to the long-term margins and growth assumed under the business-as-usual scenario. Exhibit 9 compares the nominal and real returns on invested capital under both scenarios: In the downside scenario, the returns plummet and then increase as the recovery starts. After 2010, the nominal returns even surpass those in the base case as the extreme inflation levels push up the capital turnovers. Of course, the nominal returns are artificially high, as a comparison with the real returns shows. The DCF value under the downside scenario will turn out to be only half of the base-case value. We estimated the probability of this downside scenario at 25 to 35 percent.

ESTIMATING COST OF CAPITAL IN EMERGING MARKETS

4

Calculating the cost of capital in any country can be challenging, but for emerging markets, the challenge is an order of magnitude higher. In this section, we provide our fundamental assumptions, background on the important issues, and a practical way to estimate the components of the cost of capital.

---

[11] See, for example, D. Duffie and K. Singleton, "Modeling Term Structures of Defaultable Bonds," *Review of Financial Studies* 12 (1999): 687–720; and R. Merton, "On the Pricing of Corporate Debt: The Risk Structure of Interest Rates," *Journal of Finance,* 29(2) (1974): 449–470.

[12] See J. Merrick, "Crisis Dynamics of Implied Default Recovery Ratios: Evidence from Russia and Argentina," *Journal of Banking and Finance,* 25(10) (2001): 1921–1939.

EXHIBIT 9	ConsuCo: ROIC in Downside Scenario versus Base Case

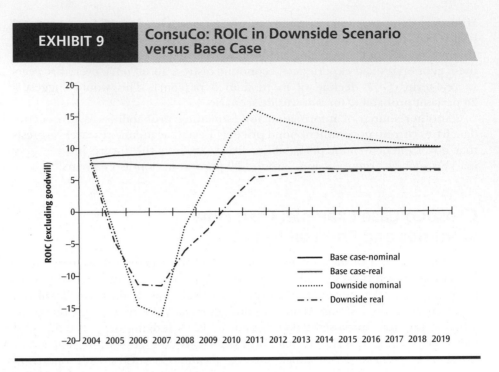

Fundamental Assumptions

Our analysis adopts the perspective of a global investor—either a multinational company or an international investor with a diversified portfolio. Of course, many emerging markets are not well integrated with the global market, and local investors may face barriers to investing outside their home market. As a result, local investors cannot always hold well-diversified portfolios, and their cost of capital may be considerably different from that of a global investor. Unfortunately, there is no established framework for estimating the capital cost for local investors. Furthermore, as long as international investors have access to local investment opportunities, local prices will be based on an international cost of capital. Finally, according to empirical research, emerging markets have become increasingly integrated into global capital markets.[13] We believe that this trend will continue and that most countries will gradually reduce foreign-investment restrictions for local investors in the long run.

Another assumption is that most country risks are diversifiable from the perspective of the global investor. We therefore need no additional risk premiums in the cost of capital for the risks encountered in emerging markets when discounting expected cash flows. Of course, if you choose to discount the cash flow from the business-as-usual scenario only, you should add a country risk premium.

Given these assumptions, the cost of capital in emerging markets should generally be close to a global cost of capital adjusted for local inflation and capital structure. It is also useful to keep some general guidelines in mind:

▶ *Use the CAPM to estimate the cost of equity in emerging markets.* The CAPM may be a less robust model for the less-integrated emerging markets, but there is no better alternative model today. Furthermore, we believe it will become a better predictor of equity returns world-wide as markets continue to become more integrated.

---

[13] See, for example, C. Harvey, "The Drivers of Expected Returns in International Markets," *Emerging Markets Quarterly* (Fall 2000): 1–17.

► *There is no one "right" answer, so be pragmatic.* In emerging markets, there are often significant information and data gaps (e.g., for estimating betas or the risk-free rate in local currency). Be flexible as you assemble the available information piece by piece to build the cost of capital, and triangulate your results with country risk premium approaches and multiples.

► *Be sure monetary assumptions are consistent.* Ground your model in a common set of monetary assumptions to ensure that the cash flow forecasts and discount rate are consistent. If you are using local nominal cash flows, the cost of capital must reflect the local inflation rate that is embedded in the cash flows. For real-terms cash flows, subtract inflation from the nominal cost of capital.

► *Allow for changes in cost of capital.* The cost of capital in an emerging-market valuation may change, based on evolving inflation expectations, changes in a company's capital structure and cost of debt, or foreseeable reforms in the tax system. For example, for valuations in Argentina during the economic and monetary crisis of 2002, the short-term inflation rate of 30 percent could not be considered a reasonable basis for a long-term cost of capital estimate because such a crisis could not be expected to last forever.[14] In such cases, estimate the cost of capital on a year-by-year basis, following the underlying set of basic monetary assumptions.

► *Don't mix approaches.* Use the cost of capital to discount the cash flows in a probability-weighted scenario approach. Do not add any risk premium, because you would be double-counting risk. If you are discounting only future cash flows in a business-as-usual scenario, add a risk premium to the discount rate.

Estimating the Cost of Equity

To estimate the components of the cost of equity, use the standard CAPM model.

Risk-Free Rate   In emerging markets, the risk-free rate is harder to estimate from government bonds than in developed markets. Three main problems arise. First, most of the government debt in emerging markets is not, in fact, risk free: The ratings on much of this debt are often well below investment grade. Second, it is difficult to find long-term government bonds that are actively traded with sufficient liquidity. Finally, the long-term debt that is traded is often in U.S. dollars, a European currency, or the Japanese yen, so it is not appropriate for discounting local nominal cash flows.

Our recommendation is to follow a very straightforward approach. Start with a risk-free rate based on the 10-year U.S. government bond yield, as in developed markets. Add to this the projected difference over time between U.S. and local inflation to develop a nominal risk-free rate in local currency.[15] Sometimes you can derive this inflation differential from the spread between local government bond yields denominated in local currency versus U.S. dollars.[16]

Beta   Sometimes practitioners calculate beta relative to the local market index. This is not only inconsistent from the perspective of a global investor, but also

---

[14] Annual consumer price inflation came down to around 5 percent in Argentina in 2004.

[15] In this way, we do not model the U.S. term structure of interest rates. Technically, this should be included as well, but it will not make a large difference in the valuation.

[16] Technically, this is correct only if the emerging-market bonds are relatively low risk, as for example for Chile and South Korea.

potentially distorted by the fact that the index in an emerging market will rarely be representative of a diversified economy. Instead, estimate industry betas relative to a well-diversified or global market index as recommended in the reading on the mortgage-backed sector of the bond market. Since equity markets in emerging economies are often small, with liquidity concentrated in a few stocks, it may be hard to find a representative sample of publicly traded local companies to estimate an industry beta. In that case, derive an industry beta from international comparables that operate in the same or a similar sector. The implicit assumption is that the fundamental drivers of systematic risk will be similar in emerging and developed markets.

For ConsuCo, we used three sources for estimates of beta in an international peer group: Bloomberg betas calculated against the FT World Index, Barra betas, and betas adjusted for the high-tech boom. Note that the unlevered beta estimates are similar for industry peers, with some exceptions, as shown in Exhibit 10. Overall, our estimate for the unlevered industry beta is 0.55, translating into an equity beta for ConsuCo of 0.8 (given a debt-to-capital target weight of 0.3, as discussed later).

Market Risk Premium   Excess returns of local equity markets over local bond returns are not a good proxy for the market risk premium. This holds even more so for emerging markets given the lack of diversification in the local equity market. Furthermore, the quality and length of available data on equity and bond market returns are usually unsuitable for making long-term estimates. To use a market risk premium that is consistent with the perspective of a global investor, use a global estimate of 4.5 to 5.5 percent.

In Exhibit 11, we summarize the nominal cost of equity calculation for ConsuCo. In the base case, we have assumed a decreasing rate of inflation for the Brazilian economy from 7.1 percent in 2004 to 4.4 percent in 2008 and beyond. This is also reflected in the cost of capital estimates going forward. For the downside scenario, inflation projections follow a different trajectory, and the cost of capital for this scenario is adjusted accordingly.

EXHIBIT 10	ConsuCo: Estimating Beta

Peers	Unlevered betas			
	Bloomberg[a]	Barra	Adjusted[b]	Average
ConsuCo	0.733	1.343	0.748	1.038
PeerCo 1	0.664	0.712	0.782	0.688
PeerCo 2	0.589	0.407	0.846	0.498
PeerCo 3	0.795	0.693	1.232	0.744
PeerCo 4	0.492	0.236	0.346	0.364
PeerCo 5	0.475	0.749	0.439	0.612
PeerCo 6	0.480	0.231	0.381	0.356
PeerCo 7	0.294	0.198	0.271	0.246
PeerCo 8	0.278	0.361	0.386	0.319
PeerCo 9	0.418	0.384	0.641	0.401
PeerCo 10	0.820	0.635	0.803	0.728
PeerCo 11	0.649	0.688	0.625	0.669
Average	**0.557**	**0.553**	**0.625**	**0.555**
Median	**0.541**	**0.521**	**0.633**	**0.531**

[a] Against FT World Index on a weekly basis over past two years.
[b] Adjusted for the high-tech boom.

Source: Bloomberg, Barra, Datastream, McKinsey analysis.

EXHIBIT 11	ConsuCo: Estimating the Nominal Cost of Equity

	2004	2005	2006	2007	2008	2009	2014	2019
United States								
Inflation (percent)	2.0	2.0	2.0	2.0	2.0	2.0	2.0	2.0
Risk-free interest rate (percent)	4.6	4.6	4.6	4.6	4.6	4.6	4.6	4.6
Brazil								
Inflation (IPCA, percent)	7.1	5.6	4.9	4.6	4.4	4.4	4.4	4.4
Risk-free interest rate (percent)[a]	9.8	8.2	7.5	7.2	7.0	7.0	7.0	7.0
Relevered beta	0.8	0.8	0.8	0.8	0.8	0.8	0.8	0.8
Market risk premium (percent)	5.0	5.0	5.0	5.0	5.0	5.0	5.0	5.0
Cost of equity (percent)	14.0	12.4	11.7	11.3	11.1	11.1	11.1	11.1

[a] Brazilian risk-free rate estimated as: $(1 + \text{U.S. risk free rate}) \times (1 + \text{Brazilian inflation}) \div (1 + \text{U.S. inflation}) - 1$.

Sources: Banco Central do Brasil, Bloomberg, EIU Viewswire, McKinsey analysis.

Estimating the After-Tax Cost of Debt

In most emerging economies, there are no liquid markets for corporate bonds, so little or no market information is available to estimate the cost of debt. However, from an international investor's perspective, the cost of debt in local currency should simply equal the sum of the dollar (or euro) risk-free rate, the systematic part of the credit spread, and the inflation differential between local currency and dollars (or euros). Most of the country risk can be diversified away in a global bond portfolio. Therefore, the systematic part of the default risk is probably no larger than that of companies in international markets, and the cost of debt should not include a separate country risk premium. This explains why the funding costs of multinationals with extensive emerging-market portfolios, companies including Coca-Cola and Colgate-Palmolive, have a cost of debt no higher than their mainly U.S.-focused competitors.

Returning to the ConsuCo example, we calculated the cost of debt in Brazilian Reais. ConsuCo does not have its own credit rating, but based on its EBITDA coverage ratios versus rated peers, we estimated that ConsuCo would probably have a B to B+ rating. ConsuCo's cost of debt can be estimated as the sum of the risk-free rate in Brazilian Reais plus the systematic credit spread for a U.S. corporate bond rated B+ versus the U.S. government bond yield as shown in Exhibit 12. Of course, the inflation assumptions underlying the estimates for cost of debt should be consistent with those for the base-case and downside scenarios.

Remember that ConsuCo's cost of debt is significantly lower than the interest rate it is currently paying because the latter represents the promised yield, not the expected yield.

The marginal tax rate in emerging markets can be very different from the effective tax rate, which often includes investment tax credits, export tax credits, taxes, equity or dividend credits, and operating loss credits. Many of these do not provide a tax shield on interest expense. Only taxes that apply to interest expense should be used in the WACC estimate. Other taxes or credits should be modeled directly in the cash flows. For ConsuCo, we used the Brazilian corporate income tax rate of 25 percent plus social contribution tax of 9 percent.

EXHIBIT 12	ConsuCo: Estimating the Nominal Cost of Debt

percent

	2004	2005	2006	2007	2008	2009	2014	2019
Risk-free interest rate	9.8	8.2	7.5	7.2	7.0	7.0	7.0	7.0
BBB credit spread	1.2	1.2	1.2	1.2	1.2	1.2	1.2	1.2
Systematic credit spread for B+	0.5	0.5	0.5	0.5	0.5	0.5	0.5	0.5
Cost of debt	11.5	9.9	9.2	8.9	8.8	8.8	8.8	8.8
Tax rate	34	34	34	34	34	34	34	34
After-tax cost of debt	7.6	6.6	6.1	5.9	5.8	5.8	5.8	5.8

Source: Standard & Poor's, McKinsey analysis.

Estimating WACC

Given the estimates for cost of equity and after-tax cost of debt, we need debt and equity weights to derive an estimate of the weighted average cost of capital. In emerging markets, many companies have unusual capital structures compared with their international peers. One reason is, of course, the country risk. The possibility of macroeconomic distress makes companies more conservative in setting their leverage. Another reason could be anomalies in the local debt or equity markets. In the long run, when the anomalies are corrected, the companies should expect to converge to a capital structure similar to that of their global competitors. You could forecast explicitly how the company evolves to a capital structure that is more similar to global standards. In that case, you should consider using the APV approach.

For the ConsuCo case, we kept the capital structure going forward at its long-term historical levels, with leverage somewhat below the peer group average at a ratio of debt to enterprise value of 0.3. Exhibit 13 summarizes the WACC estimates for both the base case and downside scenario in nominal terms. Note how the extreme inflation assumption underlying the downside scenario leads to a radically higher cost of capital in the crisis years until 2009.

Estimating the Country Risk Premium

If you are discounting business-as-usual cash flows instead of expected cash flows, you should add a country risk premium to the WACC. There is no agreed-upon approach to estimating this premium, but we have some advice.

Do Not Simply Use the Sovereign Risk Premium   The long-term sovereign risk premium equals the difference between a long-term (e.g., 10-year) U.S. government bond yield and a dollar-denominated local bond's stripped yield[17] with the same maturity. This difference will reasonably approximate the country risk premium only if the cash flows of the corporation being valued move closely in line with the payments on government bonds. This is not necessarily the case. In the consumer goods or raw-materials sector, for example, cash flows have low correlation with local government bond payments and lower volatility.

---

[17] Some emerging markets' country debt is partially guaranteed by international institutions or backed by U.S. Treasury bonds. For these bonds, you need to estimate the yield on the nonguaranteed part of the bond, the "stripped" yield. Stripped yields are available from bond data suppliers.

EXHIBIT 13	ConsuCo: Estimating Nominal WACC for ConsuCo							
	2004	2005	2006	2007	2008	2009	2014	2019
Base case								
After-tax cost of debt (percent)	7.6	6.6	6.1	5.9	5.8	5.8	5.8	5.8
Cost of equity (percent)	14.0	12.4	11.7	11.3	11.1	11.1	11.1	11.1
Debt/enterprise value	0.3	0.3	0.3	0.3	0.3	0.3	0.3	0.3
WACC (percent)	12.0	10.5	9.9	9.5	9.4	9.4	9.4	9.4
Downside								
After-tax cost of debt (percent)	7.6	37.1	105.9	37.1	19.9	6.2	5.8	5.8
Cost of equity (percent)	14.0	59.6	166.0	59.6	33.0	11.7	11.1	11.1
Debt/enterprise value	0.3	0.3	0.3	0.3	0.3	0.3	0.3	0.3
WACC (percent)	12.0	52.3	146.5	52.3	28.8	9.9	9.4	9.4

Understand Estimates from Different Sources   Estimates for country risk premiums from different sources usually fall in a very wide range because analysts use different methods.[18] But they frequently compensate for high estimates of country risk premiums by making aggressive estimates for growth and return forecasts.

An example is the valuation of a large Brazilian chemicals company that we undertook in 2002. Using a local WACC of 10 percent, we reached an enterprise value of 4.0 to 4.5 times EBITDA. A second advisor was also asked to value the company and came to a very similar valuation result—an EBITDA multiple of around 4.5—in spite of using a very high country risk premium of 11 percent on top of the WACC. The result was similar because the second advisor made performance assumptions that were extremely aggressive: real sales growth of almost 10 percent per year and a ROIC increasing to 46 percent in the long term. Such long-term performance assumptions are unrealistic for a commodity-based, competitive industry such as chemicals.

Be Careful to Avoid Setting the Country Risk Premium Too High   Make sure you understand the economic implications of a high country risk premium. We believe that a country risk premium for Brazil is far below the premiums of 5 percent and higher that analysts typically use.

One reason is that current valuations in the stock market do not support the discount rates implied by higher risk premiums. We estimated the trading multiples of enterprise value to the 2004 forecasted EBITA for the 30 largest Brazilian companies in terms of market capitalization. The median value for the multiple was 7.4 in October 2004. We estimated the implied WACC by means of a DCF valuation. We set the future long-term return on invested capital at 11 percent, approximately equal to the median historical ROIC for these companies over the past five or six years (a period after Brazil brought inflation under control, so it is indicative of a business-as-usual scenario). Assuming future long-term inflation at 4.4 percent and real growth at 3.0 percent for the Brazilian economy as a whole, the WACC for the Brazilian market implied by the EBITA multiple of 7.4 is around 10.3 percent. The WACC estimated with the CAPM method previously described is around 9.8 percent.[19] This would imply a country risk

---

[18] For an overview, see, for example, L. Pereiro, *Valuation of Companies in Emerging Markets: A Practical Approach* (New York: Wiley, 2002), 118.

[19] Based on a real risk-free rate of 2 percent, long-term inflation of 4.4 percent, a market risk premium of 5.0 percent, cost of debt of 7.6 percent, and a debt-to-capital ratio of 0.25.

premium for Brazil of around 0.5 percent. Of course, this is not a precise estimate; as the Brazilian market goes up and down, the implied WACC and country risk premium would change as well. But it does suggest a country risk premium that is far below the 5 percent that many analysts currently use.

The other reason for such a low country risk premium is that historical returns in the Brazilian stock market do not support a high premium. The average real-terms return on the Brazilian stock market over the past 10 years is 3.8 percent per year. Let's take this period as a proxy for a business-as-usual scenario: real GPD grew by around 2 percent per year on average, and inflation was moderate at around 9 percent annually. At a country risk premium of 5 percent, the expected return on a stock with a beta equal to one under a business-as-usual scenario should be around 12 percent in real terms,[20] which is far above these historical returns.

5   CALCULATING AND INTERPRETING RESULTS

Given the estimates for cash flow and the cost of capital, we can discount the free cash flows for ConsuCo under the base-case and downside scenarios. The resulting present values of operations are shown in Exhibit 14. Under each scenario, the valuation results are exactly the same for the nominal and real projections. The next step is to weight the valuation results by the scenario probabilities and derive the present value of operations. Finally, add the market value of the nonoperating assets and subtract the financial claims to get at the estimated equity value. The estimated value obtained for ConsuCo is 188 to 206 Reais per share, given a probability of economic distress of 25 to 35 percent.

ConsuCo's share price, like the Brazilian stock market in general, has been extremely volatile over recent years, as shown in Exhibit 15 on page 186. Thus, you need to be careful in comparing the valuation outcome of 188 to 206 Reais per share with the current (December 2004) share price of 230 Reais. Just four months earlier, the price was 150 Reais. At the beginning of that year it traded for 270 Reais.

Of course, in emerging markets share prices are not always reliable references for intrinsic value, for several reasons. First, free float is often limited, with large equity stakes in the hands of a small group of owners, leaving public shareholders with little or no influence. As a result, the share price in the market could well be below intrinsic value, as estimated from a DCF analysis. Also, liquidity in emerging-markets stocks is often much lower than in developed markets. Share prices may not fully reflect intrinsic value because not all information is incorporated in the market value. Finally, share prices in emerging markets are often much more volatile than in developed markets. The share price on any particular day could therefore be off from intrinsic value.

ConsuCo has a primary listing on the Brazilian stock exchange. Turnover in the stock, as measured by the number of days to trade the free float, is around 130 days, not too far above typical levels of around 100 days in the United States and Europe. Still, because of the share price volatility, triangulation of the DCF results with multiples and a country risk premium approach is important.

---

[20] Assuming a real risk-free rate of 2 percent and a market risk premium of 5 percent.

EXHIBIT 14   ConsuCo: Scenario DCF Valuation

Reais million, percent

	2004	2005	2006	2007	2008	2009	2014	2019
Base case								
Nominal projections								
Free cash flow	331	(161)	(14)	166	379	833	1,065	1,491
WACC (percent)	12.0	10.5	9.9	9.5	9.4	9.4	9.4	9.4
Real projections								
Free cash flow	309	(143)	(12)	134	293	615	633	714
WACC (percent)	4.5	4.6	4.7	4.7	4.7	4.7	4.7	4.7
Downside								
Nominal projections								
Free cash flow	135	(2,817)	(11,192)	(11,205)	(10,491)	(4,039)	(3,851)	8,004
WACC (percent)	12.0	52.3	146.5	52.3	28.8	9.9	9.4	9.4
Real projections								
Free cash flow	126	(1,753)	(2,786)	(1,859)	(1,392)	(511)	(392)	656
WACC (percent)	4.5	1.5	(1.4)	1.5	3.0	4.7	4.7	4.7

1 – p^a = 75%
(65%)

DCF value	**24,459**
Nonoperating assets	3,010
Debt and debt equivalents	(11,097)
Equity value	**16,372**
Value per share (Reais)	**253**

p^a = 25%
(35%)

DCF value	**12,427**
Nonoperating assets	3,010
Debt and debt equivalents	(11,097)
Equity value	**4,340**
Value per share (Reais)	**67**

Value per share (Reais)
206
(188)

[a] p = probability of economic distress.

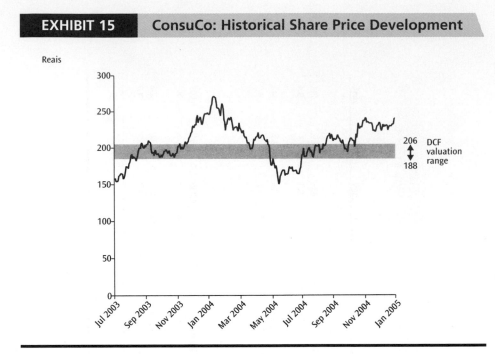

EXHIBIT 15   ConsuCo: Historical Share Price Development

Triangulating with Multiples and Country Risk Premium Approach

For triangulation with multiples, do a best-practice multiples analysis to check valuation results. For the ConsuCo example, we compared the implied multiples of enterprise value over EBITDA with those of peer companies across the world. All multiples are forward-looking multiples over EBITDA as expected for 2005, based on analyst consensus forecasts. As Exhibit 16 illustrates, the implied multiple from our ConsuCo valuation is quite similar to most of its peers, at around seven times EBITDA. Apparently, the fact that ConsuCo is domiciled in Brazil does not matter much for the relative pricing of its stock. This is another indication that any country risk premium for ConsuCo should be very small. Using the average multiple for the peer group of 8.3, the value of ConsuCo would end up at 228 Reais, as shown in Exhibit 17. Note that this is probably an aggressive estimate, given that there are some outliers in the peer group with extremely high multiples. Using the median multiple of 7.1 would lead to a valuation estimate of 176 Reais per share.

The last part of the triangulation consists of a valuation of ConsuCo using a country risk premium approach. We estimated the country risk premium for Brazil at around 0.5 percent earlier in this reading. Discounting the business-as-usual scenario at the cost of capital plus this country risk premium leads to a value per share of 167 Reais, below the result obtained in the scenario DCF approach.

Note that a risk premium of 5 percent (as typically used in Brazil) would either result in unrealistically low valuations relative to current share price and peer group multiples, or require an unrealistic, bullish forecast of future performance with returns on capital of at least 15 percent and real growth rates of at least 6 percent for many years. Given long-term returns and growth in its industry and the historical performance of ConsuCo, even taking just the good years into account, such forecasts are unreasonable.

EXHIBIT 16	ConsuCo: Multiples Analysis versus Peers

EV/EBITDA 05

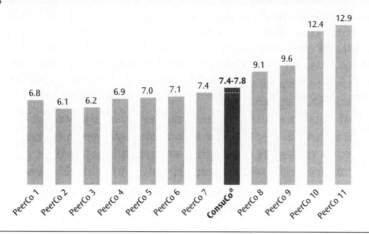

[a] Multiple of EV/EBITDA implied by DCF valuation range.

EXHIBIT 17	ConsuCo: Valuation Summary

Reais, million

	Scenario DCF valuation[a] low	Scenario DCF valuation[a] high	Average multiple valuation	Median multiple valuation	Country risk premium DCF valuation
EBITDA multiple			8.3	7.1	
EBITDA 2005			2,746	2,746	
DCF value	20,248	21,451	22,841	19,496	18,933
Nonoperating assets	3,010	3,010	3,010	3,010	3,010
Debt and debt equivalents	(11,097)	(11,097)	(11,097)	(11,097)	(11,097)
Equity value	12,161	13,364	14,754	11,409	10,846
Number of shares (million)	65	65	65	65	65
Value per share	188	206	228	176	167

[a] Shown are the probability-weighted values.

Given the inherent uncertainty in valuing emerging-market companies, it is best to use an explicit value range instead of a point estimate. For ConsuCo, we summarize the valuation findings in Exhibit 17. Based on the DCF valuation and multiples comparison, we end up with a range of about 175 to 205 Reais per share, depending on the exact scenario and probability assumptions, compared with a 12-month share price range of 150 to 270 Reais per share.

SUMMARY

To value companies in emerging markets, we use concepts similar to the ones applied to developed markets. However, the application of these concepts can be somewhat different. Inflation, which is often high in emerging markets, is factored into the cash flow projections by combining insights from both real and nominal financial analyses. Emerging market risks such as macroeconomic or political crises can be incorporated following the scenario DCF approach by developing alternative scenarios for future cash flows, discounting the cash flows at the cost of capital without country risk premium, and then weighting the DCF values by the scenario probabilities. The cost of capital estimates for emerging markets build on the assumption of a global risk-free rate, market risk premium and beta, following guidelines similar to those used for developed markets. Since the value of companies in emerging markets is often more volatile than in developed markets, we recommend triangulating the scenario DCF results with a country risk premium DCF and a multiples-based valuation.

PRACTICE PROBLEMS FOR READING 38

The following information relates to Questions 1–6[1]

Nigel Hall is an experienced equity analyst at Taurus Investment Management located in New York. Hall specializes in the analysis of emerging markets and is the primary analyst covering India at Taurus. He is currently analyzing Bharat Industries Limited (BIL), a manufacturer of components for high-quality audio and video equipment located in New Delhi, India. Hall observes that inflation in India has been escalating in recent years, and he believes inflation will be at a moderately high level into the foreseeable future.

Hall intends to perform a discounted cash flow (DCF) valuation analysis of BIL and collects the data in Exhibits 1–3. Exhibit 1 provides selected financial indicators for BIL's most recent fiscal year, 2008. Exhibit 2 displays forecasts of various financial data for BIL. Exhibit 3 displays consensus forecasts of key capital market data. Hall has estimated two equity betas for BIL:

▶ an equity beta for BIL relative to the Bombay Stock Exchange (BSE) Sensex 30, the leading local broad market equity index in India. Hall's estimate of the BSE equity beta is 1.1, which is expected to remain at that level for the foreseeable future.

▶ an equity beta for BIL relative to the FT World Index (FTWI), a more broad, global equity index. Hall's estimate of the FTWI equity beta is 0.7, which is expected to remain at that level for the foreseeable future.

Hall uses his forecasts to estimate real and nominal projections of net operating profit less adjusted taxes (NOPLAT) and free cash flow for BIL; components of these estimates are presented in Exhibit 4. Hall incorporates the additional risk of BIL operating in an emerging market into his DCF analysis by adding a country risk premium directly to BIL's weighted average cost of capital (WACC).

---

[1]Developed by Lee Dunham, CFA (Creighton University, Omaha, Nebraska).

EXHIBIT 1	Selected BIL Nominal Financial Indicators for 2008 (Total Sales, Net PPE, and Net Working Capital in Thousands)
Total sales	INR 7,671
Year-end net PPE	INR 1,500
Year-end net working capital	INR 1,100
EBITDA / Sales	5.4%
NOPLAT / Sales	4.7%
Net PPE / Sales	19.6%
Sales / Total assets	12.7%
ROIC	7.9%

EXHIBIT 2   Financial Forecasts for BIL

	2009	2010	2011 Onward
Real sales growth	6%	5%	5%
EBITDA / Sales	10%	9%	8%
Tax rate	35%	35%	35%
Net PPE (end of year) / Sales	20%	20%	20%
Working capital / Sales	15%	15%	15%
Estimated lifetime of net PPE (years)	7	7	7

EXHIBIT 3   Forecasted Inflation Rates, Interest Rates, and Cost of Capital Estimates (%)

	2009	2010	2011 Onward
India annual inflation	10	9	8
U.S. annual inflation	2.50	2.50	2.50
U.S. 10-year Treasury	3.75	3.75	3.75
India market risk premium	15	12	10
Global market risk premium	6	5.50	5.50

EXHIBIT 4	Select Real and Nominal Financial Forecasts for BIL All Data in Indian Rupees (INR'000)							
	Real Forecasts				**Nominal Forecasts**			
	2009	**2010**	**2011**	**2012**	**2009**	**2010**	**2011**	**2012**
NOPLAT:								
Real sales								
Real EBITDA								
Depreciation			244					
EBIT					680			
Taxes					238			
NOPLAT			292	304	442	445		
Free Cash Flow:								
NOPLAT			292	304	442	445		
Depreciation			244					
Capital expenditures								
Investment in WC								
FCF		93	47	47		112	61	66
Invested Capital:								
Net PPE (beginning of year)	1500				1500			
Depreciation								
Capital expenditures								
Net PPE (end of year)					1660			
Net working capital	1220				1342			
Invested capital								

1. Which of the following financial indicators provided in Exhibit 1 is *most likely* to be understated as a result of the level of India's inflation during 2008?

   A. Net PPE / Sales.

   B. NOPLAT / Sales.

   C. Sales / Total assets.

2. The projected sales, in nominal terms, for BIL in 2012 is *closest* to:

   A. INR 10,166,000.

   B. INR 10,739,000.

   C. INR 13,164,000.

3. The forecasted NOPLAT, in real terms, for BIL in 2009 is *closest* to:

   A. INR 383,000.

   B. INR 389,000.

   C. INR 402,000.

4. The forecasted capital expenditures, in nominal terms, for BIL in 2009 is *closest* to:

   A. INR 160,000.

   B. INR 375,000.

   C. INR 503,000.

5. The estimated nominal cost of equity in India in 2010 is *closest* to:

   A. 14.10%.

   B. 16.30%.

   C. 23.50%.

6. Which of the following best explains why Hall's method of incorporating emerging market risk into the analysis is incorrect?

   A. Most country risks do not generally apply uniformly to all firms in a given country.

   B. Many country risks such as expropriation and devaluation are largely not diversifiable.

   C. The investment returns of BIL are not likely highly correlated with the returns of local government debt.

SOLUTIONS FOR READING 38

1. A is correct. Operating assets (PPE) are typically carried at historical values rather than their higher replacement values during periods of high inflation.

2. C is correct.

2012 nominal sales = 2012 real sales × 2012 inflation index

2012 real sales = 7,671 × 1.06 × 1.05 × 1.05 × 1.05 = INR 9,412.95 (thousands)

2012 inflation index = 1.10 × 1.09 × 1.08 × 1.08 = 1.3985

2012 nominal sales = 9,412.95 × 1.3985 = INR 13,164,000

3. A is correct.

2009 real sales = 7,671,000 × 1.06 =	8,131,260
2009 real EBITDA = 10% of 2009 real sales =	813,126
Less: 2009 real depreciation: 1,500,000 / 7 =	214,286
Equals: 2009 real EBIT	598,840
Less: 2009 real taxes = (238,000 / 1.10) =	216,364
Equals: 2009 real NOPLAT =	382,476 (app. INR 383,000)

4. B is correct.

2009 nominal capital expenditures = 2009 real capital exp. × 2009 inflation index

2009 real cap. exp. = 2009 real net PPE (eoy) − 2009 real net PPE (boy) + 2009 real depr.

2009 real cap. exp. = 0.20 × 2009 real sales − 2009 real net PPE (boy) + 2009 real depr.

2009 real cap. exp. = (0.20 × 8,131,126) − 1,500,000 + 214,286 = 340,511

2009 nominal capital expenditures = 340,511 × 1.10 = INR 374,562 (approx. INR 375,000)

5. A is correct. India risk-free rate = U.S. 10-year Treasury rate + (difference between India and U.S. inflation rates) = 3.75% + (9.0% − 2.50%) = 10.25%

Nominal cost of equity using CAPM = 10.25% + 0.7(5.5%) = 14.10%

6. A is correct. Many country risks typically apply unequally to companies in a given country and therefore the application of a single country-level risk premium to all companies is not prudent.

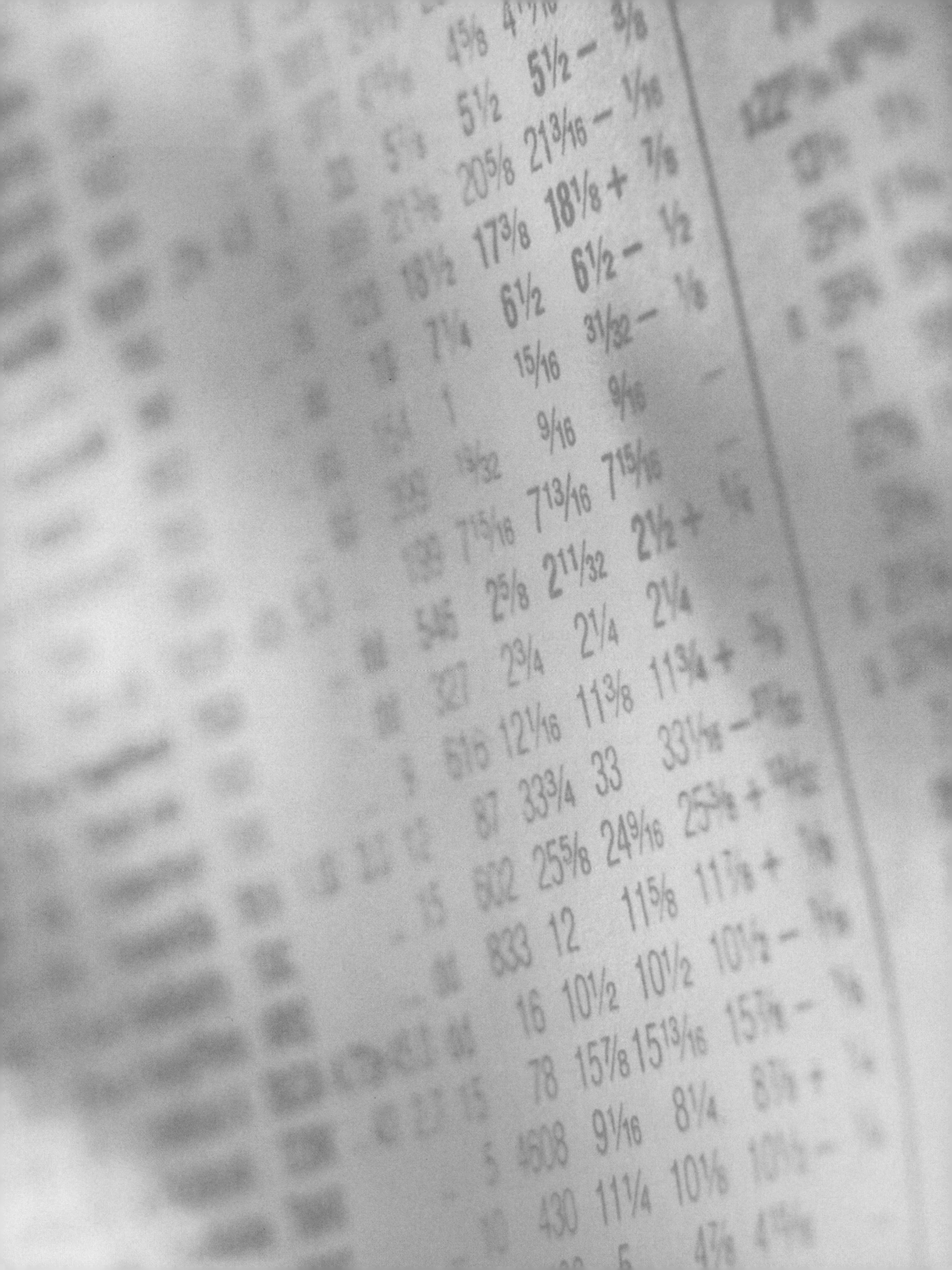

4⅝ 4⅞₁₆ − ⅜₁₆
5½ 5½ −
5½ 21¹³₁₆ − ¼₁₆
20⅝ 21¹³₁₆ − ⅞
17⅜ 18⅛ + ⅞
18½ 6½ − ½
7¼ 6½ 6½ −
15₁₆ 31₃₂ − ⅛
15₁₆ 9₁₆
9₁₆ 9₁₆
⅝₃₂ 7¹³₁₆ 7⅝₁₆
7¹⁵₁₆ 7¹³₁₆ 7⁵⁄₈
25⅝ 2¹¹₃₂ 2½ +
2¾ 2¼ 2¼
6½ 12¹⁄₁₆ 11⅜ 11¾ +
87 33¾ 33 33⅛ −
6⅛ 25⅝ 24⁹₁₆ 25⅝ +
833 12 11⅝ 11⅞ +
16 10½ 10½ 10½ −
78 15⅞ 15¹³₁₆ 15⅞ −
508 9¹⁄₁₆ 8¼ 8⅞ +
430 11¼ 10⅛ 10⅛

DISCOUNTED DIVIDEND VALUATION

by Jerald Pinto, CFA, Elaine Henry, CFA, Thomas Robinson, CFA, and John Stowe, CFA

LEARNING OUTCOMES

The candidate should be able to:	Mastery
a. compare dividends, free cash flow, and residual income as measures in discounted cash flow models, and identify investment situations for which each measure is suitable;	☐
b. calculate and interpret the value of a common stock using the dividend discount model (DDM) for one-, two-, and multiple-period holding periods;	☐
c. calculate the value of a common stock using the Gordon growth model, and explain the model's underlying assumptions;	☐
d. calculate the implied growth rate of dividends using the Gordon growth model and current stock price;	☐
e. calculate and interpret the present value of growth opportunities (PVGO) and the component of the leading price-to-earnings ratio (P/E) related to PVGO;	☐
f. calculate the justified leading and trailing P/Es using the Gordon growth model;	☐
g. calculate the value of noncallable fixed-rate perpetual preferred stock;	☐
h. describe strengths and limitations of the Gordon growth model, and justify its selection to value a company's common shares;	☐
i. explain the assumptions and justify the selection of the two-stage DDM, the H-model, the three-stage DDM, or spreadsheet modeling to value a company's common shares;	☐
j. explain the growth phase, transitional phase, and maturity phase of a business;	☐
k. describe terminal value, and explain alternative approaches to determining the terminal value in a DDM;	☐

l.	calculate and interpret the value of common shares using the two-stage DDM, the H-model, and the three-stage DDM;	☐
m.	estimate a required return based on any DDM, including the Gordon growth model and the H-model;	☐
n.	calculate and interpret the sustainable growth rate of a company, and demonstrate the use of DuPont analysis to estimate a company's sustainable growth rate;	☐
o.	demonstrate the use of spreadsheet modeling to forecast dividends and value common shares;	☐
p.	evaluate whether a stock is overvalued, fairly valued, or undervalued by the market based on a DDM estimate of value.	☐

1 INTRODUCTION

Common stock represents an ownership interest in a business. A business in its operations generates a stream of cash flows, and as owners of the business, common stockholders have an equity ownership claim on those future cash flows. Beginning with John Burr Williams (1938), analysts have developed this insight into a group of valuation models known as discounted cash flow (DCF) valuation models. DCF models—which view the intrinsic value of common stock as the present value of its expected future cash flows—are a fundamental tool in both investment management and investment research. This reading is the first of several that describe DCF models and address how to apply those models in practice.

Although the principles behind discounted cash flow valuation are simple, applying the theory to equity valuation can be challenging. Four broad steps in applying DCF analysis to equity valuation are:

► choosing the class of DCF model—equivalently, selecting a specific definition of cash flow;

► forecasting the cash flows;

► choosing a discount rate methodology; and

► estimating the discount rate.

In this reading, we take the perspective that dividends—distributions to shareholders authorized by a company's board of directors—are an appropriate definition of cash flows. The class of models based on this idea is called dividend discount models, or DDMs. The basic objective of any DDM is to value a stock. The variety of implementations corresponds to different ways to model a company's future stream of dividend payments. The steps of choosing a discount rate methodology and estimating the discount rate involve the same considerations for all DCF models, so they have been presented separately in a reading on return concepts.

The reading is organized as follows: Section 2 provides an overview of present value models. A general statement of the dividend discount model follows in Section 3. Forecasting dividends, individually and in detail, into the indefinite future is not generally practicable, so the dividend-forecasting problem is usually simplified. One approach is to assign dividends to a stylized growth pattern. The simplest pattern—dividends growing at a constant rate forever—is the constant growth (or Gordon growth) model, discussed in Section 4. For some companies, it is more appropriate to view earnings and dividends as having multiple stages of growth; multistage dividend discount models are presented in Section 5 along with spreadsheet modeling. Section 6 lays out the determinants of dividend growth rates, and the final section summarizes the reading.

PRESENT VALUE MODELS 2

Present value models as a group constitute a demanding and rigorous approach for valuing assets. In this section, we discuss the economic rationale for valuing an asset as the present value of its expected future cash flows. We also discuss alternative definitions of cash flows and present the major alternative methods for estimating the discount rate.

2.1 Valuation Based on the Present Value of Future Cash Flows

The value of an asset must be related to the benefits or returns we expect to receive from holding it. Those returns are called the asset's future cash flows (we will define *cash flow* more concretely and technically later). We also need to recognize that a given amount of money received in the future is worth less than the same amount of money received today. Money received today gives us the option of immediately spending and consuming it, so money has a time value. Therefore, when valuing an asset, before adding up the estimated future cash flows, we must **discount** each cash flow back to the present: the cash flow's value is reduced with respect to how far away it is in time. The two elements of discounted cash flow valuation—estimating the cash flows and discounting the cash flows to account for the time value of money—provide the economic rationale for discounted cash flow valuation. In the simplest case, in which the timing and amounts of future cash flows are known with certainty, if we invest an amount equal to the present value of future cash flows at the given discount rate, that investment will replicate all of the asset's cash flows (with no money left over).

For some assets, such as government debt, cash flows may be essentially known with certainty—that is, they are default risk free. The appropriate discount rate for such a risk-free cash flow is a risk-free rate of interest. For example, if an asset has a single, certain cash flow of $100 to be received in two years, and the risk-free interest rate is 5 percent a year, the value of the asset is the present value of $100 discounted at the risk-free rate, $100/(1.05)^2 = 90.70.

In contrast to risk-free debt, future cash flows for equity investments are not known with certainty—they are risky. Introducing risk makes applying the present value approach much more challenging. The most common approach to dealing with risky cash flows involves two adjustments relative to the risk-free case. First, discount the *expected* value of the cash flows, viewing the cash flows as random variables.[1] Second, adjust the discount rate to reflect the risk of the cash flows.

The following equation expresses the concept that an asset's value is the present value of its (expected) future cash flows:

$$V_0 = \sum_{t=1}^{n} \frac{CF_t}{(1 + r)^t} \tag{1}$$

where
  V_0 = the value of the asset at time $t = 0$ (today)
  n = number of cash flows in the life of the asset (n is set equal to ∞ for equities)
  CF_t = the cash flow (or the expected cash flow, for risky cash flows) at time t
  r = the discount rate or required rate of return

For simplicity, the discount rate in Equation 1 is represented as the same for all time periods (i.e., a flat term structure of discount rates is assumed). The analyst has the latitude in this model, however, to apply different discount rates to different cash flows.[2]

Equation 1 gives an asset's value from the perspective of today ($t = 0$). Likewise, an asset's value at some point in the future equals the value of all subsequent cash flows discounted back to that point in time. Example 1 illustrates these points.

EXAMPLE 1

Value as the Present Value of Future Cash Flows

An asset is expected to generate cash flows of $100 in one year, $150 in two years, and $200 in three years. The value of this asset today, using a 10 percent discount rate, is

$$V_0 = \frac{100}{(1.10)^1} + \frac{150}{(1.10)^2} + \frac{200}{(1.10)^3}$$

$$= 90.909 + 123.967 + 150.263 = \$365.14$$

The value at $t = 0$ is $365.14. The same logic is used to value an asset at a future date. The value of the asset at $t = 1$ is the present value, discounted back to $t = 1$, of all cash flows after this point. This value, V_1, is

[1] The expected value of a random quantity is the mean, or average, value of its possible outcomes, in which each outcome's weight in the average is its probability of occurrence. See DeFusco, McLeavey, Pinto, and Runkle (2004) for all statistical concepts used in this reading.

[2] Different discount rates could reflect different degrees of cash flow riskiness or different risk-free rates at different time horizons. Differences in cash flow riskiness may be caused by differences in business risk, operating risk (use of fixed assets in production), or financial risk or leverage (use of debt in the capital structure). The simple expression given, however, is adequate for this discussion.

$$V_1 = \frac{150}{(1.10)^1} + \frac{200}{(1.10)^2}$$

$$= 136.364 + 165.289 = \$301.65$$

At any point in time, the asset's value is the value of future cash flows (CF) discounted back to that point. Because V_1 represents the value of CF_2 and CF_3 at $t = 1$, the value of the asset at $t = 0$ is also the present value of CF_1 and V_1:

$$V_0 = \frac{100}{(1.10)^1} + \frac{301.653}{(1.10)^1}$$

$$= 90.909 + 274.23 = \$365.14$$

Finding V_0 as the present value of CF_1, CF_2, and CF_3 is logically equivalent to finding V_0 as the present value of CF_1 and V_1.

In the next section, we present an overview of three alternative definitions of cash flow. The selected cash flow concept defines the type of DCF model we can use: the dividend discount model, the free cash flow model, or the residual income model. We also broadly characterize the types of valuation problems for which analysts often choose a particular model. (Further details are supplied when each model is discussed individually.)

2.2 Streams of Expected Cash Flows

In present value models of stock valuation, the three most widely used definitions of returns are dividends, free cash flow, and residual income. We discuss each definition in turn.

The dividend discount model defines cash flows as dividends. The basic argument for using this definition of cash flow is that an investor who buys and holds a share of stock generally receives cash returns only in the form of dividends.[3] In practice, analysts usually view investment value as driven by earnings. Does the definition of cash flow as dividends ignore earnings not distributed to shareholders as dividends? Reinvested earnings should provide the basis for increased future dividends. Therefore, the DDM accounts for reinvested earnings when it takes all future dividends into account. Because dividends are less volatile than earnings and other return concepts, the relative stability of dividends may make DDM values less sensitive to short-run fluctuations in underlying value than alternative DCF models. Analysts often view DDM values as reflecting long-run intrinsic value.

A stock either pays dividends or does not pay dividends. A company might not pay dividends on its stock because the company is not profitable and has no cash to distribute. Also, a company might not pay dividends for the opposite reason: because it is very profitable. For example, a company may reinvest all earnings—paying no dividends—to take advantage of profitable growth opportunities. As the company matures and faces fewer attractive investment

---

[3] Corporations can also effectively distribute cash to stockholders through stock repurchases (also called buybacks). This fact, however, does not affect the argument.

opportunities, it may initiate dividends. Generally, mature, profitable companies tend to pay dividends and are reluctant to reduce the level of dividends.[4]

Dividend policy practices have international differences and change through time, even in one market. Typically, a lower percentage of companies in a given U.S. stock market index have paid dividends than have companies in a comparable European stock market index. Wanger (2007) noted a much higher propensity for European and Asian small-cap companies to pay dividends compared with U.S. companies. In addition, the following broad trends in dividend policy have been observed:

▶ The fraction of companies paying cash dividends has been in long-term decline in most developed markets (e.g., the United States, Canada, the European Union, the United Kingdom, and Japan).[5] For example, Fama and French (2001) found that although 66.5 percent of U.S. stocks paid dividends in 1978, only 20.8 percent did in 1999, with later research documenting a small rebound since 2001.[6] In the United States, the decline was caused by a reduced propensity to pay dividends (controlling for differences in profitability and growth opportunities) and by growth in the number of smaller, publicly traded companies with low profitability and large growth opportunities.[7]

▶ Since the early 1980s in the United States[8] and the early 1990s in the United Kingdom and continental Europe,[9] the fraction of companies engaging in share repurchases (an alternative way to distribute cash to shareholders) has trended upwards.

Analysts will frequently need to value non-dividend-paying shares. Can the DDM be applied to non-dividend-paying shares? In theory it can, as is illustrated later, but in practice it generally is not.

Predicting the timing of dividend initiation and the magnitude of future dividends without any prior dividend data or specifics about dividend policy to guide the analysis is generally not practical. For a non-dividend-paying company, analysts usually prefer a model that defines returns at the company level (as free cash flow or residual income—these concepts are defined shortly) rather than at the stockholder level (as dividends). Another consideration in the choice of models relates to ownership perspective. An investor purchasing a small ownership share does not have the ability to meaningfully influence the timing or magnitude of the distribution of the company's cash to shareholders. That perspective is the one taken in applying a dividend discount model. The only access to the company's value is through the receipt of dividends, and dividend policy is taken as a given. If dividends do not bear an understandable relation to value creation in the company, applying the DDM to value the stock is prone to error.

Generally, the definition of returns as dividends, and the DDM, is most suitable when:

▶ the company is dividend-paying (i.e., the analyst has a dividend record to analyze);

---

[4] See Lintner (1956) and Grullon, Paye, Underwood, and Weston (2007).

[5] See von Eije and Megginson (2008) and references therein.

[6] Julio and Ikenberry (2005).

[7] Fama and French (2001).

[8] Important in the United States was the adoption of Securities and Exchange Commission Rule 10b-18 in 1982, which relieved companies from concerns of stock manipulation in repurchasing shares so long as companies follow certain guidelines.

[9] See von Eije and Megginson (2008).

▶ the board of directors has established a dividend policy that bears an understandable and consistent relationship to the company's profitability; and

▶ the investor takes a noncontrol perspective.

Often, companies with established dividends are seasoned companies, profitable but operating outside the economy's fastest-growing subsectors. Professional analysts often apply a dividend discount model to value the common stock of such companies.

EXAMPLE 2

Coca-Cola Bottling Company and Hormel Foods: Is the DDM an Appropriate Choice?

As director of equity research at a brokerage, you have final responsibility in the choice of valuation models. An analyst covering consumer/noncyclicals has approached you about the use of a dividend discount model for valuing the equity of two companies: Coca-Cola Bottling Company Consolidated (NASDAQ: COKE) and Hormel Foods (NYSE: HRL). Exhibit 1 gives the most recent 15 years of data. (In the table, EPS is earnings per share, DPS is dividends per share, and payout ratio is DPS divided by EPS.)

EXHIBIT 1 — COKE and HRL: The Earnings and Dividends Record

	COKE			HRL		
Year	EPS ($)	DPS ($)	Payout Ratio (%)	EPS ($)	DPS ($)	Payout Ratio (%)
2006	2.55	1.00	39	2.05	0.56	27
2005	2.53	1.00	40	1.82	0.52	29
2004	2.41	1.00	41	1.65	0.45	27
2003	3.40	1.00	29	1.33	0.42	32
2002	2.56	1.00	39	1.35	0.39	29
2001	1.07	1.00	93	1.30	0.37	28
2000	0.71	1.00	141	1.20	0.35	29
1999	0.37	1.00	270	1.11	0.33	30
1998	1.75	1.00	57	0.93	0.32	34
1997	1.79	1.00	56	0.72	0.39	54
1996	1.73	1.00	58	0.52	0.30	58
1995	1.67	1.00	60	0.79	0.29	37
1994	1.52	1.00	66	0.77	0.25	32
1993	1.60	0.88	55	0.66	0.22	33
1992	(0.23)	0.88	NM*	0.62	0.18	29

*NM = Not meaningful
Source: Standard & Poor's Stock Reports, www.sec.edgar-online.com.

Answer the following questions based on the information in Exhibit 1:

1. State whether a dividend discount model is an appropriate choice for valuing COKE. Explain your answer.

2. State whether a dividend discount model is an appropriate choice for valuing HRL. Explain your answer.

Solution to 1: Based only on the data given in Exhibit 1, a DDM does not appear to be an appropriate choice for valuing COKE. COKE's dividends have been $1.00 per share since 1994. In 1994, COKE's EPS was $1.52 and EPS grew through 1997. After a steep decline in the period of 1999 through 2001, COKE's earnings re-established themselves at a level above $2.40 per share from 2002 on. In short, during the twelve year period of 1994–2006, COKE achieved compound annual growth of 4.4 percent with considerable variability while DPS were flat. Just based on the record presented, it is hard to discern an understandable and consistent relationship of dividends to earnings. Because dividends do not appear to adjust to reflect changes in profitability, applying a DDM to COKE is probably inappropriate. Valuing COKE on another basis, such as a company-level definition of cash flows, appears to be more appropriate.

Solution to 2: The historical earnings of HRL show a long-term upward trend, with the exception of 1996, 1997, and 2003. Although you might want to research those divergent payout ratios, HRL's dividends have generally followed its growth in earnings. Earnings per share and dividends per share grew at comparable compound annual growth rates of 8.9 percent and 8.4 percent during the entire period. During the most recent five year period, EPS and DPS also grew at comparable rates, reflecting a dividend payout ratio varying only between 29 percent and 32 percent. In summary, because HRL is dividend-paying and dividends bear an understandable and consistent relationship to earnings, using a DDM to value HRL is appropriate.

Valuation is a forward-looking exercise. In practice, the analyst would check for public disclosures concerning changes in dividend policy going forward.

A second definition of returns is free cash flow. The term *cash flow* has been given many meanings in different contexts. Earlier the term was used informally, referring to returns to ownership (equity). We now want to give it a more technical meaning, related to accounting usage. Over a given period of time, a company can add to cash (or use up cash) by selling goods and services. This money is cash flow from operations (for that time period). Cash flow from operations is the critical cash flow concept addressing a business's underlying economics. Companies can also generate (or use up) cash in two other ways. First, a company affects cash through buying and selling assets, including investment and disinvestment in plant and equipment. Second, a company can add to or reduce cash through its financing activities. Financing includes debt and equity. For example, issuing bonds increases cash, and buying back stock decreases cash (all else equal).[10]

---

[10] Internationally, accounting definitions may not be fully consistent with the presented concepts in distinguishing between types of sources and uses of cash. Although the implementation details are not the focus here, an example can be given. U.S. generally accepted accounting principles include a financing item, net interest payments, in *cash flow from operating activities*. So, careful analysts working with U.S. accounting data often add back after-tax net interest payments to cash flow from operating activities when calculating cash flow from operations. Under International Accounting Standards, companies may or may not include interest expense as an operating cash flow.

Assets supporting current sales may need replacement because of obsolescence or wear and tear, and the company may need new assets to take advantage of profitable growth opportunities. The concept of free cash flow responds to the reality that, for a going concern, some of the cash flow from operations is not "free" but rather needs to be committed to reinvestment and new investment in assets. **Free cash flow to the firm** (FCFF) is cash flow from operations minus capital expenditures. Capital expenditures—reinvestment in new assets, including working capital—are needed to maintain the company as a going concern, so only that part of cash flow from operations remaining after such reinvestment is "free." (This definition is conceptual; a later reading defines free cash flow concepts in detail.) FCFF is the part of the cash flow generated by the company's operations that can be withdrawn by bondholders and stockholders without economically impairing the company. Conceptually, the value of common equity is the present value of expected future FCFF—the total value of the company— minus the market value of outstanding debt.

Another approach to valuing equity works with free cash flow to equity. **Free cash flow to equity** (FCFE) is cash flow from operations minus capital expenditures, or FCFF, from which we net all payments to debtholders (interest and principal repayments net of new debt issues). Debt has a claim on the cash of the company that must be satisfied before any money can be paid to stockholders, so money paid on debt is not available to common stockholders. Conceptually, common equity can be valued as the present value of expected FCFE. FCFF is a predebt free cash flow concept; FCFE is a postdebt free cash flow concept. The FCFE model is the baseline free cash flow valuation model for equity, but the FCFF model may be easier to apply in several cases, such as when the company's leverage (debt in its capital structure) is expected to change significantly over time.

Valuation using a free cash flow concept is popular in current investment practice. Free cash flow (FCFF or FCFE) can be calculated for any company. The record of free cash flows can also be examined even for a non-dividend-paying company. FCFE can be viewed as measuring what a company can afford to pay out in dividends. Even for dividend-paying companies, a free cash flow model valuation may be preferred when dividends exceed or fall short of FCFE by significant amounts.[11] FCFE also represents cash flow that can be redeployed outside the company without affecting the company's capital investments. A controlling equity interest can effect such redeployment. As a result, free cash flow valuation is appropriate for investors who want to take a control perspective. (Even a small shareholder may want to take such a perspective when potential exists for the company to be acquired, because stock price should reflect the price an acquirer would pay.)

Just as there are cases in which an analyst would find it impractical to apply the DDM, applying the free cash flow approach is a problem in some cases. Some companies have intense capital demands and, as a result, have negative expected free cash flows far into the future. As one example, a retailer may be constantly constructing new outlets and be far from saturating even its domestic market. Even if the retailer is currently very profitable, free cash flow may be negative indefinitely because of the level of capital expenditures. The present value of a series of negative free cash flows is a negative number: The use of a free cash flow model may entail a long forecast horizon to capture the point at which expected

---

[11] In theory, when period-by-period dividends equal FCFE, the DDM and FCFE models should value stock identically, if all other assumptions are consistent. See Miller and Modigliani (1961), a classic reference for the mathematics and theory of present value models of stock value.

free cash flow turns positive. The uncertainty associated with distant forecasts may be considerable. In such cases, the analyst may have more confidence using another approach, such as residual income valuation.

Generally, defining returns as free cash flow and using the FCFE (and FCFF) models are most suitable when:

▶ the company is not dividend-paying;

▶ the company is dividend-paying but dividends significantly exceed or fall short of free cash flow to equity;

▶ the company's free cash flows align with the company's profitability within a forecast horizon with which the analyst is comfortable; and

▶ the investor takes a control perspective.

The third and final definition of returns that we will discuss in this overview is residual income. Conceptually, **residual income** for a given time period is the earnings for that period in excess of the investors' required return on beginning-of-period investment (common stockholders' equity). Suppose shareholders' initial investment is $200 million, and the required rate of return on the stock is 8 percent. The required rate of return is investors' **opportunity cost** for investing in the stock: the highest expected return available from other equally risky investments, which is the return that investors forgo when investing in the stock. The company earns $18 million in the course of a year. How much value has the company added for shareholders? A return of 0.08 × $200 million = $16 million just meets the amount investors could have earned in an equivalent-risk investment (by the definition of opportunity cost). Only the residual or excess amount of $18 million − $16 million = $2 million represents value added, or an economic gain, to shareholders. So, $2 million is the company's residual income for the period. The residual income approach attempts to match profits to the time period in which they are earned (but not necessarily realized as cash). In contrast to accounting net income (which has the same matching objective in principle), however, residual income attempts to measure the value added in excess of opportunity costs.

The residual income model states that a stock's value is book value per share plus the present value of expected future residual earnings. (**Book value per share** is common stockholders' equity divided by the number of common shares outstanding.) In contrast to the dividend and free cash flow models, the residual income model introduces a stock concept, book value per share, into the present value expression. Nevertheless, the residual income model can be viewed as a restatement of the dividend discount model, using a company-level return concept. Dividends are paid out of earnings and are related to earnings and book value through a simple expression.[12] The residual income model is a useful addition to an analyst's toolbox. Because the record of residual income can always be

---

[12] Book value of equity at t = (Book value of equity at $t − 1$) + (Earnings over $t − 1$ to t) − (Dividends paid at t), as long as anything that goes through the balance sheet (affecting book value) first goes through the income statement (reflected in earnings), apart from ownership transactions. The condition that all changes in the book value of equity other than transactions with owners are reflected in income is known as **clean surplus accounting**. U.S. and international accounting standards do not always follow clean surplus accounting; the analyst, therefore, in using this expression, must critically evaluate whether accounting-based results conform to clean surplus accounting and, if they do not, adjust them appropriately.

calculated, a residual income model can be used for both dividend-paying and non-dividend-paying stocks. Analysts may choose a residual income approach for companies with negative expected free cash flows within their comfortable forecast horizon. In such cases, a residual income valuation often brings the recognition of value closer to the present as compared with a free cash flow valuation, producing higher value estimates.

The residual income model has an attractive focus on profitability in relation to opportunity costs.[13] Knowledgeable application of the residual income model requires a detailed knowledge of accrual accounting; consequently, in cases for which the dividend discount model is suitable, analysts may prefer it as the simpler choice. Management sometimes exercises its discretion within allowable accounting practices to distort the accuracy of its financials as a reflection of economic performance. If the quality of accounting disclosure is good, the analyst may be able to calculate residual income by making appropriate adjustments (to reported net income and book value, in particular). In some cases, the degree of distortion and the quality of accounting disclosure can be such that the application of the residual income model is error-prone.

Generally, the definition of returns as residual income, and the residual income model, is most suitable when:

▶ the company is not paying dividends, as an alternative to a free cash flow model, or

▶ the company's expected free cash flows are negative within the analyst's comfortable forecast horizon.

In summary, the three most widely used definitions of returns to investors are dividends, free cash flow, and residual income. Although claims are often made that one cash flow definition is inherently superior to the rest—often following changing fashions in investment practice—a more flexible viewpoint is practical. The analyst may find that one model is more suitable to a particular valuation problem. The analyst may also develop more expertise in applying one type of model. In practice, skill in application—in particular, the quality of forecasts—is frequently decisive for the usefulness of the analyst's work.

In the next section, we present the general form of the dividend discount model as a prelude to discussing the particular implementations of the model that are suitable for different sets of attributes of the company being valued.

THE DIVIDEND DISCOUNT MODEL   3

Investment analysts use a wide range of models and techniques to estimate the value of common stock, including present value models. In Section 2.2, we discussed three common definitions of returns for use in present value analysis: dividends, free cash flow, and residual income. In this section, we develop the most general form of the dividend discount model.

---

[13] Executive compensation schemes are sometimes based on a residual income concept, including branded variations such as Economic Value Added (EVA®) from Stern Stewart & Co.

The DDM is the simplest and oldest present value approach to valuing stock. In a survey of CFA Institute[14] members by Block (1999), 42 percent of respondents viewed the DDM as "very important" or "moderately important" for determining the value of individual stocks. Beginning in 1989, the *Merrill Lynch Institutional Factor Survey* has assessed the popularity of 23 valuation factors and methods among a group of institutional investors. The highest recorded usage level of the DDM was in the first survey in 1989, when more than 50 percent of respondents reported using the DDM. Although DDMs have had five years of popularity increases since 1989 (with a notable rebound to 39 percent usage in 2002), the long-term trend has been one of decline, with usage slightly more than 20 percent in 2006—still a significant presence. Besides its continuing significant position in practice, the DDM has an important place in both academic and practitioner equity research. The DDM is, for all these reasons, a basic tool in equity valuation.

3.1 The Expression for a Single Holding Period

From the perspective of a shareholder who buys and holds a share of stock, the cash flows he or she will obtain are the dividends paid on it and the market price of the share when he or she sells it. The future selling price should in turn reflect expectations about dividends subsequent to the sale. In this section, we will show how this argument leads to the most general form of the dividend discount model. In addition, the general expression developed for a finite holding period corresponds to one practical approach to DDM valuation; in that approach, the analyst forecasts dividends over a finite horizon, as well as the terminal sales price.

If an investor wishes to buy a share of stock and hold it for one year, the value of that share of stock today is the present value of the expected dividend to be received on the stock plus the present value of the expected selling price in one year:

$$V_0 = \frac{D_1}{(1 + r)^1} + \frac{P_1}{(1 + r)^1} = \frac{D_1 + P_1}{(1 + r)^1} \qquad \textbf{(2)}$$

where

   V_0 = the value of a share of stock today, at $t = 0$
   P_1 = the expected price per share at $t = 1$
   D_1 = the expected dividend per share for Year 1, assumed to be paid at the
         end of the year at $t = 1$
   r = the required rate of return on the stock

Equation 2 applies, to a single holding period, the principle that an asset's value is the present value of its future cash flows. In this case, the expected cash flows are the dividend in one year (for simplicity, assumed to be received as one payment at the end of the year)[15] and the price of the stock in one year.

---

[14] Then called and referred to in the Block (1999) paper as the Association for Investment Management and Research. The name was changed to CFA Institute in 2004.

[15] Throughout the discussion of the DDM, we assume that dividends for a period are paid in one sum at the end of the period.

EXAMPLE 3

DDM Value with a Single Holding Period

Suppose that you expect Carrefour SA (NYSE Euronext Paris: CA) to pay a €1.10 dividend next year. You expect the price of CA stock to be €53.55 in one year. The required rate of return for CA stock is 9 percent. What is your estimate of the value of CA stock?

Discounting the expected dividend of €1.10 and the expected sales price of €53.55 at the required return on equity of 9 percent, we obtain

$$V_0 = \frac{D_1 + P_1}{(1 + r)^1} = \frac{1.10 + 53.55}{(1 + 0.09)^1} = \frac{54.65}{1.09} = 50.14$$

3.2 The Expression for Multiple Holding Periods

If an investor plans to hold a stock for two years, the value of the stock is the present value of the expected dividend in Year 1, plus the present value of the expected dividend in Year 2, plus the present value of the expected selling price at the end of Year 2.

$$V_0 = \frac{D_1}{(1 + r)^1} + \frac{D_2}{(1 + r)^2} + \frac{P_2}{(1 + r)^2} = \frac{D_1}{(1 + r)^1} + \frac{D_2 + P_2}{(1 + r)^2} \qquad \textbf{(3)}$$

The expression for the DDM value of a share of stock for any finite holding period is a straightforward extension of the expressions for one-year and two-year holding periods. For an n-period model, the value of a stock is the present value of the expected dividends for the n periods plus the present value of the expected price in n periods (at $t = n$).

$$V_0 = \frac{D_1}{(1 + r)^1} + \cdots + \frac{D_n}{(1 + r)^n} + \frac{P_n}{(1 + r)^n} \qquad \textbf{(4)}$$

If we use summation notation to represent the present value of the first n expected dividends, the general expression for an n-period holding period or investment horizon can be written as

$$V_0 = \sum_{t=1}^{n} \frac{D_t}{(1 + r)^t} + \frac{P_n}{(1 + r)^n} \qquad \textbf{(5)}$$

Equation 5 is significant in DDM application because analysts may make individual forecasts of dividends over some finite horizon (often two to five years) and then estimate the terminal price, P_n, based on one of a number of approaches. (We will discuss valuation using a finite forecasting horizon in Section 5.) Example 4 reviews the mechanics of this calculation.

EXAMPLE 4

Finding the Stock Price for a Five-Year Forecast Horizon

For the next five years, the annual dividends of a stock are expected to be $2.00, $2.10, $2.20, $3.50, and $3.75. In addition, the stock price is expected to be $40.00 in five years. If the required return on equity is 10 percent, what is the value of this stock?

The present values of the expected future cash flows can be written out as

$$V_0 = \frac{2.00}{(1.10)^1} + \frac{2.10}{(1.10)^2} + \frac{2.20}{(1.10)^3} + \frac{3.50}{(1.10)^4}$$

$$+ \frac{3.75}{(1.10)^5} + \frac{40.00}{(1.10)^5}$$

Calculating and summing these present values gives a stock value of $V_0 = 1.818 + 1.736 + 1.653 + 2.391 + 2.328 + 24.837 = \$34.76$.

The five dividends have a total present value of $9.926 and the terminal stock value has a present value of $24.837, for a total stock value of $34.76.

With a finite holding period, whether one, two, five, or some other number of years, the dividend discount model finds the value of stock as the sum of 1) the present values of the expected dividends during the holding period, and 2) the present value of the expected stock price at the end of the holding period. As the holding period is increased by one year, we have an extra expected dividend term. In the limit (i.e., if the holding period extends into the indefinite future), the stock's value is the present value of all expected future dividends.

$$V_0 = \frac{D_1}{(1 + r)^1} + \; \dots \; + \frac{D_n}{(1 + r)^n} + \; \dots \tag{6}$$

This value can be expressed with summation notation as

$$V_0 = \sum_{t=1}^{\infty} \frac{D_t}{(1 + r)^t} \tag{7}$$

Equation 7 is the general form of the dividend discount model, first presented by John Burr Williams (1938). Even from the perspective of an investor with a finite investment horizon, the value of stock depends on all future dividends. For that investor, stock value today depends *directly* on the dividends the investor expects to receive before the stock is sold and *indirectly* on the expected dividends after the stock is sold, because those future dividends determine the expected selling price.

Equation 7, by expressing the value of stock as the present value of expected dividends into the indefinite future, presents a daunting forecasting challenge. In practice, of course, analysts cannot make detailed, individual forecasts of an infinite number of dividends. To use the DDM, the forecasting problem must be simplified. Two broad approaches exist, each of which has several variations:

1. Future dividends can be forecast by assigning the stream of future dividends to one of several stylized growth patterns. The most commonly used patterns are:

▶ constant growth forever (the Gordon growth model);

▶ two distinct stages of growth (the two-stage growth model and the H-model); and

▶ three distinct stages of growth (the three-stage growth model).

The DDM value of the stock is then found by discounting the dividend streams back to the present. We present the Gordon growth model in Section 4, and the two-stage, H-model, and three-stage growth models are presented in Section 5.

2. A finite number of dividends can be forecast individually up to a terminal point, by using pro forma financial statement analysis, for example. Typically, such forecasts extend from 3 to 10 years into the future. Although some analysts apply the same horizon to all companies under analysis, the horizon selected often depends on the perceived predictability (sometimes called the **visibility**) of the company's earnings. We can then forecast either:

▶ the remaining dividends from the terminal point forward by assigning those dividends to a stylized growth pattern, or

▶ the share price at the terminal point of our dividend forecasts (**terminal share price**), by using some method (such as taking a multiple of forecasted book value or earnings per share as of that point, based on one of several methods for estimating such multiples).

The stock's DDM value is then found by discounting the dividends (and forecasted price, if any) back to the present.

Spreadsheets are particularly convenient tools for implementing a DDM with individual dividend forecasts, but are useful in all cases. We address spreadsheet modeling in Section 5.

Whether analysts are using dividends or some other definition of cash flow, they generally use one of the above forecasting approaches when valuing stock. The challenge in practice is to choose an appropriate model for a stock's future dividends and to develop quality inputs to that model.

THE GORDON GROWTH MODEL   4

The Gordon growth model, developed by Gordon and Shapiro (1956) and Gordon (1962), assumes that dividends grow indefinitely at a constant rate. This assumption, applied to the general dividend discount model (Equation 7), leads to a simple and elegant valuation formula that has been influential in investment practice. This section explores the development of the Gordon growth model and illustrates its uses.

4.1 The Gordon Growth Model Equation

The simplest pattern that can be assumed in forecasting future dividends is growth at a constant rate. In mathematical terms, this assumption can be stated as

$$D_t = D_{t-1}(1 + g)$$

where g is the expected constant growth rate in dividends and D_t is the expected dividend payable at time t. Suppose, for example, that the most recent dividend, D_0, was €10. Then, if a 5 percent dividend growth rate is forecast, the expected dividend at $t = 1$ is $D_1 = D_0(1 + g) = €10 \times 1.05 = €10.5$. For any time t, D_t also equals the $t = 0$ dividend, compounded at g for t periods:

$$D_t = D_0(1 + g)^t \qquad \text{(8)}$$

To continue the example, at the end of five years the expected dividend is $D_5 = D_0(1 + g)^5 = €10 \times (1.05)^5 = €10 \times 1.276282 = €12.76$. If $D_0(1 + g)^t$ is substituted into Equation 7 for D_t, it gives the Gordon growth model. If all of the terms are written out, they are

$$V_0 = \frac{D_0(1 + g)}{(1 + r)} + \frac{D_0(1 + g)^2}{(1 + r)^2} + \ldots + \frac{D_0(1 + g)^n}{(1 + r)^n} + \ldots \qquad \text{(9)}$$

Equation 9 is a geometric series; that is, each term in the expression is equal to the previous term times a constant, which in this case is $(1 + g)/(1 + r)$. This equation can be simplified algebraically into a much more compact equation:[16]

$$V_0 = \frac{D_0(1 + g)}{r - g}, \text{ or } V_0 = \frac{D_1}{r - g} \qquad \text{(10)}$$

Both equations are equivalent because $D_1 = D_0(1 + g)$. In Equation 10, it must be specified that the required return on equity must be greater than the expected growth rate: $r > g$. If $r = g$ or $r < g$, Equation 10 as a compact formula for value assuming constant growth is not valid. If $r = g$, dividends grow at the same rate at which they are discounted, so the value of the stock (as the undiscounted sum of all expected future dividends) is infinite. If $r < g$, dividends grow faster than they are discounted, so the value of the stock is infinite. Of course, infinite values do not make economic sense; so constant growth with $r = g$ or $r < g$ does not make sense.

To illustrate the calculation, suppose that an annual dividend of €5 has just been paid ($D_0 = €5$). The expected long-term growth rate is 5 percent and the required return on equity is 8 percent. The Gordon growth model value per share is $D_0(1 + g)/(r - g) = (€5 \times 1.05)/(0.08 - 0.05) = €5.25/0.03 = €175$. When calculating the model value, be careful to use D_1 and not D_0 in the numerator.

The Gordon growth model (Equation 10) is one of the most widely recognized equations in the field of security analysis. Because the model is based on indefinitely extending future dividends, the model's required rate of return and growth rate should reflect long-term expectations. Further, model values are very sensitive to both the required rate of return, r, and the expected dividend growth rate, g. In this model and other valuation models, it is helpful to perform a sensitivity analysis on the inputs, particularly when an analyst is not confident about the proper values.

Earlier we stated that analysts typically apply DDMs to dividend-paying stocks when dividends bear an understandable and consistent relation to the company's profitability. The same qualifications hold for the Gordon growth model.

---

[16] The simplification involves the expression for the sum of an infinite geometric progression with the first term equal to a and the growth factor equal to m with $|m| < 1$ [i.e., the sum of $a + am + am^2 + \ldots$ is $a/(1 - m)$]. Setting $a = D_1/(1 + r)$ and $m = (1 + g)/(1 + r)$, gives the Gordon growth model.

In addition, the Gordon growth model form of the DDM is most appropriate for companies with earnings expected to grow at a rate comparable to or lower than the economy's nominal growth rate. Businesses growing at much higher rates than the economy often grow at lower rates in maturity, and the horizon in using the Gordon growth model is the entire future stream of dividends.

To determine whether the company's growth rate qualifies it as a candidate for the Gordon growth model, an estimate of the economy's nominal growth rate is needed. This growth rate is usually measured by the growth in **gross domestic product** (GDP). (GDP is a money measure of the goods and services produced within a country's borders.) National government agencies as well as the World Bank (www.worldbank.org) publish GDP data, which are also available from several secondary sources. Exhibit 2 shows the recent real GDP growth record for a number of major developed markets.

EXHIBIT 2	Average Annual Real GDP Growth Rates: 1980–2006 (in Percent)		
	Time Period		
Country	**1980–89**	**1990–99**	**2000–06**
Australia	3.4%	3.3%	3.1%
Canada	3.0	2.4	3.0
Denmark	2.2	2.3	2.0
France	2.1	1.8	2.0
Germany	1.9	1.3	1.3
Italy	2.4	1.5	1.3
Japan	3.9	1.7	1.6
Netherlands	2.0	3.0	1.9
Sweden	2.4	1.8	2.9
Switzerland	1.8	1.1	1.9
United Kingdom	2.4	2.1	2.7
United States	3.1	3.1	2.6

Source: OECD, Datastream, Bloomberg.

Based on historical and/or forward-looking information, nominal GDP growth can be estimated as the sum of the estimated real growth rate in GDP plus the expected long-run inflation rate. For example, an estimate of the underlying real growth rate of the Canadian economy is 3 percent as of early 2007. By using the Bank of Canada's inflation target of 2 percent as the expected inflation rate, an estimate of the Canadian economy's nominal annual growth rate is 3 percent + 2 percent = 5 percent. Publicly traded companies constitute varying amounts of the total corporate sector, but always less than 100 percent. As a result, the overall growth rate of the public corporate sector can diverge from the nominal GDP growth rate during a long horizon; furthermore, within the public corporate sector, some subsectors may experience persistent growth rate differentials. Nevertheless, an earnings growth rate far above the nominal GDP growth rate is not sustainable in perpetuity.

When forecasting an earnings growth rate far above the economy's nominal growth rate, analysts should use a multistage DDM in which the final-stage growth rate reflects a growth rate that is more plausible relative to the economy's nominal growth rate, rather than using the Gordon growth model.

EXAMPLE 5

Valuation Using the Gordon Growth Model (1)

Joel Williams follows Sonoco Products Company (NYSE: SON), a manufacturer of paper and plastic packaging for both consumer and industrial use. SON appears to have a dividend policy of recognizing sustainable increases in the level of earnings with increases in dividends, keeping the dividend payout ratio within a range of 40 percent to 60 percent. Williams also notes:

▶ SON's most recent quarterly dividend (ex-dividend date: 15 August 2007) was $0.26, consistent with a current annual dividend of $4 \times \$0.26 = \$1.04$ per year.

▶ A forecasted dividend growth rate of 6.0 percent per year.

▶ With a beta (β_i) of 1.13, given an equity risk premium (expected excess return of equities over the risk-free rate, $E(R_M) - R_F$) of 4.5 percent and a risk-free rate (R_F) of 5 percent, SON's required return on equity is $r = R_F + \beta_i[E(R_M) - R_F] = 5.0 + 1.13(4.5) = 10.1$ percent, using the capital asset pricing model (CAPM).

Williams believes the Gordon growth model may be an appropriate model for valuing SON.

1. Calculate the Gordon growth model value for SON stock.

2. The current market price of SON stock is $30.18. Using your answer to Question 1, judge whether SON stock is fairly valued, undervalued, or overvalued.

Solution to 1: Using Equation 10,

$$V_0 = \frac{D_0(1 + g)}{r - g} = \frac{\$1.04 \times 1.06}{0.101 - 0.06} = \frac{\$1.10}{0.041} = \$26.89$$

Solution to 2: The market price of $30.18 is $3.29 or approximately 12 percent more than the Gordon growth model intrinsic value estimate of $26.89. SON appears to be overvalued, based on the Gordon growth model estimate.

The next example illustrates a Gordon growth model valuation introducing some problems the analyst might face in practice. The example refers to adjusted beta; the most common calculation adjusts raw historical beta toward the overall mean value of one for beta.

EXAMPLE 6

Valuation Using the Gordon Growth Model (2)

As an analyst for a U.S. domestic equity–income mutual fund, Roberta Kim is evaluating Middlesex Water Company (NASDAQ: MSEX), a publicly traded water utility, for possible inclusion in the approved list of investments. Kim is conducting the analysis in early 2007.

Not all countries have traded water utility stocks. In the United States, about 85 percent of the population gets its water from government entities. A group of investor-owned water utilities, however, also supplies water to the public. With a market capitalization of about $250 million as of late 2007, MSEX is among the ten largest publicly traded U.S. water utilities. MSEX's historical base is the Middlesex System, serving residential, industrial, and commercial customers in a well-developed area of central New Jersey. Through various subsidiaries, MSEX also provides water and wastewater collection and treatment services to areas of southern New Jersey and Delaware.

Net income growth during the past five years has been 7 percent, in line with the long-term growth rate of nominal U.S. GDP. During the last five years, MSEX's return on equity averaged 9 percent with relatively little variation, slightly below the 10 percent level targeted by some faster growing peer companies. Because MSEX obtains most of its revenue from the regulated business providing an important staple, water, to a relatively stable population, Kim feels confident in forecasting future earnings and dividend growth. MSEX appears to have a policy of small annual increases in the dividend rate, maintaining a dividend payout ratio of at least 80 percent. Other facts and forecasts include the following:

- ▶ MSEX's per-share dividends for 2006 (D_0) were $0.68.
- ▶ Kim forecasts a long-term earnings growth rate of 6 percent per year, somewhat below the 8 percent consensus 3–5-year earnings growth rate forecast reported by Zacks Investment Research (based on two analysts).
- ▶ MSEX's raw beta and adjusted beta are, respectively, 0.717 and 0.811 based on 60 monthly returns. The R^2 associated with beta, however, is under 10 percent.
- ▶ Kim estimates that MSEX's pretax cost of debt is 6.9 percent based on Standard & Poor's issuer rating for MSEX of A− and the current corporate yield curve.
- ▶ Kim's estimate of MSEX's required return on equity is 9.25 percent.
- ▶ MSEX's current market price is $18.39.

1. Calculate the Gordon growth model estimate of value for MSEX using Kim's required return on equity estimate.
· 2. State whether MSEX appears to be overvalued, fairly valued, or undervalued based on the Gordon growth model estimate of value.

3. Justify the selection of the Gordon growth model for valuing MSEX.

4. Calculate the CAPM estimate of the required return on equity for MSEX under the assumption that beta regresses to the mean. (Assume an equity risk premium of 4.5 percent and a risk-free rate of 5 percent as of the price quotation date.)

5. Calculate the Gordon growth estimate of value using A) the required return on equity from your answer to Question 4, and B) a bond-yield-plus-risk-premium approach with a risk premium of 3 percent.

6. Evaluate the effect of uncertainty in MSEX's required return on equity on the valuation conclusion in Question 2.

Solution to 1: From Equation 10,

$$V_0 = \frac{D_0(1 + g)}{r - g} = \frac{\$0.68(1.06)}{0.0925 - 0.06} = \$22.18$$

Solution to 2: Because the Gordon growth model estimate of $22.18 is $3.79 or about 21 percent higher than the market price of $18.39, MSEX appears to be undervalued.

Solution to 3: The Gordon growth model, which assumes that dividends grow at a stable rate in perpetuity, is a realistic model for MSEX for the following reasons:

▶ MSEX profitability is stable as reflected in its return on equity. This stability reflects predictable demand and regulated prices for its product, water.

▶ Dividends bear an understandable and consistent relationship to earnings, as evidenced by the company's policy of annual increases and predictable dividend payout ratios.

▶ Historical earnings growth, at 7 percent a year, is in line with long-term nominal annual GDP growth for the United States and is plausibly sustainable long term.

▶ Forecasted earnings growth is also in line with a plausible nominal GDP growth and does not include a period of forecasted very high or very low growth.

Solution to 4: The assumption of regression to the mean is characteristic of adjusted historical beta. The required return on equity as given by the CAPM is 5 percent + 0.811(4.5 percent) = 8.6 percent using adjusted beta, which assumes reversion to the mean of 1.0.

Solution to 5:
A. The Gordon growth value of MSEX using a required return on equity of 8.6 percent is

$$V_0 = \frac{D_0(1 + g)}{r - g} = \frac{\$0.68(1.06)}{0.086 - 0.06} = \$27.72$$

B. The bond-yield-plus-risk-premium estimate of the required return on equity is 6.9 percent + 3 percent = 9.9 percent.

$$V_0 = \frac{D_0(1 + g)}{r - g} = \frac{\$0.68(1.06)}{0.099 - 0.06} = \$18.48$$

Solution to 6: Using the CAPM estimate of the required return on equity (Question 5A), MSEX appears to be definitely undervalued. Beta explains less than 10 percent of the variation in MSEX's returns, however, according to the fact given concerning R^2. Using a bond-yield-plus-risk-premium approach, MSEX appears to be approximately fairly valued ($18.48 exceeds the market price of $18.39 by less than 1 percent). No specific evidence, however, supports the particular value of the risk premium selected in the bond-yield-plus-risk-premium approach. In this case, because of the uncertainty in the required return on equity estimate, one has less confidence that MSEX is undervalued. In particular, the analyst may view MSEX as approximately fairly valued.

As mentioned earlier, an analyst needs to be aware that Gordon growth model values can be very sensitive to small changes in the values of the required rate of return and expected dividend growth rate. Example 7 illustrates a format for a sensitivity analysis.

EXAMPLE 7

Valuation Using the Gordon Growth Model (3)

In Example 6, the Gordon growth model value for MSEX was estimated as $22.18 based on a current dividend of $0.68, an expected dividend growth rate of 6 percent, and a required return on equity of 9.25 percent. What if the estimates of r and g can each vary by 25 basis points? How sensitive is the model value to changes in the estimates of r and g? Exhibit 3 provides information on this sensitivity.

EXHIBIT 3	Estimated Price Given Uncertain Inputs		
	$g = 5.75\%$	$g = 6.00\%$	$g = 6.25\%$
$r = 9.00\%$	$22.13	$24.03	$26.27
$r = 9.25\%$	$20.55	**$22.18**	$24.08
$r = 9.50\%$	$19.18	$20.59	$22.23

A point of interest following from the mathematics of the Gordon growth model is that when the spread between r and g is the widest ($r = 9.50$ percent and $g = 5.75$ percent), the Gordon growth model value is the smallest ($19.18), and when the spread is the narrowest ($r = 9.00$

percent and $g = 6.25$ percent), the model value is the largest ($26.27).
As the spread goes to zero, in fact, the model value increases without
bound. The largest value in Exhibit 3, $26.27, is 37 percent larger than
the smallest value, $19.18. The values in Exhibit 3 all exceed MSEX's
current market price of $18.39, tending to support the conclusion that
MSEX is undervalued. In summary, the best estimate of the value of
MSEX given the assumptions is $22.18, bolded in Exhibit 3, but the esti-
mate is quite sensitive to rather small changes in inputs.

Examples 6 and 7 illustrate the application of the Gordon growth model to a
utility, a traditional source for such illustrations because of the stability afforded
by providing an essential service in a regulated environment. Before applying
any valuation model, however, analysts need to know much more about a company than industry membership. For example, another water utility, Aqua America Inc. (NYSE: WTR), is expected to be on a greater than 10 percent per year
growth path for an extended period as a result of an aggressive acquisition program. Furthermore, many utility holding companies in the United States have
major, nonregulated business subsidiaries so the traditional picture of steady and
slow growth often does not hold.

In addition to individual stocks, analysts have often used the Gordon growth
model to value broad equity market indices, especially in developed markets.
Because the value of publicly traded issues typically represents a large fraction of
the overall corporate sector in developed markets, such indices reflect average
economic growth rates. Furthermore, in such economies, a sustainable trend
value of growth may be identifiable.

The Gordon growth model can also be used to value the noncallable form
of a traditional type of preferred stock, **fixed-rate perpetual preferred stock**
(stock with a specified dividend rate that has a claim on earnings senior to the
claim of common stock, and no maturity date). Perpetual preferred stock has
been used particularly by financial institutions such as banks to obtain permanent equity capital while diluting the interests of common equity. Generally,
such issues have been callable by the issuer after a certain period, so valuation
must take account of the issuer's call option. Valuation of the noncallable form,
however, is straightforward.

If the dividend on such preferred stock is D, because payments extend into
the indefinite future a **perpetuity** (a stream of level payments extending to infinity) exists in the constant amount of D. With $g = 0$, which is true because dividends are fixed for such preferred stock, the Gordon growth model becomes

$$V_0 = \frac{D}{r} \tag{11}$$

The discount rate, r, capitalizes the amount D, and for that reason is often called
a **capitalization rate** in this expression and any other expression for the value of
a perpetuity.

EXAMPLE 8

Valuing Noncallable Fixed-Rate Perpetual Preferred Stock

Kansas City Southern Preferred 4% (NYSE: KSU.PR), issued 2 January 1963, has a par value of $25 per share. Thus, a share pays 0.04($25) = $1.00 in annual dividends. The required return on this security is estimated at 9 percent. Estimate the value of this issue.

Solution: According to the model in Equation 11, KSU.PR preferred stock is worth $D/r = 1.00/0.09 = \$11.11$.

A perpetual preferred stock has a level dividend, thus a dividend growth rate of zero. Another case is a declining dividend—a negative growth rate. The Gordon growth model also accommodates this possibility, as illustrated in Example 9.

EXAMPLE 9

Gordon Growth Model with Negative Growth

Afton Mines is a profitable company that is expected to pay a $4.25 dividend next year. Because it is depleting its mining properties, the best estimate is that dividends will decline forever at a rate of 10 percent. The required rate of return on Afton stock is 12 percent. What is the value of Afton shares?

Solution: For Afton, the value of the stock is

$$V_0 = \frac{4.25}{0.12 - (-0.10)}$$
$$= \frac{4.25}{0.22} = \$19.32$$

The negative growth results in a $19.32 valuation for the stock.

4.2 The Links Among Dividend Growth, Earnings Growth, and Value Appreciation in the Gordon Growth Model

The Gordon growth model implies a set of relationships for the growth rates of dividends, earnings, and stock value. With dividends growing at a constant rate g, stock value also grows at g as well. The current stock value is $V_0 = D_1/(r - g)$. Multiplying both sides by $(1 + g)$ gives $V_0(1 + g) = D_1(1 + g)/(r - g)$, which is

$V_1 = D_2/(r - g)$. So, both dividends and value have grown at a rate of g (holding r constant).[17] Given a constant payout ratio—a constant, proportional relationship between earnings and dividends—dividends and earnings grow at g.

To summarize, g in the Gordon growth model is the rate of value or capital appreciation (sometimes also called the capital gains yield). Some textbooks state that g is the rate of price appreciation. If prices are efficient (price equals value), price is indeed expected to grow at a rate of g. If there is mispricing (price is different from value), however, the actual rate of capital appreciation depends on the nature of the mispricing and how fast it is corrected, if at all. This topic is discussed in the reading on return concepts.

Another characteristic of the constant growth model is that the components of total return (dividend yield and capital gains yield) will also stay constant through time, given that price tracks value exactly. The dividend yield, which is D_1/P_0 at $t = 0$, will stay unchanged because both the dividend and the price are expected to grow at the same rate, leaving the dividend yield unchanged through time. For example, consider a stock selling for €50.00 with a **forward dividend yield** (a dividend yield based on the anticipated dividend during the next 12 months) of 2 percent based on an expected dividend of €1. The estimate of g is 5.50 percent per year. The dividend yield of 2 percent, the capital gains yield of 5.50 percent, and the total return of 7.50 percent are expected to be the same at $t = 0$ and at any future point in time.

4.3 Share Repurchases

An issue of increasing importance in many developed markets is share repurchases. Companies can distribute free cash flow to shareholders in the form of share repurchases (also called buybacks) as well as dividends. In the United States currently, more than half of dividend-paying companies also make regular share repurchases.[18] Clearly, analysts using DDMs need to understand share repurchases. Share repurchases and cash dividends have several distinctive features:

▶ Share repurchases involve a reduction in the number of shares outstanding, all else equal. Selling shareholders see their relative ownership position reduced compared to nonselling shareholders.

▶ Whereas many corporations with established cash dividends are reluctant to reduce or omit cash dividends, corporations generally do not view themselves as committed to maintain share repurchases at any specified level.

▶ Cash dividends tend to be more predictable in money terms and more predictable as to timing.[19] Although evidence from the United States suggests that, for companies with active repurchase programs, the amount of repurchases during two-year intervals bears a relationship to earnings,

---

[17] More formally, the fact that the value grows at a rate equal to g is demonstrated as follows:

$$\frac{V_{t+1} - V_t}{V_t} = \frac{D_{t+2}/(r - g) - D_{t+1}/(r - g)}{D_{t+1}/(r - g)} = \frac{D_{t+2} - D_{t+1}}{D_{t+1}} = 1 + g - 1 = g$$

[18] See Skinner (2007), who also finds evidence that this group of companies increasingly has tended to distribute earnings increases via share repurchases rather than cash dividends.

[19] As discussed by Wanger (2007).

companies appear to be opportunistic in timing exactly when to repurchase.[20] Thus, share repurchases are generally harder to forecast than the cash dividends of companies with an identifiable dividend policy.

▶ As a baseline case, share repurchases are neutral in their effect on the wealth of ongoing shareholders if the repurchases are accomplished at market prices.

The analyst could account for share repurchases directly by forecasting the total earnings, total distributions to shareholders (via either cash dividends or share repurchases), and shares outstanding. Experience and familiarity with such models is much less than for DDMs. Focusing on cash dividends, however, DDMs supply accurate valuations consistent with such an approach if the analyst takes account of the effect of expected repurchases on the per-share growth rates of dividends. Correctly applied, the DDM is a valid approach to common stock valuation even when the company being analyzed engages in share repurchases.

4.4 The Implied Dividend Growth Rate

Because the dividend growth rate affects the estimated value of a stock using the Gordon growth model, differences between estimated values of a stock and its actual market value might be explained by different growth rate assumptions. Given price, the expected next-period dividend, and an estimate of the required rate of return, the dividend growth rate reflected in price can be inferred assuming the Gordon growth model. (Actually, it is possible to infer the market-price-implied dividend growth based on other DDMs as well.) An analyst can then judge whether the implied dividend growth rate is reasonable, high, or low, based on what he or she knows about the company. In effect, the calculation of the implied dividend growth rate provides an alternative perspective on the valuation of the stock (fairly valued, overvalued, or undervalued). Example 10 shows how the Gordon growth model can be used to infer the market's implied growth rate for a stock.

EXAMPLE 10

The Growth Rate Implied by the Current Stock Price

Suppose a company has a beta of 1.1. The risk-free rate is 5.6 percent and the equity risk premium is 6 percent. The current dividend of $2.00 is expected to grow at 5 percent indefinitely. The price of the stock is $40.

1. Estimate the value of the company's stock.
2. Determine the constant dividend growth rate that would be required to justify the market price of $40.

---

[20] See Skinner (2007).

Solution to 1: The required rate of return is 5.6 percent + 1.1(6 percent) = 12.2 percent. The value of one share, using the Gordon growth model, is

$$V_0 = \frac{D_0(1 + g)}{r - g}$$

$$= \frac{2.00(1.05)}{0.122 - 0.05}$$

$$= \frac{2.10}{0.072} = \$29.17$$

Solution to 2: The valuation estimate of the model (\$29.17) is less than the market value of \$40.00, thus the market price must be forecasting a growth rate above the assumed 5 percent. Assuming that the model and the required return assumption are appropriate, the growth rate in dividends required to justify the \$40 stock price can be calculated by substituting all known values into the Gordon growth model equation except for g:

$$40 = \frac{2.00(1 + g)}{0.122 - g}$$

$$4.88 - 40g = 2 + 2g$$
$$42g = 2.88$$
$$g = 0.0686$$

An expected dividend growth rate of 6.86 percent is required for the stock price to be correctly valued at the market price of \$40.

4.5 The Present Value of Growth Opportunities

The value of a stock can be analyzed as the sum of 1) the value of the company without earnings reinvestment, and 2) the **present value of growth opportunities** (PVGO). PVGO, also known as the **value of growth**, sums the expected value today of opportunities to profitably reinvest future earnings.[21] In this section, we illustrate this decomposition and discuss how it may be interpreted to gain insight into the market's view of a company's business and prospects.

Earnings growth may increase, leave unchanged, or reduce shareholder wealth depending on whether the growth results from earning returns in excess of, equal to, or less than the opportunity cost of funds. Consider a company with a required return on equity of 10 percent that has earned €1 per share. The company is deciding whether to pay out current earnings as a dividend or to reinvest them at 10 percent and distribute the ending value as a dividend in one year. If it reinvests, the present value of investment is €1.10/1.10 = €1.00, equaling its cost, so the decision to reinvest has a net present value (NPV) of zero. If the company were able to earn more than 10 percent by exploiting a profitable growth

---

[21] More technically, PVGO can be defined as the forecasted total net present value of future projects. See Brealey, Myers, and Allen (2006), p. 259.

opportunity, reinvesting would have a positive NPV, increasing shareholder wealth. Suppose the company could reinvest earnings at 25 percent for one year: The per-share NPV of the growth opportunity would be €1.25/1.10 − €1 ≈ €0.14. Note that any reinvestment at a positive rate below 10 percent, although increasing EPS, is not in shareholders' interests. Increases in shareholder wealth occur only when reinvested earnings earn more than the opportunity cost of funds (i.e., investments are in positive net present value projects).[22] Thus, investors actively assess whether and to what degree companies will have opportunities to invest in profitable projects. In principle, companies without prospects for investing in positive NPV projects should distribute most or all earnings to shareholders as dividends so the shareholders can redirect capital to more attractive areas.

A company without positive expected NPV projects is defined as a **no-growth company** (a term for a company without opportunities for *profitable* growth). Such companies should distribute all their earnings in dividends because earnings cannot be reinvested profitably and earnings will be flat in perpetuity, assuming a constant return on equity (ROE). This flatness occurs because earnings equal ROE × Equity, and equity is constant because retained earnings are not added to it. E_1 is $t = 1$ earnings, which is the constant level of earnings or the average earnings of a no-growth company if return on equity is viewed as varying about its average level. The **no-growth value per share** is defined as E_1/r, which is the present value of a perpetuity in the amount of E_1 where the capitalization rate, r, is the required rate of return on the company's equity. E_1/r can also be interpreted as the per-share value of assets in place because of the assumption that the company is making no new investments because none are profitable. For any company, the actual value per share is the sum of the no-growth value per share and the present value of growth opportunities (PVGO):

$$V_0 = \frac{E_1}{r} + \text{PVGO} \qquad\qquad \textbf{(12)}$$

If prices reflect value ($P_0 = V_0$), P_0 less E_1/r gives the market's estimate of the company's value of growth, PVGO. Referring back to Example 6, suppose that MSEX is expected to have average EPS of $0.79 if it distributed all earnings as dividends. Its required return of 9.25 percent and a current price of $18.39 gives

$$\$18.39 = (\$0.79/0.0925) + \text{PVGO}$$
$$= \$8.54 + \text{PVGO}$$

where PVGO = $18.39 − $8.54 = $9.85. So, 54 percent ($9.85/$18.39 = 0.54) of the company's value, as reflected in the market price, is attributable to the value of growth.

Exhibit 4, based on data from early October 2008, illustrates that the value of growth represented about 65 percent of the market value of technology company Google; a much smaller percentage of McDonald's value; and for Macy's, the value of growth appeared to be negative. The negative value for Macy's PVGO could be explained in several ways. The value could reflect an expectation that management's investment policy would destroy value (e.g., analysts were generally negative on the company's business prospects and reinvestment in it

---

[22] We can interpret this condition of profitability as ROE > r with ROE calculated with the *market* value of equity (rather than the book value of equity) in the denominator. Book value based on historical cost accounting can present a distorted picture of the value of shareholders' investment in the company.

	EXHIBIT 4		Estimated PVGO as a Percentage of Price				
Company	**β**	**r^{23}**	**E_1**	**Price**	**E_1/r**	**PVGO**	**PVGO/ Price**
Google, Inc.	2.09	13.7%	$15.88	$332.0	115.91	216.09	65.1%
McDonald's Corp	1.04	9.0	3.45	53.35	38.33	15.02	28.2
Macy's Inc.	1.28	10.1	1.30	10.50	12.87	−2.37	−22.6

Source: Standard & Poor's Stock Reports for beta, earnings estimate, and price of each.

might not cover all costs including the cost of funds); it could indicate that this stock's price in a severe market break had lost contact with fundamentals (one month earlier the company's share price was approximately double); or it might indicate that the estimated no-growth value per share was too high because the earnings estimate was too high and/or the required return on equity estimate was too low.

What determines PVGO? One determinant is the value of a company's options to invest, captured by the word "opportunities." In addition, the flexibility to adapt investments to new circumstances and information is valuable. Thus, a second determinant of PVGO is the value of the company's options to time the start, adjust the scale, or even abandon future projects. This element is the value of the company's **real options** (options to modify projects, in this context). Companies that have good business opportunities and/or a high level of managerial flexibility in responding to changes in the marketplace should tend to have higher values of PVGO than companies that do not have such advantages. This perspective on what contributes to PVGO can provide additional understanding of the results in Exhibit 4.

As an additional aid to an analyst, Equation 12 can be restated in terms of the familiar P/E ratio based on forecasted earnings:

$$\frac{V_0}{E_1} \text{ or } \frac{P_0}{E_1} \text{ or } P/E = \frac{1}{r} + \frac{PVGO}{E_1} \tag{13}$$

The first term, $1/r$, is the value of the P/E for a no-growth company. The second term is the component of the P/E value that relates to growth opportunities. For MSEX, the P/E is $18.39/$0.79 = 23.3. The no-growth P/E is 1/0.0925 = 10.8 and is the multiple the company should sell at if it has no growth opportunities. The growth component of $9.85/$0.79 = 12.5 reflects anticipated growth opportunities. Leibowitz and Kogelman (1990) and Leibowitz (1997) have provided elaborate analyses of the drivers of the growth component of P/E as a franchise-value approach.

As analysts, the distinction between no-growth and growth values is of interest because the value of growth and the value of assets in place generally have different risk characteristics (as the interpretation of PVGO as incorporating the real options suggests).

---

[23] The required rate of return is estimated using the CAPM with the following inputs: the beta from the Standard & Poor's Stock Reports, 4.3 percent (30-year U.S. T-bond rate) for the risk-free rate of return, and 4.5 percent for the equity risk premium.

4.6 Gordon Growth Model and the Price-to-Earnings Ratio

The price-to-earnings ratio (P/E) is perhaps the most widely recognized valuation indicator, familiar to readers of newspaper financial tables and institutional research reports. Using the Gordon growth model, an expression for P/E in terms of the fundamentals can be developed. This expression has two uses:

▶ When used with forecasts of the inputs to the model, the analyst obtains a **justified (fundamental) P/E**—the P/E that is fair, warranted, or justified on the basis of fundamentals (given that the valuation model is appropriate). The analyst can then state his or her view of value in terms not of the Gordon growth model value but of the justified P/E. Because P/E is so widely recognized, this method may be an effective way to communicate the analysis.

▶ The analyst may also use the expression for P/E to weigh whether the forecasts of earnings growth built into the current stock price are reasonable. What expected earnings growth rate is implied by the actual market P/E? Is that growth rate plausible?

The expression for P/E can be stated in terms of the current (or trailing) P/E (today's market price per share divided by trailing 12 months' earnings per share) or in terms of the leading (or forward) P/E (today's market price per share divided by a forecast of the next 12 months' earnings per share, or sometimes the next fiscal year's earnings per share).

Leading and trailing justified P/E expressions can be developed from the Gordon growth model. Assuming that the model can be applied for a particular stock's valuation, the dividend payout ratio is considered fixed. Define b as the retention rate, the fraction of earnings reinvested in the company rather than paid out in dividends. The dividend payout ratio is then, by definition, $(1 - b) =$ Dividend per share/Earnings per share $= D_t/E_t$. If $P_0 = D_1/(r - g)$ is divided by next year's earnings per share, E_1, we have

$$\frac{P_0}{E_1} = \frac{D_1/E_1}{r - g} = \frac{1 - b}{r - g} \qquad \textbf{(14)}$$

This represents a leading P/E, which is current price divided by next year's earnings. Alternatively, if $P_0 = D_0(1 + g)/(r - g)$ is divided by the current-year's earnings per share, E_0, the result is

$$\frac{P_0}{E_0} = \frac{D_0(1 + g)/E_0}{r - g} = \frac{(1 - b)(1 + g)}{r - g} \qquad \textbf{(15)}$$

This expression is for trailing P/E, which is current price divided by trailing (current year) earnings.

EXAMPLE 11

The Justified P/E Based on the Gordon Growth Model

Harry Trice wants to use the Gordon growth model to find a justified P/E for the French company Carrefour SA (NYSE Euronext: CA), a global food retailer specializing in hypermarkets and supermarkets. Trice has assembled the following information:

► Current stock price = €47.46.
► Trailing annual earnings per share = €3.22.
► Current level of annual dividends = €1.03.
► Dividend growth rate = 7 percent.
► Risk-free rate = 4.4 percent.
► Equity risk premium = 6.39 percent.
► Beta versus the CAC index = 0.72.

1. Calculate the justified trailing and leading P/Es based on the Gordon growth model.

2. Based on the justified trailing P/E and the actual P/E, judge whether CA is fairly valued, overvalued, or undervalued.

Solution to 1: For CA, the required rate of return using the CAPM is

$$r_i = 4.4\% + 0.72(6.39\%)$$
$$= 9.0\%$$

The dividend payout ratio is

$$(1 - b) = D_0/E_0$$
$$= 1.03/3.22$$
$$= 0.32$$

The justified leading P/E (based on next year's earnings) is

$$\frac{P_0}{E_1} = \frac{1-b}{r-g} = \frac{0.32}{0.09 - 0.07} = 16.0$$

The justified trailing P/E (based on trailing earnings) is

$$\frac{P_0}{E_0} = \frac{(1-b)(1+g)}{r-g} = \frac{0.32(1.07)}{0.09 - 0.07} = 17.1$$

Solution to 2: Based on a current price of €47.46 and trailing earnings of €3.22, the trailing P/E is €47.46/€3.22 = 14.7. Because the actual P/E of 14.7 is smaller than the justified trailing P/E of 17.1, the conclusion is that CA appears to be undervalued. The apparent mispricing can also be expressed in terms of the Gordon growth model. Using Trice's assumptions, the Gordon growth model assigns a value of 1.03(1.07)/(0.09 − 0.07) = €55.11, which is above the current market value of €47.46. The Gordon growth model approach gives a higher stock value than the market price and a higher justified P/E than the current market P/E.

Later in the reading, we will present multistage DDMs. Expressions for the P/E can be developed in terms of the variables of multistage DDMs, but the usefulness of these expressions is not commensurate with their complexity. For multistage models, the simple way to calculate a justified leading P/E is to divide the model value directly by the first year's expected earnings. In all cases, the P/E is explained in terms of the required return on equity, expected dividend growth rate(s), and the dividend payout ratio(s). All else equal, higher prices are associated with higher anticipated dividend growth rates.

4.7 Estimating a Required Return Using the Gordon Growth Model

Under the assumption of efficient prices, the Gordon growth model has been used to estimate a stock's required rate of return, or equivalently, the market-price-implied expected return. The Gordon growth model solved for r is

$$r = \frac{D_0(1 + g)}{P_0} + g = \frac{D_1}{P_0} + g \qquad \textbf{(16)}$$

As explained in the reading on return concepts, r in Equation 16 is technically an internal rate of return (IRR). The rate r is composed of two parts; the dividend yield (D_1/P_0) and the capital gains (or appreciation) yield (g).

EXAMPLE 12

Finding the Expected Rate of Return with the Gordon Growth Model

Bob Inguigiatto, CFA, has been given the task of developing mean return estimates for a list of stocks as preparation for a portfolio optimization. On his list is FPL Group, Inc. (NYSE: FPL). On analysis, he decides that it is appropriate to model FPL using the Gordon growth model, and he takes prices as reflecting value. The company paid dividends of $2.24 during the past year, and the current stock price is $56.60. The growth rates of dividends and earnings per share have been 4.01 percent and 5.30 percent, respectively, for the past five years. Analysts' consensus estimate of the five-year earnings growth rate is 7.0 percent. Based on his own analysis, Inguigiatto has decided to use 5.50 percent as his best estimate of the long-term earnings and dividend growth rate. Next year's projected dividend, D_1, should be $2.24(1.055) − $2.363. Using the Gordon growth model, FPL's expected rate of return should be

$$r = \frac{D_1}{P_0} + g$$

$$= \frac{2.363}{56.60} + 0.055$$

$$= 0.0417 + 0.055$$

$$= 0.0967 = 9.67\%$$

The expected rate of return can be broken into two components, the dividend yield (D_1/P_0 = 4.17 percent) and the capital gains yield (g = 5.50 percent).

4.8 The Gordon Growth Model: Concluding Remarks

The Gordon growth model is the simplest practical implementation of discounted dividend valuation. The Gordon growth model is appropriate for valuing the equity of dividend-paying companies when its key assumption of a stable future dividend and earnings growth rate is expected to be satisfied. Broad equity market indices of developed markets frequently satisfy the conditions of the model fairly well; as a result, analysts have used it to judge whether an equity market is fairly valued or not and for estimating the equity risk premium associated with the current market level. In the multistage models discussed in the next section, the Gordon growth model has often been used to model the last growth stage, when a previously high growth company matures and the growth rate drops to a long-term sustainable level. In any case in which the model is applied, the analyst must be aware that the output of the model is typically sensitive to small changes in the assumed growth rate and required rate of return.

The Gordon growth model is a single-stage DDM because all future periods are grouped into one stage characterized by single growth rate. For many or even the majority of companies, however, future growth can be expected to consist of multiple stages. Multistage DDMs are the subject of the next section.

5   MULTISTAGE DIVIDEND DISCOUNT MODELS

Earlier we noted that the basic expression for the DDM (Equation 7) is too general for investment analysts to use in practice because one cannot forecast individually more than a relatively small number of dividends. The strongest simplifying assumption—a stable dividend growth rate from now into the indefinite future, leading to the Gordon growth model—is not realistic for many or even most companies. For many publicly traded companies, practitioners assume growth falls into three stages (see Sharpe, Alexander, and Bailey 1999):

► **Growth phase.** A company in its growth phase typically enjoys rapidly expanding markets, high profit margins, and an abnormally high growth rate in earnings per share (**supernormal growth**). Companies in this phase often have negative free cash flow to equity because the company invests heavily in expanding operations. Given high prospective returns on equity, the dividend payout ratios of growth-phase companies are often low or even zero. As the company's markets mature or as unusual growth opportunities attract competitors, earnings growth rates eventually decline.

► **Transition phase.** In this phase, which is a transition to maturity, earnings growth slows as competition puts pressure on prices and profit margins or as sales growth slows because of market saturation. In this phase, earnings growth rates may be above average but declining toward the growth rate for the overall economy. Capital requirements typically decline in this phase, often resulting in positive free cash flow and increasing dividend payout ratios (or the initiation of dividends).

► **Mature phase.** In maturity, the company reaches an equilibrium in which investment opportunities on average just earn their opportunity cost of capital. Return on equity approaches the required return on equity, and earnings growth, the dividend payout ratio, and the return on equity stabilize at levels that can be sustained long term. The dividend and earnings growth rate of this phase is called the **mature growth rate**. This phase, in fact, reflects the stage in which a company can properly be valued using the Gordon growth model, and that model is one tool for valuing this phase of a current high-growth company's future.

A company may attempt and succeed in restarting the growth phase by changing its strategic focuses and business mix. Technological advances may alter a company's growth prospects for better or worse with surprising rapidity. Nevertheless, this growth-phase picture of a company is a useful approximation. The growth-phase concept provides the intuition for multistage discounted cash flow (DCF) models of all types, including multistage dividend discount models. Multistage models are a staple valuation discipline of investment management firms using DCF valuation models.

In the following sections, we present three popular multistage DDMs: the two-stage DDM, the H-model (a type of two-stage model), and the three-stage DDM. Keep in mind that all these models represent stylized patterns of growth; they are attempting to identify the pattern that most accurately approximates an analyst's view of the company's future growth.

5.1 Two-Stage Dividend Discount Model

Two common versions of the two-stage DDM exist. Both versions assume constant growth at a mature growth rate (for example, 7 percent) in Stage 2. In the first version ("the general two-stage model"), the whole of Stage 1 represents a period of abnormal growth—for example, growth at 15 percent. The transition to mature growth in Stage 2 is generally abrupt.

In the second version, called the H-model, the dividend growth rate is assumed to decline from an abnormal rate to the mature growth rate during the course of Stage 1. For example, the growth rate could begin at 15 percent and decline continuously in Stage 1 until it reaches 7 percent. The second model will be presented after the general two-stage model.

The first two-stage DDM provides for a high growth rate for the initial period, followed by a sustainable and usually lower growth rate thereafter. The two-stage DDM is based on the multiple-period model

$$V_0 = \sum_{t=1}^{n} \frac{D_t}{(1 + r)^t} + \frac{V_n}{(1 + r)^n} \qquad (17)$$

where V_n is used as an estimate of P_n. The two-stage model assumes that the first n dividends grow at an extraordinary short-term rate, g_S:

$$D_t = D_0(1 + g_S)^t$$

After time n, the annual dividend growth rate changes to a normal long-term rate, g_L. The dividend at time $n + 1$ is $D_{n+1} = D_n (1 + g_L) = D_0 (1 + g_S)^n(1 + g_L)$, and this dividend continues to grow at g_L. Using D_{n+1}, an analyst can use the Gordon growth model to find V_n:

$$V_n = \frac{D_0(1 + g_S)^n(1 + g_L)}{r - g_L} \qquad (18)$$

To find the value at $t = 0$, V_0, simply find the present value of the first n dividends and the present value of the projected value at time n

$$V_0 = \sum_{t=1}^{n} \frac{D_0(1 + g_S)^t}{(1 + r)^t} + \frac{D_0(1 + g_S)^n(1 + g_L)}{(1 + r)^n(r - g_L)} \qquad (19)$$

EXAMPLE 13

Valuing a Stock Using the Two-Stage Dividend Discount Model

Carl Zeiss Meditec AG (Deutsche Börse XETRA: AFX), 65 percent owned by the Carl Zeiss Group, provides screening, diagnostic, and therapeutic systems for the treatment of ophthalmologic (vision) problems. Reviewing the issue as of the beginning of October 2007, when it is trading for €19.10, Hans Mattern, a buy-side analyst covering Meditec, forecasts that the current dividend of €0.14 will grow by 15 percent per year during the next 10 years. Thereafter, Mattern believes that the growth rate will decline to 8 percent and remain at that level indefinitely.

Mattern estimates Meditec's required return on equity as 9.7 percent based on a beta of 0.89 against the DAX, a 4.5 percent risk-free rate, and his equity risk premium estimate of 5.8 percent.

Exhibit 5 shows the calculations of the first ten dividends and their present values discounted at 9.7 percent. The terminal stock value at $t = 10$ is

$$V_{10} = \frac{D_0(1 + g_S)^n(1 + g_L)}{r - g_L}$$

$$= \frac{0.14(1.15)^{10}(1.08)}{0.097 - 0.08}$$

$$= 35.9817$$

The terminal stock value and its present value are also given.

EXHIBIT 5   **Carl Zeiss Meditec AG**

Time	Value	Calculation	D_t or V_t	Present Values $D_t/(1.097)^t$ or $V_t/(1.097)^t$
1	D_1	€0.14(1.15)	€0.1610	€0.1468
2	D_2	0.14(1.15)^2	0.1852	0.1539
3	D_3	0.14(1.15)^3	0.2129	0.1613
4	D_4	0.14(1.15)^4	0.2449	0.1691
5	D_5	0.14(1.15)^5	0.2816	0.1772
6	D_6	0.14(1.15)^6	0.3238	0.1858
7	D_7	0.14(1.15)^7	0.3724	0.1948
8	D_8	0.14(1.15)^8	0.4283	0.2042
9	D_9	0.14(1.15)^9	0.4925	0.2141
10	D_{10}	0.14(1.15)^10	0.5664	0.2244
10	V_{10}	0.14(1.15)^10(1.08)/ (0.097 − 0.08)	35.9817	14.2566
Total				€16.0882

In this two-stage model, the dividends are forecast during the first stage and then their present values are calculated. The Gordon growth model is used to derive the terminal value (the value of the dividends in the second stage as of the beginning of that stage). As shown in Exhibit 5, the terminal value is $V_{10} = D_{11}/(r - g_L)$. Ignoring rounding errors, the Period 11 dividend is €0.6117 (= $D_{10} \times 1.08 = €0.5664 \times 1.08$). By using the standard Gordon growth model, $V_{10} = €35.98 = €0.6117/(0.097 - 0.08)$. The present value of the terminal value is €14.26 = $€35.9817/1.097^{10}$. The total estimated value of Meditec is €16.09 using this model. Notice that approximately 89 percent of this value, €14.26, is the present value of V_{10}, and the balance, €16.09 − €14.26 = €1.83, is the present value of the first ten dividends. Recalling the discussion of the sensitivity of the Gordon growth model to changes in the inputs, an interval for the intrinsic value of Meditec could be calculated by varying the mature growth rate through the range of plausible values.

The two-stage DDM is useful because many scenarios exist in which a company can achieve a supernormal growth rate for a few years, after which time the growth rate falls to a more sustainable level. For example, a company may achieve supernormal growth through possession of a patent, first-mover advantage, or another factor that provides a temporary lead in a specific marketplace. Subsequently, earnings will most likely descend to a level that is more consistent with competition and growth in the overall economy. Accordingly, that is why in the two-stage model, extraordinary growth is often forecast for a few years and normal growth is forecast thereafter. A possible limitation of the two-stage model is that the transition between the initial abnormal growth period and the final steady-state growth period is abrupt.

The accurate estimation of V_n, the **terminal value of the stock** (also known as its **continuing value**) is an important part of the correct use of DDMs. In practice, analysts estimate the terminal value either by applying a multiple to a projected terminal value of a fundamental, such as earnings per share or book value per share, or they estimate V_n using the Gordon growth model. In the reading on market multiples, we will discuss using price–earnings multiples in this context.

In the examples, a single discount rate, r, is used for all phases, reflecting both a desire for simplicity and lack of a clear objective basis for adjusting the discount rate for different phases. Some analysts, however, use different discount rates for different growth phases.

The following example values E. I. DuPont de Nemours and Company by combining the dividend discount model and a P/E valuation model.

EXAMPLE 14

Combining a DDM and P/E Model to Value a Stock

An analyst is reviewing the valuation of DuPont (NYSE: DD) as of the beginning of October 2007 when DD is selling for $50. In the previous year, DuPont paid a $1.48 dividend that the analyst expects to grow at a rate of 10 percent annually for the next four years. At the end of Year 4, the analyst expects the dividend to equal 40 percent of earnings per share and the trailing P/E for DD to be 14. If the required return on DD common stock is 10.5 percent, calculate the per-share value of DD common stock.

Exhibit 6 summarizes the relevant calculations. When the dividends are growing at 10 percent, the expected dividends and the present value of each (discounted at 10.5 percent) are shown. The terminal stock price, V_4, deserves some explanation. As shown in the table, the Year 4 dividend is $1.48(1.10)^4 = 2.1669$. Because dividends at that time are assumed to be 40 percent of earnings, the EPS projection for Year 4 is $EPS_4 = D_4/0.40 = 2.1669/0.40 = 5.4172$. With a trailing P/E of 14.0, the value of DD at the end of Year 4 should be $14.0(5.4172) = \$75.84$. Discounted at 10.5 percent for four years, the present value of V_4 is $50.87.

EXHIBIT 6		Value of DuPont Common Stock		
Time	Value	Calculation	D_t or V_t	Present Values $D_t/(1.105)^t$ or $V_t/(1.105)^t$
1	D_1	$\$1.48(1.10)^1$	$\$1.6280$	$\$1.4733$
2	D_2	$1.48(1.10)^2$	1.7908	1.4666
3	D_3	$1.48(1.10)^3$	1.9699	1.4600
4	D_4	$1.48(1.10)^4$	2.1669	1.4534
4	V_4	$14 \times [1.48(1.10)^4/0.40]$ $= 14 \times [2.1669/0.40]$ $= 14 \times 5.4172$	75.8404	50.8688
Total				$\$56.72$

The present values of the dividends for Years 1 through 4 sum to $5.85. The present value of the terminal value of $75.84 is $50.87. The estimated total value of DD is the sum of these, or $56.72 per share.

5.2 Valuing a Non-Dividend-Paying Company

The fact that a stock is currently paying no dividends does not mean that the principles of the dividend discount model do not apply. Even though D_0 and/or D_1 may be zero, and the company may not begin paying dividends for some time, the present value of future dividends may still capture the value of the company. Of course, if a company pays no dividends and will never be able to distribute cash to shareholders, the stock is worthless.

To value a non-dividend-paying company using a DDM, generally an analyst can use a multistage DDM model in which the first-stage dividend equals zero. Example 15 illustrates the approach.

EXAMPLE 15

Valuing a Non-Dividend-Paying Stock

Assume that a company is currently paying no dividend and will not pay one for several years. If the company begins paying a dividend of $1.00 five years from now, and the dividend is expected to grow at 5 percent thereafter, this future dividend stream can be discounted back to find the value of the company. This company's required rate of return is 11 percent. Because the expression

$$V_n = \frac{D_{n+1}}{r - g}$$

values a stock at period n using the next period's dividend, the $t = 5$ dividend is used to find the value at $t = 4$:

$$V_4 = \frac{D_5}{r - g} = \frac{1.00}{0.11 - 0.05} = \$16.67$$

To find the value of the stock today, simply discount V_4 back for four years:

$$V_0 = \frac{V_4}{(1 + r)^4} = \frac{16.67}{(1.11)^4} = \$10.98$$

The value of this stock, even though it will not pay a dividend until Year 5, is $10.98.

If a company is not paying a dividend but is very profitable, an analyst might be willing to forecast its future dividends. Of course, for non-dividend-paying, unprofitable companies, such a forecast would be very difficult. Furthermore, as discussed in Section 2.2 (Streams of Expected Cash Flows), it is usually difficult for the analyst to estimate the timing of the initiation of dividends and the dividend policy that will then be established by the company. Thus, the analyst may prefer a free cash flow or residual income model for valuing such companies.

5.3 The H-Model

The basic two-stage model assumes a constant, extraordinary rate for the supernormal growth period that is followed by a constant, normal growth rate thereafter. The difference in growth rates may be substantial. For instance, in Example 13, the growth rate for Carl Zeiss Meditec was 15 percent annually for 10 years, followed by a drop to 8 percent growth in Year 11 and thereafter. In some cases, a smoother transition to the mature phase growth rate would be more realistic. Fuller and Hsia (1984) developed a variant of the two-stage model in which growth begins at a high rate and declines linearly throughout the supernormal growth period until it reaches a normal rate at the end. The value of the dividend stream in the H-model is

$$V_0 = \frac{D_0(1 + g_L)}{r - g_L} + \frac{D_0 H(g_S - g_L)}{r - g_L} \tag{20}$$

or

$$V_0 = \frac{D_0(1 + g_L) + D_0 H(g_S - g_L)}{r - g_L}$$

where

V_0 = value per share at $t = 0$

D_0 = current dividend

r = required rate of return on equity

H = half-life in years of the high-growth period (i.e., high-growth period = $2H$ years)

g_S = initial short-term dividend growth rate

g_L = normal long-term dividend growth rate after Year $2H$

The first term on the right-hand side of Equation 20 is the present value of the company's dividend stream if it were to grow at g_L forever. The second term is an approximation of the extra value (assuming $g_S > g_L$) accruing to the stock because of its supernormal growth for Years 1 through $2H$ (see Fuller and Hsia 1984, for technical details).[24] Logically, the longer the supernormal growth period (i.e., the larger the value of H, which is one-half the length of the supernormal growth period) and the larger the extra growth rate in the supernormal growth period (measured by g_S minus g_L), the higher the share value, all else equal. To illustrate the expression, if the analyst in Example 13 had forecast a linear decline of the growth rate from 15 percent to 8 percent over the next 10 years, his estimate of value using the H-model would have been €11.78 (rather than €16.09 as in Example 13):

$$
\begin{aligned}
V_0 &= \frac{D_0(1 + g_L) + D_0 H(g_S - g_L)}{r - g_L} \\[2mm]
&= \frac{0.14(1.08) + 0.14(5)(0.15 - 0.08)}{0.097 - 0.08} \\[2mm]
&= \frac{0.1512 + 0.0490}{0.017} \\[2mm]
&= 11.78
\end{aligned}
$$

Note that an H of 5 corresponds to the 10-year high-growth period of Example 13. Example 16 provides another illustration of the H-model.

EXAMPLE 16

Valuing a Stock with the H-Model

Françoise Delacour, a portfolio manager of a U.S.-based diversified global equity portfolio, is researching the valuation of Vinci SA (NYSE

---

[24] We can provide some intuition on the expression. On average, the expected excess growth rate in the supernormal period will be $(g_S - g_L)/2$. Through $2H$ periods, a total excess amount of dividends (compared with the level given g_L) of $2HD_0(g_S - g_L)/2 = D_0 H(g_S - g_L)$ is expected. This term is the H-model upward adjustment to the first dividend term, reflecting the extra expected dividends as growth declines from g_S to g_L during the first period. Note, however, that the timing of the individual dividends in the first period is not reflected by individually discounting them; the expression is thus an approximation.

Euronext: DG). Vinci is the world's largest construction company, operating chiefly in France (approximately two-thirds of revenue) and the rest of Europe (approximately one-quarter of revenue). Through 2003, DG paid a single regular cash dividend per fiscal year. Since 2004 it has paid two dividends per (fiscal) year, an interim dividend in December and a final dividend in May. Although during the past five years total annual dividends grew at 26 percent per year, Delacour foresees less rapid future growth.

Having decided to compute the H-model value estimate for DG, Delacour gathers the following facts and forecasts:

▶ The share price as of mid-August 2007 was €57.

▶ The current dividend is €1.37.

▶ The initial dividend growth rate is 24 percent, declining linearly during a 12-year period to a final and perpetual growth rate of 6 percent.

▶ Delacour estimates DG's required rate of return on equity as 10 percent.

1. Using the H-model and the information given, estimate the per-share value of DG.

2. Estimate the value of DG shares if its normal growth period began immediately.

3. Evaluate whether DG shares appear to be fairly valued, overvalued, or undervalued.

Solution to 1: Using the H-model expression gives

$$
\begin{aligned}
V_0 &= \frac{D_0(1 + g_L)}{r - g_L} + \frac{D_0 H(g_S - g_L)}{r - g_L} \\
&= \frac{1.37(1.06)}{0.10 - 0.06} + \frac{1.37(6)(0.24 - 0.06)}{0.10 - 0.06} \\
&= 36.31 + 36.99 = €73.30
\end{aligned}
$$

Solution to 2: If DG experienced normal growth starting now, its estimated value would be the first component of the H-model estimate, €36.31. Note that extraordinary growth adds €36.99 to its value, resulting in an estimate of €73.30 for the value of a DG share.

Solution to 3: €73.30 is approximately 30 percent greater than DG's current market price. Thus DG appears to be undervalued.

The H-model is an approximation model that estimates the valuation that would result from discounting all of the future dividends individually. In many circumstances, this approximation is very close. For a long extraordinary growth period (a high H) or for a large difference in growth rates (the difference between g_S and g_L), however, the analyst might abandon the approximation model for the more exact model. Fortunately, the many tedious calculations of the exact model are made fairly easy using a spreadsheet program.

5.4 Three-Stage Dividend Discount Models

There are two popular versions of the three-stage DDM, distinguished by the modeling of the second stage. In the first version ("the general three-stage model"), the company is assumed to have three distinct stages of growth and the growth rate of the second stage is typically constant. For example, Stage 1 could assume 20 percent growth for three years, Stage 2 could have 10 percent growth for four years, and Stage 3 could have 5 percent growth thereafter. In the second version, the growth rate in the middle (second) stage is assumed to decline linearly to the mature growth rate: essentially, the second and third stages are treated as an H-model.

The example below shows how the first type of the three-stage model can be used to value a stock, in this case IBM.

EXAMPLE 17

The Three-Stage DDM with Three Distinct Stages

IBM currently (2007) pays a dividend of $1.60 per year. A current price is $118.36. An analyst makes the following estimates:

▶ the current required return on equity for IBM is 12 percent, and

▶ dividends will grow at 14 percent for the next two years, 12 percent for the following five years, and 10.2 percent thereafter.

Based only on the information given, estimate the value of IBM using a three-stage DDM approach.

Solution: Exhibit 7 gives the calculations.

EXHIBIT 7   Estimated Value of IBM

Time	Value	Calculation	D_t or V_t	Present Values $D_t/(1.12)^t$ or $V_t/(1.12)^t$
1	D_1	$1.60(1.14)$	$1.8240	$1.6286
2	D_2	$1.60(1.14)^2$	2.0794	1.6577
3	D_3	$1.60(1.14)^2(1.12)$	2.3289	1.6577
4	D_4	$1.60(1.14)^2(1.12)^2$	2.6083	1.6577
5	D_5	$1.60(1.14)^2(1.12)^3$	2.9214	1.6577
6	D_6	$1.60(1.14)^2(1.12)^4$	3.2719	1.6577
7	D_7	$1.60(1.14)^2(1.12)^5$	3.6645	1.6577
7	V_7	$1.60(1.14)^2(1.12)^5(1.102)/$ $(0.12 - 0.102)$	$224.3515	101.4852
Total				$113.0600

Given these assumptions, the three-stage model indicates that a fair price should be $113.06, which is very close to the current market price. Characteristically, the terminal value of $101.49 constitutes the overwhelming portion (here, about 90 percent) of total estimated value.

A second version of the three-stage DDM has a middle stage similar to the first stage in the H-model. In the first stage, dividends grow at a high, constant (supernormal) rate for the whole period. In the second stage, dividends decline linearly as they do in the H-model. Finally, in Stage 3, dividends grow at a sustainable, constant growth rate. The process of using this model involves four steps:

► Gather the required inputs:
  ► the current dividend;
  ► the lengths of the first, second, and third stages;
  ► the expected growth rates for the first and third stages; and
  ► an estimate of the required return on equity.
► Compute the expected dividends in the first stage and find the sum of their present values.
► Apply the H-model expression to the second and third stages to obtain an estimate of their value as of the beginning of the second stage. Then find the present value of this H-value as of today ($t = 0$).
► Sum the values obtained in the second and third steps.

In the first step, analysts often investigate the company more deeply, making explicit, individual earnings and dividend forecasts for the near future (often 3, 5, or 10 years), rather than applying a growth rate to the current level of dividends.

EXAMPLE 18

The Three-Stage DDM with Declining Growth Rates in Stage 2

Elaine Bouvier is evaluating Energen (NYSE: EGN) for possible inclusion in a small-cap growth oriented portfolio. Headquartered in Alabama, EGN is a diversified energy company involved in oil and gas exploration through its subsidiary, Energen Resources, and in natural gas distribution through its Alabama Gas Corporation subsidiary. In light of EGN's aggressive program of purchasing oil and gas producing properties, Bouvier expects above average growth for the next five years. Bouvier establishes the following facts and forecasts (as of the beginning of October 2007):

► The current market price is $57.77.
► The current dividend is $0.46.
► Bouvier forecasts an initial 5-year period of 12 percent per year earnings and dividend growth.

► Bouvier anticipates that EGN can grow 7.5 percent per year as a mature company, and allows 10 years for the transition to the mature growth period.

► To estimate the required return on equity using the CAPM, Bouvier uses an adjusted beta of 1.11 based on 2 years of weekly observations, an estimated equity risk premium of 4.5 percent, and a risk-free rate based on the 20-year Treasury bond yield of 5 percent.

► Bouvier considers any security trading within a band of ± 20 percent of her estimate of intrinsic value to be within a "fair value range."

1. Estimate the required return on EGN using the CAPM. (Use only one decimal place in stating the result.)

2. Estimate the value of EGN using a three-stage dividend discount model with a linearly declining dividend growth rate in Stage 2.

3. Calculate the percentages of the total value represented by the first stage and by the second and third stages considered as one group.

4. Judge whether EGN is undervalued or overvalued according to Bouvier's perspective.

5. Some analysts are forecasting essentially flat EPS and dividends in the second year. Estimate the value of EGN making the assumption that EPS is flat in the second year and that 12 percent growth resumes in the third year.

Solution to 1: The required return on equity is $r = 5$ percent + $1.11(4.5$ percent$) = 10$ percent.

Solution to 2: The first step is to compute the five dividends in Stage 1 and find their present values at 10 percent. The dividends in Stages 2 and 3 can be valued with the H-model, which estimates their value at the beginning of Stage 2. This value is then discounted back to find the dividends' present value at $t = 0$.

The calculation of the five dividends in Stage 1 and their present values are given in Exhibit 8. The H-model for calculating the value of the Stage 2 and Stage 3 dividends at the beginning of Stage 2 $(t = 5)$ would be

$$V_5 = \frac{D_5(1 + g_L)}{r - g_L} + \frac{D_5 H(g_S - g_L)}{r - g_L}$$

where
$D_5 = D_0 (1 + g_S)^5 = 0.46(1.12)^5 = \$0.8107$
$g_S = 12.0\%$
$g_L = 7.5\%$
$r = 10.0\%$
$H = 5$ (the second stage lasts $2H = 10$ years)

Substituting these values into the equation for the H-model gives V_5 as:

$$V_5 = \frac{0.8107(1.075)}{0.10 - 0.075} + \frac{0.8107(5)(0.12 - 0.075)}{0.10 - 0.075}$$

$$= 34.8601 + 7.2963$$

$$= \$42.1564$$

The present value of V_5 is $\$42.1564/(1.10)^5 = \$26.1758$.

EXHIBIT 8	Energen			
Time	D_t or V_t	Explanation of D_t or V_t	Value of D_t or V_t	PV at 10%
1	D_1	$0.46(1.12)^1$	$0.5152	$0.4684
2	D_2	$0.46(1.12)^2$	0.5770	0.4769
3	D_3	$0.46(1.12)^3$	0.6463	0.4855
4	D_4	$0.46(1.12)^4$	0.7238	0.4944
5	D_5	$0.46(1.12)^5$	0.8107	0.5034
5	V_5	H-model explained above	$42.1564	26.1758
Total				$28.6044

According to the three-stage DDM model, the total value of EGN is $28.60.

Solution to 3: The sum of the first five present value amounts in the last column of Exhibit 8 is $2.4286. Thus, the first stage represents $2.4286/$28.6044 = 8.5 percent of total value. The second and third stages together represent 100% − 8.5% = 91.5 percent of total value (check: $26.1758/$28.6044 = 91.5 percent).

Solution to 4: The band Bouvier is looking at is $28.60 ± 0.20($28.60), which runs from $28.60 + $5.72 = $34.32 on the upside to $28.60 − $5.72 = $22.88 on the downside. Because $57.77 is above $34.32, Bouvier would consider EGN to be overvalued.

Solution to 5: The estimated value becomes $25.59 with no growth in Year 2 as shown in Exhibit 9. The value of the second and third stages are given by

$$V_5 = \frac{0.7238(1.075)}{0.10 - 0.075} + \frac{0.7238(5)(0.12 - 0.075)}{0.10 - 0.075} = \$37.6376$$

		EXHIBIT 9	Energen with No Growth in Year 2		
Time	D_t or V_t	Explanation of D_t or V_t		Value of D_t or V_t	PV at 10%
1	D_1	$0.46(1.12)^1$		$0.5152	$0.4684
2	D_2	No growth in Year 2		0.5152	0.4258
3	D_3	$0.46(1.12)^2$		0.5770	0.4335
4	D_4	$0.46(1.12)^3$		0.6463	0.4414
5	D_5	$0.46(1.12)^4$		0.7238	0.4494
5	V_5	H-model explained above		$37.6376	23.3700
Total					$25.5885

In Problem 5 of Example 18, the analyst examined the consequences of 12 percent growth in Year 1 and no growth in Year 2, with 12 percent growth resuming in Years 3, 4, and 5. In the first stage, analysts may forecast earnings and dividends individually for a certain number of years.

The three-stage DDM with declining growth in Stage 2 has been widely used among companies using a DDM approach to valuation. An example is the DDM adopted by Bloomberg L.P., a financial services company that provides "Bloomberg terminals" to professional investors and analysts. The Bloomberg DDM is a model that provides an estimated value for any stock that the user selects. The DDM is a three-stage model with declining growth in Stage 2. The model uses fundamentals about the company for assumed Stage 1 and Stage 3 growth rates, and then assumes that the Stage 2 rate is a linearly declining rate between the Stage 1 and Stage 3 rates. The model also makes estimates of the required rate of return and the lengths of the three stages, assigning higher growth companies shorter growth periods (i.e., first stages) and longer transition periods, and slower growth companies longer growth periods and shorter transition periods. Fixing the total length of the growth and transition phases together at 17 years, the growth stage/transition stage durations for Bloomberg's four growth classifications are 3 years/14 years for "explosive growth" equities, 5 years/12 years for "high growth" equities, 7 years/10 years for "average growth" equities, and 9 years/8 years for "slow/mature growth" equities. Analysts, by tailoring stage specifications to their understanding of the specific company being valued, should be able to improve on the accuracy of valuations compared to a fixed specification.

5.5 Spreadsheet (General) Modeling

DDMs, such as the Gordon growth model and the multistage models presented earlier, assume stylized patterns of dividend growth. With the computational power of personal computers, calculators, and personal digital assistants, however, *any* assumed dividend pattern is easily valued.

Spreadsheets allow the analyst to build complicated models that would be very cumbersome to describe using algebra. Furthermore, built-in spreadsheet functions (such as those for finding rates of return) use algorithms to get a numerical answer when a mathematical solution would be impossible or extremely challenging. Because of the widespread use of spreadsheets, several analysts can work together or exchange information by sharing their spreadsheet models. The following example presents the results of using a spreadsheet to value a stock with dividends that change substantially through time.

EXAMPLE 19

Finding the Value of a Stock Using a Spreadsheet Model

Yang Co. is expected to pay a $21.00 dividend next year. The dividend will decline by 10 percent annually for the following three years. In Year 5, Yang will sell off assets worth $100 per share. The Year 5 dividend, which includes a distribution of some of the proceeds of the asset sale, is expected to be $60. In Year 6, the dividend is expected to decrease to $40 and will be maintained at $40 for one additional year. The dividend is then expected to grow by 5 percent annually thereafter. If the required rate of return is 12 percent, what is the value of one share of Yang?

Solution: The value is shown in Exhibit 10. Each dividend, its present value discounted at 12 percent, and an explanation are included in the table. The final row treats the dividends from $t = 8$ forward as a Gordon growth model because after Year 7, the dividend grows at a constant 5 percent annually. V_7 is the value of these dividends at $t = 7$.

EXHIBIT 10   Value of Yang Co. Stock

Year	D_t or V_t	Value of D_t or V_t	Present Value at 12%	Explanation of D_t or V_t
1	D_1	$21.00	$18.75	Dividend set at $21
2	D_2	18.90	15.07	Previous dividend $\times$ 0.90
3	D_3	17.01	12.11	Previous dividend $\times$ 0.90
4	D_4	15.31	9.73	Previous dividend $\times$ 0.90
5	D_5	60.00	34.05	Set at $60
6	D_6	40.00	20.27	Set at $40
7	D_7	40.00	18.09	Set at $40
7	V_7	600.00	271.41	$V_7 = D_8/(r - g)$ $V_7 = (40.00 \times 1.05)/(0.12 - 0.05)$
Total			$399.48	

As the table in Example 19 shows, the total present value of Yang Co.'s dividends is \$399.48. In this example, the terminal value of the company (V_n) at the end of the first stage is found using the Gordon growth model and a mature growth rate of 5 percent. Several alternative approaches to estimating g are available in this context:

▶ Use the formula $g = (b$ in the mature phase$) \times ($ROE in the mature phase$)$. We will discuss the expression $g = b \times$ ROE in Section 6. Analysts estimate mature-phase ROE in several ways, such as:

  ▶ The DuPont decomposition of ROE based on forecasts for the components of the DuPont expression.

  ▶ Setting ROE $= r$, the required rate of return on equity, based on the assumption that in the mature phase companies can do no more than earn investors' opportunity cost of capital.

  ▶ Setting ROE in the mature phase equal to the median industry ROE.

▶ The analyst may estimate the growth rate, g, with other models by relating the mature growth rate to macroeconomic, including industry, growth projections.

When the analyst uses the sustainable growth expression, the earnings retention ratio, b, may be empirically based. For example, Bloomberg L.P.'s model assumes that $b = 0.55$ in the mature phase, equivalent to a dividend payout ratio of 45 percent, a long-run average payout ratio for mature dividend-paying companies in the United States. In addition, sometimes analysts project the dividend payout ratio for the company individually.

EXAMPLE 20

A Sustainable Growth Rate Calculation

In Example 17, the analyst estimated the dividend growth rate of IBM in the final stage of a three-stage model as 10.2 percent. This value was based on the expression

$$g = (b \text{ in the mature phase}) \times (\text{ROE in the mature phase})$$

Using the typical retention ratio of 85 percent for mature technology companies and assuming that in the final stage IBM achieves a ROE equal to its estimated required return on equity of 12 percent, the calculation is:

$$g = 0.85(12\%) = 10.2\%$$

5.6 Estimating a Required Return Using Any DDM

This reading has focused on finding the value of a security using assumptions for dividends, required rates of return, and expected growth rates. Given current price and all inputs to a DDM except for the required return, an IRR can be calculated. Such an IRR has been used as a required return estimate (although reusing it in a DDM is not appropriate because it risks circularity). This IRR can also be interpreted as the expected return on the issue implied by the market price—essentially, an efficient market expected return. In the following discussion, keep in mind that if price does not equal intrinsic value, the expected return will need to be adjusted to reflect the additional component of return that accrues when the mispricing is corrected, as discussed earlier.

In some cases, finding the IRR is very easy. In the Gordon growth model, $r = D_1/P_0 + g$. The required return estimate is the dividend yield plus the expected dividend growth rate. For a security with a current price of $10, an expected dividend of $0.50, and expected growth of 8 percent, the required return estimate is 13 percent.

For the H-model, the expected rate of return can be derived as[25]

$$r = \left(\frac{D_0}{P_0}\right)[(1 + g_L) + H(g_S - g_L)] + g_L \qquad\qquad (21)$$

When the short- and long-term growth rates are the same, this model reduces to the Gordon growth model. For a security with a current dividend of $1, a current price of $20, and an expected short-term growth rate of 10 percent declining over 10 years ($H = 5$) to 6 percent, the expected rate of return would be

$$r = \left(\frac{\$1}{\$20}\right)[(1 + 0.06) + 5(0.10 - 0.06)] + 0.06 = 12.3\%$$

For multistage models and spreadsheet models, finding a single equation for the rate of return can be more difficult. The process generally used is similar to that of finding the IRR for a series of varying cash flows. Using a computer or trial and error, the analyst must find the rate of return such that the present value of future expected dividends equals the current stock price.

EXAMPLE 21

Finding the Expected Rate of Return for Varying Expected Dividends

An analyst expects JNJ's (Johnson & Johnson) current dividend of $1.66 to grow by 9 percent for six years and then grow by 7 percent into perpetuity. A recent price for JNJ as of mid-October 2007 is $66.19. What is the IRR on an investment in JNJ's stock?

In performing trial and error with the two-stage model to estimate the expected rate of return, having a good initial guess is important. In this case, the expected rate of return formula from the Gordon growth model and JNJ's long-term growth rate can be used to find a first approximation: $r = (\$1.66 \times 1.07)/\$66.19 + 0.07 = 9.68$ percent. Because the growth rate in the first six years is more than the long-term growth rate of 7 percent, the estimated rate of return must be above 9.68 percent. Exhibit 11 shows the value estimate of JNJ for two discount rates, 9.68 percent and 10 percent.

---

[25] Fuller and Hsia (1984).

| | | **EXHIBIT 11** Johnson & Johnson | |

Time	D_t	Present Value of D_t and V_6 at $r = 9.68\%$	Present Value of D_t and V_6 at $r = 10\%$
1	$1.8094	$1.6497	$1.6449
2	1.9722	1.6394	1.6300
3	2.1497	1.6293	1.6151
4	2.3432	1.6192	1.6005
5	2.5541	1.6092	1.5859
6	2.7840	1.5992	1.5715
7	2.9789		
Subtotal 1	($t = 1$ to 6)	$9.75	$9.65
Subtotal 2	($t = 7$ to ∞)	$63.85	$56.05
Total		$73.60	$65.70
Market Price		$66.19	$66.19

In the exhibit, the first subtotal is the present value of the expected dividends for Years 1 through 6. The second subtotal is the present value of the terminal value, $V_6/(1 + r)^6 = [D_7/(r - g)]/(1 + r)^6$. For $r = 9.68$ percent, that present value is $[2.9789/(0.0968 - 0.07)]/(1.0968)^6 = \$63.85$. The present value for other values of r is found similarly.

Using 9.68 percent as the discount rate, the value estimate for JNJ is $73.60, which is larger than JNJ's market price. This fact indicates that the IRR is greater than 9.68 percent. With a 10 percent discount rate, the present value of $65.70 is just slightly less than the market price. Thus, the IRR is slightly less than 10 percent. The IRR can be determined to be 9.98 percent, using a calculator or spreadsheet.

5.7 Multistage DDM: Concluding Remarks

Multistage dividend discount models can accommodate a variety of patterns of future streams of expected dividends.

In general, multistage DDMs make stylized assumptions about growth based on a lifecycle view of business. The first stage of a multistage DDM frequently incorporates analysts' individual earnings and dividend forecasts for the next two to five years (sometimes longer). The final stage is often modeled using the Gordon growth model based on an assumption of the company's long-run sustainable growth rate. In the case of the H-model, the transition to the mature growth phase happens smoothly during the first stage. In the case of the standard two-stage model, the growth rate typically transitions immediately to mature growth rate in the second period. In three-stage models, the middle stage is a stage of transition. Using a spreadsheet, an analyst can model an almost limitless variety of cash flow patterns.

Multistage DDMs have several limitations. Often, the present value of the terminal stage represents more than three-quarters of the total value of shares. Terminal value can be very sensitive to the growth and required return assumptions. Furthermore, technological innovation can make the lifecycle model a crude representation.

THE FINANCIAL DETERMINANTS OF GROWTH RATES

6

In a number of examples earlier in this reading, we have implicitly used the relationship that the dividend growth rate (g) equals the earning retention ratio (b) times the return on equity (ROE). In this section, we explain this relationship and show how it can be combined with a method of analyzing return on equity, called DuPont analysis, as a simple tool for forecasting dividend growth rates.

6.1 Sustainable Growth Rate

We define the **sustainable growth rate** as the rate of dividend (and earnings) growth that can be sustained for a given level of return on equity, assuming that the capital structure is constant through time and that additional common stock is not issued. The reason for studying this concept is that it can help in estimating the stable growth rate in a Gordon growth model valuation, or the mature growth rate in a multistage DDM in which the Gordon growth formula is used to find the terminal value of the stock.

The expression to calculate the sustainable growth rate is

$$g = b \times \text{ROE} \tag{22}$$

where

g = dividend growth rate
b = earnings retention rate (1 − Dividend payout ratio)
ROE = return on equity

More precisely, in Equation 22 the retention rate should be multiplied by the rate of return expected to be earned on new investment. Analysts commonly assume that the rate of return is well approximated by the return on equity, as shown in Equation 22; however, whether that is actually the case should be investigated by the analyst on a case-by-case basis.

Example 22 is an illustration of the fact that growth in shareholders' equity is driven by reinvested earnings alone (no new issues of equity and debt growing at the rate g).[26]

---

[26] With debt growing at the rate g, the capital structure is constant. If the capital structure is not constant, ROE would not be constant in general because ROE depends on leverage.

EXAMPLE 22

Example Showing $g = b \times$ ROE

Suppose that a company's ROE is 25 percent and its retention rate is 60 percent. According to the expression for the sustainable growth rate, the dividends should grow at $g = b \times$ ROE $= 0.60 \times 25$ percent $=$ 15 percent.

To demonstrate the working of the expression, suppose that, in the year just ended, a company began with shareholders' equity of $1,000,000, earned $250,000 net income, and paid dividends of $100,000. The company begins the next year with $1,000,000 + 0.60($250,000) = $1,000,000 + $150,000 = $1,150,000 of shareholders' equity. No additions to equity are made from the sale of additional shares.

If the company again earns 25 percent on equity, net income will be $0.25 \times$ $1,150,000 $=$ $287,500, which is a $287,500 $-$ $250,000 $=$ $37,500 or a $37,500/$250,000 = 0.15 percent increase from the prior year level. The company retains 60 percent of earnings, 60 percent $\times$ $287,500 = $172,500, and pays out the other 40 percent, 40 percent $\times$ $287,500 = $115,000 as dividends. Dividends for the company grew from $100,000 to $115,000, which is exactly a 15 percent growth rate. With the company continuing to earn 25 percent each year on the 60% of earnings that is reinvested in the company, dividends would continue to grow at 15 percent.

Equation 22 implies that the higher the return on equity, the higher the dividend growth rate, all else constant. That relation appears to be reliable. Another implication of the expression is that the lower (higher) the earnings retention ratio, the lower (higher) the growth rate in dividends, holding all else constant; this relationship has been called *the dividend displacement of earnings*.[27] Of course, all else may not be equal—the return on reinvested earnings may not be constant at different levels of investment, or companies with changing future growth prospects may change their dividend policy. Arnott and Asness (2003) and Zhou and Ruland (2006), in providing U.S.-based evidence that dividend-paying companies had higher future growth rates during the period studied, indicate that caution is appropriate in assuming that dividends displace earnings.

A practical logic for defining *sustainable* in terms of growth through internally generated funds (retained earnings) is that external equity (secondary issues of stock) is considerably more costly than internal equity (reinvested earnings), for several reasons including the investment banker fees associated with secondary equity issues. In general, continuous issuance of new stock is not a

---

[27] ROE is a variable that reflects underlying profitability as well as the use of leverage or debt. The retention ratio or dividend policy, in contrast, is not a fundamental variable in the same sense as ROE. A higher dividend growth rate through a higher retention ratio (lower dividend payout ratio) is neutral for share value in and of itself. Holding investment policy (capital projects) constant, the positive effect on value from an increase in g will be offset by the negative effect from a decrease in dividend payouts in the expression for the value of the stock in any DDM. Sharpe, Alexander, and Bailey (1999) discuss this concept in more detail.

practical funding alternative for companies.[28] Growth of capital through issuance of new debt, however, can sometimes be sustained for considerable periods. Further, if a company manages its capital structure to a target percentage of debt to total capital (debt and common stock), it will need to issue debt to maintain that percentage as equity grows through reinvested earnings. (This approach is one of a variety of observed capital structure policies.) In addition, the earnings retention ratio nearly always shows year-to-year variation in actual companies. For example, earnings may have transitory components that management does not want to reflect in dividends. The analyst may thus observe actual dividend growth rates straying from the growth rates predicted by Equation 22 because of these effects, even when his or her input estimates are unbiased. Nevertheless, the equation can be useful as a simple expression for approximating the average rate at which dividends can grow over a long horizon.

6.2 Dividend Growth Rate, Retention Rate, and ROE Analysis

Thus far we have seen that a company's sustainable growth, as defined in Section 6.1, is a function of its ability to generate return on equity (which depends on investment opportunities) and its retention rate. We now expand this model by examining what drives ROE. Remember that ROE is the return (net income) generated on the equity invested in the company:

$$\text{ROE} = \frac{\text{Net income}}{\text{Shareholders' equity}} \qquad (23)$$

If a company has a ROE of 15 percent, it generates $15 of net income for every $100 invested in stockholders' equity. For purposes of analyzing ROE, it can be related to several other financial ratios. For example, ROE can be related to return on assets (ROA) and the extent of financial leverage (equity multiplier):

$$\text{ROE} = \frac{\text{Net income}}{\text{Total assets}} \times \frac{\text{Total assets}}{\text{Shareholders' equity}} \qquad (24)$$

Therefore, a company can increase its ROE either by increasing ROA or the use of leverage (assuming the company can borrow at a rate lower than it earns on its assets).

This model can be expanded further by breaking ROA into two components, profit margin and turnover (efficiency):

$$\text{ROE} = \frac{\text{Net income}}{\text{Sales}} \times \frac{\text{Sales}}{\text{Total assets}} \times \frac{\text{Total assets}}{\text{Shareholders' equity}} \qquad (25)$$

[28] As a long-term average, about 2 percent of U.S. publicly traded companies issue new equity in a given year, which corresponds to a secondary equity issue once every 50 years, on average. Businesses may be rationed in their access to secondary issues of equity because of the costs associated with informational asymmetries between management and the public. Because management has more information on the future cash flows of the company than the general public, and equity is an ownership claim to those cash flows, the public may react to additional equity issuance as possibly motivated by an intent to "share (future) misery" rather than "share (future) wealth."

The first term is the company's profit margin. A higher profit margin will result in a higher ROE. The second term measures total asset turnover, which is the company's efficiency. A turnover of one indicates that a company generates $1 in sales for every $1 invested in assets. A higher turnover will result in higher ROE. The last term is the equity multiplier, which measures the extent of leverage, as noted earlier. This relationship is widely known as the DuPont model or analysis of ROE. Although ROE can be analyzed further using a five-way analysis, the three-way analysis will provide insight into the determinants of ROE that are pertinent to our understanding of the growth rate. By combining Equations 22 and 25, it shows that the dividend growth rate is equal to the retention rate multiplied by ROE:

$$g = \frac{\text{Net income} - \text{Dividends}}{\text{Net income}} \times \frac{\text{Net income}}{\text{Sales}} \times \frac{\text{Sales}}{\text{Total assets}}$$
$$\times \frac{\text{Total assets}}{\text{Shareholders' equity}} \tag{26}$$

This expansion of the sustainable growth expression has been called the PRAT model (Higgins 2007). Growth is a function of profit margin (P), retention rate (R), asset turnover (A), and financial leverage (T). The profit margin and asset turnover determine ROA. The other two factors, the retention rate and financial leverage, reflect the company's financial policies. So, the growth rate in dividends can be viewed as determined by the company's ROA and financial policies. Analysts may use Equation 26 to forecast a company's dividend growth rate in the mature growth phase.

Theoretically, the sustainable growth rate expression and this expansion of it based on the DuPont decomposition of ROE hold exactly only when ROE is calculated using beginning-of-period shareholders' equity, as illustrated in Example 22. Such calculation assumes that retained earnings are not available for reinvestment until the end of the period. Analysts and financial databases more frequently prefer to use average total assets in calculating ROE and, practically, DuPont analysis is frequently performed using that definition.[29] The example below illustrates the logic behind this equation.

EXAMPLE 23

ROA, Financial Policies, and the Dividend Growth Rate

Baggai Enterprises has an ROA of 10 percent, retains 30 percent of earnings, and has an equity multiplier of 1.25. Mondale Enterprises also has an ROA of 10 percent, but it retains two-thirds of earnings and has an equity multiplier of 2.00.

1. What are the sustainable dividend growth rates for (A) Baggai Enterprises and (B) Mondale Enterprises?

2. Identify the drivers of the difference in the sustainable growth rates of Baggai Enterprises and Mondale Enterprises.

---

[29] See Robinson, van Greuning, Henry, and Broihahn, "Financial Analysis Techniques," (CFA Institute, 2006).

> **Solution to 1:**
> **A.** Baggai's dividend growth rate should be $g = 0.30 \times 10\% \times 1.25 = 3.75\%$.
> **B.** Mondale's dividend growth rate should be $g = (2/3) \times 10\% \times 2.00 = 13.33\%$.
>
> **Solution to 2:** Because Mondale has the higher retention rate and higher financial leverage, its dividend growth rate is much higher.

If growth is being forecast for the next five years, an analyst should use the expectations of the four factors driving growth during this five-year period. If growth is being forecast into perpetuity, an analyst should use very long-term forecasts for these variables.

To illustrate the calculation and implications of the sustainable growth rate using the expression for ROE given by the DuPont formula, assume the growth rate is $g = b \times ROE = 0.60 \,(15 \text{ percent}) = 9$ percent. The ROE of 15 percent was based on a profit margin of 5 percent, an asset turnover of 2.0, and an equity multiplier of 1.5. Given fixed ratios of sales-to-assets and assets-to-equity, sales, assets, and debt will also be growing at 9 percent. Because dividends are fixed at 40 percent of income, dividends will grow at the same rate as income, or 9 percent. If the company increases dividends faster than 9 percent, this growth rate would not be sustainable using internally generated funds. Earning retentions would be reduced, and the company would not be able to finance the assets required for sales growth without external financing.

An analyst should be careful in projecting historical financial ratios into the future when using this analysis. Although a company may have grown at 25 percent a year for the last five years, this rate of growth is probably not sustainable indefinitely. Abnormally high ROEs, which may have driven that growth, are unlikely to persist indefinitely because of competitive forces and possibly other reasons, such as adverse changes in technology or demand. In the following example, an above average terminal growth rate is plausibly forecasted because the company has positioned itself in businesses that may have relatively high margins on an ongoing basis.

EXAMPLE 24

Forecasting Growth with the PRAT Formula

International Business Machines (NYSE: IBM), which currently pays a dividend of $1.60 per share, has been the subject of two other examples in this reading. In one example, an analyst estimated IBM's mature phase growth rate at 10.2 percent, based on its mature phase ROE exactly equaling its estimated required return on equity of 12 percent. Another estimate can be made using the DuPont decomposition of ROE.

An analysis of IBM's ROE for the past four years is shown in Exhibit 12. During the period shown, EPS grew at a compound annual rate of 11.8 percent. IBM's retention ratio is 0.85.

EXHIBIT 12		IBM Corporation		
Year	ROE (%)	Profit Margin (%)	Asset Turnover	Financial Leverage
2006	30.6 =	10.30	× 0.821	× 3.62
2005	24.7 =	8.77	× 0.880	× 3.20
2004	29.3 =	8.77	× 0.910	× 3.67
2003	30.1 =	8.54	× 0.940	× 3.75

IBM achieved relatively high ROEs in the most recent period, both compared to the historical median ROE of U.S. businesses of 12.2 percent and compared to variously defined comparison groups. Take IBM's formal Global Industry Classification System (GICS) peer group, "computer hardware — large system vendors." Making a pretax comparison to avoid the factor of differing tax effective rates, IBM's pretax profit margin of 14.6 percent for 2006 exceeded the GICS peer group mean of about 7 percent.[30] Suppose the analyst accepts IBM's asset turnover and financial leverage performance as shown in Exhibit 12 as relevant to IBM's performance in its mature phase, but believes that IBM's recent superiority in profit margin in comparison to peers will be much reduced in the mature phase. The analyst forecasts a peer mean pretax profit margin of 6 percent during IBM's mature phase. With its strategy of searching for high-margined growth and its strong ability to compete in integrated hardware–software solutions for businesses, the analyst forecasts a long-run pretax profit margin of 6.5 percent for IBM, equal to a profit margin (after tax) of about 4.6 percent based on an effective tax rate of about 30 percent. Based on an asset turnover ratio of 0.8 and financial leverage of 3.6 (close to the mean values in Exhibit 12), but using a profit margin estimate of 4.6, a forecast of ROE in the maturity phase is (4.6 percent)(0.8)(3.6) = 13.2 percent. Therefore, based on this analysis, the estimate of the sustainable growth rate for IBM would be $g = (0.85)(13.2 \text{ percent}) = 11.2 \text{ percent}$.

6.3 Financial Models and Dividends

Analysts can also forecast dividends by building more complex models of the company's total operating and financial environment. Because there can be so many aspects to such a model, a spreadsheet is used to build pro forma income statements and balance sheets. The company's ability to pay dividends in the future can be predicted using one of these models. The example below shows the dividends that a highly profitable and rapidly growing company can pay when its growth rates and profit margins decline because of increasing competition over time.

---

[30] Based on Standard & Poor's Stock Report of 6 October 2007.

EXAMPLE 25

A Spreadsheet Model for Forecasting Dividends

An analyst is preparing a forecast of dividends for Hoshino Distributors for the next five years. He uses a spreadsheet model with the following assumptions:

- ► Sales are $100 million in Year 1. They grow by 20 percent in Year 2, 15 percent in Year 3, and 10 percent in Years 4 and 5.

- ► Operating profits (earnings before interest and taxes, or EBIT) are 20 percent of sales in Years 1 and 2, 18 percent of sales in Year 3, and 16 percent of sales in Years 4 and 5.

- ► Interest expenses are 10 percent of total debt for the current year.

- ► The income tax rate is 40 percent.

- ► Hoshino pays out 20 percent of earnings in dividends in Years 1 and 2, 30 percent in Year 3, 40 percent in Year 4, and 50 percent in Year 5.

- ► Retained earnings are added to equity in the next year.

- ► Total assets are 80 percent of the current year's sales in all years.

- ► In Year 1, debt is $40 million and shareholders' equity is $40 million. Debt equals total assets minus shareholders' equity. Shareholders' equity will equal the previous year's shareholders' equity plus the addition to retained earnings from the previous year.

- ► Hoshino has 4 million shares outstanding.

- ► The required return on equity is 15 percent.

- ► The value of the company at the end of Year 5 is expected to be 10.0 times earnings.

The analyst wants to estimate the current value per share of Hoshino. Exhibit 13 adheres to the modeling assumptions above. Total dividends and earnings are found at the bottom of the income statement.

| EXHIBIT 13 | Hoshino Distributors Pro Forma Financial Statements (in Millions) |

	Year 1	Year 2	Year 3	Year 4	Year 5
Income statement					
Sales	$100.00	$120.00	$138.00	$151.80	$166.98
EBIT	20.00	24.00	24.84	24.29	26.72
Interest	4.00	4.83	5.35	5.64	6.18
EBT	16.00	19.17	19.49	18.65	20.54
Taxes	6.40	7.67	7.80	7.46	8.22
Net income	9.60	11.50	11.69	11.19	12.32
Dividends	1.92	2.30	3.51	4.48	6.16

(Exhibit continued on next page . . .)

EXHIBIT 13 (continued)

	Year 1	Year 2	Year 3	Year 4	Year 5
Balance sheet					
Total assets	$80.00	$96.00	$110.40	$121.44	$133.58
Total debt	40.00	48.32	53.52	56.38	61.81
Equity	40.00	47.68	56.88	65.06	71.77

Dividing the total dividends by the number of outstanding shares gives the dividend per share for each year shown below. The present value of each dividend, discounted at 15 percent, is also shown.

	Year 1	Year 2	Year 3	Year 4	Year 5	Total
DPS	$0.480	$0.575	$0.877	$1.120	$1.540	$4.59
PV	0.417	0.435	0.577	0.640	0.766	2.84

The earnings per share in Year 5 are $12.32 million divided by 4 million shares, or $3.08 per share. Given a P/E of 10, the market price in Year 5 is predicted to be $30.80. Discounted at 15 percent, the required return on equity by assumption, the present value of this price is $15.31. Adding the present values of the five dividends, which sum to $2.84, gives a total stock value today of $18.15 per share.

SUMMARY

This reading provided an overview of DCF models of valuation, discussed the estimation of a stock's required rate of return, and presented in detail the dividend discount model.

▶ In DCF models, the value of any asset is the present value of its (expected) future cash flows

$$V_0 = \sum_{t=1}^{n} \frac{CF_t}{(1 + r)^t}$$

where V_0 is the value of the asset as of $t = 0$ (today), CF_t is the (expected) cash flow at time t, and r is the discount rate or required rate of return. For infinitely lived assets such as common stocks, n runs to infinity.

▶ Several alternative streams of expected cash flows can be used to value equities, including dividends, free cash flow, and residual income. A discounted dividend approach is most suitable for dividend-paying stocks in which the company has a discernible dividend policy that has an understandable relationship to the company's profitability, and the investor has a noncontrol (minority ownership) perspective.

▶ The free cash flow approach (FCFF or FCFE) might be appropriate when the company does not pay dividends, dividends differ substantially from FCFE, free cash flows align with profitability, or the investor takes a control (majority ownership) perspective.

▶ The residual income approach can be useful when the company does not pay dividends (as an alternative to a FCF approach) or free cash flow is negative.

▶ The DDM with a single holding period gives stock value as

$$V_0 = \frac{D_1}{(1 + r)^1} + \frac{P_1}{(1 + r)^1} = \frac{D_1 + P_1}{(1 + r)^1}$$

where D_1 is the expected dividend at time 1 and V_0 is the stock's (expected) value at time 0. Assuming that V_0 is equal to today's market price, P_0, the expected holding-period return is

$$r = \frac{D_1 + P_1}{P_0} - 1 = \frac{D_1}{P_0} + \frac{P_1 - P_0}{P_0}$$

▶ The expression for the DDM for any given finite holding period n and the general expression for the DDM are, respectively,

$$V_0 = \sum_{t=1}^{n} \frac{D_t}{(1 + r)^t} + \frac{P_n}{(1 + r)^n} \text{ and } V_0 = \sum_{t=1}^{\infty} \frac{D_t}{(1 + r)^t}$$

▶ There are two main approaches to the problem of forecasting dividends. First, an analyst can assign the entire stream of expected future dividends to one of several stylized growth patterns. Second, an analyst can forecast a finite number of dividends individually up to a terminal point and value the remaining dividends either by assigning them to a stylized growth pattern or by forecasting share price as of the terminal point of the dividend forecasts.

▶ The Gordon growth model assumes that dividends grow at a constant rate g forever, so that $D_t = D_{t-1}(1 + g)$. The dividend stream in the Gordon growth model has a value of

$$V_0 = \frac{D_0(1 + g)}{r - g}, \text{ or } V_0 = \frac{D_1}{r - g} \text{ where } r > g$$

▶ The value of noncallable fixed-rate perpetual preferred stock is $V_0 = D/r$, where D is the stock's (constant) annual dividend.

▶ Assuming that price equals value, the Gordon growth model estimate of a stock's expected rate of return is

$$r = \frac{D_0(1 + g)}{P_0} + g = \frac{D_1}{P_0} + g$$

▶ Given an estimate of the next-period dividend and the stock's required rate of return, the Gordon growth model can be used to estimate the dividend growth rate implied by the current market price (making a constant growth rate assumption).

▶ The present value of growth opportunities (PVGO) is the part of a stock's total value, V_0, that comes from profitable future growth opportunities in contrast to the value associated with assets already in place. The relationship is $V_0 = E_1/r + \text{PVGO}$, where E_1/r is defined as the no-growth value per share.

▶ The leading price-to-earnings ratio (P_0/E_1) and the trailing price-to-earnings ratio (P_0/E_0) can be expressed in terms of the Gordon growth model as, respectively,

$$\frac{P_0}{E_1} = \frac{D_1/E_1}{r - g} = \frac{1 - b}{r - g} \text{ and } \frac{P_0}{E_0} = \frac{D_0(1 + g)/E_0}{r - g} = \frac{(1 - b)(1 + g)}{r - g}$$

The above expressions give a stock's justified price-to-earnings ratio based on forecasts of fundamentals (given that the Gordon growth model is appropriate).

▶ The Gordon growth model may be useful for valuing broad-based equity indices and the stock of businesses with earnings that are expected to grow at a stable rate comparable to or lower than the nominal growth rate of the economy.

▶ Gordon growth model values are very sensitive to the assumed growth rate and required rate of return.

▶ For many companies, growth falls into phases. In the growth phase, a company enjoys an abnormally high growth rate in earnings per share, called supernormal growth. In the transition phase, earnings growth slows. In the mature phase, the company reaches an equilibrium in which such factors as earnings growth and the return on equity stabilize at levels that can be sustained long term. Analysts often apply multistage DCF models to value the stock of a company with multistage growth prospects.

▶ The two-stage dividend discount model assumes different growth rates in Stage 1 and Stage 2

$$V_0 = \sum_{t=1}^{n} \frac{D_0(1 + g_S)^t}{(1 + r)^t} + \frac{D_0(1 + g_S)^n(1 + g_L)}{(1 + r)^n(r - g_L)}$$

where g_S is the expected dividend growth rate in the first period and g_L is the expected growth rate in the second period.

▶ The terminal stock value, V_n, is sometimes found with the Gordon growth model or with some other method, such as applying a P/E multiplier to forecasted EPS as of the terminal date.

▶ The H-model assumes that the dividend growth rate declines linearly from a high supernormal rate to the normal growth rate during Stage 1, and then grows at a constant normal growth rate thereafter:

$$V_0 = \frac{D_0(1 + g_L)}{r - g_L} + \frac{D_0 H(g_S - g_L)}{r - g_L} = \frac{D_0(1 + g_L) + D_0 H(g_S - g_L)}{r - g_L}$$

▶ There are two basic three-stage models. In one version, the growth rate in the middle stage is constant. In the second version, the growth rate declines linearly in Stage 2 and becomes constant and normal in Stage 3.

▶ Spreadsheet models are very flexible, providing the analyst with the ability to value any pattern of expected dividends.

▶ In addition to valuing equities, the IRR of a DDM, assuming assets are correctly priced in the marketplace, has been used to estimate required returns. For simpler models (such as the one-period model, the Gordon growth model, and the H-model), well-known formulas may be used to calculate these rates of return. For many dividend streams, however, the rate of return must be found by trial and error, producing a discount rate that equates the present value of the forecasted dividend stream to the current market price.

▶ Multistage DDM models can accommodate a wide variety of patterns of expected dividends. Even though such models may use stylized assumptions about growth, they can provide useful approximations.

▶ Dividend growth rates can be obtained from analyst forecasts, statistical forecasting models, or company fundamentals. The sustainable growth rate depends on the ROE and the earnings retention rate, b: $g = b \times$ ROE. This expression can be expanded further, using the DuPont formula, as

$$g = \frac{\text{Net income} - \text{Dividends}}{\text{Net income}} \times \frac{\text{Net income}}{\text{Sales}}$$
$$\times \frac{\text{Sales}}{\text{Total assets}} \times \frac{\text{Total assets}}{\text{Shareholders' equity}}$$

PRACTICE PROBLEMS FOR READING 39

1. Amy Tanner is an analyst for a U.S. pension fund. Her supervisor has asked her to value the stocks of General Electric (NYSE: GE) and General Motors (NYSE: GM). Tanner wants to evaluate the appropriateness of the dividend discount model (DDM) for valuing GE and GM and has compiled the following data for the two companies for 2000 through 2007.

Year	GE			GM		
	EPS ($)	DPS ($)	Payout Ratio	EPS ($)	DPS ($)	Payout Ratio
2007	2.17	1.15	0.53	−68.45	1.00	−0.01
2006	1.99	1.03	0.52	−3.50	1.00	−0.29
2005	1.76	0.91	0.52	−18.50	2.00	−0.11
2004	1.61	0.82	0.51	4.94	2.00	0.40
2003	1.55	0.77	0.50	5.03	2.00	0.40
2002	1.51	0.73	0.48	3.35	2.00	0.60
2001	1.41	0.66	0.47	1.77	2.00	1.13
2000	1.27	0.57	0.45	6.68	2.00	0.30

Source: Compustat.

For each of the stocks, explain whether the DDM is appropriate for valuing the stock.

2. Vincent Nguyen, an analyst, is examining the stock of British Airways (London Stock Exchange: BAY) as of the beginning of 2008. He notices that the consensus forecast by analysts is that the stock will pay a £4 dividend per share in 2009 (based on 21 analysts) and a £5 dividend in 2010 (based on 10 analysts). Nguyen expects the price of the stock at the end of 2010 to be £250. He has estimated that the required rate of return on the stock is 11 percent. Assume all dividends are paid at the end of the year.

   A. Using the DDM, estimate the value of BAY stock at the end of 2009.

   B. Using the DDM, estimate the value of BAY stock at the end of 2008.

3. Justin Owens is an analyst for an equity mutual fund that invests in British stocks. At the beginning of 2008, Owens is examining domestic stocks for possible inclusion in the fund. One of the stocks that he is analyzing is British Sky Broadcasting Group (London Stock Exchange: BSY). The stock has paid dividends per share of £9, £12.20, and £15.50 at the end of 2005, 2006, and 2007, respectively. The consensus forecast by analysts is that the stock will pay a dividend per share of £18.66 at the end of 2008 (based on 19 analysts) and £20.20 at the end of 2009 (based on 17 analysts). Owens has estimated that the required rate of return on the stock is 11 percent.

    A. Compare the compound annual growth rate in dividends from 2005 to 2007 inclusive (i.e., from a beginning level of £9 to an ending level of £15.50) with the consensus predicted compound annual growth rate in dividends from 2007 to 2009, inclusive.

    B. Owens believes that BSY has matured such that the dividend growth rate will be constant going forward at half the consensus compound annual growth rate from 2007 to 2009, inclusive, computed in Part A. Using the growth rate forecast of Owens as the constant growth rate from 2007 onwards, estimate the value of the stock as of the end of 2007 given an 11 percent required rate of return on equity.

    C. State the relationship between estimated value and r and estimated value and g.

4. During the period 1960–2007, earnings of the S&P 500 Index companies have increased at an average rate of 8.18 percent per year and the dividends paid have increased at an average rate of 5.9 percent per year. Assume that:

    ▶ Dividends will continue to grow at the 1960–2007 rate.

    ▶ The required return on the index is 8 percent.

    ▶ Companies in the S&P 500 Index collectively paid $246.6 billion in dividends in 2007.

Estimate the aggregate value of the S&P 500 Index component companies at the beginning of 2008 using the Gordon growth model.

5. Great Plains Energy is a public utility holding company that listed its 4.5 percent cumulative perpetual preferred stock series E on the NYSE Euronext in March 1952 (Ticker: GXPPrE). The par value of the preferred stock is $100. If the required rate of return on this stock is 5.6 percent, estimate the value of the stock.

6. German Resources is involved in coal mining. The company is currently profitable and is expected to pay a dividend of €4 per share next year. The company has suspended exploration, however, and because its current mature operations exhaust the existing mines, you expect that the dividends paid by the company will decline forever at an 8 percent rate. The required return on German Resource's stock is 11 percent. Using the DDM, estimate the value of the stock.

7. Maspeth Robotics shares are currently selling for €24 and have paid a dividend of €1 per share for the most recent year. The following additional information is given:

   ▶ The risk-free rate is 4 percent;

   ▶ The shares have an estimated beta of 1.2; and

   ▶ The equity risk premium is estimated at 5 percent.

   Based on the above information, determine the constant dividend growth rate that would be required to justify the market price of €24.

8. You believe the Gordon (constant) growth model is appropriate to value the stock of Reliable Electric Corp. The company had an EPS of $2 in 2008. The retention ratio is 0.60. The company is expected to earn an ROE of 14 percent on its investments and the required rate of return is 11 percent. Assume that all dividends are paid at the end of the year.

   A. Calculate the company's sustainable growth rate.

   B. Estimate the value of the company's stock at the beginning of 2009.

   C. Calculate the present value of growth opportunities.

   D. Determine the fraction of the company's value which comes from its growth opportunities.

9. Stellar Baking Company in Australia has a trailing P/E of 14. Analysts predict that Stellar's dividends will continue to grow at its recent rate of 4.5 percent per year into the indefinite future. Given a current dividend and EPS of A$0.7 per share and A$2.00 per share, respectively, and a required rate of return on equity of 8 percent, determine whether Stellar Baking Company is undervalued, fairly valued, or overvalued. Justify your answer.

10. Mohan Gupta is the portfolio manager of an India-based equity fund. He is analyzing the value of Tata Chemicals Ltd. (Bombay Stock Exchange: TATACHEM). Tata Chemicals is India's leading manufacturer of inorganic chemicals, and also manufactures fertilizers and food additives. Gupta has concluded that the DDM is appropriate to value Tata Chemicals.

    During the last five years (fiscal year ending 31 March 2004 to fiscal year ending 31 March 2008), the company has paid dividends per share of Rs. 5.50, 6.50, 7.00, 8.00, and 9.00, respectively. These dividends suggest an average annual growth rate in DPS of just above 13 percent. Gupta has decided to use a three-stage DDM with a linearly declining growth rate in Stage 2. He considers Tata Chemicals to be an average growth company, and estimates Stage 1 (the growth stage) to be 6 years and Stage 2 (the transition stage) to be 10 years. He estimates the growth rate to be 14 percent in Stage 1 and 10 percent in Stage 3. Gupta has estimated the required return on equity for Tata Chemicals to be 16 percent. Estimate the current value of the stock.

11. You are analyzing the stock of Ansell Limited (Australian Stock Exchange: ANN), a healthcare company, as of late June 2008. The stock price is A$9.74. The company's dividend per share for the fiscal year ending 30 June 2008 was A$0.27. You expect the dividend to increase by 10 percent for the next three years and then increase by 8 percent per year forever. You estimate the required return on equity of Ansell Limited to be 12 percent.

    A. Estimate the value of ANN using a two-stage dividend discount model.

    B. Judge whether ANN is undervalued, fairly valued, or overvalued.

12. Sime Natural Cosmetics Ltd. has a dividend yield of 2 percent based on the current dividend and a mature phase dividend growth rate of 5 percent a year. The current dividend growth rate is 10 percent a year, but the growth rate is expected to decline linearly to its mature phase value during the next six years.

A. If Sime Natural Cosmetics is fairly priced in the marketplace, what is the expected rate of return on its shares?

B. If Sime were in its mature growth phase right now, would its expected return be higher or lower, holding all other facts constant?

13. Kazuo Uto is analyzing the stock of Brother Industries, Ltd. (Tokyo Stock Exchange: 64480), a diversified Japanese company that produces a wide variety of products. Brother distributes its products under its own name and under original-equipment manufacturer agreements with other companies. Uto has concluded that a multistage DDM is appropriate to value the stock of Brother Industries and the company will reach a mature stage in four years. The ROE of the company has declined from 16.7 percent in the fiscal year ending in 2004 to 12.7 percent in the fiscal year ending in 2008. The dividend payout ratio has increased from 11.5 percent in 2004 to 22.3 percent in 2008. Uto has estimated that in the mature phase Brother's ROE will be 11 percent, which is approximately equal to estimated required return on equity. He has also estimated that the payout ratio in the mature phase will be 40 percent, which is significantly greater than its payout ratio in 2008 but less than the average payout of about 50 percent for Japanese companies.

A. Calculate the sustainable growth rate for Brother in the mature phase.

B. With reference to the formula for the sustainable growth rate, a colleague of Uto asserts that the greater the earnings retention ratio, the greater the sustainable growth rate because g is a positive function of b. The colleague argues that Brother should decrease payout ratio. Explain the flaw in that argument.

14. An analyst following Chevron Corp. (NYSE Euronext: CVX) wants to estimate the sustainable growth rate for the company by using the PRAT model. For this purpose, the analyst has compiled the data in the following table. Assets and equity values are for the end of the year; the analyst uses averages of beginning and ending balance sheet values in computing ratios based on total assets and shareholders' equity. For example average total assets for 2007 would be computed as $(148,786 + 132,628)/2 = \$140,707$. *Note*: All numbers except for EPS and DPS are in $ millions.

Item	2007	2006	2005	2004
Net income	$18,688	$17,138	$14,099	$13,328
Sales	214,091	204,892	193,641	150,865
Total assets	148,786	132,628	125,833	93,208
Shareholders' equity	77,088	68,935	62,676	45,230
EPS	8.77	7.80	6.54	6.28
DPS	2.26	2.01	1.75	1.53

Source: Financial statements from Chevron's website.

A. Compute the average value of each PRAT component during 2005–2007.

B. Using the overall mean value of the average component values calculated in Part A, estimate the sustainable growth rate for Chevron.

C. Judge whether Chevron has reached a mature growth stage.

15. Casey Hyunh is trying to value the stock of Resources Limited. To easily see how a change in one or more of her assumptions affects the estimated value of the stock, she is using a spreadsheet model. The model has projections for the next four years based on the following assumptions.

► Sales will be $300 million in Year 1.

► Sales will grow at 15 percent in Years 2 and 3 and 10 percent in Year 4.

► Operating profits (EBIT) will be 17 percent of sales in each year.

► Interest expense will be $10 million per year.

► Income tax rate is 30 percent.

► Earnings retention ratio would stay at 0.60.

► The per-share dividend growth rate will be constant from Year 4 forward and this final growth rate will be 200 basis points less than the growth rate from Year 3 to Year 4.

The company has 10 million shares outstanding. Hyunh has estimated the required return on Resources' stock to be 13 percent.

A. Estimate the value of the stock at the end of Year 4 based on the above assumptions.

B. Estimate the current value of the stock using the above assumptions.

C. Hyunh is wondering how a change in the projected sales growth rate would affect the estimated value. Estimate the current value of the stock if the sales growth rate in Year 3 is 10 percent instead of 15 percent.

The following information relates to Questions 16–21

Jacob Daniel is the chief investment officer at a U.S. pension fund sponsor, and Steven Rae is an analyst for the pension fund who follows consumer/noncyclical stocks. At the beginning of 2009, Daniel asks Rae to value the equity of Tasty Foods Company for its possible inclusion in the list of approved investments. Tasty Foods Company is involved in the production of frozen foods that are sold under its own brand name to retailers.

Rae is considering if a dividend discount model would be appropriate for valuing Tasty Foods. He has compiled the information in the following table for the company's EPS and DPS during the last five years. The quarterly dividends paid by the company have been added to arrive at the annual dividends. Rae has also computed the dividend payout ratio for each year as DPS/EPS and the growth rates in EPS and DPS.

Year	EPS ($)	DPS ($)	Payout Ratio	Growth in EPS (%)	Growth in DPS (%)
2008	2.12	0.59	0.278	2.9	3.5
2007	2.06	0.57	0.277	2.5	5.6
2006	2.01	0.54	0.269	6.3	5.9
2005	1.89	0.51	0.270	6.2	6.3
2004	1.78	0.48	0.270		

Rae notes that the EPS of the company has been increasing at an average rate of 4.48 percent per year. The dividend payout ratio has remained fairly stable and dividends have increased at an average rate of 5.30 percent. In view of a history of dividend payments by the company and the understandable relationship dividend policy bears to the company's earnings, Rae concludes that the DDM is appropriate to value the equity of Tasty Foods. Further, he expects the moderate growth rate of the company to persist and decides to use the Gordon growth model.

Rae uses the CAPM to compute the return on equity. He uses the annual yield of 4 percent on the 10-year Treasury bond as the risk-free return. He estimates the expected U.S. equity risk premium, with the S&P 500 Index used as a proxy for the market, to be 6.5 percent per year. The estimated beta of Tasty Foods against the S&P 500 Index is 1.10. Accordingly, Rae's estimate for the required return on equity for Tasty Foods is $0.04 + 1.10(0.065) = 0.1115$ or 11.15 percent.

Using the past growth rate in dividends of 5.30 percent as his estimate of the future growth rate in dividends, Rae computes the value of Tasty Foods stock. He shows his analysis to Alex Renteria, his colleague at the pension fund who specializes in the frozen foods industry. Renteria concurs with the valuation approach used by Rae but disagrees with the future growth rate he used. Renteria believes that the stock's current price of $8.42 is the fair value of the stock.

16. Which of the following is *closest* to Rae's estimate of the stock's value?

   A. $10.08.

   B. $10.54.

   C. $10.62.

17. What is the stock's justified trailing P/E based on the stock's value estimated by Rae?

A. 5.01.

B. 5.24.

C. 5.27.

18. Rae considers a security trading within a band of ±10 percent of his estimate of intrinsic value to be within a "fair value range." By that criterion, the stock of Tasty Foods is:

A. undervalued.

B. fairly valued.

C. overvalued.

19. The beta of Tasty Foods stock of 1.10 used by Rae in computing the required return on equity was based on monthly returns for the last 10 years. If Rae uses daily returns for the last 5 years, the beta estimate is 1.25. If a beta of 1.25 is used, what would be Rae's estimate of the value of the stock of Tasty Foods?

A. $8.64.

B. $9.10.

C. $20.13.

20. Alex Renteria has suggested that the market price of Tasty Foods stock is its fair value. What is the implied growth rate of dividends given the stock's market price? Use the required return on equity based on a beta of 1.10.

A. 3.87%.

B. 5.30%.

C. 12.1%.

21. If Alex Renteria is correct that the current price of Tasty Foods stock is its fair value, what is expected capital gains yield on the stock?

A. 3.87%.

B. 4.25%.

C. 5.30%.

The following information relates to Questions 22–27

Assorted Fund, a U.K.-based globally diversified equity mutual fund, is considering adding Talisman Energy Inc. (Toronto Stock Exchange: TLM) to its portfolio. Talisman is an independent upstream oil and gas company headquartered in Calgary, Canada. It is one of the largest oil and gas companies in Canada and has operations in several countries. Brian Dobson, an analyst at the mutual fund, has been assigned the task of estimating a fair value of Talisman. Dobson is aware of several approaches that could be used for this purpose. After carefully considering the characteristics of the company and its competitors, he believes the company will have extraordinary growth for the next few years and normal growth thereafter. So, he has concluded that a two-stage DDM is the most appropriate for valuing the stock.

Talisman pays semi-annual dividends. The total dividends during 2006, 2007, and 2008 have been C$0.114, C$0.15, and C$0.175, respectively. These imply a growth rate of 32 percent in 2007 and 17 percent in 2008. Dobson believes that the growth rate will be 14 percent in the next year. He has estimated that the first stage will include the next eight years.

Dobson is using the CAPM to estimate the required return on equity for Talisman. He has estimated that the beta of Talisman, as measured against the S&P/TSX Composite Index (formerly TSE 300 Composite Index), is 0.84. The Canadian risk-free rate, as measured by the annual yield on the 10-year government bond, is 4.1 percent. The equity risk premium for the Canadian market is estimated at 5.5 percent. Based on these data, Dobson has estimated that the required return on Talisman stock is $0.041 + 0.84(0.055) = 0.0872$ or 8.72 percent. Dobson is doing the analysis in January 2009 and the stock price at that time is C\$17.

Dobson realizes that even within the two-stage DDM, there could be some variations in the approach. He would like to explore how these variations affect the valuation of the stock. Specifically, he wants to estimate the value of the stock for each of the following approaches separately.

I. The dividend growth rate will be 14 percent throughout the first stage of eight years. The dividend growth rate thereafter will be 7 percent.

II. Instead of using the estimated stable growth rate of 7 percent in the second stage, Dobson wants to use his estimate that eight years later Talisman's stock will be worth 17 times its earnings per share (trailing P/E of 17). He expects that the earnings retention ratio at that time will be 0.70.

III. In contrast to the first approach above in which the growth rate declines abruptly from 14 percent in the eighth year to 7 percent in the ninth, the growth rate would decline linearly from 14 percent in the first year to 7 percent in the ninth.

22. What is the terminal value of the stock based on the first approach?
   A. C\$17.65.
   B. C\$31.06.
   C. C\$33.09.

23. In the first approach, what proportion of the total value of the stock is represented by the value of second stage?
   A. 0.10.
   B. 0.52.
   C. 0.90.

24. What is the terminal value of the stock based on the second approach (earnings multiple)?
   A. C\$12.12.
   B. C\$28.29.
   C. C\$33.09.

25. What is the current value of the stock based on the second approach?
   A. C\$16.24.
   B. C\$17.65.
   C. C\$28.29.

26. Based on the third approach (the H-model), the stock is:
   A. undervalued.
   B. fairly valued.
   C. overvalued.

27. Dobson is wondering what the consequences would be if the duration of the first stage was assumed to be 11 years instead of 8, with all the other assumptions/estimates remaining the same. Considering this change, which of the following is true?

   A. In the second approach, the proportion of the total value of the stock represented by the second stage would not change.

   B. The total value estimated using the third approach would increase.

   C. Using this new assumption and the first approach will lead Dobson to conclude that the stock is overvalued.

SOLUTIONS FOR READING 39

1. Both companies are dividend-paying and have an established history of dividend payments that can provide some help in forecasting future dividends. In the case of GE, EPS has been increasing steadily from 2000 to 2007 and DPS has shown increases consistent with this trend. For example, EPS increased by $0.23 from 2005 to 2006 and DPS increased by $0.12. Then EPS increased by $0.18 from 2006 to 2007 and DPS increased by $0.12. The payout ratios have also been increasing gradually during the period examined. Dividends appear to be at least somewhat predictable given earnings forecasts. Overall, the DDM seems to be an appropriate model for valuing GE. In the case of GM, however, dividends do not have a discernable relationship to the company's profitability. For example, DPS was $2 in 2000 when GM was doing well and had an EPS of $6.68, but DPS continued to be $2 in 2005 when EPS was –$18.50. The company continued to pay dividends in 2007, which was the third consecutive year of a negative EPS: in 2007, EPS had fallen to –$68.45. The lack of a clear relationship of dividends to operating results suggests that the DDM is not appropriate for valuing GM.

2. **A.** Discounting the expected dividend of £5 in 2010 and the expected stock price of £250 at the end of 2010,

$$V_1 = \frac{D_2 + P_2}{(1 + r)^1} = \frac{5 + 250}{(1 + 0.11)^1} = \frac{255}{1.11} = 229.73$$

   B. One way to answer this question is to use a DDM for two holding periods. Accordingly, discounting the expected dividend of £5 in 2010 and the expected stock price of £250 at the end of 2010 for two periods, and discounting the expected dividend of £4 in 2009 for one period,

$$V_0 = \frac{D_1}{(1 + r)^1} + \frac{D_2 + P_2}{(1 + r)^2} + \frac{4}{(1 + 0.11)^1} + \frac{5 + 250}{(1 + 0.11)^2}$$

$$= \frac{4}{1.11} + \frac{255}{1.11^2} = 3.60 + 206.96 = 210.57$$

   based on full precision, or £210.56 with intermediate rounding. Another way to answer this question is to use the answer to Part A and a DDM for one holding period. Accordingly, discounting the expected dividend of £4 in 2009 and the expected stock price of £229.73 at the end of 2009 for one period,

$$V_0 = \frac{D_1 + V_1}{(1 + r)^1} = \frac{4 + 229.73}{(1 + 0.11)^1} = \frac{233.73}{1.11} = 210.57$$

3. **A.** The growth rate from 2005 to 2007 is $(15.50/9)^{1/2} - 1 = 0.312$ or 31.2 percent. The consensus predicted growth rate from 2007 to 2009 is $(20.20/15.50)^{1/2} - 1 = 0.142$ or 14.2 percent. Thus, the consensus forecast is for a sharp decline in the dividend growth rate for 2008 to 2009.

B. Half of the growth rate computed in Part A = 14.2/2 = 7.1 percent. Based on this growth rate, D_1 = £15.50(1.071) = £16.60, rounded. Using the Gordon growth model,

$$V_0 = \frac{D_1}{r - g} = \frac{16.60}{0.11 - 0.071} = 425.64$$

or 425.65 based on not rounding the numerator.

C. The estimated value of BSY would decrease as r increases and increase as g increases, all else equal.

4. Applying the Gordon growth model with the assumed 5.9 percent dividend growth rate results in an estimated value of $12,435.7 billion for the S&P 500 Index.

$$V_0 = \frac{D_1}{r - g} = \frac{246.6(1 + 0.059)}{0.08 - 0.059} = \$12,435.7 \text{ billion}$$

5. The preferred stock pays 4.5 percent of $100 or $4.50 in annual dividends. The dividend is fixed; so g = 0. Therefore, using the Gordon growth model with zero growth,

$$V_0 = \frac{D_1}{g} = \frac{4.50}{0.056} = \$80.36$$

6. This problem can be addressed using the Gordon growth model with constant expected negative growth. The estimated value of the stock is

$$V_0 = \frac{D_1}{r - g} = \frac{4}{0.11 - (-0.08)} = 21.05$$

7. Using the CAPM, the required rate of return on Maspeth Robotics shares is 4 percent + 1.2(5%) = 10 percent. Therefore, the constant dividend growth rate implied by a market price of €24 is 5.6 percent as shown below:

$$V_0 = \frac{D_0(1 + g)}{r - g}$$

$$24 = \frac{1.00(1 + g)}{0.10 - g}$$

$$2.4 - 24g = 1.00 + g$$

$$25g = 1.4$$

$$g = 0.056 \text{ or } 5.6 \text{ percent}$$

8. **A.** With b = 0.60, the dividend payout ratio = 1 − b = 1 − 0.60 = 0.40. Sustainable growth rate g = b(ROE) = 0.60(0.14) = 0.084 or 8.4 percent.

   B. The company paid a dividend per share of 1 − b(EPS) = 0.40($2) = $0.80 in 2008. The estimated value at the beginning of 2009 is

$$V_0 = \frac{D_1}{r - g} = \frac{0.80(1 + 0.0840)}{0.1100 - 0.0840} = \$33.35$$

C. If the company was a no-growth company, that is it paid out all its earnings and did not reinvest any, its earnings would stay the same. The value of such a company would be the value of a perpetuity, which is $D/r = E/r = \$2/0.11 = \$18.18$. This amount is the no-growth value per share. So, PVGO = $\$33.35 - \$18.18 = \$15.17$.

D. The fraction of the company's value that comes from its growth opportunities is $15.17/33.35 = 0.4549$ or 45.49 percent.

9. The payout ratio is A\$0.70/A\$2.00 = 0.35 = 1 − *b*, where *b* is the earnings retention ratio. Therefore, the justified trailing P/E based on fundamentals is 10.45, as shown below:

$$\frac{P_0}{E_0} = \frac{(1 - b)(1 + g)}{r - g}$$
$$= \frac{0.35(1 + 0.045)}{0.08 - 0.045}$$
$$= 10.45$$

Because the market trailing P/E of 14 is greater than 10.45, Stellar Baking Company shares appear to be overvalued (i.e., selling at a higher than warranted P/E).

10. The dividends in Stages 2 and 3 can be valued with the H-model, which estimates their value at the beginning of Stage 2. In this case, V_6 would capture the value of Stages 2 and 3 dividends. V_6 would then be discounted to the present. Also, the present values of dividends D_1 through D_6 need to be added to the present value of V_6.

$$V_6 = \frac{D_6(1 + g_L) + D_6 H(g_S - g_L)}{r - g_L}$$

where
$D_6 = D_0(1 + g_S)^6 = 9(1.14)^6 = 19.7548$
$r = 0.16$
$H = 10/2 = 5$
$g_S = 0.14$
$g_L = 0.10$

$$V_6 = \frac{19.7548(1.10) + 19.7548(5)(0.14 - 0.10)}{0.16 - 0.10} = 428.02$$
PV of $V_6 = 428.02/1.16^6 = 175.68$

PV of $D_1 = 9(1.14)/1.16 = 8.8448$
PV of $D_2 = 9(1.14)^2/1.16^2 = 8.6923$
PV of $D_3 = 9(1.14)^3/1.16^3 = 8.5425$
PV of $D_4 = 9(1.14)^4/1.16^4 = 8.3952$
PV of $D_5 = 9(1.14)^5/1.16^5 = 8.2504$
PV of $D_6 = 9(1.14)^6/1.16^6 = 8.1082$

Value of stock = 8.8448 + 8.6923 + 8.5425 + 8.3952 + 8.2504 + 8.1082 + 175.68 = Rs. 226.51

11. A. Let *r* be the required rate of return. Also let *t* = 0 indicate the middle of 2008. Because the dividend growth rate becomes constant from the middle of 2011 (*t* = 3), the value of the mature phase can be expressed as

$$V_3 = D_4/(r - g) = D_4/(r - 0.08)$$

Also,

$$D_1 = 0.27(1.10) = 0.2970$$
$$D_2 = 0.27(1.10)^2 = 0.3267$$
$$D_3 = 0.27(1.10)^3 = 0.3594$$
$$D_4 = D_3(1.08) = 0.3594(1.08) = 0.3881$$

V_0 can be expressed as

$$V_0 = 9.74 = \frac{D_1}{1 + r} + \frac{D_2}{(1 + r)^2} + \frac{D_3}{(1 + r)^3} + \frac{V_3}{(1 + r)^3}$$

$$= \frac{0.2970}{1 + 0.12} + \frac{0.3267}{(1 + 0.12)^2} + \frac{0.3594}{(1 + 0.12)^3} + \frac{0.3881}{(0.12 - 0.08)(1 + 0.12)^3}$$

$$= 0.2652 + 0.2604 + 0.2558 + 6.9064$$

$$A\$ = 7.69$$

B. Because ANN's estimated value of A\$7.69 is less than the market price of A\$9.74, ANN appears to be overvalued at the market price.

12. A. Use the H-model expression, with $H = 6/2 = 3$ and long-term and short-term dividend growth rates of 0.05 and 0.10, respectively, which gives an expected return of 7.4 percent as shown below:

$$r = \left(\frac{D_0}{P_0}\right)[(1 + g_L) + H(g_S - g_L)] + g_L$$
$$= 0.02[(1 + 0.05) + 3(0.10 - 0.05)] + 0.05$$
$$= 0.024 + 0.05$$
$$= 0.074$$

B. In this case the long- and short-term dividend growth rates are identical and the expected return is lower:

$$r = \left(\frac{D_0}{P_0}\right)[(1 + g_L) + H(g_S - g_L)] + g_L$$
$$= 0.02[(1 + 0.05) + 3(0.05 - 0.05)] + 0.05$$
$$= 0.021 + 0.05$$
$$= 0.071$$

It is intuitive that a higher dividend growth rate is associated with a higher expected return if all the other facts (such as the assumed required rate of return) are held constant.

13. A. The formula for sustainable growth rate is

$$g = (b \text{ in the mature phase}) \times (\text{ROE in the mature phase})$$

Because the dividend payout ratio in the mature phase is estimated to be 40 percent or 0.40, the retention ratio b is expected to $1 - 0.40 = 0.60$. Therefore, given the 11 percent per year forecasted ROE,

$$g = 0.60(11\%) = 6.6\%$$

B. Based on the formula for sustainable growth rate, as b increases, growth rate increases, holding all else constant. However, all else may not be constant. In particular, the return accruing to additional investments may be lower, leading to a lower overall ROE. If that is the case and Brother lowers the payout ratio to below 0.40 (thus increasing b to above 0.60), ROE would be expected to decline, which may lead to a lower growth rate.

14. A. The four components of PRAT are computed for 2007 as follows:

P (Profit margin) = NI/Sales = 18,688/214,091 = 0.0873
R (Retention)   = b = (EPS − DPS)/EPS = (8.77 − 2.26)/8.77
                  = 0.7423
A (Asset turnover) = Sales/Average total assets
                  = 214,091/0.5(148,786 + 132,628) = 1.5215
T (Leverage)   = Average total assets/Average shareholders'
                  equity = (148,786 + 132,628)/(77,088
                  + 68,935) = 1.9272

The components are similarly computed for the other years and summarized in the following table. Their average values are also included.

| Item | Needed for Solution to B | Solution to A | | |
	Average	2007	2006	2005
P (Profit margin)	0.0812	0.0873	0.0836	0.0728
R (Retention)	0.7390	0.7423	0.7423	0.7324
A (Asset turnover)	1.6250	1.5215	1.5855	1.7681
T (Leverage)	1.9736	1.9272	1.9638	2.0299

B. Using the average values for each component,

$$g = \text{PRAT} = (0.0812)(0.7390)(1.6250)(1.9736) = 0.1924 \text{ or } 19.2 \text{ percent}$$

The sustainable growth rate for Chevron based on the PRAT expression is 19.8 percent.

C. Given that the high value of g does not seem sustainable indefinitely, it appears that the company has not reached the mature phase yet.

15. A. The table on the following page provides the details from the spreadsheet model. The constant growth rate after Year 4 is 2 percent less than that in Year 4. So,

$$g = 0.1180 - 0.0200 = 0.098 \text{ or } 9.8 \text{ percent.}$$
$$V_4 = D_4(1+g)/(r - g) = 1.80(1.098)/(0.13 - 0.098) = \$61.76$$

Year	1	2	3	4
Sales ($ millions)	300.00	345.00	396.75	436.43
EBIT	51.00	58.65	67.45	74.19
Interest (%)	10.00	10.00	10.00	10.00
EBT	41.00	48.65	57.45	64.19
Taxes (30%)	12.30	14.60	17.23	19.26
Net income	28.70	34.06	40.21	44.93
Dividends	11.48	13.62	16.09	17.97
DPS	1.15	1.36	1.61	1.80
Growth rate of DPS		18.26%	18.38%	11.80%
PV of DPS	1.02	1.07	1.12	1.10
$V_4 = D_4(1+g)/(r-g)$				61.76
PV of V_4				$37.87

B. $V_0 =$ Sum of PV of DPS and PV of V_4 = 1.02 + 1.07 + 1.12 + 1.10 + 61.76/(1 + 0.13)^4 = $42.18

C. The following table provides the details if the sales growth rate in Year 3 is 10 percent:

Year	1	2	3	4
Sales ($ millions)	300.00	345.00	379.50	417.45
EBIT	51.00	58.65	64.52	70.97
Interest (%)	10.00	10.00	10.00	10.00
EBT	41.00	48.65	54.52	60.97
Taxes (%)	12.30	14.60	16.35	18.29
Net income	28.70	34.06	38.16	42.68
Dividends	11.48	13.62	15.26	17.07
DPS	1.15	1.36	1.53	1.71
Growth rate of DPS		18.26%	12.50%	11.76%
PV of DPS	1.02	1.07	1.06	1.05
$V_4 = D_4(1+g)/(r-g)$				57.93
PV of V_4				$35.53

$V_0 =$ Sum of PV of DPS and PV of V_4 = 1.02 + 1.07 + 1.06 + 1.05 + 35.53 = $39.73

16. C is correct. Using the Gordon growth model,

$$V_0 = \frac{D_1}{r-g} = \frac{0.59(1 + 0.0530)}{0.1115 - 0.0530} = \$10.62$$

17. A is correct. The justified trailing P/E or P_0/E_0 is V_0/E_0, where V_0 is the fair value based on the stock's fundamentals. The fair value V_0 computed earlier is \$10.62 and E_0 is \$2.12. So, the justified trailing P/E is $10.62/2.12 = 5.01$.

18. A is correct. Rae's estimate of the intrinsic value is \$10.62. So, the band Rae is looking at is $\$10.62 \pm 0.10(\$10.62)$, which runs from $\$10.62 + \$1.06 = \$11.68$ on the upside to $\$10.62 - \$1.06 = \$9.56$ on the downside. Because \$8.42 is below \$9.56, Rae would consider Tasty Foods to be undervalued.

19. B is correct. Using a beta of 1.25, Rae's estimate for the required return on equity for Tasty Foods is $0.04 + 1.25(0.065) = 0.1213$ or 12.13 percent. The estimated value of the stock is

$$V_0 = \frac{D_1}{r-g} = \frac{0.59 \times (1 + 0.0530)}{0.1213 - 0.0530} = \$9.10$$

20. A is correct. The price of the stock is \$8.42. If this price is also the fair value of the stock,

$$V_0 = 8.42 = \frac{D_1}{r-g} = \frac{0.59 \times (1 + g)}{0.1115 - g}$$

$$0.9388 - 8.42g = 0.59 + 0.59g$$
$$9.01g = 0.3488$$
$$g = 0.0387 \text{ or } 3.87 \text{ percent}$$

21. A is correct. If the stock is fairly priced in the market as per the Gordon growth model, the stock price is expected to increase at g, the expected growth rate in dividends. The implied growth rate in dividends, if price is the fair value, is 3.87 percent. Therefore, the expected capital gains yield is 3.87 percent.

22. B is correct. The following table provides the calculations needed to compute the value of the stock using the first approach, including the calculations for the terminal value V_8. As the table shows, the terminal value $V_8 = C\$31.0550$.

Time	Value	Calculation	D_t or V_t	Present Values $D_t/(1.0872)^t$ or $V_t/(1.0872)^t$
1	D_1	C\$0.175(1.14)	C\$0.1995	C\$0.1835
2	D_2	$0.175(1.14)^2$	0.2274	0.1924
3	D_3	$0.175(1.14)^3$	0.2593	0.2018
4	D_4	$0.175(1.14)^4$	0.2956	0.2116
5	D_5	$0.175(1.14)^5$	0.3369	0.2218
6	D_6	$0.175(1.14)^6$	0.3841	0.2326
7	D_7	$0.175(1.14)^7$	0.4379	0.2439
8	D_8	$0.175(1.14)^8$	0.4992	0.2557
8	V_8	$0.175(1.14)^8(1.07)/(0.0872 - 0.07)$	31.0550	15.9095
Total				C\$17.6528

23. C is correct. As shown in the above table, the value of the second stage = PV of V_8 = C$15.9095. The total value is C$17.6528. As a proportion, the second stage represents $15.9095/17.6528 = 0.90$ of the total value.

24. B is correct.

$V_8/E_8 = 17$
$D_8/E_8 = 1 - 0.70 = 0.30$

From the table with the calculation details for the solution to Problem 22, D_8 = C$0.4992. So, $0.4992/E_8 = 0.30$, which means that $E_8 = 0.4992/0.30 = 1.6640$.

$V_8/E_8 = 17$ implies that $V_8/1.6640 = 17$, which gives $V_8 = 17(1.6640)$
            = C$28.2880.

25. A is correct. As computed earlier, $V_8 = 17(1.6640)$ = C$28.2880.

  PV of $V_8 = 28.2880/1.0872^8 = 14.4919$

From the table with the calculation details for the solution to Problem 22,

  Sum of PV of D_1 through $D_8 = 1.7433$

So, the value of stock $V_0 = 14.4919 + 1.7433$ = C$16.2352.

26. C is correct. Using the H-model

$$V_0 = \frac{D_0(1 + g_L) + D_0 H(g_S - g_L)}{r - g_L}$$

where
  $D_0 = 0.175$
  $r = 0.0872$
  $H = 4$
  $g_S = 0.14$
  $g_L = 0.07$
  $$V_0 = \frac{0.175(1.07) + 0.175(4)(0.14 - 0.07)}{0.0872 - 0.07} = 13.7355$$

The market price is C$17, which is greater than C$13.7355. So, the stock is overvalued in the market.

27. B is correct. If the extraordinary growth rate of 14 percent is expected to continue for a longer duration, the stock's value would increase. Choice A is false because given that the first stage is longer (11 years instead of 8), the terminal value is being calculated at a later point in time. So, its present value would be smaller. Moreover, the first stage has more years and contributes more to the total value. Overall, the proportion contributed by the second stage would be smaller. Choice C is false because the intrinsic value of the stock would be higher and the appropriate conclusion would be that the stock would be undervalued to a greater extent based on the first approach.

STUDY SESSION 12
EQUITY INVESTMENTS:
Valuation Models

This study session presents additional valuation methods for estimating a company's intrinsic value. The dividend discount model discussed in Study Session 11 remains a baseline model. The free cash flow approach to valuation is an important alternative to the dividend discount model when dividends are not the best representation of a company's value. Price and enterprise multiples are among the most familiar and widely used valuation measures because of their simplicity and the ease with which they can be used and communicated. Residual income models have become common alternatives to the other models. The final reading addresses valuation issues associated with private companies.

READING ASSIGNMENTS

Reading 40   Free Cash Flow Valuation
Equity Asset Valuation, Second Edition, by Jerald Pinto, CFA,
Elaine Henry, CFA, Thomas Robinson, CFA, and John Stowe, CFA

Reading 41   Market-Based Valuation: Price and Enterprise Value Multiples
Equity Asset Valuation, Second Edition, by Jerald Pinto, CFA,
Elaine Henry, CFA, Thomas Robinson, CFA, and John Stowe, CFA

Reading 42   Residual Income Valuation
Equity Asset Valuation, Second Edition, by Jerald Pinto, CFA,
Elaine Henry, CFA, Thomas Robinson, CFA, and John Stowe, CFA

Reading 43   Private Company Valuation
by Raymond D. Rath, ASA, CFA

$23\frac{3}{8}$ 24 ...

$4\frac{5}{8}$ $4\frac{11}{16}$ $3\frac{3}{8}$

$5\frac{1}{2}$ $5\frac{1}{2}$ —

$5\frac{1}{2}$ $21\frac{3}{16}$ — $\frac{1}{16}$

$20\frac{5}{8}$ $21\frac{3}{16}$ + $\frac{7}{8}$

$17\frac{3}{8}$ $18\frac{1}{8}$ +

$13\frac{1}{2}$ $6\frac{1}{2}$ — $\frac{1}{2}$

$6\frac{1}{2}$ $6\frac{1}{2}$ —

$7\frac{1}{4}$ $31\frac{1}{32}$ — $\frac{1}{8}$

$15\frac{1}{16}$

$9\frac{1}{16}$ $9\frac{1}{8}$

$\frac{9}{32}$

$7\frac{15}{16}$ $7\frac{13}{16}$ $7\frac{15}{16}$

$25\frac{5}{8}$ $2\frac{11}{32}$ $2\frac{1}{2}$ +

$2\frac{3}{4}$ $2\frac{1}{4}$ $2\frac{1}{4}$

$12\frac{1}{16}$ $11\frac{3}{8}$ $11\frac{3}{4}$ +

87 $33\frac{3}{4}$ 33 $33\frac{1}{8}$ —

602 $25\frac{5}{8}$ $24\frac{9}{16}$ $25\frac{3}{8}$ +

833 12 $11\frac{5}{8}$ $11\frac{7}{8}$ +

16 $10\frac{1}{2}$ $10\frac{1}{2}$ $10\frac{1}{2}$ —

78 $15\frac{7}{8}$ $15\frac{13}{16}$ $15\frac{7}{8}$ —

4608 $9\frac{1}{16}$ $8\frac{1}{4}$ $8\frac{7}{8}$ —

$11\frac{1}{4}$ $10\frac{5}{8}$

FREE CASH FLOW VALUATION

by Jerald Pinto, CFA, Elaine Henry, CFA, Thomas Robinson, CFA, and John Stowe, CFA

LEARNING OUTCOMES

The candidate should be able to:	Mastery
a. compare the free cash flow to the firm (FCFF) and free cash flow to equity (FCFE) approaches to valuation;	☐
b. contrast the ownership perspective implicit in the FCFE approach to the ownership perspective implicit in the dividend discount approach;	☐
c. explain the appropriate adjustments to net income, earnings before interest and taxes (EBIT), earnings before interest, taxes, depreciation, and amortization (EBITDA), and cash flow from operations (CFO) to calculate FCFF and FCFE;	☐
d. calculate FCFF and FCFE;	☐
e. describe approaches for forecasting FCFF and FCFE;	☐
f. contrast the recognition of value in the FCFE model with recognition of value in dividend discount models;	☐
g. explain how dividends, share repurchases, share issues, and changes in leverage may affect future FCFF and FCFE;	☐
h. evaluate the use of net income and EBITDA as proxies for cash flow in valuation;	☐
i. explain the single-stage (stable-growth), two-stage, and three-stage FCFF and FCFE models, and select and justify the appropriate model given a company's characteristics;	☐
j. estimate a company's value using the appropriate free cash flow model(s);	☐
k. explain the use of sensitivity analysis in FCFF and FCFE valuations;	☐
l. describe approaches for calculating the terminal value in a multistage valuation model.	☐

INTRODUCTION TO FREE CASH FLOWS

Discounted cash flow (DCF) valuation views the intrinsic value of a security as the present value of its expected future cash flows. When applied to dividends, the DCF model is the discounted dividend approach or dividend discount model (DDM). This reading extends DCF analysis to value a company and its equity securities by valuing free cash flow to the firm (FCFF) and free cash flow to equity (FCFE). Whereas dividends are the cash flows actually paid to stockholders, free cash flows are the cash flows *available* for distribution to shareholders.

Unlike dividends, FCFF and FCFE are not readily available data. Analysts need to compute these quantities from available financial information, which requires a clear understanding of free cash flows and the ability to interpret and use the information correctly. Forecasting future free cash flows is also a rich and demanding exercise. The analyst's understanding of a company's financial statements, its operations, its financing, and its industry can pay real "dividends" as he or she addresses that task. Many analysts consider free cash flow models to be more useful than DDMs in practice. Free cash flows provide an economically sound basis for valuation.

Analysts like to use free cash flow as the return (either FCFF or FCFE) whenever one or more of the following conditions is present:

► The company does not pay dividends.

► The company pays dividends but the dividends paid differ significantly from the company's capacity to pay dividends.

► Free cash flows align with profitability within a reasonable forecast period with which the analyst is comfortable.

► The investor takes a "control" perspective. With control comes discretion over the uses of free cash flow. If an investor can take control of the company (or expects another investor to do so), dividends may be changed substantially; for example, they may be set at a level approximating the company's capacity to pay dividends. Such an investor can also apply free cash flows to uses such as servicing the debt incurred in an acquisition.

Common equity can be valued directly by using FCFE or indirectly by first using a FCFF model to estimate the value of the firm and then subtracting the value of non-common-stock capital (usually debt) from FCFF to arrive at an estimate of the value of equity. The purpose of this reading is to develop the background required to use the FCFF or FCFE approaches to value a company's equity.

Section 2 defines the concepts of free cash flow to the firm and free cash flow to equity and then presents the two valuation models based on discounting of FCFF and FCFE. We also explore the constant-growth models for valuing FCFF and FCFE, which are special cases of the general models, in this section. After reviewing the FCFF and FCFE valuation process in Section 2, we turn in Section 3 to the vital task of calculating and forecasting FCFF and FCFE. Section 4 explains multistage free cash flow valuation models and presents some of the issues associated with their application. Analysts usually value operating assets and nonoperating assets separately and then combine them to find the total value of the firm, an approach described in Section 5.

FCFF AND FCFE VALUATION APPROACHES

2

The purpose of this section is to provide a conceptual understanding of free cash flows and the valuation models based on them. A detailed accounting treatment of free cash flows and more-complicated valuation models follow in subsequent sections.

2.1 Defining Free Cash Flow

Free cash flow to the firm is the cash flow available to the company's suppliers of capital after all operating expenses (including taxes) have been paid and necessary investments in working capital (e.g., inventory) and fixed capital (e.g., equipment) have been made. FCFF is the cash flow from operations minus capital expenditures. A company's suppliers of capital include common stockholders, bondholders, and sometimes, preferred stockholders. The equations analysts use to calculate FCFF depend on the accounting information available.

Free cash flow to equity is the cash flow available to the company's holders of common equity after all operating expenses, interest, and principal payments have been paid and necessary investments in working and fixed capital have been made. FCFE is the cash flow from operations minus capital expenditures minus payments to (and plus receipts from) debtholders.

The way in which free cash flow is related to a company's net income, cash flow from operations, and measures such as EBITDA (earnings before interest, taxes, depreciation, and amortization) is important: The analyst must understand the relationship between a company's reported accounting data and free cash flow in order to forecast free cash flow and its expected growth. Although a company reports cash flow from operations (CFO) on the statement of cash flows, CFO is *not* free cash flow. Net income and CFO data can be used, however, in determining a company's free cash flow.

The advantage of FCFF and FCFE over other cash-flow concepts is that they can be used directly in a DCF framework to value the firm or to value equity. Other cash-flow- or earnings-related measures, such as CFO, net income, EBIT, and EBITDA, do not have this property because they either double-count or omit cash flows in some way. For example, EBIT and EBITDA are before-tax measures, and the cash flows available to investors (in the firm or in the equity of the firm) must be after tax. From the stockholders' perspective, EBITDA and similar measures do not account for differing capital structures (the after-tax interest expenses or preferred dividends) or for the funds that bondholders supply to finance investments in operating assets. Moreover, these measures do not account for the reinvestment of cash flows that the company makes in capital assets and working capital to maintain or maximize the long-run value of the firm.

Using free cash flow in valuation is more challenging than using dividends because in forecasting free cash flow, the analyst must integrate the cash flows from the company's operations with those from its investing and financing activities. Because FCFF is the after-tax cash flow going to all suppliers of capital to the firm, the value of the firm is estimated by discounting FCFF at the weighted average cost of capital (WACC). An estimate of the value of equity is then found by subtracting the value of debt from the estimated value of the firm. The value of equity can also be estimated directly by discounting FCFE at the required rate of return for equity (because FCFE is the cash flow going to common stockholders, the required rate of return on equity is the appropriate risk-adjusted rate for discounting FCFE).

The two free cash flow approaches, indirect and direct, for valuing equity should theoretically yield the same estimates if all inputs reflect identical assumptions. An analyst may prefer to use one approach rather than the other, however, because of the characteristics of the company being valued. For example, if the company's capital structure is relatively stable, using FCFE to value equity is more direct and simpler than using FCFF. The FCFF model is often chosen, however, in two other cases:

▶ *A levered company with negative FCFE.* In this case, working with FCFF to value the company's equity might be easiest. The analyst would discount FCFF to find the present value of operating assets (adding the value of excess cash and marketable securities and of any other significant nonoperating assets[1] to get total firm value) and then subtract the market value of debt to obtain an estimate of the intrinsic value of equity.

▶ *A levered company with a changing capital structure.* First, if historical data are used to forecast free cash flow growth rates, FCFF growth might reflect fundamentals more clearly than does FCFE growth, which reflects fluctuating amounts of net borrowing. Second, in a forward-looking context, the required return on equity might be expected to be more sensitive to changes in financial leverage than changes in the WACC, making the use of a constant discount rate difficult to justify.

Specialized DCF approaches are also available to facilitate the equity valuation when the capital structure is expected to change.[2]

---

[1] Adjustments for excess cash and marketable securities and for other nonoperating assets are discussed further in Section 5. "Excess" means excess in relation to operating needs.

[2] The **adjusted present value** (APV) approach is one example of such models. In the APV approach, firm value is calculated as the sum of 1) the value of the company under the assumption that debt is not used (i.e., unlevered firm value) and 2) the net present value of any effects of debt on firm value (such as any tax benefits of using debt and any costs of financial distress). In this approach, the analyst estimates unlevered company value by discounting FCFF (under the assumption of no debt) at the unlevered cost of equity (the cost of equity given that the firm does not use debt). For details, see Ross, Westerfield, and Jaffe (2005), who explain APV in a capital budgeting context.

In the following, we present the general form of the FCFF valuation model and the FCFE valuation model.

2.2 Present Value of Free Cash Flow

The two distinct approaches to using free cash flow for valuation are the FCFF valuation approach and the FCFE valuation approach. The general expressions for these valuation models are similar to the expression for the general dividend discount model. In the DDM, the value of a share of stock equals the present value of forecasted dividends from Time 1 through infinity discounted at the required rate of return for equity.

2.2.1 Present Value of FCFF

The FCFF valuation approach estimates the value of the firm as the present value of future FCFF discounted at the weighted average cost of capital:

$$\text{Firm value} = \sum_{t=1}^{\infty} \frac{\text{FCFF}_t}{(1 + \text{WACC})^t} \tag{1}$$

Because FCFF is the cash flow available to all suppliers of capital, using WACC to discount FCFF gives the total value of all of the firm's capital. The value of equity is the value of the firm minus the market value of its debt:

$$\text{Equity value} = \text{Firm value} - \text{Market value of debt} \tag{2}$$

Dividing the total value of equity by the number of outstanding shares gives the value per share.

The cost of capital is the required rate of return that investors should demand for a cash flow stream like that generated by the company being analyzed. WACC depends on the riskiness of these cash flows. The calculation and interpretation of WACC were discussed in the reading on return concepts—that is, WACC is the weighted average of the after (corporate) tax required rates of return for debt and equity, where the weights are the proportions of the firm's total market value from each source, debt and equity. As an alternative, analysts may use the weights of debt and equity in the firm's target capital structure when those weights are known and differ from market value weights. The formula for WACC is

$$\text{WACC} = \frac{\text{MV(Debt)}}{\text{MV(Debt)} + \text{MV(Equity)}} r_d (1 - \text{Tax rate})$$
$$+ \frac{\text{MV(Equity)}}{\text{MV(Debt)} + \text{MV(Equity)}} r \tag{3}$$

MV(Debt) and MV(Equity) are the current market values of debt and equity, not their book or accounting values, and the ratios of MV(Debt) and MV(Equity) to the total market value of debt plus equity define the weights in the WACC formula. The quantities $r_d(1 - \text{Tax rate})$ and r are, respectively, the after-tax cost of debt and the after-tax cost of equity (in the case of equity, one could just write "cost of equity" because net income, the income belonging to equity, is after tax). In Equation 3, the tax rate is in principle the marginal corporate income tax rate.

2.2.2 Present Value of FCFE

The value of equity can also be found by discounting FCFE at the required rate of return on equity, r:

$$\text{Equity value} = \sum_{t=1}^{\infty} \frac{\text{FCFE}_t}{(1 + r)^t} \tag{4}$$

Because FCFE is the cash flow remaining for equityholders after all other claims have been satisfied, discounting FCFE by r (the required rate of return on equity) gives the value of the firm's equity. Dividing the total value of equity by the number of outstanding shares gives the value per share.

2.3 Single-Stage (Constant-Growth) FCFF and FCFE Models

In the DDM approach, the Gordon (constant- or stable-growth) model makes the assumption that dividends grow at a constant rate. The assumption that free cash flows grow at a constant rate leads to a single-stage (stable-growth) FCFF or FCFE model.[3]

2.3.1 Constant-Growth FCFF Valuation Model

Assume that FCFF grows at a constant rate, g, such that FCFF in any period is equal to FCFF in the previous period multiplied by $(1 + g)$:

$$\text{FCFF}_t = \text{FCFF}_{t-1}(1 + g)$$

If FCFF grows at a constant rate,

$$\text{Firm value} = \frac{\text{FCFF}_1}{\text{WACC} - g} = \frac{\text{FCFF}_0(1 + g)}{\text{WACC} - g} \tag{5}$$

Subtracting the market value of debt from the firm value gives the value of equity.

EXAMPLE 1

Using the Constant-Growth FCFF Valuation Model

Cagiati Enterprises has FCFF of 700 million Swiss francs (CHF) and FCFE of CHF620 million. Cagiati's before-tax cost of debt is 5.7 percent, and its required rate of return for equity is 11.8 percent. The company expects a target capital structure consisting of 20 percent debt financing and 80 percent equity financing. The tax rate is 33.33 percent, and FCFF is expected to grow forever at 5.0 percent. Cagiati Enterprises has debt outstanding with a market value of CHF2.2 billion and has 200 million outstanding common shares.

---

[3] In the context of private company valuation, these constant-growth free cash flow models are often referred to as **capitalized cash flow models**.

1. What is Cagiati's weighted average cost of capital?
2. What is the value of Cagiati's equity using the FCFF valuation approach?
3. What is the value per share using this FCFF approach?

Solution to 1: From Equation 3, WACC is

$$\text{WACC} = 0.20(5.7\%)(1 - 0.3333) + 0.80(11.8\%) = 10.2\%$$

Solution to 2: The firm value of Cagiati Enterprises is the present value of FCFF discounted by using WACC. For FCFF growing at a constant 5 percent rate, the result is

$$\text{Firm value} = \frac{\text{FCFF}_1}{\text{WACC} - g} = \frac{\text{FCFF}_0(1 + g)}{\text{WACC} - g} = \frac{700(1.05)}{0.102 - 0.05}$$

$$= \frac{735}{0.052} = \text{CHF}14,134.6 \text{ million}$$

The value of equity is the value of the firm minus the value of debt:

$$\text{Equity value} = 14,134.6 - 2,200 = \text{CHF}11,934.6 \text{ million}$$

Solution to 3: Dividing CH11,934.6 million by the number of outstanding shares gives the estimated value per share, V_0:

$$V_0 = \text{CHF}11,934.6 \text{ million}/200 \text{ million shares}$$
$$= \text{CHF}59.67 \text{ per share}$$

2.3.2 Constant-Growth FCFE Valuation Model

The constant-growth FCFE valuation model assumes that FCFE grows at constant rate g. FCFE in any period is equal to FCFE in the preceding period multiplied by $(1 + g)$:

$$\text{FCFE}_t = \text{FCFE}_{t-1}(1 + g)$$

The value of equity if FCFE is growing at a constant rate is

$$\text{Equity value} = \frac{\text{FCFE}_1}{r - g} = \frac{\text{FCFE}_0(1 + g)}{r - g} \tag{6}$$

The discount rate is r, the required rate of return on equity. Note that the growth rate of FCFF and the growth rate of FCFE need not be and frequently are not the same.

In this section, we presented the basic ideas underlying free cash flow valuation and the simplest implementation, single-stage free cash flow models. The next section examines the precise definition of free cash flow and introduces the issues involved in forecasting free cash flow.

3   FORECASTING FREE CASH FLOW

Estimating FCFF or FCFE requires a complete understanding of the company and its financial statements. To provide a context for the estimation of FCFF and FCFE, we first use an extensive example to show the relationship between free cash flow and accounting measures of income.

For most of this section, we assume that the company has two sources of capital, debt and common stock. Once the concepts of FCFF and FCFE are understood for a company financed by using only debt and common stock, it is easy to incorporate preferred stock for the relatively small number of companies that actually use it (in Section 3.8 we incorporate preferred stock as a third source of capital).

3.1 Computing FCFF from Net Income

FCFF is the cash flow available to the company's suppliers of capital after all operating expenses (including taxes) have been paid and operating investments have been made. The company's suppliers of capital include bondholders and common shareholders (plus, occasionally, holders of preferred stock, which we ignore until later). Keeping in mind that a noncash charge is a charge or expense that does not involve the outlay of cash, we can write the expression for FCFF as follows:

> FCFF = Net income available to common shareholders (NI)
> Plus: Net noncash charges (NCC)
> Plus: Interest expense $\times$ (1 − Tax rate)
> Less: Investment in fixed capital[4] (FCInv)
> Less: Investment in working capital (WCInv)

This equation can be written more compactly as

$$FCFF = NI + NCC + Int(1 - \text{Tax rate}) - FCInv - WCInv \qquad \textbf{(7)}$$

Consider each component of FCFF. The starting point in Equation 7 is net income available to common shareholders—the bottom line in an income statement. It represents income after depreciation, amortization, interest expense, income taxes, and the payment of dividends to preferred shareholders (but not payment of dividends to common shareholders).

Net noncash charges represent an adjustment for noncash decreases and increases in net income. This adjustment is the first of several that analysts generally perform on a net basis. If noncash decreases in net income exceed the increases, as is usually the case, the adjustment is positive. If noncash increases exceed noncash decreases, the adjustment is negative. The most common noncash charge is depreciation expense. When a company purchases fixed capital, such as equipment, the balance sheet reflects a cash outflow at the time of the purchase. In subsequent periods, the company records depreciation expense as the asset is used. The depreciation expense reduces net income but is not a cash outflow. Depreciation expense is thus one (the most common)

---

[4] In this reading, when we refer to "investment in fixed capital" or "investment in working capital," we are referring to the investments made in the specific period for which the free cash flow is being calculated.

noncash charge that must be added back in computing FCFF. In the case of intangible assets, there is a similar noncash charge, amortization expense, which must be added back. Other noncash charges vary from company to company and are discussed in Section 3.3.

After-tax interest expense must be added back to net income to arrive at FCFF. This step is required because interest expense net of the related tax savings was deducted in arriving at net income and because interest is a cash flow available to one of the company's capital providers (i.e., the company's creditors). In the United States and many other countries, interest is tax deductible (reduces taxes) for the company (borrower) and taxable for the recipient (lender). As we explain later, when we discount FCFF, we use an after-tax cost of capital. For consistency, we thus compute FCFF by using the after-tax interest paid.[5]

Similar to after-tax interest expense, if a company has preferred stock, dividends on that preferred stock are deducted in arriving at net income available to common shareholders. Because preferred stock dividends are also a cash flow available to one of the company's capital providers, this item is added back to arrive at FCFF. Further discussion of the effects of preferred stock is in Section 3.8.

Investments in fixed capital represent the outflows of cash to purchase fixed capital necessary to support the company's current and future operations. These investments are capital expenditures for long-term assets, such as the property, plant, and equipment (PP&E) necessary to support the company's operations. Necessary capital expenditures may also include intangible assets, such as trademarks. In the case of cash acquisition of another company instead of a direct acquisition of PP&E, the cash purchase amount can also be treated as a capital expenditure that reduces the company's free cash flow (note that this treatment is conservative because it reduces FCFF). In the case of large acquisitions (and all noncash acquisitions), analysts must take care in evaluating the impact on future free cash flow. If a company receives cash in disposing of any of its fixed capital, the analyst must deduct this cash in calculating investment in fixed capital. For example, suppose we had a sale of equipment for $100,000. This cash inflow would reduce the company's cash outflows for investments in fixed capital.

The company's statement of cash flows is an excellent source of information on capital expenditures as well as on sales of fixed capital. Analysts should be aware that some companies acquire fixed capital without using cash—for example, through an exchange for stock or debt. Such acquisitions do not appear in a company's statement of cash flows but, if material, must be disclosed in the footnotes. Although noncash exchanges do not affect historical FCFF, if the capital expenditures are necessary and may be made in cash in the future, the analyst should use this information in forecasting future FCFF.

The final point to cover is the important adjustment for net increases in working capital. This adjustment represents the net investment in current assets (such as accounts receivable) less current liabilities (such as accounts payable). Analysts can find this information by examining either the company's balance sheet or its statement of cash flows.

Although working capital is often defined as current assets minus current liabilities, working capital for cash flow and valuation purposes is defined to exclude cash and short-term debt (which includes notes payable and the current portion of long-term debt). When finding the net increase in working capital for the purpose of calculating free cash flow, we define working capital to exclude

---

[5] Note that we could compute WACC on a pretax basis and compute FCFF by adding back interest paid with no tax adjustment. Whichever approach is adopted, the analyst must use mutually consistent definitions of FCFF and WACC.

cash and cash equivalents as well as notes payable and the current portion of long-term debt. Cash and cash equivalents are excluded because a change in cash is what we are trying to explain. Notes payable and the current portion of long-term debt are excluded because they are liabilities with explicit interest costs that make them financing items rather than operating items.

Example 2 shows all of the adjustments to net income required to find FCFF.

EXAMPLE 2

Calculating FCFF from Net Income

Cane Distribution, Inc., incorporated on 31 December 2007 with initial capital infusions of $224,000 of debt and $336,000 of common stock, acts as a distributor of industrial goods. The company managers immediately invested the initial capital in fixed capital of $500,000 and working capital of $60,000. Working capital initially consisted solely of inventory. The fixed capital consisted of nondepreciable property of $50,000 and depreciable property of $450,000. The depreciable property has a 10-year useful life with no salvage value. Exhibits 1, 2, and 3 provide Cane's financial statements for the three years following incorporation. Starting with net income, calculate Cane's FCFF for each year.

EXHIBIT 1   Cane Distribution, Inc. Income Statement (in Thousands)

	Years Ending 31 December		
	2008	2009	2010
Earnings before interest, taxes, depreciation, and amortization (EBITDA)	$200.00	$220.00	$242.00
Depreciation expense	45.00	49.50	54.45
Operating income	155.00	170.50	187.55
Interest expense (at 7 percent)	15.68	17.25	18.97
Income before taxes	139.32	153.25	168.58
Income taxes (at 30 percent)	41.80	45.97	50.58
Net income	$ 97.52	$107.28	$118.00

EXHIBIT 2   Cane Distribution, Inc. Balance Sheet (in Thousands)

	Years Ending 31 December			
	2007	2008	2009	2010
Cash	$ 0.00	$108.92	$228.74	$ 360.54
Accounts receivable	0.00	100.00	110.00	121.00
Inventory	60.00	66.00	72.60	79.86
Current assets	60.00	274.92	411.34	561.40
Fixed assets	500.00	500.00	550.00	605.00
Less: Accumulated depreciation	0.00	45.00	94.50	148.95
Total assets	$560.00	$729.92	$866.84	$1,017.45

(Exhibit continued on next page . . .)

EXHIBIT 2   (continued)

	Years Ending 31 December			
	2007	2008	2009	2010
Accounts payable	$ 0.00	$ 50.00	$ 55.00	$ 60.50
Current portion of long-term debt	0.00	0.00	0.00	0.00
Current liabilities	0.00	50.00	55.00	60.50
Long-term debt	224.00	246.40	271.04	298.14
Common stock	336.00	336.00	336.00	336.00
Retained earnings	0.00	97.52	204.80	322.80
Total liabilities and equity	$560.00	$729.92	$866.84	$1,017.45

EXHIBIT 3   Cane Distribution, Inc. Working Capital (in Thousands)

	Years Ending 31 December			
	2007	2008	2009	2010
Current assets excluding cash				
Accounts receivable	$ 0.00	$100.00	$110.00	$121.00
Inventory	60.00	66.00	72.60	79.86
Total current assets excluding cash	60.00	166.00	182.60	200.86
Current liabilities excluding short-term debt				
Accounts payable	0.00	50.00	55.00	60.50
Working capital	$60.00	$116.00	$127.60	$140.36
Increase in working capital		$ 56.00	$ 11.60	$ 12.76

Solution: Following the logic in Equation 7, we calculate FCFF from net income as follows: We add noncash charges (here, depreciation) and after-tax interest expense to net income, then subtract the investment in fixed capital and the investment in working capital. The format for presenting the solution follows the convention that parentheses around a number indicate subtraction. The calculation follows (in thousands):

	Years Ending 31 December		
	2008	2009	2010
Net income	$97.52	$107.28	$118.00
Noncash charges − Depreciation	45.00	49.50	54.45
Interest expense × (1 − Tax rate)	10.98	12.08	13.28
Investment in fixed capital	(0.00)	(50.00)	(55.00)
Investment in working capital	(56.00)	(11.60)	(12.76)
Free cash flow to the firm	$97.50	$107.26	$117.97

3.2 Computing FCFF from the Statement of Cash Flows

FCFF is cash flow available to all providers of capital (debt and equity). Analysts frequently use cash flow from operations, taken from the statement of cash flows, as a starting point to compute free cash flow because CFO incorporates adjustments for noncash expenses (such as depreciation and amortization) as well as for net investments in working capital.

In a statement of cash flows, cash flows are separated into three components: cash flow from operating activities (or cash flow from operations), cash flow from investing activities, and cash flow from financing activities. Cash flow from operations is the net amount of cash provided by the company's operating activities. The operating section of the statement of cash flows shows such cash flows as cash received from customers and cash paid to suppliers. Cash flow from investing activities includes the company's investments in (or sales of) long-term assets—for example, PP&E and long-term investments in other companies. Cash flow from financing activities relates to the company's activities in raising or repaying capital. International Financial Reporting Standards (IFRS) allow the company to classify interest paid as either an operating or financing activity. Furthermore, IFRS allow dividends paid to be classified as either an operating or financing activity. Interestingly, under U.S. generally accepted accounting principles (GAAP), interest expense paid to providers of debt capital must be classified as part of cash flow from operations (as is interest income) but payment of dividends to providers of equity capital is classified as a financing activity.

Exhibit 4 summarizes IFRS and U.S. GAAP treatment of interest and dividends.

EXHIBIT 4	IFRS versus U.S. GAAP Treatment of Interest and Dividends	
	IFRS	**U.S. GAAP**
Interest received	Operating or Investing	Operating
Interest paid	Operating or Financing	Operating
Dividends received	Operating or Investing	Operating
Dividends paid	Operating or Financing	Financing

To estimate FCFF by starting with CFO, we must recognize the treatment of interest paid. If the after-tax interest expense was taken out of net income and out of CFO, as with U.S. GAAP, then after-tax interest expense must be added back to get FCFF. In the case of U.S. GAAP, FCFF can be estimated as follows:

Free cash flow to the firm = Cash flow from operations
 Plus: Interest expense × (1 − Tax rate)
 Less: Investment in fixed capital

or

$$FCFF = CFO + Int(1 - Tax\ rate) - FCInv \qquad (8)$$

To reiterate, the after-tax interest expense is added back because it was previously taken out of net income. The investment in working capital does not appear in Equation 8 because CFO already includes investment in working capital. Example 3 illustrates the use of CFO to calculate FCFF. In this example, the calculation of CFO begins with calculating net income, an approach known as the "indirect" method.[6]

EXAMPLE 3

Calculating FCFF from CFO

Use the information from the statement of cash flows given in Exhibit 5 to calculate FCFF for the three years 2008–2010. The tax rate (as given in Exhibit 1) is 30 percent.

EXHIBIT 5	Cane Distribution, Inc. Statement of Cash Flows: Indirect Method (in Thousands)		
	Years Ending 31 December		
	2008	**2009**	**2010**
Cash flow from operations			
Net income	$ 97.52	$107.28	$118.00
Plus: Depreciation	45.00	49.50	54.45
Increase in accounts receivable	(100.00)	(10.00)	(11.00)
Increase in inventory	(6.00)	(6.60)	(7.26)
Increase in accounts payable	50.00	5.00	5.50
Cash flow from operations	86.52	145.18	159.69
Cash flow from investing activities			
Purchases of PP&E	0.00	(50.00)	(55.00)
Cash flow from financing activities			
Borrowing (repayment)	22.40	24.64	27.10
Total cash flow	108.92	119.82	131.80
Beginning cash	0.00	108.92	228.74
Ending cash	$108.92	$228.74	$360.54
Notes:			
Cash paid for interest	($15.68)	($17.25)	($18.97)
Cash paid for taxes	($41.80)	($45.98)	($50.57)

---

[6] See Robinson, van Greuning, Henry, and Broihahn, "Understanding the Cash Flow Statement" (2007) for a discussion of the indirect and direct cash flow statement formats.

Solution: As shown in Equation 8, FCFF equals CFO plus after-tax interest minus the investment in fixed capital:

	Years Ending 31 December		
	2008	**2009**	**2010**
Cash flow from operations	$86.52	$145.18	$159.69
Interest expense × (1 − Tax rate)	10.98	12.08	13.28
Investment in fixed capital	(0.00)	(50.00)	(55.00)
Free cash flow to the firm	$97.50	$107.26	$117.97

3.3 Noncash Charges

The best place to find historical noncash charges is in the company's statement of cash flows. If an analyst wants to use an add-back method, as in FCFF = NI + NCC + Int(1 − Tax rate) − FCInv − WCInv, the analyst should verify the noncash charges to ensure that the FCFF estimate provides a reasonable basis for forecasting. For example, restructuring charges may involve cash expenditures and noncash charges. Severance pay for laid-off employees could be a cash restructuring charge, but a write-down in the value of assets as part of a restructuring charge is a noncash item. Example 4 illustrates noncash restructuring charges that must be added back to net income to obtain CFO. Note in the example that (noncash) gains from the sale of assets in restructuring are subtracted from net income to obtain CFO.

EXAMPLE 4

An Examination of Noncash Charges

Alberto-Culver Company (NYSE:ACV) develops, manufactures, distributes, and markets branded beauty care products and branded food and household products in more than 100 countries. Jane Everett wants to value Alberto-Culver by using the FCFF method. She collects information from the company's 10-K for the fiscal year ended 30 September 2007.

Note that the statement of cash flows in Exhibit 6 uses a presentation convention that follows the logic that "minus a minus equals a plus," so in this convention, "Less: . . . 50" means "subtract 50" and "Less: . . . (50)" means "add 50." An analyst may also encounter in practice, however, "Less: . . . (50)" interpreted as "subtract 50."

| EXHIBIT 6 | Consolidated Statements of Cash Flows
Alberto-Culver Company and Subsidiaries (in US$ Thousands) |

	2007	2006	2005
Cash Flows from Operating Activities:			
Net earnings	78,264	205,321	210,901
Less: Earnings (loss) from discontinued operations	(2,963)	125,806	141,062
Earnings from continuing operations	81,227	79,515	69,839

(Exhibit continued on next page . . .)

EXHIBIT 6	(continued)			
		2007	**2006**	**2005**
Adjustments to reconcile earnings from continuing operations to net cash provided by operating activities:				
Depreciation		28,824	24,642	23,420
Amortization of other assets and unearned compensation		2,811	3,403	2,774
Restructuring and other noncash charges (note 4)		14,053	—	—
Restructuring and other—gain on sale of assets (note 4)		(5,894)	—	—
Noncash charge related to conversion to one class of common stock (note 5)		—	4	10,456
Stock option expense (note 9)		3,741	10,763	—
Deferred income taxes		(21,064)	2,196	677
Cash effects of changes in (excluding acquisitions and divestitures):				
Receivables, net		(26,635)	(15,270)	(24,223)
Inventories		4,168	(13,424)	(13,751)
Other current assets		2,842	(5,497)	(1,665)
Accounts payable and accrued expenses		15,096	4,761	(14,386)
Income taxes		4,657	(905)	9,137
Other assets		(897)	(2,786)	(8,595)
Other liabilities		(3,914)	3,736	15,192
Net cash provided by operating activities		99,015	91,138	68,875

Everett notices that the reconciliation amounts in the statement of cash flows for restructuring charges differ from the $34,645 restructuring charge recorded in the income statement. She finds the following discussion of restructuring charges in the management discussion and analysis (MD&A) section.

EXHIBIT 7	Excerpt from Management Discussion and Analysis

Restructuring and other expenses during the fiscal year ended September 30, 2007 consist of the following (in thousands):

Severance and other exit costs	$17,056
Non-cash charges related to the acceleration of vesting of stock options and restricted shares in connection with the Separation	12,198
Contractual termination benefits for the former President and Chief Executive Officer in connection with the Separation	9,888
Non-cash charge for the recognition of foreign currency translation loss in connection with the liquidation of a foreign legal entity	1,355
Legal fees and other expenses incurred to assign the company's trademarks following the closing of the Separation	42
Gain on sale of assets	(5,894)
	$34,645

Severance and Other Exit Costs

On November 27, 2006, the company committed to a plan to terminate employees as part of a reorganization following the Separation. In connection with this reorganization plan, on December 1, 2006 the company announced that it expects to close its manufacturing facility in Dallas, Texas. The company's worldwide workforce is being reduced by approximately 225 employees as a result of the reorganization plan, including 125 employees from the Dallas, Texas manufacturing facility. The changes primarily affect corporate functions or the Consumer Packaged Goods business segment. The company expects to record additional pre-tax restructuring charges of approximately $1.5 million related to this plan in fiscal year 2008, primarily during the first half. These amounts exclude the effect of the sale of the manufacturing facility in Dallas, Texas. Cash payments related to this plan are expected to be substantially completed by the end of the second quarter of fiscal year 2008.

The following table reflects the activity related to the restructuring plan during the fiscal year ended September 30, 2007 (in thousands):

	Initial Charges	Cash Payments & Other Settlements	Liability at September 30, 2007
Severance	$15,405	(12,774)	2,631
Contract termination costs	237	(237)	—
Other	1,414	(1,321)	93
	$17,056	(14,332)	2,724

Using the information about Alberto-Culver provided, answer the following questions:

1. Why is there a difference in the amount shown for restructuring charges in the income statement and the amount shown for restructuring charges in the statement of cash flows?

2. How should the restructuring charges be treated when forecasting future cash flows?

Solution to 1: The difference between restructuring charges in the income statement and restructuring charges in the statement of cash flows arises because some of the restructuring charges were paid in cash and others were not. The statement of cash flows shows the noncash restructuring charges ($14,053) as an amount added back to net income in the process of arriving at net cash provided by operating activities.

Note that Exhibit 7 discloses two noncash charges, which total $12,198 + $1,355 = $13,553, but the statement of cash flows shows restructuring and other noncash charges of $14,053. The MD&A provides no explanation for the balance of $14,053 − $13,553 = $500; thus, the MD&A disclosure of information is incomplete.

Solution to 2: Restructuring charges are generally unpredictable and are not typically part of a forecast. In Alberto-Culver's case, however, $2,724 of restructuring-related liabilities remain (consisting mostly of liabilities for severance pay), which the company expects to pay in early 2008. Therefore, the forecast for 2008 should reflect these cash expenditures that will be made.

Noncash restructuring charges may also cause an increase in net income in some circumstances—for example when a company reverses part or all of a previous accrual. Gains and losses (e.g., of operating assets) are another noncash item that may increase or decrease net noncash charges. If a company sells a piece of equipment with a book value of €60,000 for €100,000, it reports the

€40,000 gain as part of net income. The €40,000 gain is not a cash flow, however, and must be subtracted in arriving at FCFF. Note that the €100,000 *is* a cash flow and is part of the company's net investment in fixed capital. A loss reduces net income and thus must be added back in arriving at FCFF. Aside from depreciation, gains and losses are the most commonly seen noncash charges that require an adjustment to net income. Analysts should examine the company's statement of cash flows to identify items particular to a company and to determine what adjustments the analyst might need to make for the accounting numbers to be useful for forecasting purposes.

Exhibit 8 summarizes the common noncash charges that affect net income and indicates for each item whether to add it to or subtract it from net income in arriving at FCFF.

The item deferred taxes requires special attention because deferred taxes result from differences in the timing of reporting income and expenses in the company's financial statements and the company's tax return. The income tax expense deducted in arriving at net income for financial reporting purposes is not the same as the amount of cash taxes paid. Over time, these differences between book income and taxable income should offset each other and have no impact on aggregate cash flows. Generally, if the analyst's purpose is forecasting and, therefore, identifying the persistent components of FCFF, then the analyst should not add back deferred tax changes that are expected to reverse in the near future. In some circumstances, however, a company may be able to consistently defer taxes until a much later date. If a company is growing and has the ability to indefinitely defer its tax liability, adding back deferred taxes to net income is warranted. Nevertheless, an acquirer must be aware that these taxes may be payable at some time in the future.

Companies often record expenses (e.g., restructuring charges) for financial reporting purposes that are not deductible for tax purposes. In this case, current tax payments are higher than taxes reported in the income statement, resulting in a deferred tax *asset* and a subtraction from net income to arrive at cash flow in the statement of cash flows. If the deferred tax asset is expected to reverse in the near future (e.g., through tax depreciation deductions), to avoid underestimating future cash flows, the analyst should not subtract the deferred tax asset in

EXHIBIT 8	**Noncash Items and FCFF**

Noncash Item	Adjustment to NI to Arrive at FCFF
Depreciation	Added back
Amortization and impairment of intangibles	Added back
Restructuring charges (expense)	Added back
Restructuring charges (income resulting from reversal)	Subtracted
Losses	Added back
Gains	Subtracted
Amortization of long-term bond discounts	Added back
Amortization of long-term bond premiums	Subtracted
Deferred taxes	Added back but calls for special attention

a cash flow forecast. If the company is expected to have these charges on a continual basis, however, a subtraction that will lower the forecast of future cash flows is warranted.

Employee share-based compensation (stock options) provides another challenge to the forecaster. Under IFRS and U.S. GAAP, companies must record in the income statement an expense for options provided to employees. The granting of options themselves does not result in a cash outflow and is thus a noncash charge; however, the granting of options has long-term cash flow implications. When the employee exercises the option, the company receives some cash related to the exercise price of the option at the strike price. This cash flow is considered a financing cash flow. Also, in some cases, a company receives a tax benefit from issuing options, which could increase operating cash flow but not net income. Both IFRS and U.S. GAAP require that a portion of the tax effect be recorded as a financing cash flow rather than an operating cash flow in the statement of cash flows. Analysts should review the statement of cash flows and footnotes to determine the impact of options on operating cash flows. If these cash flows are not expected to persist in the future, analysts should not include them in their forecasts of cash flows. Analysts should also consider the impact of stock options on the number of shares outstanding. When computing equity value, analysts may want to use the number of shares *expected* to be outstanding (based on the exercise of employee stock options) rather than the number currently outstanding.

Example 5 illustrates that when forecasting cash flows for valuation purposes, analysts should consider the sustainability of historical working capital effects on free cash flow.

EXAMPLE 5

Sustainability of Working Capital Effects on Free Cash Flow

Ryanair Holdings PLC (LSE: RYAOF) operates a low-fares scheduled passenger airline serving short-haul, point-to-point routes between Ireland, the United Kingdom, Continental Europe, and Morocco. The operating activities section of its statement of cash flows and a portion of the investing activities section are presented in Exhibit 9. The statement of cash flows was prepared in accordance with IFRS.

EXHIBIT 9	Ryan Holdings PLC Excerpt from Statement of Cash Flows (Euros in Thousands)		
	Year Ended 31 March		
	2007	**2006**	**2005**
Operating activities			
Profit before tax	451,037	338,888	309,196
Adjustments to reconcile profits before tax to net cash provided by operating activities			
Depreciation	143,503	124,405	110,357
Decrease (increase) in inventories	1,002	(962)	(424)
Decrease (increase) in trade receivables	6,497	(9,265)	(5,712)

(Exhibit continued on next page . . .)

EXHIBIT 9	(continued)			
		Year Ended 31 March		
		2007	**2006**	**2005**
Decrease (increase) in other current assets		(30,849)	(882)	(4,855)
(Decrease) increase in trade payables		(24,482)	(12,835)	24,182
(Decrease) increase in accrued expenses		233,839	150,083	89,406
(Decrease) increase in other creditors		75,351	11,403	(10,986)
Increase in maintenance provisions		11,997	9,486	714
Loss (gain) on disposal of property, plant, and equipment		(91)	(815)	(47)
Decrease (increase) in interest receivable		48	(3,959)	(505)
(Decrease) increase in interest payable		2,671	1,159	3,420
Retirement costs		589	507	167
Share based payments		3,935	2,921	488
Income tax		(5,194)	436	(4,198)
Net cash provided by operating activities		869,853	610,570	511,203
Investing activities				
Capital expenditure (purchase of property, plant, and equipment)		(494,972)	(546,225)	(631,994)

Analysts predict that as Ryanair grows in coming years, depreciation expense will increase substantially. Based on the information given, address the following:

1. Contrast reported depreciation expense to reported capital expenditures and describe the implications of future growth in depreciation expense (all else being equal) for future net income and future cash from operating activities.

2. Explain the effects on free cash flow to equity of changes in 2007 in working capital accounts, such as inventory, accounts receivable, and accounts payable, and comment on the long-term sustainability of such changes.

Solution to 1: In the 2005–2007 period, depreciation expense was a small fraction of capital expenditures. For example, in 2007, capital expenditures of €495 million were 3.5 times as large as the €143.5 million depreciation expense.

In calculating net income, depreciation is a deduction. Therefore, as depreciation expense increases in coming years, net income will decrease. Specifically, net income will be reduced by (depreciation expense) × (1 − Tax rate). In calculating CFO, however, depreciation is added back in full to net income. The difference between depreciation expense—the amount added back to net income to calculate CFO—and the amount by which net income is reduced by depreciation expense is (tax rate) × (depreciation expense), which represents a positive increment to CFO. Thus, the projected increase in depreciation expense is a negative for future net income but a positive for future CFO. (At worst, if the company operates at a loss, depreciation is neutral for CFO.)

Solution to 2: In 2007, the decreases in inventory and accounts receivable ("trade receivables") resulted in positive adjustments to net income (i.e., the changes increased cash flow relative to net income). The adjustments are positive because decreases in these accounts (the sale of inventory and collection of accounts receivable) are a source of cash. On the current liabilities side, the increase in accrued expenses and increase in "other creditors" are also added back to net income and are sources of cash because such increases represent increased amounts for which cash payments have yet to be made. The negative adjustment for accounts payable, however, indicates that the accounts payable balance declined in 2007: Ryanair spent cash to reduce the amount of trade credit being extended to it by suppliers during the year, resulting in a reduction in cash. Because CFO is a component of FCFE, the items that had a positive (negative) effect on CFO also have a positive (negative) effect on FCFE.

Declining balances for assets, such as inventory, or for liabilities, such as accounts payable, are not sustainable indefinitely. In the extreme case, the balance declines to zero and no further reduction is possible. Given the growth in its net income and the expansion of PP&E evidenced by capital expenditures, Ryanair appears to be growing and investors should expect its working capital requirements to grow accordingly. Thus, the components of 2007 FCFE attributable to reduction in inventory and accounts receivable balances are probably not relevant in forecasting future FCFE.

3.4 Computing FCFE from FCFF

FCFE is cash flow available to equityholders only. To find FCFE, therefore, we must reduce FCFF by the after-tax value of interest paid to debtholders and add net borrowing (which is debt issued less debt repaid over the period for which one is calculating free cash flow):

Free cash flow to equity = Free cash flow to the firm
Less: Interest expense $\times$ (1 − Tax rate)
Plus: Net borrowing

or

$$\text{FCFE} = \text{FCFF} - \text{Int}(1 - \text{Tax rate}) + \text{Net borrowing} \tag{9}$$

As Equation 9 shows, FCFE is found by starting from FCFF, subtracting after-tax interest expenses, and adding net new borrowing. The analyst can also find FCFF from FCFE by making the opposite adjustments—by adding after-tax interest expenses and subtracting net borrowing: FCFF = FCFE + Int(1 − Tax rate) − Net borrowing.

Exhibit 10 uses the values for FCFF for Cane Distribution calculated in Example 3 to show the calculation of FCFE when starting with FCFF. To calculate FCFE in this manner, we subtract after-tax interest expense from FCFF and then add net borrowing (equal to new debt borrowing minus debt repayment).

To reiterate, FCFE is the cash flow available to common stockholders—the cash flow remaining after all operating expenses (including taxes) have been paid, capital investments have been made, and other transactions with other suppliers of capital have been carried out. The company's other capital suppliers include creditors, such as bondholders, and preferred stockholders. The cash

EXHIBIT 10	Calculating FCFE from FCFF		
	Years Ending 31 December		
	2008	**2009**	**2010**
Free cash flow to the firm	97.50	107.26	117.97
Interest paid × (1 − Tax rate)	(10.98)	(12.08)	(13.28)
New debt borrowing	22.40	24.64	27.10
Debt repayment	(0)	(0)	(0)
Free cash flow to equity	108.92	119.82	131.79

flows (net of taxes) that arise from transactions with creditors and preferred stockholders are deducted from FCFF to arrive at FCFE.

FCFE is the amount that the company can afford to pay out as dividends. In actuality, for various reasons companies often pay out substantially more or substantially less than FCFE, so FCFE often differs from dividends paid. One reason for this difference is that the dividend decision is a discretionary decision of the board of directors. Most corporations "manage" their dividends; they prefer to raise them gradually over time, partly because they do not want to cut dividends. Many companies raise dividends slowly even when their earnings are increasing rapidly, and companies often maintain their current dividends even when their profitability has declined. Consequently, earnings are much more volatile than dividends.

In Equations 7 and 8, we show the calculation of FCFF starting with, respectively, net income and cash flow from operations. As Equation 9 shows, FCFE = FCFF − Int(1 − Tax rate) + Net borrowing. By subtracting after-tax interest expense and adding net borrowing to Equations 7 and 8, we have equations to calculate FCFE starting with, respectively, net income and CFO:

$$FCFE = NI + NCC - FCInv - WCInv + Net\ borrowing \tag{10}$$

$$FCFE = CFO - FCInv + Net\ borrowing \tag{11}$$

Example 6 illustrates how to adjust net income or CFO to find FCFF and FCFE.

EXAMPLE 6

Adjusting Net Income or CFO to Find FCFF and FCFE

The balance sheet, income statement, and statement of cash flows for the Pitts Corporation are shown in Exhibit 11. Note that the statement of cash flows follows a convention according to which the positive numbers of $400 million and $85 million for "cash *used for* investing activities" and "cash *used for* financing activities," respectively, indicate outflows and thus amounts to be *subtracted*. Analysts will also encounter a convention in which the value "(400)" for "cash provided by (used for) investing activities" would be used to indicate a subtraction of $400.

EXHIBIT 11	Financial Statements for Pitts Corporation (in Millions, except for Per-Share Data)

	Year Ended 31 December	
Balance Sheet	**2006**	**2007**
Assets		
Current assets		
Cash and equivalents	$ 190	$ 200
Accounts receivable	560	600
Inventory	410	440
Total current assets	1,160	1,240
Gross fixed assets	2,200	2,600
Accumulated depreciation	(900)	(1,200)
Net fixed assets	1,300	1,400
Total assets	$2,460	$2,640
Liabilities and shareholders' equity		
Current liabilities		
Accounts payable	$ 285	$ 300
Notes payable	200	250
Accrued taxes and expenses	140	150
Total current liabilities	625	700
Long-term debt	865	890
Common stock	100	100
Additional paid-in capital	200	200
Retained earnings	670	750
Total shareholders' equity	970	1,050
Total liabilities and shareholders' equity	$2,460	$2,640

Statement of Income Year Ended 31 December	**2007**
Total revenues	$3,000
Operating costs and expenses	2,200
EBITDA	800
Depreciation	300
Operating income (EBIT)	500
Interest expense	100
Income before tax	400

(Exhibit continued on next page . . .)

EXHIBIT 11	(continued)

Statement of Income
Year Ended 31 December	2007
Taxes (at 40 percent)	160
Net income	240
Dividends	160
Change in retained earnings	80
Earnings per share (EPS)	$0.48
Dividends per share	$0.32

Statement of Cash Flows
Year Ended 31 December	2007
Operating activities	
Net income	$240
Adjustments	
Depreciation	300
Changes in working capital	
Accounts receivable	(40)
Inventories	(30)
Accounts payable	15
Accrued taxes and expenses	10
Cash provided by operating activities	$495
Investing activities	
Purchases of fixed assets	400
Cash used for investing activities	$400
Financing activities	
Notes payable	(50)
Long-term financing issuances	(25)
Common stock dividends	160
Cash used for financing activities	$ 85
Cash and equivalents increase (decrease)	10
Cash and equivalents at beginning of year	190
Cash and equivalents at end of year	$200
Supplemental cash flow disclosures	
Interest paid	$100
Income taxes paid	$160

Note that the Pitts Corporation had net income of $240 million in 2007. In the following, show the calculations required to do each of the following:

1. Calculate FCFF starting with the net income figure.
2. Calculate FCFE starting from the FCFF calculated in Part 1.
3. Calculate FCFE starting with the net income figure.
4. Calculate FCFF starting with CFO.
5. Calculate FCFE starting with CFO.

Solution to 1: The analyst can use Equation 7 to find FCFF from net income (amounts are in millions):

Net income available to common shareholders	$240
Plus: Net noncash charges	300
Plus: Interest expense × (1 − Tax rate)	60
Less: Investment in fixed capital	400
Less: Investment in working capital	45
Free cash flow to the firm	$155

In the format shown and throughout the solutions, "Less: . . . x" is interpreted as "subtract x."

This equation can also be written as

$$FCFF = NI + NCC + Int(1 − Tax\ rate) − FCInv − WCInv$$
$$= 240 + 300 + 60 − 400 − 45 = \$155\ million$$

Some of these items need explanation. Capital spending is $400 million, which is the increase in gross fixed assets shown on the balance sheet and in capital expenditures shown as an investing activity in the statement of cash flows. The increase in working capital is $45 million, which is the increase in accounts receivable of $40 million ($600 million − $560 million) plus the increase in inventories of $30 million ($440 million − $410 million) minus the increase in accounts payable of $15 million ($300 million − $285 million) minus the increase in accrued taxes and expenses of $10 million ($150 million − $140 million). When finding the increase in working capital, we ignore cash because the change in cash is what we are calculating. We also ignore short-term debt, such as notes payable, because such debt is part of the capital provided to the company and is not considered an operating item. The after-tax interest cost is the interest expense times (1 − Tax rate): $100 million × (1 − 0.40) = $60 million. The values of the remaining items in Equation 7 can be taken directly from the financial statements.

Solution to 2: Finding FCFE from FCFF can be done with Equation 9:

Free cash flow to the firm	$155
Less: Interest expense × (1 − Tax rate)	60
Plus: Net borrowing	75
Free cash flow to equity	$170

Or by using the equation

$$FCFE = FCFF - Int(1 - Tax\ rate) + Net\ borrowing$$
$$= 155 - 60 + 75 = \$170\ million$$

Solution to 3: The analyst can use Equation 10 to find FCFE from NI.

Net income available to common shareholders	$240
Plus: Net noncash charges	300
Less: Investment in fixed capital	400
Less: Investment in working capital	45
Plus: Net borrowing	75
Free cash flow to equity	$170

Or by using the equation

$$FCFE = NI + NCC - FCInv - WCInv + Net\ borrowing$$
$$= 240 + 300 - 400 - 45 + 75 = \$170\ million$$

Because notes payable increased by $50 million ($250 million − $200 million) and long-term debt increased by $25 million ($890 million − $865 million), net borrowing is $75 million.

Solution to 4: Equation 8 can be used to find FCFF from CFO:

Cash flow from operations	$495
Plus: Interest expense × (1 − Tax rate)	60
Less: Investment in fixed capital	400
Free cash flow to the firm	$155

or

$$FCFF = CFO + Int(1 - Tax\ rate) - FCInv$$
$$= 495 + 60 - 400 = \$155\ million$$

Solution to 5: Equation 11 can be used to find FCFE from CFO:

Cash flow from operations	$495
Less: Investment in fixed capital	400
Plus: Net borrowing	75
Free cash flow to equity	$170

or

$$FCFE = CFO - FCInv + Net\ borrowing$$
$$= 495 - 400 + 75 = \$170\ million$$

FCFE is usually less than FCFF. In this example, however, FCFE ($170 million) exceeds FCFF ($155 million) because external borrowing was large during this year.

3.5 Finding FCFF and FCFE from EBIT or EBITDA

FCFF and FCFE are most frequently calculated from a starting basis of net income or CFO (as shown in Sections 3.1 and 3.2). Two other starting points are EBIT and EBITDA from the income statement.

To show the relationship between EBIT and FCFF, we start with Equation 7 and assume that the only noncash charge (NCC) is depreciation (Dep):

$$FCFF = NI + Dep + Int(1 - Tax\ rate) - FCInv - WCInv$$

Net income (NI) can be expressed as

$$NI = (EBIT - Int)(1 - Tax\ rate) = EBIT(1 - Tax\ rate) - Int(1 - Tax\ rate)$$

Substituting this equation for NI in Equation 7, we have

$$FCFF = EBIT(1 - Tax\ rate) + Dep - FCInv - WCInv \qquad \textbf{(12)}$$

To get FCFF from EBIT, we multiply EBIT by $(1 - Tax\ rate)$, add back depreciation, and then subtract the investments in fixed capital and working capital.

The relationship between FCFF and EBITDA can also be easily shown. Net income can be expressed as

$$NI = (EBITDA - Dep - Int)(1 - Tax\ rate) = EBITDA(1 - Tax\ rate) \\ - Dep(1 - Tax\ rate) - Int(1 - Tax\ rate)$$

Substituting this equation for NI in Equation 7 results in

$$FCFF = EBITDA(1 - Tax\ rate) + Dep(Tax\ rate) \qquad \textbf{(13)} \\ - FCInv - WCInv$$

FCFF equals EBITDA times $(1 - Tax\ rate)$ plus depreciation times the tax rate minus investments in fixed capital and working capital. In comparing Equations 12 and 13, note the difference in how depreciation is handled.

Many adjustments for noncash charges that are required to calculate FCFF when starting from net income are not required when starting from EBIT or EBITDA. In the calculation of net income, many noncash charges are made after computing EBIT or EBITDA, so they do not need to be added back when calculating FCFF based on EBIT or EBITDA. Another important consideration is that some noncash charges, such as depreciation, are tax deductible. A noncash charge that affects taxes must be accounted for.

In summary, in calculating FCFF from EBIT or EBITDA, whether an adjustment for a noncash charge is needed depends on where in the income statement the charge has been deducted; furthermore, the form of any needed adjustment depends on whether the noncash charge is a tax-deductible expense.

We can also calculate FCFE (instead of FCFF) from EBIT or EBITDA. An easy way to obtain FCFE based on EBIT or EBITDA is to use Equation 12 (the expression for FCFF in terms of EBIT) or Equation 13 (the expression for FCFF in terms of EBITDA), respectively, and then subtract $Int(1 - Tax\ rate)$ and add net borrowing because FCFE is related to FCFF as follows (see Equation 9):

$$FCFE = FCFF - Int(1 - Tax\ rate) + Net\ borrowing$$

Example 7 uses the Pitts Corporation financial statements to find FCFF and FCFE from EBIT and EBITDA.

EXAMPLE 7

Adjusting EBIT and EBITDA to Find FCFF and FCFE

The Pitts Corporation (financial statements provided in Example 6) had EBIT of $500 million and EBITDA of $800 million in 2007. Show the adjustments that would be required to find FCFF and FCFE:

1. Starting from EBIT.
2. Starting from EBITDA.

Solution to 1: To get FCFF from EBIT using Equation 12, we carry out the following (in millions):

EBIT$(1 - $ Tax rate$) = 500(1 - 0.40)$	$300
Plus: Net noncash charges	300
Less: Net investment in fixed capital	400
Less: Net increase in working capital	45
Free cash flow to the firm	$155

or

$$FCFF = EBIT(1 - \text{Tax rate}) + Dep - FCInv - WCInv$$
$$= 500(1 - 0.40) + 300 - 400 - 45 = \$155 \text{ million}$$

To obtain FCFE, make the appropriate adjustments to FCFF:

$$FCFE = FCFF - Int(1 - \text{Tax rate}) + \text{Net borrowing}$$
$$= 155 - 100(1 - 0.40) + 75 = \$170 \text{ million}$$

Solution to 2: To obtain FCFF from EBITDA using Equation 13, we do the following (in millions):

EBITDA$(1 - $ Tax rate$) = \$800(1 - 0.40)$	$480
Plus: Dep(Tax rate) $= \$300(0.40)$	120
Less: Net investment in fixed capital	400
Less: Net increase in working capital	45
Free cash flow to the firm	$155

or

$$FCFF = EBITDA(1 - \text{Tax rate}) + Dep(\text{Tax rate}) - FCInv - WCInv$$
$$= 800(1 - 0.40) + 300(0.40) - 400 - 45 = \$155 \text{ million}$$

Again, to obtain FCFE, make the appropriate adjustments to FCFF:

$$FCFE = FCFF - Int(1 - \text{Tax rate}) + \text{Net borrowing}$$
$$= 155 - 100(1 - 0.40) + 75 = \$170 \text{ million}$$

3.6 FCFF and FCFE on a Uses-of-Free-Cash-Flow Basis

Prior sections illustrated the calculation of FCFF and FCFE from various income or cash flow starting points (e.g., net income or cash flow from operations). Those approaches to calculating free cash flow can be characterized as showing the *sources* of free cash flow. An alternative perspective examines the *uses* of free cash flow. In the context of calculating FCFF and FCFE, analyzing free cash flow on a uses basis serves as a consistency check on the sources calculation and may reveal information relevant to understanding a company's capital structure policy or cash position.

In general, a firm has the following alternative uses of positive FCFF: 1) retain the cash and thus increase the firm's balances of cash and marketable securities; 2) use the cash for payments to providers of debt capital (i.e., interest payments and principal payments in excess of new borrowings); and 3) use the cash for payments to providers of equity capital (i.e., dividend payments and/or share repurchases in excess of new share issuances). Similarly, a firm has the following general alternatives for covering negative free cash flows: draw down cash balances, borrow additional cash, or issue equity.

The effects on the company's capital structure of its transactions with capital providers should be noted. For a simple example, assume that free cash flows are zero and that the company makes no change to its cash balances. Obtaining cash via net new borrowings and using the cash for dividends or net share repurchases will increase the company's leverage, whereas obtaining cash from net new share issuances and using that cash to make principal payments in excess of new borrowings will reduce leverage.

We calculate uses of FCFF as follows:

Uses of FCFF =

>   Increases (or minus decreases) in cash balances
>
>   Plus: Net payments to providers of debt capital, which are calculated as:
>
>   ► Plus: Interest expense × (1 − Tax rate).
>
>   ► Plus: Repayment of principal in excess of new borrowing (or minus new borrowing in excess of debt repayment if new borrowing is greater).
>
>   Plus: Payments to providers of equity capital, which are calculated as:
>
>   ► Plus: Cash dividends.
>
>   ► Plus: Share repurchases in excess of share issuance (or minus new share issuance in excess of share repurchases if share issuance is greater).

Uses of FCFF must equal sources of FCFF as previously calculated.

Free cash flows to equity reflect free cash flows to the firm net of the cash used for payments to providers of debt capital. Accordingly, we can calculate FCFE as follows:

Uses of FCFE =

>   Plus: Increases (or minus decreases) in cash balances
>
>   Plus: Payments to providers of equity capital, which are calculated as:
>
>   ► Plus: Cash dividends.
>
>   ► Plus: Share repurchases in excess of share issuance (or minus new share issuance in excess of share repurchases if share issuance is greater).

Again, the uses of FCFE must equal the sources of FCFE (calculated previously).

To illustrate the equivalence of sources and uses of FCFF and FCFE for the Pitts Corporation, whose financial statements are given in Exhibit 11 in Example 6, note the following for 2007:

▶ The increase in the balance of cash and equivalents was $10, calculated as $200 – $190.

▶ After-tax interest expense was $60, calculated as interest expense ×
$(1 − \text{Tax rate}) = \$100 × (1 − 0.40)$.

▶ Net borrowing was $75, calculated as increase in borrowing minus repayment of debt = $50 (increase in notes payable) + $25 (increase in long-term debt).

▶ Cash dividends totaled $160.

▶ Share repurchases and issuance both equaled $0.

FCFF, previously calculated, was $155. Pitts Corporation used the FCFF as follows:

Increase in balance of cash and cash equivalents		$ 10
Plus:	After-tax interest payments to providers of debt capital	$ 60
Minus:	New borrowing[7]	($ 75)
Plus:	Payments of dividends to providers of equity capital	$160
Plus:	Share repurchases in excess of share issuances (or minus new share issuance in excess of share repurchases)	$ 0
Total uses of FCFF		$155

FCFE, previously calculated, was $170. Pitts Corporation used the FCFE as follows:

Increase in balance of cash and cash equivalents		$ 10
Plus:	Payments of dividends to providers of equity capital	$160
Plus:	Share repurchases in excess of share issuances (or minus new share issuance in excess of share repurchases)	$ 0
Total uses of FCFE		$170

In summary, an analysis of the uses of free cash flows shows that Pitts Corporation was using free cash flows to manage its capital structure by increasing debt. The additional debt was not needed to cover capital expenditures; the statement of cash flows showed that the company's operating cash flows of $495 were more than adequate to cover its capital expenditures of $400. Instead, the additional debt was used, in part, to make dividend payments to the company's shareholders.

3.7 Forecasting FCFF and FCFE

Computing FCFF and FCFE from historical accounting data is relatively straightforward. In some cases, these data are used directly to extrapolate free cash flow growth in a single-stage free cash flow valuation model. On other occasions,

---

[7] Payments of principal to providers of debt capital in excess of new borrowings are a use of free cash flow. Here, the corporation did not use its free cash flow to repay debt; rather, it borrowed new debt, which increased the cash flows available to be used for providers of equity capital.

however, the analyst may expect that the future free cash flows will not bear a simple relationship to the past. The analyst who wishes to forecast future FCFF or FCFE directly for such a company must forecast the individual components of free cash flow. This section extends our previous presentation on *computing* FCFF and FCFE to the more complex task of *forecasting* FCFF and FCFE.

One method for forecasting free cash flow involves applying some constant growth rate to a current level of free cash flow (possibly adjusted). The simplest basis for specifying the future growth rate is to assume that a historical growth rate will also apply to the future. This approach is appropriate if a company's free cash flow has tended to grow at a constant rate and if historical relationships between free cash flow and fundamental factors are expected to continue. Example 8 asks that the reader apply this approach to the Pitts Corporation based on 2007 FCFF of $155 million as calculated in Examples 6 and 7.

EXAMPLE 8

Constant Growth in FCFF

Use Pitts Corporation data to compute its FCFF for the next three years. Assume that growth in FCFF remains at the historical levels of 15 percent a year. The answer is (in millions):

	2007 Actual	2008 Estimate	2009 Estimate	2010 Estimate
FCFF	155.00	178.25	204.99	235.74

A more complex approach is to forecast the components of free cash flow. This approach is able to capture the complex relationships among the components. One popular method[8] is to forecast the individual components of free cash flow—EBIT(1 − Tax rate), net noncash charges, investment in fixed capital, and investment in working capital. EBIT can be forecasted directly or by forecasting sales and the company's EBIT margin based on an analysis of historical data and the current and expected economic environment. Similarly, analysts can base forecasts of capital needs on historical relationships between increases in sales and investments in fixed and working capital.

In this discussion, we illustrate a simple sales-based forecasting method for FCFF and FCFE based on the following major assumption:

> Investment in fixed capital in excess of depreciation (FCInv − Dep) and investment in working capital (WCInv) both bear a constant relationship to forecast increases in the size of the company as measured by increases in sales.

In addition, for FCFE forecasting, we assume that the capital structure represented by the debt ratio (DR)—debt as a percentage of debt plus equity—is constant. Under that assumption, DR indicates the percentage of the investment

---

[8] See Rappaport (1997) for a variation of this model.

in fixed capital in excess of depreciation (also called "net new investment in fixed capital") and in working capital that will be financed by debt. This method involves a simplification because it considers depreciation as the only noncash charge, so the method does not work well when that approximation is not a good assumption.

If depreciation reflects the annual cost for maintaining the existing capital stock, the difference between fixed capital investment and depreciation—incremental FCInv—should be related to the capital expenditures required for growth. In this case, the following inputs are needed:

▶ forecasts of sales growth rates;

▶ forecasts of the after-tax operating margin (for FCFF forecasting) or profit margin (for FCFE forecasting);

▶ an estimate of the relationship of incremental FCInv to sales increases;

▶ an estimate of the relationship of WCInv to sales increases; and

▶ an estimate of DR.

In the case of FCFF forecasting, FCFF is calculated by forecasting EBIT(1 − Tax rate) and subtracting incremental fixed capital expenditures and incremental working capital expenditures.[9] To estimate FCInv and WCInv, we multiply their past proportion to sales increases by the forecasted sales increases. Incremental fixed capital expenditures as a proportion of sales increases are computed as follows:

$$\frac{\text{Capital expenditures} - \text{Depreciation expense}}{\text{Increase in sales}}$$

Similarly, incremental working capital expenditures as a proportion of sales increases are

$$\frac{\text{Increase in working capital}}{\text{Increase in sales}}$$

When depreciation is the only significant net noncash charge, this method yields the same results as the previous equations for estimating FCFF or FCFE. Rather than adding back all depreciation and subtracting all capital expenditures when starting with EBIT(1 − Tax rate), this approach simply subtracts the net capital expenditures in excess of depreciation.

Although the recognition may not be obvious, this approach recognizes that capital expenditures have two components: those expenditures necessary to maintain existing capacity (fixed capital replacement) and those incremental expenditures necessary for growth. In forecasting, the expenditures to maintain capacity are likely to be related to the current level of sales and the expenditures for growth are likely to be related to the forecast of sales growth.

When forecasting FCFE, analysts often make an assumption that the financing of the company involves a "target" debt ratio. In this case, they assume that a specified percentage of the sum of 1) net new investment in fixed capital (new fixed capital minus depreciation expense) and 2) increase in working capital is financed based on a target DR. This assumption leads to a simplification of FCFE calculations. If we assume that depreciation is the only noncash

---

[9] See Rappaport (1997).

charge, Equation 10, which is FCFE = NI + NCC − FCInv − WCInv + Net borrowing, becomes

$$\text{FCFE} = \text{NI} - (\text{FCInv} - \text{Dep}) - \text{WCInv} + \text{Net borrowing} \qquad (14)$$

Note that FCInv − Dep represents the incremental fixed capital expenditure net of depreciation. By assuming a target DR, we eliminated the need to forecast net borrowing and can use the expression

$$\text{Net borrowing} = \text{DR}(\text{FCInv} - \text{Dep}) + \text{DR}(\text{WCInv})$$

By using this expression, we do not need to forecast debt issuance and repayment on an annual basis to estimate net borrowing. Equation 14 then becomes

$$\text{FCFE} = \text{NI} - (\text{FCInv} - \text{Dep}) - \text{WCInv} + (\text{DR})(\text{FCInv} - \text{Dep}) + (\text{DR})(\text{WCInv})$$

or

$$\text{FCFE} = \text{NI} - (1 - \text{DR})(\text{FCInv} - \text{Dep}) - (1 - \text{DR})(\text{WCInv}) \qquad (15)$$

Equation 15 says that FCFE equals NI minus the amount of fixed capital expenditure (net of depreciation) and working capital investment that is financed by equity. Again for Equation 15, we have assumed that the only noncash charge is depreciation.

Examples 9 and 10 illustrate this sales-based method for forecasting free cash flow to the firm.

EXAMPLE 9

Free Cash Flow Tied to Sales

Carla Espinosa is an analyst following Pitts Corporation at the end of 2007. From the data in Example 6, she can see that the company's sales for 2007 were $3,000 million, and she assumes that sales grew by $300 million from 2006 to 2007. Espinosa expects Pitts Corporation's sales to increase by 10 percent a year thereafter. Pitts Corporation is a fairly stable company, so Espinosa expects it to maintain its historical EBIT margin and proportions of incremental investments in fixed and working capital. Pitts Corporation's EBIT for 2007 is $500 million; its EBIT margin is 16.67 percent (500/3,000), and its tax rate is 40 percent.

Note from Pitts Corporation's 2007 statement of cash flows (Exhibit 11) the amount for "purchases of fixed assets" (i.e., capital expenditures) of $400 million and depreciation of $300 million. Thus, incremental fixed capital investment in 2007 was

$$\frac{\text{Capital expenditures} - \text{Depreciation expense}}{\text{Increase in sales}}$$
$$= \frac{400 - 300}{300} = 33.33\%$$

Incremental working capital investment in the past year was

$$\frac{\text{Increase in working capital}}{\text{Increase in sales}} = \frac{45}{300} = 15\%$$

So, for every $100 increase in sales, Pitts Corporation invests $33.33 in new equipment in addition to replacement of depreciated equipment and $15 in working capital. Espinosa forecasts FCFF for 2008 as follows (dollars in millions):

Sales	$3,300	Up 10 percent
EBIT	550	16.67 percent of sales
EBIT(1 − Tax rate)	330	Adjusted for 40 percent tax rate
Incremental FC	(100)	33.33 percent of sales increase
Incremental WC	(45)	15 percent of sales increase
FCFF	$ 185	

This model can be used to forecast multiple periods and is flexible enough to allow varying sales growth rates, EBIT margins, tax rates, and rates of incremental capital increases.

EXAMPLE 10

Free Cash Flow Growth Tied to Sales Growth

Continuing her work, Espinosa decides to forecast FCFF for the next five years. She is concerned that Pitts Corporation will not be able to maintain its historical EBIT margin and that the EBIT margin will decline from the current 16.67 percent to 14.5 percent in the next five years. Exhibit 12 summarizes her forecasts.

EXHIBIT 12 Free Cash Flow Growth for Pitts Corporation (Dollars in Millions)

	Year 1	Year 2	Year 3	Year 4	Year 5
Sales growth	10.00%	10.00%	10.00%	10.00%	10.00%
EBIT margin	16.67%	16.00%	15.50%	15.00%	14.50%
Tax rate	40.00%	40.00%	40.00%	40.00%	40.00%
Incremental FC investment	33.33%	33.33%	33.33%	33.33%	33.33%
Incremental WC investment	15.00%	15.00%	15.00%	15.00%	15.00%
Prior-year sales	$3,000.00				
Sales forecast	$3,300.00	$3,630.00	$3,993.00	$4,392.30	$4,831.53
EBIT forecast	550.00	580.80	618.92	658.85	700.57
EBIT(1 − Tax rate)	330.00	348.48	371.35	395.31	420.34
Incremental FC	(100.00)	(110.00)	(121.00)	(133.10)	(146.41)
Incremental WC	(45.00)	(49.50)	(54.45)	(59.90)	(65.88)
FCFF	$185.00	$188.98	$195.90	$202.31	$208.05

The model need not begin with sales; it could start with net income, cash flow from operations, or EBITDA.

A similar model can be designed for FCFE, as shown in Example 11. In the case of FCFE, the analyst should begin with net income and must also forecast any net new borrowing or net preferred stock issue.

EXAMPLE 11

Finding FCFE from Sales Forecasts

Espinosa decides to forecast FCFE for the year 2008. She uses the same expectations derived in Example 9. Additionally, she expects the following:

▶ the profit margin will remain at 8 percent (= 240/3,000), and

▶ the company will finance incremental fixed and working capital investments with 50 percent debt—the target DR. Espinosa's forecast for 2008 is as follows (dollars in millions):

Sales	$3,300	Up 10 percent
NI	264	8.0 percent of sales
Incremental FC	(100)	33.33 percent of sales increase
Incremental WC	(45)	15 percent of sales increase
Net borrowing	72.50	(100 FCInv + 45 WCInv) × 50%
FCFE	$ 191.50	

When the company being analyzed has significant noncash charges other than depreciation expense, the approach we have just illustrated will result in a less accurate estimate of FCFE than one obtained by forecasting all the individual components of FCFE. In some cases, the analyst will have specific forecasts of planned components, such as capital expenditures. In other cases, the analyst will study historical relationships, such as previous capital expenditures and sales levels, to develop a forecast.

3.8 Other Issues in Free Cash Flow Analysis

We have already presented a number of practical issues that arise in using free cash flow valuation models. Other issues relate to analyst adjustments to CFO, the relationship between free cash flow and dividends, and valuation with complicated financial structures.

3.8.1 Analyst Adjustments to CFO

Although many corporate financial statements are straightforward, some are not transparent (i.e., the quality of the reported numbers and of disclosures is not high). Sometimes, difficulties in analysis arise because the companies and their transactions are more complicated than the Pitts Corporation example we just provided.

For instance, in many corporate financial statements, the changes in balance sheet items (the increase in an asset or the decrease in a liability) differ from the changes reported in the statement of cash flows. Similarly, depreciation in the statement of cash flows may differ from depreciation expense in the income statement. How do such problems arise?

Factors that can cause discrepancies between changes in balance sheet accounts and the changes reported in the statement of cash flows include acquisitions or divestitures and the presence of nondomestic subsidiaries. For example, an increase in an inventory account may result from purchases from suppliers (which is an operating activity) or from an acquisition or merger with another company that has inventory on its balance sheet (which is an investing activity). Discrepancies may also occur from currency translations of the earnings of nondomestic subsidiaries.

Because the CFO figure from the statement of cash flows may be contaminated by cash flows arising from financing and/or investing activities, when analysts use CFO in a valuation context, ideally they should remove such contaminations. The resulting analyst-adjusted CFO is then the starting point for free cash flow calculations.

3.8.2 Free Cash Flow versus Dividends and Other Earnings Components

Many analysts have a strong preference for free cash flow valuation models over dividend discount models. Although one type of model may have no theoretical advantage over another type, legitimate reasons to prefer one model can arise in the process of applying free cash flow models versus DDMs. First, many corporations pay no, or very low, cash dividends. Using a DDM to value these companies is difficult because they require forecasts about when dividends will be initiated, the level of dividends at initiation, and the growth rate or rates from that point forward. Second, dividend payments are at the discretion of the corporation's board of directors. Therefore, they may imperfectly signal the company's long-run profitability. Some corporations clearly pay dividends that are substantially less than their free cash flow, and others pay dividends that are substantially more. Finally, as mentioned earlier, dividends are the cash flow actually going to shareholders whereas free cash flow to equity is the cash flow available to be distributed to shareholders without impairing the company's value. If a company is being analyzed because it is a target for takeover, free cash flow is the appropriate cash flow measure; once the company is taken over, the new owners will have discretion over how free cash flow is used (including its distribution in the form of dividends).

We have defined FCFF and FCFE and presented alternative (equivalent) ways to calculate both of them. So, the reader should have a good idea of what is included in FCFF or FCFE but may wonder why some cash flows are not included. Specifically, what role do dividends, share repurchases, share issuance, or changes in leverage have on FCFF and FCFE? The simple answer is: not much. Recall the formulas for FCFF and FCFE:

$$FCFF = NI + NCC + Int(1 - Tax\ rate) - FCInv - WCInv$$

and

$$FCFE = NI + NCC - FCInv - WCInv + Net\ borrowing$$

Notice that dividends and share repurchases and issuance are absent from the formulas. The reason is that FCFF and FCFE are the cash flows *available* to investors or to stockholders; dividends and share repurchases are *uses* of these cash flows. So, the simple answer is that transactions between the company and its shareholders (through cash dividends, share repurchases, and share issuances) do not affect free cash flow. Leverage changes, such as the use of more debt financing, have some impact because they increase the interest tax shield (reduce corporate taxes because of the tax deductibility of interest) and reduce the cash flow available to equity. In the long run, the investing and financing decisions made today will affect future cash flows.

If all the inputs were known and mutually consistent, a DDM and a FCFE model would result in identical valuations for a stock. One possibility would be that FCFE equals cash dividends each year. Then, both cash flow streams would be discounted at the required return for equity and would have the same present value.

Generally, however, FCFE and dividends will differ, but the same economic forces that lead to low (high) dividends lead to low (high) FCFE. For example, a rapidly growing company with superior investment opportunities will retain a high proportion of earnings and pay low dividends. This same company will have high investments in fixed capital and working capital and have a low FCFE (which is clear from the expression FCFE = NI + NCC − FCInv − WCInv + Net borrowing). Conversely, a mature company that is investing relatively little might have high dividends and high FCFE. In spite of this tendency, however, FCFE and dividends will usually differ.

FCFF and FCFE, as defined in this reading, are measures of cash flow designed for valuation of the firm or its equity. Other definitions of "free cash flow" frequently appear in textbooks, articles, and vendor-supplied databases of financial information on public companies. In many cases, these other definitions of free cash flow are not designed for valuation purposes and thus should not be used for valuation. Using numbers supplied by others without knowing exactly how they are defined increases the likelihood of making errors in valuation. As consumers and producers of research, analysts should understand (if consumers) or make clear (if producers) the definition of free cash flow being used.

Because using free cash flow analysis requires considerable care and understanding, some practitioners erroneously use earnings components such as NI, EBIT, EBITDA, or CFO in a discounted cash flow valuation. Such mistakes may lead the practitioner to systematically overstate or understate the value of a stock. Shortcuts can be costly.

A common shortcut is to use EBITDA as a proxy for the cash flow to the firm. Equation 13 clearly shows the differences between EBITDA and FCFF:

$$\text{FCFF} = \text{EBITDA}(1 - \text{Tax rate}) + \text{Dep(Tax rate)} - \text{FCInv} - \text{WCInv}$$

Depreciation charges as a percentage of EBITDA differ substantially for different companies and industries, as does the depreciation tax shield (the depreciation charge times the tax rate). Although FCFF captures this difference, EBITDA does not. EBITDA also does not account for the investments a company makes in fixed capital or working capital. Hence, EBITDA is a poor measure of the cash flow available to the company's investors. Using EBITDA (instead of free cash flow) in a DCF model has another important aspect as well: EBITDA is a before-tax measure, so the discount rate applied to EBITDA would be a before-tax rate. The WACC used to discount FCFF is an after-tax cost of capital.

EBITDA is a poor proxy for free cash flow to the firm because it does not account for the depreciation tax shield and the investment in fixed capital and working capital, but it is an even poorer proxy for free cash flow to equity. From a stockholder's perspective, additional defects of EBITDA include its failure to account for the after-tax interest costs or cash flows from new borrowing or debt repayments. Example 12 shows the mistakes sometimes made in discussions of cash flows.

EXAMPLE 12

The Mistakes of Using Net Income for FCFE and EBITDA for FCFF

A recent job applicant made some interesting comments about FCFE and FCFF: "I don't like the definitions for FCFE and FCFF because they are unnecessarily complicated and confusing. The best measure of FCFE, the funds available to pay dividends, is simply net income. You take the net income number straight from the income statement and don't need to make any further adjustments. Similarly, the best measure of FCFF, the funds available to the company's suppliers of capital, is EBITDA. You can take EBITDA straight from the income statement, and you don't need to consider using anything else."

How would you respond to the job applicant's definition of 1) FCFE and 2) FCFF?

Solution to 1: The FCFE is the cash generated by the business's operations less the amount it must reinvest in additional assets plus the amounts it is borrowing. Equation 10, which starts with net income to find FCFE, shows these items:

Free cash flow to equity = Net income available to common
shareholders
Plus: Net noncash charges
Less: Investment in fixed capital
Less: Investment in working capital
Plus: Net borrowing

Net income does not include several cash flows. So, net income tells only part of the overall story. Investments in fixed or working capital reduce the cash available to stockholders, as do loan repayments. New borrowing increases the cash available. FCFE, however, includes the cash generated from operating the business and also accounts for the investing and financing activities of the company. Of course, a special case exists in which net income and FCFE are the same. This case occurs when new investments exactly equal depreciation and the company is not investing in working capital or engaging in any net borrowing.

Solution to 2: Assuming that EBITDA equals FCFF introduces several possible mistakes. Equation 13 highlights these mistakes:

Free cash flow to the firm = EBITDA(1 − Tax rate)
Plus: Depreciation(Tax rate)
Less: Investment in fixed capital
Less: Investment in working capital

The applicant is ignoring taxes, which obviously reduce the cash available to the company's suppliers of capital.

3.8.3 Free Cash Flow and Complicated Capital Structures

For the most part, the discussion of FCFF and FCFE so far has assumed the company has a simple capital structure with two sources of capital, namely, debt and equity. Including preferred stock as a third source of capital requires the analyst to add terms to the equations for FCFF and FCFE to account for the dividends paid on preferred stock and for the issuance or repurchase of preferred shares. Instead of including those terms in all of the equations, we chose to leave preferred stock out because only a few corporations use preferred stock. For companies that do have preferred stock, however, the effects of the preferred stock can be incorporated in the valuation models.

For example, in Equation 7, which calculates FCFF starting with net income available to common shareholders, preferred dividends paid would be added to the cash flows to obtain FCFF. In Equation 10 which calculates FCFE starting with net income available to common shareholders, if preferred dividends were already subtracted when arriving at net income, no further adjustment for preferred dividends would be required. Issuing (redeeming) preferred stock increases (decreases) the cash flow available to common stockholders, however, so this term would have to be added in. The existence of preferred stock in the capital structure has many of the same effects as the existence of debt, except that unlike interest payments on debt, preferred stock dividends paid are not tax deductible.

Example 13 shows how to calculate WACC, FCFE, and FCFF when the company has preferred stock.

EXAMPLE 13

FCFF Valuation with Preferred Stock in the Capital Structure

Welch Corporation uses bond, preferred stock, and common stock financing. The market value of each of these sources of financing and the before-tax required rates of return for each are given in Exhibit 13:

EXHIBIT 13	Welch Corporation Capital Structure (Dollars in Millions)	
	Market Value ($)	**Required Return (%)**
Bonds	400	8.0
Preferred stock	100	8.0
Common stock	500	12.0
Total	1,000	

Other financial information (dollars in millions):

▶ Net income available to common shareholders = $110.

▶ Interest expenses = $32.

▶ Preferred dividends = $8.

▶ Depreciation = $40.

▶ Investment in fixed capital = $70.

▶ Investment in working capital = $20.

▶ Net borrowing = $25.

▶ Tax rate = 30 percent.

▶ Stable growth rate of FCFF = 4.0 percent.

▶ Stable growth rate of FCFE = 5.4 percent.

1. Calculate Welch Corporation's WACC.

2. Calculate the current value of FCFF.

3. Based on forecasted Year 1 FCFF, what is the total value of Welch Corporation and the value of its equity?

4. Calculate the current value of FCFE.

5. Based on forecasted Year 1 FCFE, what is the value of equity?

Solution to 1: Based on the weights and after-tax costs of each source of capital, the WACC is

$$\text{WACC} = \frac{400}{1,000}8\%(1 - 0.30) + \frac{100}{1,000}8\% + \frac{500}{1,000}12\% = 9.04\%$$

Solution to 2: If the company did not issue preferred stock, FCFF would be

$$\text{FCFF} = \text{NI} + \text{NCC} + \text{Int}(1 - \text{Tax rate}) - \text{FCInv} - \text{WCInv}$$

If preferred stock dividends have been paid (and net income is income available to common shareholders), the preferred dividends must be added back just as after-tax interest expenses are. The modified equation (including preferred dividends) for FCFF is

$$\text{FCFF} = \text{NI} + \text{NCC} + \text{Int}(1 - \text{Tax rate}) + \text{Preferred dividends}$$
$$- \text{FCInv} - \text{WCInv}$$

For Welch Corporation, FCFF is

$$\text{FCFF} = 110 + 40 + 32(1 - 0.30) + 8 - 70 - 20 = \$90.4 \text{ million}$$

Solution to 3: The total value of the firm is

$$\text{Firm value} = \frac{\text{FCFF}_1}{\text{WACC} - g} = \frac{90.4(1.04)}{0.0904 - 0.04}$$

$$= \frac{94.016}{0.0504} = \$1,865.40 \text{ million}$$

The value of (common) equity is the total value of the company minus the value of debt and preferred stock:

$$\text{Equity} = 1,865.40 - 400 - 100 = \$1,365.40 \text{ million}$$

Solution to 4: With no preferred stock, FCFE is

$$\text{FCFE} = \text{NI} + \text{NCC} - \text{FCInv} - \text{WCInv} + \text{Net borrowing}$$

> If the company has preferred stock, the FCFE equation is essentially the same. Net borrowing in this case is the total of new debt borrowing and net issuances of new preferred stock. For Welch Corporation, FCFE is
>
> $$FCFE = 110 + 40 - 70 - 20 + 25 = \$85 \text{ million}$$
>
> **Solution to 5:** Valuing FCFE, which is growing at 5.4 percent, produces a value of equity of
>
> $$\text{Equity} = \frac{FCFE_1}{r - g} = \frac{85(1.054)}{0.12 - 0.054} = \frac{89.59}{0.066} = \$1,357.42 \text{ million}$$

Paying cash dividends on common stock does not affect FCFF or FCFE, which are the amounts of cash *available* to all investors or to common stock-holders. It is simply a use of the available cash. Share repurchases of common stock also do not affect FCFF or FCFE. Share repurchases are, in many respects, a substitute for cash dividends. Similarly, issuing shares of common stock does not affect FCFF or FCFE.

Changing leverage, however (changing the amount of debt financing in the company's capital structure), does have some effects on FCFE particularly. An increase in leverage will not affect FCFF (although it might affect the calculations used to arrive at FCFF). An increase in leverage affects FCFE in two ways. In the year the debt is issued, it increases the FCFE by the amount of debt issued. After the debt is issued, FCFE is then reduced by the after-tax interest expense.

In Section 3, we have discussed the concepts of FCFF and FCFE and their estimation. The next section presents additional valuation models that use forecasts of FCFF or FCFE to value the firm or its equity. These free cash flow models are similar in structure to dividend discount models, although the analyst must face the reality that estimating free cash flows is more time-consuming than estimating dividends.

4   FREE CASH FLOW MODEL VARIATIONS

Section 4 presents several extensions of the free cash flow models presented earlier. In many cases, especially when inflation rates are volatile, analysts will value real cash flows instead of nominal values. As with dividend discount models, free cash flow models are sensitive to the data inputs, so analysts routinely perform sensitivity analyses of their valuations.

In Section 2.3, we presented the single-stage free cash flow model, which has a constant growth rate. In the following, we use the single-stage model to address selected valuation issues; we then present multistage free cash flow models.

4.1 An International Application of the Single-Stage Model

Valuation by using real (inflation-adjusted) values instead of nominal values has much appeal when inflation rates are high and volatile. Many analysts use this adaptation for both domestic and nondomestic stocks, but the use of real values is especially helpful for valuing international stocks. Special challenges to valuing equities from multiple countries include 1) incorporating economic factors—such as interest rates, inflation rates, and growth rates—that differ among countries and 2) dealing with varied accounting standards. Furthermore, performing analyses in multiple countries challenges the analyst—particularly a team of analysts—to use *consistent* assumptions for all countries.

Several securities firms have adapted the single-stage FCFE model to address some of the challenges of international valuation. They choose to analyze companies by using real cash flows and real discount rates instead of nominal values. To estimate real discount rates, they use a modification of the build-up method mentioned in the reading on return concepts. Starting with a "country return," which is a real required rate of return for stocks from a particular country, they then make adjustments to the country return for the stock's industry, size, and leverage:

Country return (real)	x.xx%
+/− Industry adjustment	x.xx%
+/− Size adjustment	x.xx%
+/− Leverage adjustment	x.xx%
Required rate of return (real)	x.xx%

The adjustments in the model should have sound economic justification. They should reflect factors expected to affect the relative risk and return associated with an investment.

The securities firms making these adjustments predict the growth rate of FCFE also in real terms. The firms supply their analysts with estimates of the real economic growth rate for each country, and each analyst chooses a real growth rate for the stock being analyzed that is benchmarked against the real country growth rate. This approach is particularly useful for countries with high or variable inflation rates.

The value of the stock is found with an equation essentially like Equation 6 except that all variables in the equation are stated in real terms:

$$V_0 = \frac{\text{FCFE}_0(1 + g_{\text{real}})}{r_{\text{real}} - g_{\text{real}}}$$

Whenever real discount rates and real growth rates can be estimated more reliably than nominal discount rates and nominal growth rates, this method is worth using. Example 14 shows how this procedure can be applied.

EXAMPLE 14

Using Real Cash Flows and Discount Rates for International Stocks

YPF Sociedad Anonima (NYSE: YPF) is an integrated oil and gas company headquartered in Buenos Aires, Argentina. Although the company's cash flows have been volatile, an analyst has estimated a per-share normalized FCFE of 1.05 Argentine pesos (ARS) for the year just ended. The real country return for Argentina is 7.30 percent; adjustments to the country return for YPF S.A. are an industry adjustment of +0.80 percent, a size adjustment of −0.33 percent, and a leverage adjustment of −0.12 percent. The long-term real growth rate for Argentina is estimated to be 3.0 percent, and the real growth rate of YPF S.A. is expected to be about 0.5 percent below the country rate. The real required rate of return for YPF S.A. is

Country return (real)	7.30%
Industry adjustment	+0.80%
Size adjustment	−0.33%
Leverage adjustment	−0.12%
Required rate of return	7.65%

The real growth rate of FCFE is expected to be 2.5 percent (3.0 percent − 0.5 percent), so the value of one share is

$$V_0 = \frac{FCFE_0(1 + g_{real})}{r_{real} - g_{real}} = \frac{1.05(1.025)}{0.0765 - 0.025} = \frac{1.07625}{0.0515} = ARS20.90$$

4.2 Sensitivity Analysis of FCFF and FCFE Valuations

In large measure, growth in FCFF and in FCFE depends on a company's future profitability. Sales growth and changes in net profit margins dictate future net profits. Sales growth and profit margins depend on the growth phase of the company and the profitability of the industry. A highly profitable company in a growing industry can enjoy years of profit growth. Eventually, however, its profit margins are likely to be eroded by increased competition; sales growth is also likely to abate because of fewer opportunities for expansion of market size and market share. Growth rates and the duration of growth are difficult to forecast.

The base-year values for the FCFF or FCFE growth models are also critical. Given the same required rates of return and growth rates, the value of the firm or the value of equity will increase or decrease proportionately with the initial value of FCFF or FCFE used.

To examine how sensitive the final valuation is to changes in each of a valuation model's input variables, analysts can perform a sensitivity analysis. Some input variables have a much larger impact on stock valuation than others. Example 15 shows the sensitivity of the valuation of Petroleo Brasileiro to four input variables.

EXAMPLE 15

Sensitivity Analysis of a FCFE Valuation

Steve Bono is valuing the equity of Petroleo Brasileiro (NYSE: PBR), commonly known as Petrobras, in early 2007 by using the single-stage (constant-growth) FCFE model. Estimated FCFE for 2006 is 6.15 Brazilian reais (BRL). Bono's best estimates of input values for the analysis are as follows:

▶ The FCFE growth rate is 7.3 percent.
▶ The risk-free rate is 10.0 percent.
▶ The equity risk premium is 5.5 percent.
▶ Beta is 1.0.

Using the capital asset pricing model (CAPM), Bono estimates that the required rate of return for Petrobras is

$$r = E(R_i) = R_F + \beta_i[E(R_M) - R_F] = 10\% + 1.0(5.5\%) = 15.5\%$$

The estimated value per share is

$$V_0 = \frac{\text{FCFE}_0(1 + g)}{r - g} = \frac{6.15(1.073)}{0.155 - 0.073} = \text{BRL}80.48$$

Exhibit 14 shows Bono's base case and the highest and lowest reasonable alternative estimates. The column "Valuation with Low Estimate" gives the estimated value of Petrobras based on the low estimate for the variable on the same row of the first column and the base-case estimates for the remaining three variables. "Valuation with High Estimate" performs a similar exercise based on the high estimate for the variable at issue.

EXHIBIT 14	Sensitivity Analysis for Petrobras Valuation				
Variable	Base-Case Estimate	Low Estimate	High Estimate	Valuation with Low Estimate	Valuation with High Estimate
Beta	1	0.75	1.25	BRL96.69	BRL68.92
Risk-free rate	10.00%	8.00%	12.00%	BRL106.43	BRL64.70
Equity risk premium	5.50%	4.50%	6.50%	BRL91.65	BRL71.73
FCFE growth rate	7.3%	5.00%	9.00%	BRL61.50	BRL103.13

As Exhibit 14 shows, the value of Petrobras is very sensitive to the inputs. Of the four variables presented, the stock valuation is least sensitive to the range of estimates for the equity risk premium and beta. The range of estimates for these variables produces the smallest ranges of stock values (from BRL71.73 to BRL91.65 for the equity risk premium and from BRL68.92 to BRL96.69 for beta). The stock value is most sensitive to the extreme values for the risk-free rate and for the FCFE growth rate. Of course, the variables to which a stock price is most sensitive vary from case to case. A sensitivity analysis gives the analyst a guide as to which variables are most critical to the final valuation.

4.3 Two-Stage Free Cash Flow Models

Several two-stage and multistage models exist for valuing free cash flow streams, just as several such models are available for valuing dividend streams. The free cash flow models are much more complex than the dividend discount models because to find FCFF or FCFE, the analyst usually incorporates sales, profitability, investments, financing costs, and new financing.

In two-stage free cash flow models, the growth rate in the second stage is a long-run sustainable growth rate. For a declining industry, the second-stage growth rate could be slightly below the GDP growth rate. For an industry that is expected to grow in the future faster than the overall economy, the second-stage growth rate could be slightly greater than the GDP growth rate.

The two most popular versions of the two-stage FCFF and FCFE models are distinguished by the pattern of the growth rates in Stage 1. In one version, the growth rate is constant in Stage 1 before dropping to the long-run sustainable rate in Stage 2. In the other version, the growth rate declines in Stage 1 to reach the sustainable rate at the beginning of Stage 2. This second type of model is like the H-model for discounted dividend valuation, in which dividend growth rates decline in Stage 1 and are constant in Stage 2.

Unlike multistage DDMs, in which the growth rates are consistently dividend growth rates, in free cash flow models, the "growth rate" may refer to different variables (which variables should be stated or should be clear from the context). The growth rate could be the growth rate for FCFF or FCFE, the growth rate for income (either net income or operating income), or the growth rate for sales. If the growth rate is for net income, the changes in FCFF or FCFE also depend on investments in operating assets and the financing of these investments. When the growth rate in income declines, such as between Stage 1 and Stage 2, investments in operating assets probably decline at the same time. If the growth rate is for sales, changes in net profit margins as well as investments in operating assets and financing policies will determine FCFF and FCFE.

A general expression for the two-stage FCFF valuation model is

$$\text{Firm value} = \sum_{t=1}^{n} \frac{\text{FCFF}_t}{(1 + \text{WACC})^t} + \frac{\text{FCFF}_{n+1}}{(\text{WACC} - g)} \frac{1}{(1 + \text{WACC})^n} \quad \textbf{(16)}$$

The summation gives the present value of the first n years of FCFF. The terminal value of the FCFF from Year $n + 1$ forward is $\text{FCFF}_{n+1}/(\text{WACC} - g)$, which is discounted at the WACC for n periods to obtain its present value. Subtracting the value of outstanding debt gives the value of equity. The value per share is then found by dividing the total value of equity by the number of outstanding shares.

The general expression for the two-stage FCFE valuation model is

$$\text{Equity value} = \sum_{t=1}^{n} \frac{\text{FCFE}_t}{(1 + r)^t} + \frac{\text{FCFE}_{n+1}}{r - g} \frac{1}{(1 + r)^n} \quad \textbf{(17)}$$

In this case, the summation is the present value of the first n years of FCFE and the terminal value of $\text{FCFE}_{n+1}/(r - g)$ is discounted at the required rate of return on equity for n years. The value per share is found by dividing the total value of equity by the number of outstanding shares.

In Equation 17, the terminal value of the stock at $t = n$, TV_n, is found by using the constant-growth FCFE model. In this case, $\text{TV}_n = \text{FCFE}_{n+1}/(r - g)$. (Of course, the analyst might choose to estimate terminal value another way, such as using a P/E multiplied by the company's forecasted EPS.) The terminal value estimation is critical for a simple reason: The present value of the terminal value is often a substantial portion of the total value of the stock. For example, in Equation 17, when the analyst is calculating the total present value of the first n cash flows (FCFE) and the present value of the terminal value, the present value of the terminal value is often substantial. In the examples that follow, the terminal value usually represents a substantial part of total estimated value. The same is true in practice.

4.3.1 Fixed Growth Rates in Stage 1 and Stage 2

The simplest two-stage FCFF or FCFE growth model has a constant growth rate in each stage. Example 16 finds the value of a firm that has a 20 percent sales growth rate in Stage 1 and a 6 percent sales growth rate in Stage 2.

EXAMPLE 16

A Two-Stage FCFE Valuation Model with a Constant Growth Rate in Each Stage

Uwe Henschel is doing a valuation of TechnoSchaft on the basis of the following information:

- Year 0 sales per share = €25.
- Sales growth rate = 20 percent annually for three years and 6 percent annually thereafter.
- Net profit margin = 10 percent forever.
- Net investment in fixed capital (net of depreciation) = 50 percent of the sales increase.
- Annual increase in working capital = 20 percent of the sales increase.
- Debt financing = 40 percent of the net investments in capital equipment and working capital.
- TechnoSchaft beta = 1.20; the risk-free rate of return = 7 percent; the equity risk premium = 4.5 percent.

The required rate of return for equity is

$$r = E(R_i) = R_F + \beta_i[E(R_M) - R_F] = 7\% + 1.2(4.5\%) = 12.4\%$$

Exhibit 15 shows the calculations for FCFE.

EXHIBIT 15   **FCFE Estimates for TechnoSchaft (in Euros)**

	Year					
	1	2	3	4	5	6
Sales growth rate	20%	20%	20%	6%	6%	6%
Sales per share	30.000	36.000	43.200	45.792	48.540	51.452
Net profit margin	10%	10%	10%	10%	10%	10%
EPS	3.000	3.600	4.320	4.579	4.854	5.145
Net FCInv per share	2.500	3.000	3.600	1.296	1.374	1.456
WCInv per share	1.000	1.200	1.440	0.518	0.550	0.582
Debt financing per share	1.400	1.680	2.016	0.726	0.769	0.815
FCFE per share	0.900	1.080	1.296	3.491	3.700	3.922
Growth rate of FCFE		20%	20%	169%	6%	6%

In Exhibit 15, sales are shown to grow at 20 percent annually for the first three years and then at 6 percent thereafter. Profits, which are 10 percent of sales, grow at the same rates. The net investments in fixed capital and working capital are, respectively, 50 percent of the increase in sales and 20 percent of the increase in sales. New debt financing equals 40 percent of the total increase in net fixed capital and working capital. FCFE is EPS minus the net investment in fixed capital per share minus the investment in working capital per share plus the debt financing per share.

Notice that FCFE grows by 20 percent annually for the first three years (i.e., between $t = 0$ and $t = 3$). Then, between Year 3 and Year 4, when the sales growth rate drops from 20 percent to

6 percent, FCFE increases substantially. In fact, FCFE increases by 169 percent from Year 3 to Year 4. This large increase in FCFE occurs because profits grow at 6 percent but the investments in capital equipment and working capital (and the increase in debt financing) drop substantially from the previous year. In Years 5 and 6 in Exhibit 15, sales, profit, investments, financing, and FCFE are all shown to grow at 6 percent.

The stock value is the present value of the first three years' FCFE plus the present value of the terminal value of the FCFE from Years 4 and later. The terminal value is

$$TV_3 = \frac{FCFE_4}{r - g} = \frac{3.491}{0.124 - 0.06} = €54.55$$

The present values are

$$V_0 = \frac{0.900}{1.124} + \frac{1.080}{(1.124)^2} + \frac{1.296}{(1.124)^3} + \frac{54.55}{(1.124)^3}$$

$$= 0.801 + 0.855 + 0.913 + 38.415 = €40.98$$

The estimated value of this stock is €40.98 per share.

As mentioned previously, the terminal value may account for a large portion of the value of a stock. In the case of TechnoSchaft, the present value of the terminal value is €38.415 out of a total value of €40.98. The present value (PV) of the terminal value is almost 94 percent of the total value of TechnoSchaft stock.

4.3.2 Declining Growth Rate in Stage 1 and Constant Growth in Stage 2

Growth rates usually do not drop precipitously as they do between the stages in the two-stage model just described, but growth rates can decline over time for many reasons. Sometimes, a small company has a high growth rate that is not sustainable as its market share increases. A highly profitable company may attract competition that makes it harder for the company to sustain its high profit margins.

In this section, we present two examples of the two-stage model with declining growth rates in Stage 1. In the first example, the growth rate of EPS declines during Stage 1. As a company's profitability declines and the company is no longer generating high returns, the company will usually reduce its net new investment in operating assets. The debt financing accompanying the new investments will also decline. Many highly profitable, growing companies have negative or low free cash flows. Later, when growth in profits slows, investments will tend to slow and the company will experience positive cash flows. Of course, the negative cash flows incurred in the high-growth stage help determine the cash flows that occur in future years.

Example 17 models FCFE per share as a function of EPS that declines constantly during Stage 1. Because of declining earnings growth rates, the company in the example also reduces its new investments over time. The value of the company depends on these free cash flows, which are substantial after the high-growth (and high-profitability) period has largely elapsed.

EXAMPLE 17

A Two-Stage FCFE Valuation Model with Declining Net Income Growth in Stage 1

Vishal Noronha needs to prepare a valuation of Sindhuh Enterprises. Noronha has assembled the following information for his analysis. It is now the first day of 2008.

▶ EPS for 2007 is $2.40.
▶ For the next five years, the growth rate in EPS is given in the following table. After 2012, the growth rate will be 7 percent.

	2008	2009	2010	2011	2012
Growth rate for EPS	30%	18%	12%	9%	7%

▶ Net investments in fixed capital (net of depreciation) for the next five years are given in the following table. After 2012, capital expenditures are expected to grow at 7 percent annually.

	2008	2009	2010	2011	2012
Net capital expenditure per share	$3.00	$2.50	$2.00	$1.50	$1.00

▶ The investment in working capital each year will equal 50 percent of the net investment in capital items.
▶ Thirty percent of the net investment in fixed capital and investment in working capital will be financed with new debt financing.
▶ Current market conditions dictate a risk-free rate of 6.0 percent, an equity risk premium of 4.0 percent, and a beta of 1.10 for Sindhuh Enterprises.

1. What is the per-share value of Sindhuh Enterprises on the first day of 2008?

2. What should be the trailing P/E on the first day of 2008 and the first day of 2012?

Solution to 1: The required return for Sindhuh should be

$$r = E(R_i) = R_F + \beta_i [E(R_M) - R_F] = 6\% + 1.1 \ (4\%) = 10.4\%$$

The FCFEs for the company for years 2008 through 2012 are given in Exhibit 16.

EXHIBIT 16	FCFE Estimates for Sindhuh Enterprises (Per-Share Data in U.S. Dollars)				

	Year				
	2008	2009	2010	2011	2012
Growth rate for EPS	30%	18%	12%	9%	7%
EPS	3.120	3.682	4.123	4.494	4.809
Net FCInv per share	3.000	2.500	2.000	1.500	1.000
WCInv per share	1.500	1.250	1.000	0.750	0.500
Debt financing per share[a]	1.350	1.125	0.900	0.675	0.450
FCFE per share[b]	−0.030	1.057	2.023	2.919	3.759
PV of FCFE discounted at 10.4%	−0.027	0.867	1.504	1.965	

[a] 30 percent of (Net FCInv + WCInv).

[b] EPS − Net FCInv per share − WCInv per share + Debt financing per share.

Earnings are \$2.40 in 2007. Earnings increase each year by the growth rate given in the table. Net capital expenditures (capital expenditures minus depreciation) are the amounts that Noronha assumed. The increase in working capital each year is 50 percent of the increase in net capital expenditures. Debt financing is 30 percent of the total outlays for net capital expenditures and working capital each year. The FCFE each year is net income minus net capital expenditures minus increase in working capital plus new debt financing. Finally, for years 2008 through 2011, the present value of FCFE is found by discounting FCFE by the 10.4 percent required rate of return for equity.

After 2011, FCFE will grow by a constant 7 percent annually, so the constant growth FCFE valuation model can be used to value this cash flow stream. At the end of 2011, the value of the future FCFE is

$$V_{2011} = \frac{FCFE_{2012}}{r - g} = \frac{3.759}{0.104 - 0.07} = \$110.56 \text{ per share}$$

To find the present value of V_{2011} as of the end of 2007, V_{2007}, we discount V_{2011} at 10.4 percent for four years:

$$PV = 110.56/(1.104)^4 = \$74.425 \text{ per share}$$

The total present value of the company is the present value of the first four years' FCFE plus the present value of the terminal value, or

$$V_{2007} = -0.027 + 0.867 + 1.504 + 1.965 + 74.42 = \$78.73 \text{ per share}$$

Solution to 2: Using the estimated \$78.73 stock value, we find that the trailing P/E at the beginning of 2008 is

$$P/E = 78.73/2.40 = 32.8$$

At the beginning of 2012, the expected stock value is \$110.56 and the previous year's EPS is \$4.494, so the trailing P/E at this time would be

$$P/E = 110.56/4.494 = 24.6$$

After its high-growth phase has ended, the P/E for the company declines substantially.

The FCFE in Example 17 was based on forecasts of future EPS. Analysts often model a company by forecasting future sales and then estimating the profits, investments, and financing associated with those sales levels. For large companies, analysts may estimate the sales, profitability, investments, and financing for each division or large subsidiary. Then, they aggregate the free cash flows for all of the divisions or subsidiaries to get the free cash flow for the company as a whole.

Example 18 is a two-stage FCFE model with declining sales growth rates in Stage 1, with profits, investments, and financing keyed to sales. In Stage 1, the growth rate of sales and the profit margin on sales both decline as the company matures and faces more competition and slower growth.

EXAMPLE 18

A Two-Stage FCFE Valuation Model with Declining Sales Growth Rates

Medina Werks, a manufacturing company headquartered in Canada, has a competitive advantage that will probably deteriorate over time. Analyst Flavio Torino expects this deterioration to be reflected in declining sales growth rates as well as declining profit margins. To value the company, Torino has accumulated the following information:

▶ Current sales are C$600 million. Over the next six years, the annual sales growth rate and the net profit margin are projected to be as follows:

	Year 1 (%)	Year 2 (%)	Year 3 (%)	Year 4 (%)	Year 5 (%)	Year 6 (%)
Sales growth rate	20	16	12	10	8	7
Net profit margin	14	13	12	11	10.5	10

Beginning in Year 6, the 7 percent sales growth rate and 10 percent net profit margin should persist indefinitely.

▶ Capital expenditures (net of depreciation) in the amount of 60 percent of the sales increase will be required each year.

▶ Investments in working capital equal to 25 percent of the sales increase will also be required each year.

▶ Debt financing will be used to fund 40 percent of the investments in net capital items and working capital.

▶ The beta for Medina Werks is 1.10; the risk-free rate of return is 6.0 percent; the equity risk premium is 4.5 percent.

▶ The company has 70 million outstanding shares.

1. What is the estimated total market value of equity?

2. What is the estimated value per share?

Solution to 1: The required return for Medina is

$$r = E(R_i) = R_F + \beta_i[E(R_M) - R_F] = 6\% + 1.10(4.5\%) = 10.95\%$$

The annual sales and net profit can be readily found as shown in Exhibit 17.

EXHIBIT 17   **FCFE Estimates for Medina Werks (C$ in Millions)**

	Year					
	1	2	3	4	5	6
Sales growth rate	20%	16%	12%	10%	8%	7%
Net profit margin	14%	13%	12%	11%	10.50%	10%
Sales	720.000	835.200	935.424	1028.966	1111.284	1189.074
Net profit	100.800	108.576	112.251	113.186	116.685	118.907
Net FCInv	72.000	69.120	60.134	56.125	49.390	46.674
WCInv	30.000	28.800	25.056	23.386	20.579	19.447
Debt financing	40.800	39.168	34.076	31.804	27.988	26.449
FCFE	39.600	49.824	61.137	65.480	74.703	79.235
PV of FCFE at 10.95%	35.692	40.475	44.763	43.211	44.433	

As can be seen, sales are expected to increase each year by a declining sales growth rate. Net profit each year is the year's net profit margin times the year's sales. Capital investment (net of depreciation) equals 60 percent of the sales increase from the previous year. The investment in working capital is 25 percent of the sales increase from the previous year. The debt financing each year is equal to 40 percent of the total net investment in capital items and working capital for that year. FCFE is net income minus the net capital investment minus the working capital investment plus the debt financing. The present value of each year's FCFE is found by discounting FCFE at the required rate of return for equity, 10.95 percent.

In Year 6 and beyond, Torino predicts sales to increase at 7 percent annually. Net income will be 10 percent of sales, so net profit will also grow at a 7 percent annual rate. Because they are pegged to the 7 percent sales increase, the investments in capital items and working capital and debt financing will also grow at the same 7 percent rate. The amounts in Year 6 for net income, investment in capital items, investment in working capital, debt financing, and FCFE will grow at 7 percent.

The terminal value of FCFE in Year 6 and beyond is

$$TV_5 = \frac{FCFE_6}{r - g} = \frac{79.235}{0.1095 - 0.07} = C\$2,005.95 \text{ million}$$

The present value of this amount is

$$PV \text{ of } TV_5 = \frac{2,005.95}{(1.1095)^5} = C\$1,193.12 \text{ million}$$

The estimated total market value of the firm is the present value of FCFE for Years 1 through 5 plus the present value of the terminal value:

$$MV = 35.692 + 40.475 + 44.763 + 43.211 + 44.433 + 1,193.12 = C\$1,401.69 \text{ million}$$

Solution to 2: Dividing C$1,401.69 million by the 70 million outstanding shares gives the estimated value per share of C$20.02.

4.4 Three-Stage Growth Models

Three-stage models are a straightforward extension of the two-stage models. One common version of a three-stage model is to assume a constant growth rate in each of the three stages. The growth rates could be for sales, profits, and investments in fixed and working capital; external financing could be a function of the level of sales or changes in sales. A simpler model would apply the growth rate to FCFF or FCFE.

A second common model is a three-stage model with constant growth rates in Stages 1 and 3 and a declining growth rate in Stage 2. Again, the growth rates could be applied to sales or to FCFF or FCFE. Although future FCFF and FCFE are unlikely to follow the assumptions of either of these three-stage growth models, analysts often find such models to be useful approximations.

Example 19 is a three-stage FCFF valuation model with declining growth rates in Stage 2. The model directly forecasts FCFF instead of deriving FCFF from a more complicated model that estimates cash flow from operations and investments in fixed and working capital.

EXAMPLE 19

A Three-Stage FCFF Valuation Model with Declining Growth in Stage 2

Charles Jones is evaluating Reliant Home Furnishings by using a three-stage growth model. He has accumulated the following information:

▶ Current FCFF = $745 million.

▶ Outstanding shares = 309.39 million.

▶ Equity beta = 0.90, risk-free rate = 5.04 percent; equity risk premium = 5.5 percent.

▶ Cost of debt = 7.1 percent.

▶ Marginal tax rate = 34 percent.

▶ Capital structure = 20 percent debt, 80 percent equity.

▶ Long-term debt = $1.518 billion.

▶ Growth rate of FCFF =

   ▶ 8.8 percent annually in Stage 1, Years 1–4.

   ▶ 7.4 percent in Year 5, 6.0 percent in Year 6, 4.6 percent in Year 7.

   ▶ 3.2 percent in Year 8 and thereafter.

From the information that Jones has accumulated, estimate the following:

1. WACC.
2. Total value of the firm.
3. Total value of equity.
4. Value per share.

Solution to 1: The required return for equity is

$$r = E(R_i) = R_F + \beta_i[E(R_M) - R_F] = 5.04\% + 0.9(5.5\%) = 9.99\%$$

WACC is

$$WACC = 0.20(7.1\%)(1 - 0.34) + 0.80(9.99\%) = 8.93\%$$

Solution to 2: Exhibit 18 displays the projected FCFF for the next eight years and the present value of each FCFF discounted at 8.93 percent:

EXHIBIT 18	Forecasted FCFF for Reliant Home Furnishings							

	Year							
	1	**2**	**3**	**4**	**5**	**6**	**7**	**8**
Growth rate	8.80%	8.80%	8.80%	8.80%	7.40%	6.00%	4.60%	3.20%
FCFF	811	882	959	1,044	1,121	1,188	1,243	1,283
PV at 8.93%	744	743	742	741	731	711	683	

The terminal value at the end of Year 7 is

$$TV_7 = \frac{FCFF_8}{WACC - g} = \frac{1,283}{0.0893 - 0.032} = \$22,391 \text{ million}$$

The present value of this amount discounted at 8.93 percent for seven years is

$$PV \text{ of } TV_7 = \frac{22,391}{(1.0893)^7} = \$12,304 \text{ million}$$

The total present value of the first seven years of FCFF is $5,097 million. The total value of the firm is 12,304 + 5,097 = $17,401 million.

Solution to 3: The value of equity is the value of the firm minus the market value of debt:

$$17,401 - 1,518 = \$15,883 \text{ million}$$

Solution to 4: Dividing the equity value by the number of shares yields the value per share:

$$\$15,883 \text{ million}/309.39 \text{ million} = \$51.34$$

The next section discusses an important technical issue, the treatment of nonoperating assets in valuation.

NONOPERATING ASSETS AND FIRM VALUE $\qquad$ 5

Free cash flow valuation focuses on the value of assets that generate or are needed to generate operating cash flows. If a company has significant nonoperating assets, such as excess cash,[10] excess marketable securities, or land held for investment, then analysts often calculate the value of the firm as the value of its operating assets (e.g., as estimated by FCFF valuation) plus the value of its nonoperating assets:

$$\text{Value of firm} = \text{Value of operating assets} + \text{Value of nonoperating assets} \tag{18}$$

In general, if any company asset is excluded from the set of assets being considered in projecting a company's future cash flows, the analyst should add that omitted asset's estimated value to the cash-flows-based value estimate. Some companies have substantial noncurrent investments in stocks and bonds that are not operating subsidiaries but, rather, financial investments. These investments should be reflected at their current market value. Those securities reported at book values on the basis of accounting conventions should be revalued to market values.

---

[10] In this case, "excess" is in relation to what is needed for generating operating cash flows. Estimating what constitutes excess cash may be difficult; for example, an analyst could consider as excess cash any amount in excess of the amount predicted by multiplying total assets by the industry median level of the ratio of cash to total assets.

SUMMARY

Discounted cash flow models are widely used by analysts to value companies.

▶ Free cash flow to the firm (FCFF) and free cash flow to equity (FCFE) are the cash flows available to, respectively, all of the investors in the company and to common stockholders.

▶ Analysts like to use free cash flow (either FCFF or FCFE) as the return:
  ▶ if the company is not paying dividends;
  ▶ if the company pays dividends but the dividends paid differ significantly from the company's capacity to pay dividends;
  ▶ if free cash flows align with profitability within a reasonable forecast period with which the analyst is comfortable; or
  ▶ if the investor takes a control perspective.

▶ The FCFF valuation approach estimates the value of the firm as the present value of future FCFF discounted at the weighted average cost of capital:

$$\text{Firm value} = \sum_{t=1}^{\infty} \frac{\text{FCFF}_t}{(1 + \text{WACC})^t}$$

The value of equity is the value of the firm minus the value of the firm's debt:

$$\text{Equity value} = \text{Firm value} - \text{Market value of debt}$$

Dividing the total value of equity by the number of outstanding shares gives the value per share.

The WACC formula is

$$\text{WACC} = \frac{\text{MV(Debt)}}{\text{MV(Debt)} + \text{MV(Equity)}} r_d (1 - \text{Tax rate})$$
$$+ \frac{\text{MV(Equity)}}{\text{MV(Debt)} + \text{MV(Equity)}} r$$

▶ The value of the firm if FCFF is growing at a constant rate is

$$\text{Firm value} = \frac{\text{FCFF}_1}{\text{WACC} - g} = \frac{\text{FCFF}_0 (1 + g)}{\text{WACC} - g}$$

▶ With the FCFE valuation approach, the value of equity can be found by discounting FCFE at the required rate of return on equity, r:

$$\text{Equity value} = \sum_{t=1}^{\infty} \frac{\text{FCFE}_t}{(1 + r)^t}$$

Dividing the total value of equity by the number of outstanding shares gives the value per share.

▶ The value of equity if FCFE is growing at a constant rate is

$$\text{Equity value} = \frac{\text{FCFE}_1}{r - g} = \frac{\text{FCFE}_0 (1 + g)}{r - g}$$

▶ FCFF and FCFE are frequently calculated by starting with net income:

FCFF = NI + NCC + Int(1–Tax rate) − FCInv − WCInv

FCFE = NI + NCC − FCInv − WCInv + Net borrowing

▶ FCFF and FCFE are related to each other as follows:

FCFE = FCFF − Int(1 − Tax rate) + Net borrowing

▶ FCFF and FCFE can be calculated by starting from cash flow from operations:

FCFF = CFO + Int(1 − Tax rate) − FCInv

FCFE = CFO − FCInv + Net borrowing

▶ FCFF can also be calculated from EBIT or EBITDA:

FCFF = EBIT(1 − Tax rate) + Dep − FCInv − WCInv

FCFF = EBITDA(1 − Tax rate) + Dep(Tax rate) − FCInv − WCInv

FCFE can then be found by using FCFE = FCFF − Int(1 − Tax rate) + Net borrowing.

▶ Finding CFO, FCFF, and FCFE may require careful interpretation of corporate financial statements. In some cases, the needed information may not be transparent.

▶ Earnings components such as net income, EBIT, EBITDA, and CFO should not be used as cash flow measures to value a firm. These earnings components either double-count or ignore parts of the cash flow stream.

▶ FCFF or FCFE valuation expressions can be easily adapted to accommodate complicated capital structures, such as those that include preferred stock.

▶ A general expression for the two-stage FCFF valuation model is

$$\text{Firm value} = \sum_{t=1}^{n} \frac{\text{FCFF}_t}{(1 + \text{WACC})^t} + \frac{\text{FCFF}_{n+1}}{(\text{WACC} - g)} \frac{1}{(1 + \text{WACC})^n}$$

▶ A general expression for the two-stage FCFE valuation model is

$$\text{Equity value} = \sum_{t=1}^{n} \frac{\text{FCFE}_t}{(1 + r)^t} + \frac{\text{FCFE}_{n+1}}{r - g} \frac{1}{(1 + r)^n}$$

▶ One common two-stage model assumes a constant growth rate in each stage, and a second common model assumes declining growth in Stage 1 followed by a long-run sustainable growth rate in Stage 2.

▶ To forecast FCFF and FCFE, analysts build a variety of models of varying complexity. A common approach is to forecast sales, with profitability, investments, and financing derived from changes in sales.

▶ Three-stage models are often considered to be good approximations for cash flow streams that, in reality, fluctuate from year to year.

▶ Nonoperating assets, such as excess cash and marketable securities, noncurrent investment securities, and nonperforming assets, are usually segregated from the company's operating assets. They are valued separately and then added to the value of the company's operating assets to find total firm value.

PRACTICE PROBLEMS FOR READING 40

1. Indicate the effect on this period's FCFF and FCFE of a change in each of the items listed here. Assume a $100 increase in each case and a 40 percent tax rate.

   A. Net income.

   B. Cash operating expenses.

   C. Depreciation.

   D. Interest expense.

   E. EBIT.

   F. Accounts receivable.

   G. Accounts payable.

   H. Property, plant, and equipment.

   I. Notes payable.

   J. Cash dividends paid.

   K. Proceeds from issuing new common shares.

   L. Common shares repurchased.

2. LaForge Systems, Inc. has net income of $285 million for the year 2008. Using information from the company's financial statements given here, show the adjustments to net income that would be required to find:

   A. FCFF.

   B. FCFE.

   C. In addition, show the adjustments to FCFF that would result in FCFE.

LaForge Systems, Inc. Balance Sheet (in Millions)

Years Ended 31 December	2007	2008
Assets		
Current assets		
Cash and equivalents	$ 210	$ 248
Accounts receivable	474	513
Inventory	520	564
Total current assets	1,204	1,325
Gross fixed assets	2,501	2,850
Accumulated depreciation	(604)	(784)
Net fixed assets	1,897	2,066
Total assets	$3,101	$3,391
Liabilities and shareholders' equity		
Current liabilities		
Accounts payable	$ 295	$ 317
Notes payable	300	310
Accrued taxes and expenses	76	99
Total current liabilities	671	726

(Table continued on next page . . .)

(continued)

Years Ended 31 December	2007	2008
Long-term debt	1,010	1,050
Common stock	50	50
Additional paid-in capital	300	300
Retained earnings	1,070	1,265
Total shareholders' equity	1,420	1,615
Total liabilities and shareholders' equity	$3,101	$3,391

Statement of Income
In Millions, except Per-Share Data   **31 December 2008**

Total revenues	$2,215
Operating costs and expenses	1,430
EBITDA	785
Depreciation	180
EBIT	605
Interest expense	130
Income before tax	475
Taxes (at 40 percent)	190
Net income	285
Dividends	90
Addition to retained earnings	195

Statement of Cash Flows
In Millions   **31 December 2008**

Operating activities	
Net income	$285
Adjustments	
Depreciation	180
Changes in working capital	
Accounts receivable	(39)
Inventories	(44)
Accounts payable	22
Accrued taxes and expenses	23
Cash provided by operating activities	$427
Investing activities	
Purchases of fixed assets	349
Cash used for investing activities	$349

(Table continued on next page . . .)

(continued)

Statement of Cash Flows In Millions	31 December 2008
Financing activities	
Notes payable	$(10)
Long-term financing issuances	(40)
Common stock dividends	90
Cash used for financing activities	$ 40
Cash and equivalents increase (decrease)	38
Cash and equivalents at beginning of year	210
Cash and equivalents at end of year	$248
Supplemental cash flow disclosures	
Interest paid	$130
Income taxes paid	$190

Note: The statement of cash flows shows the use of a convention by which the positive numbers of $349 and $40 for cash used for investing activities and cash used for financing activities, respectively, are understood to be subtractions, because "cash used" is an outflow.

3. For LaForge Systems, whose financial statements are given in Problem 2, show the adjustments from the current levels of CFO (which is $427 million), EBIT ($605 million), and EBITDA ($785 million) to find:

   A. FCFF.

   B. FCFE.

4. The term "free cash flow" is frequently applied to cash flows that differ from the definition for FCFF that should be used to value a firm. Two such definitions of free cash flow are given below. Compare these two definitions for free cash flow with the technically correct definition of FCFF used in the reading.

   A. FCF = Net income + Depreciation and amortization − Cash dividends − Capital expenditures.

   B. FCF = Cash flow from operations (from the statement of cash flows) − Capital expenditures.

5. Proust Company has FCFF of $1.7 billion and FCFE of $1.3 billion. Proust's WACC is 11 percent, and its required rate of return for equity is 13 percent. FCFF is expected to grow forever at 7 percent, and FCFE is expected to grow forever at 7.5 percent. Proust has debt outstanding of $15 billion.

   A. What is the total value of Proust's equity using the FCFF valuation approach?

   B. What is the total value of Proust's equity using the FCFE valuation approach?

6. Quinton Johnston is evaluating TMI Manufacturing Company, Ltd., which is headquartered in Taiwan. In 2008, when Johnston is performing his analysis, the company is unprofitable. Furthermore, TMI pays no dividends on its common shares. Johnston decides to value TMI Manufacturing by using his forecasts of FCFE. Johnston gathers the following facts and assumptions:

   ▶ The company has 17.0 billion shares outstanding.

   ▶ Sales will be $5.5 billion in 2009, increasing at 28 percent annually for the next four years (through 2013).

   ▶ Net income will be 32 percent of sales.

   ▶ Investment in fixed assets will be 35 percent of sales; investment in working capital will be 6 percent of sales; depreciation will be 9 percent of sales.

   ▶ 20 percent of the net investment in assets will be financed with debt.

   ▶ Interest expenses will be only 2 percent of sales.

   ▶ The tax rate will be 10 percent. TMI Manufacturing's beta is 2.1; the risk-free government bond rate is 6.4 percent; the equity risk premium is 5.0 percent.

   ▶ At the end of 2013, Johnston projects TMI terminal stock value at 18 times earnings.

   What is the value of one ordinary share of TMI Manufacturing Company?

7. Do Pham is evaluating Phaneuf Accelerateur by using the FCFF and FCFE valuation approaches. Pham has collected the following information (currency in euros):

   ▶ Phaneuf has net income of €250 million, depreciation of €90 million, capital expenditures of €170 million, and an increase in working capital of €40 million.

   ▶ Phaneuf will finance 40 percent of the increase in net fixed assets (capital expenditures less depreciation) and 40 percent of the increase in working capital with debt financing.

   ▶ Interest expenses are €150 million. The current market value of Phaneuf's outstanding debt is €1,800 million.

   ▶ FCFF is expected to grow at 6.0 percent indefinitely, and FCFE is expected to grow at 7.0 percent.

   ▶ The tax rate is 30 percent.

   ▶ Phaneuf is financed with 40 percent debt and 60 percent equity. The before-tax cost of debt is 9 percent, and the before-tax cost of equity is 13 percent.

   ▶ Phaneuf has 10 million outstanding shares.

   A. Using the FCFF valuation approach, estimate the total value of the firm, the total market value of equity, and the per-share value of equity.

   B. Using the FCFE valuation approach, estimate the total market value of equity and the per-share value of equity.

8. PHB Company currently sells for $32.50 per share. In an attempt to determine whether PHB is fairly priced, an analyst has assembled the following information:

▶ The before-tax required rates of return on PHB debt, preferred stock, and common stock are, respectively, 7.0 percent, 6.8 percent, and 11.0 percent.

▶ The company's target capital structure is 30 percent debt, 15 percent preferred stock, and 55 percent common stock.

▶ The market value of the company's debt is $145 million, and its preferred stock is valued at $65 million.

▶ PHB's FCFF for the year just ended is $28 million. FCFF is expected to grow at a constant rate of 4 percent for the foreseeable future.

▶ The tax rate is 35 percent.

▶ PHB has 8 million outstanding common shares.

What is PHB's estimated value per share? Is PHB's stock underpriced?

9. Watson Dunn is planning to value BCC Corporation, a provider of a variety of industrial metals and minerals. Dunn uses a single-stage FCFF approach. The financial information Dunn has assembled for his valuation is as follows:

▶ The company has 1,852 million shares outstanding.

▶ The market value of its debt is $3.192 billion.

▶ The FCFF is currently $1.1559 billion.

▶ The equity beta is 0.90; the equity risk premium is 5.5 percent; the risk-free rate is 5.5 percent.

▶ The before-tax cost of debt is 7.0 percent.

▶ The tax rate is 40 percent.

▶ To calculate WACC, he will assume the company is financed 25 percent with debt.

▶ The FCFF growth rate is 4 percent.

Using Dunn's information, calculate the following:

A. WACC.

B. Value of the firm.

C. Total market value of equity.

D. Value per share.

10. Kenneth McCoin is valuing McInish Corporation and performing a sensitivity analysis on his valuation. He uses a single-stage FCFE growth model. The base-case values for each of the parameters in the model are given, together with possible low and high estimates for each variable, in the following table.

Variable	Base-Case Value	Low Estimate	High Estimate
Normalized $FCFE_0$	$0.88	$0.70	$1.14
Risk-free rate	5.08%	5.00%	5.20%
Equity risk premium	5.50%	4.50%	6.50%
Beta	0.70	0.60	0.80
FCFE growth rate	6.40%	4.00%	7.00%

A. Use the base-case values to estimate the current value of McInish Corporation.

B. Calculate the range of stock prices that would occur if the base-case value for $FCFE_0$ were replaced by the low estimate and the high estimate for $FCFE_0$. Similarly, using the base-case values for all other variables, calculate the range of stock prices caused by using the low and high values for beta, the risk-free rate, the equity risk premium, and the growth rate. Based on these ranges, rank the sensitivity of the stock price to each of the five variables.

11. An aggressive financial planner who claims to have a superior method for picking undervalued stocks is courting one of your clients. The planner claims that the best way to find the value of a stock is to divide EBITDA by the risk-free bond rate. The planner is urging your client to invest in NewMarket, Inc. The planner says that NewMarket's EBITDA of $1,580 million divided by the long-term government bond rate of 7 percent gives a total value of $22,571.4 million. With 318 million outstanding shares, NewMarket's value per share found by using this method is $70.98. Shares of NewMarket currently trade for $36.50.

A. Provide your client with an alternative estimate of NewMarket's value per share based on a two-stage FCFE valuation approach. Use the following assumptions:

▶ Net income is currently $600 million. Net income will grow by 20 percent annually for the next three years.

▶ The net investment in operating assets (capital expenditures less depreciation plus investment in working capital) will be $1,150 million next year and grow at 15 percent for the following two years.

▶ Forty percent of the net investment in operating assets will be financed with net new debt financing.

▶ NewMarket's beta is 1.3; the risk-free bond rate is 7 percent; the equity risk premium is 4 percent.

▶ After three years, the growth rate of net income will be 8 percent and the net investment in operating assets (capital expenditures minus depreciation plus increase in working capital) each year will drop to 30 percent of net income.

▶ Debt is, and will continue to be, 40 percent of total assets.

▶ NewMarket has 318 million shares outstanding.

B. Criticize the valuation approach that the aggressive financial planner used.

12. Bron has EPS of $3.00 in 2002 and expects EPS to increase by 21 percent in 2003. EPS are expected to grow at a decreasing rate for the following five years, as shown in the following table.

	2003	2004	2005	2006	2007	2008
Growth rate for EPS	21%	18%	15%	12%	9%	6%
Net capital expenditures per share	$5.00	$5.00	$4.50	$4.00	$3.50	$1.50

In 2008, the growth rate will be 6 percent and is expected to stay at that rate thereafter. Net capital expenditures (capital expenditures minus depreciation) will be $5.00 per share in 2002 and then follow the pattern predicted in the table. In 2008, net capital expenditures are expected to be $1.50 and will then grow at 6 percent annually. The investment in working capital parallels the increase in net capital expenditures and is predicted to equal 25 percent of net capital expenditures each year. In 2008, investment in working capital will be $0.375 and is predicted to grow at 6 percent thereafter. Bron will use debt financing to fund 40 percent of net capital expenditures and 40 percent of the investment in working capital. The required rate of return for Bron is 12 percent.

Estimate the value of a Bron share using a two-stage FCFE valuation approach.

13. The management of Telluride, an international diversified conglomerate based in the United States, believes that the recent strong performance of its wholly owned medical supply subsidiary, Sundanci, has gone unnoticed. To realize Sundanci's full value, Telluride has announced that it will divest Sundanci in a tax-free spin-off.

Sue Carroll, CFA, is director of research at Kesson and Associates. In developing an investment recommendation for Sundanci, Carroll has gathered the information shown in Exhibits 1 and 2.

EXHIBIT 1	Sundanci Actual 2007 and 2008 Financial Statements for Fiscal Years Ending 31 May (Dollars in Millions except Per-Share Data)	

Income Statement	2007	2008
Revenue	$474	$598
Depreciation	20	23
Other operating costs	368	460
Income before taxes	86	115
Taxes	26	35
Net income	60	80
Dividends	18	24
EPS	$0.714	$0.952
Dividends per share	$0.214	$0.286
Common shares outstanding	84.0	84.0

Balance Sheet	2007	2008
Current assets (includes $5 cash in 2007 and 2008)	$201	$326
Net property, plant, and equipment	474	489
Total assets	675	815
Current liabilities (all non-interest-bearing)	57	141
Long-term debt	0	0
Total liabilities	57	141
Shareholders' equity	618	674
Total liabilities and equity	675	815
Capital expenditures	34	38

EXHIBIT 2	Selected Financial Information
Required rate of return on equity	14%
Industry growth rate	13%
Industry P/E	26

Abbey Naylor, CFA, has been directed by Carroll to determine the value of Sundanci's stock by using the FCFE model. Naylor believes that Sundanci's FCFE will grow at 27 percent for two years and at 13 percent thereafter. Capital expenditures, depreciation, and working capital are all expected to increase proportionately with FCFE.

A. Calculate the amount of FCFE per share for 2008 by using the data from Exhibit 1.

B. Calculate the current value of a share of Sundanci stock based on the two-stage FCFE model.

C. Describe limitations that the two-stage DDM and FCFE models have in common.

14. John Jones, CFA, is head of the research department of Peninsular Research. One of the companies he is researching, Mackinac Inc., is a U.S.-based manufacturing company. Mackinac has released the June 2007 financial statements shown in Exhibits 1, 2, and 3.

EXHIBIT 1	Mackinac Inc. Annual Income Statement 30 June 2007 (in Thousands, except Per-Share Data)
Sales	$250,000
Cost of goods sold	125,000
Gross operating profit	125,000
Selling, general, and administrative expenses	50,000
EBITDA	75,000
Depreciation and amortization	10,500
EBIT	64,500
Interest expense	11,000
Pretax income	53,500
Income taxes	16,050
Net income	$ 37,450
Shares outstanding	13,000
EPS	$2.88

EXHIBIT 2	Mackinac Inc. Balance Sheet 30 June 2007 (in Thousands)

Current Assets

Cash and equivalents	$20,000	
Receivables	40,000	
Inventories	29,000	
Other current assets	23,000	
Total current assets		$112,000

Noncurrent Assets

Property, plant, and equipment	$145,000		
Less: Accumulated depreciation	43,000		
Net property, plant, and equipment		102,000	
Investments		70,000	
Other noncurrent assets		36,000	
Total noncurrent assets			208,000
Total assets			$320,000

Current Liabilities

Accounts payable	$41,000	
Short-term debt	12,000	
Other current liabilities	17,000	
Total current liabilities		$ 70,000

Noncurrent Liabilities

Long-term debt	100,000	
Total noncurrent liabilities		100,000
Total liabilities		170,000

Shareholders' Equity

Common equity	40,000	
Retained earnings	110,000	
Total equity		150,000
Total liabilities and equity		$320,000

EXHIBIT 3	Mackinac Inc. Statement of Cash Flows 30 June 2007 (in Thousands)

Cash Flow from Operating Activities

Net income	$37,450
Depreciation and amortization	10,500

(Exhibit continued on next page . . .)

EXHIBIT 3	(continued)

Change in Working Capital

(Increase) decrease in receivables	($5,000)	
(Increase) decrease in inventories	(8,000)	
Increase (decrease) in payables	6,000	
Increase (decrease) in other current liabilities	1,500	
Net change in working capital		(5,500)
Net cash from operating activities		$42,450

Cash Flow from Investing Activities

Purchase of property, plant, and equipment	($15,000)	
Net cash from investing activities		($15,000)

Cash Flow from Financing Activities

Change in debt outstanding	$4,000	
Payment of cash dividends	(22,470)	
Net cash from financing activities		(18,470)
Net change in cash and cash equivalents		$8,980
Cash at beginning of period		11,020
Cash at end of period		$20,000

Mackinac has announced that it has finalized an agreement to handle North American production of a successful product currently marketed by a company headquartered outside North America. Jones decides to value Mackinac by using the DDM and FCFE models. After reviewing Mackinac's financial statements and forecasts related to the new production agreement, Jones concludes the following:

▶ Mackinac's earnings and FCFE are expected to grow 17 percent a year over the next three years before stabilizing at an annual growth rate of 9 percent.

▶ Mackinac will maintain the current payout ratio.

▶ Mackinac's beta is 1.25.

▶ The government bond yield is 6 percent, and the market equity risk premium is 5 percent.

A. Calculate the value of a share of Mackinac's common stock by using the two-stage DDM.

B. Calculate the value of a share of Mackinac's common stock by using the two-stage FCFE model.

C. Jones is discussing with a corporate client the possibility of that client acquiring a 70 percent interest in Mackinac. Discuss whether the DDM or FCFE model is more appropriate for this client's valuation purposes.

15. SK Telecom Company is a cellular telephone paging and computer communication services company in Seoul, South Korea. The company is traded on the Korea, New York, and London stock exchanges (NYSE: SKM). Sol Kim has estimated the normalized FCFE for SK Telecom to be 1,300 Korean won (per share) for the year just ended. The real country return for South Korea is 6.50 percent. To estimate the required return for SK Telecom, Kim makes the following adjustments to the real country return: an industry adjustment of +0.60 percent, a size adjustment of −0.10 percent, and a leverage adjustment of +0.25 percent. The long-term real growth rate for South Korea is estimated to be 3.5 percent, and Kim expects the real growth rate of SK Telecom to track the country rate.

   A. What is the real required rate of return for SK Telecom?

   B. Using the single-stage FCFE valuation model and real values for the discount rate and FCFE growth rate, estimate the value of one share of SK Telecom.

16. Lawrence McKibben is preparing a valuation of QuickChange Auto Centers, Inc. McKibben has decided to use a three-stage FCFE valuation model and the following estimates. The FCFE per share for the current year is $0.75. The FCFE is expected to grow at 10 percent for next year, then at 26 percent annually for the following three years, and then at 6 percent in Year 5 and thereafter. QuickChange's estimated beta is 2.00, and McKibben believes that current market conditions dictate a 4.5 percent risk-free rate of return and a 5.0 percent equity risk premium. Given McKibben's assumptions and approach, estimate the value of a share of QuickChange.

17. Clay Cooperman has valued the operating assets of Johnson Extrusion at $720 million. The company also has short-term cash and securities with a market value of $60 million that are not needed for Johnson's operations. The noncurrent investments have a book value of $30 million and a market value of $45 million. The company also has an overfunded pension plan, with plan assets of $210 million and plan liabilities of $170 million. Johnson Extrusion has $215 million of notes and bonds outstanding and 100 million outstanding shares. What is the value per share of Johnson Extrusion stock?

The following information relates to Questions 18–23

Ryan Leigh is preparing a presentation that analyzes the valuation of the common stock of two companies under consideration as additions to his firm's recommended list, Emerald Corporation and Holt Corporation. Leigh has prepared preliminary valuations of both companies using a FCFE model and is also preparing a value estimate for Emerald using a dividend discount model. Holt's 2007 and 2008 financial statements, contained in Exhibits 1 and 2, are prepared in accordance with U.S. GAAP.

EXHIBIT 1	Holt Corporation Consolidated Balance Sheets (US$ Millions)

		As of 31 December		
		2008		2007
Assets				
Current assets				
Cash and cash equivalents		$ 372		$ 315
Accounts receivable		770		711
Inventories		846		780
Total current assets		1,988		1,806
Gross fixed assets	4,275		3,752	
Less: Accumulated depreciation	1,176	3,099	906	2,846
Total assets		$5,087		$4,652
Liabilities and shareholders' equity				
Current liabilities				
Accounts payable		$ 476		$ 443
Accrued taxes and expenses		149		114
Notes payable		465		450
Total current liabilities		1,090		1,007
Long-term debt		1,575		1,515
Common stock		525		525
Retained earnings		1,897		1,605
Total liabilities and shareholders' equity		$5,087		$4,652

EXHIBIT 2	Holt Corporation Consolidated Income Statement for the Year Ended 31 December 2008 (US$ Millions)

Total revenues	$3,323
Cost of goods sold	1,287
Selling, general, and administrative expenses	858
Earnings before interest, taxes, depreciation, and amortization (EBITDA)	1,178
Depreciation expense	270
Operating income	908
Interest expense	195
Pretax income	713
Income tax (at 32 percent)	228
Net income	$ 485

Leigh presents his valuations of the common stock of Emerald and Holt to his supervisor, Alice Smith. Smith has the following questions and comments:

1. "I estimate that Emerald's long-term expected dividend payout rate is 20 percent and its return on equity is 10 percent over the long term."
2. "Why did you use a FCFE model to value Holt's common stock? Can you use a DDM instead?"
3. "How did Holt's FCFE for 2008 compare with its FCFF for the same year? I recommend you use a FCFF model to value Holt's common stock instead of using a FCFE model because Holt has had a history of leverage changes in the past."
4. "In the last three years, about 5 percent of Holt's growth in FCFE has come from decreases in inventory."

Leigh responds to each of Smith's points as follows:

1. "I will use your estimates and calculate Emerald's long-term, sustainable dividend growth rate."
2. "There are two reasons why I used the FCFE model to value Holt's common stock instead of using a DDM. The first reason is that Holt's dividends have differed significantly from its capacity to pay dividends. The second reason is that Holt is a takeover target and once the company is taken over, the new owners will have discretion over the uses of free cash flow."
3. "I will calculate Holt's FCFF for 2008 and estimate the value of Holt's common stock using a FCFF model."
4. "Holt is a growing company. In forecasting either Holt's FCFE or FCFF growth rates, I will not consider decreases in inventory to be a long-term source of growth."

18. Which of the following long-term FCFE growth rates is *most* consistent with the facts and stated policies of Emerald?
    A. 5 percent or lower.
    B. 2 percent or higher.
    C. 8 percent or higher.

19. Do the reasons provided by Leigh support his use of the FCFE model to value Holt's common stock instead of using a DDM?
    A. Yes.
    B. No, because Holt's dividend situation argues in favor of using the DDM.
    C. No, because FCFE is not appropriate for investors taking a control perspective.

20. Holt's FCFF (in millions) for 2008 is *closest* to:
    A. $308.
    B. $370.
    C. $422.

21. Holt's FCFE (in millions) for 2008 is *closest* to:

   A. $175.

   B. $250.

   C. $364.

22. Leigh's comment about not considering decreases in inventory to be a source of long-term growth in free cash flow for Holt is:

   A. inconsistent with a forecasting perspective.

   B. mistaken because decreases in inventory are a use rather than a source of cash.

   C. consistent with a forecasting perspective because inventory reduction has a limit, particularly for a growing firm.

23. Smith's recommendation to use a FCFF model to value Holt is:

   A. logical, given the prospect of Holt changing capital structure.

   B. not logical because a FCFF model is used only to value the total firm.

   C. not logical because FCFE represents a more direct approach to free cash flow valuation.

SOLUTIONS FOR READING 40

1.

For a $100 increase in:	Change in FCFF (in U.S. Dollars)	Change in FCFE (in U.S. Dollars)
A. Net income	+100	+100
B. Cash operating expenses	−60	−60
C. Depreciation	+40	+40
D. Interest expense	0	−60
E. EBIT	+60	+60
F. Accounts receivable	−100	−100
G. Accounts payable	+100	+100
H. Property, plant, and equipment	−100	−100
I. Notes payable	0	+100
J. Cash dividends paid	0	0
K. Proceeds from new shares issued	0	0
L. Share repurchases	0	0

2. A. Free cash flow to the firm, found with Equation 7, is

$$FCFF = NI + NCC + Int(1 - Tax\ rate) - FCInv - WCInv$$
$$FCFF = 285 + 180 + 130(1 - 0.40) - 349 - (39 + 44 - 22 - 23)$$
$$FCFF = 285 + 180 + 78 - 349 - 38 = \$156\ million$$

   B. Free cash flow to equity, found with Equation 10, is

$$FCFE = NI + NCC - FCInv - WCInv + Net\ borrowing$$
$$FCFE = 285 + 180 - 349 - (39 + 44 - 22 - 23) + (10 + 40)$$
$$FCFE = 285 + 180 - 349 - 38 + 50 = \$128\ million$$

   C. To find FCFE from FCFF, one uses the relationship in Equation 9:

$$FCFE = FCFF - Int(1 - Tax\ rate) + Net\ borrowing$$
$$FCFE = 156 - 130(1 - 0.40) + (10 + 40)$$
$$FCFE = 156 - 78 + 50 = \$128\ million$$

3. A. To find FCFF from CFO, EBIT, or EBITDA, the analyst can use Equations 8, 12, and 13.

   To find FCFF from CFO:

$$FCFF = CFO + Int(1 - Tax\ rate) - FCInv$$
$$FCFF = 427 + 130(1 - 0.40) - 349 = 427 + 78 - 349 = \$156\ million$$

To find FCFF from EBIT:

$$\text{FCFF} = \text{EBIT}(1 - \text{Tax rate}) + \text{Dep} - \text{FCInv} - \text{WCInv}$$
$$\text{FCFF} = 605(1 - 0.40) + 180 - 349 - 38$$
$$\text{FCFF} = 363 + 180 - 349 - 38 = \$156 \text{ million}$$

Finally, to obtain FCFF from EBITDA:

$$\text{FCFF} = \text{EBITDA}(1 - \text{Tax rate}) + \text{Dep}(\text{Tax rate}) - \text{FCInv} - \text{WCInv}$$
$$\text{FCFF} = 785(1 - 0.40) + 180(0.40) - 349 - 38$$
$$\text{FCFF} = 471 + 72 - 349 - 38 = \$156 \text{ million}$$

B. The simplest approach is to calculate FCFF from CFO, EBIT, or EBITDA as was done in Part A and then to find FCFE by making the appropriate adjustments to FCFF:

$$\text{FCFE} = \text{FCFF} - \text{Int}(1 - \text{Tax rate}) + \text{Net borrowing.}$$
$$\text{FCFE} = 156 - 130(1 - 0.40) + 50 = 156 - 78 + 50 = \$128 \text{ million}$$

The analyst can also find FCFE by using CFO, EBIT, or EBITDA directly. Starting with CFO and using Equation 11, FCFE is found to be

$$\text{FCFE} = \text{CFO} - \text{FCInv} + \text{Net borrowing}$$
$$\text{FCFE} = 427 - 349 + 50 = \$128 \text{ million}$$

Starting with EBIT, on the basis of Equations 9 and 12, FCFE is

$$\text{FCFE} = \text{EBIT}(1 - \text{Tax rate}) + \text{Dep} - \text{Int}(1 - \text{Tax rate}) - \text{FCInv}$$
$$- \text{WCInv} + \text{Net borrowing}$$
$$\text{FCFE} = 605(1 - 0.40) + 180 - 130(1 - 0.40) - 349 - 38 + 50$$
$$\text{FCFE} = 363 + 180 - 78 - 349 - 38 + 50 = \$128 \text{ million}$$

Finally, starting with EBITDA, on the basis of Equations 9 and 13, FCFE is

$$\text{FCFE} = \text{EBITDA}(1 - \text{Tax rate}) + \text{Dep}(\text{Tax rate})$$
$$- \text{Int}(1 - \text{Tax rate}) - \text{FCInv} - \text{WCInv} + \text{Net borrowing}$$
$$\text{FCFE} = 785(1 - 0.40) + 180(0.40) - 130(1 - 0.40) - 349 - 38 + 50$$
$$\text{FCFE} = 471 + 72 - 78 - 349 - 38 + 50 = \$128 \text{ million}$$

4. A. FCF = Net income + Depreciation and amortization − Cash dividends − Capital expenditures. This definition of free cash flow is sometimes used to determine how much "discretionary" cash flow management has at its disposal. Management discretion concerning dividends is limited by investor expectations that dividends will be maintained. Comparing this definition with Equation 7, FCFF = NI + NCC + Int(1 − Tax rate) − FCInv − WCInv, we find that FCFF includes a reduction for investments in working capital and the addition of after-tax interest expense. Common stock dividends are not subtracted from FCFF because dividends represent a distribution of the cash available to investors. (If a company pays preferred dividends and they were previously taken out when net income available to common shareholders was calculated, they are added back in Equation 7 to include them in FCFF.)

B. FCF = Cash flow from operations (from the statement of cash flows) − Capital expenditures. Comparing this definition of free cash flow with Equation 8, FCFF = CFO + Int(1 − Tax rate) − FCInv, highlights the relationship of CFO to FCFF: The primary point is that when Equation 8 is used, after-tax interest is added back to CFO to arrive at the cash flow to all investors. Then FCInv is subtracted to arrive at the amount of that cash flow that is "free" in the sense of available for distribution to those investors after taking care of capital investment needs. If preferred dividends were subtracted to obtain net income (in CFO), they would also have to be added back in. This definition is commonly used to approximate FCFF, but it generally understates the actual FCFF by the amount of after-tax interest expense.

5. A. The firm value is the present value of FCFF discounted at the WACC, or

$$\text{Firm value} = \frac{\text{FCFF}_1}{\text{WACC} - g} = \frac{\text{FCFF}_0(1 + g)}{\text{WACC} - g} = \frac{1.7(1.07)}{0.11 - 0.07}$$

$$= \frac{1.819}{0.04} = \$45.475 \text{ billion}$$

The market value of equity is the value of the firm minus the value of debt:

$$\text{Equity} = 45.475 - 15 = \$30.475 \text{ billion}$$

B. Using the FCFE valuation approach, we find the present value of FCFE discounted at the required rate of return on equity to be

$$\text{PV} = \frac{\text{FCFE}_1}{r - g} = \frac{\text{FCFE}_0(1 + g)}{r - g} = \frac{1.3(1.075)}{0.13 - 0.075}$$

$$= \frac{1.3975}{0.055} = \$25.409 \text{ billion}$$

The value of equity using this approach is \$25.409 billion.

6. The required rate of return found with the CAPM is

$$r = E(R_i) = R_F + \beta_i[E(R_M) - R_F] = 6.4\% + 2.1\,(5.0\%) = 16.9\%$$

The following table shows the values of sales, net income, capital expenditures less depreciation, and investments in working capital. FCFE equals net income less the investments financed with equity:

FCFE = Net income − (1 − DR)(Capital expenditures − Depreciation) − (1 − DR)(Investment in working capital)

where DR is the debt ratio (debt financing as a percentage of debt and equity). Because 20 percent of net new investments are financed with debt, 80 percent of the investments are financed with equity, which reduces FCFE by 80 percent of (Capital expenditures − Depreciation) and 80 percent of the investment in working capital.

(All Data in Billions of Taiwan Dollars)	2009	2010	2011	2012	2013
Sales (growing at 28%)	5.500	7.040	9.011	11.534	14.764
Net income = 32% of sales	1.760	2.253	2.884	3.691	4.724
FCInv − Dep = (35% − 9%) × Sales	1.430	1.830	2.343	2.999	3.839
WCInv = (6% of Sales)	0.330	0.422	0.541	0.692	0.886
0.80 × (FCInv − Dep + WCInv)	1.408	1.802	2.307	2.953	3.780
FCFE = NI − 0.80 × (FCInv − Dep + WCInv)	0.352	0.451	0.577	0.738	0.945
PV of FCFE discounted at 16.9%	0.301	0.330	0.361	0.395	0.433
Terminal stock value		85.032			
PV of terminal value discounted at 16.9%		38.950			
Total PV of FCFE		1.820			
Total value of equity		40.770			

The terminal stock value is 18.0 times the earnings in 2013, or $18 \times 4.724 =$ \$85.03 billion. The present value of the terminal value (\$38.95 billion) plus the present value of the first five years' FCFE (\$1.82 billion) is \$40.77 billion. Because TMI Manufacturing has 17 billion outstanding shares, the value per ordinary share is \$2.398.

7. A. The FCFF is (in euros)

$$FCFF = NI + NCC + Int(1 - \text{Tax rate}) - FCInv - WCInv$$
$$FCFF = 250 + 90 + 150(1 - 0.30) - 170 - 40$$
$$FCFF = 250 + 90 + 105 - 170 - 40 = 235 \text{ million}$$

The weighted-average cost of capital is

$$WACC = 9\%(1 - 0.30)(0.40) + 13\%(0.60) = 10.32\%$$

The value of the firm (in euro) is

$$\text{Firm value} = \frac{FCFF_1}{WACC - g} = \frac{FCFF_0(1 + g)}{WACC - g} = \frac{235(1.06)}{0.1032 - 0.06}$$
$$= \frac{249.1}{0.0432} = 5{,}766.20 \text{ million}$$

The total value of equity is the total firm value minus the value of debt, Equity = €5,766.20 million − €1,800 million = €3,966.20 million. Dividing by the number of shares gives the per share estimate of V_0 = €3,966.20 million/10 million = €396.62 per share.

B. The free cash flow to equity is

$$FCFE = NI + NCC - FCInv - WCInv + \text{Net borrowing}$$
$$FCFE = 250 + 90 - 170 - 40 + 0.40(170 - 90 + 40)$$
$$FCFE = 250 + 90 - 170 - 40 + 48 = €178 \text{ million.}$$

Because the company is borrowing 40 percent of the increase in net capital expenditures $(170 - 90)$ and working capital (40), net borrowing is €48 million.

The total value of equity is the FCFE discounted at the required rate of return of equity,

$$\text{Equity value} = \frac{\text{FCFE}_1}{r - g} = \frac{\text{FCFE}_0(1 + g)}{r - g} = \frac{178(1.07)}{0.13 - 0.07}$$

$$= \frac{190.46}{0.06} = \text{€3,174.33 million}$$

The value per share is $V_0 = $ €3,174.33 million/10 million = €317.43 per share.

8. The WACC for PHB Company is

$$\text{WACC} = 0.30(7.0\%)(1 - 0.35) + 0.15(6.8\%) + 0.55(11.0\%)$$
$$= 8.435\%$$

The firm value is

Firm value = $\text{FCFF}_0(1 + g)/(\text{WACC} - g)$
Firm value = $28(1.04)/(0.08435 - 0.04) = 29.12/0.04435$
          = \$656.60 million

The value of equity is the firm value minus the value of debt minus the value of preferred stock: Equity = $656.60 - 145 - 65 = $ \$446.60 million. Dividing this amount by the number of shares gives the estimated value per share of \$446.60 million/8 million shares = \$55.82.

The estimated value for the stock is greater than the market price of \$32.50, so the stock appears to be undervalued.

9. A. The required return on equity is

$$r = E(R_i) = R_F + \beta_i[E(R_M) - R_F] = 5.5\% + 0.90(5.5\%) = 10.45\%$$

The weighted-average cost of capital is

$$\text{WACC} = 0.25(7.0\%)(1 - 0.40) + 0.75(10.45\%) = 8.89\%$$

B. Firm value $= \dfrac{\text{FCFF}_0(1 + g)}{\text{WACC} - g}$

Firm value $= \dfrac{1.1559(1.04)}{0.0889 - 0.04} = $ \$24.583

C. Equity value = Firm value − Market value of debt
Equity value = $24.583 - 3.192 = $ \$21.391 billion

D. Value per share = Equity value/Number of shares
Value per share = \$21.391 billion /1.852 billion = \$11.55

10. A. The required rate of return for McInish found with the CAPM is

$$r = E(R_i) = R_F + \beta_i[E(R_M) - R_F] = 5.08\% + 0.70(5.50\%) = 8.93\%$$

The value per share is

$$V_0 = \frac{\text{FCFE}_0(1 + g)}{r - g} = \frac{0.88(1.064)}{0.0893 - 0.064} = \$37.01$$

B. The following table shows the calculated price for McInish based on the base-case values for all values except the variable being changed from the base-case value.

Variable	Estimated Price with Low Value ($)	Estimated Price with High Value ($)	Range (Rank) ($)
Normalized FCFE$_0$	29.44	47.94	18.50 (3)
Risk-free rate	38.22	35.33	2.89 (5)
Equity risk premium	51.17	28.99	22.18 (2)
Beta	47.29	30.40	16.89 (4)
FCFE growth rate	18.56	48.79	30.23 (1)

As the table shows, the value of McInish is most sensitive to the changes in the FCFE growth rate, with the price moving over a wide range. McInish's stock price is least sensitive to alternative values of the risk-free rate. Alternative values of beta, the equity risk premium, or the initial FCFE value also have a large impact on the value of the stock, although the effects of these variables are smaller than the effect of the growth rate.

11. A. Using the CAPM, the required rate of return for NewMarket is

$$r = E(R_i) = R_F + \beta_i[E(R_M) - R_F] = 7\% + 1.3(4\%) = 12.2\%$$

To estimate FCFE, we use Equation 15:

$$\text{FCFE} = \text{Net income} - (1 - \text{DR})(\text{FCInv} - \text{Depreciation}) \\ - (1 - \text{DR})(\text{WCInv})$$

which can be written

$$\text{FCFE} = \text{Net income} - (1 - \text{DR})(\text{FCInv} - \text{Depreciation} + \text{WCInv}) \\ = \text{Net income} - (1 - \text{DR})(\text{Net investment in operating assets})$$

The following table shows that net income grows at 20 percent annually for Years 1, 2, and 3 and then grows at 8 percent for Year 4. The net investment in operating assets is $1,150 million in Year 1 and grows at 15 percent annually for Years 2 and 3. Debt financing is 40 percent of this investment. FCFE is NI − Net investment in operating assets + New debt financing. Finally, the present value of FCFE for Years 1, 2, and 3 is found by discounting at 12.2 percent.

(in $ Millions)	Year			
	1	2	3	4
Net income	720.00	864.00	1,036.80	1,119.74
Net investment in operating assets	1,150.00	1,322.50	1,520.88	335.92
New debt financing	460.00	529.00	608.35	134.37
FCFE	30.00	70.50	124.27	918.19
PV of FCFE discounted at 12.2%	26.74	56.00	87.98	

In Year 4, net income is 8 percent larger than in Year 3. In Year 4, the investment in operating assets is 30 percent of net income and debt financing is 40 percent of this investment. The FCFE in Year 4 is $918.19 million. The value of FCFE after Year 3 is found by using the constant-growth model:

$$V_3 = \frac{FCFE_4}{r - g} = \frac{918.19}{0.122 - 0.08} = \$21{,}861.67 \text{ million}$$

The present value of V_3 discounted at 12.2 percent is $15,477.64 million. The total value of equity, the present value of the first three years' FCFE plus the present value of V_3, is $15,648.36 million. Dividing this by the number of outstanding shares (318 million) gives a value per share of $49.21. For the first three years, NewMarket has a small FCFE because of the large investments it is making during the high-growth phase. In the normal-growth phase, FCFE is much larger because the investments required are much smaller.

B. The planner's estimate of the share value of $70.98 is much higher than the FCFE model estimate of $49.21 for several reasons. First, taxes and interest expenses have a prior claim to the company's cash flow and should be taken out of the cash flows used in estimating the value of equity because these amounts are not available to equityholders. The planner did not do this.

Second, EBITDA does not account for the company's reinvestments in operating assets. So, EBITDA overstates the funds available to stockholders if reinvestment needs exceed depreciation charges, which is the case for growing companies such as NewMarket.

Third, EBITDA does not account for the company's capital structure. Using EBITDA to represent a benefit to stockholders (as opposed to stockholders and bondholders combined) is a mistake.

Finally, dividing EBITDA by the bond rate commits a major error. The risk-free bond rate is an inappropriate discount rate for risky equity cash flows; the proper measure is the required rate of return on the company's equity. Dividing by a fixed rate also assumes, erroneously, that the cash flow stream is a fixed perpetuity. EBITDA cannot be a perpetual stream because if it were distributed, the stream would eventually decline to zero (lacking capital investments). NewMarket is actually a growing company, so assuming it to be a nongrowing perpetuity is a mistake.

12. The following table develops the information to calculate FCFE per share (amounts are in U.S. dollars).

	2003	2004	2005	2006	2007	2008
Growth rate for EPS	21%	18%	15%	12%	9%	6%
EPS	3.630	4.283	4.926	5.517	6.014	6.374
Capital expenditure per share	5.000	5.000	4.500	4.000	3.500	1.500
Investment in WC per share	1.250	1.250	1.125	1.000	0.875	0.375
New debt financing = 40% of (Capital expenditure + WCInv)	2.500	2.500	2.250	2.000	1.750	0.750
FCFE = NI − Capital expenditure − WCInv + New debt financing	−0.120	0.533	1.551	2.517	3.389	5.249
PV of FCFE discounted at 12%	−0.107	0.425	1.104	1.600	1.923	

Earnings per share for 2002 are $3.00, and the EPS estimates for 2003 through 2008 in the table are found by increasing the previous year's EPS by that year's growth rate. The net capital expenditures each year were specified by the analyst. The increase in working capital per share is equal to 25 percent of net capital expenditures. Finally, debt financing is 40 percent of that year's total net capital expenditures and investment in working capital. For example, in 2003, the per-share amount for net capital expenditures plus investment in working capital is $5.00 + $1.25 = $6.25. Debt financing is 40 percent of $6.25, or $2.50. Debt financing for 2004 through 2008 is found in the same way.

FCFE equals net income minus net capital expenditures minus investment in working capital plus new debt financing. Notice that FCFE is negative in 2003 because of large capital investments and investments in working capital. As these investments decline relative to net income, FCFE becomes positive and substantial.

The present values of FCFE from 2003 through 2007 are given in the bottom row of the table. These five present values sum to $4.944 per share. Because FCFE from 2008 onward will grow at a constant 6 percent, the constant-growth model can be used to value these cash flows.

$$V_{2007} = \frac{FCFE_{2008}}{r - g} = \frac{5.249}{0.12 - 0.06} = \$87.483$$

The present value of this stream is $87.483/(1.12)^5 = 49.640. The value per share is the present value of the first five FCFEs (2003–2007) plus the present value of the FCFE after 2007, or $4.944 + $49.640 = $54.58.

13. A. FCFE is defined as the cash flow remaining after the company meets all financial obligations, including debt payment, and covers all capital expenditure and working capital needs. Sundanci's FCFE for the year 2008 is calculated as follows:

Net income	= $80 million
Plus: Depreciation expense	= 23
Less: Capital expenditures	= 38
Less: Investment in WC	= 41
Equals: FCFE	= $24 million

Thus, FCFE per share equals ($24 million)/(84 million shares) = $0.286.

B. The FCFE model requires forecasts of FCFE for the high-growth years (2009 and 2010) plus a forecast for the first year of stable growth (2011) to allow for an estimate of the terminal value in 2010 based on constant perpetual growth. Because all of the components of FCFE are expected to grow at the same rate, the values can be obtained by projecting the FCFE at the common rate. (Alternatively, the components of FCFE can be projected and aggregated for each year.)

The following table provides the process for estimating Sundanci's current value on a per-share basis.

Free Cash Flow to Equity

Base assumptions:

Shares outstanding (millions)	84
Required return on equity, r	14%

			Actual 2008		Projected 2009	Projected 2010	Projected 2011
					$g = 27\%$	$g = 27\%$	$g = 13\%$
			Total	Per share			
Earnings after tax			$80	$0.952	$1.2090	$1.5355	$1.7351
Plus: Depreciation expense			$23	$0.274	$0.3480	$0.4419	$0.4994
Less: Capital expenditures			$38	$0.452	$0.5740	$0.7290	$0.8238
Less: Increase in net working capital			$41	$0.488	$0.6198	$0.7871	$0.8894
Equals: FCFE			$24	$0.286	$0.3632	$0.4613	$0.5213
Terminal value[a]						$52.1300	
Total cash flows to equity[b]					$0.3632	$52.5913	
Discounted value[c]					$0.3186	$40.4673	
Current value per share[d]			$40.7859				

[a] Projected 2010 terminal value = Projected 2011 FCFE/$(r - g)$.

[b] Projected 2010 total cash flows to equity = Projected 2010 FCFE + Projected 2010 terminal value.

[c] Discounted values obtained by using $r = 14$ percent.

[d] Current value per share = Discounted value 2009 + Discounted value 2010.

C. The following limitations of the DDM *are* addressed by the FCFE model: The DDM uses a strict definition of cash flow to equity; that is, cash flows to equity are the dividends on the common stock. The FCFE model expands the definition of cash flow to include the balance of residual cash flows after all financial obligations and investment needs have been met. Thus, the FCFE model explicitly recognizes the company's investment and financing policies as well as its dividend policy. In instances of a change of corporate control, and thus the possibility of changing dividend policy, the FCFE model provides a better estimate of value.

Both two-stage valuation models allow for two distinct phases of growth—an initial finite period when the growth is abnormal followed by a stable growth period that is expected to last forever. These two-stage models share the same limitations with respect to the growth assumptions:

First, the analyst must confront the difficulty of defining the duration of the extraordinary growth period. A long period of high growth will produce a higher valuation, and the analyst may be tempted to assume an unrealistically long period of extraordinary growth.

Second, the analyst must realize that assuming a sudden shift from high growth to lower, stable growth is unrealistic. The transformation is more likely to occur gradually over time.

Third, because value is quite sensitive to the steady-state growth assumption, overestimating or underestimating this rate can lead to large errors in value.

The two models also share other limitations—notably, difficulties in accurately estimating required rates of return.

14. A. When a two-stage DDM is used, the value of a share of Mackinac, dividends per share (DPS), is calculated as follows:

$$DPS_0 = \text{Cash dividends/Shares outstanding} = \$22,470/13,000$$
$$= \$1.7285$$
$$DPS_1 = DPS_0 \times 1.17 = \$2.0223$$
$$DPS_2 = DPS_0 \times 1.17^2 = \$2.3661$$
$$DPS_3 = DPS_0 \times 1.17^3 = \$2.7683$$
$$DPS_4 = DPS_0 \times 1.17^3 \times 1.09 = \$3.0175$$

When the CAPM is used, the required return on equity, r, is

$$r = \text{Government bond rate} + (\text{Beta} \times \text{Equity risk premium})$$
$$= 0.06 + (1.25 \times 0.05) = 0.1225 \text{ or } 12.25 \text{ percent}$$

$$\text{Value per share} = DPS_1/(1 + r) + DPS_2/(1 + r)^2 + DPS_3/(1 + r)^3 + [DPS_4/(r - g_{\text{stable}})]/(1 + r)^3$$

$$\text{Value per share} = \$2.0223/1.1225 + \$2.3661/1.1225^2 + \$2.7683/1.1225^3 + [\$3.0175/(0.1225 - 0.09)]/1.1225^3$$
$$= \$1.8016 + \$1.8778 + \$1.9573 + \$65.6450$$
$$= \$71.28$$

B. When the two-stage FCFE model is used, the value of a share of Mackinac is calculated as follows (in $ thousands except per-share data):

Net income = $37,450

Depreciation = $10,500

Capital expenditures = $15,000

Change in working capital = $5,500

New debt issuance − Principal repayments = Change in debt outstanding = $4,000

$FCFE_0$ = Net income + Depreciation − Capital expenditures − Change in working capital − Principal repayments + New debt issues

$FCFE_0$ = $37,450 + $10,500 − $15,000 − $5,500 + $4,000
= $31,450

$FCFE_0$ per share = $31,450/13,000 = $2.4192

$FCFE_1 = FCFE_0 \times 1.17 = \$2.8305$

$FCFE_2 = FCFE_0 \times 1.17^2 = \$3.3117$

$FCFE_3 = FCFE_0 \times 1.17^3 = \$3.8747$

$FCFE_4 = FCFE_0 \times 1.17^3 \times 1.09 = \$4.2234$

From the answer to A, r = 12.25 percent.

Value per share = $FCFE_1/(1 + r) + FCFE_2/(1 + r)^2 + FCFE_3/(1 + r)^3 + [FCFE_4/(r - g_{stable})]/(1 + r)^3$

Value per share = $2.8305/1.1225 + $3.3117/1.1225^2 + $3.8747/1.1225^3 + [$4.2234/(0.1225 − 0.09)]/1.1225^3
= $2.5216 + $2.6283 + $2.7395 + $91.8798
= $99.77

C. The FCFE model is best for valuing companies for takeovers or in situations that have a reasonable chance of a change in corporate control. Because controlling stockholders can change the dividend policy, they are interested in estimating the maximum residual cash flow after meeting all financial obligations and investment needs. The DDM is based on the premise that the only cash flows received by stockholders are dividends. FCFE uses a more expansive definition to measure what a company can afford to pay out as dividends.

15. A. The real required rate of return for SK Telecom is

Country return (real)	6.50%
Industry adjustment	+0.60%
Size adjustment	−0.10%
Leverage adjustment	+0.25%
Required rate of return	7.25%

B. The real growth rate of FCFE is expected to be the same as the country rate of 3.5 percent. The value of one share is

$$V_0 = \frac{FCFE_0(1 + g_{real})}{r_{real} - g_{real}} = \frac{1,300(1.035)}{0.0725 - 0.035} = 35,880 \text{ Korean won}$$

16. The required return for QuickChange, found by using the CAPM, is $r = E(R_i) = R_F + \beta_i[E(R_M) - R_F] = 4.5\% + 2.0(5.0\%) = 14.5\%$. The estimated future values of FCFE are given in the following exhibit (amounts in U.S. dollars):

Year t	Variable	Calculation	Value in Year t	Present Value at 14.5%
1	$FCFE_1$	0.75(1.10)	0.825	0.721
2	$FCFE_2$	0.75(1.10)(1.26)	1.040	0.793
3	$FCFE_3$	0.75(1.10)(1.26)²	1.310	0.873
4	$FCFE_4$	0.75(1.10)(1.26)³	1.650	0.960
4	TV_4	$FCFE_5/(r - g)$	20.580	11.974
		$= 0.75(1.10)(1.26)^3(1.06)/(0.145{-}0.06)$		
		$= 1.749/0.085$		
0		Total value = PV of FCFE for Years 1–4		
		+ PV of Terminal value		15.32

The FCFE grows at 10 percent for Year 1 and then at 26 percent for Years 2–4. These calculated values for FCFE are shown in the exhibit. The present values of the FCFE for the first four years discounted at the required rate of return are given in the last column of the table. After Year 4, FCFE will grow at 6 percent forever, so the constant-growth FCFE model is used to find the terminal value at Time 4, which is $TV_4 = FCFE_5/(r - g)$. TV_4 is discounted at the required return for four periods to find its present value, as shown in the table. Finally, the total value of the stock, $15.32, is the sum of the present values of the first four years' FCFE per share plus the present value of the terminal value per share.

17. The total value of nonoperating assets is

$60 million short-term securities
$45 million market value of noncurrent assets
$40 million pension fund surplus
―――――
$145 million nonoperating assets

The total value of the firm is the value of the operating assets plus the value of the nonoperating assets, or $720 million plus $145 million = $865 million. The equity value is the value of the firm minus the value of debt, or $865 million − $215 million = $650 million. The value per share is $650 million/100 million shares = $6.50 per share.

18. C is correct. The sustainable growth rate is return on equity (ROE) multiplied by the retention ratio. ROE is 10 percent, and the retention ratio is 1 − Payout ratio, or 1.0 − 0.2 = 0.8. The sustainable growth rate is 0.8 × 10% = 8%. Because Emerald's policy states that dividend growth will not exceed FCFE growth, FCFE growth should be at least 8 percent per year in the long term.

19. A is correct. Justifications for choosing the FCFE model over the DDM include:

▶ The company pays dividends but its dividends differ significantly from the company's capacity to pay dividends (the first reason given by Leigh).

▶ The investor takes a control perspective (the second reason given by Leigh).

20. A is correct. FCFF = NI + NCC + Interest expense (1 − Tax rate) − FCInv −WCInv. In this case:

NI = $485 million

NCC = Depreciation expense = $270 million

Interest expense (1 − Tax rate) = 195 (1 − 0.32) = $132.6 million

FCInv = Net purchase of fixed assets = Increase in gross fixed assets
= 4,275 − 3,752 = $523 million

WCInv = Increase in accounts receivable + Increase in inventory
− Increase in accounts payable − Increase in accrued
liabilities = (770 − 711) + (846 − 780) − (476 − 443)
− (149 − 114) = $57 million

FCFF = 485 + 270 + 132.6 − 523 − 57 = 307.6, or $308 million

21. B is correct. FCFE = NI + NCC − FCInv − WCInv + Net borrowing. In this case:

NI	= $485 million
NCC	= Depreciation expense = $270 million
FCInv	= Net purchase of fixed assets = Increase in gross fixed assets
	= 4,275 − 3,752 = $523 million
WCInv	= Increase in accounts receivable + Increase in inventory − Increase in accounts payable − Increase in accrued liabilities
	= (770 − 711) + (846 − 780) − (476 − 443) − (149 − 114)
	= $57 million
Net borrowing	= Increase in notes payable + Increase in long-term debt
	= (465 − 450) + (1,575 − 1,515) = $75 million
FCFE	= 485 + 270 − 523 − 57 + 75 = $250 million

An alternative calculation is

FCFE = FCFF − Int(1 − Tax rate) + Net borrowing

FCFE = 307.6 − 195 (1 − 0.32) + (15 + 60) = $250 million

22. C is correct. Inventory cannot be reduced below zero. Furthermore, sales growth tends to increase inventory.

23. A is correct. The FCFF model is often selected when the capital structure is expected to change because FCFF estimation may be easier than FCFE estimation in the presence of changing financial leverage.

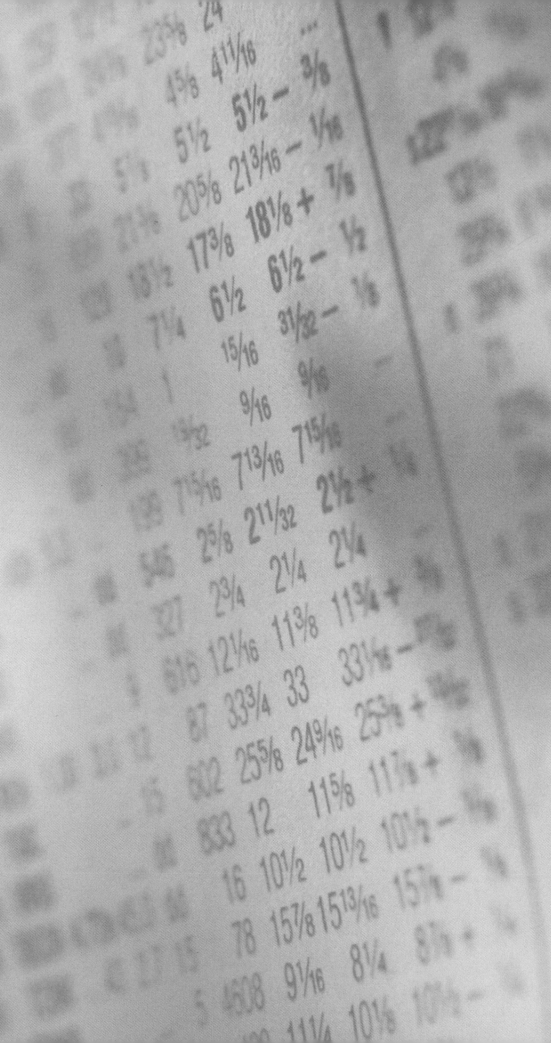

MARKET-BASED VALUATION: PRICE AND ENTERPRISE VALUE MULTIPLES

by Jerald Pinto, CFA, Elaine Henry, CFA, Thomas Robinson, CFA, and John Stowe, CFA

LEARNING OUTCOMES

The candidate should be able to:	Mastery
a. distinguish between the method of comparables and the method based on forecasted fundamentals as approaches to using price multiples in valuation, and explain economic rationales for each approach;	☐
b. interpret a justified price multiple;	☐
c. describe rationales for and possible drawbacks to using price multiples (including P/E, P/B, P/S, P/CF) and dividend yield in valuation;	☐
d. calculate and interpret alternative price multiples and dividend yield;	☐
e. calculate and interpret underlying earnings, explain methods of normalizing EPS, and calculate normalized EPS;	☐
f. explain and justify the use of earnings yield (E/P);	☐
g. describe fundamental factors that influence alternative price multiples and dividend yield;	☐
h. calculate and interpret the justified price-to-earnings ratio (P/E), price-to-book ratio (P/B), and price-to-sales ratio (P/S) for a stock, based on forecasted fundamentals;	☐
i. calculate and interpret a predicted P/E, given a cross-sectional regression on fundamentals, and explain limitations to the cross-sectional regression methodology;	☐
j. evaluate a stock by the method of comparables, and explain the importance of fundamentals in using the method of comparables;	☐
k. calculate and interpret the P/E-to-growth ratio (PEG), and explain its use in relative valuation;	☐
l. calculate and explain the use of price multiples in determining terminal value in a multistage discounted cash flow (DCF) model;	☐

Equity Asset Valuation, Second Edition, by Jerald Pinto, CFA, Elaine Henry, CFA, Thomas Robinson, CFA, and John Stowe, CFA. Copyright © 2009 by CFA Institute. Reprinted with permission.

m. explain alternative definitions of cash flow used in price and enterprise value multiples, and describe limitations of each definition;	☐
n. calculate and interpret enterprise value multiples, and evaluate the use of EV/EBITDA;	☐
o. explain sources of differences in cross-border valuation comparisons;	☐
p. describe momentum indicators and their use in valuation;	☐
q. evaluate whether a stock is overvalued, fairly valued, or undervalued based on comparisons of multiples;	☐
r. explain the use of the arithmetic mean, the harmonic mean, the weighted harmonic mean, and the median to describe the central tendency of a group of multiples.	☐

1 INTRODUCTION

Among the most familiar and widely used valuation tools are price and enterprise value multiples. **Price multiples** are ratios of a stock's market price to some measure of fundamental value per share. **Enterprise value multiples**, by contrast, relate the total market value of all sources of a company's capital to a measure of fundamental value for the entire company.

The intuition behind price multiples is that investors evaluate the price of a share of stock—judge whether it is fairly valued, overvalued, or undervalued—by considering what a share buys in terms of per share earnings, net assets, cash flow or some other measure of value (stated on a per share basis). The intuition behind enterprise value multiples is similar; investors evaluate the market value of an entire enterprise relative to the amount of earnings before interest, taxes, depreciation, and amortization (EBITDA), sales, or operating cash flow it generates. As valuation indicators (measures or indicators of value), multiples have the appealing qualities of simplicity in use and ease in communication. A multiple summarizes in a single number the relationship between the market value of a company's stock (or of its total capital) and some fundamental quantity, such as earnings, sales, or **book value** (owners' equity based on accounting values).

Among the questions we will study in this reading for answers that will help in making correct use of multiples as valuation tools are the following:

► What accounting issues affect particular price and enterprise value multiples, and how can analysts address them?
► How do price multiples relate to fundamentals, such as earnings growth rates, and how can analysts use this information when making valuation comparisons among stocks?

▶ For which types of valuation problems is a particular price or enterprise value multiple appropriate or inappropriate?

▶ What challenges arise in applying price and enterprise value multiples internationally?

Multiples may be viewed as valuation indicators relating to individual securities. Another type of valuation indicator used in securities selection is **momentum indicators**. They typically relate either price or a fundamental (such as earnings) to the time series of its own past values or, in some cases, to its expected value. The logic behind the use of momentum indicators is that such indicators may provide information on future patterns of returns over some time horizon. Because the purpose of momentum indicators is to identify potentially rewarding investment opportunities, they can be viewed as a class of valuation indicators with a focus that is different from and complementary to the focus of price and enterprise value multiples.

This reading is organized as follows. In Section 2, we put the use of price and enterprise value multiples in an economic context and present certain themes common to the use of any price or enterprise value multiple. Section 3 presents price multiples; a subsection is devoted to each multiple. The treatment of each multiple follows a common format: usage considerations, the relationship of the multiple to investors' expectations about fundamentals, and using the multiple in valuation based on comparables. Section 4 presents enterprise value multiples and is organized similarly to Section 3. Section 5 presents international considerations in using multiples. A treatment of momentum indicators follows in Section 6. Section 7 discusses several practical issues that arise in using valuation indicators. We then summarize the reading, and the reading concludes with practice problems.

PRICE AND ENTERPRISE VALUE MULTIPLES IN VALUATION

2

In practice, two methods underpin analysts' use of price and enterprise value multiples: the method of comparables and the method based on forecasted fundamentals. Each of these methods relates to a definite economic rationale. In this section, we introduce the two methods and their associated economic rationales.

2.1 The Method of Comparables

The **method of comparables** refers to the valuation of an asset based on multiples of comparable (similar) assets—that is, valuation based on multiples benchmarked to the multiples of similar assets. The similar assets may be referred to as the **comparables**, the **comps**, or the **guideline assets** (or in the case of equity valuation, **guideline companies**). For example, multiplying a benchmark value of the price-to-earnings (P/E) multiple by an estimate of a company's earnings per share (EPS) provides a quick estimate of the value of the company's stock that can be compared with the stock's market price. Equivalently, comparing a stock's actual price multiple with a relevant benchmark multiple should lead the analyst to the same conclusion on whether the stock is relatively fairly valued, relatively undervalued, or relatively overvalued.

The idea behind price multiples is that a stock's price cannot be evaluated in isolation. Rather, it needs to be evaluated in relation to what it buys in terms of earnings, net assets, or some other measure of value. Obtained by dividing price by a measure of value per share, a price multiple gives the price to purchase one unit of value in whatever way value is measured. For example, a P/E of 20 means that it takes 20 units of currency (for example, €20) to buy one unit of earnings (for example, €1 of earnings). This scaling of price per share by value per share also makes possible comparisons among various stocks. For example, an investor pays more for a unit of earnings for a stock with a P/E of 25 than for another stock with a P/E of 20. Applying the method of comparables, the analyst would reason that if the securities are otherwise closely similar (if they have similar risk, profit margins, and growth prospects, for example), the security with the P/E of 20 is undervalued relative to the one with the P/E of 25.

The word *relative* is necessary. An asset may be undervalued relative to a comparison asset or group of assets, and an analyst may thus expect the asset to outperform the comparison asset or assets on a relative basis. If the comparison asset or assets themselves are not efficiently priced, however, the stock may not be undervalued—it could be fairly valued or even overvalued (on an absolute basis, i.e., in relation to its intrinsic value). Example 1 presents the method of comparables in its simplest application.

EXAMPLE 1

The Method of Comparables at Its Simplest

Company A's EPS is $1.50. Its closest competitor, Company B, is trading at a P/E of 22. Assume the companies have a similar operating and financial profile.

1. If Company A's stock is trading at $37.50, what does that indicate about its value relative to Company B?

2. If we assume that Company A's stock should trade at about the same P/E as Company B's stock, what will we estimate as an appropriate price for Company A's stock?

Solution to 1: If Company A's stock is trading at $37.50, its P/E will be 25 ($37.50 divided by $1.50). If the companies are similar, this P/E would indicate that Company A is overvalued relative to Company B.

Solution to 2: If we assume that Company A's stock should trade at about the same P/E as Company B's stock, we will estimate that an appropriate price for Company A's stock is $33 ($1.50 times 22).

The method of comparables applies also to enterprise value multiples. In this application, we would evaluate the market value of an entire company in relation to some measure of value relevant to all providers of capital, not only providers of equity capital. For example, multiplying a benchmark multiple of enterprise value (EV) to earnings before interest, taxes, depreciation, and amortization (EBITDA) times an estimate of a company's EBITDA provides a quick estimate of the value of the entire company. Similarly, comparing a company's actual enterprise value multiple with a relevant benchmark multiple allows an assessment of whether the company is relatively fairly valued, relatively undervalued, or relatively overvalued.

Many choices for the benchmark value of a multiple have appeared in valuation methodologies, including the multiple of a closely matched individual stock and the average or median value of the multiple for the stock's industry peer group. The economic rationale underlying the method of comparables is the **law of one price**—the economic principle that two identical assets should sell at the same price.[1] The method of comparables is perhaps the most widely used approach for analysts *reporting* valuation judgments on the basis of price multiples. For this reason, the use of multiples in valuation is sometimes viewed solely as a type of relative-valuation approach; however, multiples can also be derived from, and expressed in terms of, fundamentals, as discussed in the next section.

2.2 The Method Based on Forecasted Fundamentals

The **method based on forecasted fundamentals**[2] refers to the use of multiples that are derived from forecasted fundamentals—characteristics of a business related to profitability, growth, or financial strength. Fundamentals drive cash flows, and we can relate multiples to company fundamentals through a discounted cash flow (DCF) model. Algebraic expressions of price multiples in terms of fundamentals facilitate an examination of how valuation differences among stocks relate to different expectations for those fundamentals. We illustrated this concept in the reading on discounted dividend valuation, where we explained P/E in terms of perhaps the simplest DCF model, the Gordon growth dividend discount model, in an expression that includes (among other variables) the expected dividend growth rate.

One process for relating multiples to forecasted fundamentals begins with a valuation based on a DCF model. Recall that DCF models estimate the intrinsic value of a firm or its equity as the present value of expected cash flows, and that fundamentals drive cash flows. Multiples are stated with respect to a single value of a fundamental, but any price or enterprise value multiple relates to the entire future stream of expected cash flows through its DCF value.

We can illustrate this concept by first taking the present value of the stream of expected future cash flows and then expressing the result relative to a forecasted fundamental. For example, if the DCF value of a U.K. stock is £10.20 and its forecasted EPS is £1.2, the forward P/E multiple consistent with the DCF value is £10.20/£1.2 = 8.5. (The term **forward P/E** refers to a P/E calculated on the basis of a forecast of EPS and is discussed in further detail later in this reading.) This exercise of relating a valuation to a price multiple applies to any definition of price multiple and any DCF model or residual income model.[3]

---

[1] In practice, analysts can match characteristics among companies or across time only approximately. Nevertheless, the law of one price is the idea driving the method of comparables. To keep our classification simple, we will discuss comparisons with a market index or with historical values of a stock's multiple under the rubric of the method of comparables.

[2] For brevity, we sometimes use the phrase "based on fundamentals" in describing multiples derived using this approach.

[3] Recall that residual income models estimate the intrinsic value of a share of common stock as the sum of book value per share and the present value of expected future per-share residual income. Residual income equals net income minus a deduction for the cost of equity capital.

In summary, we can approach valuation by using multiples from two perspectives. First, we can use the method of comparables, which involves comparing an asset's multiple to a standard of comparison. Similar assets should sell at similar prices. Second, we can use the method based on forecasted fundamentals, which involves forecasting the company's fundamentals rather than making comparisons with other companies. The price multiple of an asset should be related to its expected future cash flows. We can also incorporate the insights from the method based on forecasted fundamentals in explaining valuation differences based on comparables, because we seldom (if ever) find exact comparables. In the sections covering each multiple, we will present the method based on forecasted fundamentals first so we can refer to it when using the method of comparables.

Using either method, how can an analyst communicate a view about the value of a stock? Of course, the analyst can offer simply a qualitative judgment about whether the stock appears to be fairly valued, overvalued, or undervalued (and offer specific reasons for the view). The analyst may also be more precise by communicating a **justified price multiple** for the stock. The justified price multiple is the estimated fair value of that multiple, which can be justified on the basis of the method of comparables or the method of forecasted fundamentals.

For an example of a justified multiple based on the method of comparables, suppose we use the price-to-book (P/B) multiple in a valuation and find that the median P/B for the company's peer group, which would be the standard of comparison, is 2.2.[4] The stock's justified P/B based on the method of comparables is 2.2 (without making any adjustments for differences in fundamentals). We can compare the justified P/B with the actual P/B based on market price to form an opinion about value. If the justified P/B is larger (smaller) than the actual P/B, the stock may be undervalued (overvalued). We can also, on the assumption that the comparison assets are fairly priced, translate the justified P/B based on comparables into an estimate of absolute fair value of the stock. If the current book value per share is $23, then the fair value of the stock is $2.2 \times \$23 = \$50.60$, which can be compared with its market price.

For an example of a justified multiple based on fundamentals, suppose that we are using a residual income model and estimate that the value of the stock is $46. Then, the justified P/B based on forecasted fundamentals is $\$46/\$23 = 2.0$, which we can again compare with the actual value of the stock's P/B. We can also state our estimate of the stock's absolute fair value as $2 \times \$23 = \$46$. (Note that the analyst could report valuation judgments related to a DCF model in terms of the DCF value directly; price multiples are a familiar form, however, in which to state valuations.) Furthermore, we can incorporate the insights from the method based on fundamentals to explain differences from results based on comparables.

In the next section, we begin a discussion of specific price and enterprise value multiples used in valuation.

3   PRICE MULTIPLES

In this section, we first discuss the most familiar price multiple, the price-to-earnings ratio. In the context of that discussion, we introduce a variety of practical issues that have counterparts for most other multiples. These issues include

---

[4] Note we are using the median, rather than the mean, value of the peer group's multiple to avoid distortions by outliers. This issue is often important when dealing with peer groups because they frequently consist of a small number of companies. An alternative is to use the harmonic mean, which we describe and illustrate in a later section.

analyst adjustments to the denominator of the ratio for accuracy and comparability and the use of inverse price multiples. Then, we discuss four other major price multiples from the same practical perspective.

3.1 Price to Earnings

In the first edition of *Security Analysis* (1934, p. 351), Benjamin Graham and David L. Dodd described common stock valuation based on P/Es as the standard method of that era, and the P/E is still the most familiar valuation measure today.

We begin our discussion with rationales offered by analysts for the use of P/E and with the possible drawbacks of its use. We then define the two chief variations of the P/E: the trailing P/E and the forward P/E (also called the "leading P/E"). The multiple's numerator, market price, is (as in other multiples) definitely determinable; it presents no special problems of interpretation. But the denominator, EPS, is based on the complex rules of accrual accounting and presents significant interpretation issues. We discuss those issues and the adjustments analysts can make to obtain more-meaningful P/Es. Finally, we conclude the section by examining how analysts use P/Es to value a stock using the method of forecasted fundamentals and the method of comparables. As mentioned earlier, we discuss fundamentals first so that we can draw insights from that discussion when using comparables.

Several rationales support the use of P/E multiples in valuation:

▶ Earning power is a chief driver of investment value, and EPS, the denominator in the P/E ratio, is perhaps the chief focus of security analysts' attention.[5] In a 2007 survey of CFA Institute members, P/E ranked first among price multiples used in market-based valuation.[6]

▶ The P/E ratio is widely recognized and used by investors.

▶ Differences in stocks' P/Es may be related to differences in long-run average returns on investments in those stocks, according to empirical research.[7]

Potential drawbacks to using P/Es derive from the characteristics of EPS:

▶ EPS can be zero, negative, or insignificantly small relative to price, and P/E does not make economic sense with a zero, negative, or insignificantly small denominator.

▶ The ongoing or recurring components of earnings that are most important in determining intrinsic value can be practically difficult to distinguish from transient components.

---

[5] U.S.-based empirical research tends to show that valuations derived from earnings-based multiples are closer to actual market prices than valuations derived from multiples based on other fundamentals (Liu, Nissim, and Thomas 2002, 2007). If shares are efficiently priced on average, such findings support the importance of earnings in the pricing of common shares.

[6] See Pinto, Marmorstein, Robinson, Stowe, and McLeavey (2008) for more details.

[7] Chan and Lakonishok (2004) summarize and update academic empirical evidence of superior returns to value investing—that is, investing focused on stocks with low price multiples (e.g., P/E)—in most of the 13 countries they examined. O'Shaughnessy (2005) provides empirical evidence of superior returns to long-term value investing in the U.S. market since 1951, although returns to a low-P/E strategy were dominated by returns to low-P/B, low price-to-sales, and low price-to-cash-flow strategies. In general, debate continues about whether long-run average superior returns to value investing are attributable to higher risk in value than in growth stocks and about other elements in the interpretation of the evidence.

▶ The application of accounting standards requires corporate managers to choose among acceptable alternatives and to use estimates in reporting. In making such choices and estimates, managers may distort EPS as an accurate reflection of economic performance. Such distortions may affect the comparability of P/Es among companies.

Methods to address these potential drawbacks will be discussed later in the reading. In the next section, we discuss alternative definitions of P/E based on alternative specifications of earnings.

3.1.1 Alternative Definitions of P/E

In calculating a P/E, the numerator most commonly used is the current price of the common stock, which is generally easily obtained and unambiguous for publicly traded companies. Selecting the appropriate EPS figure to be used in the denominator is not as straightforward. The following two issues must be considered:

▶ the time horizon over which earnings are measured, which results in alternative definitions of P/E, and

▶ adjustments to accounting earnings that the analyst may make so that P/Es for various companies can be compared.

Common alternative definitions of P/E are trailing P/E and forward P/E.

▶ A stock's **trailing P/E** (sometimes referred to as a current P/E[8]) is its current market price divided by the most recent four quarters' EPS. In such calculations, EPS is sometimes referred to as "trailing 12 month (TTM) EPS."

▶ The **forward P/E** (also called the **leading P/E** or **prospective P/E**) is a stock's current price divided by next year's expected earnings. Trailing P/E is the P/E usually presented first in stock profiles that appear in financial databases, but most databases also provide the forward P/E. In practice, the forward P/E has a number of important variations that depend on how "next year" is defined, as discussed in Section 3.1.3.

Other names and time-horizon definitions for P/E exist. For example, Thomson First Call[9] provides various P/Es, including ratios that have as the denominator a stock's trailing twelve months EPS, last reported annual EPS, and EPS forecasted for one year to three years ahead. Another example is Value Line's company reports which display a median P/E, which is a rounded average of the four middle values of the range of annual average P/Es over the past 10 years.

In using the P/E, an analyst should apply the same definition to all companies and time periods under examination. Otherwise, the P/Es are not comparable, for a given company over time or for various companies at a specific point in time. One reason is that the differences in P/Es calculated by different methods may be systematic (as opposed to random). For example, for companies with rising earnings, the forward P/E will be smaller than the trailing P/E because the denominator in the forward P/E calculation will be larger.

---

[8] However, *The Value Line Investment Survey* uses "current P/E" to mean a P/E based on EPS for the most recent six months plus the projected EPS for the coming six months. That calculation blends historical and forward looking elements.

[9] Thomson First Call is now part of Reuters; the Reuters and Thomson First Call databases are separate, however, so these estimates continue to be referred to as Thomson First Call estimates.

Valuation is a forward-looking process, so analysts usually focus on the forward P/E when earnings forecasts are available. For large public companies, an analyst can develop earnings forecasts and/or obtain consensus earnings forecasts from a commercial database. When earnings are not readily predictable, however, a trailing P/E (or another valuation metric) may be more appropriate than forward P/E. Furthermore, logic sometimes indicates that a particular definition of the P/E is not relevant. For example, a major acquisition or divestiture or a significant change in financial leverage may change a company's operating or financial risk so much that the trailing P/E based on past EPS is not informative about the future and thus not relevant to a valuation. In such a case, the forward P/E is the appropriate measure. In the following sections, we address issues that arise in calculating trailing and forward P/Es.

Trailing P/Es and forward P/Es are based on a single year's EPS. If that number is negative or viewed as unrepresentative of a company's earning power, however, an analyst may base the P/E calculation on a longer run expected average EPS value. P/Es based on such normalized EPS data may be called **normalized P/Es**. Because the denominators in normalized P/Es are typically based on historical information, they are covered in the next section on calculating the trailing P/E.

3.1.2 Calculating the Trailing P/E

When using trailing earnings to calculate a P/E, the analyst must take care in determining the EPS to be used in the denominator. The analyst must consider the following:

▶ potential dilution of EPS;[10]

▶ transitory, nonrecurring components of earnings that are company specific;

▶ transitory components of earnings ascribable to cyclicality (business or industry cyclicality); and

▶ differences in accounting methods (when different companies' stocks are being compared).

Among the considerations mentioned, potential dilution of EPS generally makes the least demands on analysts' accounting expertise because companies are themselves required to present both basic EPS and diluted EPS. **Basic earnings per share** data reflect total earnings divided by the weighted average number of shares actually outstanding during the period. **Diluted earnings per share** reflects division by the number of shares that would be outstanding if holders of securities such as executive stock options, equity warrants, and convertible bonds exercised their options to obtain common stock. The diluted EPS measure also reflects the effect of such conversion on the numerator, earnings.[11] Because companies present both EPS numbers, the analyst does not need to make the computation. Companies also typically report details of the EPS computation in a footnote to the financial statements. Example 2, illustrating the first bullet point, shows the typical case in which the P/E based on diluted EPS is higher than the P/E based on basic EPS.

---

[10] **Dilution** refers to a reduction in proportional ownership interest as a result of the issuance of new shares.

[11] For example, conversion of a convertible bond affects both the numerator (earnings) and the denominator (number of shares) in the EPS calculation. If the holder of a convertible bond exercises the option to convert the bond into common shares, the issuer no longer has an obligation to pay interest on the bond, which affects the amount of earnings, and the issuer issues the required number of shares, which, all else being equal, increases the total number of shares outstanding.

EXAMPLE 2

Basic versus Diluted EPS

For the fiscal year ended 31 December 2007, WPP Group PLC (London: WPP) reported basic EPS of £39.6 and diluted EPS of £38.0. Based on a closing stock price of £596.5 on 29 February 2008, the day on which the company issued its earnings press release, WPP's trailing P/E is 15.1 if basic EPS is used and 15.7 if diluted EPS is used.

When comparing companies, analysts generally prefer to use diluted EPS so that the EPS of companies with differing amounts of dilutive securities are on a comparable basis. The other bulleted considerations frequently lead to analyst adjustments to reported earnings numbers and are discussed in order below.

3.1.2.1 Analyst Adjustments for Nonrecurring Items   Items in earnings that are not expected to recur in the future are generally removed by analysts because valuation concentrates on future cash flows. The analyst's focus is on estimating **underlying earnings** (other names for this concept include **persistent earnings**, **continuing earnings**, and **core earnings**)—that is, earnings that exclude nonrecurring items. An increase in underlying earnings reflects an increase in earnings that the analyst expects to persist into the future. Companies may disclose "adjusted earnings," which may be called non-IFRS (not reportable under International Financial Reporting Standards) earnings, non-GAAP (not reportable under U.S. generally accepted accounting principles) earnings, pro forma earnings, adjusted earnings, or, as in Example 3, core earnings. All of these terms indicate that the earnings number differs in some way from that presented in conformity with accounting standards. Example 3 shows the calculation of EPS and P/E before and after analyst adjustments for nonrecurring items.

EXAMPLE 3

Calculating Trailing 12 Months EPS and Adjusting EPS for Nonrecurring Items

You are calculating a trailing P/E for AstraZeneca PLC (NYSE, LSE: AZN) as of 24 April 2008, when the share price closed at $41.95 in New York (£21.19 in London). In its first quarter of 2008, ended 31 March, AZN reported EPS according to IFRS of $1.03, which included $0.06 of restructuring costs, $0.07 of amortization of intangibles arising from acquisitions, and $0.12 of impairment charges taken to reflect the negative impact of a competing generic product on the value of one of the company's patented products. Adjusting for all of these items, AZN reported "core EPS" of $1.28 for the first quarter of 2008, compared with core EPS of $1.07 for the first quarter of 2007. Because the core EPS differed from the EPS calculated under IFRS, the company provided a reconciliation of the two EPS figures.

Other data for AZN as of April 2008 are given below. The trailing 12 months EPS includes one quarter in 2008 and three quarters in 2007.

Measure	Full Year 2007 (a)	Less 1st Quarter 2007 (b)	Three Quarters of 2007 (c = a − b)	Plus 1st Quarter 2008 (d)	Trailing 12 Months EPS (e = c + d)
Reported EPS	$3.74	$1.02	$2.72	$1.03	$3.75
Core EPS	$4.38	$1.07	$3.31	$1.28	$4.59
EPS excluding 1st quarter 2008 impairment	$3.74	$1.02	$2.72	$1.15	$3.87

Based on the table and information about AZN, address the following:

1. Based on the company's reported EPS, determine the trailing P/E of AZN as of 24 April 2008.

2. Determine the trailing P/E of AZN as of 24 April 2008 using core earnings as determined by AZN.

Suppose you expect the amortization charges to continue for some years and note that, although AZN excluded restructuring charges from its core earnings calculation, AZN has reported restructuring charges in previous years. After reviewing all relevant data, you conclude that, in this instance only, the asset impairment should be viewed as clearly nonrecurring.

3. Determine the trailing P/E based on your adjustment to EPS.

Solution to 1: Based on reported EPS and without any adjustments for nonrecurring items, the trailing P/E is $41.95/$3.75 = 11.2.

Solution to 2: Using the company's reported core earnings, you find that the trailing EPS would be $4.59 and the trailing P/E would be $41.95/$4.59 = 9.1.

Solution to 3: The trailing EPS excluding only what you consider to be nonrecurring items is $3.87 and the trailing P/E on that basis is $41.95/$3.87 = 10.8.

Example 3 makes several important points:

▶ By any of its various names, underlying earnings or core earnings is a non-IFRS concept without prescribed rules for its calculation.

▶ An analyst's calculation of underlying earnings may well differ from that of the company supplying the earnings numbers. Company-reported core earnings may not be comparable among companies because of differing bases of calculation. Analysts should thus always carefully examine the calculation and, generally, should not rely on such company-reported core earnings numbers.

▶ In general, the P/E that an analyst uses in valuation should reflect the analyst's judgment about the company's underlying earnings and should be calculated on a consistent basis among all stocks under review.

The identification of nonrecurring items often requires detailed work—in particular, examination of the income statement, the footnotes to the income statement, and the management discussion and analysis section. The analyst cannot rely on income statement classifications alone to identify nonrecurring components of earnings. Nonrecurring items (for example, gains and losses from the sale of assets, asset write-downs, goodwill impairment, provisions for future losses, and changes in accounting estimates) often appear in the income from continuing operations portion of a business's income statement.[12] An analyst may decide not to exclude income/loss from discontinued operations when assets released from discontinued operations are redirected back into the company's earnings base. An analyst who takes income statement classifications at face value may draw incorrect conclusions in a valuation.

This discussion does not exhaust the analysis that may be necessary to distinguish earnings components that are expected to persist into the future from those that are not. For example, earnings may be decomposed into cash flow and accrual components.[13] The broad implication of research is that the cash flow component of earnings should receive a greater weight than the accrual component of earnings in valuation.[14] And analysts may attempt to reflect that conclusion in the earnings used in calculating P/Es.

3.1.2.2 Analyst Adjustments for Business-Cycle Influences   In addition to company-specific effects, such as restructuring costs, transitory effects on earnings can come from business-cycle or industry-cycle influences. These effects are somewhat different from company-specific effects. Because business cycles repeat, business-cycle effects, although transitory, can be expected to recur in subsequent cycles.

Because of cyclical effects, the most recent four quarters of earnings may not accurately reflect the average or long-term earning power of the business, particularly for **cyclical businesses**—those with high sensitivity to business- or industry-cycle influences, such as automobile and steel manufacturers. Trailing EPS for such stocks are often depressed or negative at the bottom of a cycle and unusually high at the top of a cycle. Empirically, P/Es for cyclical companies are often highly volatile over a cycle even without any change in business prospects: High P/Es on depressed EPS at the bottom of the cycle and low P/Es on unusually high EPS at the top of the cycle reflect the countercyclical property of P/Es known as the **Molodovsky effect**.[15] Analysts address this problem by normalizing EPS—that is, estimating the level of EPS that the business could be expected to achieve under mid-cyclical conditions (**normalized EPS** or **normal EPS**).[16] Two of several available methods to calculate normalized EPS are as follows:

---

[12] An asset **write-down** is a reduction in the value of an asset as stated in the balance sheet. The timing and amount of write-downs often are, at least in part, discretionary. **Accounting estimates** include the useful (depreciable) lives of assets, warranty costs, and the amount of uncollectible receivables.

[13] See Richardson and Tuna (2008) summarizing research by Sloan (1996) and others. The accrual component of earnings is the difference between a cash measure of earnings and a measure of earnings under the relevant set of accounting standards (e.g., IFRS or U.S. GAAP). For example, a cash measure of revenues for a period equals only those amounts collected during the period. In contrast, an accrual measure of revenues includes all revenues earned during the period (both the amounts collected during the period and amounts expected to be collected in future periods, which are, therefore, still in the accounts receivable section at the end of the period.) Additionally, accrual revenues are adjusted for estimated returns and allowances, and accounts receivable are adjusted for estimated uncollectibles.

[14] See Richardson and Tuna (2008).

[15] This effect was named after Nicholas Molodovsky, who wrote on this subject in the 1950s and referred to using averaged earnings as a simple starting point for understanding a company's underlying earning power. We can state the Molodovsky effect another way: P/Es may be negatively related to the recent earnings growth rate but positively related to the anticipated future growth rate because of expected rebounds in earnings.

[16] Here, we are using the term "normalized earnings" to refer to earnings adjusted for the effects of a business cycle. Some sources use the term "normalized earnings" also to refer to earnings adjusted for nonrecurring items.

► The method of *historical average EPS*, in which normalized EPS is calculated as average EPS over the most recent full cycle.

► The method of *average return on equity*, in which normalized EPS is calculated as the average return on equity (ROE) from the most recent full cycle, multiplied by current book value per share.

The first method is one of several possible statistical approaches to the problem of cyclical earnings; however, this method does not account for changes in a business's size. The second alternative, by using recent book value per share, reflects more accurately the effect on EPS of growth or shrinkage in the company's size. For that reason, the method of average ROE is sometimes preferred.[17] When reported current book value does not adequately reflect company size in relation to past values (because of items such as large write-downs), the analyst can make appropriate accounting adjustments. The analyst can also estimate normalized earnings by multiplying total assets by an estimate of the long-run return on total assets[18] or by multiplying shareholders' equity by an estimate of the long-run return on total shareholders' equity. These methods are particularly useful for a period in which a cyclical company has reported a loss.

Example 4 illustrates this concept. The example uses data for an **American Depositary Receipt** (ADR) but is applicable to any equity security. An ADR is intended to facilitate U.S. investment in non-U.S. companies. It is a negotiable certificate issued by a depositary bank that represents ownership in a non-U.S. company's deposited equity (i.e., equity held in custody by the depositary bank in the company's home market). One ADR may represent more than one, or fewer than one, deposited share. The number of, or fraction of, deposited securities represented by one ADR is referred to as the "ADR ratio."

EXAMPLE 4

Normalizing EPS for Business-Cycle Effects

You are researching the valuation of Taiwan Semiconductor Manufacturing Company (NYSE: TSM, TAIEX: 2330), the world's largest dedicated semiconductor foundry (www.tsmc.com). Your research is for a U.S. investor who is interested in the company's ADRs rather than the company's shares listed on the Taiwan Stock Exchange. On 28 February 2008, the closing price of TSM, the NYSE listed ADR, was $10.01. The semiconductor industry is notably cyclical, so you decide to normalize earnings as part of your analysis. You believe that data from 2001 reasonably captures the beginning of the most recent business cycle, and you want to evaluate a normalized P/E. Exhibit 1 supplies data on EPS for one TSM ADR, book value per share (BVPS) for one ADR, and the company's ROE.[19]

---

[17] This approach has appeared in valuation research; for example, Michaud (1999) calculated a normalized earnings yield (that is, EPS divided by price) rather than a normalized P/E.

[18] An example of the application of this method is the study of the intrinsic value of the Dow Jones Industrial Average (the U.S. equities index) by Lee, Myers, and Swaminathan (1999). The authors used 6 percent of total assets as a proxy for normal earnings to estimate a payout ratio for periods in which a company's earnings were negative. According to the authors, the long-run return on total assets in the United States is approximately 6 percent.

[19] This example involves a single company. When the analyst compares multiple companies on the basis of P/Es based on normalized EPS and uses this normalization approach, the analyst should be sure that the ROEs are being calculated consistently by the subject companies. In this example, ROE for each year is being calculated by using ending BVPS and, essentially, trailing earnings are being normalized.

EXHIBIT 1	Taiwan Semiconductor Manufacturing Company (Currency in U.S. Dollars)						
Measure	2001	2002	2003	2004	2005	2006	2007
EPS (ADR)	$0.08	$0.12	$0.28	$0.58	$0.59	$0.74	$0.63
BVPS (ADR)	$1.58	$1.64	$1.94	$2.50	$2.67	$3.03	$3.34
ROE	5.2%	7.3%	14.4%	23.1%	21.0%	24.7%	19.0%

Source: *The Value Line Investment Survey.*

Using the data in Exhibit 1:

1. Calculate a normalized EPS for TSM by the method of historical average EPS and then calculate the P/E based on that estimate of normalized EPS.
2. Calculate a normalized EPS for TSM by the method of average ROE and the P/E based on that estimate of normalized EPS.
3. Explain the source of the differences in the normalized EPS calculated by the two methods, and contrast the impact on the estimate of a normalized P/E.

Solution to 1: Averaging EPS over the 2001–2007 period, you would find it to be ($0.08 + $0.12 + $0.28 + $0.58 + $0.59 + $0.74 + 0.63)/ 7 = $0.43. Thus, according to the method of historical average EPS, TSM's normalized EPS is $0.43. The P/E based on this estimate is $10.01/$0.43 = 23.3.

Solution to 2: Average ROE over the 2001–2007 period is (5.2% + 7.3% + 14.4% + 23.1% + 21.0% + 24.7% + 19.0%)/7 = 16.39%. Based on the current BVPS of $3.34, the method of average ROE gives 0.1639 × $3.34 = $0.55 as normalized EPS. The P/E based on this estimate is $10.01/$0.55 = 18.2.

Solution to 3: From 2001 to 2007, BVPS increased from $1.58 to $3.34, an increase of about 111 percent. The estimate of normalized EPS of $0.55 from the average ROE method reflects the use of information on the current size of the company better than does the $0.43 calculated from the historical average EPS method. Because of that difference, TSM appears more conservatively valued (as indicated by a lower P/E) when the method based on average ROE is used.

3.1.2.3 Analyst Adjustments for Comparability with Other Companies   Analysts adjust EPS for differences in accounting methods between the company and companies it is being compared with so that the P/Es will be comparable. For example, if an analyst is comparing a company that uses the last-in, first-out (LIFO) method of inventory accounting as permitted by U.S. GAAP (but not by IFRS) with another company that uses the first-in, first-out (FIFO) method, the analyst should adjust earnings to provide comparability in all ratio and valuation analyses. In general, any adjustment made to a company's reported financials for purposes of financial statement analysis should be incorporated into an analysis of P/E and other multiples.

3.1.2.4 Dealing with Extremely Low, Zero, or Negative Earnings   Having addressed the challenges that arise to calculating P/E because of nonrecurring items, business-cycle influences, and for comparability among companies, we present in this section the methods analysts have developed for dealing with extremely low, zero, or negative earnings.

Stock selection disciplines that use P/Es or other price multiples often involve ranking stocks from highest value of the multiple to lowest value of the multiple. The security with the lowest positive P/E has the lowest purchase cost per currency unit of earnings among the securities ranked. Zero earnings and negative earnings pose a problem if the analyst wishes to use P/E as the valuation metric. Because division by zero is undefined, P/Es cannot be calculated for zero earnings.

A P/E can technically be calculated in the case of negative earnings. Negative earnings, however, result in a negative P/E. A negative-P/E security will rank below the lowest positive-P/E security but, because earnings are negative, the negative-P/E security is actually the most costly in terms of earnings purchased. Thus, negative P/Es are not meaningful.

In some cases, an analyst might handle negative EPS by using normalized EPS instead. Also, when trailing EPS are negative, the year-ahead EPS and thus the forward P/E may be positive. An argument in favor of either of these approaches based on positive earnings is that if a company is appropriately treated as a going concern, losses cannot be the usual operating result.

If the analyst is interested in a ranking, however, one solution (applicable to any ratio involving a quantity that can be negative or zero) is the use of an **inverse price ratio**—that is, the reciprocal of the original ratio, which places price in the denominator. The use of inverse price multiples addresses the issue of consistent ranking because price is never negative.[20] In the case of the P/E, the inverse price ratio is earnings to price (E/P), known as the **earnings yield**. Ranked by earnings yield from highest to lowest, the securities are correctly ranked from cheapest to most costly in terms of the amount of earnings one unit of currency buys.

Exhibit 2 illustrates these points for a group of beer companies, two of which have negative EPS. When reporting a P/E based on negative earnings, analysts should report such P/Es as "NM" (not meaningful).

---

[20] Earnings yield can be based on normalized EPS, expected next-year EPS, or trailing EPS. In these cases also, earnings yield provides a consistent ranking.

EXHIBIT 2	P/E and E/P for Five Beer Companies (as of 16 June 2008; in U.S. Dollars)			
Company	**Current Price**	**Diluted EPS (TTM)**	**Trailing P/E**	**E/P (%)**
Molson Coors Brewing Co. (NYSE: TAP)	57.72	2.90	19.9	5.02
Anheuser-Busch Cos. (NYSE: BUD)	61.12	2.83	21.6	4.63
Boston Beer Co. (NYSE: SAM)	40.34	0.90	44.8	2.23
Redhook Ale Brewery (NASDAQGM: HOOK)	4.50	−0.14	NM	−3.11
Pyramid Breweries (NASDAQGM: PMID)	2.57	−0.42	NM	−16.34

Source: Yahoo! Finance.

In addition to zero and negative earnings, extremely low earnings can pose problems when using P/Es—particularly for evaluating the distribution of P/Es of a group of stocks under review. In this case, again, inverse price ratios can be useful. The P/E of a stock with extremely low earnings may, nevertheless, be extremely high because an earnings rebound is anticipated. An extremely high P/E—an outlier P/E—can swamp the effect of the other P/Es in the calculation of the mean P/E. Although the use of median P/Es and other techniques can mitigate the problem of skewness caused by outliers, the distribution of inverse price ratios is inherently less susceptible to outlier-induced skewness.

As mentioned, earnings yield is but one example of an inverse price ratio— that is, the reciprocal of a price ratio. Exhibit 3 summarizes inverse price ratios for all the price ratios we discuss in this reading.

EXHIBIT 3	Summary of Price and Inverse Price Ratios	
Price Ratio	**Inverse Price Ratio**	**Comments**
Price-to-earnings (P/E)	Earnings yield (E/P)	Both forms commonly used.
Price-to-book (P/B)	Book-to-market (B/P)[21]	Book value is less commonly negative than EPS. Book-to-market is favored in research but not common in practitioner usage.
Price-to-sales (P/S)	Sales-to-price (S/P)	S/P is rarely used except when all other ratios are being stated in the form of inverse price ratios; sales is not zero or negative in practice for going concerns.
Price-to-cash flow (P/CF)	Cash flow yield (CF/P)	Both forms are commonly used.

(Exhibit continued on next page . . .)

---

[21] "Book-to-*market*" is probably more common usage than "book-to-*price*." Book-to-market is variously abbreviated B/M, BV/MV (for "book value" and "market value"), or B/P.

EXHIBIT 3	(continued)	
Price Ratio	**Inverse Price Ratio**	**Comments**
Price-to-dividends (P/D)	Dividend yield (D/P)	Dividend yield is much more commonly used because P/D is not calculable for non-dividend-paying stocks, but both D/P and P/D are used in discussing index valuation.

Note: B, S, CF, and D are in per-share terms.

3.1.3 Forward P/E

The forward P/E is a major and logical alternative to the trailing P/E because valuation is naturally forward looking. In the definition of forward P/E, analysts have interpreted "next year's expected earnings" as expected EPS for:

▶ the next four quarters;

▶ the next 12 months; or

▶ the next fiscal year.

In this section, unless otherwise stated, we use the first definition of forward P/E (i.e., the next four quarters), which is closest to how cash flows are dated in our discussion of DCF valuation.[22] To illustrate the calculation, suppose the current market price of a stock is $15 as of 1 March 2008 and the most recently reported quarterly EPS (for the quarter ended 31 December 2007) is $0.22. Our forecasts of EPS are as follows:

▶ $0.15 for the quarter ending 31 March 2008;

▶ $0.18 for the quarter ending 30 June 2008;

▶ $0.18 for the quarter ending 30 September 2008; and

▶ $0.24 for the quarter ending 31 December 2008.

The sum of the forecasts for the next four quarters is $0.15 + $0.18 + $0.18 + $0.24 = $0.75, and the forward P/E for this stock is $15/$0.75 = 20.0.

Another important concept related to the forward P/E is the next twelve month (NTM) P/E, which corresponds in a forward-looking sense to the TTM P/E concept of trailing P/E. A stock's **NTM P/E** is its current market price divided by an estimated next twelve months EPS, which typically combines the annual EPS estimates from two fiscal years, weighted to reflect the relative proximity of the fiscal year. For example, assume that in August 2008, an analyst is looking at Microsoft Corporation (NASDAQGS: MSFT). Microsoft has a June fiscal year end, so at the time of the analyst's scrutiny, there were 10 months remaining until the end of the company's 2009 fiscal year (i.e., September 2008 through June 2009, inclusive). The estimated next twelve months EPS for Microsoft would be calculated as $[(10/12) \times \text{FY09E EPS}] + [(2/12) \times \text{FY10E EPS}]$. NTM P/E is useful because it facilitates comparison of companies with different fiscal year-ends without the need to use quarterly estimates, which for many companies are not available.

---

[22] Analysts have developed DCF expressions that incorporate fractional time periods. In practice, uncertainty in forecasts reduces accuracy more than any other factor in estimating justified P/Es.

Applying the fiscal-year concept, Thomson First Call reports a stock's "forward P/E" in two ways: first, based on the mean of analysts' *current fiscal year* (FY1 = Fiscal Year 1) forecasts, for which analysts may have actual EPS in hand for some quarters; second, based on analysts' *following fiscal year* (FY2 = Fiscal Year 2) forecasts, which must be based entirely on forecasts. For Thomson First Call, "forward P/E" contrasts with "current P/E," which is based on the last reported annual EPS.

Clearly, analysts must be consistent in the definition of forward P/E when comparing stocks. Examples 5 and 6 illustrate two ways of calculating forward P/E.

EXAMPLE 5

Calculating a Forward P/E (1)

A market price for the common stock of IBM (NYSE: IBM) in mid-June 2008 was $126.15. IBM's fiscal year coincides with the calendar year. According to data from Thomson First Call, the consensus EPS forecast for 2008 (FY1) as of June 2008 was $8.54. The consensus EPS forecast for 2009 (FY2) as of June 2008 was $9.59.

1. Calculate IBM's forward P/E based on a fiscal-year definition per Thomson First Call and FY1 consensus forecasted EPS.

2. Calculate IBM's forward P/E based on a fiscal-year definition and FY2 consensus forecasted EPS.

Solution to 1: IBM's forward P/E is $126.15/$8.54 = 14.8 based on FY1 forecasted EPS. Note that this EPS number involves the forecast of three remaining quarters as of mid-June 2008.

Solution to 2: IBM's forward P/E is $126.15/$9.59 = 13.2 based on FY2 forecasted EPS.

In Example 5, the company's EPS was expected to increase by slightly more than 12 percent, so the forward P/Es based on the two different EPS specifications differed from one another somewhat but not dramatically. Example 6 presents the calculation of forward P/Es for a company with volatile earnings.

EXAMPLE 6

Calculating a Forward P/E (2)

In this example, we use alternative definitions of "forward" to compute forward P/Es. Exhibit 4 presents actual and forecasted EPS for Alcatel-Lucent (Euronext Paris: ALU; NYSE: ALU), a telecommunications equipment manufacturer formed by the merger of a French company (Alcatel) with a U.S. company (Lucent). ALU is based in France. The company's ADRs trade on the NYSE. The company's recent results reflect a slowdown in equipment purchases by many telecom operators and the incurring of additional expenses related to integrating operations following the merger.

EXHIBIT 4	Quarterly EPS for Alcatel-Lucent ADR (in U.S. Dollars; Excluding Nonrecurring Items)				

Year	31 March	30 June	30 September	31 December	Annual Estimate
2007	(0.28)	(0.09)	(0.16)	E(0.03)	−0.56
2008	E(0.02)	E0.02	E0.10	E0.20	0.30

Source: The Value Line Investment Survey.

On 21 November 2007, the company's ADRs closed at $7.37. ALU's fiscal year ends on 31 December. As of 21 November 2007, solve the following problems by using the information in Exhibit 4:

1. Calculate ALU's forward P/E based on the next four quarters of forecasted EPS.
2. Calculate ALU's NTM P/E.
3. Calculate ALU's forward P/E based on a fiscal-year definition and current fiscal year (2007) forecasted EPS.
4. Calculate ALU's forward P/E based on a fiscal-year definition and next fiscal year (2008) forecasted EPS.

Solution to 1: We sum forecasted EPS as follows:

4Q:2007 EPS (estimate)	($0.03)
1Q:2008 EPS (estimate)	($0.02)
2Q:2008 EPS (estimate)	$0.02
3Q:2008 EPS (estimate)	$0.10
Sum	$0.07

The forward P/E by this definition is $7.37/$0.07 = 105.3.

Solution to 2: As of 21 November 2007, approximately one month remained in FY2007. Therefore, the estimated next twelve months EPS for ALU would be based on annual estimates in the last column of Exhibit 4: $[(1/12) \times FY07E\ EPS] + [(11/12) \times FY08E\ EPS] = (1/12)(-0.56) + (11/12)(0.30) = 0.228$. The NTM P/E would be $7.37/0.228 = 32.3.

Solution to 3: We sum EPS as follows:

1Q:2007 EPS (actual)	($0.28)
2Q:2007 EPS (actual)	($0.09)
3Q:2007 EPS (actual)	($0.16)
4Q:2007 EPS (estimate)	($0.03)
Sum	($0.56)

The forward P/E is $7.37/($0.56) = −13.2, which is not meaningful. Note that because this example assumes that financial results for 9 of the 12 months of the fiscal year have been reported, this forward P/E is nearly the same as a trailing P/E.

Solution to 4: We sum EPS as follows:

1Q:2008 EPS (estimate)	($0.02)
2Q:2008 EPS (estimate)	$0.02
3Q:2008 EPS (estimate)	$0.10
4Q:2008 EPS (estimate)	$0.20
Sum	$0.30

The forward P/E by this definition is $7.37/$0.30 = 24.6.

As illustrated in Example 6, for companies with volatile earnings, forward P/Es and thus valuations based on forward P/Es can vary dramatically depending on the definition of earnings. The analyst would probably be justified in normalizing EPS for the Alcatel-Lucent ADR.

Having explored the issues involved in calculating P/Es, we turn to using them in valuation.

3.1.4 Valuation Based on Forecasted Fundamentals

The analyst who understands DCF valuation models can use them not only in developing an estimate of the justified P/E for a stock but also to gain insight into possible sources of valuation differences when the method of comparables is used. Linking P/Es to a DCF model helps us address what value the market should place on a dollar of EPS when we are given a particular set of expectations about the company's profitability, growth, and cost of capital.

3.1.4.1 Justified P/E The simplest of all DCF models is the Gordon (constant) growth form of the dividend discount model (DDM). Presentations of discounted dividend valuation commonly show that the P/E of a share can be related to the value of a stock as calculated in the Gordon growth model through the expressions

$$\frac{P_0}{E_1} = \frac{D_1/E_1}{r - g} = \frac{1 - b}{r - g} \tag{1}$$

for the forward P/E, and for the trailing P/E,

$$\frac{P_0}{E_0} = \frac{D_0(1 + g)/E_0}{r - g} = \frac{(1 - b)(1 + g)}{r - g}$$

(2)

where

   P = price
   E = earnings
   D = dividends
   r = required rate of return
   g = dividend growth rate
   b = retention rate

Under the assumption of constant dividend growth, the first expression gives the justified forward P/E and the second gives the justified trailing P/E. Note that both expressions state P/E as a function of two fundamentals: the stock's required rate of return, r, which reflects its risk, and the expected (stable) dividend growth rate, g. The dividend payout ratio, $1 - b$, also enters into the expressions.

A particular value of the P/E is associated with a set of forecasts of the fundamentals and the dividend payout ratio. This value is the stock's justified P/E based on forecasted fundamentals (that is, the P/E justified by fundamentals). All else being equal, the higher the expected dividend growth rate or the lower the stock's required rate of return, the higher the stock's intrinsic value and the higher its justified P/E.

This intuition carries over to more-complex DCF models. Using any DCF model, all else being equal, justified P/E is:

▶ inversely related to the stock's required rate of return, and

▶ positively related to the growth rate(s) of future expected cash flows, however defined.

We illustrate the calculation of a justified forward P/E in Example 7.

EXAMPLE 7

Forward P/E Based on Fundamental Forecasts (1)

BP p.l.c. (London: BP) is one of the world's largest integrated oil producers. Jan Unger, an energy analyst, forecasts a long-term earnings retention rate, b, for BP of 15 percent and a long-term growth rate of 6 percent. Unger also calculates a required rate of return of 9.5 percent. Based on Unger's forecasts of fundamentals and Equation 1, BP's justified forward P/E is

$$\frac{P_0}{E_1} = \frac{1 - b}{r - g} = \frac{1 - 0.15}{0.095 - 0.06} = 24.3$$

When using a complex DCF model to value the stock (e.g., a model with varying growth rates and varying assumptions about dividends), the analyst may not be able to express the P/E as a function of fundamental, constant variables. In such cases, the analyst can still calculate a justified P/E by dividing the value per share (that results from a DCF model) by estimated EPS, as illustrated in Example 8. Approaches similar to this one can be used to develop other justified multiples.

EXAMPLE 8

Forward P/E Based on Fundamental Forecasts (2)

Toyota Motor Corporation (TYO: 7203; NYSE: TM) is one of the world's largest vehicle manufacturers. The company's most recent fiscal year ended on 31 March 2008. In early May 2008, you are valuing Toyota stock, which closed at ¥5,480 on the previous day. You have used a free cash flow to equity (FCFE) model to value the company stock and have obtained a value of ¥6,122 for the stock. For ease of communication, you want to express your valuation in terms of a forward P/E based on your forecasted fiscal year 2009 EPS of ¥580. Toyota's fiscal year 2009 is from April 2008 through March 2009.

1. What is Toyota's justified P/E based on forecasted fundamentals?

2. Based on a comparison of the current price of ¥5,480 with your estimated intrinsic value of ¥6,122, the stock appears to be slightly undervalued. Use your answer to Part 1 to state this evaluation in terms of P/Es.

Solution to 1:
Value of the stock derived from FCFE = ¥6,122
Forecasted EPS = ¥580
¥6,122/¥580 = 10.6 is the justified forward P/E.

Solution to 2: The justified P/E of 10.6 is slightly higher than the forward P/E based on current market price, ¥5,480/¥580 = 9.4.

The next section illustrates another, but less commonly used, approach to relating price multiples to fundamentals.

3.1.4.2 Predicted P/E Based on Cross-Sectional Regression   A predicted P/E, which is conceptually similar to a justified P/E, can be estimated from cross-sectional regressions of P/E on the fundamentals believed to drive security valuation. Kisor and Whitbeck (1963) and Malkiel and Cragg (1970) pioneered this approach. The studies measured P/Es for a group of stocks and the characteristics thought to determine P/E: growth rate in earnings, payout ratio, and a measure of volatility, such as standard deviation of earnings changes or beta. An analyst can conduct such cross-sectional regressions by using any set of explanatory variables considered to determine investment value; the analyst must bear in mind, however, potential distortions that can be introduced by multicollinearity among independent variables. Example 9 illustrates the prediction of P/E using cross-sectional regression.

EXAMPLE 9

Predicted P/E Based on a Cross-Sectional Regression

You are valuing a food company with a beta of 0.9, a dividend payout ratio of 0.45, and an earnings growth rate of 0.08. The estimated regression for a group of other stocks in the same industry is

$$\text{Predicted P/E} = 12.12 + (2.25 \times \text{DPR}) - (0.20 \times \text{Beta}) + (14.43 \times \text{EGR})$$

where DPR is the dividend payout ratio and EGR is the five-year earnings growth rate.

1. Based on this cross-sectional regression, what is the predicted P/E for the food company?
2. If the stock's actual trailing P/E is 18, is the stock fairly valued, overvalued, or undervalued?

Solution to 1: Predicted P/E = $12.12 + (2.25 \times 0.45) - (0.20 \times 0.9) + (14.43 \times 0.08) = 14.1$. The predicted P/E is 14.1.

Solution to 2: Because the predicted P/E of 14.1 is less than the actual P/E of 18, the stock appears to be overvalued. That is, it is selling at a higher multiple than is justified by its fundamentals.

A cross-sectional regression summarizes a large amount of data in a single equation and can provide a useful additional perspective on a valuation. It is not frequently used as a main tool, however, because it is subject to at least three limitations:

► The method captures valuation relationships only for the specific stock (or sample of stocks) over a particular time period. The predictive power of the regression for a different stock and different time period is not known.
► The regression coefficients and explanatory power of the regressions tend to change substantially over a number of years. The relationships between P/E and fundamentals may thus change over time. Empirical evidence based on data for 1987–1991 suggest that the relationships between P/Es and such characteristics as earnings growth, dividend payout, and beta are not stable over time (Damodaran 1996). Furthermore, because distributions of multiples change over time, the predictive power of results from a regression at any point in time can be expected to diminish with the passage of time (Damodaran 2006).
► Because regressions based on this method are prone to the problem of multicollinearity (correlation within linear combinations of the independent variables), interpreting individual regression coefficients is difficult.

Overall, rather than examining the relationship between a stock's P/E multiple and economic variables, the bulk of capital market research examines the relationship between companies' stock prices (and returns on the stock) and explanatory variables, one of which is often earnings (or unexpected earnings). A classic example of such research is the Fama and French (1992) study showing that, used alone, a number of factors explained cross-sectional stock returns in the 1963–1990 period; the factors were E/P, size, leverage, and the book-to-market multiples. When these variables were used in combination, however, size and book-to-market had explanatory power that absorbed the roles of the other variables in explaining cross-sectional stock returns. Research building on that study eventually resulted in the Fama–French three-factor model (with the factors of size, book-to-market, and beta). Another classic academic study providing evidence that accounting variables appear to have predictive power for stock returns is Lakonishok, Shleifer, and Vishny (1994), which also provided evidence that value strategies—buying stocks with low prices relative to earnings, book value, cash flow, and sales growth—produced superior five-year buy-and-hold returns in the 1968–1990 period without involving greater fundamental risk than a strategy of buying growth stocks.

3.1.5 Valuation Based on Comparables

The most common application of the P/E approach to valuation is to estimate the value of a company's stock by applying a benchmark multiple to the company's actual or forecasted earnings. An essentially equivalent approach is to compare a stock's actual price multiple with a benchmark value of the multiple. This section explores these comparisons for P/Es. Using any multiple in the method of comparables involves the following steps:

► Select and calculate the price multiple that will be used in the comparison.

► Select the comparison asset or assets and calculate the value of the multiple for the comparison asset(s). For a group of comparison assets, calculate a median or mean value of the multiple for the assets. The result in either case is the **benchmark value of the multiple**.

► Use the benchmark value of the multiple, possibly subjectively adjusted for differences in fundamentals, to estimate the value of a company's stock. (Equivalently, compare the subject stock's actual multiple with the benchmark value.)

► When feasible, assess whether differences between the estimated value of the company's stock and the current price of the company's stock are explained by differences in the fundamental determinants of the price multiple and modify conclusions about relative valuation accordingly. (An essentially equivalent approach is to assess whether differences between a company's actual multiple and the benchmark value of the multiple can be explained by differences in fundamentals.)

These bullet points provide the structure for this reading's presentation of the method of comparables. The first price multiple that will be used in the comparison is the P/E. Practitioners' choices for the comparison assets and the benchmark value of the P/E derived from these assets include the following:

► the average or median value of the P/E for the company's peer group of companies within an industry, including an average past value of the P/E for the stock relative to this peer group;

▶ the average or median value of the P/E for the company's industry or sector, including an average past value of the P/E for the stock relative to the industry or sector;

▶ the P/E for a representative equity index, including an average past value of the P/E for the stock relative to the equity index; and

▶ an average past value of the P/E for the stock.

To illustrate the first bullet point, the company's P/E (say, 15) may be compared to the median P/E for the peer companies currently (say, 10), or the ratio 15/10 = 1.5 may be compared to its average past value. The P/E of the most closely matched individual stock can also be used as a benchmark; because of averaging, however, using a group of stocks or an equity index is typically expected to generate less valuation error than using a single stock. In Section 3.3, we illustrate a comparison with a single closely matched individual stock.

Economists and investment analysts have long attempted to group companies by similarities and differences in their business operations. A country's economy overall is typically grouped most broadly into **economic sectors** or large industry groupings. These groupings differ depending on the source of the financial information, and an analyst should be aware of differences among data sources. Classifications often attempt to group companies by what they supply (e.g., energy, consumer goods), by demand characteristics (e.g., consumer discretionary), or by financial market or economic "theme" (e.g., consumer cyclical, consumer noncyclical).

Two classification systems that are widely used in equity analysis are the Global Industry Classification System (GICS) sponsored by Standard & Poor's and MSCI Barra, and the Industrial Classification Benchmark (ICB) developed by Dow Jones and FTSE, which in 2006 replaced the FTSE Global Classification System. Many other classification schemes developed by commercial and governmental organizations and by academics are also in use.[23]

The GICS structure assigns each company to one of 154 subindustries, an industry (68 in total), an industry group (24 in total), and an economic sector (10 in total: consumer discretionary, consumer staples, energy, financials, health care, industrials, information technology, materials, telecommunication services, and utilities).[24] The assignment is made by a judgment as to the company's principal business activity, which is based primarily on sales. Because a company is classified on the basis of one business activity, a given company appears in just one group at each level of the classification. A classification ("industrial conglomerates") is available under the economic sector of industrials for companies that cannot be assigned to a principal business activity.

The ICB, like GICS, has four levels, but the terminology of ICB uses "sector" and "industry" in nearly opposite senses. At the bottom of the four levels are 114 subsectors, each of which belongs to one of 41 sectors; each sector belongs to one of 19 supersectors; and each supersector belongs to one of 10 industries at the highest level of classification.[25] The industries are oil and gas, basic materials,

---

[23] The most notable academic industrial classification was developed by Fama and French. Bhojraj, Lee, and Oler (2002) and Chan, Lakonishok, and Swaminathan (2007) provide some information of the relative performance of these various systems in an investments context.

[24] The numbers in the groups are current as of 8 August 2008; changes are made to the classifications from time to time. See www.gics.standardandpoors.com for details.

[25] The numbers in the groups are current as of 8 August 2008; changes are made to the classification from time to time. See www.icbenchmark.com for details.

industrials, consumer goods, health care, consumer services, telecommunications, utilities, financials, and technology.[26]

For these classification systems, analysts often choose the narrowest grouping (i.e., subindustry for GICS and subsector for ICB) as an appropriate starting point for comparison asset identification. For example, the company Continental AG (Xetra Level 1: 543900, also traded as an ADR; NASDAQ: CTTAY), a manufacturer of tires headquartered in Hanover, Germany, appears in the ICB subsector "tires." This subsector also includes Michelin (NYSE Euronext Paris: 4588364), Goodyear Tire & Rubber Company (NYSE: GT), Bridgestone (Tokyo Stock Exchange: 5810; also traded as an ADR with ticker BRDCY), and Cooper Tire and Rubber (NYSE: CTB). One level up, the sector automobiles and parts includes, in addition to tire companies, such disparate companies as automobile manufacturers and their nontire parts suppliers. To narrow the list of comparables in the subsector, an analyst might use information on company size (as measured by revenue or market value of equity) and information on the specific markets served.

Analysts should be aware that, although different organizations often group companies in a broadly similar fashion, sometimes they differ sharply. For example, Reuters Company Research places GATX Corporation (NYSE: GMT), which has several distinct business units, under miscellaneous transportation (within a transportation sector), GICS places it under trading companies and distributors (within its industrials sector), and BNY Jaywalk and Yahoo! Finance place it under rental and leasing services (in a services sector); the lists of peer companies or competitors given by each are, as a result, quite distinct.[27]

The comparable companies—selected by using any of the choices described previously—provide the basis for calculating a benchmark value of the multiple. In analyzing differences between the subject company's multiple and the benchmark value of the multiple, financial ratio analysis serves as a useful tool. Financial ratios can point out:

▶ a company's ability to meet short-term financial obligations (liquidity ratios);

▶ the efficiency with which assets are being used to generate sales (asset turnover ratios);

▶ the use of debt in financing the business (leverage ratios);

▶ the degree to which fixed charges, such as interest on debt, are being met by earnings or cash flow (coverage ratios); and

▶ profitability (profitability ratios).

With this understanding of terms in hand, we turn to using the method of comparables. We begin with cross-sectional P/Es derived from industry peer groups and move to P/Es derived from comparison assets that are progressively less closely matched to the stock. We then turn to using historical P/Es—that is, P/Es derived from the company's own history. Finally, we sketch how

---

[26] One of the chief contrasts between the ICB and GICS systems is that the ICB makes a distinction between goods and services (in GICS, both consumer discretionary and consumer staples include both goods and services components). The two systems also have some similarities that they do not share with other systems—for example, 10 groups at the highest level and an avoidance of a cyclical versus noncyclical distinction in their nomenclature.

[27] Reuters Company Research Report and S&P Stock Report dated 4 August 2008, BNY Jaywalk Consensus Report of 6 August 2008, and Yahoo! Finance accessed 6 August 2008. Yahoo! Finance information is sourced to Hemscott Americas.

both fundamentals- and comparables-driven models for P/Es can be used to calculate the terminal value in a multistage DCF valuation.

3.1.5.1 Peer-Company Multiples   Companies operating in the same industry as the subject company (i.e., its peer group) are frequently used as comparison assets. The advantage of using a peer group is that the constituent companies are typically similar in their business mix to the company being analyzed. This approach is consistent with the idea underlying the method of comparables—that similar assets should sell at similar prices. The subject stock's P/E is compared with the median or mean P/E for the peer group to arrive at a relative valuation. Equivalently, multiplying the benchmark P/E by the company's EPS provides an estimate of the stock's value that can be compared with the stock's market price. The value estimated in this way represents an estimate of intrinsic value if the comparison assets are efficiently (fairly) priced.

In practice, analysts often find that the stock being valued has some significant differences from the median or mean fundamental characteristics of the comparison assets. In applying the method of comparables, analysts usually attempt to judge whether differences from the benchmark value of the multiple can be explained by differences in the fundamental factors believed to influence the multiple. The following relationships for P/E hold, all else being equal:

► If the subject stock has higher-than-average (or higher-than-median) expected earnings growth, a higher P/E than the benchmark P/E is justified.

► If the subject stock has higher-than-average (or higher-than-median) risk (operating or financial), a lower P/E than the benchmark P/E is justified.

Another perspective on these two points is that for a group of stocks with comparable relative valuations, the stock with the greatest expected growth rate (or the lowest risk) is, all else equal, the most attractively valued. Example 10 illustrates a simple comparison of a company with its peer group.

EXAMPLE 10

A Simple Peer-Group Comparison

As a telecommunications industry analyst at a brokerage firm, you are valuing Verizon Communications, Inc. (NYSE: VZ), the second largest U.S. telecommunications service provider. The valuation metric that you have selected is the trailing P/E. You are evaluating the P/E using the median trailing P/E of peer-group companies as the benchmark value. According to GICS, VZ is in the telecommunications services sector and, within it, the integrated telecommunication services subindustry. Exhibit 5 presents the relevant data. (Note that although BCE Inc. is a Canadian company, it is classified in this peer group.)

EXHIBIT 5	Trailing P/Es of Telecommunications Services Companies (as of 19 June 2008)
Company	**Trailing P/E**
AT&T (NYSE: T)	17.35
BCE Inc. (NYSE: BCE; TSE: BCE)	7.71
Centurytel (NYSE: CTL)	8.34
Cincinnati Bell (NYSE: CBB)	19.61
Citizens Communications Co. (NYSE: CZN)	19.22
Equinix (NASDAQGS: EQIX)	702.61
Qwest Communications International (NYSE: Q)	2.73
Verizon Communications (NYSE: VZ)	18.30
Windstream Corp. (NYSE: WIN)	6.51
Mean	89.15
Median	17.35

Source: Thomson Financial.

Based on the data in Exhibit 5, address the following:

1. Given the definition of the benchmark stated above, determine the most appropriate benchmark value of the P/E for VZ.

2. State whether VZ is relatively fairly valued, relatively overvalued, or relatively undervalued, assuming no differences in fundamentals among the peer group companies. Justify your answer.

3. Identify the stocks in this group of telecommunication companies that appear to be relatively undervalued when the median trailing P/E is used as a benchmark. Explain what further analysis might be appropriate to confirm your answer.

Solution to 1: As stated earlier, the use of median values mitigates the effect of outliers on the valuation conclusion. In this instance, the P/E for EQIX is clearly an outlier. Therefore, the median trailing P/E for the group, 17.35, is more appropriate than the mean trailing P/E of 89.15 for use as the benchmark value of the P/E. *Note*: When a group includes an odd number of companies, as here, the median value will be the middle value when the values are ranked (in either ascending or descending order). When the group includes an even number of companies, the median value will be the average of the two middle values.

Solution to 2: If you assume no differences in fundamentals among the peer group companies, VZ appears to be overvalued because its P/E is greater than the median P/E of 17.35.

> **Solution to 3:** Q, WIN, BCE, and CTL appear to be undervalued
> relative to their peers because their trailing P/Es are lower than the
> median P/E. T appears to be relatively fairly valued because its P/E
> equals the median P/E. To confirm the valuation conclusion, you
> should analyze the companies for differences in risk and expected
> growth rates. Specifically, a relatively low P/E may reflect greater risk
> and/or lower expected earnings growth than the benchmark. Financial
> ratio analysis is one tool to help analysts determine the dimensions
> along which companies may differ in risk, growth, or profitability.

A metric that appears to address the impact of earnings growth on P/E is the P/E-to-growth (**PEG**) ratio. PEG is calculated as the stock's P/E divided by the expected earnings growth rate in percent. The ratio, in effect, is a calculation of a stock's P/E per percentage point of expected growth. Stocks with lower PEGs are more attractive than stocks with higher PEGs, all else being equal. Some consider that a PEG ratio less than 1 is an indicator of an attractive value level. PEG is useful but must be used with care for several reasons:

▶ PEG assumes a linear relationship between P/E and growth. The model for P/E in terms of the DDM shows that, in theory, the relationship is not linear.

▶ PEG does not factor in differences in risk, an important determinant of P/E.

▶ PEG does not account for differences in the duration of growth. For example, dividing P/Es by short-term (five-year) growth forecasts may not capture differences in long-term growth prospects.

The way in which fundamentals can add insight to comparables is illustrated in Example 11.

EXAMPLE 11

A Peer-Group Comparison Modified by Fundamentals

Continuing with the valuation of telecommunication service providers, you gather information on selected fundamentals related to risk (beta), profitability (five-year earnings growth forecast), and valuation (trailing and forward P/Es).[28] These data are reported in Exhibit 6, which lists companies in order of descending earnings growth forecast. The use of forward P/Es recognizes that differences in trailing P/Es could be the result of transitory effects on earnings.

---

[28] In comparables work, analysts may also use other measures of risk, such as financial leverage, and of profitability, such as return on assets.

EXHIBIT 6		Valuation Data for Telecommunications Services Companies (as of 19 June 2008)		
Company	Trailing P/E	Forward P/E	Five-Year EPS Growth Forecast	Forward PEG	Beta
EQIX	702.6	49.1	49.00%	1.00	1.40
Q	2.7	8.6	21.00	0.41	1.25
T	17.4	10.2	13.00	0.78	1.00
BCE	7.7	14.8	6.00	2.47	0.80
CZN	19.2	16.0	6.00	2.67	0.90
WIN	6.5	11.7	6.00	1.95	NM
CBB	19.6	9.2	4.50	2.05	1.35
VZ	18.3	12.2	3.50	3.49	0.95
CTL	8.3	9.4	1.00	9.39	0.85
Mean	89.2	15.7	12.22%	2.69	1.06
Median	17.4	11.7	6.00	2.05	0.98

Notes: NM = not meaningful. WIN was formed in 2006 through the spin-off of Alltel's landline business and merger with VALOR Telecom. Thus, WIN lacks a sufficiently long operating history to calculate a meaningful value of beta.
Sources: Yahoo! Finance for P/Es; *The Value Line Investment Survey* for growth forecasts and betas.

Based on the data in Exhibit 6, answer the following questions:

1. In Example 10, Part 3, Q, WIN, BCE, and CTL were identified as possibly relatively undervalued compared with the peer group as a whole, and T was identified as relatively fairly valued. What does the additional information in Exhibit 6 relating to profitability and risk suggest about the relative valuation of these stocks?

2. T has a consensus year-ahead EPS forecast of $3.42. Suppose the median P/E of 11.72 for the peer group is subjectively adjusted upward to 12.00 to reflect T's superior profitability and below-average risk. Estimate T's intrinsic value.

3. T's current market price is $35.15. State whether T appears to be fairly valued, overvalued, or undervalued when compared with the intrinsic value estimated in answer to Part 2 above.

Solution to 1: According to the profitability data and PEG given in Exhibit 6, among the stocks Q, WIN, BCE, and CTL, Q appears to represent the greatest undervaluation. Of the four stocks, Q has:

► the highest five-year consensus earnings growth forecast, and
► the lowest PEG based on forward P/E.

Of the four stocks, Q has the highest level of risk based on its beta, however, and thus does not clearly dominate the other three stocks. Q's expectations of faster growth are accompanied by expectations of higher risk.

Some analysts consider a PEG ratio below 1 to be attractive, implying that T is attractive when judged by expected earnings growth. In addition to its attractive growth expectations, T's level of risk, as measured by beta, is approximately the same as the median for the peer group.

Solution to 2: $3.42 × 12 = $41.04 is an estimate of intrinsic value.

Solution to 3: Because the estimated intrinsic value of $41.04 is greater than the current market price of $35.15, T appears to be undervalued by the market on an absolute basis.

In Problem 2 of the above example, a peer median P/E of 11.72 was subjectively adjusted upward to 12.00. Depending on the context, the justification for using the specific value of 12.00 as the relevant benchmark rather than some other value, such as 11.75, 12.25, or 13.00, could be raised. To avoid that issue, one way to express the analysis and results would be as follows: Given its above-average growth and similar risk, T should trade at a premium to the median P/E (11.72) of its peer group.

Analysts frequently compare a stock's multiple with the median or mean value of the multiple for larger sets of assets than a company's peer group. The next sections examine comparisons with these larger groups.

3.1.5.2 **Industry and Sector Multiples**   Median or mean P/Es for industries and for economic sectors are frequently used in relative valuations. Although median P/Es have the advantage that they are insensitive to outliers, some databases report only mean values of multiples for industries.

The mechanics of using industry multiples are identical to those used for peer-group comparisons. Taking account of relevant fundamental information, we compare a stock's multiple with the median or mean multiple for the company's industry.

Using industry and sector data can help an analyst explore whether the peer-group comparison assets are themselves appropriately priced. Comparisons with broader segments of the economy can potentially provide insight about whether the relative valuation based on comparables accurately reflects intrinsic value. For example, Value Line reports a relative P/E that is calculated as the stock's current P/E divided by the median P/E of all issues under Value Line review. The less closely matched the stock is to the comparison assets, the more dissimilarities are likely to be present to complicate the analyst's interpretation of the data. Arguably, however, the larger the number of comparison assets, the more likely that mispricing of individual assets cancel out. In some cases, we may be able to draw inferences about an industry or sector overall. For example, during the 1998–2000 internet bubble, comparisons of an individual internet stock's value with the overall market would have been more likely to point to overvaluation than comparisons of relative valuation only among internet stocks.

3.1.5.3 Overall Market Multiple Although the logic of the comparables approach suggests the use of industry and peer companies as comparison assets, equity market indices also have been used as comparison assets. The mechanics of using the method of comparables do not change in such an approach, although the user should be cognizant of any size differences between the subject stock and the stocks in the selected index.

The question of whether the overall market is fairly priced has captured analyst interest throughout the entire history of investing. We mentioned one approach to market valuation (using a DDM) in an earlier reading.

Example 12 shows a valuation comparison to the broad equity market on the basis of P/E.

EXAMPLE 12

Valuation Relative to the Market

You are analyzing three large-cap U.S. stock issues with approximately equal earnings growth prospects and risk. As one step in your analysis, you have decided to check valuations relative to the S&P 500 Composite Index. Exhibit 7 provides the data.

EXHIBIT 7	Comparison with an Index Multiple (Prices and EPS in U.S. Dollars; as of 12 June 2008)			
Measure	Stock A	Stock B	Stock C	S&P 500
Current price	23	50	80	1339.87
P/E 2008E	12.5	25.5	12.5	14.9
Five-year average P/E (as percent of S&P 500 P/E)	80	120	105	

Source: Standard & Poor's *The Outlook* (18 June 2008) for S&P 500 data.

Based only on the data in Exhibit 7, address the following:

1. Explain which stock appears relatively undervalued when compared with the S&P 500.

2. State the assumption underlying the use of five-year average P/E comparisons.

Solution to 1: Stock C appears to be undervalued when compared to the S&P 500. Stock A and Stock C are both trading at a P/E of 12.5 relative to 2008 estimated earnings, versus a P/E of 14.9 for the S&P 500. But the last row of Exhibit 7 indicates that Stock A has historically traded at a P/E reflecting a 20 percent discount to the S&P 500 (which, based on the current level of the S&P 500, would imply a P/E of 0.8 × 14.9 = 11.9). In contrast, Stock C has usually traded at a premium to the S&P 500 P/E but now trades at a discount to it. Stock B is trading at a high P/E, even higher than its historical relationship to the S&P 500's P/E ($1.2 \times 14.9 = 17.9$).

Solution to 2: Using historical relative-value information in investment decisions relies on an assumption of stable underlying economic relationships (that is, that the past is relevant for the future).

Because many equity indices are market-capitalization weighted, financial databases often report the average market P/E with the individual P/Es weighted by the company's market capitalization. As a consequence, the largest constituent stocks heavily influence the calculated P/E. If P/Es differ systematically by market capitalization, however, differences in a company's P/E multiple from the index's multiple may be explained by that effect. Therefore, particularly for stocks in the middle-cap range, the analyst should favor using the median P/E for the index as the benchmark value of the multiple.

As with other comparison assets, the analyst may be interested in whether the equity index itself is efficiently priced. A common comparison is the index's P/E in relation to historical values. Siegel (2002) noted that P/Es in 2001 were more than twice as high as the average P/E for U.S. stocks over a 130-year period (1871–2001) of 14.5. Potential justifications for a higher-than-average P/E include lower-than-average interest rates and/or higher-than-average expected growth rates. An alternative hypothesis in a situation such as that noted by Siegel is that the market as a whole is overvalued or, alternatively, that earnings are abnormally low.

The time frame for comparing average multiples is important. For example, at the end of the second quarter of 2008, the P/E for the S&P 500, based on 2008 earnings estimates, was 17.6. That value, although higher than the 15.8 historical average since 1935, fell below the historical average for the previous 5-, 10-, and 20-year time periods, when the P/E ranged between 20 and 26. The use of past data relies on the key assumption that the past (sometimes the distant past) is relevant for the future.

We end this section with an introduction to valuation of the equity market itself on the basis of P/E. A well-known comparison is the earnings yield (the E/P) on a group of stocks and the interest yield on a bond. The so-called Fed Model, based on a paper written by three analysts at the U.S. Federal Reserve, predicts the return on the S&P 500 on the basis of the relationship between forecasted earnings yields and yields on bonds (Lander, Orphanides, and Douvogiannis 1997). Example 13 illustrates the Fed Model.

EXAMPLE 13

The Fed Model

One of the main drivers of P/E for the market as a whole is the level of interest rates. The inverse relationship between value and interest rates can be seen from the expression of P/E in terms of fundamentals, because the risk-free rate is one component of the required rate of return that is inversely related to value. The Fed Model relates the earnings yield on the S&P 500 to the yield to maturity on 10-year U.S. Treasury bonds. As we have defined it, the earnings yield (E/P) is the inverse of the P/E; the Fed Model uses expected earnings for the next 12 months in calculating the ratio.

Based on the premise that the two yields should be closely linked, on average, the trading rule based on the Fed Model considers the stock market to be overvalued when the market's current earnings yield is less than the 10-year Treasury bond (T-bond) yield. The intuition is that when risk-free T-bonds offer a yield that is higher than stocks—which are a riskier investment—stocks are an unattractive investment.

According to the model, the justified or fair-value P/E for the S&P 500 is the reciprocal of the 10-year T-bond yield. As of 2 July 2008, according to the model, with a 10-year T-bond yielding 3.79 percent, the justified P/E on the S&P 500 was 1/0.0379 = 26.4. The forward P/E based on 2009 earnings estimates for the S&P 500 as of same date was 18.3.

We previously presented an expression for the justified P/E in terms of the Gordon growth model. That expression indicates that the expected growth rate in dividends or earnings is a variable that enters into the intrinsic value of a stock (or an index of stocks). A concern in considering the Fed Model is that this variable is lacking in the model.[29] Example 14 presents a valuation model for the equity market that incorporates the expected growth rate in earnings.

EXAMPLE 14

The Yardeni Model

Yardeni (2000) developed a model that incorporates the expected growth rate in earnings—a variable that is missing in the Fed Model.[30] Yardeni's model is

$$CEY = CBY - b \times LTEG + Residual$$

where CEY is the current earnings yield on the market index, CBY is the current Moody's Investors Service A-rated corporate bond yield, and LTEG is the consensus five-year earnings growth rate forecast for the market index. The coefficient b measures the weight the market gives to five-year earnings projections. (Recall that the expression for P/E in terms of the Gordon growth model is based on the long-term sustainable growth rate and that five-year forecasts of growth may not be sustainable.) Although CBY incorporates a default risk premium relative to T-bonds, it does not incorporate an equity risk premium per se. For

---

[29] The earnings yield is, in fact, the expected rate of return on a no-growth stock (under the assumption that price equals value). With PVGO the present value of growth opportunities and setting price equal to value, we obtain $P_0 = E_1/r + PVGO$. Setting the present value of growth opportunities equal to zero and rearranging, we obtain $r = E_1/P_0$.

[30] This model is presented as one example of more-complex models than the Fed Model. Economic analysts at many investment firms have their own models that incorporate growth and historical relationships of market indices with government bonds.

example, in the bond yield plus risk premium model for the cost of equity, an analyst typically adds 300–400 basis points to a corporate bond yield.

Yardeni found that, historically, the coefficient b has averaged 0.10. Noting that CEY is E/P and taking the inverse of both sides of this equation, Yardeni obtained the following expression for the justified P/E on the market:

$$\frac{P}{E} = \frac{1}{CBY - b \times LTEG}$$

Consistent with valuation theory, in Yardeni's model, higher current corporate bond yields imply a lower justified P/E and higher expected long-term growth results in a higher justified P/E.

Critics of the Fed Model point out that the model inadequately reflects the effects of inflation and incorrectly incorporates the differential effects of inflation on earnings and interest payments (e.g., Siegel 2002; Ritter and War 2002). Some empirical evidence has shown that prediction of future returns based on simple P/E outperforms prediction based on the Fed Model's differential with bond yields (for the U.S. market, see Asness 2003; for nine other markets, see Aubert and Giot 2007).

Another drawback to the Fed Model is that the relationship between interest rates and earnings yields is not a linear one. This drawback is most noticeable at low interest rates. For example, in August 2008, the yield on 10-year Japanese government bonds was 1.42 percent, which, according to the Fed Model, implied an unreasonably high justified P/E of 70.4 for the Nikkei 225 (1/0.0142 = 70.4) at that time. Furthermore, small changes in interest rates and/or corporate profits can significantly alter the justified P/E predicted by the model. Overall, an analyst should look to the Fed Model only as one tool for calibrating the overall value of the stock market and should avoid overreliance on the model as a predictive method, particularly in periods of low inflation and low interest rates.

3.1.5.4 Own Historical P/E   As an alternative to comparing a stock's valuation with that of other stocks, one traditional approach uses past values of the stock's own P/E as a basis for comparison. Underlying this approach is the idea that a stock's P/E may regress to historical average levels.

An analyst can obtain a benchmark value in a variety of ways with this approach. Value Line reports as a "P/E median" a rounded average of four middle values of a stock's average annual P/E for the previous 10 years. The five-year average trailing P/E is another reasonable metric. In general, trailing P/Es are more commonly used than forward P/Es in such computations. In addition to "higher" and "lower" comparisons with this benchmark, justified price based on this approach may be calculated as follows:

Justified price = (Benchmark value of own historical P/Es)   **(3)**
              × (Most recent EPS)

Normalized EPS replaces most recent EPS in this equation when EPS is negative and whenever otherwise appropriate.

Example 15 illustrates the use of past values of the stock's own P/E as a basis for reaching a valuation conclusion.

EXAMPLE 15

Valuation Relative to Own Historical P/Es

As of mid-2008, you are valuing Honda Motor Company (TSE: 72670; NYSE ADR: HMC), Japan's second largest auto maker in terms of sales, assets, and market capitalization. You are applying the method of comparables using HMC's five-year average P/E as the benchmark value of the multiple. Exhibit 8 presents the data.

EXHIBIT 8			Historical P/Es for HMC				
2007	**2006**	**2005**	**2004**	**2003**	**Mean**	**Median**
11.7	12.7	9.8	10.0	8.8	10.6	10.0

Sources: The Value Line Investment Survey for average annual P/Es; calculations for mean and median P/Es.

1. State a benchmark value for Honda's P/E.
2. Given EPS for the year ended 31 March 2008 of ¥330.54, calculate and interpret a justified price for Honda.
3. Compare the justified price with the stock's recent price of ¥3,590.

Solution to 1: From Exhibit 8, the benchmark value based on the median P/E value is 10.0 and based on the mean P/E value is 10.6.

Solution to 2: The calculation is $10.0 \times ¥330.54 = ¥3,305$ when the median-based benchmark P/E is used and $10.6 \times ¥330.54 = ¥3,504$ when the mean-based benchmark P/E is used.

Solution to 3: The stock's recent price is 8.6 percent (calculated as 3,590/3,305 − 1) more than the justified price of the stock based on median historical P/E but only 2.5 percent (calculated as 3,590/3,504 − 1) more than the justified price of the stock based on mean historical P/Es. The stock may be overvalued but misvaluation, if present, appears slight.

In using historical P/Es for comparisons, analysts should be alert to the impact on P/E levels of changes in a company's business mix and leverage over time. If the company's business has changed substantially within the time period being examined, the method based on a company's own past P/Es is prone to error. Shifts in the use of financial leverage may also impair comparability based on average own past P/E.

Changes in the interest rate environment and economic fundamentals over different time periods can be another limitation to using an average past value of P/E for a stock as a benchmark. A specific caution is that inflation can distort the economic meaning of reported earnings. Consequently, if the inflationary environments reflected in current P/E and average own past P/E are different, a comparison between the two P/Es may be misleading. Changes in a company's ability to pass through cost inflation to higher prices over time may also affect the reliability of such comparisons, as illustrated in Example 16 in the next section.

3.1.6 P/Es in Cross-Country Comparisons

When comparing the P/Es of companies in different countries, the analyst should be aware of the following effects that may influence the comparison:

▶ the effect on EPS of differences in accounting standards. Comparisons (without analyst adjustments) among companies preparing financial statements based on different accounting standards may be distorted. Such distortions may occur when, for example, the accounting standards differ as to permissible recognition of revenues, expenses, or gains.

▶ the effect on marketwide benchmarks of differences in their macroeconomic contexts. Differences in macroeconomic contexts may distort comparisons of benchmark P/E levels among companies operating in different markets.

A specific case of the second bullet point is differences in inflation rates and in the ability of companies to pass through inflation in their costs in the form of higher prices to their customers. For two companies with the same pass-through ability, the company operating in the environment with higher inflation will have a lower justified P/E; if the inflation rates are equal but pass-through rates differ, the justified P/E should be lower for the company with the lower pass-through rate. Example 16 provides analysis in support of these conclusions.

EXAMPLE 16

An Analysis of P/Es and Inflation[31]

Assume a company with no real earnings growth, such that its earnings growth can result only from inflation, will pay out all its earnings as dividends. Based on the Gordon (constant growth) DDM, the value of a share is:

$$P_0 = \frac{E_0(1 + I)}{r - I}$$

where:

P_0 = current price, which is substituted for the intrinsic value, V_0, for purposes of analyzing a justified P/E

E_0 = current EPS, which is substituted for current dividends per share, D_0, because the assumption in this example is that all earnings are paid out as dividends

---

[31] This example follows the analysis of Solnik and McLeavey (2004, pp. 289–290).

I = rate of inflation, which is substituted for expected growth, g, because of the assumption in this example that the company's only growth is from inflation

r = required return

Suppose the company has the ability to pass on some or all inflation to its customers and let λ represent the percentage of inflation in costs that the company can pass through to revenue. The company's earnings growth may then be expressed as λI and the equation becomes

$$P_0 = \frac{E_0(1 + \lambda I)}{r - \lambda I} = \frac{E_1}{r - \lambda I}$$

Now, introduce a real rate of return, defined here as r minus I and represented as ρ. The value of a share and the justified forward P/E can now be expressed, respectively, as follows:[32]

$$P_0 = \frac{E_1}{\rho + (1 - \lambda)I}$$

and

$$\frac{P_0}{E_1} = \frac{1}{\rho + (1 - \lambda)I}$$

If a company can pass through all inflation, so that $\lambda = 1$ (100 percent), then the P/E is equal to $1/\rho$. But if the company can pass through no inflation, so that $\lambda = 0$, then the P/E is equal to $1/(\rho + I)$—that is, $1/r$.

You are analyzing two companies, Company M and Company P. The real rate of return required on the shares of Company M and Company P is 3 percent per year. Using the analytic framework provided, address the following:

1. Suppose both Company M and Company P can pass through 75 percent of cost increases. Cost inflation is 6 percent for Company M but only 2 percent for Company P.

   A. Estimate the justified P/E for each company.
   B. Interpret your answer to Part A.

2. Suppose both Company M and Company P face 6 percent a year inflation. Company M can pass through 90 percent of cost increases, but Company P can pass through only 70 percent.

   A. Estimate the justified P/E for each company.
   B. Interpret your answer to Part A.

---

[32] The denominator of this equation is derived from the previous equation as follows: $r - \lambda I = r - I + I - I\lambda = (r - I) + (1 - \lambda)I = \rho - (1 - \lambda)I$.

Solution to 1:

A. For Company M, $\dfrac{1}{0.03 + (1 - 0.75)0.06} = 22.2$

For Company P, $\dfrac{1}{0.03 + (1 - 0.75)0.02} = 28.6$

B. With less than 100 percent cost pass-through, the justified P/E is inversely related to the inflation rate.

Solution to 2:

A. For Company M, $\dfrac{1}{0.03 + (1 - 0.90)0.06} = 27.8$

For Company P, $\dfrac{1}{0.03 + (1 - 0.70)0.06} = 20.8$

B. For equal inflation rates, the company with the higher pass-through rate has a higher justified P/E.

Example 16 illustrates that with less than 100 percent cost pass-through, the justified P/E is inversely related to the inflation rate (with complete cost pass-through, the justified P/E should not be affected by inflation). The higher the inflation rate, the greater the impact of incomplete cost pass-through on P/E. From Example 16, one can also infer that the higher the inflation rate, the more serious the effect on justified P/E of a pass-through rate that is less than 100 percent.

3.1.7 Using P/Es to Obtain Terminal Value in Multistage Dividend Discount Models

In using a DDM to value a stock, whether applying a multistage model or modeling within a spreadsheet (forecasting specific cash flows individually up to some horizon), estimation of the terminal value of the stock is important. The key condition that must be satisfied is that terminal value reflects earnings growth that the company can sustain in the long run. Analysts frequently use price multiples—in particular, P/Es and P/Bs—to estimate terminal value. We can call such multiples **terminal price multiples**. Choices for the terminal multiple, with a terminal P/E multiple used as the example, include the following:

Terminal Price Multiple Based on Fundamentals   As illustrated earlier, analysts can restate the Gordon growth model as a multiple by, for example, dividing both sides of the model by EPS. For terminal P/E multiples, dividing both sides of the Gordon growth model by EPS at time n, where n is the point in time at which the final stage begins (i.e., E_n), gives a trailing terminal price multiple; dividing both sides by EPS at time $n + 1$ (i.e., E_{n+1}) gives a leading terminal price multiple. Of course, an analyst can use the Gordon growth model to estimate terminal value and need not go through the process of deriving a terminal price multiple and then multiplying by the same value of the fundamental to estimate terminal value. Because of their familiarity, however, multiples may be useful in communicating an estimate of terminal value.

Terminal Price Multiple Based on Comparables   Analysts have used various choices for the benchmark value, including:

▶ median industry P/E;

▶ average industry P/E; and

▶ average of own past P/Es.

Having selected a terminal multiple, the expression for terminal value when using a terminal P/E multiple is

$$V_n = \text{Benchmark value of trailing terminal P/E} \times E_n$$

or

$$V_n = \text{Benchmark value of forward terminal P/E} \times E_{n+1}$$

where
V_n = terminal value at time n

The use of a comparables approach has the strength that it is entirely grounded in market data. In contrast, the Gordon growth model calls for specific estimates (the required rate of return, the dividend payout ratio, and the expected mature growth rate), and the model's output is very sensitive to changes in those estimates. A possible disadvantage to the comparables approach is that when the benchmark value reflects mispricing (over- or under-valuation), so will the estimate of terminal value. Example 17 illustrates the use of P/Es and the Gordon growth model to estimate terminal value.

EXAMPLE 17

Using P/Es and the Gordon Growth Model to Value the Mature Growth Phase

As an energy analyst, you are valuing the stock of an oil exploration company. You have projected earnings and dividends three years out (to $t = 3$), and you have gathered the following data and estimates:

▶ Required rate of return = 0.10.

▶ Average dividend payout rate for mature companies in the market = 0.45.

▶ Industry average ROE = 0.13.

▶ E_3 = $3.00.

▶ Industry average P/E = 14.3.

On the basis of this information, carry out the following:

1. Calculate terminal value based on comparables, using your estimated industry average P/E as the benchmark.

2. Contrast your answer in Part 1 to an estimate of terminal value using the Gordon growth model.

Solution to 1: V_n = Benchmark value of P/E $\times E_n$ = 14.3 $\times$ \$3.00
= \$42.90.

> **Solution to 2:** Recall that the Gordon growth model expresses intrinsic value, V, as the present value of dividends divided by the required rate of return, r, minus the growth rate, g: $V_0 = D_0(1 + g)/(r - g)$. Here we are estimating terminal value, so the relevant expression is $V_n = D_n(1 + g)/(r - g)$. You would estimate that the dividend at $t = 3$ will equal earnings in Year 3 of $3.00 times the average payout ratio of 0.45, or $D_n = \$3.00 \times 0.45 = \$1.35$. Recall also the sustainable growth rate expression—that is, $g = b \times ROE$, where b is the retention rate and equivalent to 1 minus the dividend payout ratio. In this example, $b = (1 - 0.45) = 0.55$, and you can use $ROE = 0.13$ (the industry average). Therefore, $g = b \times ROE = 0.55 \times 0.13 = 0.0715$. Given the required rate of return of 0.10, you obtain the estimate $V_n = (\$1.35)(1 + 0.0715)/(0.10 - 0.0715) = \$50.76$. In this example, therefore, the Gordon growth model estimate of terminal value is 18.3 percent higher than the estimate based on comparables calculated in Part 1 (i.e., $0.1832 = \$50.76/\$42.90 - 1$).

3.2 Price to Book Value

The ratio of market price per share to book value per share (P/B), like P/E, has a long history of use in valuation practice (as discussed in Graham and Dodd 1934). According to the 2007 *Merrill Lynch Institutional Factor Survey* of factors used by institutional investors in stock selection, from 1989 through 2005, P/B was only slightly less popular than P/E as a factor; in 2006, P/B was equally popular.

In the P/E multiple, the measure of value (EPS) in the denominator is a flow variable relating to the income statement. In contrast, the measure of value in the P/B's denominator (book value per share) is a stock or level variable coming from the balance sheet. (*Book* refers to the fact that the measurement of value comes from accounting records or books, in contrast to market value.) Intuitively, therefore, we note that book value per share attempts to represent, on a per-share basis, the investment that common shareholders have made in the company. To define book value per share more precisely, we first find **shareholders' equity** (total assets minus total liabilities). Because our purpose is to value common stock, we subtract from shareholders' equity any value attributable to preferred stock to obtain common shareholders' equity, or the **book value of equity** (often called simply **book value**).[33] Dividing book value by the number of common stock shares outstanding, we obtain **book value per share**, the denominator in P/B.

In the balance of this section, we present the reasons analysts have offered for using P/B and possible drawbacks to its use. We then illustrate the calculation of P/B and discuss the fundamental factors that drive P/B. We end the section by showing the use of P/B based on the method of comparables.

Analysts have offered several rationales for the use of P/B; some specifically compare P/B with P/E:

▶ Because book value is a cumulative balance sheet amount, book value is generally positive even when EPS is zero or negative. An analyst can generally use P/B when EPS is zero or negative, whereas P/E based on a zero or negative EPS is not meaningful.

---

[33] If we were to value a company as a whole, rather than value only the common stock, we would not exclude the value of preferred stock from the computation.

► Because book value per share is more stable than EPS, P/B may be more meaningful than P/E when EPS is abnormally high or low or is highly variable.

► As a measure of net asset value per share, book value per share has been viewed as appropriate for valuing companies composed chiefly of liquid assets, such as finance, investment, insurance, and banking institutions (Wild, Bernstein, and Subramanyam 2001, p. 233). For such companies, book values of assets may approximate market values. When information on individual corporate assets is available, analysts may adjust reported book values to market values where they differ.

► Book value has also been used in the valuation of companies that are not expected to continue as a going concern (Martin 1998, p. 22).

► Differences in P/Bs may be related to differences in long-run average returns, according to empirical research.[34]

Possible drawbacks of P/Bs in practice include the following:

► Assets in addition to those recognized in financial statements may be critical operating factors. For example, in many service companies, **human capital**—the value of skills and knowledge possessed by the workforce—is more important than physical capital as an operating factor, but it is not reflected as an asset on the balance sheet. Similarly, the good reputation that a company develops by consistently providing high-quality goods and services is not reflected as an asset on the balance sheet.

► P/B may be misleading as a valuation indicator when the levels of assets used by the companies under examination differ significantly. Such differences may reflect differences in business models.

► Accounting effects on book value may compromise how useful book value is as a measure of the shareholders' investment in the company. In general, intangible assets that are generated internally (as opposed to being acquired) are not shown as assets on a company's balance sheet. For example, companies account for advertising and marketing as expenses, so the value of internally generated brands, which are created and maintained by advertising and marketing activities, do not appear as assets on a company's balance sheet under IFRS or U.S. GAAP. Similarly, when accounting standards require that research and development (R&D) expenditures be treated as expenses, the value of internally developed patents do not appear as assets. Certain R&D expenditures can be capitalized, although rules vary among accounting standards. Accounting effects such as these may impair the comparability of P/B among companies and countries unless appropriate analyst adjustments are made.

► In the accounting of many countries, including the United States, book value largely reflects the historical purchase costs of assets, net of the accumulated accounting depreciation expenses. Inflation and technological change eventually drive a wedge, however, between the book value and the market value of assets. As a result, book value per share often poorly reflects the value of shareholders' investments. Significant differences in the average age of assets among companies being compared may weaken the comparability of P/Bs among companies.

► Share repurchases or issuances may distort historical comparisons.

---

[34] See Bodie, Kane, and Marcus (2008) for a brief summary of the empirical research.

As an example of the effects of share repurchases, consider Colgate-Palmolive Company (NYSE: CL). As of 31 December 2007, CL's trailing P/E and P/B were, respectively, 22.5 and 19.0. Ten years earlier (as of 31 December 1997), CL's trailing P/E and P/B were 32.5 and 12.1. In other words, the company's P/E narrowed by 31 percent (= 22.5/32.5 − 1) while its P/B widened by 57 percent (= 19.0/12.1 − 1). The majority of the difference in changes in these two multiples can be attributed to the substantial amount of shares that CL repurchased over those 10 years, as reflected in the 18 percent compounded annual growth rate (CAGR) of its treasury stock. Because of those share repurchases and the dramatic growth in treasury stock, CL's total shareholders' equity grew at a rate of only 0.5 percent despite the 13 percent CAGR in retained earnings. In summary, when a company repurchases shares at a price higher than the current book value per share, it lowers the overall book value per share for the company. All else being equal, the effect is to make the stock appear more expensive on a P/B basis than it would appear if historical levels of P/B were used.

Example 18 illustrates another potential limitation to using P/B in valuation.

EXAMPLE 18

Differences in Business Models Reflected in Differences in P/Bs

Dell Computer Corporation competes in the personal computer industry. Exhibit 9 gives Dell's P/B and P/Bs of its industry peers as of mid-2008.

EXHIBIT 9	P/Bs for Dell and Industry
Entity	**P/B**
Dell	10.14
Peer mean	5.06
Peer median	2.71

Source: Thompson One Banker.

With a P/B that is 3.7 times higher than the peer median, Dell appears to be substantially overvalued (at least if we assume that profitability is comparable). However, consideration of Dell's business model shows that this conclusion may be mistaken. Dell is an assembler rather than a manufacturer, uses a just-in-time inventory system for parts needed in assembly, and sells built-to-order computers directly to the end consumer. Just-in-time inventory systems attempt to minimize the amount of time that parts needed for building computers are held in inventory. How can these practices explain the much higher P/B of Dell compared with the P/Bs of peer-group stocks?

Because Dell assembles parts manufactured elsewhere, it requires smaller investments in fixed assets than it would if it were a manufacturer;

this business strategy translates into a smaller book value per share. The just-in-time inventory system reduces Dell's required investment in working capital. Because Dell does not need to respond to the inventory needs of large resellers, its need to invest in working capital is reduced.

The overall effect of this business model is that Dell generates its sales on a comparatively small base of assets. So, Dell's higher P/B is explained by its business model. Because Dell's P/B is not directly comparable with those of its peer group, using an average or median P/B as the benchmark for estimating the value of Dell would be misleading.

3.2.1 Determining Book Value

In this section, we illustrate how to calculate book value and how to adjust book value to improve the comparability of P/Bs among companies. To compute book value per share, we need to refer to the business's balance sheet, which has a shareholders' (or stockholders') equity section. The computation of book value is as follows:

▶ (Shareholders' equity) − (Total value of equity claims that are senior to common stock) = Common shareholders' equity.

▶ (Common shareholders' equity)/(Number of common stock shares outstanding) = Book value per share.

Possible claims senior to the claims of common stock, which would be subtracted from shareholders' equity, include the value of preferred stock and the dividends in arrears on preferred stock.[35] Example 19 illustrates the calculation.

EXAMPLE 19

Computing Book Value per Share

The Allstate Corporation (NYSE: ALL), a U.S.-based insurance company, reported the balance sheet given in Exhibit 10 for its fiscal year ending 31 December 2007.

EXHIBIT 10	Allstate Corporation and Subsidiaries Consolidated Statements of Financial Position ($ in Millions, except Par Value Data)

Assets

Investments

Fixed-income securities, at fair value (amortized cost $93,495)	$94,451
Equity securities, at fair value (cost $4,267)	5,257

(Exhibit continued on next page . . .)

---

[35] Some preferred stock issues have the right to premiums (liquidation premiums) if they are liquidated. If present, these premiums should also be deducted.

EXHIBIT 10 (continued)

Mortgage loans	10,830
Limited partnership interests	2,501
Short-term	3,058
Other	2,883
Total investments	118,980
Cash	422
Premium installment receivables, net	4,879
Deferred policy acquisition costs	5,768
Reinsurance recoverables, net	5,817
Accrued investment income	1,050
Deferred income taxes	467
Property and equipment, net	1,062
Goodwill	825
Other assets	2,209
Separate accounts	14,929
Total assets	$156,408

Liabilities

Reserve for property-liability insurance claims and claims expense	$18,865
Reserve for life-contingent contract benefits	13,212
Contractholder funds	61,975
Unearned premiums	10,409
Claim payments outstanding	748
Other liabilities and accrued expenses	8,779
Short-term debt	0
Long-term debt	5,640
Separate accounts	14,929
Total liabilities	134,557
Commitments and contingent liabilities (Notes 6, 7, and 13)	

Shareholders' equity

Preferred stock, $1 par value, 25 million shares authorized, none issued	0
Common stock, $.01 par value, 2.0 billion shares authorized and 900 million issued, 563 million shares outstanding	9
Additional capital paid in	3,052
Retained income	32,796
Deferred ESOP expense	(55)
Treasury stock, at cost (337 million)	(14,574)

(Exhibit continued on next page . . .)

EXHIBIT 10   **(continued)**

Total accumulated other comprehensive income	623
Total shareholders' equity	21,851
Total liabilities and shareholders' equity	$156,408

Note: ESOP = employee stock option plan.

The entries in the balance sheet should be familiar. Treasury stock results from share repurchases (or buybacks) and is a reduction in total shareholders' equity.

1. Using the data in Exhibit 10, calculate book value per share as of 31 December 2007.

2. Given a closing price per share for ALL of $47.00 as of 13 February 2008 and your answer to Part 1, calculate ALL's P/B as of 13 February 2008.

Solution to 1: The divisor is the number of shares outstanding. As shown in the line labeled "Common stock . . ." in Exhibit 10, the number of shares outstanding (563 million) is equal to the number of shares issued (900 million) minus the number of shares held in treasury stock (337 million), which appears in the line labeled "Treasury stock . . ." Therefore, (Common shareholders' equity)/(Number of common stock shares outstanding) = $21,851/563 = $38.81.

Solution to 2: P/B = $47.00/$38.81 = 1.21.

Example 19 illustrated the calculation of book value per share without any adjustments. Adjusting P/B has two purposes: 1) to make the book value per share more accurately reflect the value of shareholders' investment and 2) to make P/B more useful for making comparisons among different stocks. Some adjustments are as follows:

▶ Some services and analysts report a **tangible book value per share**. Computing tangible book value per share involves subtracting reported intangible assets on the balance sheet from common shareholders' equity. The analyst should be familiar with the calculation. From the viewpoint of financial theory, however, the general exclusion of all intangibles may not be warranted. In the case of individual intangible assets, such as patents, which can be separated from the entity and sold, exclusion may not be justified. Exclusion may be appropriate, however, for goodwill from acquisitions, particularly for comparative purposes. **Goodwill** represents the excess of the purchase price of an acquisition beyond the fair value of acquired tangible assets and specifically identifiable intangible assets. Many analysts believe that goodwill does not represent an asset because it is not separable and may reflect overpayment for an acquisition.

▶ Certain adjustments may be appropriate for enhancing comparability. For example, one company may use FIFO whereas a peer company uses LIFO, which in an inflationary environment will generally understate inventory values. To accurately assess the relative valuation of the two companies, the analyst should restate the book value of the company using LIFO to what it would be based on FIFO. For a more complete discussion of adjustments to balance sheet amounts, refer to the readings on financial statement analysis.

▶ For book value per share to most accurately reflect current values, the balance sheet should be adjusted for significant off-balance sheet assets and liabilities. An example of an off-balance sheet liability is a guarantee to pay a debt of another company in the event of that company's default. U.S. accounting standards require companies to disclose off-balance sheet liabilities.

Example 20 illustrates adjustments an analyst might make to a financial firm's P/B to obtain an accurate firm value.

EXAMPLE 20

Adjusting Book Value

Edward Stavros is a junior analyst at a major U.S. pension fund. Stavros is researching Discover Financial Services (NYSE: DFS) for his fund's Credit Services portfolio and is preparing background information prior to an upcoming meeting with the company. Stavros is particularly interested in Discover's P/B and in assessing the impact of recently introduced fair-value accounting disclosures. He obtains the condensed balance sheet and selected footnote excerpts for Discover for the first quarter of 2008 from SEC filings; these data are shown in Exhibit 11.

EXHIBIT 11 — Discover Financial Services Condensed Consolidated Balance Sheet (in Thousands except Per-Share Amounts)

	February 29, 2008 (Unaudited)	November 30, 2007
Assets		
Cash and cash equivalents	$8,286,290	$8,085,467
Investment securities:		
Available-for-sale (amortized cost of $809,497 and $425,681 at February 29, 2008 and November 30, 2007, respectively)	792,979	420,837
Held-to-maturity (market value $91,881 and $100,769 at February 29, 2008 and November 30, 2007, respectively)	99,527	104,602
Net loan receivables	20,182,303	20,071,192
Accrued interest receivable	122,765	123,292
Amounts due from asset securitization	2,935,494	3,041,215
Premises and equipment, net	567,475	575,229
Goodwill	255,421	255,421

(Exhibit continued on next page . . .)

	February 29, 2008 (Unaudited)	November 30, 2007
Intangible assets, net	57,900	59,769
Other assets	922,578	712,678
Assets of discontinued operations	3,105,327	3,926,403
Total assets	$37,328,059	$37,376,105
Liabilities and Stockholders' Equity		
Liabilities [detail omitted]		
Total liabilities	31,673,718	31,776,683
Stockholders' Equity:		
Preferred stock, par value $0.01 per share; 200,000,000 shares authorized; none issued or outstanding	0	0
Common stock, par value $0.01 per share; 2,000,000,000 shares authorized; 479,269,154 and 477,762,018 shares issued at February 29, 2008 and November 30, 2007, respectively	4,793	4,777
Additional paid-in capital	2,885,610	2,846,127
Retained earnings	2,761,159	2,717,905
Accumulated other comprehensive income	5,191	32,032
Treasury stock, at cost; 142,245 and 73,795 shares at February 29, 2008 and November 30, 2007, respectively	−2,412	−1,419
Total stockholders' equity	5,654,341	5,599,422
Total liabilities and stockholders' equity	$37,328,059	$37,376,105

Excerpt from Footnotes to the Discover Financial Services Financial Statements

Assets and Liabilities Measured at Fair Value on a Recurring Basis at February 29, 2008 (Dollars in Thousands)

	Quoted Prices in Active Markets for Identical Assets (Level 1)	Significant Other Observable Inputs (Level 2)	Significant Unobservable Inputs (Level 3)	Balance at February 29, 2008
Assets				
Investment securities—available for sale	$536	$792,443	$0	$792,979
Amounts due from asset securitization*	0	0	1,952,901	1,952,901

(continued on next page . . .)

(continued)

Assets and Liabilities Measured at Fair Value on a Recurring Basis at February 29, 2008 (Dollars in Thousands)

	Quoted Prices in Active Markets for Identical Assets (Level 1)	Significant Other Observable Inputs (Level 2)	Significant Unobservable Inputs (Level 3)	Balance at February 29, 2008
Derivative financial instruments	0	11,695	0	11,695
Liabilities				
Derivative financial instruments	0	1,655	0	1,655

* *Amounts due from asset securitization*. Carrying values of the portion of amounts due from asset securitization that are short term in nature approximate their fair values. Fair values of the remaining assets recorded in amounts due from asset securitization reflect the present value of estimated future cash flows utilizing management's best estimate of key assumptions with regard to credit card receivable performance and interest rate environment projections.

Stavros computes book value per share initially by dividing total shareholders' equity ($5,654,341,000) by the number of shares outstanding at 29 February 2008 (479,126,909). The resulting book value per share is $11.80.

Stavros then computes tangible book value per share as $11.15 (calculated as $5,654,341,000 minus $255,421,000 of goodwill and $57,900,000 of other intangibles = $5,341,020,000 net tangible assets, which is then divided by 479,126,909 shares). Based on a price of $17.40 shortly after the end of the first quarter, Discover has a P/B of $17.40/$11.15 = 1.6.

Stavros then turns to the footnotes to examine the fair-value data. In particular, he is interested in the amount of assets that are measured by using Level 3 inputs. The level of input refers to how observable the inputs used by management to assess fair value are, and Level 3 would contain the least observable (and thus the most sensitive to management's judgment).[36] An asset valued using Level 1 inputs is based on a market quote for an identical asset in a liquid market, and an asset valued on Level 2 inputs uses significant other observable inputs. In some cases, if an analyst has concern about the estimated inputs or the valuation methodology, it may be appropriate for the analyst to apply a discount to Level 3 assets and liabilities and to adjust ratios accordingly.

For Discover, Stavros notes that the total amount of assets measured using Level 3 inputs is $1,952,901,000. This amount is 71 percent of the company's assets measured at fair value and 5 percent of the company's total assets. Its materiality suggests that the amount merits additional attention. From the financial statement footnotes, Stavros sees that the value of the Level 3 assets is based on management's projections of credit card receivable performance and the interest rate environment. Stavros concludes that it will be very important for him to understand how management makes those projections, and he will thus give particular attention to the discussion of the topic at the upcoming meeting with the firm. At present, he has no reason to disagree with the fair values and will thus proceed with the tangible book value per share as calculated.

---

[36] U.S. GAAP Statement of Financial Accounting Standards No. 157 defines valuation input levels and the required disclosures.

An analyst should also be aware of differences in accounting standards related to how assets and liabilities are valued in financial statements. Accounting standards currently require companies to report some assets and liabilities at fair value[37] and others at historical cost (with some adjustments).

Financial assets, such as investments in marketable securities, are usually reported at fair market value. Investments classified as "held to maturity" and reported on a historical cost basis are an exception. Some financial liabilities also are reported at fair value.

Nonfinancial assets, such as land and equipment, are generally reported at their historical acquisition costs, and in the case of equipment, the assets are depreciated over their useful lives. The value of these assets may have increased over time, however, or the value may have decreased more than is reflected in the accumulated depreciation. When the reported amount of an asset—i.e., its carrying value—exceeds its recoverable amount, both international accounting (IFRS) and U.S. accounting standards (GAAP) require companies to reduce the reported amount of the asset and show the reduction as an impairment loss.[38] U.S. GAAP, however, prohibit revaluing assets upward, whereas IFRS allow companies to report either a revalued amount or an amount based on historical cost. When assets are reported at fair value, P/Bs become more comparable among companies; for this reason, P/Bs are considered to be more comparable for companies with significant amounts of financial assets.

3.2.2 Valuation Based on Forecasted Fundamentals

We can use forecasts of a company's fundamentals to estimate a stock's justified P/B. For example, assuming the Gordon growth model and using the expression $g = b \times \text{ROE}$ for the sustainable growth rate, the expression for the justified P/B based on the most recent book value (B_0) is[39]

$$\frac{P_0}{B_0} = \frac{\text{ROE} - g}{r - g} \qquad \textbf{(4)}$$

For example, if a business's ROE is 12 percent, its required rate of return is 10 percent, and its expected growth rate is 7 percent, then its justified P/B based on fundamentals is $(0.12 - 0.07)/(0.10 - 0.07) = 1.67$.

Equation 4 states that the justified P/B is an increasing function of ROE, all else equal. Because the numerator and denominator are differences of, respectively, ROE and r from the same quantity, g, what determines the justified P/B in Equation 4 is ROE in relation to the required rate of return r. The larger ROE is in relation to r, the higher is the justified P/B based on fundamentals.[40]

---

[37] **Fair value** is defined in international accounting standards as "the amount for which an asset could be exchanged, or a liability settled, between knowledgeable, willing parties in an arm's length transaction" and is defined in U.S. GAAP as "the price that would be received to sell an asset or paid to transfer a liability in an orderly transaction between market participants at the measurement date" (www.iasb.org and www.fasb.org as of July 2008).

[38] The two sets of standards differ in the measurement of impairment losses.

[39] According to the Gordon growth model, $V_0 = E_1 \times (1 - b)/(r - g)$. Defining ROE as E_1/B_0 so $E_1 = B_0 \times \text{ROE}$ and substituting for E_1 into the prior expression, we have $V_0 = B_0 \times \text{ROE} \times (1 - b)/(r - g)$, giving $V_0/B_0 = \text{ROE} \times (1 - b)/(r - g)$. The sustainable growth rate expression is $g = b \times \text{ROE}$. Substituting $b = g/\text{ROE}$ into the expression just given for V_0/B_0, we have $V_0/B_0 = (\text{ROE} - g)/(r - g)$. Because justified price is intrinsic value, V_0, we obtain Equation 4.

[40] This relationship can be seen clearly if we set g equal to 0 (the no-growth case): $P_0/B_0 = \text{ROE}/r$.

A practical insight from Equation 4 is that we cannot conclude whether a particular value of the P/B reflects undervaluation without taking into account the business's profitability. Equation 4 also suggests that if we are evaluating two stocks with the same P/B, the one with the higher ROE is relatively undervalued, all else equal. These relationships have been confirmed through cross-sectional regression analyses.[41]

Further insight into P/B comes from the residual income model, which is discussed in detail in another reading. The expression for the justified P/B based on the residual income valuation is[42]

$$\frac{P_0}{B_0} = 1 + \frac{\text{Present value of expected future residual earnings}}{B_0} \qquad (5)$$

Equation 5, which makes no special assumptions about growth, states the following:

▶ If the present value of expected future residual earnings is zero—for example, if the business just earns its required return on investment in every period—the justified P/B is 1.

▶ If the present value of expected future residual earnings is positive (negative), the justified P/B is greater than (less than) 1.

3.2.3 Valuation Based on Comparables

To use the method of comparables for valuing stocks using a P/B, we follow the steps given in Section 3.1.5. In contrast to EPS, however, analysts' forecasts of book value are not aggregated and widely disseminated by financial data vendors; in practice, most analysts use trailing book value in calculating P/Bs.[43] Evaluation of relative P/Bs should consider differences in ROE, risk, and expected earnings growth. The use of P/Bs in the method of comparables is illustrated in Example 21.

EXAMPLE 21

P/B Comparables Approach

You are working on a project to value an independent securities brokerage firm. Although you are aware that significant changes occurred in the industry in 2008, as part of the analysis, you decide to review 2007

---

[41] Harris and Marston (1994) performed a regression of book value to market value (MV), which is the inverse of P/B, against variables for growth (mean analyst forecasts) and risk (beta) for a large sample of companies over the period July 1982 through December 1989. The estimated regression was $B/P = 1.172 - 4.15 \times \text{Growth} + 0.093 \times \text{Risk}$ (with $R^2 = 22.9\%$). The coefficient of -4.15 indicates that expected growth was negatively related to B/P and, as a consequence, positively related to P/B. Risk was positively related to B/P and thus negatively related to P/B. Both variables were statistically significant, with growth having the greatest impact. Fairfield (1994) also found that P/Bs are related to future expectations of ROE in the predicted fashion.

[42] Noting that $(\text{ROE} - r) \times B_0$ would define a level residual income stream, we can show that Equation 4 is consistent with Equation 5 (a general expression) as follows. In $P_0/B_0 = (\text{ROE} - g)/(r - g)$, we can successively rewrite the numerator $(\text{ROE} - g) + r - r = (r - g) + (\text{ROE} - r)$, so $P_0/B_0 = [(r - g) + (\text{ROE} - r)]/(r - g) = 1 + (\text{ROE} - r)/(r - g)$, which can be written $P_0/B_0 = 1 + [(\text{ROE} - r)/(r - g)] \times B_0/B_0 = 1 + [(\text{ROE} - r) \times B_0/(r - g)]/B_0$; the second term in the final expression is the present value of residual income divided by B_0 as in Equation 5.

[43] Because equity in successive balance sheets is linked by net income from the income statement, however, the analyst could, given dividend forecasts, translate EPS forecasts into corresponding book value forecasts while taking account of any anticipated ownership transactions.

data on three firms that, at that time, were independent securities brokerage firms: Goldman Sachs (NYSE: GS), Merrill Lynch (formerly NYSE: MER), and Morgan Stanley (NYSE: MS). Exhibit 12 presents information on these firms.[44]

EXHIBIT 12   P/B Comparables

| | Price to Book Value | | | | | | | | |
| | | | | | | Five-Year | | Forecasted | |
Firm	2003	2004	2005	2006	2007	Average	Current	ROE	Beta
GS	1.8	1.9	1.9	2.1	1.8	1.9	1.4	14.0%	1.54
MS	2.0	2.1	2.0	2.1	2.4	2.1	1.5	16.5	1.67
MER	1.6	1.7	1.7	1.9	2.5	1.9	1.5	13.5	1.91
Investment/ Brokerage industry (mean value)							2.0	13.8	

Sources: *The Value Line Investment Survey* (25 April 2008); Yahoo! Finance for industry average; www.Reuters.com for beta.

Based only on the information in Exhibit 12, discuss the valuation of MER relative to the industry and peer companies.

Solution: MER was selling at a P/B that was 75 percent of the industry mean P/B. At the same time, its expected ROE was roughly equivalent to the industry's. Solely on the basis of the data given, MER appears to be slightly undervalued relative to the industry benchmark. Based on the data given, however, it appears to be overvalued with respect to MS and GS. Specifically:

▶ Compared with MS, MER has the same P/B but a lower expected ROE and higher risk, as judged by beta.

▶ Compared with GS, MER has a higher P/B but a lower expected ROE and higher risk, as judged by beta.

3.3 Price to Sales

Certain types of privately held companies, including investment management companies and many types of companies in partnership form, have long been valued by a multiple of annual revenues. In recent decades, the ratio of price to sales has become well known as a valuation indicator for the equity of publicly traded companies as well. Based on U.S. data, O'Shaughnessy (2005) characterized P/S as the best ratio for selecting undervalued stocks. According to the *Merrill Lynch Institutional Factor Survey*, from 1989 through 2006, almost 20 percent of respondents, on average, consistently used P/S in their investment process. Analysts have offered the following rationales for using P/S:

---

[44] Forecasted ROE refers to forecasts for 2004 to 2006.

► Sales are generally less subject to distortion or manipulation than are other fundamentals, such as EPS or book value. For example, through discretionary accounting decisions about expenses, company managers can distort EPS as a reflection of economic performance. In contrast, total sales, as the top line in the income statement, is prior to any expenses.

► Sales are positive even when EPS is negative. Therefore, analysts can use P/S when EPS is negative, whereas the P/E based on a zero or negative EPS is not meaningful.

► Because sales are generally more stable than EPS, which reflects operating and financial leverage, P/S is generally more stable than P/E. P/S may be more meaningful than P/E when EPS is abnormally high or low.

► P/S has been viewed as appropriate for valuing the stocks of mature, cyclical, and zero-income companies (Martin 1998).

► Differences in P/S multiples may be related to differences in long-run average returns, according to empirical research.[45]

Possible drawbacks of using P/S in practice include the following:

► A business may show high growth in sales even when it is not operating profitably as judged by earnings and cash flow from operations. To have value as a going concern, a business must ultimately generate earnings and cash.

► Share price reflects the effect of debt financing on profitability and risk. In the P/S multiple, however, price is compared with sales, which is a pre-financing income measure—a logical mismatch. For this reason, some experts use a ratio of enterprise value to sales because enterprise value incorporates the value of debt.

► P/S does not reflect differences in cost structures among different companies.

► Although P/S is relatively robust with respect to manipulation, revenue recognition practices have the potential to distort P/S.

Despite the contrasts between P/S to P/E, the ratios have a relationship with which analysts should be familiar. The fact that (Sales) × (Net profit margin) = Net income means that (P/E) × (Net profit margin) = P/S. For two stocks with the same positive P/E, the stock with the higher P/S has a higher (actual or forecasted) net profit margin, calculated as the ratio of P/S to P/E.

3.3.1 Determining Sales

P/S is calculated as price per share divided by annual net sales per share (net sales is total sales minus returns and customer discounts). Analysts usually use annual sales from the company's most recent fiscal year in the calculation, as illustrated in Example 22. Because valuation is forward looking in principle, the analyst may also develop and use P/S multiples based on forecasts of next year's sales.

---

[45] Nathan, Sivakumar, and Vijayakumar (2001); O'Shaughnessy (2005); Senchack and Martin (1987).

EXAMPLE 22

Calculating P/S

Stora Enso Oyj (Helsinki Stock Exchange: STEAV) is an integrated paper, packaging, and forest products company headquartered in Finland. In 2007, Stora Enso reported net sales of €13,373.6 million and had 788,619,987 shares outstanding. Calculate the P/S for Stora Enso based on a closing price of €8.87 on 12 February 2008.

Solution: Sales per share = €13,373.6 million/788,619,987 shares = €16.96. So, P/S = €8.87/€16.96 = 0.523.

Although the determination of sales is more straightforward than the determination of earnings, the analyst should evaluate a company's revenue recognition practices—in particular those tending to speed up the recognition of revenues—before relying on the P/S multiple. An analyst using a P/S approach who does not also assess the quality of accounting for sales may place too high a value on the company's shares. Example 23 illustrates the problem.

EXAMPLE 23

Revenue Recognition Practices (1)

Analysts label stock markets "bubbles" when market prices appear to lose contact with intrinsic values. To many analysts, the run-up in the prices of internet stocks in the U.S. market in the 1998–2000 period represented a bubble. During that period, many analysts adopted P/S as a metric for valuing the many internet stocks that had negative earnings and cash flow. Perhaps at least partly as a result of this practice, some internet companies engaged in questionable revenue recognition practices to justify their high valuations. To increase sales, some companies engaged in bartering website advertising with other internet companies. For example, InternetRevenue.com might barter $1,000,000 worth of banner advertising with RevenueIsUs.com. Each could then show $1,000,000 of revenue and $1,000,000 of expenses. Although neither had any net income or cash flow, each company's revenue growth and market valuation was enhanced (at least temporarily). In addition the value placed on the advertising was frequently questionable.

As a result of these and other questionable activities, the U.S. SEC issued a stern warning to companies and formalized revenue recognition practices for barter in Staff Accounting Bulletin No. 101. Similarly, international accounting standard setters issued Standing Interpretations Committee Interpretation 31 to define revenue recognition principles for barter transactions involving advertising services. The analyst should review footnote disclosures to assess whether a company may be recognizing revenue prematurely or otherwise aggressively.

Example 24 illustrates another classic instance in which an analyst should look behind the accounting numbers.

EXAMPLE 24

Revenue Recognition Practices (2)

Sales on a **bill-and-hold basis** involve selling products but not delivering those products until a later date.[46] Sales on this basis have the effect of accelerating sales into an earlier reporting period. The following is a typical case. In its Form 10-K filed 6 March 1998, for the fiscal year ended 28 December 1997, Sunbeam Corporation provided the following footnote:

1. OPERATIONS AND SIGNIFICANT ACCOUNTING POLICIES
REVENUE RECOGNITION
The Company recognizes revenues from product sales principally at the time of shipment to customers. In limited circumstances, at the customer's request the Company may sell seasonal product on a bill and hold basis provided that the goods are completed, packaged and ready for shipment, such goods are segregated and the risks of ownership and legal title have passed to the customer. The amount of such bill and hold sales at 29 December 1997 was approximately 3 percent of consolidated revenues. Net sales are comprised of gross sales less provisions for expected customer returns, discounts, promotional allowances and cooperative advertising.

After internal and SEC investigations, the company restated its financial results and revenue recognition policy:

REVENUE RECOGNITION
The Company recognizes sales and related cost of goods sold from product sales when title passes to the customers which is generally at the time of shipment. Net sales is comprised of gross sales less provisions for estimated customer returns, discounts, promotional allowances, cooperative advertising allowances and costs incurred by the Company to ship product to customers. Reserves for estimated returns are established by the Company concurrently with the recognition of revenue. Reserves are established based on a variety of factors, including historical return rates, estimates of customer inventory levels, the market for the product and projected economic conditions. The Company monitors these reserves and makes adjustment to them when management believes that actual returns or costs to be incurred differ from amounts recorded. In some situations, the Company has shipped product with the right of return where the Company is unable to reasonably estimate the level of returns and/or the sale is contingent upon the resale of the product. In these situations, the Company does not recognize revenue upon product shipment, but rather when it is reasonably expected the product will not be returned.

---

[46] For companies whose reports must conform to U.S. SEC accounting regulations, revenue from bill-and-hold sales cannot be reported unless the risk of loss on the products transfers to the buyer and additional criteria are met. (SEC Staff Accounting Bulletin No. 101 specifies the criteria.)

The company had originally reported revenue of $1,168,182,000 for the fiscal year ended 31 December 1997. After restatement, the company reported revenue of $1,073,000,000 for the same period—a more than 8 percent reduction in revenue. The analyst reading the footnote in the original report would have noted the bill-and-hold practices and reduced revenue by 3 percent. This company engaged in other accounting practices tending to inflate revenue that did not come to light until the investigation.

Examples 23 and 24 dealt with situations that occurred some years ago. It should not be assumed, however, that all aggressive revenue recognition practices have now been eliminated. Example 25 briefly summarizes a more recent example.

EXAMPLE 25

Revenue Recognition Practices (3)

In February 2008, Diebold Inc., a manufacturer of security systems, automated teller machines, and voting machines announced that it had determined that "its previous, long-standing method of accounting for bill and hold transactions was in error, representing a misapplication of generally accepted accounting principles, and that it would discontinue its use of bill and hold as a method of revenue recognition in its North America and International businesses" (from Diebold's Form 8-K filed with the SEC on 8 February 2008). The company announced it would restate its financial statements back to fiscal year 2003.

Sometimes, as in the Sunbeam example, even when a company discloses its revenue recognition practices, the analyst cannot determine precisely by how much sales may be overstated. If a company is engaging in questionable revenue recognition practices and the amount being manipulated is unknown, the analyst might do well to suggest avoiding investment in that company's securities. At the very least, the analyst should be skeptical and assign the company a higher risk premium than otherwise, which would result in a lower justified P/S.

3.3.2 Valuation Based on Forecasted Fundamentals

Like other multiples, P/S can be linked to DCF models. In terms of the Gordon growth model, we can state P/S as[47]

$$\frac{P_0}{S_0} = \frac{(E_0/S_0)\,(1 - b)\,(1 + g)}{r - g}$$

(6)

---

[47] The Gordon growth model is $P_0 = D_0\,(1 + g)/(r - g)$. Substituting $D_0 = E_0\,(1 - b)$ into the previous equation produces $P_0 = E_0\,(1 - b)(1 + g)/(r - g)$. Dividing both sides by S_0 gives $P_0/S_0 = (E_0/S_0)(1 - b)(1 + g)/(r - g)$.

where E_0/S_0 is the business's profit margin. Although the profit margin is stated in terms of trailing sales and earnings, the analyst may use a long-term forecasted profit margin in Equation 6. Equation 6 states that the justified P/S is an increasing function of the profit margin and earnings growth rate, and the intuition behind Equation 6 generalizes to more-complex DCF models.

Profit margin is a determinant of the justified P/S not only directly but also through its effect on *g*. We can illustrate this concept by restating the equation for the sustainable growth rate [$g =$ (Retention rate, b) $\times$ ROE], as follows:

$$g = b \times \text{PM}_0 \times \frac{\text{Sales}}{\text{Total assets}} \times \frac{\text{Total assets}}{\text{Shareholders' equity}}$$

where PM_0 is profit margin and the last three terms come from the DuPont analysis of ROE. An increase (decrease) in the profit margin produces a higher (lower) sustainable growth rate as long as sales do not decrease (increase) proportionately.[48] Example 26 illustrates the use of justified P/S and how to apply it in valuation.

EXAMPLE 26

Justified P/S Based on Forecasted Fundamentals

As a health care analyst, you are valuing the stocks of three medical equipment manufacturers, including the Swedish company Getinge AB (Stockholm: GETI) in July 2008. Based on an average of estimates obtained from a capital asset pricing model (CAPM) and a bond yield plus risk premium, you estimate that GETI's required rate of return is 11 percent. Your other forecasts are as follows:

- ▶ long-term profit margin = 8.2 percent;
- ▶ dividend payout ratio = 30 percent; and
- ▶ earnings growth rate = 10 percent.

Although GETI's profit margin in the most recent year was 7.7 percent, the company's average profit margin over the previous five years was 8.8 percent. An earnings growth rate of 10 percent is close to the median analyst forecast, according to Thomson First Call. To obtain a first estimate of GETI's justified P/S based on forecasted fundamentals, you use Equation 6.

1. Based on these data, calculate GETI's justified P/S.
2. Given a forecast of GETI's sales per share (in Swedish krona) for 2008 of SEK64.40, estimate the intrinsic value of GETI stock.
3. Given a market price for GETI of SEK138 on 9 July 2008 and your answer to Part 2, state whether GETI stock appears to be fairly valued, overvalued, or undervalued.

---

[48] That is, an increase (decrease) in the profit margin could be offset by a decrease (increase) in total asset turnover (sales/assets).

Solution to 1: From Equation 6, GETI's justified P/S is calculated as follows:

$$\frac{P_0}{S_0} = \frac{(E_0/S_0)\,(1 - b)\,(1 + g)}{r - g} = \frac{0.082 \times 0.30 \times 1.10}{0.11 - 0.10} = 2.7$$

Solution to 2: An estimate of the intrinsic value of GETI stock is $2.7 \times$ SEK64.40 = SEK173.88.

Solution to 3: GETI stock appears to be undervalued because its current market value of SEK138 is less than its estimated intrinsic value of SEK173.88.

3.3.3 Valuation Based on Comparables

Using P/S in the method of comparables to value stocks follows the steps given in Section 3.1.5. As mentioned earlier, P/S ratios are usually reported on the basis of trailing sales. Analysts may also base relative valuations on P/S multiples calculated on forecasted sales. In doing so, analysts may make their own sales forecasts or may use forecasts supplied by data vendors.[49] In valuing stocks using the method of comparables, analysts should also gather information on profit margins, expected earnings growth, and risk. As always, the quality of accounting also merits investigation. Example 27 illustrates the use of P/S in the comparables approach.

EXAMPLE 27

P/S Comparables Approach

Continuing with the project to value Getinge AB, you have compiled the information on GETI and peer companies Smith & Nephew PLC (London: SN) and CR Bard Inc. (NYSE: BCR) given in Exhibit 13.

EXHIBIT 13   P/S Comparables (as of 9 July 2008)

Measure	GETI	SN	BCR
Price to sales (current close)	1.9	2.9	4.0
Prior-year profit margin	7.7%	9.4%	18.5%
Forecasted profit margin	8.2%	13.1%	18.7%
Median analyst long-term growth forecast	10.0%	9.0%	14.0%
Beta	0.83	0.81	0.74

Source: Thomson First Call.

---

[49] Although sales forecasts have historically been less readily available than earnings forecasts, several leading vendors of U.S. market data currently provide forecasts of sales as well as such quantities as cash flow per share and dividends per share.

Use the data in Exhibit 13 to address the following:

1. Based on the P/S (calculated from the current close) but referring to no other information, assess GETI's relative valuation.

2. State whether GETI is more closely comparable to SN or to BCR. Justify your answer.

Solution to 1: Because the P/S for GETI, 1.9, is the lowest of the three P/S multiples, if no other information is referenced, GETI appears to be relatively undervalued.

Solution to 2: On the basis of the information given, GETI appears to be more closely matched to SN than BCR. The profit margin, the growth rate, and risk are key fundamentals in the P/S approach, and GETI's profit margin and expected growth rate are closer to those of SN. Furthermore, the risk of GETI stock as measured by beta is closer to SN than to BCR.

3.4 Price to Cash Flow

Price to cash flow is a widely reported valuation indicator. According to the *Merrill Lynch Institutional Factor Survey*, price to cash flow on average, was more widely used in investment practice than P/E, P/B, P/S, or dividend yield in the 1989–2005 period among the institutional investors surveyed; in 2006, the use of price to cash flow was approximately the same as P/E and P/B but was still higher than P/S or dividend yield.

In this section, we present price to cash flow based on alternative major cash flow concepts.[50] Because of the wide variety of cash flow concepts in use, the analyst should be especially careful to understand (and communicate) the exact definition of "cash flow" that is the basis for the analysis.

Analysts have offered the following rationales for the use of price to cash flow:

▶ Cash flow is less subject to manipulation by management than earnings.

▶ Because cash flow is generally more stable than earnings, price to cash flow is generally more stable than P/E.

▶ Using price to cash flow rather than P/E addresses the issue of differences in accounting conservatism between companies (differences in the quality of earnings).

▶ Differences in price to cash flow may be related to differences in long-run average returns, according to empirical research.[51]

Possible drawbacks to the use of price to cash flow include the following:

▶ When cash flow from operations is defined as EPS plus noncash charges, items affecting actual cash flow from operations, such as noncash revenue

---

[50] "Price to cash flow" is used to refer to the ratio of share price to any one of these definitions of cash flow. P/CF is reserved for the ratio of price to the earnings plus noncash charges definition of cash flow, explained subsequently.
[51] For example, see O'Shaughnessy (2004).

and net changes in working capital, are ignored. So, for example, aggressive recognition of revenue (front-end loading) would not be accurately captured in the earnings-plus-noncash-charges definition because the measure would not reflect the divergence between revenues as reported and actual cash collections related to that revenue.

▶ Theory views free cash flow to equity (FCFE) rather than cash flow as the appropriate variable for price-based valuation multiples. We can use P/FCFE but FCFE does have the possible drawback of being more volatile than cash flow for many businesses. FCFE is also more frequently negative than cash flow.

▶ As analysts' use of cash flow has increased over time, some companies have increased their use of accounting methods that enhance cash flow measures. Operating cash flow, for example, can be enhanced by securitizing accounts receivable to speed up a company's operating cash inflow or by outsourcing the payment of accounts payable to slow down the company's operating cash outflow (while the outsource company continues to make timely payments and provides financing to cover any timing differences). Mulford and Comiskey (2005) describe a number of opportunistic accounting choices that companies can make to increase their reported operating cash flow.

One approximation of cash flow in practical use is EPS plus depreciation, amortization, and depletion. Even this simple approximation can be used to highlight issues of interest to the analyst in valuation, as Example 28 shows.

EXAMPLE 28

Accounting Methods and Cash Flow

Consider two hypothetical companies, Company A and Company B, that have constant cash revenues and cash expenses (as well as a constant number of shares outstanding) in 2007, 2008, and 2009. In addition, both companies incur total depreciation of $15.00 per share during the three-year period and both use the same depreciation method for tax purposes. The two companies use different depreciation methods, however, for financial reporting. Company A spreads the depreciation expense evenly over the three years (straight-line depreciation, SLD). Because its revenues, expenses, and depreciation are constant over the period, Company A's EPS is also constant. In this example Company A's EPS is assumed to be $10 each year, as shown in Column 1 in Exhibit 14.

Company B is identical to Company A except that it uses accelerated depreciation. Company B's depreciation is 150 percent of SLD in 2007 and declines to 50 percent of SLD in 2009, as shown in Column 5.

	EXHIBIT 14		**Earnings Growth Rates and Cash Flow (All Amounts per Share)**			
	Company A			**Company B**		
Year	**Earnings (1)**	**Depreciation (2)**	**Cash Flow (3)**	**Earnings (4)**	**Depreciation (5)**	**Cash Flow (6)**
2007	$10.00	$ 5.00	$15.00	$ 7.50	$ 7.50	$15.00
2008	10.00	5.00	15.00	10.00	5.00	15.00
2009	10.00	5.00	15.00	12.50	2.50	15.00
Total		$15.00			$15.00	

Because of the different depreciation methods used by Company A and Company B for financial reporting purposes, Company A's EPS is flat at $10.00 (Column 1) whereas Company B's EPS (Column 4) shows 29 percent compound growth: $(\$12.50/\$7.50)^{1/2} - 1.00 = 0.29$. Thus, Company B appears to have positive earnings momentum. Analysts comparing Companies A and B might be misled by using the EPS numbers as reported instead of putting EPS on a comparable basis. For both companies, however, cash flow per share is level at $15.

Depreciation may be the simplest noncash charge to understand; write-offs and other noncash charges may offer more latitude for the management of earnings.

3.4.1 Determining Cash Flow

In practice, analysts and data vendors often use simple *approximations* of cash flow from operations in calculating cash flow for price to cash flow analysis. For many companies, depreciation and amortization are the major noncash charges regularly added to net income in the process of calculating cash flow from operations by the add-back method, so the approximation focuses on them. A representative approximation specifies cash flow per share as EPS plus per-share depreciation, amortization, and depletion.[52] We call this estimation the "earnings-plus-noncash-charges" definition and in this section, use the acronym CF for it. Keep in mind, however, that this definition is only one commonly used in calculating price to cash flow, not a technically accurate definition from an accounting perspective. We will also describe more technically accurate cash flow concepts: cash flow from operations, free cash flow to equity, and EBITDA (an estimate of pre-interest, pretax operating cash flow).[53]

Most frequently, trailing price to cash flows are reported. A trailing price to cash flow is calculated as the current market price divided by the sum of the most recent four quarters' cash flow per share. A fiscal-year definition is also possible, as in the case of EPS.

---

[52] This representation is the definition of cash flow in Value Line, for example: " the total of net income plus non-cash charges (depreciation, amortization, and depletion) minus preferred dividends (if any)." (This definition appears in the Value Line online glossary—current as of July 2008.) To obtain cash flow per share, total cash flow is divided by the number of shares outstanding. Note that *depletion* is an expense only for natural resource companies.

[53] Grant and Parker (2001) point out that EBITDA as a cash flow approximation assumes that changes in working capital accounts are immaterial. The EPS-plus-noncash-charges definition makes the same assumption (it is, essentially, earnings before depreciation and amortization).

Example 29 illustrates the calculation of P/CF with cash flow defined as earnings plus noncash charges.

EXAMPLE 29

Calculating Price to Cash Flow with Cash Flow Defined as Earnings plus Noncash Charges

In 2007, Koninklijke Philips Electronics N.V. (AEX: PHIA and NYSE: PHG) reported net income from continuing operations of €4,728 million, equal to EPS of €4.30. The company's depreciation and amortization was €1,083 million, or €0.99 per share. An AEX price for PHIA as of early March 2008 was €25.90. Calculate the P/CF for PHIA.

Solution: CF (defined as EPS plus per-share depreciation, amortization, and depletion) is €4.30 + €0.99 = €5.29 per share. Thus, P/CF = €25.90/€5.29 = 4.9.

Rather than use an approximate EPS-plus-noncash charges concept of cash flow, analysts can use cash flow from operations (CFO) in a price multiple. CFO is to be found in the statement of cash flows. Similar to the adjustments to normalize earning, adjustments to CFO for components not expected to persist into future time periods may also be appropriate. In addition, adjustments to CFO may be required when comparing companies that use different accounting standards. For example, under IFRS, companies can classify interest payments either as operating cash flows or as financing cash flows, but U.S. GAAP requires companies to classify interest payments as operating cash flows.

As an alternative to CF and CFO, the analyst can relate price to FCFE, the cash flow concept with the strongest link to valuation theory. Because the amounts of capital expenditures in proportion to CFO generally differ among companies being compared, the analyst may find that rankings by price to cash flow from operations (P/CFO) and by P/CF will differ from rankings by P/FCFE. Period-by-period FCFE may be more volatile than CFO (or CF), however, so a trailing P/FCFE is not necessarily more informative in a valuation. For example, consider two similar businesses with the same CFO and capital expenditures over a two-year period. If the first company times its capital expenditures to fall toward the beginning of the period and the second times its capital expenditures to fall toward the end of the period, the P/FCFEs for the two stocks may differ sharply without representing a meaningful economic difference.[54] This concern can be addressed, at least in part, by using price to average free cash flow, as in Hackel, Livnat, and Rai (1994).

Another cash flow concept used in multiples is EBITDA (earnings before interest, taxes, depreciation, and amortization).[55] To forecast EBITDA, analysts usually start with their projections of EBIT and simply add depreciation and amortization to arrive at an estimate for EBITDA. In calculating EBITDA from historical numbers, one can start with earnings from continuing operations,

---

[54] The analyst could, however, appropriately use the FCFE discounted cash flow model value, which incorporates all expected future free cash flows to equity.

[55] Another concept that has become popular is cash earnings, which has been defined in various ways, such as earnings plus amortization of intangibles or EBITDA minus net financial expenses.

excluding nonrecurring items. To that earnings number, interest, taxes, depreciation, and amortization are added.

In practice, both EV/EBITDA and P/EBITDA have been used by analysts as valuation metrics. EV/EBITDA has been the preferred metric, however, because its numerator includes the value of debt; therefore, it is the more appropriate method because EBITDA is pre-interest and is thus a flow to both debt and equity. EV/EBITDA is discussed in detail in a later section.

3.4.2 Valuation Based on Forecasted Fundamentals

The relationship between the justified price to cash flow and fundamentals follows from the familiar mathematics of the present value model. The justified price to cash flow, all else being equal, is inversely related to the stock's required rate of return and positively related to the growth rate(s) of expected future cash flows (however defined). We can find a justified price to cash flow based on fundamentals by finding the value of a stock using the most suitable DCF model and dividing that number by cash flow (based on our chosen definition of cash flow). Example 30 illustrates the process.

EXAMPLE 30

Justified Price to Cash Flow Based on Forecasted Fundamentals

As a technology analyst, you are working on the valuation of Western Digital (NYSE: WDC), a manufacturer of hard disk drives. As a first estimate of value, you are applying a FCFE model under the assumption of a stable long-term growth rate in FCFE:

$$V_0 = \frac{(1 + g)\,\text{FCFE}_0}{r - g}$$

where g is the expected growth rate of FCFE. You estimate trailing FCFE at \$1.34 per share and trailing CF (based on the earnings plus noncash charges definition) at \$5.43. Your other estimates are a 11.5 percent required rate of return and an 8.0 percent expected growth rate of FCFE.

1. What is the intrinsic value of WDC according to a constant-growth FCFE model?
2. What is the justified P/CF based on forecasted fundamentals?
3. What is the justified P/FCFE based on forecasted fundamentals?

Solution to 1: Calculate intrinsic value as $(1.080 \times \$1.34)/$ $(0.115 - 0.080) = \$41.35$.

Solution to 2: Calculate a justified P/CF based on forecasted fundamentals as $\$41.35/\$5.43 = 7.6$.

Solution to 3: The justified P/FCFE is $\$41.35/\$1.34 = 30.9$.

3.4.3 Valuation Based on Comparables

The method of comparables for valuing stocks based on price to cash flow follows the steps given previously and illustrated for P/E, P/B, and P/S. Example 31 is a simple exercise in the comparable method based on price to cash flow measures.

EXAMPLE 31

Price to Cash Flow and Comparables

Exhibit 15 provides information on P/CF, P/FCFE, and selected fundamentals as of 16 April 2008 for two hypothetical companies. Using the information in Exhibit 15, compare the valuations of the two companies.

EXHIBIT 15   Comparison of Two Companies (All Amounts per Share)

Company	Current Price (£)	Trailing CF per Share (£)	P/CF	Trailing FCFE per Share (£)	P/FCFE	Consensus Five-Year CF Growth Forecast (%)	Beta
Company A	17.98	1.84	9.8	0.29	62	13.4	1.50
Company B	15.65	1.37	11.4	−.99	NM	10.6	1.50

Company A is selling at a P/CF (9.8) approximately 14 percent smaller than the P/CF of Company B (11.4). Based on that comparison, we expect that, all else equal, investors would anticipate a higher growth rate for Company B. Contrary to that expectation, however, the consensus five-year earnings growth forecast for Company A is 280 basis points higher than it is for Company B. As of the date of the comparison, Company A appears to be relatively undervalued compared with Company B, as judged by P/CF and expected growth. The information in Exhibit 15 on FCFE supports the proposition that Company A may be relatively undervalued. The positive FCFE for Company A indicates that operating cash flows and new debt borrowing are more than sufficient to cover capital expenditures. Negative FCFE for Company B suggests the need for external funding of growth.

3.5 Price to Dividends and Dividend Yield

The total return on an equity investment has a capital appreciation component and a dividend yield component. Dividend yield data are frequently reported to provide investors with an estimate of the dividend yield component in total return. Dividend yield is also used as a valuation indicator. According to the 2007 *Merrill Lynch Institutional Factor Survey*, from 1989 to 2006, on average, slightly more than one-quarter of respondents reported using dividend yield as a factor in the investment process.

Analysts have offered the following rationales for using dividend yields in valuation:

▶ Dividend yield is a component of total return.

▶ Dividends are a less risky component of total return than capital appreciation.

Possible drawbacks of using dividend yields include the following:

▶ Dividend yield is only one component of total return; not using all information related to expected return is suboptimal.

▶ Investors may trade off future earnings growth to receive higher current dividends. That is, holding return on equity constant, dividends paid now displace earnings in all future periods (a concept known as the **dividend displacement of earnings**).[56]

▶ The argument about the relative safety of dividends presupposes that market prices reflect in a biased way differences in the relative risk of the components of return.

3.5.1 Calculation of Dividend Yield

This reading so far has presented multiples with market price (or market capitalization) in the numerator. P/Ds have sometimes appeared in valuation, particularly with respect to indices. Many stocks, however, do not pay dividends, and the P/D ratio is undefined with zero in the denominator. For such non-dividend-paying stocks, dividend yield *is* defined: It is equal to zero. For practical purposes, then, dividend yield is the preferred way to present this multiple.

Trailing dividend yield is generally calculated by using the dividend rate divided by the current market price per share. The annualized amount of the most recent dividend is known as the **dividend rate**. For companies paying quarterly dividends, the dividend rate is calculated as four times the most recent quarterly per-share dividend. (Some data sources use the dividends in the last four quarters as the dividend rate for purposes of a trailing dividend yield.) For companies that pay semiannual dividends comprising an interim dividend that typically differs in magnitude from the final dividend, the dividend rate is usually calculated as the most recent annual per-share dividend.

The dividend rate indicates the annual amount of dividends per share under the assumption of no increase or decrease over the year. The analyst's forecast of leading dividends could be higher or lower and is the basis of the leading dividend yield. The **leading dividend yield** is calculated as forecasted dividends per share over the next year divided by the current market price per share. Example 32 illustrates the calculation of dividend yield.

EXAMPLE 32

Calculating Dividend Yield

Exhibit 16 gives quarterly dividend data for Procter & Gamble (NYSE: PG) and semiannual dividend data for the ADRs of Unilever PLC (NYSE:UL).

---

[56] Arnott and Asness (2003) and Zhou and Ruland (2006), however, show that caution must be exercised in assuming that dividends displace future earnings in practice, because dividend payout may be correlated with future profitability.

	EXHIBIT 16	**Dividends Paid per Share for Procter & Gamble and for Unilever ADRs**	

Period	PG ($)	UL ADR ($)
3Q:2006	0.31	
4Q:2006	0.31	0.298
1Q:2007	0.31	
2Q:2007	0.35	0.636
Total	1.28	0.934
3Q:2007	0.35	
4Q:2007	0.35	0.352
1Q:2008	0.35	
2Q:2008	0.40	0.668
Total	1.45	1.020

Source: Value Line.

1. Given a price per share for PG of $62.86, calculate this company's trailing dividend yield.
2. Given a price per ADR for UL of $33.62, calculate the trailing dividend yield for the ADRs.

Solution to 1: The dividend rate for PG is $0.40 × 4 = $1.60. The dividend yield is $1.60/$62.86 = 0.0255 or 2.5 percent.

Solution to 2: Because UL pays semiannual dividends that differ in magnitude between the interim and final dividends, the dividend rate for UL's ADR is the total dividend in the most recent year, $1.020. The dividend yield is $1.020/$33.62 = 0.0303 or 3.0 percent.

3.5.2 Valuation Based on Forecasted Fundamentals

The relationship of dividend yield to fundamentals can be illustrated in the context of the Gordon growth model. From that model, we obtain the expression

$$\frac{D_0}{P_0} = \frac{r - g}{1 + g} \tag{7}$$

Equation 7 shows that dividend yield is negatively related to the expected rate of growth in dividends and positively related to the stock's required rate of return. The first point implies that the selection of stocks with relatively high dividend yields is consistent with an orientation to a value rather than growth investment style.

3.5.3 Valuation Based on Comparables

Using dividend yield with comparables is similar to the process that has been illustrated for other multiples. An analyst compares a company with its peers to determine whether it is attractively priced, considering its dividend yield and risk. The analyst should examine whether differences in expected growth explain the differences in dividend yield. Another consideration used by some investors is the security of the dividend (the probability that it will be reduced or eliminated). A useful metric in assessing the safety of the dividend is the payout ratio: A high payout relative to other companies operating in the same industry may indicate a less secure dividend because the dividend is less well covered by earnings. Balance sheet metrics are equally important in assessing the safety of the dividend, and relevant ratios to consider include the interest coverage ratio and the ratio of net debt to EBITDA. Example 33 illustrates use of the dividend yield in the method of comparables.

EXAMPLE 33

Dividend Yield Comparables

William Leiderman is a portfolio manager for a U.S. pension fund's domestic equity portfolio. The portfolio is exempt from taxes, so any differences in the taxation of dividends and capital gains are not relevant. Leiderman's client requires high current income. Leiderman is considering the purchase of utility stocks for the fund in July 2008. He has narrowed down his selection to four large-cap U.S. electric utilities. Exhibit 17 presents selected information on the stocks.

EXHIBIT 17	Using Dividend Yield to Compare Stocks			
Company	Consensus Growth Forecast (%)	Beta	Dividend Yield (%)	Payout Ratio (%)
Progress Energy (NYSE:PGN)	5.96	0.53	5.9	76
Pepco Holdings (NYSE: POM)	10.50	0.72	4.2	62
Portland General Electric Co. (NYSE:POR)	6.48	0.83	4.3	54
PPL Corp. (NYSE:PPL)	17.02	0.33	2.6	41

Source: Yahoo! Finance.

All of the securities exhibit similar low market risk; they each have a beta less than 1.00. Although PGN has the highest dividend yield, it also has the lowest expected growth rate. PGN's dividend payout ratio of 76 percent, the highest of the group, also suggests that its dividend may be subject to greater risk. Leiderman determines that PPL provides the greatest combination of dividend yield and expected growth—nearly 20 percent.

4   ENTERPRISE VALUE MULTIPLES

Enterprise value multiples are multiples that relate the enterprise value of a company to some measure of value (typically, a pre-interest income measure). Perhaps the most frequently advanced argument for using enterprise value multiples rather than price multiples in valuation is that enterprise value multiples are relatively less sensitive to the effects of financial leverage than price multiples when one is comparing companies that use differing amounts of leverage. Enterprise value multiples, in defining the numerator as they do, take a control perspective (discussed in more detail later). Thus, even where leverage differences are not an issue, enterprise value multiples may complement the perspective of price multiples. Indeed, although some analysts strictly favor one type of multiple, other analysts report both price and enterprise value multiples.

4.1 Enterprise Value to EBITDA

Enterprise value to EBITDA is by far the most widely used enterprise value multiple.

Earlier, EBITDA was introduced as an estimate of pre-interest, pretax operating cash flow. Because EBITDA is a flow to both debt and equity, as noted, defining an EBITDA multiple by using a measure of total company value in the numerator, such as EV, is appropriate. Recall that **enterprise value** is total company value (the market value of debt, common equity, and preferred equity) minus the value of cash and short-term investments. Thus, EV/EBITDA is a valuation indicator for the overall company rather than solely its common stock. If, however, the analyst can assume that the business's debt and preferred stock (if any) are efficiently priced, the analyst can use EV/EBITDA to draw an inference about the valuation of common equity. Such an inference is often reasonable.

Analysts have offered the following rationales for using EV/EBITDA:

▶ EV/EBITDA is usually more appropriate than P/E alone for comparing companies with different financial leverage (debt), because EBITDA is a pre-interest earnings figure, in contrast to EPS, which is postinterest.

▶ By adding back depreciation and amortization, EBITDA controls for differences in depreciation and amortization among businesses, in contrast to net income, which is postdepreciation and postamortization. For this reason, EV/EBITDA is frequently used in the valuation of capital-intensive businesses (for example, cable companies and steel companies). Such businesses typically have substantial depreciation and amortization expenses.

▶ EBITDA is frequently positive when EPS is negative.

Possible drawbacks to using EV/EBITDA include the following:[57]

▶ EBITDA will overestimate cash flow from operations if working capital is growing. EBITDA also ignores the effects of differences in revenue recognition policy on cash flow from operations.

▶ Free cash flow to the firm (FCFF), which directly reflects the amount of the company's required capital expenditures, has a stronger link to valuation theory than does EBITDA. Only if depreciation expenses match capital expenditures do we expect EBITDA to reflect differences in businesses' capital programs. This qualification to EBITDA comparisons may be particularly meaningful for the capital-intensive businesses to which EV/EBITDA is often applied.

4.1.1 Determining Enterprise Value

We illustrated the calculation of EBITDA previously. As discussed, analysts commonly define enterprise value as follows:

Market value of common equity	(Number of shares outstanding × Price per share)
Plus:	Market value of preferred stock (if any)[58]
Plus:	Market value of debt
Less:	Cash and investments (specifically: cash, cash equivalents, and short-term investments)[59]
Equals:	Enterprise value

Cash and investments (sometimes termed **nonearning assets**) are subtracted because EV is designed to measure the net price an acquirer would pay for the company as a whole. The acquirer must buy out current equity and debt providers but then receives access to the cash and investments, which lower the net cost of the acquisition. (For example, cash and investments can be used to pay off debt or loans used to finance the purchase.) The same logic explains the use of market values: In repurchasing debt, an acquirer has to pay market prices. Some debt, however, may be private and it does not trade; some debt may be publicly traded but trade infrequently. When analysts do not have market values, they often use book values obtained from the balance sheet.[60] Example 34 illustrates the calculation of EV/EBITDA.

---

[57] See Moody's Investors Service (2000) and Grant and Parker (2001) for additional issues and concerns.

[58] Minority interest, if any, usually should be added back unless it is already included elsewhere. **Minority interest** appears in the consolidated financial statements of a parent company that owns more than 50 percent but not 100 percent of a subsidiary; minority interest refers to that portion of equity in the subsidiary that is not owned by the parent.

[59] Some analysts attempt to distinguish between cash and investments that are or are not needed in the operations of the company, subtracting only the nonoperating part in this calculation. However, making such a distinction is not always practical.

[60] However, using so-called matrix price estimates of debt market values in such cases, where they are available, may be more accurate. Matrix price estimates are based on characteristics of the debt issue and information on how the marketplace prices those characteristics.

EXAMPLE 34

Calculating EV/EBITDA

Western Digital Corporation (NYSE: WDC) manufactures hard disk drives. Exhibit 18 presents the company's consolidated balance sheet as of 28 March 2008.

EXHIBIT 18	Western Digital Corporation Condensed Consolidated Balance Sheets (in Millions except Par Values; Unaudited)

ASSETS

Current assets:

Cash and cash equivalents	$ 917
Short-term investments	32
Accounts receivable, net	1,014
Inventories	455
Advances to suppliers	36
Other current assets	175
Total current assets	2,629
Property and equipment, net	1,529
Goodwill and other intangible assets, net	187
Other noncurrent assets	198
Total assets	$4,543

LIABILITIES AND SHAREHOLDERS' EQUITY

Current liabilities:

Accounts payable	$1,144
Customer advances	28
Accrued expenses	226
Accrued warranty	85
Current portion of long-term debt	11
Total current liabilities	1,494
Long-term debt	503
Other liabilities	129
Total liabilities	2,126

Commitments and contingencies (Note 6)

Shareholders' equity:

Preferred stock, $0.01 par value; authorized—5 shares; outstanding—none	—
Common stock, $0.01 par value; authorized —450 shares; outstanding—225 shares	2

(Exhibit continued on next page . . .)

EXHIBIT 18	(continued)	
Additional paid-in capital		821
Accumulated comprehensive income (loss)		43
Retained earnings		1,609
Treasury stock—common shares at cost		(58)
Total shareholders' equity		2,417
Total liabilities and shareholders' equity		$4,543

The balance sheet is labeled as unaudited because it is a quarterly balance sheet and U.S. companies are required to have audits only for their annual financial statements.

The income statement and statement of cash flows for the year ended 29 June 2007 and for the nine months ended 28 March 2008 and 30 March 2007 gave the following items (in millions):

Item	Source	Year Ended 29 June 2007	Nine Months Ended 28 March 2008	Nine Months Ended 30 March 2007
Net income	Income statement	$564	$654	$352
Interest	Income statement	4	44	3
Taxes	Income statement	121	90	4
Depreciation and amortization	Statement of cash flows	210	300	149

The company's share price as of 11 July 2008 was $33.06. Based on the above information, calculate EV/EBITDA.

Solution:

► For EV, we first calculate the total value of WDC's equity: 225 million shares outstanding times $33.06 price per share equals $7,439 million market capitalization.

WDC has only one class of common stock, no preferred shares, and no minority interest. For companies that have multiple classes of common stock, market capitalization includes the total value of all classes of common stock. Similarly, for companies that have preferred stock and/or minority interest, the market value of preferred stock and the amount of minority interest are added to market capitalization.

EV also includes the value of long-term debt. Per WDC's balance sheet, the amount of long-term debt is $514 million ($503 million plus the current portion of $11 million). Typically, the book value of long-term debt is used in EV. If, however, the market value of the debt is readily available and materially different from the book value, the market value should be used.

EV excludes cash, cash equivalents, and short-term investments. Per WDC's balance sheet, the total of cash equivalents and short-term investments is $917 million + $32 million = $949 million.

So, WDC's EV is $7,439 million + $514 million − $949 million = $7,004 million.

► For EBITDA, we first calculate the trailing 12 month (TTM) information using the first nine months of the current fiscal year plus the last three months of the prior fiscal year. For example, the TTM net income equals $654 million from the first nine months ending 28 March 2008 plus $212 million from the last three months of the previous fiscal year ($564 million minus $352 million.) EBITDA is calculated as net income plus interest plus taxes plus depreciation and amortization. The TTM EBITDA totals $1,479 million. These calculations are summarized as follows:

EBITDA Component	Year Ended 29 June 2007	9 Months Ended 28 March 2008	9 Months Ended 30 March 2007	Total (TTM)
Net income	$564	$ 654	$352	$ 866
Interest	4	44	3	45
Taxes	121	90	4	207
Depreciation and amortization	210	300	149	361
EBITDA	$899	$1,088	$508	$1,479

WDC does not have preferred equity. Companies that do have preferred equity typically present in their financial statements net income available to common shareholders. In those cases, the EBITDA calculation uses net income available to *both* preferred and common equityholders.

We conclude that EV/EBITDA = ($7,004 million)/($1,479 million) = 4.7.

4.1.2 Valuation Based on Forecasted Fundamentals

As with other multiples, intuition about the fundamental drivers of enterprise value to EBITDA can help when applying the method of comparables. All else being equal, the justified EV/EBITDA based on fundamentals should be positively related to the expected growth rate in free cash flow to the firm, positively related to expected profitability as measured by return on invested capital, and negatively related to the business's weighted average cost of capital. **Return on**

invested capital (ROIC) is calculated as operating profit after tax divided by total invested capital. In analyzing ratios such as EV/EBITDA, ROIC is the relevant measure of profitability because EBITDA flows to all providers of capital.

4.1.3 *Valuation Based on Comparables*

All else equal, a lower EV/EBITDA value relative to peers indicates that a company is relatively undervalued. An analyst's recommendations, however, are usually not completely determined by relative EV/EBITDA; from an analyst's perspective, EV/EBITDA is simply one piece of information to consider.

Example 35 presents a comparison of enterprise value multiples for four peer companies. The example includes a measure of total firm value, **total invested capital** (TIC), sometimes also known as the **market value of invested capital**, that is an alternative to enterprise value. Similar to EV, TIC includes the market value of equity and debt, but does not deduct cash and investments.

EXAMPLE 35

Comparable Enterprise Value Multiples

Exhibit 19 presents EV multiples for four companies in the data storage device industry: Western Digital Corporation (NYSE: WDC), NetApp (NASDAQGS: NTAP), EMC Corporation (NYSE: EMC), and Seagate Technology (NYSE: STX).

EXHIBIT 19   **Enterprise Value Multiples for Industry Peers**

Measure	WDC	NTAP	EMC	STX
Price	$ 33.06	$ 21.94	$ 12.73	$ 17.00
Times: shares outstanding (millions)	225	329.9	2,070	484.7
Equals: equity market cap	7,439	7,238	26,351	8,240
Plus: Debt (most recent quarter)	514	173	3,450	2,030
Plus: Preferred stock	—	—	—	—
Equals: Total Invested Capital (TIC)	7,953	7,411	29,801	10,270
Less: cash	949	1,160	5,610	1,280
Equals: Enterprise Value (EV)	$7,004	$6,251	$24,191	$8,990
EBITDA (TTM)	$1,479	$ 458	$ 2,790	$2,350
TIC/EBITDA	5.4	16.2	10.7	4.4
EV/EBITDA	4.7	13.6	8.7	3.8
Debt/Equity	21.3%	10.2%	27.9%	43.5%
ROIC (TTM)	6.90%	2.50%	3.73%	8.65%
Quarterly revenue growth (year over year)	49.7%	17.0%	16.6%	9.8%

Sources: Companies' annual reports; Yahoo! Finance; calculations.

1. Exhibit 19 provides two alternative enterprise value multiples, TIC/EBITDA and EV/EBITDA. The ranking of the companies' multiples is identical by both multiples. In general, what could cause the rankings to vary?

2. Each EBITDA multiple incorporates a comparison with enterprise value. How do these multiples differ from price to cash flow multiples?

3. Based solely on the information in Exhibit 19, how does the valuation of WDC compare with that of the other three companies?

Solution to 1: The difference between TIC and EV is that EV excludes cash, cash equivalents, and marketable securities. So, a material variation among companies in cash, cash equivalents, or marketable securities relative to EBITDA could cause the rankings to vary.

Solution to 2: These multiples differ from price to cash flow multiples in that the numerator is a measure of firm value rather than share price, to match the denominator which is a pre-interest measure of earnings. These multiples thus provide a more appropriate comparison than price to cash flow when companies have significantly different capital structures.

Solution to 3: Based on its lower TIC/EBITDA and EV/EBITDA multiples of 5.4 and 4.7, respectively, WDC appears undervalued relative to NTAP and EMC. In addition, WDC has a higher ROIC and higher revenue growth than NTAP and EMC, which supports the appearance of undervaluation relative to these two companies. Compared with STX, the enterprise value multiples of WDC are slightly higher despite it being somewhat less profitable than STX (ROIC of 6.90 percent versus 8.65 percent). However, WDC's lower leverage (a debt-to-equity ratio of 21.3 percent versus 43.5 percent) and faster growth rate (49.7 percent versus 9.8 percent) suggest that WDC's higher enterprise value multiple is justified. The comparison between WDC and STX is inconclusive.

4.2 Other Enterprise Value Multiples

Although EV/EBITDA is the most widely known and used enterprise value multiple, other enterprise value multiples are used together with or in place of EV/EBITDA—either in a broad range of applications or for valuations in a specific industry. EV/FCFF is an example of a broadly used multiple; an example of a special-purpose multiple is EV/EBITDAR (where R stands for rent expense), which is favored by airline industry analysts. This section reviews the most common such multiples (except EV/sales, which is covered in the next section). In each case, a valuation metric could be formulated in terms of TIC rather than EV.

Major alternatives to using EBITDA in the denominator of enterprise value multiples include FCFF (free cash flow to the firm), EBITA (earnings before interest, taxes, and amortization), and EBIT (earnings before interest and taxes). Exhibit 20 summarizes the components of each of these measurements and how they relate to net income. Note that, in practice, analysts typically forecast EBITDA by forecasting EBIT and adding depreciation and amortization.

EXHIBIT 20	Alternative Denominators in Enterprise Value Multiples

		plus	minus			less	less
Free Cash Flow to the Firm =	Net Income	Interest Expense	Tax Savings on Interest	plus Depreciation	plus Amortization	Investment in Working Capital	Investment in Fixed Capital
EBITDA =	Net Income	plus Interest Expense	plus Taxes	plus Depreciation	plus Amortization		
EBITA =	Net Income	plus Interest Expense	plus Taxes		plus Amortization		
EBIT =	Net Income	plus Interest Expense	plus Taxes				

Note that the calculation of all the measures given in Exhibit 20 add interest back to net income, which reflects that these measures are flows relevant to all providers of both debt and equity capital. As one moves down the rows of Exhibit 20, the measures incorporate increasingly less precise information about a company's tax position and its capital investments, although each measure has a rationale. For example, EBITA may be chosen in cases in which amortization (associated with intangibles) but not depreciation (associated with tangibles) is a major expense for companies being compared. EBIT may be chosen where neither depreciation nor amortization is a major item.

In addition to enterprise value multiples based on financial measures, in some industries or sectors, the analyst may find it appropriate to examine enterprise value multiples based on a nonfinancial measurement that is specific to that industry or sector. For example, for satellite and cable TV broadcasters, an analyst might usefully examine EV to subscribers. For a resource-based company, a multiple based on reserves of the resource may be appropriate.

Regardless of the specific denominator used in an enterprise value multiple, the concept remains the same—namely, to relate the market value of the total company to some fundamental financial or nonfinancial measure of the company's value.

4.3 Enterprise Value to Sales

Enterprise value to sales is a major alternative to the price-to-sales ratio. The P/S multiple has the conceptual weakness that it fails to recognize that for a debt-financed company, not all sales belong to a company's equity investors. Some of the proceeds from the company's sales will be used to pay interest and principal to the providers of the company's debt capital. For example, a P/S for a company with little or no debt would not be comparable to a P/S for a company that is largely financed with debt. EV/S would be the basis for a valid comparison in such a case. In summary, EV/S is an alternative sales-based ratio that is particularly useful when comparing companies with diverse capital structures. Example 36 illustrates the calculation of EV/S multiples.

EXAMPLE 36

Calculating Enterprise Value to Sales

As described in Example 22, Stora Enso Oyj (Helsinki Stock Exchange: STEAV) reported net sales of €13,373.6 million for 2007. Based on 788,619,987 shares outstanding and a stock price of €8.87 on 12 February 2008, the total market value of the company's equity was €6,995.1 million. The company reported debt of €4,441.5 million, minority interest of €71.9 million, and cash of €970.7 million. Assume that the market value of the company's debt is equal to the amount reported. Calculate the company's EV/S.

Solution: Enterprise value = €6,995.1 million + €4,441.5 million + €71.9 million − €970.7 million = €10,537.8 million. So, EV/S = €10,537.8 million/€13,373.6 million = 0.79.

4.4 Price and Enterprise Value Multiples in a Comparable Analysis: Some Illustrative Data

In previous sections, we explained the major price and enterprise value multiples. Analysts using multiples and a benchmark based on closely similar companies should be aware of the range of values for multiples for peer companies and should track the fundamentals that may explain differences. For the sake of illustration Exhibit 21 shows, for fiscal year 2007, the median value of various multiples by GICS economic sector, the median dividend payout ratio, and median values of selected fundamentals:

▶ ROE and its determinants (net profit margin, asset turnover, and financial leverage).

▶ The compound average growth rate in operating margin for the three years ending with FY 2007 (shown in the last column under "3-Year CAGR Op Margin").

Exhibit 21 is based on the Standard & Poor's Super 1500 Composite Index for U.S. equities consisting of the S&P 500, the S&P Midcap 400 Index, and the S&P SmallCap 600 Index. GICS was previously described in Section 3.1.5.

At the level of aggregation shown in Exhibit 21, the data are, arguably, most relevant to relative sector valuation. For the purposes of valuing individual companies, analysts would most likely use more narrowly defined industry or sector classification.

5   INTERNATIONAL CONSIDERATIONS WHEN USING MULTIPLES

Clearly, to perform a relative-value analysis, an analyst must use comparable companies and underlying financial data prepared by applying comparable methods. Therefore, using relative-valuation methods in an international setting is difficult. Comparing companies across borders frequently involves differences in

EXHIBIT 21 Fundamental and Valuation Statistics by GICS Economic Sector: Median Values from S&P 1500, FY2007

GICS Sector (count)	Valuation Statistics							Fundamental Statistics						
	Trailing P/E	P/B	P/S	P/CF	Dividend Yield (%)	EV/ EBITDA	EV/S	Net Profit Margin (%)	Asset Turnover	Financial Leverage	ROE (%)	Dividend Payout Ratio (%)	3-Year CAGR Operating Margin (%)
Energy (85)	14.406	2.531	2.186	8.622	0.4	7.733	2.64	13.942	0.573	2.103	19.688	4.024	12.035
Materials (85)	15.343	2.254	0.888	9.588	1.4	7.686	1.095	5.568	0.995	2.465	15.728	17.874	4.157
Industrials (207)	17.275	2.578	1.045	11.642	1.0	8.979	1.209	6.089	1.139	2.143	15.262	16.066	5.337
Consumer Discretionary (279)	15.417	2.254	0.789	9.986	0.7	7.634	0.928	4.777	1.383	2.12	13.289	0	−2.682
Consumer Staples (80)	19.522	3.048	1.122	13.379	1.4	10.66	1.237	5.306	1.351	2.208	17.264	23.133	−0.88
Health Care (167)	23.027	3.088	2.061	15.762	0	11.623	2.274	6.637	0.83	1.854	12.399	0	−1.708
Financials (257)	14.648	1.559	1.888	11.186	3.1	9.482	4.017	13.113	0.113	5.848	10.348	41.691	−4.124
Information Technology (252)	20.205	2.444	2.162	45.073	0	11.594	1.811	7.929	0.743	1.587	10.444	0	1.254
Telecommuni- cation Services (13)	19.585	2.485	1.527	5.266	0.8	6.681	2.345	7.109	0.471	2.367	5.43	6.862	−2.421
Utilities (75)	16.682	1.784	1.151	8.405	3.1	9.056	1.903	7.21	0.439	3.52	11.853	52.738	0.361
Overall (1,500)	17.148	2.246	1.398	11.328	0.8	9.108	1.626	7.318	0.839	2.227	12.701	8.051	0.181

Source: Standard & Poor's Research Insight.

accounting methods, cultural differences, economic differences, and resulting differences in risk and growth opportunities. P/Es for individual companies in the same industry but in different countries have been found to vary widely.[61] Furthermore, P/Es of different national markets often vary substantially at any single point in time.

Although international accounting standards are converging, significant differences still exist across borders, sometimes making comparisons difficult. Even when harmonization of accounting principles is achieved, the need to adjust accounting data for comparability will remain. As we showed in earlier sections, even within a single country's accounting standards, differences between companies result from accounting choices (e.g., FIFO versus LIFO). Prior to 2008, the U.S. SEC required non-U.S. companies whose securities trade in U.S. markets to provide a reconciliation between their earnings from home-country accounting principles to U.S. GAAP. This requirement not only assisted the analyst in making necessary adjustments but also provided some insight into appropriate adjustments for other companies not required to provide this data. In December 2007, however, the SEC eliminated the reconciliation requirement for non-U.S. companies that use IFRS. Research analyzing reconciliations by EU companies with U.S. listings shows that most of those companies reported net income under IFRS that was higher than they would have reported under U.S. GAAP and lower shareholders' equity than they would have under U.S. GAAP, with a result that more of the sample companies reported higher ROE under IFRS than under U.S. GAAP (Henry, Lin, and Yang 2008).

Exhibit 22 presents a reconciliation from IFRS to U.S. GAAP for Nokia Corporation (NYSE: NOK).

In a study of companies filing such reconciliations to U.S. GAAP, Harris and Muller (1999) classified common differences into seven categories, as shown in Exhibit 23.

EXHIBIT 22	Principal Differences between IFRS and U.S. GAAP for Nokia Corporation (Years Ended 31 December; Euros in Millions)		
Measure		**2006**	**2005**
Profit attributable to equityholders of the parent reported under IFRS		€ 4,306	€ 3,616
U.S. GAAP adjustments:			
Pensions		(1)	(3)
Development costs		(55)	10
Share-based compensation expense		(8)	(39)
Cash flow hedges		—	(12)
Other differences		22	(1)
Deferred tax effect of U.S. GAAP adjustments		11	11
Net income under U.S. GAAP		€ 4,275	€ 3,582
Total equity reported under IFRS		€12,060	€12,514
Less minority interests		(92)	(205)

(Exhibit continued on next page . . .)

---

[61] Copeland, Koller, and Murrin (1994, p. 375) provide an interesting example.

EXHIBIT 22	(continued)	

Measure	2006	2005
Capital and reserves attributable to equityholders of the parent under IFRS	€11,968	€12,309
U.S. GAAP adjustments:		
Pensions	(276)	(65)
Development costs	(102)	(47)
Share issue premium	143	135
Share-based compensation	(143)	(135)
Amortization of identifiable intangible assets acquired	(62)	(62)
Impairment of identifiable intangible assets acquired	(47)	(47)
Amortization of goodwill	432	432
Impairment of goodwill	255	255
Translation of goodwill	(231)	(242)
Other differences	29	6
Deferred tax effect of U.S. GAAP adjustments	146	83
Total shareholders' equity under U.S. GAAP	€12,112	€12,622

Source: Nokia Corporation Annual Report in SEC Form 20-F, 2006.

EXHIBIT 23	Reconciliation of IFRS to U.S. GAAP: Average Adjustment

Category	Earnings	Equity
Differences in the treatment of goodwill	Minus	Plus
Deferred income taxes	Plus	Plus
Foreign exchange adjustments	Plus	Minus
Research and development costs	Minus	Minus
Pension expense	Minus	Plus
Tangible asset revaluations	Plus	Minus
Other	Minus	Minus

The list in Exhibit 23 provides the analyst with some insight into areas where differences commonly arise. Although the *average* adjustments are presented here, however, adjustments for individual companies may vary considerably.

International accounting differences affect the comparability of all price multiples. Of the price multiples examined in this reading, P/CFO and P/FCFE will generally be least affected by accounting differences. P/B, P/E, and multiples based on such concepts as EBITDA, which start from accounting earnings, will generally be the most affected.

6

MOMENTUM VALUATION INDICATORS

The valuation indicators we call momentum indicators relate either price or a fundamental, such as earnings, to the time series of their own past values or, in some cases, to the fundamental's expected value. One style of growth investing uses positive momentum in various senses as a selection criterion, and practitioners sometimes refer to such strategies as "growth/momentum investment strategies." Momentum indicators based on price, such as the relative-strength indicator we will discuss here, have also been referred to as **technical indicators**. According to the *Merrill Lynch Institutional Factor Survey*, momentum indicators were among the most popular valuation indicators in use between 1989 and 2006.[62] In this section, we review three representative momentum indicators: earnings surprise, standardized unexpected earnings, and relative strength.

To define standardized unexpected earnings, we define **unexpected earnings** (also called **earnings surprise**) as the difference between reported earnings and expected earnings:

$$UE_t = \text{EPS}_t - E(\text{EPS}_t)$$

where UE_t is the unexpected earnings for quarter t, EPS_t is the reported EPS for quarter t, and $E(\text{EPS}_t)$ is the expected EPS for the quarter.

For example, a stock with reported quarterly earnings of \$1.05 and expected earnings of \$1.00 would have a positive earnings surprise of \$0.05. Often, the percent earnings surprise (i.e., earnings surprise divided by expected EPS) is reported by data providers; in this example, the percent earning surprise would be \$0.05/\$1.00 = 0.05 or 5 percent. When used directly as a valuation indicator, earnings surprise is generally scaled by a measure reflecting the variability or range in analysts' EPS estimates. The principle is that the less disagreement among analysts' forecasts, the more meaningful the EPS forecast error of a given size in relation to the mean. A way to accomplish such scaling is to divide unexpected earnings by the standard deviation of analysts' earnings forecasts, which we refer to as the **scaled earnings surprise**. Example 37 illustrates the calculation of such a scaled earnings surprise.

EXAMPLE 37

Calculating Scaled Earnings Surprise by Using Analysts' Forecasts

As of July 2008, the mean consensus earnings forecast for Koninklijke Philips Electronics (AEX: PHIA; NYSE: PHG) for the fiscal year ending December 2008 was €1.53. Of the 35 estimates, the low forecast was €1.02, the high forecast was €2.40, and the standard deviation was €0.28.

If actual reported earnings for 2008 come in equal to the high forecast, what would be the measure of the earnings surprise for Koninklijke Philips scaled to reflect the dispersion in analysts' forecasts?

Solution: In this case, scaled earnings surprise would be (€2.40 − €1.53)/€0.28 = 3.11.

---

[62] During the period 1989 to 2005, the percentages of respondents who indicated that they used earnings surprise (surprise relative to consensus forecasts), earnings momentum (defined as TTM EPS divided by year-ago TTM EPS), and relative strength (defined as the difference between 3-month and 12-month price performance) were, respectively, 49 percent, 43 percent, and 38 percent. In 2006, the percentage of respondents using the measures was approximately 40 percent for each.

The rationale behind using earnings surprise is the thesis that positive surprises may be associated with persistent positive abnormal returns, or alpha. The same rationale lies behind a momentum indicator that is closely related to earnings surprise but more highly researched, namely, **standardized unexpected earnings** (SUE). The SUE measure is defined as

$$SUE_t = \frac{EPS_t - E(EPS_t)}{\sigma[EPS_t - E(EPS_t)]}$$

where

EPS_t	= actual EPS for time t
$E(EPS_t)$	= expected EPS for time t
$\sigma[EPS_t - E(EPS_t)]$	= standard deviation of $[EPS_t - E(EPS_t)]$ over some historical time period

In words, the numerator is the unexpected earnings at time t and the denominator is the standard deviation of past unexpected earnings over some period prior to time t—for example, the 20 quarters prior to t as in Latané and Jones (1979), the article that introduced the SUE concept.[63] In SUE, the magnitude of unexpected earnings is scaled by a measure of the size of historical forecast errors or surprises. The principle is that the smaller (larger) the historical size of forecast errors, the more (less) meaningful a given size of EPS forecast error.

Suppose that for a stock with a $0.05 earnings surprise, the standard deviation of past surprises is $0.20. The $0.05 surprise is relatively small compared with past forecast errors, which would be reflected in a SUE score of $0.05/$0.20 = 0.25. If the standard error of past surprises were smaller—say, $0.07—the SUE score would be $0.05/$0.07 = 0.71. Example 38 applies analysis of SUE to two electronics companies.

EXAMPLE 38

Unexpected Earnings

Exhibits 24 and 25 provide information about the earnings surprise history for two companies: Sony Corporation (Tokyo: 6758; NYSE: SNE) and Koninklijke Philips Electronics (AEX: PHIA; NYSE: PHG).

EXHIBIT 24   **Earnings Surprise History for Sony (in Japanese Yen)**

Quarter Ending	EPS Release Date	Mean Consensus EPS Forecast	Actual EPS	% Surprise	Std. Dev.	SUE Score
Mar 2008	14 May 2008	−6.300	28.950	−559.524	8.341	4.225
Dec 2007	1 Feb 2008	182.433	199.600	9.410	49.912	0.344
Sep 2007	26 Oct 2007	73.633	73.500	−0.181	4.629	−0.029
Jun 2007	27 Jul 2007	34.200	66.290	93.830	7.495	4.282

---

[63] For a summary of the research on SUE, see Reilly and Brown (2006) or Brown (1997).

EXHIBIT 25		Earnings Surprise History for Koninklijke Philips				
Quarter Ending	EPS Release Date	Mean Consensus EPS Forecast	Actual EPS	% Surprise	Std. Dev.	SUE Score
Mar 2008	14 Apr 2008	0.317	0.221	−30.284	0.089	−1.079
Dec 2007	21 Jan 2008	0.588	0.688	17.007	0.126	0.794
Sep 2007	15 Oct 2007	0.322	0.308	−4.348	0.057	−0.246
Jun 2007	17 Jul 2007	0.333	0.324	−2.703	0.059	−0.153

Source: Thomson Surprise Report.

1. Explain how Sony's SUE score of 4.225 for the quarter ending March 2008 is calculated.

2. Based on these exhibits, for which company were the consensus forecasts less accurate over the past four quarters?

3. Interpret the amount of Sony's "% Surprise" for the quarter ending March 2008 and explain why the sign of "% Surprise" differs from the sign of "SUE Score."

Solution to 1: The amount of Sony's unexpected earnings (i.e., its earnings surprise) for the quarter ending March 2008 was ¥28.950 − (−¥6.300) = ¥35.250. Dividing by the standard deviation of ¥8.344 gives a SUE score of 4.225.

Solution to 2: Over the past four quarters, the consensus forecasts were much less accurate for Sony than for Koninklijke Philips. The largest earnings surprise for Koninklijke Philips was for the quarter ending March 2008, in which the company's actual EPS was 30.3 percent lower than the consensus forecast and the SUE score was −1.079. For Sony, the company's actual earnings for the quarter ending June 2007 were almost twice as high as the consensus forecast (percent surprise of 93.8 percent) and the SUE score was 4.282. For the quarter ending March 2008, Sony's SUE score was 4.225.

Solution to 3: For the quarter ending March 2008, Sony reported earnings whereas the consensus forecast had been for a loss. Thus, the earnings surprise was positive; the company had much better results than anticipated, earning ¥35.250 more than the consensus forecast. The percent surprise is a negative number, however, because it shows the surprise as a percentage of the forecast (i.e., ¥35.250 divided by −¥6.300).

Another set of indicators, **relative-strength** indicators, compares a stock's performance during a particular period either with its own past performance or with the performance of some group of stocks. The simplest relative-strength indicator that compares a stock's performance during a period with its past performance is the stock's compound rate of return over some specified time horizon, such as six months or one year. This indicator has also been referred to as **price momentum** in the academic literature. Despite its simplicity, this measure has been used in numerous studies.[64] The rationale behind its use is the thesis

---

[64] Chan, Jegadeesh, and Lakonishok (1999) and Lee and Swaminathan (2000).

that patterns of persistence or reversal exist in stock returns that may be shown empirically to depend on the investor's time horizon (Lee and Swaminathan 2000).

Other definitions of relative strength relate a stock's return over a recent period to its return over a longer period that includes the more recent period. For example, a classic study of technical momentum indicators (Brock, Lakonishok, and LeBaron 1992) examined trading strategies based on two technical rules—namely, a moving-average oscillator and a trading-range break (i.e., resistance and support levels)—in which buy and sell signals are determined by the relationship between a short period's moving average and a longer period's moving average (and bands around those averages). The reader should keep in mind that research on patterns of historical stock returns is notoriously vulnerable to data snooping and hindsight biases. Furthermore, investing strategies based purely on technical momentum indicators are viewed as inherently self-destructing, in that "once a useful technical rule (or price pattern) is discovered, it ought to be invalidated when the mass of traders attempts to exploit it" (Bodie, Kane, and Marcus 2005, p. 377). Yet, the possibility of discovering a profitable trading rule and exploiting it prior to mass use continues to motivate research.

A simple relative-strength indicator of the second type (i.e., the stock's performance relative to the performance of some group of stocks) is the stock's performance divided by the performance of an equity index. If the value of this ratio increases, the stock price increases relative to the index and displays positive relative strength. Often, the relative-strength indicator is scaled to 1.0 at the beginning of the study period. If the stock goes up at a higher (lower) rate than the index, then relative strength will be above (below) 1.0. Relative strength in this sense is often calculated for industries and individual stocks. Example 39 explores this indicator.

EXAMPLE 39

Relative Strength in Relation to an Equity Index

Exhibit 26 shows the values of the S&P 500 and three exchange-traded funds (ETFs) for the end of each of 18 months from February 2007 through July 2008. The ETFs are for gold, the U.S. financial services sector, and U.S. utilities. SPDR stands for Standard & Poor's Depositary Receipt, which is the ETF representing the S&P 500 Index.

EXHIBIT 26	NYSE Indices		
Date	S&P 500 Index	SPDR Gold Shares (GLD)	Financial Select Sector SPDR (XLF)	Utilities Select Sector SPDR (XLU)
1 Feb 2007	1,406.82	66.48	34.48	36.96
1 Mar 2007	1,420.86	65.74	34.28	38.29
2 Apr 2007	1,482.37	67.09	35.60	40.17
1 May 2007	1,530.62	65.54	36.46	40.36
1 Jun 2007	1,503.35	64.27	35.00	38.44

(Exhibit continued on next page . . .)

Date	S&P 500 Index	SPDR Gold Shares (GLD)	Financial Select Sector SPDR (XLF)	Utilities Select Sector SPDR (XLU)
2 Jul 2007	1,455.27	65.79	31.82	36.91
1 Aug 2007	1,473.99	66.52	32.65	37.49
4 Sep 2007	1,526.75	73.51	33.44	38.93
1 Oct 2007	1,549.38	78.62	32.87	41.52
1 Nov 2007	1,481.14	77.32	30.21	41.79
3 Dec 2007	1,468.36	82.46	28.45	41.72
2 Jan 2008	1,378.55	91.40	28.65	38.65
1 Feb 2008	1,330.63	96.18	25.40	37.07
3 Mar 2008	1,322.70	90.41	24.65	37.66
1 Apr 2008	1,385.59	86.65	26.38	39.59
1 May 2008	1,400.38	87.45	24.54	41.01
2 Jun 2008	1,280.00	91.40	20.26	40.70
1 Jul 2008	1,239.49	95.16	18.68	40.46

EXHIBIT 26   (continued)

To produce the information for Exhibit 27, we divided each ETF value by the S&P 500 value for the same month and then scaled those results so that the value of the relative-strength indicator (RSTR) for February 2007 would equal 1.0. To illustrate, on 1 February 2007, the value of GLD divided by the S&P 500 was 66.48/1,406.82 = 0.0473. The RSTR for GLD on that date, by design, is then 0.0473/0.0473 = 1.0. In March, the value of GLD divided by the S&P 500 was 65.74/1,420.86 = 0.0463, which we scaled by the February number. The RSTR for 1 March 2007 for GLD is 0.0463/0.0473 = 0.9789, shown in Exhibit 27 as 0.979.

EXHIBIT 27   Relative-Strength Indicators

Date	RSTR SPDR Gold Shares (GLD)	RSTR Financial Select Sector SPDR (XLF)	RSTR Utilities Select Sector SPDR (XLU)
1 Feb 2007	1.000	1.000	1.000
1 Mar 2007	0.979	0.984	1.026
2 Apr 2007	0.958	0.980	1.031
1 May 2007	0.906	0.972	1.004
1 Jun 2007	0.905	0.950	0.973

(Exhibit continued on next page . . .)

EXHIBIT 27   (continued)

Date	RSTR SPDR Gold Shares (GLD)	RSTR Financial Select Sector SPDR (XLF)	RSTR Utilities Select Sector SPDR (XLU)
2 Jul 2007	0.957	0.892	0.965
1 Aug 2007	0.955	0.904	0.968
4 Sep 2007	1.019	0.894	0.971
1 Oct 2007	1.074	0.866	1.020
1 Nov 2007	1.105	0.832	1.074
3 Dec 2007	1.188	0.791	1.081
2 Jan 2008	1.403	0.848	1.067
1 Feb 2008	1.530	0.779	1.060
3 Mar 2008	1.446	0.760	1.084
1 Apr 2008	1.323	0.777	1.088
1 May 2008	1.321	0.715	1.115
2 Jun 2008	1.511	0.646	1.210
1 Jul 2008	1.625	0.615	1.242

On the basis of Exhibits 26 and 27, address the following:

1. State the relative strength of gold, financial services, and utilities over the entire time period February 2007 through July 2008. Interpret the relative strength for each sector over that period.

2. Discuss the relative performance of the financial services ETF and the utilities ETF in the month of December 2007.

Solution to 1: The relative-strength indicator for gold is 1.625. This number represents $1.625 - 1.000 = 0.625$, or 62.5 percent over-performance relative to the S&P 500 over the time period. The relative-strength indicator for the financial services ETF is 0.615. This number represents $1.000 - 0.615 = 0.385$, or 38.5 percent underperformance relative to the S&P 500 over the time period. The relative-strength indicator for the utilities ETF is 1.242, indicating that the utilities ETF outperformed the S&P 500 by 24.2 percent over the time frame.

Solution to 2: The January 2008 RSTR for the financials ETF, at 0.848, is higher than in the prior month, whereas the utilities' RSTR, at 1.067, is lower than in the prior month. In December 2007, the financials ETF outperformed the utilities ETF. The relative performance for that one month differs from the relative performance over the entire period, during which the utilities ETF significantly outperformed the financial services ETF.

Overall, momentum indicators have a substantial following among professional investors. Some view momentum indicators as signals that should prompt an analyst to consider whether a stock price is moving successively *farther from* or successively *closer to* the fundamental valuations derived from models and multiples. In other words, an analyst might be correct about the intrinsic value of a firm and the momentum indicators might provide a clue about when the market price will converge with that intrinsic value. The use of such indicators continues to be a subject of active research in industry and in business schools.

7   VALUATION INDICATORS: ISSUES IN PRACTICE

All the valuation indicators discussed in this reading are quantitative aids but not necessarily solutions to the problem of security selection. In this section, we discuss some issues that arise in practice when averages are used to establish benchmark multiples and then illustrate the use of multiple valuation indicators.

7.1 Averaging Multiples: The Harmonic Mean

The harmonic mean and the weighted harmonic mean are often applied to average a group of price multiples.

Consider a hypothetical portfolio that contains two stocks. For simplicity, assume the portfolio owns 100 percent of the shares of each stock. One stock has a market capitalization of €715 million and earnings of €71.5 million, giving it a P/E of 10. The other stock has a market capitalization of €585 million and earnings of €29.25 million, for a P/E of 20. Note that the P/E for the portfolio is calculated directly by aggregating the companies' market capitalizations and earnings: (€715 + €585)/(€71.50 + €29.25) = €1,300/€100.75 = 12.90. The question that will be addressed is: What calculation of portfolio P/E, based on the individual stock P/Es, best reflects the value of 12.90?

If the ratio of an individual holding is represented by X_i, the expression for the simple **harmonic mean** of the ratio is

$$X_H = \frac{n}{\sum_{i=1}^{n}(1/X_i)} \tag{8}$$

which is the reciprocal of the arithmetic mean of the reciprocals.

The expression for the **weighted harmonic mean** is

$$X_{WH} = \frac{1}{\sum_{i=1}^{n}(w_i/X_i)} \tag{9}$$

where the w_i are portfolio value weights (summing to 1) and $X_i > 0$ for $i = 1$, $2, \ldots, n$.

Exhibit 28 displays the calculation of the hypothetical portfolio's simple arithmetic mean P/E, weighted mean P/E, (simple) harmonic mean P/E, and weighted harmonic mean P/E.

The weighted harmonic mean P/E precisely corresponds to the portfolio P/E value of 12.90. This example explains why index fund vendors frequently use the weighted harmonic mean to calculate the "average" P/E or average value

| EXHIBIT 28 | Alternative Mean P/Es |

| Security | Market Cap | | Earnings (€ Millions) | Stock P/E | (1) | (2) | (3) | (4) |
	(€ Millions)	Percent						
Stock 1	715	55	71.50	10	0.5×10	0.55×10	0.5×0.1	0.55×0.1
Stock 2	585	45	29.25	20	0.5×20	0.45×20	0.5×0.05	0.45×0.05
					15	14.5	0.075	0.0775
Arithmetic mean P/E (1)					**15**			
Weighted mean P/E (2)						**14.5**		
Harmonic mean P/E (3)							$1/0.075 =$ **13.33**	
Weighted harmonic mean P/E (4)								$1/0.0775 =$ **12.90**

of other price multiples for indices. In some applications, an analyst might not want or be able to incorporate the market value weight information needed to calculate the weighted harmonic mean. In such cases, the simple harmonic mean can still be calculated.

Note that the simple harmonic mean P/E is smaller than the arithmetic mean and closer to the directly calculated value of 12.90 in this example. The harmonic mean inherently gives less weight to higher P/Es and more weight to lower P/Es. In general, unless all the observations in a data set have the same value, the harmonic mean is less than the arithmetic mean.

As explained and illustrated earlier in this reading, using the median rather than the arithmetic mean to derive an average multiple mitigates the effect of outliers. The harmonic mean is sometimes also used to reduce the impact of large outliers—which are typically the major concern in using the arithmetic mean multiple—but not the impact of small outliers (i.e., those close to zero). The harmonic mean tends to mitigate the impact of large outliers. The harmonic mean may aggravate the impact of small outliers, but such outliers are bounded by zero on the downside.

We can use the group of telecommunications companies examined earlier in the reading (see Exhibit 5) to illustrate differences between the arithmetic mean and harmonic mean. This group includes a large outlier for P/E, Equinix at a P/E of 702.61. Qwest's P/E of 2.73 appears to be a small outlier. Exhibit 29 shows mean values including and excluding the outliers.

Note that for the entire group, the mean (89.15) is far higher than the median (17.35) because of Equinix. The harmonic mean (9.13) is much closer to the median and more plausible as representing central tendency, although it is influenced by the P/E of Qwest, as shown by its higher value of 11.32 when outliers are eliminated.

This example illustrates the importance for the analyst of understanding how an average has been calculated, particularly when the analyst is reviewing information prepared by another analyst, and the usefulness of examining several summary statistics.

EXHIBIT 29	Arithmetic versus Harmonic Mean	

Company	Trailing P/E (with Outliers)	Trailing P/E (No Outliers)
AT&T (NYSE: T)	17.35	17.35
BCE Inc. (NYSE: BCE, TSE: BCE)	7.71	7.71
Centurytel (NYSE: CTL)	8.34	8.34
Cincinnati Bell (NYSE: CBB)	19.61	19.61
Citizens Communications Co. (NYSE: CZN)	19.22	19.22
Equinix (NASDAQGS: EQIX)	702.61	
Qwest Communications International (NYSE: Q)	2.73	
Verizon Communications (NYSE: VZ)	18.3	18.3
Windstream Corp. (NYSE: WIN)	6.51	6.51
Arithmetic mean	89.15	13.86
Median	17.35	17.35
Harmonic mean	9.13	11.32

7.2 Using Multiple Valuation Indicators

Because each carefully selected and calculated price multiple, momentum indicator, or fundamental may supply some piece of the puzzle of stock valuation, many investors and analysts use more than one valuation indicator (in addition to other criteria) in stock valuation and selection. Example 40 illustrates the use of multiple indicators.

EXAMPLE 40	

Multiple Indicators in Stock Valuation

The following excerpts from equity analyst reports illustrate the use of multiple ratios in communicating views about a stock's value. In the first excerpt, from a report on Colorpak Ltd. (Australia: CKL), the analyst has used a discounted cash flow valuation as the preferred methodology but notes that the stock is also attractive when a price-to-earnings ratio (PER in the report) is used. In the second excerpt, from a report on Jurong Technologies (Singapore: JTL), the analysts evaluate the stock price by using two multiples, price to book value (P/BV) and EV/EBITDA, and then summarize the company's operational issues that contributed to their negative view.

    Colorpak Ltd. (Australia: CKL)
    Our DCF for CKL is A$0.82ps, which represents a 44% prem. to the current price. Whilst the DCF valuation is our preferred methodology, we recognise that CKL also looks attractive on different metrics.

Applying a mid-cycle PER multiple of 10.5× (30% disc to mkt) to FY08 EPS of 7.6cps, we derive a valuation of A$0.80. Importantly, were the stock to reach our target of A$0.75ps in 12mths, CKL would be trading on a fwd PER of 9.1×, which we do not view as demanding. At current levels, the stock is also offering an attractive dividend yield of 5.7% (fully franked). [*Note*: "fully franked" is a concept specific to the Australian market and refers to tax treatment of the dividend.]

Mario Maia, CFA
Merrill Lynch (Australia)

Jurong Technologies (Singapore: JTL)
Our target price of S$0.35 (S$0.37 previously) implies a P/BV of 0.7× and an EV/EBITDA of 5.0× on our fresh earnings forecast for FY08. Despite valuations being at an all-time low, macro difficulties and woes at key customer Motorola suggest a lack of upside catalysts. We believe Jurong Tech needs to diversify away from Motorola, de-gear or lengthen the duration of its debt profile, and boost productivity metrics for a sustained re-rating.

Patrick Yau, CFA, and Valerie Law, CFA
Macquarie Research Equities

In selecting stocks, institutional investors surveyed in the *Merrill Lynch Institutional Factor Surveys* from 1989 to 2006 used an average of 8.5 factors in selecting stocks (depending on the year, 23–25 factors were included in the survey). The survey factors included not only price multiples, momentum indicators, and the DDM but also the fundamentals ROE, debt to equity, projected five-year EPS growth, EPS variability, EPS estimate dispersion, size, beta, foreign exposure, low price, and neglect. Exhibit 30 lists the factors classified by percentage of investors indicating that they use that factor in making investment decisions.

An issue concerning the use of ratios in an investing strategy is look-ahead bias. **Look-ahead bias** is the use of information that was not contemporaneously available in computing a quantity. Investment analysts often use historical data to back test an investment strategy that involves stock selection based on price multiples or other factors. When back testing, an analyst should be aware that time lags in the reporting of financial results create the potential for look-ahead bias in such research. For example, as of early January 2008, most companies had not reported EPS for the last quarter of 2007, so at that time, a company's trailing P/E would be based on EPS for the first, second, and third quarters of 2007 and the last quarter of 2006. Any investment strategy based on a trailing P/E that used actual EPS for the last quarter of 2007 could be implemented only after the data became available. Thus, if an analysis assumed that an investment was made in early January 2008 based on full-year 2007 data, the analysis would involve look-ahead bias. To avoid this bias an analyst would calculate the trailing P/E based on the most recent four quarters of EPS then being reported. The same principle applies to other multiples calculated on a trailing basis.

The application of a set of criteria to reduce an investment universe to a smaller set of investments is called **screening**. Stock screens often include not only criteria based on the valuation measures discussed in this reading but also on fundamental criteria that may explain differences in such measures. Computerized

| EXHIBIT 30 | Frequency of Investor Usage of Factors in Making Investment Decisions |

High (●) >30%; Med (◈) >10%<30%; Low (○) <10%*

Factor	2002	2003	2004	2005	2006
Estimate revision	●	●	●	●	●
P/B	●	●	●	●	●
P/CF	●	●	●	●	●
ROE	●	●	●	●	●
PEG	NA	●	●	●	●
D/E**	●	●	●	●	◈
EPS momentum	●	◈	●	●	●
EPS surprise	●	◈	●	●	●
P/E	●	◈	●	●	●
Relative strength	●	●	◈	●	●
Dividend yield	◈	●	●	●	◈
EPS variability	●	◈	●	●	◈
Neglect	◈	◈	●	●	◈
P/S	●	◈	◈	●	◈
EV/EBITDA	NA	●	●	●	◈
DDM	●	◈	◈	◈	◈
Beta	◈	◈	◈	◈	◈
Projected 5-year growth	◈	◈	◈	◈	◈
Rating revision	◈	◈	◈	◈	◈
Size	◈	◈	◈	◈	◈
Foreign exposure	○	◈	◈	◈	○
EPS dispersion	◈	○	○	◈	○
Low price	◈	○	○	◈	○
EPS torpedo	◈	○	○	○	○
Duration	○	○	○	○	○

* The survey presents actual percentages rather than high, medium, and low as defined here.

** For years 2004–2006, the survey reported high debt to equity (D/E) as a separate factor from low D/E.

Note: NA = not applicable

Source: *Merrill Lynch Institutional Factor Surveys.*

stock screening is an efficient way to narrow a search for investments and is a part of many stock selection disciplines. The limitations to many commercial databases and screening tools usually include lack of control by the user of the calculation of important inputs (such as EPS); the absence of qualitative factors in most databases is another important limitation. Example 41 illustrates the use of a screen in stock selection.

EXAMPLE 41

Using Screens to Find Stocks for a Portfolio

Janet Larsen manages an institutional portfolio and is currently looking for new stocks to add to the portfolio. Larsen has a commercial database with information on U.S. stocks. She has designed several screens to select stocks with low P/Es and low EV/CFO multiples. Because Larsen is aware that screening for low P/E and low EV/CFO multiples may identify stocks with low expected growth, she also wants stocks that have a PEG less than 1.0. She decides to screen for stocks with a dividend yield of at least 2.5 percent and a total market capitalization between $1 billion and $5 billion. Exhibit 31 shows the number of stocks that successively met each of the five criteria as of July 2008 (so, the number of stocks that met all five criteria is 24).

EXHIBIT 31 Stock Screen

Criterion	Stocks Meeting Each Criterion Successively
P/E ≤ 20.0	2,052
EV/CFO ≤ 10.0	693
PEG ≤ 1.0	462
Dividend yield ≥ 2.5%	113
Market capitalization from $1 billion to $5 billion	24

Other information:

▶ The screening database indicates that the P/E of the S&P 500 was 20.5 as of the date of the screen.

▶ S&P's *U.S. Style Indices*[65] indicates that the style indices measure growth and value by the following seven factors, which S&P standardizes and uses to compute growth and value scores for each company:

Three Growth Factors

Five-year EPS growth rate

Five-year sales per share growth rate

Five-year internal growth rate
        (Internal growth rate = ROE × Earnings retention rate)

Four Value Factors

P/BV

P/CF

P/S

Dividend yield

---

[65] From www2.standardandpoors.com/spf/pdf/index/faq_style_updtd_mfm%20edits.pdf.

> ► S&P uses the following guidelines for size indices (in U.S. dollars): Unadjusted market capitalization of $4 billion or more for the S&P 500, $1 billion to $4.5 billion for the S&P MidCap 400, and $250 million to $1.5 billion for the S&P SmallCap 600.[66]

Using the information supplied, answer the following questions:

1. What type of valuation indicators does Larsen *not* include in her stock screen?
2. Characterize the overall orientation of Larsen as to investment style.
3. State two limitations of Larsen's stock screen.

Solution to 1: Larsen has not included momentum indicators in the screen.

Solution to 2: Larsen can be characterized as a mid-cap value investor, based on the specified market capitalization. Although her screen does include a PEG, it excludes explicit growth rate criteria, such as those used by S&P, and it excludes momentum indicators usually associated with a growth orientation, such as positive earnings surprise. Larsen also uses a cutoff for P/E that is less than the average P/E for the S&P 500. Note that her criteria for multiples are all "less than" criteria.

Solution to 3: Larsen does not include any profitability criteria or risk measurements. These omissions are a limitation because a stock's expected low profitability or high risk may explain its low P/E. Another limitation of her screen is that the computations of the value indicators in a commercial database may not reflect the appropriate adjustments to inputs. The absence of qualitative criteria is also a possible limitation.

Investors also apply all the metrics that we have illustrated in terms of individual stocks to industries and economic sectors. For example, average price multiples and momentum indicators can be used in sector rotation strategies to determine relatively under- or overvalued sectors.[67] (A sector rotation strategy is an investment strategy that overweights economic sectors that are anticipated to outperform or lead the overall market.)

---

[66] Size guidelines are as of October 2008. Information is from: www2.standardandpoors.com/spf/pdf/index/SP_500_Factsheet.pdf; www2.standardandpoors.com/spf/pdf/index/SP_MidCap_400_Factsheet.pdf; and www2.standardandpoors.com/spf/pdf/index/SP_SmallCap_600_Factsheet.pdf.

[67] See Salsman (1997) for an example.

SUMMARY

In this reading, we have defined and explained the most important valuation indicators in professional use and illustrated their application to a variety of valuation problems.

► Price multiples are ratios of a stock's price to some measure of value per share.

► Price multiples are most frequently applied to valuation in the method of comparables. This method involves using a price multiple to evaluate whether an asset is relatively undervalued, fairly valued, or overvalued in relation to a benchmark value of the multiple.

► The benchmark value of the multiple may be the multiple of a similar company or the median or average value of the multiple for a peer group of companies, an industry, an economic sector, an equity index, or the company's own median or average past values of the multiple.

► The economic rationale for the method of comparables is the law of one price.

► Price multiples may also be applied to valuation in the method based on forecasted fundamentals. Discounted cash flow (DCF) models provide the basis and rationale for this method. Fundamentals also interest analysts who use the method of comparables because differences between a price multiple and its benchmark value may be explained by differences in fundamentals.

► The key idea behind the use of price-to-earnings ratios (P/Es) is that earning power is a chief driver of investment value and earnings per share (EPS) is probably the primary focus of security analysts' attention. The EPS figure, however, is frequently subject to distortion, often volatile, and sometimes negative.

► The two alternative definitions of P/E are trailing P/E, based on the most recent four quarters of EPS, and forward P/E, based on next year's expected earnings.

► Analysts address the problem of cyclicality by normalizing EPS—that is, calculating the level of EPS that the business could achieve currently under midcyclical conditions (normalized EPS).

► Two methods to normalize EPS are the method of historical average EPS (calculated over the most recent full cycle) and the method of average return on equity (ROE = average ROE multiplied by current book value per share).

► Earnings yield (E/P) is the reciprocal of the P/E. When stocks have zero or negative EPS, a ranking by earnings yield is meaningful whereas a ranking by P/E is not.

► Historical trailing P/Es should be calculated with EPS lagged a sufficient amount of time to avoid look-ahead bias. The same principle applies to other multiples calculated on a trailing basis.

► The fundamental drivers of P/E are the expected earnings growth rate and the required rate of return. The justified P/E based on fundamentals bears a positive relationship to the first factor and an inverse relationship to the second factor.

► PEG (P/E to growth) is a tool to incorporate the impact of earnings growth on P/E. PEG is calculated as the ratio of the P/E to the consensus growth forecast. Stocks with low PEGs are, all else equal, more attractive than stocks with high PEGs.

► We can estimate terminal value in multistage DCF models by using price multiples based on comparables. The expression for terminal value, V_n, is (using P/E as the example)

$$V_n = \text{Benchmark value of trailing P/E} \times E_n$$

or

$$V_n = \text{Benchmark value of forward P/E} \times E_{n+1}$$

► Book value per share is intended to represent, on a per-share basis, the investment that common shareholders have in the company. Inflation, technological change, and accounting distortions, however, may impair the use of book value for this purpose.

► Book value is calculated as common shareholders' equity divided by the number of shares outstanding. Analysts adjust book value to accurately reflect the value of the shareholders' investment and to make P/B (the price-to-book ratio) more useful for comparing different stocks.

► The fundamental drivers of P/B are ROE and the required rate of return. The justified P/B based on fundamentals bears a positive relationship to the first factor and an inverse relationship to the second factor.

► An important rationale for using the price-to-sales ratio (P/S) is that sales, as the top line in an income statement, are generally less subject to distortion or manipulation than other fundamentals, such as EPS or book value. Sales are also more stable than earnings and are never negative.

► P/S fails to take into account differences in cost structure between businesses, may not properly reflect the situation of companies losing money, and may be subject to manipulation through revenue recognition practices.

► The fundamental drivers of P/S are profit margin, growth rate, and the required rate of return. The justified P/S based on fundamentals bears a positive relationship to the first two factors and an inverse relationship to the third factor.

► Enterprise value (EV) is total company value (the market value of debt, common equity, and preferred equity) minus the value of cash and investments.

► The ratio of EV to total sales is conceptually preferable to P/S because EV/S facilitates comparisons among companies with varying capital structures.

► A key idea behind the use of price to cash flow is that cash flow is less subject to manipulation than are earnings. Price to cash flow multiples are often more stable than P/E. Some common approximations to cash flow from operations have limitations, however, because they ignore items that may be subject to manipulation.

► The major cash flow (and related) concepts used in multiples are earnings plus noncash charges (CF), cash flow from operations (CFO), free cash flow to equity (FCFE), and earnings before interest, taxes, depreciation, and amortization (EBITDA).

► In calculating price to cash flow, the earnings-plus-noncash-charges concept is traditionally used, although FCFE has the strongest link to financial theory.

► CF and EBITDA are not strictly cash flow numbers because they do not account for noncash revenue and net changes in working capital.

► The fundamental drivers of price to cash flow, however defined, are the expected growth rate of future cash flow and the required rate of return. The justified price to cash flow based on fundamentals bears a positive relationship to the first factor and an inverse relationship to the second.

► EV/EBITDA is preferred to P/EBITDA because EBITDA, as a preinterest number, is a flow to all providers of capital.

► EV/EBITDA may be more appropriate than P/E for comparing companies with different amounts of financial leverage (debt).

► EV/EBITDA is frequently used in the valuation of capital-intensive businesses.

► The fundamental drivers of EV/EBITDA are the expected growth rate in free cash flow to the firm, profitability, and the weighted average cost of capital. The justified EV/EBITDA based on fundamentals bears a positive relationship to the first two factors and an inverse relationship to the third.

► Dividend yield has been used as a valuation indicator because it is a component of total return and is less risky than capital appreciation.

► Trailing dividend yield is calculated as four times the most recent quarterly per-share dividend divided by the current market price.

► The fundamental drivers of dividend yield are the expected growth rate in dividends and the required rate of return.

► Comparing companies across borders frequently involves dealing with differences in accounting methods, cultural differences, economic differences, and resulting differences in risk and growth opportunities.

► Momentum indicators relate either price or a fundamental to the time series of the price or fundamental's own past values (in some cases, to their expected values).

► Momentum valuation indicators include earnings surprise, standardized unexpected earnings (SUE), and relative strength.

► Unexpected earnings (or earnings surprise) equals the difference between reported earnings and expected earnings.

► SUE is unexpected earnings divided by the standard deviation in past unexpected earnings.

► Relative-strength indicators allow comparison of a stock's performance during a period either with its own past performance (first type) or with the performance of some group of stocks (second type). The rationale for using relative strength is the thesis that patterns of persistence or reversal in returns exist.

► Screening is the application of a set of criteria to reduce an investment universe to a smaller set of investments and is a part of many stock selection disciplines. In general, limitations of such screens include the lack of control in vendor-provided data of the calculation of important inputs and the absence of qualitative factors.

PRACTICE PROBLEMS FOR READING 41

1. As of February 2008, you are researching Jonash International, a hypothetical company subject to cyclical demand for its services. Jonash shares closed at $57.98 on 2 February 2007. You believe the 2003–2006 period reasonably captures average profitability:

Measure	2007	2006	2005	2004	2003
EPS	E$3.03	$1.45	$0.23	$2.13	$2.55
BV per share	E$19.20	$16.21	$14.52	$13.17	$11.84
ROE	E16.0%	8.9%	1.6%	16.3%	21.8%

    A. Define normalized EPS.

    B. Calculate a normalized EPS for Jonash based on the method of historical average EPS and then calculate the P/E based on normalized EPS.

    C. Calculate a normalized EPS for Jonash based on the method of average ROE and the P/E based on normalized EPS.

2. An analyst plans to use P/E and the method of comparables as a basis for recommending purchasing shares of one of two peer-group companies in the business of manufacturing personal digital assistants. Neither company has been profitable to date, and neither is expected to have positive EPS over the next year. Data on the companies' prices, trailing EPS, and expected growth rates in sales (five-year compounded rates) are given in the following table:

Company	Price	Trailing EPS	P/E	Expected Growth (Sales)
Hand	$22	−$2.20	NM	45%
Somersault	$10	−$1.25	NM	40%

Unfortunately, because the earnings for both companies have been negative, their P/Es are not meaningful. On the basis of this information, address the following:

    A. Discuss how the analyst might make a relative valuation in this case.

    B. State which stock the analyst should recommend.

Practice Problems and Solutions: *Equity Asset Valuation*, Second Edition, by Jerald Pinto, CFA, Elaine Henry, CFA, Thomas Robinson, CFA, and John Stowe, CFA. Copyright © 2009 by CFA Institute. Reprinted with permission.

3. May Stewart, CFA, a retail analyst, is performing a P/E-based comparison of two hypothetical jewelry stores as of early 2009. She has the following data for Hallwhite Stores (HS) and Ruffany (RUF).

▶ HS is priced at $44. RUF is priced at $22.50.

▶ HS has a simple capital structure, earned $2.00 per share (basic and diluted) in 2008, and is expected to earn $2.20 (basic and diluted) in 2009.

▶ RUF has a complex capital structure as a result of its outstanding stock options. Moreover, it had several unusual items that reduced its basic EPS in 2008 to $0.50 (versus the $0.75 that it earned in 2007).

▶ For 2009, Stewart expects RUF to achieve net income of $30 million. RUF has 30 million shares outstanding and options outstanding for an additional 3,333,333 shares.

   A. Which P/E (trailing or forward) should Stewart use to compare the two companies' valuation?

   B. Which of the two stocks is relatively more attractive when valued on the basis of P/Es (assuming that all other factors are approximately the same for both stocks)?

4. You are researching the valuation of the stock of a company in the food-processing industry. Suppose you intend to use the mean value of the forward P/Es for the food-processing industry stocks as the benchmark value of the multiple. This mean P/E is 18.0. The forward or expected EPS for the next year for the stock you are studying is $2.00. You calculate 18.0 × $2.00 = $36, which you take to be the intrinsic value of the stock based only on the information given here. Comparing $36 with the stock's current market price of $30, you conclude the stock is undervalued.

   A. Give two reasons why your conclusion that the stock is undervalued may be in error.

   B. What additional information about the stock and the peer group would support your original conclusion?

5. Suppose an analyst uses an equity index as a comparison asset in valuing a stock. In making a decision to recommend purchase of an individual stock, which price multiple(s) would cause concern about the impact of potential overvaluation of the equity index?

6. Christie Johnson, CFA, has been assigned to analyze Sundanci. Johnson assumes that Sundanci's earnings and dividends will grow at a constant rate of 13 percent. Exhibits 1 and 2 provide financial statements for the most recent two years (2007 and 2008) and other information for Sundanci.

EXHIBIT 1	Sundanci Actual 2007 and 2008 Financial Statements for Fiscal Years Ending 31 May (in Millions except Per-Share Data)	
Income Statement	**2007**	**2008**
Revenue	$474	$598
Depreciation	20	23
Other operating costs	368	460
Income before taxes	86	115
Taxes	26	35
Net income	60	80
Dividends	18	24
Earnings per share	$0.714	$0.952
Dividends per share	$0.214	$0.286
Common shares outstanding	84.0	84.0
Balance Sheet	**2007**	**2008**
Current assets	$201	$326
Net property, plant, and equipment	474	489
Total assets	675	815
Current liabilities	57	141
Long-term debt	0	0
Total liabilities	57	141
Shareholders' equity	618	674
Total liabilities and equity	675	815
Other Information		
Capital expenditures	34	38

EXHIBIT 2	Selected Financial Information
Required rate of ROE	14%
Growth rate of industry	13%
Industry P/E	26

   A. Based on information in Exhibits 1 and 2 and on Johnson's assumptions for Sundanci, calculate justified trailing and forward P/Es for this company.

   B. Identify, within the context of the constant dividend growth model, how *each* of the following fundamental factors would affect the P/E:

     i. The risk (beta) of Sundanci increases substantially.

     ii. The estimated growth rate of Sundanci's earnings and dividends increases.

     iii. The equity risk premium increases.

     Note: A change in a fundamental factor is assumed to happen in isolation; interactive effects between factors are ignored. That is, every other item of the company is unchanged.

7. Tom Smithfield is valuing the stock of a food-processing business. He feels confident explicitly projecting earnings and dividends to three years (to $t = 3$). Other information and estimates are as follows:

   ▶ Required rate of return = 0.09.

   ▶ Average dividend payout rate for mature companies in the market = 0.45.

   ▶ Industry average ROE = 0.10.

   ▶ E_3 = \$3.00.

   ▶ Industry average P/E = 12.

On the basis of this information, answer the following questions:

   A. Compute terminal value (V_3) based on comparables.

   B. Contrast your answer in Part A to an estimate of terminal value based on the Gordon growth model.

8. Discuss three types of stocks or investment situations for which an analyst could appropriately use P/B in valuation.

9. Aratatech is a multinational distributor of semiconductor chips and related products to businesses. Its leading competitor around the world is Trymye Electronics. Aratatech has a current market price of \$10.00, 20 million shares outstanding, annual sales of \$1 billion, and a 5 percent profit margin. Trymye has a market price of \$20.00, 30 million shares outstanding, annual sales of \$1.6 billion, and a profit margin of 4.9 percent. Based on the information given, answer the following questions:

   A. Which of the two companies has a more attractive valuation based on P/S?

   B. Identify and explain one advantage of P/S over P/E as a valuation tool.

10. Wilhelm Müller, CFA, has organized the selected data on four food companies that appear below (TTM stands for trailing 12 months):

Measure	Hoppelli Foods	Telli Foods	Drisket Co.	Whiteline Foods
Stock price	$25.70	$11.77	$23.65	$24.61
Shares outstanding (thousands)	138,923	220,662	108,170	103,803
Market cap ($ millions)	3,570	2,597	2,558	2,555
Enterprise value ($ millions)	3,779	4,056	3,846	4,258
Sales ($ millions)	4,124	10,751	17,388	6,354
Operating income ($ millions)	285	135	186	396
Operating profit margin	6.91%	1.26%	1.07%	6.23%
Net income ($ millions)	182	88	122	252
TTM EPS	$1.30	$0.40	$1.14	$2.43
Return on equity	19.20%	4.10%	6.40%	23.00%
Net profit margin	4.41%	0.82%	0.70%	3.97%

On the basis of the data given, answer the following questions:

A. Calculate the trailing P/E and EV/Sales for each company.

B. Explain, on the basis of fundamentals, why these stocks have different EV/S multiples.

11. John Jones, CFA, is head of the research department at Peninsular Research. Peninsular has a client who has inquired about the valuation method best suited for comparing companies in an industry with the following characteristics:

▶ Principal competitors within the industry are located in the United States, France, Japan, and Brazil.

▶ The industry is currently operating at a cyclical low, with many companies reporting losses.

Jones recommends that the client consider the following valuation ratios:

1. P/E.
2. P/B.
3. EV/S.

Determine which *one* of the three valuation ratios is most appropriate for comparing companies in this industry. Support your answer with *one* reason that makes that ratio superior to either of the other two ratios in this case.

12. Giantin Growing AG (GG) is currently selling for €38.50, with TTM EPS and dividends per share of €1.36 and €0.91, respectively. The company's P/E is 28.3, P/B is 7.1, and P/S is 2.9. The ROE is 27.0 percent, and the profit margin on sales is 10.24 percent. The Treasury bond rate is 4.9 percent, the equity risk premium is 5.5 percent, and GG's beta is 1.2.

   A. What is GG's required rate of return, based on the capital asset pricing model (CAPM)?

   B. Assume that the dividend and earnings growth rates are 9 percent. What trailing P/E, P/B, and P/S multiples would be justified in light of the required rate of return in Part A and current values of the dividend payout ratio, ROE, and profit margin?

   C. Given that the assumptions and constant growth model are appropriate, state and justify whether GG, based on fundamentals, appears to be fairly valued, overvalued, or undervalued.

13. Jorge Zaldys, CFA, is researching the relative valuation of two companies in the aerospace/defense industry, NCI Heavy Industries (NCI) and Relay Group International (RGI). He has gathered relevant information on the companies in the following table.

EBITDA Comparisons (in € Millions except Per-Share and Share-Count Data)

Company	RGI	NCI
Price per share	150	100
Shares outstanding	5 million	2 million
Market value of debt	50	100
Book value of debt	52	112
Cash and investments	5	2
Net income	49.5	12
Net income from continuing operations	49.5	8
Interest expense	3	5
Depreciation and amortization	8	4
Taxes	2	3

Using the information in the table, answer the following questions:

   A. Calculate P/EBITDA for NCI and RGI.

   B. Calculate EV/EBITDA for NCI and RGI.

   C. Which company should Zaldys recommend as relatively undervalued? Justify the selection.

14. Define the major alternative cash flow concepts, and state one limitation of each.

15. Data for two hypothetical companies in the pharmaceutical industry, DriveMed and MAT Technology, are given in the following table. For both companies, expenditures on fixed capital and working capital during the previous year reflect anticipated average expenditures over the foreseeable horizon.

Measure	DriveMed	MAT Technology
Current price	$46.00	$78.00
Trailing CF per share	$3.60	$6.00
P/CF	12.8	13.0
Trailing FCFE per share	$1.00	$5.00
P/FCFE	46.0	15.6
Consensus five-year growth forecast	15%	20%
Beta	1.25	1.25

On the basis of the information supplied, discuss the valuation of MAT Technology relative to DriveMed. Justify your conclusion.

16. Your value-oriented investment management firm recently hired a new analyst, Bob Westard, because of his expertise in the life sciences and biotechnology areas. At the firm's weekly meeting, during which each analyst proposes a stock idea for inclusion in the firm's approved list, Westard recommends Hitech Clothing International (HCI). He bases his recommendation on two considerations. First, HCI has pending patent applications but a P/E that he judges to be low in light of the potential earnings from the patented products. Second, HCI has had high relative strength versus the S&P 500 over the past month.

   A. Explain the difference between Westard's two approaches—that is, the use of price multiples and the relative-strength approach.

   B. State which, if any, of the bases for Westard's recommendation is consistent with the investment orientation of your firm.

17. Kirstin Kruse, a portfolio manager, has an important client who wants to alter the composition of her equity portfolio, which is currently a diversified portfolio of 60 global common stocks. Because of concerns about the economy and based on the thesis that the consumer staples sector will be less hurt than others in a recession, the client wants to add a group of stocks from the consumer staples sector. In addition, the client wants the stocks to meet the following criteria:

► Stocks must be considered large cap (i.e., have a large market capitalization).

► Stocks must have a dividend yield of at least 4.0 percent.

► Stocks must have a forward P/E no greater than 15.

The following table shows how many stocks satisfied each screen, which was run in July 2008.

Screen	Number Satisfying
Consumer staples sector	277
Large cap (> $9.7 billion in this database)	446
Dividend yield of at least 4.0%	1,609
P/E less than 15	2,994
All four screens	6

The stocks meeting all four screens were Altria Group, Inc.; British American Tobacco (the company's ADR); Reynolds American, Inc.; Tesco PLC (the ADR); Unilever N.V. (the ADR); and Unilever PLC (the ADR).

A. Critique the construction of the screen.

B. Do these criteria identify appropriate additions to this client's portfolio?

SOLUTIONS FOR READING 41

1. A. Normalized EPS is the level of earnings per share that the company could currently achieve under midcyclical conditions.

B. Averaging EPS over the 2003–2006 period, we find that ($2.55 + $2.13 + $0.23 + $1.45)/4 = $1.59. According to the method of historical average EPS, Jonash's normalized EPS is $1.59. The P/E based on this estimate is $57.98/1.59 = 36.5.

C. Averaging ROE over the 2003–2006 period, we find that (0.218 + 0.163 + 0.016 + 0.089)/4 = 0.1215. For current BV per share, you would use the estimated value of $19.20 for year-end 2007. According to the method of average ROE, 0.1215 × $19.20 = $2.33 is the normalized EPS. The P/E based on this estimate is $57.98/$2.33 = 24.9.

2. A. The analyst can rank the two stocks by earnings yield (E/P). Whether EPS is positive or negative, a lower E/P reflects a richer (higher) valuation and a ranking from high to low E/P has a meaningful interpretation.

In some cases, an analyst might handle negative EPS by using normalized EPS in its place. Neither business, however, has a history of profitability. When year-ahead EPS is expected to be positive, forward P/E is positive. Thus, the use of forward P/Es sometimes addresses the problem of trailing negative EPS. Forward P/E is not meaningful in this case, however, because next year's earnings are expected to be negative.

B. Hand has an E/P of −0.100, and Somersault has an E/P of −0.125. A higher earnings yield has an interpretation that is similar to that of a lower P/E, so Hand appears to be relatively undervalued. The difference in earnings yield cannot be explained by differences in sales growth forecasts. In fact, Hand has a higher expected sales growth rate than Somersault. Therefore, the analyst should recommend Hand.

3. A. Because investing looks to the future, analysts often favor forward P/E when earnings forecasts are available, as they are here. A specific reason to use forward P/Es is the fact given that RUF had some unusual items affecting EPS for 2008. The data to make appropriate adjustments to RUF's 2008 EPS are not given. In summary, Stewart should use forward P/Es.

B. Because RUF has a complex capital structure, the P/Es of the two companies must be compared on the basis of diluted EPS.

For HS, forward P/E = $44/2.20 = 20.

For RUF, forward P/E per diluted share
= $22.50/(30,000,000/33,333,333) = 25.

Therefore, HS has the more attractive valuation at present.

The problem illustrates some of the considerations that should be taken into account in using P/Es and the method of comparables.

4. A. Your conclusion may be in error because of the following:

▶ The peer-group stocks themselves may be overvalued; that is, the mean P/E of 18 may be too high in terms of intrinsic value. If so, using 18 as a multiplier of the stock's expected EPS will lead to an estimate of stock value in excess of intrinsic value.

▶ The stock's fundamentals may differ from those of the mean food-processing industry stock. For example, if the stock's expected growth rate is lower than the mean industry growth rate and its risk is higher than the mean, the stock may deserve a lower P/E than the industry mean.

In addition, mean P/E may be influenced by outliers.

B. The following additional evidence would support the original conclusion:

▶ Evidence that stocks in the industry are, at least on average, fairly valued (that stock prices reflect fundamentals).

▶ Evidence that no significant differences exist in the fundamental drivers of P/E for the stock being compared and the average industry stock.

5. In principle, the use of any price multiple for valuation is subject to the concern stated. If the stock market is overvalued, an asset that appears to be fairly or even undervalued in relation to an equity index may also be overvalued.

6. A. The formula for calculating the justified forward P/E for a stable-growth company is the payout ratio divided by the difference between the required rate of return and the growth rate of dividends. If the P/E is being calculated on trailing earnings (Year 0), the payout ratio is increased by 1 plus the growth rate. According to the 2007 income statement, the payout ratio is $18/60 = 0.30$; the 2008 income statement gives the same number ($24/80 = 0.30$). Thus,

P/E based on trailing earnings:

$$\text{P/E} = [\text{Payout ratio} \times (1 + g)]/(r - g)$$
$$= (0.30 \times 1.13)/(0.14 - 0.13) = 33.9$$

P/E based on next year's earnings:

$$\text{P/E} = \text{Payout ratio}/(r - g)$$
$$= 0.30/(0.14 - 0.13) = 30$$

B.

Fundamental Factor	Effect on P/E	Explanation (Not Required in Question)
The risk (beta) of Sundanci increases substantially.	Decrease	P/E is a decreasing function of risk—that is, as risk increases, P/E decreases. Increases in the risk of Sundanci stock would be expected to lower its P/E.

(continued on next page . . .)

Fundamental Factor	Effect on P/E	Explanation (Not Required in Question)
The estimated growth rate of Sundanci's earnings and dividends increases.	Increase	P/E is an increasing function of the growth rate of the company— that is, the higher the expected growth, the higher the P/E. Sundanci would command a higher P/E if the market price were to incorporate expectations of a higher growth rate.
The equity risk premium increases.	Decrease	P/E is a decreasing function of the equity risk premium. An increased equity risk premium increases the required rate of return, which lowers the price of a stock relative to its earnings. A higher equity risk premium would be expected to lower Sundanci's P/E.

7. **A.** V_n = Benchmark value of P/E $\times E_n$ = 12 $\times$ \$3.00 = \$36.0.

   B. In the expression for sustainable growth rate $g = b \times$ ROE, you can use $(1 - 0.45) = 0.55 = b$, and ROE = 0.10 (the industry average), obtaining 0.55 $\times$ 0.10 = 0.055. Given the required rate of return of 0.09, you obtain the estimate \$3.00(0.45)(1.055)/(0.09 − 0.055) = \$40.69. In this case, the estimate of terminal value obtained from the Gordon growth model is higher than the estimate based on multiples. The two estimates may differ for a number of reasons, including the sensitivity of the Gordon growth model to the values of the inputs.

8. Although the measurement of book value has a number of widely recognized shortcomings, P/B may still be applied fruitfully in several circumstances:

   ► The company is not expected to continue as a going concern. When a company is likely to be liquidated (so ongoing earnings and cash flow are not relevant), the value of its assets less its liabilities is of utmost importance. Naturally, the analyst must establish the fair value of these assets.

   ► The company is composed mainly of liquid assets, which is the case for finance, investment, insurance, and banking institutions.

   ► The company's EPS is highly variable or negative.

9. **A.** Aratatech: P/S = (\$10 price per share)/[(\$1 billion sales)/(20 million shares)] = \$10/(\$1,000,000,000/20,000,000) = 0.2

   Trymye: P/S = (\$20 price per share)/[(\$1.6 billion sales)/(30 million shares)] = \$20/(\$1,600,000,000/30,000,000) = 0.375

   Aratatech has a more attractive valuation than Trymye based on its lower P/S but comparable profit margin.

   B. One advantage of P/S over P/E is that companies' accounting decisions typically have a much greater impact on reported earnings than they are likely to have on reported sales. Although companies are able to make a number of legitimate business and accounting decisions that affect earnings, their discretion over reported sales (revenue recognition) is limited. Another advantage is that sales are almost always positive, so using P/S eliminates issues that arise when EPS is zero or negative.

10. **A.** The P/Es are:

Hoppelli	$25.70/1.30 = 19.8$
Telli	$11.77/0.40 = 29.4$
Drisket	$23.65/1.14 = 20.7$
Whiteline	$24.61/2.43 = 10.1$

The EV/S multiples for each company are:

Hoppelli	$3,779/4,124 = 0.916$
Telli	$4,056/10,751 = 0.377$
Drisket	$3,846/17,388 = 0.221$
Whiteline	$4,258/6,354 = 0.670$

B. The data for the problem include measures of profitability, such as operating profit margin, ROE, and net profit margin. Because EV includes the market values of both debt and equity, logically the ranking based on EV/S should be compared with a pre-interest measure of profitability, namely, operating profit margin. The ranking of the stocks by EV/S from highest to lowest and the companies' operating margins are:

Company	EV/S	Operating Profit Margin (%)
Hoppelli	0.916	6.91
Whiteline	0.670	6.23
Telli	0.377	1.26
Drisket	0.221	1.07

The differences in EV/S appear to be explained, at least in part, by differences in cost structure as measured by operating profit margin.

11. For companies in the industry described, EV/S would be superior to either of the other two ratios. Among other considerations, EV/S is:

▶ more useful than P/E in valuing companies with negative earnings;

▶ better than either P/E or P/B for comparing companies in different countries that are likely to use different accounting standards (a consequence of the multinational nature of the industry);

▶ less subject to manipulation than earnings (i.e., through aggressive accounting decisions by management, who may be more motivated to manage earnings when a company is in a cyclical low, rather than in a high, and thus likely to report losses).

12. **A.** Based on the CAPM, the required rate of return is $4.9\% + 1.2 \times 5.5\% = 11.5\%$.

B. The dividend payout ratio is €0.91/€1.36 = 0.669. The justified values for the three valuation ratios should be

$$\frac{P_0}{E_0} = \frac{(1-b) \times (1+g)}{r-g} = \frac{0.669 \times 1.09}{0.115 - 0.09} = \frac{0.7293}{0.025} = 29.2$$

$$\frac{P_0}{B_0} = \frac{ROE - g}{r-g} = \frac{0.27 - 0.09}{0.115 - 0.09} = \frac{0.18}{0.025} = 7.2$$

$$\frac{P_0}{S_0} = \frac{PM \times (1-b) \times (1+g)}{r-g} = \frac{0.1024 \times 0.669 \times 1.09}{0.115 - 0.09}$$

$$= \frac{0.0747}{0.025} = 3.0$$

C. The justified trailing P/E is higher than the trailing P/E (29.2 versus 28.3), the justified P/B is higher than the actual P/B (7.2 versus 7.1), and the justified P/S is higher than the actual P/S (3.0 versus 2.9). Therefore, based on these three measures, GG appears to be slightly undervalued.

13. A. EBITDA = Net income (from continuing operations) + Interest expense + Taxes + Depreciation + Amortization

EBITDA for RGI = €49.5 million + €3 million + €2 million + €8 million = €62.5 million

Per-share EBITDA = (€62.5 million)/(5 million shares) = €12.5

P/EBITDA for RGI = €150/€12.5 = 12

EBITDA for NCI = €8 million + €5 million + €3 million + €4 million = €20 million

Per-share EBITDA = (€20 million)/(2 million shares) = €10

P/EBITDA for NCI = €100/€10 = 10

B. For RGI:

Market value of equity = €150 × 5 million = €750 million

Market value of debt = €50

Total market value = €750 million + €50 = €800 million

EV = €800 million − €5 million (cash and investments) = €795 million

Now, Zaldys would divide EV by total (as opposed to per-share) EBITDA:

EV/EBITDA for RGI = (€795 million)/(€62.5 million) = 12.72

For NCI:

Market value of equity = €100 × 2 million = €200 million

Market value of debt = €100

Total market value = €200 million + €100 = €300 million

EV = €300 million − €2 million (cash and investments) = €298 million

Now, Zaldys would divide EV by total (as opposed to per-share) EBITDA:

EV/EBITDA for NCI = (€298 million)/(€20 million) = 14.9

C. Zaldys should select RGI as relatively undervalued.

First, it is correct that NCI *appears* to be relatively undervalued based on P/EBITDA, because NCI has a lower P/EBITDA multiple:

▶ P/EBITDA = €150/€12.5 = 12 for RGI.

▶ P/EBITDA = €100/€10 = 10 for NCI.

RGI is relatively undervalued on the basis of EV/EBITDA, however, because RGI has the lower EV/EBITDA multiple:

▶ EV/EBITDA = (€795 million)/(€62.5 million) = 12.72 for RGI.

▶ EV/EBITDA = (€298 million)/(€20 million) = 14.9 for NCI.

EBITDA is a pre-interest flow; therefore, it is a flow to both debt and equity and the EV/EBITDA multiple is more appropriate than the P/EBITDA multiple. Zaldys would rely on EV/EBITDA to reach his decision if the two ratios conflicted. Note that P/EBITDA does not take into account differences in the use of financial leverage. Substantial differences in leverage exist in this case (NCI uses much more debt), so the preference for using EV/EBITDA rather than P/EBITDA is supported.

14. The major concepts are as follows:

▶ EPS plus per-share depreciation, amortization, and depletion (CF)

Limitation: Ignores changes in working capital and noncash revenue; not a free cash flow concept.

▶ Cash flow from operations (CFO)

Limitation: Not a free cash flow concept, so not directly linked to theory.

▶ Free cash flow to equity (FCFE)

Limitation: Often more variable and more frequently negative than other cash flow concepts.

▶ Earnings before interest, taxes, depreciation, and amortization (EBITDA)

Limitation: Ignores changes in working capital and noncash revenue; not a free cash flow concept. Relative to its use in P/EBITDA, EBITDA is mismatched with the numerator because it is a pre-interest concept.

15. MAT Technology is relatively undervalued compared with DriveMed on the basis of P/FCFE. MAT Tech's P/FCFE multiple is 34 percent the size of DriveMed's FCFE multiple (15.6/46 = 0.34, or 34 percent). The only comparison slightly in DriveMed's favor, or approximately equal for both companies, is the comparison based on P/CF (i.e., 12.8 for DriveMed versus 13.0 for MAT Technology). However, FCFE is more strongly grounded in valuation theory than P/CF. Because DriveMed's and MAT Technology's expenditures for fixed capital and working capital during the previous year reflected anticipated average expenditures over the foreseeable horizon, you would have additional confidence in the P/FCFE comparison.

16. A. Relative strength is based strictly on price movement (a technical indicator). As used by Westard, the comparison is between the returns on HCI and the returns on the S&P 500. In contrast, the price multiple approaches are based on the relationship of current price, not to past prices, but to some measure of value such as EPS, book value, sales, or cash flow.

B. Only the reference to the P/E in relationship to the pending patent applications in Westard's recommendation is consistent with the company's value orientation. High relative strength would be relevant for a portfolio managed with a growth/momentum investment style.

17. A. As a rule, a screen that includes a maximum P/E ratio should include criteria requiring positive earnings; otherwise, the screen could select companies with negative P/E ratios. The screen may be too narrowly focused on value measures. It did not include criteria related to expected growth, required rate of return, risk, or financial strength.

B. The screen results in a very concentrated portfolio. The screen selected both of the parent companies of the Unilever Group: Unilever NV and Unilever PLC, which operate as a single business entity despite having separate legal identities and separate stock exchange listings. Thus, owning both stocks would provide no diversification benefits. In addition, the screen selected three tobacco companies, which typically pay high dividends. Again, owning all three stocks would provide little diversification.

RESIDUAL INCOME VALUATION

by Jerald Pinto, CFA, Elaine Henry, CFA, Thomas Robinson, CFA, and John Stowe, CFA

LEARNING OUTCOMES

The candidate should be able to:	Mastery
a. calculate and interpret residual income, economic value added, and market value added;	☐
b. describe the uses of residual income models;	☐
c. calculate the intrinsic value of a common stock using the residual income model, and contrast the recognition of value in the residual income model to value recognition in other present value models;	☐
d. explain fundamental determinants of residual income;	☐
e. explain the relation between residual income valuation and the justified price-to-book ratio based on forecasted fundamentals;	☐
f. calculate and interpret the intrinsic value of a common stock using single-stage (constant-growth) and multistage residual income models;	☐
g. calculate the implied growth rate in residual income, given the market price-to-book ratio and an estimate of the required rate of return on equity;	☐
h. explain continuing residual income, and justify an estimate of continuing residual income at the forecast horizon, given company and industry prospects;	☐
i. compare residual income models to dividend discount and free cash flow models;	☐
j. explain strengths and weaknesses of residual income models;	☐
k. justify the selection of a residual income model to value a company's common stock;	☐
l. describe accounting issues in applying residual income models;	☐
m. evaluate whether a stock is overvalued, fairly valued, or undervalued based on a residual income model.	☐

Equity Asset Valuation, Second Edition, by Jerald Pinto, CFA, Elaine Henry, CFA, Thomas Robinson, CFA, and John Stowe, CFA. Copyright © 2009 by CFA Institute. Reprinted with permission.

1

INTRODUCTION

Residual income models of equity value have become widely recognized tools in both investment practice and research. Conceptually, residual income is net income less a charge (deduction) for common shareholders' opportunity cost in generating net income. It is the residual or remaining income after considering the costs of all of a company's capital. The appeal of residual income models stems from a shortcoming of traditional accounting. Specifically, although a company's income statement includes a charge for the cost of debt capital in the form of interest expense, it does not include a charge for the cost of equity capital. A company can have positive net income but may still not be adding value for shareholders if it does not earn more than its cost of equity capital. Residual income models explicitly recognize the costs of all the capital used in generating income.

As an economic concept, residual income has a long history, dating back to Alfred Marshall in the late 1800s.[1] As far back as the 1920s, General Motors used the concept in evaluating business segments.[2] More recently, residual income has received renewed attention and interest, sometimes under names such as economic profit, abnormal earnings, or economic value added. Although residual income concepts have been used in a variety of contexts, including the measurement of internal corporate performance, this reading will focus on the residual income model for estimating the intrinsic value of common stock. Among the questions we will study to help us apply residual income models are the following:

► How is residual income measured, and how can an analyst use residual income in valuation?
► How does residual income relate to fundamentals, such as return on equity and earnings growth rates?
► How is residual income linked to other valuation methods, such as a price-multiple approach?
► What accounting-based challenges arise in applying residual income valuation?

---

[1] Alfred Marshall, Book Two: Some Fundamental Notions, Chapter 4, "Income, Capital," in *Principles of Economics* (London; Macmillan and Co., Ltd., 1890).

[2] See, for example, Young (1999) and Lo and Lys (2000).

The reading is organized as follows: Section 2 develops the concept of residual income, introduces the use of residual income in valuation, and briefly presents alternative measures used in practice. Section 3 presents the residual income model and illustrates its use in valuing common stock. This section also shows practical applications, including the single-stage (constant-growth) residual income model and a multistage residual income model. Section 4 describes the relative strengths and weaknesses of residual income valuation compared to other valuation methods. Section 5 addresses accounting issues in the use of residual income valuation. The final section summarizes the reading and practice problems conclude.

RESIDUAL INCOME 2

Traditional financial statements, particularly the income statement, are prepared to reflect earnings available to owners. As a result, the income statement shows net income after deducting an expense for the cost of debt capital, that is, interest expense. The income statement does not, however, deduct dividends or other charges for equity capital. Thus, traditional financial statements essentially let the owners decide whether earnings cover their opportunity costs. Conversely, the economic concept of residual income explicitly deducts the estimated cost of equity capital, the finance concept that measures shareholders' opportunity costs. The cost of equity is the marginal cost of equity, which is also referred to as the required rate of return on equity. The cost of equity is a marginal cost because it represents the cost of additional equity, whether generated internally or by selling more equity interests. Example 1 illustrates, in a stylized setting, the calculation and interpretation of residual income.[3]

EXAMPLE 1

Calculation of Residual Income

Axis Manufacturing Company, Inc. (AXCI), a very small company in terms of market capitalization, has total assets of €2 million financed 50 percent with debt and 50 percent with equity capital. The cost of debt is 7 percent before taxes; this example assumes that interest is tax deductible, so the after-tax cost of debt is 4.9 percent.[4] The cost of equity capital is 12 percent. The company has earnings before interest and

---

[3] To simplify this introduction, we assume that net income accurately reflects *clean surplus accounting*, which will be explained later in this reading. The discussions in this reading assume that companies' financing only consists of common equity and debt. In the case of a company that also has preferred stock financing, the calculation of residual income would reflect the deduction of preferred stock dividends from net income.

[4] In countries where corporate interest is not tax deductible, the after-tax cost of debt would equal the pretax cost of debt.

taxes (EBIT) of €200,000 and a tax rate of 30 percent. Net income for AXCI can be determined as follows:

EBIT	€200,000
Less: Interest Expense	70,000
Pretax Income	€130,000
Less: Income Tax Expense	39,000
Net Income	€ 91,000

With earnings of €91,000, AXCI is clearly profitable in an accounting sense. But was the company's profitability adequate return for its owners? Unfortunately, it was not. To incorporate the cost of equity capital, compute residual income. One approach to calculating residual income is to deduct an **equity charge** (the estimated cost of equity capital in money terms) from net income. Compute the equity charge as follows:

$$\text{Equity charge} = \text{Equity capital} \times \text{Cost of equity capital}$$
$$= €1,000,000 \times 12\%$$
$$= €120,000.$$

As stated, residual income is equal to net income minus the equity charge:

Net Income	€ 91,000
Less: Equity Charge	120,000
Residual Income	€(29,000)

AXCI did not earn enough to cover the cost of equity capital. As a result, it has negative residual income. Although AXCI is profitable in an accounting sense, it is not profitable in an economic sense.

In Example 1, residual income is calculated based on net income and a charge for the cost of equity capital. Analysts will also encounter another approach to calculating residual income that yields the same results under certain assumptions. In this second approach, which takes the perspective of all providers of capital (both debt and equity), a **capital charge** (the company's total cost of capital in money terms) is subtracted from the company's after-tax operating profit. In the case of AXCI in Example 1, the capital charge is €169,000:

Equity charge	$0.12 \times €1,000,000 =$	€120,000
Debt charge	$0.07(1 - 0.30) \times €1,000,000 =$	49,000
Total capital charge		€169,000

The company's net operating profit after taxes (NOPAT) is €140,000 (€200,000 − 30% taxes). The capital charge of €169,000 is higher than the after-tax operating profit of €140,000 by €29,000, the same figure obtained in Example 1.

As illustrated in the following table, both approaches yield the same results in this case because of two assumptions. First, this example assumes that the marginal cost of debt equals the current cost of debt, that is, the cost used to determine net income. Specifically, in this instance, the after-tax interest expense incorporated in net income [€49,000 = €70,000 × (1 − 30%)] is equal to the after-tax cost of debt incorporated into the capital charge. Second, this example assumes that the weights used to calculate the capital charge are derived from the book value of debt and equity. Specifically, it uses the weights of 50 percent debt and 50 percent equity.

Approach 1		Reconciliation	Approach 2	
Net income	€ 91,000	Plus the after-tax interest expense of €49,000	Net operating profit after tax	€140,000
Less: Equity charge	120,000	Plus the after-tax capital charge for debt of €49,000	Less: Capital charge	169,000
Residual income	€(29,000)		Residual income	€(29,000)

That the company is not profitable in an economic sense can also be seen by comparing the company's cost of capital to its return on capital. Specifically, the company's capital charge is greater than its after-tax return on total assets or capital. The after-tax net operating return on total assets or capital is calculated as profits divided by total assets (or total capital). In this example, the after-tax net operating return on total assets is 7 percent (€140,000/€2,000,000), which is 1.45 percentage points less than the company's effective capital charge of 8.45 percent (€169,000/€2,000,000).[5]

2.1 The Use of Residual Income in Equity Valuation

A company that is generating more income than its cost of obtaining capital— that is, one with positive residual income—is creating value. Conversely, a company that is not generating enough income to cover its cost of capital—that is, a company with negative residual income—is destroying value. Thus, all else equal, higher (lower) residual income should be associated with higher (lower) valuations.

To illustrate the effect of residual income on equity valuation using the case of AXCI presented in Example 1, assume the following:

▶ Initially, AXCI equity is selling for book value or €1 million with 100,000 shares outstanding. Thus, AXCI's book value per share and initial share price are both €10.

▶ Earnings per share (EPS) is €0.91 (€91,000/100,000 shares).

▶ Earnings will continue at the current level indefinitely.

▶ All net income is distributed as dividends.

Because AXCI is not earning its cost of equity, as shown in Example 1, the company's share price should fall. Given the information, AXCI is destroying €29,000 of value per year, which equals €0.29 per share (€29,000/100,000 shares). Discounted at 12 percent cost of equity, the present value of the perpetuity is €2.42 (€0.29/12%). The current share price minus the present value of the value being destroyed equals €7.58 (€10 − €2.42).

---

[5] After-tax net operating profits as a percent of total assets or capital has been called **return on invested capital** (ROIC). Residual income can also be calculated as (ROIC − Effective capital charge) × Beginning capital.

Another way to look at these data is to note that the earnings yield (E/P) for a no-growth company is an estimate of the expected rate of return. Therefore, when price reaches the point at which E/P equals the required rate of return on equity, an investment in the stock is expected to just cover the stock's required rate of return. With EPS of €0.91, the earnings yield is exactly 12 percent (AXCI's cost of equity) when its share price is €7.58333 (i.e., €0.91/€7.58333 = 12%). At a share price of €7.58333, the total market value of AXCI's equity is €758,333. When a company has negative residual income, shares are expected to sell at a discount to book value. In this example, AXCI's price-to-book ratio (P/B) at this level of discount from book value would be 0.7583. In contrast, if AXCI were earning positive residual income, then its shares should sell at a premium to book value. In summary, higher residual income is expected to be associated with higher market prices (and higher P/Bs), all else being equal.

Residual income (RI) models have been used to value both individual stocks[6] and the Dow Jones Industrial Average.[7] The models have also been proposed as a solution to measuring goodwill impairment by accounting standard setters (American Accounting Association Financial Accounting Standards Committee 2001). Recall that **impairment** in an accounting context means downward adjustment, and **goodwill** is an intangible asset that may appear on a company's balance sheet as a result of its purchase of another company.

Residual income and residual income models have been referred to by a variety of names. Residual income has sometimes been called **economic profit** because it is an estimate of the profit of the company after deducting the cost of all capital: debt and equity. In forecasting future residual income, the term **abnormal earnings** is also used. Under the assumption that in the long term the company is expected to earn its cost of capital (from all sources), any earnings in excess of the cost of capital can be termed abnormal earnings. The residual income model has also been called the **discounted abnormal earnings model** and the **Edwards–Bell–Ohlson model** after the names of researchers in the field. This reading focuses on a general residual income model that can be used by analysts using publicly available data and nonproprietary accounting adjustments. A number of commercial implementations of the approach, however, are also very well known. Before returning to the general residual income model in Section 3, we briefly discuss one such commercial implementation and the related concept of market value added.

2.2 Commercial Implementations

One example of several competing commercial implementations of the residual income concept is **economic value added** (EVA).[8] The previous section illustrated a calculation of residual income starting from net operating profit after taxes, and economic value added takes the same broad approach. Specifically, economic value added is computed as

$$\text{EVA} = \text{NOPAT} - (\text{C\%} \times \text{TC}) \tag{1}$$

---

[6] See Fleck, Craig, Bodenstab, Harris, and Huh (2001).

[7] See Lee and Swaminathan (1999) and Lee, Myers, and Swaminathan (1999).

[8] The acronym is trademarked by Stern Stewart & Company and is generally associated with a specific set of adjustments proposed by Stern Stewart & Co. The goal of these adjustments is to produce a value that is a good approximation of economic profit. For a complete discussion, see Stern (1991) and Peterson and Peterson (1996).

where NOPAT is the company's net operating profit after taxes, C% is the cost of capital, and TC is total capital. In this model, both NOPAT and TC are determined under generally accepted accounting principles and adjusted for a number of items.[9] Some of the more common adjustments include the following:

► Research and development (R&D) expenses are capitalized and amortized rather than expensed (i.e., R&D expense is added back to earnings to compute NOPAT).

► In the case of strategic investments that are not expected to generate an immediate return, a charge for capital is suspended until a later date.

► Goodwill is capitalized and not amortized (i.e., amortization expense is added back in when calculating NOPAT, and accumulated amortization is added back to capital).

► Deferred taxes are eliminated such that only cash taxes are treated as an expense.

► Any inventory LIFO (last in, first out) reserve is added back to capital, and any increase in the LIFO reserve is added in when calculating NOPAT.

► Operating leases are treated as capital leases, and nonrecurring items are adjusted.

Because of the adjustments made in calculating EVA, a different numerical result will be obtained, in general, than that resulting from the use of the simple computation presented in Example 1. In practice, general (nonbranded) residual income valuation also considers the effect of accounting methods on reported results. Analysts' adjustments to reported accounting results in estimating residual income, however, will generally reflect some differences from the set specified for EVA. Section 5 of this reading will explore accounting considerations in more detail.

Over time, a company must generate economic profit for its market value to increase. A concept related to economic profit (and EVA) is market value added (MVA):

$$MVA = \text{Market value of the company} - \text{Accounting book value of total capital} \qquad \textbf{(2)}$$

A company that generates positive economic profit should have a market value in excess of the accounting book value of its capital.

Research on the ability of value-added concepts to explain equity value and stock returns has reached mixed conclusions. Peterson and Peterson (1996) found that value-added measures are slightly more highly correlated with stock returns than traditional measures, such as return on assets and return on equity. Bernstein and Pigler (1997) and Bernstein, Bayer, and Pigler (1998) found that value-added measures are no better at predicting stock performance than are such measures as earnings growth.

A variety of commercial models related to the residual income concept have been marketed by other major accounting and consulting firms. Interestingly, the application focus of these models is not, in general, equity valuation. Rather, these implementations of the residual income concept are marketed primarily for measuring internal corporate performance and determining executive compensation.

---

[9] See, for example, Ehrbar (1998).

3

THE RESIDUAL INCOME MODEL

In Section 2, we discussed the concept of residual income and briefly introduced the relationship of residual income to equity value. In the long term, companies that earn more than the cost of capital should sell for more than book value, and companies that earn less than the cost of capital should sell for less than book value. The **residual income model** of valuation analyzes the intrinsic value of equity as the sum of two components:

▶ the current book value of equity, and

▶ the present value of expected future residual income.

Note that when the change is made from valuing total shareholders' equity to directly valuing an individual common share, earnings per share rather than net income is used. According to the residual income model, the intrinsic value of common stock can be expressed as follows:

$$V_0 = B_0 + \sum_{t=1}^{\infty} \frac{\text{RI}_t}{(1+r)^t} = B_0 + \sum_{t=1}^{\infty} \frac{E_t - rB_{t-1}}{(1+r)^t} \qquad (3)$$

where

V_0 = value of a share of stock today ($t = 0$)
B_0 = current per-share book value of equity
B_t = expected per-share book value of equity at any time t
r = required rate of return on equity investment (cost of equity)
E_t = expected EPS for period t
RI_t = expected per-share residual income, equal to $E_t - rB_{t-1}$

The per-share residual income in period t, RI_t, is the EPS for the period, E_t, minus the per-share equity charge for the period, which is the required rate of return on equity times the book value per share at the beginning of the period, or rB_{t-1}. Whenever earnings per share exceed the per-share cost of equity, per-share residual income is positive; and whenever earnings are less, per-share residual income is negative. Example 2 illustrates the calculation of per-share residual income.

EXAMPLE 2

Per-Share Residual Income Forecasts

David Smith is evaluating the expected residual income as of the end of September 2007 of Carrefour SA (NYSE Euronext Paris: FR0000120172), a France-based operator of hypermarkets and other store formats in Europe, the Americas, and Asia. Using an adjusted beta of 0.72 relative to the CAC 40 Index, a 10-year government bond yield of 4.3 percent, and an estimated equity risk premium of 7 percent, Smith uses the capital asset pricing model (CAPM) to estimate Carrefour's required rate of return, r, at 9.3 percent [4.3 percent + 0.72(7 percent)]. Smith obtains the following data from Bloomberg as of the close on 24 September 2007:

Current market price	€48.83
Book value per share as of 31 December 2006	€13.46
Consensus annual earnings estimates	
FY 2007 (ending December)	€2.71
FY 2008	€2.86
Annualized dividend per share forecast	
FY 2007	€1.03
FY 2008	€1.06

What is the forecast residual income for fiscal years ended December 2007 and December 2008?

Solution: Forecasted residual income and calculations are shown in Exhibit 1.

EXHIBIT 1	Carrefour SA	
Year	**2007**	**2008**
Forecasting book value per share		
Beginning book value (B_{t-1})	€13.46	€15.14
Earnings per share forecast (E_t)	€2.71	€2.86
Less dividend forecast (D_t)	1.03	1.06
Add Change in retained earnings $(E_t - D_t)$	1.68	1.80
Forecast ending book value per share ($B_{t-1} + E_t - D_t$)	€15.14	€16.94
Calculating the equity charge		
Beginning ending book value per share	€13.46	€15.14
Multiply cost of equity	× 0.093	× 0.093
Per-share equity charge ($r \times B_{t-1}$)	€1.25	€1.41
Estimating per share residual income		
EPS forecast	€2.71	€2.86
Less equity charge	1.25	1.41
Per-share residual income	€1.46	€1.45

The use of Equation 3, the expression for the estimated intrinsic value of common stock, is illustrated in Example 3.

EXAMPLE 3

Using the Residual Income Model (1)

Bugg Properties' expected EPS is $2.00, $2.50, and $4.00 for the next three years. Analysts expect that Bugg will pay dividends of $1.00, $1.25, and $12.25 for the three years. The last dividend is anticipated to be a liquidating dividend; analysts expect Bugg will cease operations after Year 3. Bugg's current book value is $6.00 per share, and its required rate of return on equity is 10 percent.

1. Calculate per-share book value and residual income for the next three years.

2. Estimate the stock's value using the residual income model given in Equation 3:

$$V_0 = B_0 + \sum_{t=1}^{\infty} \frac{E_t - rB_{t-1}}{(1+r)^t}$$

3. Confirm your valuation estimate in Part 2 using the discounted dividend approach (i.e., estimating the value of a share as the present value of expected future dividends).

Solution to 1: The book value and residual income for the next three years are shown in Exhibit 2.

EXHIBIT 2

Year	1	2	3
Beginning book value per share (B_{t-1})	$6.00	$7.00	$8.25
Net income per share (EPS)	2.00	2.50	4.00
Less dividends per share (D)	1.00	1.25	12.25
Change in retained earnings (EPS − D)	1.00	1.25	−8.25
Ending book value per share (B_{t-1} + EPS − D)	$7.00	$8.25	$0.00
Net income per share (EPS)	2.00	2.50	4.000
Less per-share equity charge (rB_{t-1})	0.60	0.70	0.825
Residual income (EPS − Equity charge)	$1.40	$1.80	$3.175

Solution to 2: The value using the residual income model is

$$V_0 = 6.00 + \frac{1.40}{(1.10)} + \frac{1.80}{(1.10)^2} + \frac{3.175}{(1.10)^3}$$

$$= 6.00 + 1.2727 + 1.4876 + 2.3854$$

$$= \$11.15$$

Solution to 3: The value using a discounted dividend approach is

$$V_0 = \frac{1.00}{(1.10)} + \frac{1.25}{(1.10)^2} + \frac{12.25}{(1.10)^3}$$

$$= 0.9091 + 1.0331 + 9.2036$$

$$= \$11.15$$

Example 3 illustrates two important points about residual income models. First, the RI model is fundamentally similar to other valuation models, such as the dividend discount model (DDM), and given consistent assumptions will yield equivalent results. Second, recognition of value typically occurs earlier in RI models than in DDM. In Example 3, the RI model attributes $6.00 of the $11.15 total value to the *first* time period. In contrast, the DDM model attributes $9.2036 of the $11.15 total value to the *final* time period. The rest of Section 3 develops the most familiar general expression for the RI model and illustrates the model's application.

3.1 The General Residual Income Model

The residual income model has a clear relationship to other valuation models, such as the dividend discount model. In fact, the residual income model given in Equation 3 can be derived from the DDM. The general expression for the DDM is

$$V_0 = \frac{D_1}{(1+r)^1} + \frac{D_2}{(1+r)^2} + \frac{D_3}{(1+r)^3} + \cdots$$

The **clean surplus relation** states the relationship among earnings, dividends, and book value as follows:

$$B_t = B_{t-1} + E_t - D_t$$

In other words, the ending book value of equity equals the beginning book value plus earnings minus dividends, apart from ownership transactions. The condition that income (earnings) reflects all changes in the book value of equity other than ownership transactions is known as clean surplus accounting. By rearranging the clean surplus relation, the dividend for each period can be viewed as the net income minus the earnings retained for the period, or net income minus the increase in book value:

$$D_t = E_t - (B_t - B_{t-1}) = E_t + B_{t-1} - B_t$$

Substituting $E_t + B_{t-1} - B_t$ for D_t in the expression for V_0 results in:

$$V_0 = \frac{E_1 + B_0 - B_1}{(1 + r)^1} + \frac{E_2 + B_1 - B_2}{(1 + r)^2} + \frac{E_3 + B_2 - B_3}{(1 + r)^3} + \cdots$$

This equation can be rewritten as follows:

$$V_0 = B_0 + \frac{E_1 - rB_0}{(1 + r)^1} + \frac{E_2 - rB_1}{(1 + r)^2} + \frac{E_3 - rB_2}{(1 + r)^3} + \cdots$$

Expressed with summation notation, the following equation restates the residual income model given in Equation 3:

$$V_0 = B_0 + \sum_{t=1}^{\infty} \frac{RI_t}{(1 + r)^t} = B_0 + \sum_{t=1}^{\infty} \frac{E_t - rB_{t-1}}{(1 + r)^t}$$

According to the expression, the value of a stock equals its book value per share plus the present value of expected future per-share residual income. Note that when the present value of expected future per-share residual income is positive (negative), intrinsic value, V_0, is greater (smaller) than book value per share, B_0.

The residual income model used in practice today has its origins largely in the academic work of Ohlson (1995) and Feltham and Ohlson (1995) along with the earlier work of Edwards and Bell (1961), although in the United States this method has been used to value small businesses in tax cases since the 1920s.[10] The general expression for the residual income model based on this work[11] can also be stated as:

$$V_0 = B_0 + \sum_{t=1}^{\infty} \frac{(ROE_t - r)\, B_{t-1}}{(1 + r)^t} \tag{4}$$

Equation 4 is equivalent to the expressions for V_0 given earlier because in any year, t, $RI_t = (ROE_t - r)B_{t-1}$. Other than the required rate of return on common stock, the inputs to the residual income model come from accounting data. Note that return on equity (ROE) in this context uses beginning book value of equity in the denominator, whereas in financial statement analysis ROE is frequently calculated using the average book value of equity in the denominator. Example 4 illustrates the estimation of value using Equation 4.

EXAMPLE 4

Using the Residual Income Model (2)

To recap the data from Example 3, Bugg Properties has expected earnings per share of $2.00, $2.50, and $4.00 and expected dividends per share of $1.00, $1.25, and $12.25 for the next three years. Analysts expect that the last dividend will be a liquidating dividend and that Bugg

---

[10] In tax valuation, the method is known as the **excess earnings method**. For example, see Hitchner (2006) and U.S. IRS Revenue Ruling 68-609.

[11] See, for example, Hirst and Hopkins (2000).

will cease operating after Year 3. Bugg's current book value per share is $6.00, and its estimated required rate of return on equity is 10 percent.

Using the above data, estimate the value of Bugg Properties' stock using a residual income model of the form:

$$V_0 = B_0 + \sum_{t=1}^{\infty} \frac{(ROE_t - r)\, B_{t-1}}{(1 + r)^t}$$

Solution: To value the stock, forecast residual income. Exhibit 3 illustrates the calculation of residual income. (Note that Exhibit 3 arrives at the same estimates of residual income as Exhibit 2 in Example 3.)

EXHIBIT 3

Year	1	2	3
Earnings per share	$2.00	$2.50	$4.00
Divided by beginning book value per share	÷6.00	÷7.00	÷8.25
ROE	0.3333	0.3571	0.4848
Less required rate of return on equity	−0.1000	−0.1000	−0.1000
Abnormal rate of return (ROE − r)	0.2333	0.2571	0.3848
Multiply by beginning book value per share	×6.00	×7.00	×8.25
Residual income (ROE − r) × Beginning BV	$1.400	$1.800	$3.175

Estimate the stock value as follows:

$$V_0 = 6.00 + \frac{1.40}{(1.10)} + \frac{1.80}{(1.10)^2} + \frac{3.175}{(1.10)^3}$$

$$= 6.00 + 1.2727 + 1.4876 + 2.3854$$

$$= \$11.15$$

Note that the value is identical to the estimate obtained using Equation 3, as illustrated in Example 3, because the assumptions are the same and Equations 3 and 4 are equivalent expressions:

$$V_0 = \underbrace{B_0 + \sum_{t=1}^{\infty} \frac{E_t - rB_{t-1}}{(1 + r)^t}}_{\text{Equation 3}} = \underbrace{B_0 + \sum_{t=1}^{\infty} \frac{(ROE_t - r)\, B_{t-1}}{(1 + r)^t}}_{\text{Equation 4}}$$

Example 4 showed that residual income value can be estimated using current book value, forecasts of earnings, forecasts of book value, and an estimate of the required rate of return on equity. The forecasts of earnings and book value translate into ROE forecasts.

EXAMPLE 5

Valuing a Company Using the General Residual Income Model

Robert Sumargo, an equity analyst, is considering the valuation of Cisco Systems (NASDAQGS:CSCO), which closed at $28.02 on 11 December 2007. Sumargo notes that in general CSCO had a fairly high ROE during the past 10 years and that consensus analyst forecasts for EPS for the next two fiscal years reflect an expected ROE of around 29 percent. Sumargo expects that a high ROE may not be sustainable in the future. Sumargo usually takes a present value approach to valuation. As of the date of the valuation, CSCO does not pay dividends; although a discounted dividend valuation is possible, Sumargo does not feel confident about predicting the date of a dividend initiation. He decides to apply the residual income model to value CSCO, and uses the following data and assumptions:

► According to the CAPM, CSCO has a required rate of return of approximately 10.5 percent.

► CSCO's book value per share on 28 July 2007 was $5.02.

► ROE is expected to be 29 percent for fiscal year-end July 2008. Because of competitive pressures, Sumargo expects CSCO's ROE to decline in the following years and incorporates an assumed decline of slightly less than 1 percent (0.9 percent) each year until it reaches the CAPM required rate of return.

► CSCO does not currently pay a dividend. Sumargo does not expect the company to pay a dividend in the foreseeable future, so all earnings will be reinvested. In addition, Sumargo expects that share repurchases will approximately offset new share issuances.

Compute the value of CSCO using the residual income model (Equation 4).

Solution: Book value per share is initially $5.02. Based on a ROE forecast of 29 percent in the first year, the forecast EPS would be $1.46. Because no dividends are paid and the clean surplus relation is assumed to hold, book value at the end of the period is forecast to be $6.48 ($5.02 + $1.46). For 2008, residual income is measured as projected EPS of $1.46 minus an equity charge of $0.53, or $0.93. This is equivalent to the beginning book value per share of $5.02 times the difference between ROE of 29 percent and r of 10.5 percent [i.e., $5.02(0.29 − 0.105) = $0.93]. The present value of $0.93 at 10.5 percent for one year is $0.84. This process is continued year by year as presented in Exhibit 4. The value of CSCO using this residual income model would be the present value of each year's residual income plus the current book value per share. Because residual income is zero starting in 2029, no forecast is required beyond that period. The estimated value under this model is $27.79, as shown in Exhibit 4.

| EXHIBIT 4 | Valuation of CSCO Using the Residual Income Model |

Year	Projected Income EPS	Projected Dividend per Share	Book Value per Share	Forecast ROE (Based on Beginning Book Value)	Cost of Equity	Equity Charge	Residual Income (RI)	PV of BV and RI
	[Plus]	[Minus]	$5.02					$5.02
2008	$1.46	$0.00	6.48	29.0%	10.5%	$0.53	$0.93	0.84
2009	1.82	0.00	8.30	28.1	10.5	0.68	1.14	0.93
2010	2.26	0.00	10.56	27.2	10.5	0.87	1.39	1.03
2011	2.78	0.00	13.34	26.3	10.5	1.11	1.67	1.12
2012	3.39	0.00	16.73	25.4	10.5	1.40	1.99	1.21
2013	4.10	0.00	20.83	24.5	10.5	1.76	2.34	1.29
2014	4.91	0.00	25.74	23.6	10.5	2.19	2.73	1.36
2015	5.84	0.00	31.58	22.7	10.5	2.70	3.14	1.41
2016	6.89	0.00	38.47	21.8	10.5	3.32	3.57	1.45
2017	8.04	0.00	46.51	20.9	10.5	4.04	4.00	1.47
2018	9.30	0.00	55.81	20.0	10.5	4.88	4.42	1.47
2019	10.66	0.00	66.47	19.1	10.5	5.86	4.80	1.45
2020	12.10	0.00	78.57	18.2	10.5	6.98	5.12	1.40
2021	13.59	0.00	92.16	17.3	10.5	8.25	5.34	1.32
2022	15.11	0.00	107.28	16.4	10.5	9.68	5.44	1.22
2023	16.63	0.00	123.91	15.5	10.5	11.26	5.36	1.09
2024	18.09	0.00	142.00	14.6	10.5	13.01	5.08	0.93
2025	19.45	0.00	161.45	13.7	10.5	14.91	4.54	0.75
2026	20.67	0.00	182.11	12.8	10.5	16.95	3.71	0.56
2027	21.67	0.00	203.79	11.9	10.5	19.12	2.55	0.35
2028	22.42	0.00	226.20	11.0	10.5	21.40	1.02	0.13
2029	23.75	0.00	249.95	10.5	10.5	23.75	0.00	0.00
Total								$27.79

Note: PV is present value and BV is book value. This table was created in Excel, so numbers may differ from what will be obtained using a calculator, because of rounding.

Example 5 refers to the assumption of clean surplus accounting. The residual income model, as stated earlier, assumes clean surplus accounting. The clean surplus accounting assumption is illustrated in Exhibit 4, for example, in which ending book value per share is computed as beginning book value plus net income minus dividends. Under International Financial Reporting Standards (IFRS) and U.S. generally accepted accounting principles (U.S. GAAP), several items of income and expense occurring during a period, such as changes in the market value of certain securities, bypass the income statement and affect a company's book value of equity directly.[12] Strictly speaking, residual income models involve all items of income and expense (income under clean surplus accounting). If an analyst can reliably estimate material differences from clean surplus accounting expected in the future, an adjustment to net income may be appropriate. Section 5.1 explores violations of the clean surplus accounting assumption in more detail.

3.2 Fundamental Determinants of Residual Income

In general, the residual income model makes no assumptions about future earnings and dividend growth. If constant earnings and dividend growth are assumed, a version of the residual income model that usefully illustrates the fundamental drivers of residual income can be derived. The following expression is used for justified price-to-book ratio (P/B) based on forecasted fundamentals, assuming the Gordon (constant growth) DDM and the sustainable growth rate equation, $g = b \times \text{ROE}$:[13]

$$\frac{P_0}{B_0} = \frac{\text{ROE} - g}{r - g}$$

which is mathematically equivalent to:

$$\frac{P_0}{B_0} = 1 + \frac{\text{ROE} - r}{r - g}$$

The justified price is the stock's intrinsic value ($P_0 = V_0$). Therefore, using the previous equation and remembering that residual income is earnings less the cost of equity, or $(\text{ROE} \times B_0) - (r \times B_0)$, a stock's intrinsic value under the residual income model, assuming constant growth, can be expressed as:

$$V_0 = B_0 + \frac{\text{ROE} - r}{r - g} B_0 \qquad \textbf{(5)}$$

Under this model, the estimated value of a share is the book value per share (B_0) plus the present value $[(\text{ROE} - r)B_0/(r - g)]$ of the expected stream of residual income. In the case of a company for which ROE exactly equals the cost of equity, the intrinsic value is equal to the book value per share. Equation 5 is considered a single-stage (or constant-growth) residual income model.

In an ideal world, where the book value of equity represents the fair value of net assets and clean surplus accounting prevails, the term B_0 reflects the value of assets owned by the company less its liabilities. The second term, $(\text{ROE} - r)B_0/(r - g)$, represents additional value expected because of the company's ability to generate returns in excess of its cost of equity; the second term is the present value of the company's expected economic profits. Unfortunately, both U.S. and international accounting rules allow companies to exclude some liabilities from their balance sheets, and neither set of rules reflects the fair value of many cor-

---

[12] Under IFRS, income and expense items that bypass the income statement include revaluation surpluses, particularly gains and losses arising from translating the financial statements of a foreign operation, and gains or losses on remeasuring available-for-sale financial assets. In U.S. financial statements, items that bypass the income statement (dirty surplus items) are referred to as **other comprehensive income** (OCI). The relationship is Comprehensive income = Net income + Other comprehensive income.

[13] Note that the sustainable growth rate formula itself can be derived from the clean surplus relation.

porate assets. Internationally, however, a move toward fair value accounting is occurring, particularly for financial assets. Further, controversies, such as the failure of Enron Corporation in the United States, have highlighted the importance of identifying off-balance-sheet financing techniques.

The residual income model is most closely related to the P/B ratio. A stock's justified P/B ratio is directly related to expected future residual income. Another closely related concept is **Tobin's q**, the ratio of the market value of debt and equity to the replacement cost of total assets:[14]

$$\text{Tobin's } q = \frac{\text{Market value of debt and equity}}{\text{Replacement cost of total assets}}$$

Although similar to P/B, Tobin's q also has some obvious differences. The numerator includes the market value of total capital (debt as well as equity). The denominator uses total assets rather than equity. Further, assets are valued at replacement cost rather than at historical accounting cost; replacement costs take into account the effects of inflation. All else equal, Tobin's q is expected to be higher the greater the productivity of a company's assets.[15] One difficulty in computing Tobin's q is the lack of information on the replacement cost of assets. If available, market values of assets or replacement costs can be more useful in a valuation than historical costs.

3.3 Single-Stage Residual Income Valuation

The single-stage (constant-growth) residual income model assumes that a company has a constant return on equity and constant earnings growth rate through time. This model was given in Equation 5:

$$V_0 = B_0 + \frac{\text{ROE} - r}{r - g} B_0$$

EXAMPLE 6

Single-Stage Residual Income Model (1)

Joseph Yoh is evaluating a purchase of Canon, Inc. (NYSE: CAJ). Current book value per share is $18.81, and the current price per share is $51.90 (from Value Line, 2 November 2007). Yoh expects long-term ROE to be 16 percent and long-term growth to be 8 percent. Assuming a cost of equity of 11 percent, what is the intrinsic value of Canon stock calculated using a single-stage residual income model?

Solution:

$$V_0 = \$18.81 + \frac{0.16 - 0.11}{0.11 - 0.08} \$18.81$$

$$= \$50.16$$

---

[14] See Tobin (1969) or more recent work such as Landsman and Shapiro (1995).

[15] Tobin theorized that q would average to 1 for all companies because the economic rents or profits earned by assets would average to zero.

Similar to the Gordon growth DDM, the single-stage RI model can be used to assess the market expectations of residual income growth—that is, an implied growth rate—by inputting the current price into the model and solving for g.

EXAMPLE 7

Single-Stage Residual Income Model (2)

Joseph Yoh is curious about the market-perceived growth rate, given that he is comfortable with his other inputs. By using the current price per share of $51.90 for Canon, Yoh solves the following equation for g:

$$\$51.90 = \$18.81 + \frac{0.16 - 0.11}{0.11 - g}\$18.81$$

He finds an implied growth rate of 8.16 percent.

In Examples 6 and 7, the company was valued at more than twice its book value because its ROE exceeded its cost of equity. If ROE was equal to the cost of equity, the company would be valued at book value. If ROE was lower than the cost of equity, the company would have negative residual income and be valued at less than book value. (When a company has no prospect of being able to cover its cost of capital, a liquidation of the company and redeployment of assets may be appropriate.)

In many applications, a drawback to the single-stage model is that it assumes the excess ROE above the cost of equity will persist indefinitely. More likely, a company's ROE will revert to a mean value of ROE over time, and at some point, the company's residual income will be zero. If a company or industry has an abnormally high ROE, other companies will enter the marketplace thus increasing competition and lowering returns for all companies. Similarly, if an industry has a low ROE, companies will exit the industry (through bankruptcy or otherwise) and ROE will tend to rise over time. As with the single-stage DDM, the single-stage residual income model also assumes a constant growth rate through time. In light of these considerations, the residual income model has been adapted in practice to handle declining residual income. For example, Lee and Swaminathan (1999) and Lee, Myers, and Swaminathan (1999) used a residual income model to value the Dow 30 by assuming that ROE fades (reverts) to the industry mean over time. Lee and Swaminathan found that the residual income model had more ability than traditional price multiples to predict future returns. Fortunately, other models are available that enable analysts to relax the assumption of indefinite persistence of excess returns. The following section describes a multistage residual income model.

3.4 Multistage Residual Income Valuation

As with other valuation approaches, such as DDM and free cash flow, a multistage residual income approach can be used to forecast residual income for a certain time horizon and then estimate a terminal value based on continuing residual income at the end of that time horizon. **Continuing residual income** is residual income after the forecast horizon. As with other valuation models, the forecast horizon for the initial stage should be based on the ability to explicitly forecast inputs in the model. Because ROE has been found to revert to mean levels over time and may decline to the cost of equity in a competitive environment, residual income approaches often model ROE fading toward the cost of equity. As ROE approaches the cost of equity, residual income approaches zero. An ROE equal to the cost of equity would result in residual income of zero.

In residual income valuation, the current book value often captures a large portion of total value and the terminal value may not be a large component of total value because book value is larger than the periodic residual income and because ROE may fade over time toward the cost of equity. This contrasts with other multistage approaches (DDM and DCF), in which the present value of the terminal value is frequently a significant portion of total value.

Analysts make a variety of assumptions concerning continuing residual income. Frequently, one of the following assumptions is made:

▶ residual income continues indefinitely at a positive level;

▶ residual income is zero from the terminal year forward;

▶ residual income declines to zero as ROE reverts to the cost of equity through time; or

▶ residual income reflects the reversion of ROE to some mean level.

The following examples illustrate several of these assumptions.

One finite-horizon model of residual income valuation assumes that at the end of time horizon T, a certain premium over book value ($P_T - B_T$) exists for the company, in which case, current value equals the following:[16]

$$V_0 = B_0 + \sum_{t=1}^{T} \frac{(E_t - rB_{t-1})}{(1 + r)^t} + \frac{P_T - B_T}{(1 + r)^T} \qquad \textbf{(6)}$$

Alternatively,

$$V_0 = B_0 + \sum_{t=1}^{T} \frac{(\text{ROE}_t - r)B_{t-1}}{(1 + r)^t} + \frac{P_T - B_T}{(1 + r)^T} \qquad \textbf{(7)}$$

The last component in both specifications represents the premium over book value at the end of the forecast horizon. The longer the forecast period, the greater the chance that the company's residual income will converge to zero. For long forecast periods, this last term may be treated as zero. For shorter forecast periods, a forecast of the premium should be calculated.

EXAMPLE 8

Multistage Residual Income Model (1)

Diana Rosato, CFA, is considering an investment in Taiwan Semiconductor Manufacturing Ltd., a manufacturer and marketer of integrated circuits. Listed on the Taiwan Stock Exchange (Code: 2330), the company's stock is also traded on the New York Stock Exchange (NYSE: TSM). Rosato obtained the following facts and estimates as of early 2007:

---

[16] See Bauman (1999).

▶ Current price equals TWD62.9.

▶ Cost of equity equals 15 percent.

▶ Taiwan Semiconductor's ROE has ranged from 18.4 percent to 22.7 percent during the period 2004–2006, which reflects a recovery from the difficult period of 2001–2003, when ROE averaged 7.1 percent.

▶ In 2005 the company instituted a cash dividend of TWD2.9846 for 2006.

▶ Book value per share was TWD19.59 at the end of 2006.

▶ Rosato's forecasts of EPS are TWD4.256 for 2007 and TWD5.556 for 2008. She expects dividends of TWD3.000 for 2007 and TWD3.284 for 2008.

▶ Rosato expects Taiwan Semiconductor's ROE to be 25 percent from 2009 through 2016 and then decline to 20 percent through 2026.

▶ For the period after 2008, Rosato assumes an earnings retention ratio of 70 percent.

▶ Rosato assumes that after 2026, ROE will be 15 percent and residual income will be zero; therefore, the terminal value would be zero. Rosato's residual income model is shown in Exhibit 5.

EXHIBIT 5	Taiwan Semiconductor							
Year	Book Value (TWD)	Projected Income (TWD)	Dividend per Share (TWD)	Forecasted ROE (Beg. Equity, %)	COE (%)	COE (TWD)	Residual Income (TWD)	Present Value of Residual Income (TWD)
2006	19.5900							19.59
2007	20.8460	4.2560	3.0000	21.73	15.00	2.9385	1.3175	1.15
2008	23.1180	5.5560	3.2840	26.65	15.00	3.1269	2.4291	1.84
2009	27.1637	5.7795	1.7339	25.00	15.00	3.4677	2.3118	1.52
2010	31.9173	6.7909	2.0373	25.00	15.00	4.0745	2.7164	1.55
2011	37.5028	7.9793	2.3938	25.00	15.00	4.7876	3.1917	1.59
2012	44.0658	9.3757	2.8127	25.00	15.00	5.6254	3.7503	1.62
2013	51.7773	11.0164	3.3049	25.00	15.00	6.6099	4.4066	1.66
2014	60.8385	12.9443	3.8833	25.00	15.00	7.7666	5.1777	1.69
2015	71.4851	15.2096	4.5629	25.00	15.00	9.1258	6.0838	1.73
2016	83.9950	17.8713	5.3614	25.00	15.00	10.7228	7.1485	1.77
2017	95.7543	16.7990	5.0397	20.00	15.00	12.5992	4.1997	0.90
2018	109.1598	19.1509	5.7453	20.00	15.00	14.3631	4.7877	0.89
2019	124.4422	21.8320	6.5496	20.00	15.00	16.3740	5.4580	0.89
2020	141.8641	24.8884	7.4665	20.00	15.00	18.6663	6.2221	0.88
2021	161.7251	28.3728	8.5118	20.00	15.00	21.2796	7.0932	0.87
2022	184.3666	32.3450	9.7035	20.00	15.00	24.2588	8.0863	0.86
2023	210.1779	36.8733	11.0620	20.00	15.00	27.6550	9.2183	0.86
2024	239.6029	42.0356	12.6107	20.00	15.00	31.5267	10.5089	0.85
2025	273.1473	47.9206	14.3762	20.00	15.00	35.9404	11.9801	0.84
2026	311.3879	54.6295	16.3888	20.00	15.00	40.9721	13.6574	0.83

Present value TWD 44.38

Terminal Premium = 0.00

The market price of TWD62.9 exceeds the estimated value of TWD44.38. The market price reflects higher forecasts of residual income during the period to 2026, a higher terminal premium than Rosato forecasts, and/or a lower cost of equity. If Rosato is confident in her forecasts she may conclude that the company is overvalued in the current marketplace.

Lee and Swaminathan (1999) and Lee, Myers, and Swaminathan (1999) have presented a residual income model based on explicit forecasts of residual income for three years. Thereafter, ROE is forecast to fade to the industry mean value of ROE. The terminal value at the end of the forecast horizon (T) is estimated as the terminal-year residual income discounted in perpetuity. Lee and Swaminathan stated that this assumes any growth in earnings after T is value neutral. Exhibit 6 presents sector ROE data from Hemscott Americas, retrieved from Yahoo.com. (ROE data for specific industries can be retrieved from the same source.) In forecasting a fading ROE, the analyst should also consider any trends in industry ROE.

EXHIBIT 6	U.S. Sector ROEs
Sectors	**ROE (%)**
Basic Materials	23.21
Conglomerates	20.10
Consumer Goods	20.83
Financial	20.22
Healthcare	15.49
Industrial Goods	17.37
Services	14.55
Technology	14.37
Utilities	14.44

Source: Based on Hemscott Americas data retrieved from http://biz.yahoo.com on 22 January 2008.

EXAMPLE 9

Multistage Residual Income Model (2)

Rosato's supervisor questions her assumption that Taiwan Semiconductor will have no premium at the end of her forecast period. Rosato assesses the effect of a terminal value based on a perpetuity of Year 2026 residual income. She computes the following terminal value:

TV = TWD13.6574/0.15 = TWD91.0491

The present value of this terminal value is as follows:

PV = TWD91.04901/$(1.15)^{20}$ = TWD5.5631

Adding TWD5.56 to the previous value of TWD44.38 (for which the terminal value was zero) yields a total value of TWD49.94. Because the current market price of TWD62.9 is greater than TWD49.94, market participants expect a positive continuing residual income at an even higher level than her new assumptions and/or are forecasting a higher interim ROE. Again, if Rosato is confident in her forecasts, she may conclude that the company is overvalued.

Another multistage model assumes that ROE fades over time to the cost of equity. In this approach, ROE can be explicitly forecast each period until reaching the cost of equity. The forecast would then end and the terminal value would be zero.

Dechow, Hutton, and Sloan (1998) presented an analysis of a residual income model in which residual income fades over time:[17]

$$V_0 = B_0 + \sum_{t=1}^{T-1} \frac{(E_t - rB_{t-1})}{(1 + r)^t} + \frac{E_T - rB_{T-1}}{(1 + r - \omega)(1 + r)^{T-1}} \qquad (8)$$

This model adds a persistence factor, ω, which is between zero and one. A persistence factor of one implies that residual income will not fade at all; rather it will continue at the same level indefinitely (i.e., in perpetuity). A persistence factor of zero implies that residual income will not continue after the initial forecast horizon. The higher the value of the persistence factor, the higher the stream of residual income in the final stage, and the higher the valuation, all else being equal. Dechow et al. found that in a large sample of company data from 1976 to 1995, the persistence factor equaled 0.62, which was interpreted by Bauman (1999) as equivalent to residual income decaying at an average rate of 38 percent a year. The persistence factor considers the long-run mean-reverting nature of ROE, assuming that in time ROE regresses toward r and that resulting residual income fades toward zero. Clearly, the persistence factor varies from company to company. For example, a company with a strong market leadership position would have a lower expected rate of decay (Bauman, 1999). Dechow et al. provided insight into some characteristics, listed in Exhibit 7, that can indicate a lower or higher level of persistence.

EXHIBIT 7	Final-Stage Residual Income Persistence
Lower Residual Income Persistence	**Higher Residual Income Persistence**
Extreme accounting rates of return (ROE)	Low dividend payout
Extreme levels of special items (e.g., nonrecurring items)	High historical persistence in the industry
Extreme levels of accounting accruals	

---

[17] See Dechow, Hutton, and Sloan (1998) and Bauman (1999).

Example 10 illustrates the assumption that continuing residual income will decline to zero as ROE approaches the required rate of return on equity.

EXAMPLE 10

Multistage Residual Income Model (3)

Rosato extends her analysis to consider the possibility that ROE will slowly decay toward r in 2027 and beyond, rather than using a perpetuity of Year 2026 residual income. Rosato estimates a persistence parameter of 0.60. The present value of the terminal value is determined as

$$\frac{E_T - rB_{T-1}}{(1 + r - \omega)(1 + r)^{T-1}}$$

with T equal to 21 and 2027 residual income equal to 15.5714 (13.6574 × 1.14), in which the 1.14 growth factor reflects a 14 percent growth rate calculated as the retention ratio times ROE, or (0.70)(20%) = 0.14.

$$\frac{15.57}{(1 + 0.15 - 0.60)(1.15)^{20}} = 1.73$$

Total value is TWD46.11 calculated by adding the present value of the terminal value, TWD1.73, to TWD44.38. Rosato concludes that if Taiwan Semiconductor's residual income does not persist at a stable level past 2026 and deteriorates through time, the shares are even more overvalued.

RESIDUAL INCOME VALUATION IN RELATION TO OTHER APPROACHES

4

Before addressing accounting issues in using the residual income model, we briefly summarize the relationship of the residual income model to other valuation models.

Valuation models based on discounting dividends or on discounting free cash flows are as theoretically sound as the residual income model. Unlike the residual income model, however, the discounted dividend and free cash flow models forecast future cash flows and find the value of stock by discounting them back to the present by using the required return. Recall that the required return is the cost of equity for both the DDM and the free cash flows to equity (FCFE) model. For the free cash flow to the firm (FCFF) model, the required return is the overall weighted average cost of capital. The RI model approaches this process differently. It starts with a value based on the balance sheet, the book value of equity, and adjusts this value by adding the present values of expected future residual income. Thus, in theory, the recognition of value is different, but the total present value, whether using expected dividends, expected free cash flow, or book value plus expected residual income, should be consistent.[18]

---

[18] See, for example, Shrieves and Wachowicz (2001).

Example 11 again illustrates the important point that the recognition of value in residual income models typically occurs earlier than in dividend discount models. In other words, residual income models tend to assign a relatively small portion of a security's total present value to the earnings that occur in later years. Note also that this example makes use of the fact that the present value of a perpetuity in the amount of X can be calculated as X/r.

EXAMPLE 11

Valuing a Perpetuity with the Residual Income Model

Assume the following data:

► A company will earn $1.00 per share forever.
► The company pays out all earnings as dividends.
► Book value per share is $6.00.
► The required rate of return on equity (or the percent cost of equity) is 10 percent.

1. Calculate the value of this stock using the DDM.
2. Calculate the level amount of per-share residual income that will be earned each year.
3. Calculate the value of the stock using a RI model.
4. Create a table summarizing the year-by-year valuation using the DDM and the RI model.

Solution to 1: Because the dividend, D, is a perpetuity, the present value of D can be calculated as D/r.

$$V_0 = D/r = \$1.00/0.10 = \$10.00 \text{ per share}$$

Solution to 2: Because each year all net income is paid out as dividends, book value per share will be constant at $6.00. Therefore, with a required rate of return on equity of 10 percent, for all future years, per-share residual income will be as follows:

$$\text{RI}_t = E_t - rB_{t-1} = \$1.00 - 0.10(\$6.00) = \$1.00 - \$0.60 = \$0.40$$

Solution to 3: Using a residual income model, the estimated value equals the current book value per share plus the present value of future expected residual income (which in this example can be valued as a perpetuity):

$$
\begin{aligned}
V_0 &= \text{Book value} + \text{PV of expected future per-share residual income} \\
&= \$6.00 + \$0.40/0.10 \\
&= \$6.00 + \$4.00 = \$10.00
\end{aligned}
$$

Solution to 4: Exhibit 8 summarizes the year-by-year valuation using the DDM and the RI models.

EXHIBIT 8	Value Recognition in the DDM and the RI Model			
Dividend Discount Model			**Residual Income Model**	
Year	D_t	PV of D_t	B_0 or RI_t	PV of B_0 or RI_t
0			$6.00	$6.000
1	$1.00	$0.909	0.40	0.364
2	1.00	0.826	0.40	0.331
3	1.00	0.751	0.40	0.301
4	1.00	0.683	0.40	0.273
5	1.00	0.621	0.40	0.248
6	1.00	0.564	0.40	0.226
7	1.00	0.513	0.40	0.205
8	1.00	0.467	0.40	0.187
⋮	⋮	⋮	⋮	⋮
Total		$10.00		$10.00

In the RI model, most of the total value of the stock is attributed to the earlier periods. Specifically, the current book value of $6.00 represents 60 percent of the stock's total present value of $10.

In contrast, in the DDM, value is derived from the receipt of dividends, and typically, a smaller proportion of value is attributed to the earlier periods. Less than $1.00 of the total $10 derives from the first year's dividend, and collectively, the first five years' dividends ($0.909 + $0.826 + $0.751 + $0.683 + $0.621 = $3.79) contribute only about 38 percent of the total present value of $10.

As shown earlier and illustrated again in Example 11, the dividend discount and residual income models are in theory mutually consistent. Because of the real world uncertainty in forecasting distant cash flows, however, the earlier recognition of value in a residual income approach relative to other present value approaches is a practical advantage. In the dividend discount and free cash flow models, a stock's value is often modeled as the sum of the present value of individually forecasted dividends or free cash flows up to some terminal point plus the present value of the expected terminal value of the stock. In practice, a large fraction of a stock's total present value, in either the discounted dividend or free cash flow models, is represented by the present value of the expected terminal value. Substantial uncertainty, however, often surrounds the terminal value. In contrast, residual income valuations typically are less sensitive to terminal value estimates. (In some residual income valuation contexts the terminal value may actually be set equal to zero.) The derivation of value from the earlier portion of a forecast horizon is one reason residual income valuation can be a useful analytical tool.

4.1 Strengths and Weaknesses of the Residual Income Model

Now that the implementation of the residual income model has been illustrated with several examples, a summary of the strengths and weaknesses of the residual income approach follows:

The strengths of residual income models include the following:

► Terminal values do not make up a large portion of the total present value, relative to other models.
► RI models use readily available accounting data.
► The models can be readily applied to companies that do not pay dividends or to companies that do not have positive expected near-term free cash flows.
► The models can be used when cash flows are unpredictable.
► The models have an appealing focus on economic profitability.

The potential weaknesses of residual income models include the following:

► The models are based on accounting data that can be subject to manipulation by management.
► Accounting data used as inputs may require significant adjustments.
► The models require that the clean surplus relation holds, or that the analyst makes appropriate adjustments when the clean surplus relation does not hold. Section 5.1 discusses the clean surplus relation (or clean surplus accounting).
► The residual income model's use of accounting income assumes that the cost of debt capital is reflected appropriately by interest expense.

4.2 Broad Guidelines for Using a Residual Income Model

The above list of potential weaknesses helps explain the reading's focus in the following section on accounting considerations. In light of its strengths and weaknesses, the following are broad guidelines for using a residual income model in common stock valuation.

A residual income model is most appropriate when:

► a company does not pay dividends, or its dividends are not predictable;
► a company's expected free cash flows are negative within the analyst's comfortable forecast horizon; or
► great uncertainty exists in forecasting terminal values using an alternative present value approach.

Residual income models are least appropriate when:

► significant departures from clean surplus accounting exist, or
► significant determinants of residual income, such as book value and ROE, are not predictable.

Because various valuation models can be derived from the same underlying theoretical model, when fully consistent assumptions are used to forecast earnings, cash flow, dividends, book value, and residual income through a full set of pro forma (projected) financial statements, and the same required rate of return on equity is used as the discount rate, the same estimate of value should result when using each model. Practically speaking, however, it may not be possible to forecast each of these items with the same degree of certainty.[19] For example, if a company has near-term negative free cash flow and forecasts for the terminal value are uncertain, a residual income model may be more appropriate. But a company with positive, predictable cash flow that does not pay a dividend would be well suited for a discounted free cash flow valuation.

Residual income models, just like the discounted dividend and free cash flow models, can also be used to establish justified market multiples, such as price-to-earnings ratio (P/E) or P/B. For example, the value can be determined by using a residual income model and dividing by earnings to arrive at a justified P/E.

A residual income model can also be used in conjunction with other models to assess the consistency of results. If a wide variation of estimated value is found and each model appears appropriate, the inconsistency may lie with the assumptions used in the models. The analyst would need to perform additional work to determine whether the assumptions are mutually consistent and which model is most appropriate for the subject company.

ACCOUNTING AND INTERNATIONAL CONSIDERATIONS

5

To most accurately apply the residual income model in practice, the analyst may need to adjust book value of common equity for off-balance sheet items and adjust reported net income to obtain **comprehensive income** (all changes in equity other than contributions by, and distributions to, owners). In this section, we will discuss issues relating to these tasks.

Bauman (1999) has noted that the strength of the residual income model is that the two components (book value and future earnings) of the model have a balancing effect on each other, provided that the clean surplus relationship is followed:

> All other things held constant, companies making aggressive (conservative) accounting choices will report higher (lower) book values and lower (higher) future earnings. In the model, the present value of differences in future income is exactly offset by the initial differences in book value. (Bauman 1999, page 31)

Unfortunately, this argument has several problems in practice because the clean surplus relationship does not prevail, and analysts often use past earnings to predict future earnings. IFRS and U.S. GAAP permit a variety of items to bypass the income statement and be reported directly in stockholders' equity. Further, off-balance sheet liabilities or nonoperating and nonrecurring items of income may obscure a company's financial performance. The analyst must thus be aware of such items when evaluating the book value of equity and return on equity to be used as inputs into a residual income model.

---

[19] For a lively debate on this issue, see Penman and Sougiannis (1998), Penman (2001), Lundholm and O'Keefe (2001a), and Lundholm and O'Keefe (2001b).

With regard to the possibility that aggressive accounting choices will lead to lower reported future earnings, consider an example in which a company chooses to capitalize an expenditure in the current year rather than expense it. Doing so overstates current-year earnings as well as current book value. If an analyst uses current earnings (or ROE) naively in predicting future residual earnings, the RI model will overestimate the value of the company. Take, for example, a company with $1,000,000 of book value and $200,000 of earnings before taxes, after expensing an expenditure of $50,000. Ignoring taxes, this company has a ROE of 20 percent. If the company capitalized the expenditure rather than expensing it immediately, it would have a ROE of 23.81 percent ($250,000/$1,050,000). Although at some time in the future this capitalized item will likely be amortized or written off, thus reducing realized future earnings, analysts' expectations often rely on historical data. If capitalization of expenditures persists over time for a stable size company, ROE can decline because net income will normalize over the long term, but book value will be overstated. For a growing company, for which the expenditure in question is increasing, ROE can continue at high levels over time. In practice, because the RI model uses primarily accounting data as inputs, the model can be sensitive to accounting choices, and aggressive accounting methods (e.g., accelerating revenues or deferring expenses) can result in valuation errors. The analyst must, therefore, be particularly careful in analyzing a company's reported data for use in a residual income model.

Two principal drivers of residual earnings are ROE and book value. Analysts must understand how to use historical reported accounting data for these items to the extent they use historical data in forecasting future ROE and book value. Other readings have explained the DuPont analysis of ROE, which can be used as a tool in forecasting, and discussed the calculation of book value. We extend these discussions below with specific application to residual income valuation, particularly in addressing the following accounting considerations:

▶ violations of the clean surplus relationship;

▶ balance sheet adjustments for fair value;

▶ intangible assets;

▶ nonrecurring items;

▶ aggressive accounting practices; and

▶ international considerations.

In any valuation, close attention must be paid to the accounting practices of the company being valued. The following sections address the above issues as they particularly affect residual income valuation.

5.1 Violations of the Clean Surplus Relationship

One potential accounting issue in applying a residual income model is a violation of clean surplus accounting. Violations may occur when accounting standards permit charges directly to stockholders' equity, bypassing the income statement. An example is the case of changes in the market value of available-for-sale investments. Under both IFRS (IAS 39, paragraph 55b) and U.S. GAAP (SFAS No. 115, paragraph 13), investments considered to be "available for sale" are shown on the balance sheet at market value. Any change in their market value, however, is reflected directly in stockholders' equity rather than as income on the income statement.

As stated earlier, comprehensive income is defined in U.S. GAAP as all changes in equity other than contributions by, and distributions to, owners.

Comprehensive income includes net income reported on the income statement and *other comprehensive income*, which is the result of other events and transactions that result in a change to equity but are not reported on the income statement. Items that commonly bypass the income statement include:[20]

- ▶ foreign currency translation adjustments;
- ▶ certain pension adjustments; and
- ▶ fair value changes of some financial instruments.

An identical concept exists in IFRS, although the terminology "other comprehensive income" is not used. Under both international and U.S. standards, such items as fair value changes for some financial instruments and foreign currency translation adjustments bypass the income statement. In addition, under IFRS, which unlike U.S. GAAP permits revaluation of fixed assets (IAS 16, paragraph 39–42), some changes in the fair value of fixed assets also bypass the income statement and directly affect equity.

In all of these cases in which items bypass the income statement, the book value of equity is stated accurately, but net income is not from the perspective of residual income valuation. The analyst should be most concerned with the effect of these items on forecasts of net income and ROE (which has net income in the numerator), and hence residual income.[21] Because some items (including those listed above) bypass the income statement, they are excluded from historical ROE data. As noted by Frankel and Lee (1999), bias will be introduced into the valuation only if the present expected value of the clean surplus violations do not net to zero. In other words, reductions in income from some periods may be offset by increases from other periods. The analyst must examine the equity section of the balance sheet and the related statements of shareholders' equity and comprehensive income carefully for items that have bypassed the income statement. The analyst can then assess whether amounts are likely to be offsetting and can assess the effect on future ROE.

EXAMPLE 12

Evaluating Clean Surplus Violations

Excerpts from two companies' statements of changes in stockholders' equity are shown in Exhibits 9 and 10. The first statement, prepared under IFRS as of 31 December 2006, is for Nokia Corporation (NYSE: NOK), a leading manufacturer of mobile phones headquartered in Finland and with operations in four business segments: mobile phones, multimedia, enterprise solutions, and networks. The second statement, prepared under U.S. GAAP as of 31 December 2006, is for SAP AG (NYSE: SAP), which is headquartered in Germany and is a worldwide provider of enterprise application software, including enterprise resource planning, customer relationship management, and supply chain management software.

---

[20] See Frankel and Lee (1999).

[21] The analyst should more precisely calculate historical ROE at the aggregate level (e.g., as net income divided by shareholders' equity) rather than as earnings per share divided by book value per share, because such actions as share issuance and share repurchases can distort ROE calculated on a per-share basis.

EXHIBIT 9   Nokia Corporation Statement of Changes in Stockholders' Equity (excerpt) (€ Millions)

Group	Share Capital	Share Issue Premium	Treasury Shares	Translation Differences	Fair Value and Other Reserves	Retained Earnings	Before Minority Interests	Minority Interests	Total
Balance at 31 December 2005	266	2,458	−3,616	69	−176	13,308	12,309	205	12,514
Tax benefit on stock options exercised		23					23		23
Excess tax benefit on share-based compensation		14					14		14
Translation differences				−141			−141	−13	−154
Net investment hedge gains, net of tax				38			38		38
Cash flow hedges, net of tax					171		171		171
Available-for-sale investments, net of tax					−9		−9		−9
Other decrease, net						−52	−52	−1	−53
Profit						4,306	4,306	60	4,366
Total recognized income and expense	0	37	0	−103	162	4,254	4,350	46	4,396
Total of other equity movements	−20	212	1,556	0	0	−6,439	−4,691	−159	−4,850
Balance at 31 December 2006	246	2,707	−2,060	−34	−14	11,123	11,968	92	12,060

EXHIBIT 10

SAP AG and Subsidiaries
Consolidated Statements of Shareholders' Equity and Comprehensive Income (excerpt) (€ Thousands)

	Additional Paid-In Capital	Retained Earnings	Accumulated Other Comprehensive Income/Loss					Treasury Stock	Total
			Foreign Currency Translation Adjustment	Unrealized Gains/Losses on Marketable Securities	Unrecognized Pension Plan Cost	Unrealized Gains/Losses on Hedges	Currency Effects from Inter-Company Long-Term Investment Transactions		
31 December 2005	372,767	5,986,186	−202,260	11,168	−9,975	42,449	40,763	−775,318	5,782,238
Net income		1,871,377							1,871,377
Other comprehensive income/loss, net of tax			−148,568	−6,692		−28,420	−26,022		−209,702
Total comprehensive income/loss									1,661,675
Stock-based compensation	17,611								17,611
Dividends		−447,219							−447,219
Treasury stock transactions	44,434							−966,492	−922,058
Convertible bonds and stock options exercised	48,940								49,366
Issuance of common stock	−134,768	−815,885							0
Other	3,658	350							4,008
Impact of first-time adoption of SFAS 158					−9,766				−9,766
31 December 2006	352,642	6,594,809	−350,828	4,476	−19,741	14,029	14,741	−1,741,810	6,135,855

Source: www.sap.com/about/investor/index.epx.

For Nokia, items that have bypassed the income statement in 2006 are those that are summed to obtain "Total recognized income and expense" in the columns labeled "Share issue premium," "Translation differences," and "Fair value and other reserves." For SAP, the amounts that bypassed the income statement in 2006 appear in the five columns below the heading "Accumulated other comprehensive income/loss."

To illustrate the issues in interpreting these items, consider the columns "Translation differences" (Nokia) and "Foreign currency translation adjustment" (SAP). The amounts in these columns reflect currency translation adjustments to equity that have bypassed the income statement. For Nokia, the adjustment for the year 2006 was −€103 million. Because this is a negative adjustment to stockholders' equity, this item would have decreased income if it had been reported on the income statement. The balance is not increasing, however; it appears to be reversing to zero over time. For SAP, the translation adjustment for the year 2006 was −€148 million. Again, because this is a negative adjustment to stockholders' equity, this item would have decreased income if it had been reported on the income statement. In this case, the negative balance appears to be accumulating: It does not appear to be reversing (netting to zero) over time. If the analyst expects this trend to continue and has used historical data as the basis for initial estimates of ROE to be used in residual income valuation, a downward adjustment in that estimated future ROE might be warranted. It is possible, however, that future exchange rate movements will reverse this accumulation.

The examples in this reading have used the actual beginning equity and a forecasted level of ROE (return on beginning equity) to compute the forecasted net income. Because equity includes accumulated other comprehensive income (AOCI), the assumptions about future other comprehensive income (OCI) will affect forecasted net income and thus residual income. To illustrate, Exhibit 11 shows a hypothetical company's financials for a single previous year, labeled year $t-1$, followed by three different forecasts for the following two years. In year $t-1$, the company reports net income of $120, which is a 12 percent return on beginning equity of $1,000. The company paid no dividends, so ending retained earnings equal $120. In year $t-1$, the company also reports OCI of −$100, a loss, so the ending amount shown in AOCI is a −$100. (Companies typically label this line item "accumulated other comprehensive income (loss)," indicating that the amount is an accumulated loss when given in parentheses.)

All three forecasts in Exhibit 11 assume that ROE will be 12 percent and use this assumption to forecast net income for year t and $t+1$ by using the expression $0.12 \times$ Beginning book value. Each forecast, however, incorporates different assumptions about future OCI. Forecast A assumes that the company will have no OCI in year t or year $t+1$, so the amount of AOCI does not change. Forecast B assumes that the company will continue to have the same amount of OCI in year t and year $t+1$ as it had in the prior year, so the amount of AOCI becomes more negative each year. Forecast C assumes that the company's OCI will reverse in year t, so at the end of year t, AOCI will be zero. As shown, because the forecasts use the assumed ROE to compute forecasted net income, the forecasts for net income and residual income in year $t+1$ vary significantly.

Because this example assumes all earnings are retained, a forecast of 12 percent ROE also implies that net income and residual income will grow at 12 percent. Only the year t to year $t+1$ under Forecast A, which assumes no future OCI,

	Actual	Forecast A		Forecast B		Forecast C	
Year	t–1	t	t+1	t	t+1	t	t+1
Beginning Balance Sheet							
Assets	$1,000.00	$1,020.00	$1,142.40	$1,020.00	$1,042.40	$1,020.00	$1,242.40
Liabilities	—	—	—	—	—	—	—
Common stock	1,000.00	1,000.00	1,000.00	1,000.00	1,000.00	1,000.00	1,000.00
Retained earnings	—	120.00	242.40	120.00	242.40	120.00	242.40
AOCI	—	(100.00)	(100.00)	(100.00)	(200.00)	(100.00)	—
Total equity	1,000.00	1,020.00	1,142.40	1,020.00	1,042.40	1,020.00	1,242.40
Total liabilities and total equity	$1,000.00	$1,020.00	$1,142.40	$1,020.00	$1,042.40	$1,020.00	$1,242.40
Net income	120.00	122.40	137.09	122.40	125.09	122.40	149.09
Dividends	—	—	—	—	—	—	—
Other comprehensive income	(100.00)	—	—	(100.00)	(100.00)	100.00	—
Ending Balance Sheet							
Assets	$1,020.00	$1,142.40	$1,279.49	$1,042.40	$1,067.49	$1,242.40	$1,391.49
Liabilities	—	—	—	—	—	—	—
Common stock	1,000.00	1,000.00	1,000.00	1,000.00	1,000.00	1,000.00	1,000.00
Retained earnings	120.00	242.40	379.49	242.40	367.49	242.40	391.49
AOCI	(100.00)	(100.00)	(100.00)	(200.00)	(300.00)	—	—
Total equity	$1,020.00	$1,142.40	$1,279.49	$1,042.40	$1,067.49	$1,242.40	$1,391.49
Total liabilities and total equity	$1,020.00	$1,142.40	$1,279.49	$1,042.40	$1,067.49	$1,242.40	$1,391.49
Residual income calculation based on beginning total equity							
Net income	120.00	122.40	137.09	122.40	125.09	122.40	149.09
Equity charge at 10 percent	100.00	102.00	114.24	102.00	104.24	102.00	124.24
Residual income	$20.00	$20.40	$22.85	$20.40	$20.85	$20.40	$24.85

EXHIBIT 11 Hypothetical Company — Alternative Forecasts with Different Assumptions about Comprehensive Income

correctly reflects that relationship. Specifically, in Forecast A, both net income and residual income increase by 12 percent from year t to year t+1. Net income grows from $122.40 to $137.09, an increase of 12 percent [($137.09/$122.40) − 1]; and residual income grows from $20.40 to $22.85, an increase of 12 percent [($22.85/$20.40) − 1]. In contrast to Forecast A, neither Forecast B nor Forecast C correctly reflects the relationship between ROE and growth in income (net and residual). Growth in residual income from year t to year t+1 was 2.2 percent under Forecast B and 21.8 percent under Forecast C.

If, alternatively, the forecasts of future ROE and the residual income computation had incorporated total comprehensive income (net income plus OCI), the results of the residual income computation would have differed significantly. For example, suppose that in Forecast B, which assumes the company will continue to have the same amount of OCI, the estimated future ROE was 2.0

percent, using total comprehensive income [($120 − $100)/$1,000 = $20/$1,000]. If the residual income computation had then also used forecasted total comprehensive income at time t, the amount of residual income would be negative. Specifically, for time t, forecast comprehensive income would be $22.40 (ROE of 2.0 percent times beginning equity of $1,020), the equity charge would be $102 (required return of 10 percent times beginning equity of $1,020), and residual income would be −$79.86 (comprehensive income of $22.40 minus equity charge of $102). Clearly, residual income on this basis significantly falls short of the positive $20.40 when the violation of clean surplus is ignored. As this example demonstrates, using an ROE forecast or a net income forecast that ignores violations of clean surplus accounting will distort estimates of residual income. Unless the present value of such distortions net to zero, using those forecasts will also distort valuations.

What are the implications for implementing a residual-income-based valuation? If future OCI is expected to be significant relative to net income and if the year-to-year amounts of OCI are not expected to net to zero, the analyst should attempt to incorporate these items so that residual income forecasts are closer to what they would be if the clean surplus relation held. Specifically, when possible, the analyst should incorporate explicit assumptions about future amounts of OCI.

Example 13 illustrates, by reference to the DDM value, the error that results when OCI is omitted from residual income calculations (assuming an analyst has a basis for forecasting future amounts of OCI).[22] The example also shows that the growth rate in residual income is generally not equal to the growth rate of net income or dividends.

EXAMPLE 13

Incorporating Adjustments in the Residual Income Model

Exhibit 12 gives per-share forecasts for Mannistore, Inc., a hypothetical company operating a chain of retail stores. The company's cost of capital is 10 percent.

EXHIBIT 12   Forecasts for Mannistore, Inc.

	Year				
Variable	1	2	3	4	5
Shareholders' equity $_{t-1}$	$8.58	$10.32	$11.51	$14.68	$17.86
Plus net income	2.00	2.48	3.46	3.47	4.56
Less dividends	0.26	0.29	0.29	0.29	0.38
Less other comprehensive income	0.00	1.00	0.00	0.00	0.00
Equals shareholders' equity$_t$	$10.32	$11.51	$14.68	$17.86	$22.04

---

[22] See Lundholm and O'Keefe (2001), who show how RI model and DDM valuations will differ when the analyst fails to include OCI in residual income calculations or makes inconsistent assumptions about the growth rates of net income, dividends, and residual income.

1. Assuming the forecasted terminal price of Mannistore's shares at the end of year 5 (time $t = 5$) is $68.40, estimate the value per share of Mannistore using the DDM.

2. Given that the forecast terminal price of Mannistore's shares at the end of year 5 (time $t = 5$) is $68.40, estimate the value of a share of Mannistore using the RI model and calculate residual income based on:

   A. net income without adjustment, and

   B. net income plus other comprehensive income.

3. Interpret your answers to Parts 2A and 2B.

4. Assume that a forecast of the terminal price of Mannistore's shares at the end of year 5 (time $t = 5$) is not available. Instead, an estimate of terminal price based on the Gordon growth model is appropriate. You estimate that the growth in net income and dividends from $t = 5$ to $t = 6$ will be 8 percent. Predict residual income for year 6, and based on that 8 percent growth estimate, determine the growth rate in forecasted residual income from $t = 5$ to $t = 6$.

Solution to 1: The estimated value using the DDM is:

$$V_0 = \frac{\$0.26}{(1.10)^1} + \frac{\$0.29}{(1.10)^2} + \frac{\$0.29}{(1.10)^3} + \frac{\$0.29}{(1.10)^4} + \frac{\$0.38}{(1.10)^5}$$
$$+ \frac{\$68.40}{(1.10)^5} = \$43.59$$

Solution to 2:

A. Calculating residual income as net income (NI) minus the equity charge, which is beginning shareholders' equity (SE) times the cost of equity capital (r), gives the following for years 1 through 5:

	Year				
	1	**2**	**3**	**4**	**5**
$RI = NI - (SE_{t-1} \times r)$	1.14	1.45	2.30	2.00	2.77

So, the estimated value using the RI model (using Equation 6), with residual income calculated based on net income, is:

$$V_0 = \$8.58 + \frac{\$1.14}{(1.10)^1} + \frac{\$1.45}{(1.10)^2} + \frac{\$2.30}{(1.10)^3} + \frac{\$2.00}{(1.10)^4} + \frac{\$2.77}{(1.10)^5}$$
$$+ \frac{\$68.40 - \$22.04}{(1.10)^5}$$
$$V_0 = \$8.58 + 35.84 = \$44.42$$

B. Calculating residual income as net income adjusted for OCI (NI + OCI) minus the equity charge, which equals beginning shareholders' equity (SE) times the cost of equity capital (r), gives the following for years 1 through 5:

	Year				
	1	**2**	**3**	**4**	**5**
RI = (NI + OCI) − (SE$_{t-1}$ × r)	$1.14	$0.45	$2.30	$2.00	$2.77

So, the estimated value using the RI model, with residual income based on net income adjusted for OCI, is:

$$V_0 = \$8.58 + \frac{\$1.14}{(1.10)^1} + \frac{\$.45}{(1.10)^2} + \frac{\$2.30}{(1.10)^3} + \frac{\$2.00}{(1.10)^4} + \frac{\$2.77}{(1.10)^5}$$
$$+ \frac{\$68.40 - \$22.04}{(1.10)^5}$$
$$V_0 = \$8.58 + 35.01 = \$43.59$$

Solution to 3: The first calculation (2A) incorrectly omits an adjustment for a violation of the clean surplus relation. The second calculation (2B) includes an adjustment and yields the correct value estimate, which is consistent with the DDM estimate.

Solution to 4: Given the estimated 8 percent growth in net income and dividends in year 6, the estimated year 6 net income is $4.92 ($4.56 × 1.08), and the estimated amount of year 6 dividends is $0.42 ($0.38 × 1.08).

Residual income will then equal $2.72 (which is net income of $4.92 minus the equity charge of beginning book value of $22.04 times the cost of capital of 10 percent). So, the growth rate in residual income is negative at approximately −2 percent ($2.72/$2.77 − 1).

Lacking a basis for explicit assumptions about future amounts of OCI, the analyst should nonetheless be aware of the potential effect of OCI on residual income and adjust ROE accordingly. Finally, as noted above, the analyst may decide that an alternative valuation model is more appropriate.

5.2 Balance Sheet Adjustments for Fair Value

To have a reliable measure of book value of equity, an analyst should identify and scrutinize significant off-balance sheet assets and liabilities. Additionally, reported assets and liabilities should be adjusted to fair value when possible. Off-balance sheet assets and liabilities may become apparent through an examination of the financial statement footnotes. Examples include the use of operating leases and the use of special purpose entities to remove both debt and assets from the balance sheet. Some items, such as operating leases, may not affect the amount of equity (because leases involve both off-balance sheet assets that offset the off-balance sheet liabilities) but can affect an assessment of future earnings for the residual income component of value. Other assets and liabilities may be stated at values other than fair value. For example, inventory may be stated at LIFO and require adjustment to restate to current value. (LIFO is not permitted under IFRS.) The following are some common items to review for balance sheet adjustments. Note, however, that this list is not inclusive:[23]

- ► inventory;
- ► deferred tax assets and liabilities;
- ► operating leases;
- ► special-purpose entities;
- ► reserves and allowances (for example, bad debts); and
- ► intangible assets.

Additionally, the analyst should examine the financial statements and footnotes for items unique to the subject company.

5.3 Intangible Assets

Intangible assets can have a significant effect on book value. In the case of specifically identifiable intangibles that can be separated from the entity (e.g., sold), it is appropriate to include these in the determination of book value of equity. If these assets are wasting (declining in value over time), they will be amortized over time as an expense. Intangible assets, however, require special consideration because they are often not recognized as an asset unless they are obtained in an acquisition. For example, advertising expenditures can create a highly valuable brand, which is clearly an intangible asset. Advertising expenditures, however, are shown as an expense and the value of a brand would not appear as an asset on the financial statements unless the company owning the brand was acquired.

To demonstrate this, consider a simplified example involving two companies, Alpha and Beta, with the following summary financial information (all amounts in thousands, except per-share data):

	Alpha	Beta
Cash	€1,600	€ 100
Property, plant, and equipment	3,400	900
Total assets	€5,000	€1,000
Equity	5,000	1,000
Net income	€ 600	€ 150

Each company pays out all net income as dividends (no growth), and the clean surplus relation holds. Alpha has a 12 percent ROE and Beta has a 15 percent ROE, both expected to continue indefinitely. Each has a 10 percent required rate of return. The fair market value of each company's property, plant, and equipment is the same as its book value. What is the value of each company in a residual income framework?

---

[23] See also Chapter 17 of White, Sondhi, and Fried (1998).

Using total book value rather than per-share data, the value of Alpha would be €6,000, determined as follows:[24]

$$V_0 = B_0 + \frac{\text{ROE} - r}{r - g} B_0 = 5,000 + \frac{0.12 - 0.10}{0.10 - 0.00} 5,000 = 6,000$$

Similarly, the value of Beta would be €1,500:

$$V_0 = B_0 + \frac{\text{ROE} - r}{r - g} B_0 = 1,000 + \frac{0.15 - 0.10}{0.10 - 0.00} 1,000 = 1,500$$

The value of the companies on a combined basis would be €7,500. Note that both companies are valued more highly than the book value of equity because they have ROE in excess of the required rate of return. Absent an acquisition transaction, the financial statements of Alpha and Beta do not reflect this value. If either is acquired, however, an acquirer would allocate the purchase price to the acquired assets, with any excess of the purchase price above the acquired assets shown as goodwill.

Suppose Alpha acquires Beta by paying Beta's former shareholders €1,500 in cash. Alpha has just paid €500 in excess of the value of Beta's total reported assets of €1,000. Assume that Beta's property, plant and equipment is already shown at its fair market value of €1,000, and that the €500 is considered to be the fair value of a license owned by Beta, say an exclusive right to provide a service. Assume further that the original cost of obtaining the license was an immaterial application fee, which does not appear on Beta's balance sheet, and that the license covers a period of 10 years. Because the entire purchase price of €1,500 is allocated to identifiable assets, no goodwill is reported. The balance sheet of Alpha immediately after the acquisition would be:[25]

	Alpha
Cash	€ 200
Property, plant, and equipment	4,300
License	500
Total assets	€5,000
Equity	€5,000

Note that the total book value of Alpha's equity did not change, because the acquisition was made for cash and thus did not require Alpha to issue any new shares.

Making the assumption that the license is amortized over a 10-year period, the combined company's expected net income would be €700 (€600 + €150 − €50 amortization). If this net income number is used to derive expected ROE, the expected ROE would be 14 percent. Under a residual income model, with no adjustment for amortization, the value of the combined company would be:

$$V_0 = B_0 + \frac{\text{ROE} - r}{r - g} B_0 = 5,000 + \frac{0.14 - 0.10}{0.10 - 0.00} 5,000 = 7,000$$

---

[24] Results would be the same if calculated on a per-share basis.

[25] For example, cash of €200 is calculated as €1,600 (cash of Alpha) + €100 (cash of Beta) − €1,500 (purchase price of Beta).

Why would the combined company be worth less than the two separate companies? If the assumption is made that a fair price was paid to Beta's former shareholders, the combined value should not be lower. The lower value using the residual income model results from a reduction in ROE as a result of the amortization of the intangible license asset. If this asset were not amortized (or if the amortization expense was added back before computing ROE), net income would be €750 and ROE would be 15 percent. The value of the combined entity would be:

$$V_0 = B_0 + \frac{\text{ROE} - r}{r - g} B_0 = 5{,}000 + \frac{0.15 - 0.10}{0.10 - 0.00} 5{,}000 = 7{,}500$$

This amount, €7,500, is the same as the sum of the values of the companies on a separate basis.

Would the answer be different if the acquiring company used newly issued stock rather than cash in the acquisition? The form of currency used to pay for the transaction should not impact the total value. If Alpha used €1,500 of newly issued stock to acquire Beta, its balance sheet would be

	Alpha
Cash	€1,700
Property, plant, and equipment	4,300
License	500
Total assets	€6,500
Equity	€6,500

Projected earnings, excluding the amortization of the license, would be €750, and projected ROE would be 11.538 percent. Value under the residual income model would be:

$$V_0 = B_0 + \frac{\text{ROE} - r}{r - g} B_0 = 6{,}500 + \frac{0.11538 - 0.10}{0.10 - 0.00} 6{,}500 = 7{,}500$$

The overall value remains unchanged. The book value of equity is higher but offset by the effect on ROE. Once again, this example assumes that the buyer paid a fair value for the acquisition. If an acquirer overpays for an acquisition, the overpayment should become evident in a reduction in future residual income.

Research and development (R&D) costs provide another example of an intangible asset that must be given careful consideration. Under U.S. GAAP, R&D is generally expensed to the income statement directly (except in certain cases such as SFAS No. 87 which permits the capitalization of R&D expenses related to software development after product feasibility has been established). Also, under IFRS, some R&D costs can be capitalized and amortized over time. R&D expenditures are reflected in a company's ROE, and hence residual income, over the long term. If a company engages in unproductive R&D expenditures, these will lower residual income through the expenditures made. If a company engages in productive R&D expenditures, these should result in higher revenues to offset the expenditures over time. In summary, on a continuing basis for a mature company, ROE should reflect the productivity of R&D expenditures.

IFRS and U.S. GAAP differ in accounting for in-process R&D, which can be recognized as an acquired finite-life intangible asset or as part of goodwill under IFRS, but must be expensed immediately under U.S. GAAP. Does the difference matter? Bauman (1999) found that when purchased in-process R&D is capitalized and then amortized in a short period, overall value is not affected compared with the immediate expensing of R&D in a residual income framework. Further, Lundholm and Sloan (2007) explain that including and subsequently amortizing an asset that was omitted from a company's reported assets has no affect on valuation under a residual income model. Such an adjustment would increase the estimated equity value by adding the asset to book value at time zero but decrease the estimated value by an equivalent amount, which would include a) the present value of the asset when amortized in the future and b) the present value of a periodic capital charge based on the amount of the asset times the cost of equity. Expensing R&D, however, results in an immediately lower ROE vis-à-vis capitalizing R&D. But expensing R&D will result in a slightly higher ROE relative to capitalizing R&D in future years because this capitalized R&D is amortized.[26] Because ROE is used in a number of expressions derived from the residual income model and may also be used in forecasting net income, the analyst should carefully consider a company's R&D expenditures and their effect on long-term ROE.

5.4 Nonrecurring Items

In applying a residual income model, it is important to develop a forecast of future residual income based on recurring items. Companies often report nonrecurring charges as part of earnings or classify nonoperating income (e.g., sale of assets) as part of operating income. These misclassifications can lead to overestimates and underestimates of future residual earnings if no adjustments are made. No adjustments to book value are necessary for these items, however, because nonrecurring gains and losses are reflected in the value of assets in place. Hirst and Hopkins (2000) noted that nonrecurring items sometimes result from accounting rules and at other times result from "strategic" management decisions. Regardless, they highlighted the importance of examining the financial statement notes and other sources for items that may warrant adjustment in determining recurring earnings, such as:

► unusual items;

► extraordinary items;

► restructuring charges;

► discontinued operations; and

► accounting changes.

In some cases, management may record restructuring or unusual charges in every period. In these cases, the item may be considered an ordinary operating expense and may not require adjustment.

Companies sometimes inappropriately classify nonoperating gains as a reduction in operating expenses (such as selling, general, and administrative expenses). If material, this inappropriate classification can usually be uncovered by a careful reading of financial statement footnotes and press releases. Analysts should consider whether these items are likely to continue and contribute to residual income in time. More likely, they should be removed from operating earnings when forecasting residual income.

---

[26] See Henry and Gordon "Long-lived Assets" (2008), particularly the case of NOW Inc. in Example 1, for an illustration of the principles involved.

5.5 Other Aggressive Accounting Practices

Companies may engage in accounting practices that result in the overstatement of assets (book value) and/or overstatement of earnings. We discussed many of these practices in the preceding sections. Other activities that a company may engage in include accelerating revenues to the current period or deferring expenses to a later period.[27] Both activities simultaneously increase earnings and book value. For example, a company might ship unordered goods to customers at year-end, recording revenues and a receivable. As another example, a company could capitalize rather than expense a cash payment, resulting in lower expenses and an increase in assets.

Conversely, companies have also been criticized for the use of "cookie jar" reserves (reserves saved for future use), in which excess losses or expenses are recorded in an *earlier* period (for example, in conjunction with an acquisition or restructuring) and then used to reduce expenses and increase income in future periods. The analyst should carefully examine the use of reserves when assessing residual earnings. Overall, the analyst must evaluate a company's accounting policies carefully and consider the integrity of management when assessing the inputs in a residual income model.

5.6 International Considerations

Accounting standards differ internationally. These differences result in different measures of book value and earnings internationally and suggest that valuation models based on accrual accounting data might not perform as well as other present value models in international contexts. It is interesting to note, however, that Frankel and Lee (1999) found that the residual income model works well in valuing companies on an international basis. Using a simple residual income model without any of the adjustments discussed in this reading, they found that their residual income valuation model accounted for 70 percent of the cross-sectional variation of stock prices among 20 countries. Exhibit 13 shows the model's explanatory power by country.

EXHIBIT 13	International Application of Residual Income Models
Explanatory Power	**Country**
40–50 percent	Germany
	Japan (Parent company reporting)
60–70 percent	Australia
	Canada
	Japan (Consolidated reporting)
	United Kingdom
More than 70 percent	France
	United States

Source: Frankel and Lee (1999).

---

[27] See, for example, Schilit (1993).

Germany had the lowest explanatory power. Japan had low explanatory power for companies reporting only parent company results; the explanatory power for Japanese companies reporting on a consolidated basis was considerably higher. Explanatory power was highest in France, the United Kingdom, and the United States. Frankel and Lee concluded that there are three primary considerations in applying a residual income model internationally:

▶ the availability of reliable earnings forecasts;

▶ systematic violations of the clean surplus assumption; and

▶ "poor quality" accounting rules that result in delayed recognition of value changes.

Analysts should expect the model to work best in situations in which earnings forecasts are available, clean surplus violations are limited, and accounting rules do not result in delayed recognition. Because Frankel and Lee found good explanatory power for a residual income model using unadjusted accounting data, one expects that if adjustments are made to the reported data to correct for clean surplus and other violations, international comparisons should result in comparable valuations. For circumstances in which clean surplus violations exist, accounting choices result in delayed recognition, or accounting disclosures do not permit adjustment, the residual income model would not be appropriate and the analyst should consider a model less dependent on accounting data, such as a FCFE model.

It should be noted, however, that IFRS is increasingly becoming widely used. By 2011, the number of countries that either require or permit the use of IFRSs in preparation of financial statements in their countries is expected to reach 150. Furthermore, standard setters in numerous countries have started to work toward convergence between IFRS and home-country GAAP. In time, concerns about the use of different accounting standards should become less severe. Nonetheless, even within a single set of accounting standards, companies make choices and estimates that can affect valuation.

SUMMARY

This reading has discussed the use of residual income models in valuation. Residual income is an appealing economic concept because it attempts to measure economic profit, which are profits after accounting for all opportunity costs of capital.

▶ Residual income is calculated as net income minus a deduction for the cost of equity capital. The deduction is called the equity charge and is equal to equity capital multiplied by the required rate of return on equity (the cost of equity capital in percent).

▶ Economic value added (EVA) is a commercial implementation of the residual income concept. EVA = NOPAT − (C% × TC), where NOPAT is net operating profit after taxes, C% is the percent cost of capital, and TC is total capital.

▶ Residual income models (including commercial implementations) are used not only for equity valuation but also to measure internal corporate performance and for determining executive compensation.

▶ We can forecast per-share residual income as forecasted earnings per share minus the required rate of return on equity multiplied by beginning book value per share. Alternatively, per-share residual income can be forecasted as beginning book value per share multiplied by the difference between forecasted ROE and the required rate of return on equity.

▶ In the residual income model, the intrinsic value of a share of common stock is the sum of book value per share and the present value of expected future per-share residual income. In the residual income model, the equivalent mathematical expressions for intrinsic value of a common stock are

$$V_0 = B_0 + \sum_{t=1}^{\infty} \frac{\text{RI}_t}{(1+r)^t} = B_0 + \sum_{t=1}^{\infty} \frac{E_t - rB_{t-1}}{(1+r)^t}$$

$$= B_0 + \sum_{t=1}^{\infty} \frac{(\text{ROE}_t - r)B_{t-1}}{(1+r)^t}$$

where
V_0 = value of a share of stock today ($t = 0$)
B_0 = current per-share book value of equity
B_t = expected per-share book value of equity at any time t
r = required rate of return on equity (cost of equity)
E_t = expected earnings per share for period t
RI_t = expected per-share residual income, equal to $E_t - rB_{t-1}$
or to $(\text{ROE} - r) \times B_{t-1}$

▶ In most cases, value is recognized earlier in the residual income model compared with other present value models of stock value, such as the dividend discount model.

▶ Strengths of the residual income model include the following:

▶ Terminal values do not make up a large portion of the value relative to other models.

▶ The models use readily available accounting data.

▶ The models can be used in the absence of dividends and near-term positive free cash flows.

▶ The models can be used when cash flows are unpredictable.

► Weaknesses of the residual income model include the following:

  ► The models are based on accounting data that can be subject to manipulation by management.

  ► Accounting data used as inputs may require significant adjustments.

  ► The models require that the clean surplus relation holds, or that the analyst makes appropriate adjustments when the clean surplus relation does not hold.

► The residual income model is most appropriate in the following cases:

  ► A company is not paying dividends or if it exhibits an unpredictable dividend pattern.

  ► A company has negative free cash flow many years out but is expected to generate positive cash flow at some point in the future.

  ► A great deal of uncertainty exists in forecasting terminal values.

► The fundamental determinants or drivers of residual income are book value of equity and return on equity.

► Residual income valuation is most closely related to P/B. When the present value of expected future residual income is positive (negative), the justified P/B based on fundamentals is greater than (less than) one.

► When fully consistent assumptions are used to forecast earnings, cash flow, dividends, book value, and residual income through a full set of pro forma (projected) financial statements, and the same required rate of return on equity is used as the discount rate, the same estimate of value should result from a residual income, dividend discount, or free cash flow valuation. In practice, however, analysts may find one model easier to apply and possibly arrive at different valuations using the different models.

► Continuing residual income is residual income after the forecast horizon. Frequently, one of the following assumptions concerning continuing residual income is made:

  ► Residual income continues indefinitely at a positive level. (One variation of this assumption is that residual income continues indefinitely at the rate of inflation, meaning it is constant in real terms.)

  ► Residual income is zero from the terminal year forward.

  ► Residual income declines to zero as ROE reverts to the cost of equity over time.

  ► Residual income declines to some mean level.

► The residual income model assumes the clean surplus relation of $B_t = B_{t-1} + E_t - D_t$. In other terms, the ending book value of equity equals the beginning book value plus earnings minus dividends, apart from ownership transactions.

► In practice, to apply the residual income model most accurately, the analyst may need to:

  ► adjust book value of common equity for:

    ► off-balance sheet items;

    ► discrepancies from fair value; or

    ► the amortization of certain intangible assets.

  ► adjust reported net income to reflect clean surplus accounting.

  ► adjust reported net income for nonrecurring items misclassified as recurring items.

PRACTICE PROBLEMS FOR READING 42

1. Based on the following information, determine whether Vertically Integrated Manufacturing (VIM) earned any residual income for its shareholders:

   ▶ VIM had total assets of $3,000,000, financed with twice as much debt capital as equity capital.

   ▶ VIM's pretax cost of debt is 6 percent and cost of equity capital is 10 percent.

   ▶ VIM had EBIT of $300,000 and was taxed at a rate of 40 percent.

   Calculate residual income by using the method based on deducting an equity charge.

2. Use the following information to estimate the intrinsic value of VIM's common stock using the residual income model:

   ▶ VIM had total assets of $3,000,000, financed with twice as much debt capital as equity capital.

   ▶ VIM's pretax cost of debt is 6 percent and cost of equity capital is 10 percent.

   ▶ VIM had EBIT of $300,000 and was taxed at a rate of 40 percent. EBIT is expected to continue at $300,000 indefinitely.

   ▶ VIM's book value per share is $20.

   ▶ VIM has 50,000 shares of common stock outstanding.

3. Palmetto Steel, Inc. (PSI) maintains a dividend payout ratio of 80 percent because of its limited opportunities for expansion. Its return on equity is 15 percent. The required rate of return on PSI equity is 12 percent, and its long-term growth rate is 3 percent. Compute the justified P/B based on forecasted fundamentals, consistent with the residual income model and a constant growth rate assumption.

4. Because New Market Products (NMP) markets consumer staples, it is able to make use of considerable debt in its capital structure; specifically, 90 percent of the company's total assets of $450,000,000 are financed with debt capital. Its cost of debt is 8 percent before taxes, and its cost of equity capital is 12 percent. NMP achieved a pretax income of $5.1 million in 2006 and had a tax rate of 40 percent. What was NMP's residual income?

5. In 2007, Smithson–Williams Investments (SWI) achieved an operating profit after taxes of €10 million on total assets of €100 million. Half of its assets were financed with debt with a pretax cost of 9 percent. Its cost of equity capital is 12 percent, and its tax rate is 40 percent. Did SWI achieve a positive residual income?

6. Calculate the economic value added (EVA) or residual income, as requested, for each of the following:

   A. NOPAT = $100

      Beginning book value of debt = $200

      Beginning book value of equity = $300

      WACC = 11 percent

      Calculate EVA.

Practice Problems and Solutions: *Equity Asset Valuation*, Second Edition, by Jerald Pinto, CFA, Elaine Henry, CFA, Thomas Robinson, CFA, and John Stowe, CFA. Copyright © 2009 by CFA Institute. Reprinted with permission.

   B. Net income = €5.00

   Dividends = €1.00

   Beginning book value of equity = €30.00

   Required rate of return on equity = 11 percent

   Calculate residual income.

   C. Return on equity = 18 percent

   Required rate of return on equity = 12 percent

   Beginning book value of equity = €30.00

   Calculate residual income.

7. Jim Martin is using economic value added (EVA) and market value added (MVA) to measure the performance of Sundanci. Martin uses the fiscal year 2000 information below for his analysis.

   ▶ Adjusted net operating profit after tax (NOPAT) is $100 million.

   ▶ Total capital is $700 million (no debt).

   ▶ Closing stock price is $26.

   ▶ Total shares outstanding is 84 million.

   ▶ The cost of equity is 14 percent.

   Calculate the following for Sundanci. Show your work.

   A. EVA for fiscal year 2000.

   B. MVA as of fiscal year-end 2000.

8. Protected Steel Corporation (PSC) has a book value of $6 per share. PSC is expected to earn $0.60 per share forever and pays out all of its earnings as dividends. The required rate of return on PSC's equity is 12 percent. Calculate the value of the stock using the following:

   A. Dividend discount model.

   B. Residual income model.

9. Notable Books (NB) is a family controlled company that dominates the retail book market. NB has book value of $10 per share, is expected to earn $2.00 forever, and pays out all of its earnings as dividends. Its required return on equity is 12.5 percent. Value the stock of NB using the following:

   A. Dividend discount model.

   B. Residual income model.

10. Simonson Investment Trust International (SITI) is expected to earn $4.00, $5.00, and $8.00 for the next three years. SITI will pay annual dividends of $2.00, $2.50, and $20.50 in each of these years. The last dividend includes a liquidating payment to shareholders at the end of Year 3 when the trust terminates. SITI's book value is $8 per share and its required return on equity is 10 percent.

   A. What is the current value per share of SITI according to the dividend discount model?

   B. Calculate per-share book value and residual income for SITI for each of the next 3 years and use those results to find the stock's value using the residual income model.

   C. Calculate return on equity and use it as an input to the residual income model to calculate SITI's value.

11. Foodsco Incorporated (FI), a leading distributor of food products and materials to restaurants and other institutions, has a remarkably steady track record in terms of both return on equity and growth. At year-end 2007, FI had a book value of $30 per share. For the foreseeable future, the company is expected to achieve a ROE of 15 percent (on trailing book value) and to pay out one-third of its earnings in dividends. The required return is 12 percent. Forecast FI's residual income for the year ending 31 December 2012.

12. Lendex Electronics (LE) had a great deal of turnover of top management for several years and was not followed by analysts during this period of turmoil. Because the company's performance has been improving steadily for the past three years, technology analyst Steve Kent recently reinitiated coverage of LE. A meeting with management confirmed Kent's positive impression of LE's operations and strategic plan. Kent decides LE merits further analysis.

   Careful examination of LE's financial statements revealed that the company had negative other comprehensive income from changes in the value of available-for-sale securities in each of the past five years. How, if at all, should this observation about LE's other comprehensive income affect the figures that Kent uses for the company's ROE and book value for those years?

13. Retail fund manager Seymour Simms is considering the purchase of shares in upstart retailer Hot Topic Stores (HTS). The current book value of HTS is $20 per share, and its market price is $35. Simms expects long-term ROE to be 18 percent, long-term growth to be 10 percent, and cost of equity to be 14 percent. What conclusion would you expect Simms to arrive at if he uses a single-stage residual income model to value these shares?

14. Dayton Manufactured Homes (DMH) builds prefabricated homes and mobile homes. Favorable demographics and the likelihood of slow, steady increases in market share should enable DMH to maintain its ROE of 15 percent and growth rate of 10 percent through time. DMH has a book value of $30 per share and the required rate of return on its equity is 12 percent. Compute the value of its equity using the single-stage residual income model.

15. Use the following inputs and the finite horizon form of the residual income model to compute the value of Southern Trust Bank (STB) shares as of 31 December 2007:

   ► ROE will continue at 15 percent for the next five years (and 10 percent thereafter) with all earnings reinvested (no dividends paid).

   ► Cost of equity equals 10 percent.

   ► $B_0 = \$10$ per share (at year-end 2007).

   ► Premium over book value at the end of five years will be 20 percent.

16. Shunichi Kobayashi is valuing United Parcel Service (NYSE: UPS). Kobayashi has made the following assumptions:

▶ Book value per share is estimated at $9.62 on 31 December 2007.

▶ EPS will be 22 percent of the beginning book value per share for the next eight years.

▶ Cash dividends paid will be 30 percent of EPS.

▶ At the end of the eight-year period, the market price per share will be three times the book value per share.

▶ The beta for UPS is 0.60, the risk-free rate is 5.00 percent, and the equity risk premium is 5.50 percent.

The current market price of UPS is $59.38, which indicates a current P/B of 6.2.

A. Prepare a table that shows the beginning and ending book values, net income, and cash dividends annually for the eight-year period.

B. Estimate the residual income and the present value of residual income for the eight years.

C. Estimate the value per share of UPS stock using the residual income model.

D. Estimate the value per share of UPS stock using the dividend discount model. How does this value compare with the estimate from the residual income model?

17. Boeing Company (NYSE: BA) has a current stock price of $49.86. It also has a P/B of 3.57 and book value per share of $13.97. Assume that the single-stage growth model is appropriate for valuing the company. Boeing's beta is 0.80, the risk-free rate is 5.00 percent, and the equity risk premium is 5.50 percent.

A. If the growth rate is 6 percent and the ROE is 20 percent, what is the justified P/B for Boeing?

B. If the growth rate is 6 percent, what ROE is required to yield Boeing's current P/B?

C. If the ROE is 20 percent, what growth rate is required for Boeing to have its current P/B?

SOLUTIONS FOR READING 42

1. Yes, VIM earned a positive residual income of $8,000.

EBIT	$ 300,000	
Interest	120,000	($2,000,000 × 6%)
Pretax income	$180,000	
Tax expense	72,000	
Net income	$108,000	

$$
\begin{aligned}
\text{Equity charge} &= \text{Equity capital} \times \text{Required return on equity} \\
&= (1/3)(\$3,000,000) \times 0.10 \\
&= \$1,000,000 \times 0.10 = \$100,000
\end{aligned}
$$

$$
\begin{aligned}
\text{Residual income} &= \text{Net income} - \text{Equity charge} \\
&= \$108,000 - \$100,000 = \$8,000
\end{aligned}
$$

2. According to the residual income model, the intrinsic value of a share of common stock equals book value per share plus the present value of expected future per-share residual income. Book value per share was given as $20. Noting that debt is $2,000,000 [(2/3)($3,000,000)] so that interest is $120,000 ($2,000,000 × 6%), VIM's residual income is $8,000, which is calculated (as in Problem 1) as follows:

$$
\begin{aligned}
\text{Residual income} &= \text{Net income} - \text{Equity charge} \\
&= [(\text{EBIT} - \text{Interest})(1 - \text{Tax rate})] \\
&\quad - [(\text{Equity capital})(\text{Required return on equity})] \\
&= [(\$300,000 - \$120,000)(1 - 0.40)] \\
&\quad - [(\$1,000,000)(0.10)] \\
&= \$108,000 - \$100,000 \\
&= \$8,000
\end{aligned}
$$

Therefore, residual income per share is $0.16 per share ($8,000/50,000 shares). Because EBIT is expected to continue at the current level indefinitely, the expected per-share residual income of $0.16 is treated as a perpetuity. The present value of $0.16 is discounted at the required return on equity of 10 percent, so the present value of the residual income is $1.60 ($0.16/0.10).

$$
\begin{aligned}
\text{Intrinsic value} &= \text{Book value per share} + \text{PV of expected future} \\
&\qquad \text{per-share residual income} \\
&= \$20 + \$1.60 = \$21.60
\end{aligned}
$$

3. With $g = b \times \text{ROE} = (1 - 0.80)(0.15) = (0.20)(0.15) = 0.03$,

$$
\begin{aligned}
\text{P/B} &= (\text{ROE} - g)/(r - g) \\
&= (0.15 - 0.03)/(0.12 - 0.03) \\
&= 0.12/0.09 = 1.33 \\
&\text{or} \\
\text{P/B} &= 1 + (\text{ROE} - r)/(r - g) \\
&= 1 + (0.15 - 0.12)/(0.12 - 0.03) \\
&= 1.33
\end{aligned}
$$

4. In this problem (unlike Problems 1 and 2), interest expense has already been deducted in arriving at NMP's pretax income of $5.1 million. Therefore,

$$\begin{aligned}
\text{Net income} &= \text{Pretax income} \times (1 - \text{Tax rate}) \\
&= \$5.1 \text{ million} \times (1 - 0.4) \\
&= \$5.1 \times 0.6 = \$3.06 \text{ million}
\end{aligned}$$

$$\begin{aligned}
\text{Equity charge} &= \text{Total equity} \times \text{Cost of equity capital} \\
&= (0.1 \times \$450 \text{ million}) \times 12\% \\
&= \$45 \text{ million} \times 0.12 = \$5,400,000
\end{aligned}$$

$$\begin{aligned}
\text{Residual income} &= \text{Net income} - \text{Equity charge} \\
&= \$3,060,000 - \$5,400,000 = -\$2,340,000
\end{aligned}$$

NMP had negative residual income of –$2,340,000.

5. To achieve a positive residual income, a company's net operating profit after taxes as a percentage of its total assets can be compared with its weighted average cost of capital (WACC). For SWI,

$$\begin{aligned}
\text{NOPAT/Assets} &= €10 \text{ million}/€100 \text{ million} = 10\% \\
\text{WACC} &= \text{Percent of debt} \times \text{After-tax cost of debt} \\
&\quad + \text{Percent of equity} \times \text{Cost of equity} \\
&= (0.5)(0.09)(0.6) + (0.5)(0.12) \\
&= (0.5)(0.054) + (0.5)(0.12) = 0.027 + 0.06 = 0.087 \\
&= 8.7\%
\end{aligned}$$

Therefore, SWI's residual income was positive. Specifically, residual income equals €1.3 million $[(0.10 - 0.087) \times €100 \text{ million}]$.

6. A. EVA = NOPAT − WACC × Beginning book value of assets
= $100 − (11\%) × ($200 + $300) = $100 − (11\%)($500) = $45

B. $\text{RI}_t = E_t - rB_{t-1}$
= €5.00 − (11\%)(€30.00) = €5.00 − €3.30 = €1.70

C. $\text{RI}_t = (\text{ROE}_t - r) \times B_{t-1}$
= (18\% − 12\%) × (€30) = €1.80

7. A. Economic value added = Net operating profit after taxes − (Cost of capital × Total capital) = $100 million − (14% × $700 million) = $2 million. In the absence of information that would be required to calculate the weighted average cost of debt and equity, and given that Sundanci has no long-term debt, the only capital cost used is the required rate of return on equity of 14 percent.

B. Market value added = Market value of capital − Total capital
$26 stock price × 84 million shares − $700 million = $1.48 billion

8. A. Because the dividend is a perpetuity, the no-growth form of the DDM is applied as follows:

$$\begin{aligned}
V_0 &= D/r \\
&= \$0.60/0.12 = \$5 \text{ per share}
\end{aligned}$$

B. According to the residual income model, V_0 = Book value per share + Present value of expected future per-share residual income.

Residual income is calculated as:

$$RI_t = E - rB_{t-1}$$
$$= \$0.60 - (0.12)(\$6) = -\$0.12$$

Present value of perpetual stream of residual income is calculated as:

$$RI_t/r = -\$0.12/0.12 = -\$1.00$$

The value is calculated as:

$$V_0 = \$6.00 - \$1.00 = \$5.00 \text{ per share}$$

9. A. According to the DDM, $V_0 = D/r$ for a no-growth company.

$$V_0 = \$2.00/0.125 = \$16 \text{ per share}$$

B. Under the residual income model, $V_0 = B_0 +$ Present value of expected future per-share residual income.

Residual income is calculated as:

$$RI_t = E - rB_{t-1}$$
$$= \$2 - (0.125)(\$10) = \$0.75$$

Present value of stream of residual income is calculated as:

$$RI_t/r = 0.75/0.125 = \$6$$

The value is calculated as:

$$V_0 = \$10 + \$6 = \$16 \text{ per share}$$

10. A. $V_0 =$ Present value of the future dividends
$$= \$2/1.10 + \$2.50/(1.1)^2 + \$20.50/(1.1)^3$$
$$= \$1.818 + \$2.066 + \$15.402 = \$19.286$$

B. The book values and residual incomes for the next three years are as follows:

Year	1	2	3
Beginning book value	$ 8.00	$10.00	$12.50
Retained earnings (Net income − Dividends)	2.00	2.50	(12.50)
Ending book value	$10.00	$12.50	$ 0.00
Net income	$ 4.00	$ 5.00	$ 8.00
Less equity charge ($r \times$ Book value)	0.80	1.00	1.25
Residual income	$ 3.20	$ 4.00	$ 6.75

Under the residual income model,

$V_0 = B_0 +$ Present value of expected future per-share residual income

$V_0 = \$8.00 + \$3.20/1.1 + \$4.00/(1.1)^2 + \$6.75/(1.1)^3$

$V_0 = 8.00 + \$2.909 + \$3.306 + \$5.071 = \$19.286$

C.

Year	1	2	3
Net income (NI)	$4.00	$5.00	$8.00
Beginning book value (BV)	8.00	10.00	12.50
Return on equity (ROE) = NI/BV	50%	50%	64%
ROE − r	40%	40%	54%
Residual income (ROE − r) × BV	$3.20	$4.00	$6.75

Under the residual income model,

$V_0 = B_0 +$ Present value of expected future per-share residual income

$V_0 = \$8.00 + \$3.20/1.1 + \$4.00/(1.1)^2 + \$6.75/(1.1)^3$

$V_0 = 8.00 + \$2.909 + \$3.306 + \$5.071 = \$19.286$

Note: Because the residual incomes for each year are necessarily the same in Parts B and C, the results for stock valuation are identical.

11.

Year	2008	2009	2012
Beginning book value	$30.00	$33.00	$43.92
Net income = ROE × Book value	4.50	4.95	6.59
Dividends = payout × Net income	1.50	1.65	2.20
Equity charge (r × Book value)	3.60	3.96	5.27
Residual income = Net income − Equity charge	0.90	0.99	1.32
Ending book value	$33.00	$36.30	$48.32

The table shows that residual income in Year 2008 is $0.90, which equals Beginning book value × (ROE − r) = $30 × (0.15 − 0.12). The Year 2009 column shows that residual income grew by 10 percent to $0.99, which follows from the fact that growth in residual income relates directly to the growth in net income as this example is configured. When both net income and dividends are a function of book value and return on equity is constant, then growth, g, can be predicted from (ROE)(1 − Dividend payout ratio). In this case, $g = 0.15 × (1 − 0.333) = 0.10$ or 10 percent. Net income and residual income will grow by 10 percent annually.

Therefore, residual income in Year 2012 = (Residual income in Year 2008) × $(1.1)^4 = 0.90 × 1.4641 = \$1.32$.

12. When such items as changes in the value of available-for-sale securities bypass the income statement, they are generally assumed to be nonoperating items that will fluctuate from year to year, although averaging to zero in a period of years. The evidence suggests, however, that changes in the value of available-for-sale securities are not averaging to zero but are persistently negative. Furthermore, these losses are bypassing the income statement. It appears that the company is either making an inaccurate assumption or misleading investors in one way or another. Accordingly, Kent might adjust LE's income downward by the amount of loss for other comprehensive income for each of those years. ROE would then decline commensurately. LE's book value would *not* be misstated because the decline in the value of these securities was already recognized and appears in the shareholders' equity account "Accumulated Other Comprehensive Income."

13. $V_0 = B_0 + (\text{ROE} - r)B_0/(r - g)$
$= \$20 + (0.18 - 0.14)(\$20)/(0.14 - 0.10)$
$= \$20 + \$20 = \$40$

Given the current market price is \$35 and the estimated value is \$40, Simms will probably conclude that the shares are somewhat undervalued.

14. $V_0 = B_0 + (\text{ROE} - r)B_0/(r - g)$
$= \$30 + (0.15 - 0.12)(\$30)/(0.12 - 0.10)$
$= \$30 + \$45 = \$75$ per share

15.

Year	Net Income (Projected)	Ending Book Value	ROE (%)	Equity Charge (in Currency)	Residual Income	PV of RI
2007		$10.00				
2008	$1.50	11.50	15	$1.00	$0.50	$0.45
2009	1.73	13.23	15	1.15	0.58	0.48
2010	1.99	15.22	15	1.32	0.67	0.50
2011	2.29	17.51	15	1.52	0.77	0.53
2012	2.63	20.14	15	1.75	0.88	0.55
						$2.51

Using the finite horizon form of residual income valuation,

$V_0 = B_0 +$ Sum of discounted RIs + Premium (also discounted to present)
$= \$10 + \$2.51 + (0.20)(20.14)/(1.10)^5$
$= \$10 + \$2.51 + \$2.50 = \$15.01$

16. A. Columns (a) through (d) in the table show calculations for beginning book value, net income, dividends, and ending book value.

Year	(a) Beginning Book Value	(b) Net Income	(c) Dividends	(d) Ending Book Value	(e) Residual Income	(f) PV of RI
1	$9.620	$2.116	$0.635	$11.101	$1.318	$1.217
2	11.101	2.442	0.733	12.811	1.521	1.297
3	12.811	2.818	0.846	14.784	1.755	1.382
4	14.784	3.252	0.976	17.061	2.025	1.472
5	17.061	3.753	1.126	19.688	2.337	1.569
6	19.688	4.331	1.299	22.720	2.697	1.672
7	22.720	4.998	1.500	26.219	3.113	1.781
8	26.219	5.768	1.730	30.257	3.592	1.898
Total						$12.288

For each year, net income is 22 percent of beginning book value. Dividends are 30 percent of net income. The ending book value equals the beginning book value plus net income minus dividends.

B. Column (e) shows Residual income, which equals Net income − Cost of equity (%) × Beginning book value.

To find the cost of equity, use the CAPM:

$$r = R_F + \beta_i[E(R_M) - R_F] = 5\% + (0.60)(5.5\%) = 8.30\%$$

For Year 1 in the table above,

$$\text{Residual income} = RI_t = E - rB_{t-1}$$
$$= 2.116 - (8.30\%)(9.62)$$
$$= 2.116 - 0.798 = \$1.318$$

This same calculation is repeated for Years 2 through 8.

The final column of the table, (f), gives the present value of the calculated residual income, discounted at 8.30 percent.

C. To find the stock value with the residual income method, use this equation:

$$V_0 = B_0 + \sum_{t=1}^{T} \frac{(E_t - rB_{t-1})}{(1 + r)^t} + \frac{P_T - B_T}{(1 + r)^T}$$

▶ In this equation, B_0 is the current book value per share of $9.62.

▶ The second term, the sum of the present values of the eight years' residual income is shown in the table, $12.288.

▶ To estimate the final term, the present value of the excess of the terminal stock price over the terminal book value, use the assumption that the terminal stock price is assumed to be 3.0 times the terminal book value. So, by assumption, the terminal stock price is $90.771 [$P_T = 3.0(30.257)$]. $P_T - B_T$ is $60.514 (90.771 − 30.257), and the present value of this amount discounted at 8.30 percent for eight years is $31.976.

▶ Summing the relevant terms gives a stock price of $53.884 ($V_0 = 9.62 + 12.288 + 31.976$).

D. The appropriate DDM expression expresses the value of the stock as the sum of the present value of the dividends plus the present value of the terminal value:

$$V_0 = \sum_{t=1}^{T} \frac{D_t}{(1 + r)^t} + \frac{P_T}{(1 + r)^T}$$

Discounting the dividends from the table shown in the solution to Part A above at 8.30 percent gives:

Year	Dividend	PV of Dividend
1	$0.635	$0.586
2	0.733	0.625
3	0.846	0.666
4	0.976	0.709
5	1.126	0.756
6	1.299	0.805
7	1.500	0.858
8	1.730	0.914
All		$5.919

▶ The present value of the eight dividends is $5.92. The estimated terminal stock price, calculated in the solution to Part C above is $90.771, which equals $47.964 discounted at 8.30 percent for eight years.

▶ The value for the stock, the present value of the dividends plus the present value of the terminal stock price, is $V_0 = 5.92 + 47.964 = $53.884.

▶ The stock values estimated with the residual income model and the dividend discount model are identical. Because they are based on similar financial assumptions, this equivalency is expected. Even though the two models differ in their timing of the recognition of value, their final results are the same.

17. A. The justified P/B can be found with the following formula:

$$\frac{P_0}{B_0} = 1 + \frac{\text{ROE} - r}{r - g}$$

ROE is 20 percent, g is 6 percent, and r is 9.4% [$R_F + \beta_i[E(R_M) - R_F]$ = 5% + (0.80)(5.5%)]. Substituting in the values gives a justified P/B of

$$\frac{P_0}{B_0} = 1 + \frac{0.20 - 0.094}{0.094 - 0.06} = 4.12$$

The assumed parameters give a justified P/B of 4.12, slightly above the current P/B of 3.57.

B. To find the ROE that would result in a P/B of 3.57, we substitute 3.57, r, and g into the following equation:

$$\frac{P_0}{B_0} = 1 + \frac{\text{ROE} - r}{r - g}$$

This yields

$$3.57 = 1 + \frac{\text{ROE} - 0.094}{0.094 - 0.06}$$

Solving for ROE requires several steps to finally derive a ROE of 0.18138 or 18.1 percent. This value of ROE is consistent with a P/B of 3.57.

C. To find the growth rate that would result with a P/B of 3.57, use the expression given in Part B, but solve for g instead of ROE:

$$\frac{P_0}{B_0} = 1 + \frac{\text{ROE} - r}{r - g}$$

Substituting in the values gives:

$$3.57 = 1 + \frac{0.20 - 0.094}{0.094 - g}$$

The growth rate g is 0.05275 or 5.3 percent. Assuming that the single-stage growth model is applicable to Boeing, the current P/B and current market price can be justified with values for ROE or g that are not much different from the starting values of 20 percent and 6 percent, respectively.

PRIVATE COMPANY VALUATION

by Raymond D. Rath, ASA, CFA

LEARNING OUTCOMES

The candidate should be able to:	Mastery
a. compare public and private company valuation;	☐
b. describe uses of private business valuation, and explain applications of greatest concern to financial analysts;	☐
c. explain alternative definitions of value, and demonstrate how different definitions can lead to different estimates of value;	☐
d. explain the income, market, and asset-based approaches to private company valuation and factors relevant to the selection of each approach;	☐
e. explain cash flow estimation issues related to private companies and adjustments required to estimate normalized earnings;	☐
f. demonstrate the free cash flow, capitalized cash flow, and excess earnings methods of private company valuation;	☐
g. explain factors that require adjustment when estimating the discount rate for private companies;	☐
h. compare models used to estimate the required rate of return to private company equity (for example, the CAPM, the expanded CAPM, and the build-up approach);	☐
i. demonstrate the market approaches to private company valuation (for example, guideline public company method, guideline transaction method, and prior transaction method), and describe advantages and disadvantages of each;	☐
j. demonstrate the asset-based approach to private company valuation;	☐
k. explain and evaluate the effects on private company valuations of discounts and premiums based on control and marketability;	☐
l. describe the role of valuation standards in valuing private companies.	☐

1   INTRODUCTION

The valuation of the equity of private companies is a major field of application for equity valuation.[1] Increasingly, generalist investment practitioners need to be apprised of the issues associated with such valuations. Many public companies have start-up or other operations that can best be valued as if they were private companies. Companies may grow through the acquisition of competitors, including private companies, and analysts must be prepared to evaluate the price paid in such transactions. Furthermore, acquisitions often result in significant balances of intangible assets, including goodwill, that are reported on the balance sheets of acquiring companies. Goodwill balances require annual impairment testing under International Financial Reporting Standards (IFRS) and U.S. generally accepted accounting principles (GAAP). Impairment testing and other financial reporting initiatives increasingly result in the use of fair value estimates in financial statements. The concepts and methods discussed in this reading play important roles in this aspect of financial reporting. In addition, issues addressed in this reading arise in the types of investment held by venture capital and other types of private equity funds that constitute a significant allocation in many investors' portfolios. An expanded focus on the reported values of the investments held by private equity funds is leading to greater scrutiny of the valuation processes used and resulting value estimates.

This reading presents and illustrates key elements associated with the valuation of private companies and is organized as follows: Section 2 provides some background for understanding private company valuation, including typical contrasts between public and private companies and the major purposes for which private valuations are performed. Section 3 discusses the different definitions of value used in private company valuations and the idea that the valuation must address the definition of value relevant to the particular case. Section 4 discusses earnings normalization and cash flow estimation, introduces the three major approaches recognized in private company valuation, valuation discounts and premiums, and business valuation standards and practices. We then summarize the reading and practice problems conclude.

2   THE SCOPE OF PRIVATE COMPANY VALUATION

Private companies range from single-employee, unincorporated businesses to formerly public companies that have been taken private in management buyouts or other transactions. Numerous large, successful companies also exist that have remained private since inception, such as IKEA and Bosch in Europe and Cargill

---

[1] The term "appraisal" is often used in place of "valuation" in the contexts discussed in this reading. Appraisal and valuation are synonymous, as are appraiser and valuator.

and Bechtel in the United States. The diverse characteristics of private companies have encouraged the development of diverse valuation practices.

2.1 Private and Public Company Valuation: Similarities and Contrasts

We can gain some insight into the challenges of private company valuation by examining company- and stock-specific factors that mark key differences between private and public companies.

2.1.1 Company-Specific Factors

Company-specific factors are those that characterize the company itself, including its lifecycle stage, size, markets, and the goals and characteristics of management.

▶ *Stage in lifecycle.* Private companies include companies at the earliest stages of development whereas public companies are typically further advanced in their lifecycle. Private companies may have minimal capital, assets, or employees. Private companies, however, also include large, stable, going concerns and failed companies in the process of liquidation. The stage of lifecycle influences the valuation process for a company.

▶ *Size.* Relative size—whether measured by income statement, balance sheet, or other measures—frequently distinguishes public and private companies; private companies in a given line of business tend to be smaller. Size has implications for the level of risk and, hence, relative valuation. Small size typically increases risk levels, and risk premiums for small size have often been applied in estimating required rates of return for private companies. For some private companies, small size may reduce growth prospects by reducing access to capital to fund growth of operations. The public equity markets are generally the best source for such funding. Conversely, for small companies, the costs of operating as a public company including compliance costs may outweigh any financing benefits.

▶ *Overlap of shareholders and management.* For many private companies, and in contrast to most public companies, top management has a controlling ownership interest. Therefore, they may not face the same pressure from external investors as public companies. Agency issues may also be mitigated in private companies.[2] For that reason, private company management may be able to take a longer term perspective in their decisions than public company management.

▶ *Quality/depth of management.* A small private company, especially if it has limited growth potential, would be expected to be less attractive to management candidates and have less management depth than a typical public company. The smaller scale of operation might also lead to less management depth compared with a public company. To the extent these considerations apply, they may increase risk and reduce growth for the private company.

---

[2] **Agency issues** refer to such issues as monitoring costs arising from the sometimes conflicting interests of owners (principals) and managers (agents). See Aggarwal, Harrington, Kobor, and Drake (2007) for more information.

▶ *Quality of financial and other information.* Public companies are required to meet detailed requirements for the timely disclosure of financial and other information. Investment analysts may place significant demands on the management of a public company for high quality information. The more limited availability of financial and other information for private companies results in an increased burden for the prospective investor considering an equity investment or loan. This type of information difference presumably leads to greater uncertainty and, hence, risk. All else equal, the higher risk should lead to a relatively lower valuation. Although that may be the baseline case, note that in certain private company valuations, such as fairness opinions prepared in the context of an acquisition, the analyst usually has unlimited access to books, records, contracts, and other information that would not be available to the public stock analyst.

▶ *Pressure from short-term investors.* Earnings consistency and growth rates are often perceived as critical to the stock price performance of public companies. Continued management employment and levels of incentive compensation are often linked to stock price performance but many investors' interests may be of a trading or short-term nature. As a result, management may be motivated to try to support share price in the short term.[3] According to some observers, private companies typically do not experience similar stock price performance pressure and such companies can take a longer term investment focus.

▶ *Tax concerns.* Reduction of reported taxable income and corporate tax payments may be a more important goal for private companies compared with public companies because of greater benefit to the owners.

2.1.2 Stock-Specific Factors

In addition to company-specific factors, the characteristics of the stock of a private company frequently differ markedly from that of public companies.

▶ *Liquidity of equity interests in business.* Stock in private companies is generally much less liquid than otherwise similar interests in public companies. Private companies typically have fewer shareholders. Shares of a private company have not been registered for sale in the public stock markets. The limited number of existing and potential buyers reduces the value of the shares in private companies.

▶ *Concentration of control.*[4] Control of private companies is often concentrated in one or in very few investors. This concentration of control may lead to actions by a corporation that benefits some shareholders at the cost of other shareholders. Transactions with entities related to a control group at above-market prices would transfer value away from the noncontrolling shareholders of the corporation. Above-market compensation to a controlling shareholder is a typical perquisite.

▶ *Potential agreements restricting liquidity.* Private companies may have shareholder agreements in place that restrict the ability to sell shares. These agreements may reduce the marketability of equity interests.

---

[3] See *Breaking the Short-term Cycle*, CFA Institute Centre Publications (July 2006).

[4] This factor could also be placed under company-specific factors.

Generally, stock-specific factors are a negative for private company valuation whereas company-specific factors are potentially positive or negative. The range of differences observed in private companies is such that the spectrum of risk and, therefore, the spectrum of return requirements are typically wider than for public companies. Another consequence is that the range of valuation methods and assumptions applied to private companies is typically more varied.

2.2 Reasons for Performing Valuations

Valuations of private businesses or equity interests therein fall into three groups: transaction-related, compliance-related, and litigation-related.

Transactions encompass events affecting the ownership or financing of a business and represent a primary area of private company valuation. A variety of transaction types exist.

▶ *Private financing.* Raising capital is critical to development stage companies. To reduce risk and maintain influence, **venture capital investors** (as equity investors in such companies are known) typically invest through multiple rounds of financing tied to the achievement of key developments ("milestones"). A high level of uncertainty concerning expected future cash flows results in valuations that are often informal and based on negotiations between the company and investors.

▶ *Initial public offering (IPO).* An IPO is one liquidity option for a private company. Investment banking firms prepare valuations as part of the IPO process. A key element of an IPO-related valuation is frequently the identification of any public companies that are similar to the one going public.

▶ *Acquisition.* Acquisition can be an attractive liquidity option for development stage or mature companies. Acquisition related valuations may be performed (and negotiated) by management of the target and/or buyer. Many transactions are handled by investment banking firms.

▶ *Bankruptcy.* For companies operating under bankruptcy protection, valuations of the business and its underlying assets may help assess whether a company is more valuable as a going concern or in liquidation. For viable going concerns operating in bankruptcy, insights from valuation may be critical to the restructuring of an overleveraged capital structure.

▶ *Share-based payment (compensation).* Share-based payments can be viewed as transactions between a company and its employees. These transactions often have accounting and tax implications to the issuer and the employee. Share-based payments can include stock option grants, restricted stock grants, and transactions involving an employee stock ownership plan (ESOP) in the United States and equivalent structures in other countries. Providing an incentive for improved employee performance is an important goal of such compensation mechanisms.

Compliance encompasses actions required by law or regulation. Compliance valuations are a second key area of valuation practice. Financial reporting and tax reporting are the two primary focuses of this type of valuation.

▶ *Financial reporting.* Financial reporting valuations are increasing in importance. Goodwill impairment is one of the most frequent financial reporting valuations that a securities analyst might observe.[5] Goodwill impairment tests require a business valuation for a cash-generating unit (IFRS)[6] of an entity or a reporting unit (U.S. GAAP). Essentially, components of public companies are valued using private company valuation techniques. For private companies, stock option grants will frequently require valuations.[7]

▶ *Tax reporting.* Tax reporting is a longstanding area that requires valuations of private companies. Tax-related reasons for valuations include corporate and individual tax reporting. A variety of corporate activities, such as corporate restructurings, transfer pricing, and property tax matters, may require valuations. Estate and gift taxation are examples of individual tax requirements that may generate private company valuations.

Litigation—legal proceedings including those related to damages, lost profits, shareholder disputes, and divorce—often requires valuations. Litigation may affect public or private companies or may be between shareholders with no effect at the corporate level.

As the above descriptions make clear, each of the three major practice areas requires specialized knowledge and skills. This fact has led many valuation professionals to focus their efforts in one of these areas. Transactions, for example, often involve investment bankers. Compliance valuations are best performed by valuation professionals with knowledge of the relevant accounting or tax regulations. Litigation-related valuations require effective presentations in a legal setting.

Having provided an overview of the field of private company valuation, we can proceed to discussing how valuations are done. Logically, before developing an estimate of value, the valuator must understand the context of the valuation and its requirements. An important element in that process is knowledge of the definition(s) of value that the valuation must address (the subject of the next section).

3   DEFINITIONS (STANDARDS) OF VALUE

A **definition of value** (or **standard of value**) specifies how value is understood and, therefore, specifies a type of value. Identification of the correct definition of value to apply in a given valuation is a key step in developing a good value estimate. The status of the company (in the sense of whether it is assumed to be a going concern or not)[8] and the use of the valuation are key elements in determining the definition of value to apply.

---

[5] Under IFRS, IAS 36, "Impairment of Assets," or IAS 38, "Intangible Assets," and under U.S. GAAP, SFAS No. 142, "Goodwill and Other Intangible Assets," are the relevant accounting guidance. For U.S. GAAP, SFAS No. 157, "Fair Value Measurements," provides additional guidance on measuring fair value. As of late 2008, the International Accounting Standards Board (IASB) was developing guidance similar to SFAS No. 157.

[6] IFRS 36, "Impairment of Assets," defines a **cash-generating unit** as the smallest identifiable group of assets that generates cash inflows that are largely independent of the cash inflows of other assets or groups of assets. SFAS No. 142, "Goodwill and Other Intangible Assets," defines a **reporting unit** as an operating segment or one level below an operating segment (referred to as a component). A component of an operating segment is a reporting unit if the component constitutes a business for which discrete financial information is available and segment management regularly reviews the operating results of that component.

[7] For IFRS, IFRS 2, "Share-Based Payment," and for U.S. GAAP, SFAS No. 123R, "Share-Based Payment," are the relevant accounting guidance.

[8] This assumption is sometimes referred to as the **premise of value**.

The major definitions of value may be summarized as follows.[9]

► **Fair market value**. This term can be defined as the price, expressed in terms of cash equivalents, at which a property (asset) would change hands between a hypothetical willing and able buyer and a hypothetical willing and able seller, acting at "arm's length" in an open and unrestricted market, when neither is under compulsion to buy or sell and when both have reasonable knowledge of the relevant facts. Fair market value is most often used in a tax reporting context in the United States.

► **Market value**. The International Valuation Standards Committee (IVSC)[10] defines market value as "the estimated amount for which a property should exchange on the date of valuation between a willing buyer and a willing seller in an arm's-length transaction after proper marketing wherein the parties had each acted knowledgeably, prudently, and without compulsion."[11] Market value is a definition of value often used in real estate and tangible asset appraisals when money is borrowed against the value of such assets.

► **Fair value** (financial reporting). Fair value is the definition of value used in financial reporting. Fair value shares many similarities with (fair) market value. The definition of fair value includes references to an arm's-length transaction (i.e., neither party is acting under duress) as well as the parties to a transaction being knowledgeable. Under IFRS, fair value is defined as "the price that would be received for an asset or paid to transfer a liability in a current transaction between marketplace participants in the reference market for the asset or liability."[12] Under U.S. GAAP, SFAS No. 157, "Fair Value Measurements," defines fair value as "the price that would be received to sell an asset or paid to transfer a liability in an orderly transaction between market participants at the measurement date."

► **Fair value** (litigation). Fair value is also a valuation definition as set forth in the United States by state statutes and legal precedent in certain litigation matters. Although definitions and interpretations may vary, the definition of fair value in a litigation context is generally similar to the previously given definitions for financial reporting.

► **Investment value**. Investment value can be defined as the value to a particular investor based on the investor's investment requirements and expectations. Investment value is important in the sale of a private

---

[9] Definitions of fair market value, investment value, and intrinsic value are included in the International Glossary of Business Valuation Terms (IGBVT). The IGBVT was jointly developed by the American Institute of Certified Public Accountants, American Society of Appraisers, Canadian Institute of Chartered Business Valuators, National Association of Certified Valuation Analysts, and The Institute of Business Appraisers to improve appraisal practice through the use of consistent terminology.

[10] The IVSC is an international body that develops and maintains standards for the development, reporting, and disclosure of valuations, especially those that will be relied on by investors and other third-party stakeholders.

[11] Some definitions of market value refer to value essentially on a cash equivalent basis. For example, real property is sometimes acquired with cash and seller financing (notes) in which the interest rate is different than the market rate. The cash equivalent value of the transaction would be its value if the note's value were adjusted to reflect a market interest rate. Another issue is contingent consideration, i.e., payments that are dependent on the occurrence of specified events (a more detailed definition is in Section 4.3.2), which may be an important component of certain acquisition payment structures. SFAS No. 141R has expanded rules for the inclusion of contingent consideration in determining the total price paid in business acquisitions.

[12] IASB 25 May 2006 Board Minutes on Fair Value Measurements Project (Agenda Paper 8A).

company. The value of a company or asset may differ to different buyers as a result of differing perspectives on future earnings power and the level of risk of the company or asset, differing return requirements and financing costs of prospective buyers, and potential synergies of the acquisition with other assets owned by a prospective buyer. Investment value differs from the preceding value definitions in its greater focus on a specific buyer rather than value in a "market" context.

► **Intrinsic value.** Intrinsic value is often used in investment analysis. Intrinsic value can be defined as the value that an investor considers, on the basis of an evaluation or available facts, to be the "true" or "real" value that will become the market value when other investors reach the same conclusion. This definition attempts to capture the value of an asset absent any short-term pricing aberrations perceived as resulting in an asset value that is over- or understated.

Different definitions of value can lead to different value estimates. To take a simple example, the investment value of an asset to a specific investor might be €100. This amount is not necessarily the same as the fair market value, market value, or fair value of the asset. Assume several other investors have investment values of €150 as a result of synergies or other factors and that it is believed that no other investors have investment values above €150. With sufficient investor interest at a value of €150, a fair market value estimate could be €150, recognizing the demand and supply schedules of buyers and sellers in the market.

A complexity facing valuators is that different organizations may have different perspectives on what a given standard or definition of value means. A notable example is the U.S. GAAP fair value definition as set forth in SFAS No. 157, "Fair Value Measurements."[13] Under SFAS No. 157, fair value is estimated as the price *received* to sell an asset or transfer a liability, which is an **exit price**.[14] An exit price should be less than or at most equal to the price paid to establish a position (an **entry price**). Other definitions of value (including fair value under IFRS) typically do not specify either an entry or exit price perspective.

An appraisal (valuation) should generally not be relied on for other than its intended purpose. Many private company valuations are performed for a specific purpose and reference a specific definition of value and valuation date that may not be relevant for another purpose. Prospective users must always consider whether a specific valuation and its definition of value are relevant for their situation.

To illustrate the point, consider an investor investigating the purchase of a controlling interest in a private company. The investor has access to a valuation prepared for tax reporting purposes of a small block of shares in the company. The value estimate in that report may not be relevant to this investor because it probably does not reflect the normalized earnings of the enterprise from the perspective of a majority shareholder who can influence corporate activities.[15]

---

[13] As of late 2008, the IASB had not released final guidance similar to SFAS No. 157. Two discussion papers on Fair Value Measurements were released for comment in April 2007. According to the IASB, the current project plan calls for the release of an IFRS providing fair value measurement guidance in 2010. Additional information can be found on the IASB website (www.IASB.org).

[14] Market turmoil in early 2008 led to dramatically reduced liquidity in auction rate securities and large declines in quoted market prices. Some indicated that the exit price requirement of SFAS No. 157 resulted in significant asset markdowns and the reporting of unrealized losses as securities were marked to market. Public discussion of the implications of the exit price requirement under SFAS No. 157 and the impact of short-term market inefficiencies on asset pricing resulted from this turmoil.

[15] Loosely, normalized earnings reflect adjustment for items that lessen the usefulness of the earnings number as a basis for comparison or forecasting. A more precise definition of normalized earnings is given in Section 4.1.1.

The valuation of the small block may include minority and/or marketability discounts that may not be appropriate in other contexts. A prospective buyer of the company relying on this valuation may miss an attractive acquisition candidate as expense adjustments and synergies may not have been considered. The valuation assumptions from the tax valuation would also require possible adjustments for use in a financial reporting context.

PRIVATE COMPANY VALUATION APPROACHES 4

Private company valuation experts distinguish three major approaches to valuation.

▶ The **income approach** values an asset as the present discounted value of the income expected from it. The income approach has several variations depending on the assumptions the valuator makes.

▶ The **market approach** values an asset based on pricing multiples from sales of assets viewed as similar to the subject asset.

▶ The **asset-based approach** values a private company based on the values of the underlying assets of the entity less the value of any related liabilities.

Valuation approaches for private companies are conceptually similar to those used for public companies although the labels used for them by experts in each field and the details of application may differ. The income approach corresponds to what are referred to as discounted cash flow models or present value models by public equities analysts. Along with asset-based models, discounted cash flow models are classified as absolute valuation models. By contrast, analysts use a relative valuation model when they apply a market-based approach in evaluating price and enterprise multiples relative to the value of a comparable.

Analysts select approach(es) depending on specific factors. The nature of operations and stage in lifecycle are important considerations. For a development stage company with the potential to operate as a successful large public company, the valuation methods may change over time. At the earliest stages of development, the company may best be valued using an asset-based approach because the going-concern premise of value may be uncertain and/or future cash flows may be extremely difficult to predict. With progress to a development stage company in a high growth mode, the company might be valued using a free cash flow method, which in private business appraisal is known as an income approach. A stable, mature company might be best valued on the basis of the market approach. Specific facts and circumstances may suggest different valuation methods.

Size is an important criterion in assessing valuation approaches and valuation methods. Multiples from public companies may not be appropriate for a small, relatively mature private company with very limited growth prospects. Comparisons to public companies are not a good basis of valuation for a private company if risk and growth prospects differ materially.

Public and private companies may consist of a variety of operating and nonoperating assets. Nonoperating assets are defined as assets not necessary to the ongoing operations of the business enterprise. Excess cash and investment balances are typical examples of nonoperating assets. In principle, the value of a company is the sum of the value of operating assets and the value of nonoperating assets. Thus, nonoperating assets should be included in the valuation of an enterprise regardless of the valuation approach or method being used.

Before we illustrate the application of the three approaches to valuation, we need to address certain typical issues relating to valuation model inputs that arise when valuing private companies.

4.1 Earnings Normalization and Cash Flow Estimation Issues

The next two sections cover earnings normalization and cash flow estimation in the context of private company valuation. Potential acquirers of private companies may find that current earnings reflect inefficiencies or redundancies that detract from their relevance as a baseline for forecasting future earnings under new ownership. In such cases, the earnings should be adjusted or "normalized" to a basis that is relevant for forecasting future results, given that the firm is acquired. Essentially, the valuator is seeking to understand accurately the earnings and cash flow capacity of the business enterprise if it is acquired and run efficiently.

4.1.1 Earnings Normalization Issues for Private Companies

Private company valuations may require significant adjustments to estimate the normalized earnings of the company. As defined in the International Glossary of Business Valuation Terms, **normalized earnings** are "economic benefits adjusted for nonrecurring, non-economic, or other unusual items to eliminate anomalies and/or facilitate comparisons." As a result of the concentration of control in many private businesses, reported earnings may reflect discretionary expenses or expenses that are not at arm's-length amounts. Tax and other motivations may also result in reporting earnings that may differ from the normalized earnings of a private company. The smaller size of many private companies potentially increases the relative impact on value of discretionary expenses.

When comparing the reported earnings of private companies with public companies, a key area of difference is the possible effect of transactions between the company and owners working in the business or with entities controlled by controlling shareholders. Many adjustments required to normalize earnings involve items that reduce the reported earnings of a profitable, private company. The controlling or sole shareholder is often active in the business and controls the Board of Directors and all policy and operating decisions. Above-market compensation or other expenses would reduce taxable income and income tax expense at the corporate level and subsequent taxes upon the payment of dividends to the controlling shareholder and other shareholders. Above-market expenses can also result in the controlling shareholder receiving a disproportionate return in relation to other shareholders.

Compensation expense is a key area requiring possible adjustment. Profitable, private companies may report compensation expense to owner/employees above amounts that would be paid to a nonowner employee. Family members may also be included as employees and paid amounts above the market value of their services. For private companies with limited profits or reported losses, expenses may actually be understated with the reported income of the entity overstated. Owners active in the business may not take compensation commensurate with market levels required by an employee for similar activities.

A number of other areas exist for consideration for possible adjustments. Personal expenses may be included as expenses of the private company. Personal-use assets and excess entertainment expenses are areas for consideration. Personal residences, aircraft, and luxury or excessive use of corporate vehicles for personal use may require an adjustment. Life insurance and loans to shareholders merit review.

Real estate used by the private company is also an area for consideration. When a private company owns real estate, some analysts separate the real estate from the operating company. This separation consists of removing any revenues and expenses associated with the real estate from the income statement. If the company is using the real property in its business operations, adding a market rental charge for the use of the real estate to the expenses of the company would produce a more accurate estimate of the earnings of the business operations. This approach would produce a value of the business operations excluding the owned real estate. Because the real estate is still owned by the entity, its value would represent a nonoperating asset of the entity.

Without these adjustments, real estate used in the operations that is owned by the private company may lead to a misstatement of the appraised value of the private company. Rent charges for the use of real estate include return "of" and "on" investment components. Depreciation reflects return "of" investment. If real property is owned, depreciation expense would reflect the historical acquisition cost rather than current replacement cost. For owned real estate, the return "on" component of the rental charge would not be included at a market level charge. Application of a capitalization rate for the business operations to an earnings figure that includes some of the benefit from the owned real estate may misvalue the private company. The business operations and real estate may have different levels of risk and expected future growth that require separate valuation. If real estate is leased to the private company by a related entity, the level of expense may require an adjustment to a market rental rate.

Example 1 illustrates a case in which a prospective buyer of a private business would need to make adjustments to reported financial results for a more accurate picture of the company's normalized earnings and value under new ownership.

EXAMPLE 1

Able Manufacturing: Normalized Earnings Adjustments

John Smith is the sole shareholder and CEO of Able Manufacturing, Inc. Smith has put Able up for sale in advance of his retirement. James Duvall, a manager in the corporate venturing unit of a public company, is evaluating the purchase of Able. Duvall notes the following facts affecting the most recent fiscal year's reported results:

► Smith's compensation for the year was $1.5 million. Duvall's executive compensation consultant believes a normalized compensation expense of $500,000 for a CEO of a company like Able is appropriate. Compensation is included in selling, general, and administrative expenses (SG&A).

► Certain corporate assets including ranch property and a condominium are in Duvall's judgment not required for the core operations of the company. Fiscal year expenses associated with the ranch and condominium were $400,000, including $300,000 of such operating expenses as property upkeep, property taxes, and insurance reflected in SG&A expenses, and depreciation expense of $100,000. All other asset balances (including cash) are believed to be at normal levels required to support current operations.

► Able's debt balance of $2,000,000 (interest rate of 7.5 percent) was lower than the optimal level of debt expected for the company. As reported interest expense did not reflect an optimal charge, Duvall believes the use of an earnings figure that excludes interest expense altogether, specifically operating income after taxes, will facilitate the assessment of Able.

Duvall uses the reported income statement to show the derivation of reported operating income after taxes, as given below.

Able Manufacturing, Inc.
Operating Income after Taxes

As of 31 December 2007	As Reported
Revenues	$50,000,000
Cost of goods sold	30,000,000
Gross profit	20,000,000
Selling, general, and admin. expenses	5,000,000
EBITDA	15,000,000
Depreciation and amortization	1,000,000
Earnings before interest and taxes	14,000,000
Pro forma taxes (at 40.0 percent)	5,600,000
Operating income after taxes	$ 8,400,000

Based only on the information given, address the following:

1. Identify the adjustments that Duvall would make to reported financials to estimate normalized operating income after taxes; that is, what the operating income after taxes would have been under ownership by Duvall's unit.

2. Based on your answer to Part 1, construct a pro forma statement of normalized operating income after taxes for Able.

Solution to 1: First, SG&A should be reduced by $1,500,000 − $500,000 = $1,000,000 to reflect the expected level of salary expense under professional management. Second, the ranch and condominium are nonoperating assets—they are not needed to generate revenues— so expense items should be adjusted to reflect their removal (e.g., through a sale). Two income statement lines are affected: SG&A expenses should be reduced by $300,000 and depreciation and amortization reduced by $100,000.

Solution to 2: The pro forma statement of normalized operating income after taxes would be:

Able Manufacturing, Inc.
Pro Forma Normalized Operating Income after Taxes

As of 31 December 2007	Pro Forma
Revenues	$50,000,000
Cost of goods sold	30,000,000
Gross profit	20,000,000
Selling, general, and admin. expenses	3,700,000
EBITDA	16,300,000
Depreciation and amortization	900,000
Earnings before interest and taxes	15,400,000
Pro forma taxes (at 40.0 percent)	6,160,000
Operating income after taxes	$ 9,240,000

In addition to the various adjustments noted above, a variety of other areas exist for possible adjustment that are similar for the valuation of public and private companies (e.g., adjustments related to inventory accounting methods, depreciation assumptions, and capitalization versus expensing of various costs). Private companies may have their financial statements reviewed rather than audited. **Reviewed financial statements** provide an opinion letter with representations and assurances by the reviewing accountant that are less than those in audited financial statements. The preparation of reviewed rather than audited financial statements and other factors suggest a potentially greater need for analyst adjustments to the reported financials of some private companies. **Compiled financial statements** (that are not accompanied by an auditor's opinion letter) suggest an even greater need for analytical adjustments.

4.1.2 Cash Flow Estimation Issues for Private Companies

In addition to earnings normalization, cash flow estimation is an important element of the valuation process. Free cash flow (FCF) is the relevant concept of cash flow in this context. Free cash flow to the firm (FCFF) represents free cash flow at the business enterprise level and is used to value the firm or, indirectly, the firm's equity.[16] Alternatively, free cash flow to equity (FCFE) can be used to value equity directly.

Cash flow estimation for private companies raises some important challenges, including those related to the nature of the interest being valued, potentially acute uncertainties regarding future operations, and managerial involvement in forecasting.

---

[16] Some variation in terminology exists. Net cash flow and debt free net cash flow are variations of free cash flow to the firm.

The nature of assumptions in cash flow estimates depends on a variety of factors. The equity interest appraised and the intended use of the appraisal are key in determining the appropriate definition of value for a specific valuation. The assumptions included in cash flow estimates may differ if a small minority equity interest is appraised rather than the total equity of a business. For example, an investment value standard may lead to different cash flow estimates than a fair value standard related to a financial reporting valuation assignment.

In assessing future cash flow estimates, uncertainty regarding a potentially wide range of future cash flow possibilities also creates challenges for valuation using FCF. Many development stage companies and some mature companies are subject to significant uncertainties regarding future operations and cash flows. One possible solution involves projecting the different possible future scenarios. For a privately held development stage company, the possible scenarios could include initial public offering, acquisition, continued operation as a private company, or bankruptcy. For a larger, mature company, the scenarios might be chosen to cover the range of possible levels of growth and profitability.

In valuing an individual scenario, the discount rate chosen should reflect the risk of achieving the projected cash flows in that scenario. The probability of the occurrence of each scenario must also be estimated. The overall value estimate for a company is then a probability-weighted average of the company's estimated scenario values. Alternatively, the expected future cash flows based on the scenarios could be discounted using a conventional, single discount rate to obtain an overall value estimate. Although the trend is generally to more robust models, in current practice private company valuation more frequently reflects an average or most likely scenario than an explicit multiple scenario analysis.

Managers of private companies generally command much more information about their business than outside analysts. Management may develop cash flow forecasts to be used in a valuation with appraiser input, or appraisers may develop their own forecasts consulting management as needed. The appraiser should be aware of potential managerial biases, such as to possibly overstate values in the case of goodwill impairment testing or understate values in the case of incentive stock option grants. Appraisers should also pay attention to whether projections adequately capture capital needs.

The process for estimating FCFF and FCFE is similar for private and public companies. Revenues and expenses are generally adjusted to reflect the normalized earnings capacity of the private company. For FCFF, operating income after taxes is estimated by removing interest expense on debt and including a pro forma estimate of income taxes on operating income (i.e., EBIT minus estimated taxes, based on normalized earnings). Depreciation expense is added back because it is a noncash expense. A provision for capital expenditures required to replace the existing assets is subtracted to support the current level of operations. A provision for any additional capital expenditures required to fund future growth is also subtracted. A provision for incremental working capital required to fund revenue growth is also calculated and subtracted to arrive at FCFF. FCFE is found by subtracting after-tax interest expense from FCFF and adding net new borrowing.

Appraisers may choose between a FCFF and a FCFE approach based on the facts of the case. Some analysts believe that FCFF valuation is practically more robust than FCFE valuation when substantial capital structure changes are in view because the weighted average cost of capital (WACC), the discount rate used in a FCFF approach, is typically less sensitive than the cost of equity, the discount rate used in a FCFE approach, to changes in financial leverage. Apart from such considerations, there may be a tendency for appraisers at the largest firms and investment bankers to favor using FCFF and for appraisers at small firms to favor using FCFE.

EXAMPLE 2

Able Manufacturing: Pro Forma Free Cash Flow to the Firm

Duvall, the manager of the corporate venturing unit introduced in Example 1, has decided to make a bid for Able Manufacturing. Duvall has decided to take an income approach to value Able. As stated in Example 1, Able's debt is $2,000,000. Considering the nature of Able's business, its size, and the financial leverage used by competitors, Duvall has concluded that Able has a low level of debt relative to its capacity and that it will be optimal to increase its debt if Duvall's unit succeeds in purchasing Able. Because of that anticipated change in leverage, Duvall has decided to use a FCFF approach rather than FCFE to value Able.

Based on available information, Duvall makes the following assumptions:

▶ Long-term growth of revenues and after-tax operating income is 3 percent annually.

▶ The gross profit margin will remain at 40 percent.

▶ Depreciation will remain at 1.8 percent of sales.

▶ SG&A expenses can be maintained at the prior year's level of $3,700,000 at least for two years.

▶ Working capital equal to 10 percent of revenues is required (e.g., if the increase in revenues is $X from the prior year, additional working capital of 0.10 × $X would be needed).

▶ Capital expenditures are expected to equal projected depreciation expense (to support current operations) plus 5 percent of incremental revenues (to support future growth).

1. Should Duvall use reported earnings or normalized earnings in estimating FCFF for Able? Explain.

2. Forecast FCFF for Able for the upcoming year (from the perspective of a knowledgeable buyer).

Solution to 1: For the valuation of Able in a purchase transaction, the normalized earnings of Able should be used to estimate FCFF. Normalized earnings would more accurately reflect the income expected by a willing buyer of Able than reported earnings.

Solution to 2: Duvall assumed long-term growth of 3 percent into the foreseeable future. With the $50 million revenue base from the prior year and the 3 percent annual revenue growth, a $1.5 million increase in revenues is forecast when moving from the last historical year to the year ahead. Given depreciation of $927,000 and incremental sales of $1,500,000, forecast capital expenditure sum to $927,000 + 0.05($1,500,000) = $927,000 + $75,000 = $1,002,000. A requirement for incremental working capital of 10 percent of the increase in revenues equates to a $150,000 deduction in calculating free cash flow. Based on these assumptions, free cash flow to the firm of $9,358,800 was calculated as follows.

Able Manufacturing, Inc.
Calculation of Next Year's Free Cash Flow to Firm

Revenues ($50,000,000 × 1.03 =)	$51,500,000
Cost of goods sold	30,900,000
Gross profit (0.40 × Revenues =)	20,600,000
SG&A expenses (maintained at 2007 level)	3,700,000
Pro forma EBITDA	16,900,000
Deprec. and amort. (0.018 × $51,500,000 =)	927,000
Pro forma earnings before interest and taxes	15,973,000
Pro forma taxes on EBIT (at 40.0 percent)	6,389,200
Operating income after tax	9,583,800
Plus: Depreciation and amortization	927,000
Less: Capital expenditures[a]	1,002,000
Less: Increase in working capital[b]	150,000
Free cash flow to firm	$ 9,358,800

[a] As explained in text, $927,000 + 0.05($1,500,000).

[b] 0.10($51,500,000 − $50,000,000).

4.2 Income Approach Methods of Private Company Valuation

The income approach obtains its conceptual support from the assumption that value is based on expectations of future income and cash flows. The income approach converts future economic benefits into a present value equivalent. For IFRS and U.S. GAAP, assets are defined as probable future economic benefits. This definition provides strong support for the application of the income approach to valuation of an interest in a public or private company.

The three forms of income approach include the **free cash flow method** (often referred to as the **discounted cash flow method** in the appraisal community), the **capitalized cash flow method**, and **residual income method** (frequently referred to as the **excess earnings method** in the valuation community).[17]

▶ The free cash flow method values an asset based on estimates of future cash flows that are discounted to present value by using a discount rate reflective of the risks associated with the cash flows. For a going concern, this method frequently includes a series of discrete cash flow projections followed by an estimate of the value of the business enterprise as a going concern at the end of the projection period.

▶ The capitalized cash flow method (also referred to as the **capitalized income method** or **capitalization of earnings method**) values a private company by

---

[17] The residual income method is sometimes categorized under the asset approach because it involves marking the tangible assets to market and estimating the value of intangible assets including goodwill.

using a single representative estimate of economic benefits and dividing that by an appropriate capitalization rate to derive an indication of value.

▶ For the valuation of a business enterprise, the excess earnings method consists of estimating the value of all of the intangible assets of the business by capitalizing future earnings in excess of the estimated return requirements associated with working capital and fixed assets. The value of the intangible assets is added to the values of working capital and fixed assets to arrive at the value of the business enterprise.

Whichever income approach method is used, an appropriate required rate of return estimate is needed for discounting expected future cash flows.

4.2.1 Required Rate of Return: Models and Estimation Issues

A variety of factors make estimating a required rate of return for a private company challenging.

▶ *Application of size premiums.* In assessing private company valuations, size premiums are frequently used in developing equity return requirements by private company appraisers. This practice seems to be less prevalent in the valuation of public companies.[18] Furthermore, size premium estimates based on public company data for the smallest cap segments can capture premiums for distress that may not be relevant.

▶ *Use of the CAPM.* Some parties have questioned whether the capital asset pricing model (CAPM) is appropriate for developing discount rate estimates for small private company valuations. In the United States, tax court cases involving private companies with little expectation of ever operating as public companies were one area where the CAPM was rejected. The perceived differences between the typically larger public companies and the smaller private company were key considerations. Small companies that have little prospect of going public or being acquired by a public company may be viewed as not comparable to the public companies for which market-data-based beta estimates are available.

▶ *Expanded CAPM.* The **expanded CAPM**[19] is an adaptation of the CAPM that adds to the CAPM a premium for small size and company-specific risk.

▶ *Elements of the build-up approach.* The build-up approach was introduced in the reading on return concepts. When **guideline public companies** (public-company comparables for the company being valued) are not available or of questionable comparability, appraisers may rely on a build-up method rather than the CAPM or other models. The build-up method is similar to the expanded CAPM but excludes the application of beta to the equity risk premium. Many view betas that are different from 1.0 as substantially reflecting industry risk factors and thus do not include an industry risk premium in the expanded CAPM. In the build-up model, in which beta is implicitly assumed equal to 1.0, an argument exists to include an industry risk premium, although there are challenges in measuring industry risk premiums. As the baseline implementation of the build-up model, we take the model with an industry risk premium.

---

[18] Size premiums and other issues associated with the development of discount rates are discussed in depth in Pratt and Grabowski (2008).

[19] Pratt and Grabowski, p. 84.

▶ *Relative debt availability and cost of debt.* Correct estimation of the debt capacity of a private company is another valuation challenge. In calculating a WACC for a valuation based on FCFF, analysts should note that a private company may have less access to debt financing than a similar public company. This lesser access means the private company may need to rely more on equity financing, which would tend to increase its WACC. Furthermore, a private company's typically smaller size could lead to greater operating risk and a higher cost of debt.

▶ *Discount rates in an acquisition context.* In evaluating an acquisition, some buyers erroneously use their own cost of capital rather than a cost of capital consistent with the riskiness of the target's cash flows. Also, some buyers mistakenly use their capital structure rather than the likely capital structure of the target in developing a WACC. In the context of acquisitions made by larger more mature companies of smaller riskier target companies, the buyer would be expected to have a lower cost of capital than the target. Both of these practices in general incorrectly transfer value from the buyer to the seller because the buyer would be paying the seller for possible value it brings to a transaction.[20]

▶ *Discount rate adjustment for projection risk.* Any lesser amount of information concerning a private company's operations or business model compared with a similar public company introduces greater uncertainty into projections that may lead to a higher required rate of return. As a second area of concern, management of a private company (on whom analysts may need to rely for forecasts) may have less experience forecasting future financial performance. Projections may reflect excessive optimism or pessimism. Any adjustments to a discount rate to account for projection risk or managerial inexperience in forecasting, however, would typically be highly judgmental.

EXAMPLE 3

Developing a Discount Rate for a Private Company

Duvall and his advisers have decided to use an income approach to value Able Manufacturing.

Because of its years of operating successfully and its owner's conservative nature, Able operated with little debt. Smith explored various sources of debt financing to operate Able with a lower overall cost of capital. Analysis of public companies in Able's industry indicated several guideline public companies for possible use in estimating a discount rate for Able. Duvall and his advisers agreed on the following estimates:

▶ Risk free rate: Estimated at 4.8 percent.

▶ Equity risk premium: The parties agreed that a 5 percent equity risk premium was appropriate.[21]

▶ Beta: A beta of 1.1 was estimated based on publicly traded companies in the same industry.

[20] Damodaran (2002).

[21] See the reading on return concepts and Chapter 9 of Pratt and Grabowski (2008) for further discussion of the equity risk premium.

▶ Small stock premium: The smaller size and less diversified operations suggest greater risk for Able relative to public companies. A small stock premium of 3 percent was included in the equity return calculation for these expected risks.[22]

▶ Company-specific risk premium: Assessment of Able indicated that beyond Smith's key role at the company, no other unusual elements created additional risk. A 1 percent company-specific risk adjustment was included.[23]

▶ Industry risk premium (build-up method only): The industry risk premium was 0 percent because no industry related factors were viewed as materially affecting the overall required return on equity estimate.

▶ Pretax cost of debt: Estimated at 7.5 percent.

▶ Ratio of debt to total capital for public companies in the same industry: Estimated at 20 percent.

▶ Optimal ratio of debt to total capital: The ratio was estimated at 10 percent based on discussions with various sources of financing. Able would not be able to achieve the industry capital structure based on its smaller size compared to public companies and the greater risk of its operations as a standalone company.

▶ Actual ratio of debt to total capital: For Able, the actual ratio was 2 percent.

▶ Combined corporate tax rate: Estimated at 40 percent.

Based only on the information given, address the following:

1. Calculate the required return on equity for Able using the CAPM.

2. Calculate the required return on equity for Able using the expanded CAPM.

3. Calculate the required return on equity for Able using the build-up method.

4. Discuss the selection of the capital structure weights to use in determining the weighted average cost of capital for Able.

5. Calculate the WACC for Able using the current capital structure and a 14 percent cost of equity.

6. Calculate the WACC for Able based on the optimal capital structure for Able and a 14 percent cost of equity.

Solution to 1: According to the CAPM, Required return on share i = Current expected risk-free return + β_i (Equity risk premium) = 4.8% + 1.1(5%) = 10.30 percent.

---

[22] If the CAPM were used to develop the equity required rate of return and similar risks were anticipated for the guideline public companies as for a smaller private company being valued, a small stock premium might not be warranted. As just described, the risk would likely be captured in the betas of the guideline public companies.

[23] Estimation of company-specific risk has been a very subjective element of the valuation process. Several valuation professionals have presented methodologies to develop quantitative estimates of company-specific risk. These tools are being vetted in the valuation community.

Solution to 2: The required rate of return is 14.3 percent, which is shown in the following tabular format.

Able Manufacturing, Inc.
Expanded CAPM: Required Rate of Return on Equity

Risk-free rate	4.8%
Plus: Equity risk premium adjusted for beta[a]	5.5
Plus: Small stock premium	3.0
Plus: Company-specific risk adjustment	1.0
Indicated required return on equity	14.3%

[a] 1.1 beta × 5 percent equity risk premium = 5.5 percent.

Solution to 3: The required rate of return is 13.8 percent. Note the absence of a beta adjustment. Note too that the fact that beta (1.1) is close to 1.0 possibly suggests any industry risk adjustment that could be made would be small in magnitude.

Able Manufacturing, Inc.
Build-Up Method: Required Rate of Return on Equity

Risk-free rate	4.8%
Plus: Equity risk premium	5.0
Plus: Small stock premium	3.0
Plus: Industry risk premium	0.0
Plus: Company-specific risk adjustment	1.0
Indicated return on equity	13.8%

Solution to 4: For valuation concerning the possible sale of Able, it is appropriate to assume the weights in the optimal capital structure in calculating WACC because an acquirer would be able and motivated to establish the optimum. The current capital structure of Able involves less debt than the optimal one; thus Able's WACC is currently higher than it needs to be. Note, however, that the weight on debt of similar large public companies may be higher than what is optimal for Able. Large public companies would be expected to have better access to public debt markets. Also, the small size of Able increases its risk relative to larger public companies. These two factors would tend to increase Able's cost of debt relative to a large public comparable and lead to a lower optimal weight of debt compared with such a public company.[24]

Solution to 5: The cost of capital for Able based on the existing capital structure was calculated as follows:

Able Manufacturing, Inc.
Calculation of Weighted Average Cost of Capital
Current Capital Structure

Pre-tax cost of debt	7.5%	
Tax rate complement (1 − Tax rate)	0.60	
After-tax cost of debt	4.5%	
Weight	×0.02	
Weighted cost of debt		0.1%
Cost of equity	14.0%	
Weight	×0.98	
Weighted cost of equity		13.7%
Weighted average cost of capital		13.8%

Solution to 6: The overall cost of capital using the optimal capital structure for Able reflected a higher level of debt financing. The WACC was calculated as follows:

Able Manufacturing, Inc.
Calculation of Weighted Average Cost of Capital
Optimal Capital Structure

Pre-tax cost of debt	7.5%	
Tax rate complement (1 − Tax rate)	0.60	
After-tax cost of debt	4.5%	
Weight	0.10	
Weighted cost of debt		0.5%
Cost of equity	14.0%	
Weight	0.90	
Weighted cost of equity		12.6%
Weighted average cost of capital		13.1%

[24] The AICPA practice aid, *Valuation of Privately-Held-Company Equity Securities Issued as Compensation*, (hereafter referred to as the "Stock Practice Aid") was released to provide technical guidance for the valuation of stock in the context of stock option grants and other share-based payments. Paragraph 119 notes that "one of the objectives and benefits of becoming a public enterprise is the ability to access the public capital markets, with the associated benefits of a lower cost of both equity and debt capital."

For early stage development companies, discount rate estimation concerns are magnified. Very high levels of company-specific risk, for example, may make use of the CAPM problematic. Several lifecycle stages exist with perceived broad ranges of absolute rate of return requirements for companies operating in each stage. Further, there can be uncertainty in classifying a company in a specific lifecycle stage.[25]

4.2.2 Free Cash Flow Method

Free cash flow valuation for private and public companies is substantially similar. For example, in the case of Able Manufacturing, a FCF valuation might involve projecting individually free cash flows for a number of years, finding the present value of those projected free cash flows, followed by finding the present value of a terminal value estimate that captures the business enterprise value at the end of the initial projection period. In principle, discrete free cash flow forecasts should be made until cash flows are expected to stabilize at a constant growth rate. Many practical implementations involve discrete cash flow projections for a period of five years.

To value the business enterprise at the end of the initial projection period, the capitalized cash flow method incorporating a sustainable long-term growth rate is a theoretically preferred method. Some appraisers, however, will calculate the terminal value using price multiples developed in the market approach. For a company in a high growth industry, market multiples would be expected to capture rapid growth in the near future and "normal" growth into the indefinite future. Using these multiples to estimate terminal value, the residual enterprise value may not be appropriate as rapid growth was incorporated twice: once in the cash flow projections over the projection period and also in the market multiple used in calculating the residual enterprise value.

4.2.3 Capitalized Cash Flow Method

The capitalized cash flow method (CCM) estimates value based on the expression for the value of a growing perpetuity and is essentially a stable growth (single stage) free cash flow model.[26] The CCM is only occasionally seen in the valuation of private companies—most often for the valuation of smaller private companies. The CCM is rarely used for the valuation of public companies, larger private companies, or in the context of acquisitions or financial reporting. The CCM may be appropriate, however, for valuing a private company in which no projections are available and an expectation of stable future operations exists. If market pricing evidence from public companies or transactions is limited, a CCM valuation may also be a feasible alternative.

For companies that are not expected to grow at a constant rate, FCF valuation using a series of discrete cash flow projections is theoretically preferable to the CCM. The CCM could provide assistance in assessing the discount rate or growth assumptions embedded in value indications from the market approach.

---

[25] The AICPA practice aids *Assets Acquired in a Business Combination to Be Used in Research and Development Activities: A Focus on Software, Electronic Devices, and Pharmaceutical Industries* (hereafter referred to as the "IPRD Practice Aid") and the "Stock Practice Aid" provide descriptive information on various stages in the early lifecycle of development stage companies and estimated return requirements. See pages 92 and 95 of the "IPRD Practice Aid" and various pages of the "Stock Practice Aid," including pages 13, 14, 41–43, and 49.

[26] See Pratt and Grabowski, pp. 29–30, for further discussion.

At the firm level, the formula for the capitalized cash flow to the firm is

$$V_f = \text{FCFF}_1 / (\text{WACC} - g_f) \qquad \qquad (1)$$

where
V_f = Value of the firm
FCFF_1 = Free cash flow to the firm for next twelve months
WACC = Weighted average cost of capital
g_f = Sustainable growth rate of free cash flow to the firm

The value of equity is found as the value of the company less the market value of debt or $V_f -$ (Market value of debt). An implicit assumption in using WACC for discounting FCFF in Equation 1 is that a constant capital structure at market values in the future exists.

The capitalized cash flow method can also be used to value equity directly. In this instance, the inputs for free cash flow would reflect FCFE and the equity return requirement would be substituted for the WACC:

$$V = \text{FCFE}_1 / (r - g) \qquad \qquad (2)$$

where r is the required return on equity and g is the sustainable growth rate of free cash flow to equity. In Equations 1 and 2 the denominator is known as the **capitalization rate**. Thus, the estimate of value in each is calculated as the forecasted Year 1 FCF divided by the capitalization rate. Example 4 illustrates the application of the CCM.

EXAMPLE 4

Valuation Using the Capitalized Cash Flow Method

Duvall and his team are comfortable with the normalized earnings, growth, and discount rate estimated for Able. Detailed projections for Able are not developed by management. Suppose that free cash flow to the firm is expected to grow at 3 percent per year going forward from the level of $9,358,800 forecast in Example 2.

1. Explain the rationale for the use of the capitalized cash flow method in this case.

2. Calculate the value of the equity of Able using the capitalized cash flow method and a WACC of 13.1 percent based on Able's optimal capital structure.

3. Calculate the value of the equity of Able using the WACC of 13.8 percent based on the existing capital structure.

4. Discuss factors leading to the difference in the computed values.

Solution to 1: The capitalized cash flow method is appropriate given the assumption that free cash flow to the firm grows at a constant rate (here 3 percent) is accurate. Otherwise, at best it provides a rough value estimate.

Solution to 2: With the estimated free cash flow to the firm, a capitalization rate of 10.1 percent (13.1 percent − 3 percent) was applied to derive a valuation indication for the business enterprise. Able's debt balance was subtracted to arrive at an equity value calculated as follows.

Able Manufacturing, Inc.
Capitalized Cash Flow Method—Optimal Capital Structure

Free cash flow to firm		$ 9,358,800
Weighted average cost of capital	13.1%	
Long-term growth rate	3.0%	
Capitalization rate		10.1%
Indicated value of invested capital		92,661,386
Less: Debt capital (actual, assumed to equal market value)		2,000,000
Indicated value of equity		$90,661,386

Solution to 3: This calculation is similar to the one in the Solution to 2 except for the use of a capitalization rate of 10.8 percent (13.8 percent − 3 percent).

Able Manufacturing, Inc.
Capitalized Cash Flow Method—Existing Capital Structure

Free cash flow to firm		$ 9,358,800
Weighted average cost of capital	13.8%	
Long-term growth rate	3.0%	
Capitalization rate		10.8%
Indicated value of invested capital		86,655,556
Less: Debt capital		2,000,000
Indicated value of equity		$84,655,556

Solution to 4: The low level of debt in the existing capital structure results in a higher WACC and a lower valuation conclusion for Able relative to the optimal capital structure.

4.2.4 Excess Earnings Method

In a business valuation context, the excess earnings method (EEM) involves estimating the earnings remaining after deducting amounts that reflect the required returns to working capital and fixed assets (i.e., the tangible assets). This residual amount of earnings (i.e., "excess earnings") is capitalized by using the growing perpetuity formula from the CCM to obtain an estimate of the value of intangible assets. Generally, the EEM has been used to value intangible assets and very small businesses when other such market approach methods are not feasible. For valuing the entire business, the values of working capital and fixed assets are added to the capitalized value of intangibles.

Applying the EEM to value a business enterprise would involve the following steps:

1. Estimate values of working capital and fixed assets (typically, fair value estimates are used). Suppose these are €200,000 and €800,000, respectively.

2. Determine the normalized earnings of the business enterprise. Suppose normalized earnings are €100,000 for the year just ended.

3. Develop discount rates for working capital and fixed assets. Working capital is viewed as the lowest risk and most liquid asset with the lowest required rate of return. Fixed assets require a somewhat greater rate of return. Intangible assets, given their limited liquidity and high risk, often require the highest return. Suppose the required returns on working capital and fixed assets are 5 percent and 11 percent, respectively.

4. Calculate required returns associated with working capital and fixed assets and subtract the required returns on working capital and fixed assets from the normalized earnings of the business enterprise to estimate the residual income; this residual income, if any, must reflect the value associated with intangible assets. In this case, residual income is €100,000 − 0.05(€200,000) − 0.11(€800,000) = €2,000. Assume that residual income grows at 3 percent per year.

5. Estimate discount rate and capitalization rate required for the valuation of the intangible assets.[27] This estimate typically represents all intangible assets.[28] The details of such a calculation are outside the scope of this reading; assume the discount rate is 12 percent.

6. Value intangible assets of the enterprise using the formula for a growing perpetuity. The total value of intangible assets is (1.03)(€2,000)/(0.12 − 0.03) ≈ €22,889. (Because €2,000 is associated with normalized income for the most recent year, it is increased by its assumed 3 percent growth rate to obtain a forecast of the year ahead residual income.)

7. Total of working capital, fixed assets, and intangibles equals the value of the business. The EEM estimate would be €22,889 + €200,000 + €800,000 = €1,022,889.

As mentioned, the EEM is only rarely used in pricing entire private businesses, and then only small ones. Some have viewed the specific return requirements

---

[27] Significant judgment is associated with many of these estimates. If a weighted average cost of capital for the business enterprise has been calculated, a discount rate for intangible assets can be estimated. With values for working capital and fixed assets, discrete return requirements can be developed for these asset groups based on market return levels, borrowing costs, and other factors. With the WACC known and estimates for discount rates on working capital and fixed assets, the discount rate for intangible assets can be estimated as the amount that equates the WACC with the weighted values of working capital, fixed assets, and intangible assets. The "IPRD Practice Aid" provides further discussion of this process.

[28] Valuations under SFAS No. 141R and IAS 3R will typically consider separate intangible assets, such as customer relationships, technology, trade names, and the assembled work force, among others. Typically, only one or two intangible assets are valued based on residual income. Also, acquired intangible assets are valued based on their economic life rather than into perpetuity. Although overall customer relationships may grow over time, the customers acquired at the time of acquisition will decline over time.

for working capital, tangible assets, and the residual income associated with intangible assets as not readily measurable.[29]

For financial reporting, the concept of residual income is an important element of intangible asset valuations and has wide acceptance. Residual income is the subject of significant discussion among appraisers who perform purchase price allocation valuations of intangible assets pursuant to IFRS 3R or SFAS No. 141R.[30] An analyst considering intangible asset amortization and goodwill impairment issues would benefit from an understanding of residual income concepts. Interested readers are referred to the "IPRD Practice Aid" for further explanation of the concept and the valuation of intangible assets using residual income.

4.3 Market Approach Methods of Private Company Valuation

The market approach uses direct comparisons to public companies and acquired enterprises to estimate the fair value of an equity interest in a private company. Three major variations of the market approach exist:

▶ The **guideline public company method** (GPCM) establishes a value estimate based on the observed multiples from trading activity in the shares of public companies viewed as reasonably comparable to the subject private company. The multiples from the public companies are adjusted to reflect differences in the relative risk and growth prospects of the subject private company compared with the guideline public companies.

▶ The **guideline transactions method** (GTM) establishes a value estimate based on pricing multiples derived from the acquisition of control of entire public or private companies that were acquired. Whereas GPCM uses a multiple that could be associated with trades of any size, GTM uses a multiple that specifically relates to sales of entire companies.

▶ The **prior transaction method** (PTM) considers actual transactions in the stock of the subject private company.

Because the market approach relies on data generated in actual market transactions, some consider it to be conceptually preferable to the income- and asset-based approaches for private company valuation. In the United States, tax courts assessing private company valuations have generally stated a preference for valuation based on market transactions although they often accept valuations based on the income approach. SFAS No. 157 also presents a fair value hierarchy

---

[29] Valuation professionals performing valuations of intangible assets for IAS 38 or SFAS No. 141 often estimate return requirements for the various assets of a business enterprise. Individual discount rate estimates for each asset class can be compared to the WACC for an enterprise to confirm the reasonableness of the individual estimates. For further discussion, see AICPA practice aid *Assets Acquired in a Business Combination to Be Used in Research and Development Activities: A Focus on Software, Electronic Devices, and Pharmaceutical Industries.*

[30] See 10 June 2008 discussion draft, "The Identification of Contributory Assets and the Calculation of Economic Rents," issued by the Best Practices for Valuations for Financial Reporting: Intangible Asset Working Group organized by The Appraisal Foundation.

that gives the highest priority to market based evidence.[31] The primary assumption of the market approach is that transactions providing pricing evidence are reasonably comparable to the subject company.

A primary challenge in using the market approach is finding comparable companies and accurately assessing their pricing. All of the company-specific factors noted previously may lead to different levels of expected risk and growth for a private company relative to a public company. Market multiples reflect both expected risk and growth. Risk and growth assumptions should be extracted and multiples adjusted to reflect any differences of the subject company vis-à-vis the chosen comparable(s). The stock-specific factors associated with private companies may create additional uncertainties regarding levels of risk and growth.

The pricing of stock in public companies reflects stock price volatility as a result of, in part, the ready liquidity. Interests in private companies have much more limited marketability. These differences create uncertainty in the determination of a pricing multiple and a final value conclusion for an interest in a private company.

Factors for the identification of guideline companies are similar for public and private companies. Key factors include industry membership, form of operations, trends, and current operating status, among others. As previously noted, lifecycle and size differences may create significant challenges in applying the market approach.

Public and private company analysis may differ in the financial metrics used in the valuation process. Price-to-earnings methods are frequently cited in the valuation of public companies, with other multiples considered as well. For larger mature private companies, pricing multiples based on EBITDA and/or EBIT are frequently seen. EBITDA is best compared with the **market value of invested capital** (MVIC),[32] defined as the market value of debt and equity, in forming the valuation metric. With a calculation of MVIC for a private company, the value of debt can be subtracted to produce an estimate of equity value. As current transaction market values for debt are not available in many cases, some estimate of the market value of debt is needed. The use of the face value of debt as an estimate may be acceptable in many situations in which debt represents a small fraction of overall financing and operations are stable. For companies with highly leveraged financial conditions and/or significant volatility expected in future financial performance, the valuation of equity as the residual obtained by subtracting the face value of debt from the value of the business enterprise is

---

[31] Paragraph 22 of SFAS No. 157 states that "To increase consistency and comparability in fair value measurements and related disclosures, the fair value hierarchy prioritizes the inputs to valuation techniques used to measure fair value into three broad levels. The fair value hierarchy gives the highest priority to quoted prices (unadjusted) in active markets for identical assets or liabilities (Level 1) and the lowest priority to unobservable inputs (Level 3)." Paragraph 23 notes that "The availability of inputs relative to the asset or liability and the relative reliability of the inputs might affect the selection of the valuation technique. However, the fair value hierarchy prioritizes the inputs to valuation techniques, not the valuation techniques." This last statement would suggest that the appropriate valuation approach would be dependent on the facts and circumstances unique to a particular valuation.

[32] In addition to MVIC, other similar terms include enterprise value (EV), business enterprise value (BEV), and firm value. Definitions for enterprise value vary but most frequently start with MVIC and subtract any cash and cash equivalents. BEV is typically synonymous with EV.

frequently not appropriate.[33] Estimates of market value based on debt characteristics, known as matrix prices, are an alternative in such cases.

For many very small private companies with limited asset bases, net income based multiples may be more commonly used than EBITDA multiples. For extremely small companies, multiples of revenue may even be commonly applied. This convention considers the likely absence of meaningful financial data and the greater impact and subjectivity associated with such items as owner compensation.

Nonfinancial metrics may be an appropriate means of valuation for certain industries. These metrics would probably best be used in addition to financial metrics. Significant reliance on these metrics would be appropriate only if the nonfinancial measure is generally accepted within the industry. Examples of nonfinancial metrics include price per subscriber in cable and price per bed for hospital and skilled nursing and other healthcare facilities.

4.3.1 Guideline Public Company Method

In private company valuation as has been noted, valuation based on multiples of similar public companies is often referred to as the guideline public company method (GPCM). The valuation process is essentially similar for a public or a private company. A group of public companies is identified, the relevant pricing multiples for the guideline companies are derived, and adjustments to the multiples reflecting the relative risk and growth prospects of the subject company relative to the publicly traded companies are made. For a private company, this method would lead to a conclusion of value. For a public company, application of this method helps assess over- or under-valuation of a company relative to similar companies at a specific point in time.

The primary advantage of this method is the potentially large pool of guideline companies and the significant descriptive, financial, and trading information available to the analyst/appraiser. Disadvantages include possible issues regarding comparability and subjectivity in the risk and growth adjustments to the pricing multiple.

Control premiums may be used in the valuation of a controlling interest in a company. Defined in the International Glossary of Business Valuation Terms (IGBVT), a **control premium** is an amount or a percentage by which the pro rata value of a controlling interest exceeds the pro rata value of a noncontrolling interest in a business enterprise, to reflect the power of control. For the valuation of a controlling interest, a control premium is viewed as necessary if the value is derived from the GPCM. The trading of interests in public companies reflects small blocks without control of the entity. Given this information, many but not all believe the resulting pricing multiples do not reflect control of the entity.

A control premium adjustment may be appropriate depending on the specific facts. Control premiums are estimated based on transactions in which pub-

---

[33] As noted in the "Stock Practice Aid" and observed in the capital markets, debt may not always be worth its face or par value because of repayment risk. Highly leveraged companies and/or companies with significant volatility of financial performance may have debt valued at significant discounts from face value. In these cases, option pricing theory can be used to value each debt and equity instrument as a separate call option on the business enterprise value of the company. Debt would be a senior call option with priority to payment of the business enterprise up to its face value and any unpaid interest. Preferred stock, common stock, and options would all represent different options with a call on the enterprise value. This concept is discussed in some depth in the "Stock Practice Aid."

lic companies were acquired. Several factors require careful consideration in estimating a control premium.

- ▶ *Type of transaction.* Some transaction databases classify acquisitions as either financial or strategic transactions. A **strategic transaction** involves a buyer that would benefit from certain synergies associated with owning the target firm. These synergies could include enhanced revenues, cost savings, or other possible benefits. A **financial transaction** involves a buyer having essentially no material synergies with the target. As examples, the purchase of a private company by a company in an unrelated industry or by a private equity firm would typically be a financial transaction. Compared with financial transactions, in a strategic transaction acquisition premiums are typically larger because of the expected synergies.

- ▶ *Industry factors.* Industry sectors with acquisition activity are considered to be "in-play" at a valuation date; that is, pricing of public companies in the sector may reflect some part of a possible control premium in the share prices. Control premiums measured at a date significantly before a valuation date might reflect a different industry environment from that of the valuation date.

- ▶ *Form of consideration.* Transactions involving the exchange of significant amounts of stock (as opposed to all cash transactions) might be less relevant as a basis of measuring a control premium because of the possibility that acquiring companies time such transactions during periods when their management perceives that shares of their company are overvalued in the marketplace.

The multiple resulting from applying a control premium to pricing multiples from publicly-traded companies should be assessed for reasonableness.[34] Suppose that a public company, which is viewed as comparable to a private company being appraised, was acquired at an 8x pricing multiple. A control premium of 30 percent control is paid based on the stock's price prior to the acquisition. Pricing multiples for guideline public companies, however, are 10x at the valuation date. The application of a 30 percent control premium would suggest a 13x pricing multiple. The dramatically different value indications resulting from applying a 8x transaction multiple and a 13x multiple suggest the need for further investigation before accepting the 13x multiple. Comparability issues or dramatic pricing changes may be factors leading to this material difference.

EXAMPLE 5

Valuation Using Guideline Public Company Method

Duvall decides to use the GPCM to develop value indication for Able that is independent of the FCF indication he is also pursuing. Duvall believes that many acquirors apply a multiple of market value of invested

---

[34] Appraisers performing private company valuations incorporate the control premium into the valuation calculation in a variety of different presentations. Many appraisers would not adjust the pricing multiple for a control premium. Rather, appraisers often use a multiple based on the guideline public companies and include a separate addition of the control premium in the calculation for the value estimate. The approach incorporating a control premium adjustment to the pricing multiple facilitates reconciliation of pricing multiples from public companies to those observed in transactions.

capital to EBITDA to value companies in Able's industry. A search for comparable public companies indicated several companies that might serve as guidelines or benchmarks for valuing Able; however, all of these were much larger than Able. Duvall's research on guideline public companies indicates the following:

▶ The MVIC to EBITDA multiples of such public companies averages 7.0.

▶ A combined downward adjustment of 15 percent for relative risk and growth characteristics of Able compared with the guideline public companies suggests an adjusted MVIC to EBITDA multiple of 5.95, rounded to 6, for Able.

▶ A control premium of 20 percent was reported in a single strategic acquisition from several years ago. The transaction involved an exchange of stock with no cash consideration paid.

▶ Duvall is not aware of any strategic buyers that might incorporate synergies into their valuation of Able.

▶ Normalized EBITDA is $16,900,000.

▶ Market value of debt capital is $2,000,000.

1. Explain the elements included in the calculation of a pricing multiple for Able.

2. Calculate the pricing multiple appropriate for Able including a control premium adjustment.

3. Calculate the value of Able using the guideline public company method.

Solution to 1: The value of Able in relation to a possible acquisition is desired. Pricing multiples from guideline public companies provide a starting point for the development of a pricing multiple. The pricing multiples for the guideline public companies must be adjusted to reflect any differences in risk and growth expectations for Able compared with the guideline public companies. As a final element, the pricing multiple should consider the inclusion of a control premium given the possible sale of Able.

Solution to 2: Estimation of control premiums is a challenging area given measurement issues and uncertainties associated with the comparability of transactions in which control premiums were measured. Considering the absence of any strategic buyers, in the present instance a control premium of 0 percent is a reasonable baseline. There was a single strategic transaction for the acquisition of a public company several years prior to the acquisition. The age of the transaction, however, creates concern regarding the relevance of the indicated control premium.

Based on the information provided, the MVIC to EBITDA multiple for Able can be taken to approximately 6, reflecting no control premium adjustment.

**Able Manufacturing, Inc.
Development of Pricing Multiple
for Guideline Public Company Method**

Initial MVIC to EBITDA from public companies		7.0
Relative risk and growth adjustment for Able	−15%	(1.05)
Multiple before control adjustment		5.95
Control premium adjustment[35]	0%	0
Multiple after control adjustment		5.95
Rounded to		6.0

Solution to 3:

**Able Manufacturing, Inc.
Valuation Using Guideline Public Company Method**

Normalized EBITDA	$16,900,000
Pricing multiple	6.0
Indicated value of invested capital	101,400,000
Less: Debt capital	2,000,000
Indicated value of equity	$99,400,000

4.3.2 Guideline Transactions Method

The guideline transactions method (GTM) is conceptually similar to the guideline public company method. Unlike the GPCM, the GTM uses pricing multiples derived from acquisitions of public or private companies. Transaction data available on publicly reported acquisitions is compiled from public filings by parties to the transaction with the regulatory bodies such as the Financial Services Authority in the United Kingdom or the Securities and Exchange Commission (SEC) in the United States. Data on transactions not subject to public disclosure may be available from certain transaction databases. As information may be limited and is generally not readily confirmed, many appraisers challenge the reliability of this data. All other things equal, transaction multiples would be the most relevant evidence for valuation of a controlling interest in a private company.

---

[35] Control premiums are measured based on the value of the equity of public companies before and after an acquisition. As many valuations in a transaction setting are performed on an MVIC rather than equity basis, an adjustment to an equity control premium would be required for a valuation using MVIC multiples. In the example, no control premium was concluded to be appropriate. Assuming an equity control premium of 30 percent was deemed appropriate based on different facts, a normalized capital structure of one-third debt and two-thirds equity would suggest a 20 percent control premium (two-thirds of 30 percent) if applied to an MVIC-multiple-based value from guideline public companies. Control premium data vary markedly and divergence in practice exists in this area of valuation.

A number of factors need to be considered in assessing transaction-based pricing multiples.

▶ *Synergies.* The pricing of strategic acquisitions may include payment for anticipated synergies. The relevance of payments for synergies to the case at hand merits consideration.

▶ *Contingent consideration.* **Contingent consideration** represents potential future payments to the seller that are contingent on the achievement of certain agreed on occurrences. Obtaining some form of regulatory approval or achieving a targeted level of EBITDA are two types of contingencies. Contingent consideration may be included in the structure of acquisition. The inclusion of contingent consideration in the purchase price paid for an enterprise introduces uncertainty. SFAS No. 141R has changed the requirements for contingent consideration in the context of a business combination.

▶ *Noncash consideration.* Many acquisitions include stock in the consideration. The cash equivalent value of a large block of stock may create uncertainty regarding the transaction price. For example, the 2001 merger of America Online (AOL) and Time Warner Corporation was a stock swap that occurred at a time when AOL stock was trading based on expectations of significant future growth. In 2002, the combined company reported two charges for goodwill impairment expense totaling $99 billion. The level of this impairment expense raises questions regarding whether the initial transaction price reflected temporary overvaluation of AOL stock relative to its intrinsic value.

▶ *Availability of transactions.* Meaningful transactions for a specific private company may be limited. The relevance of pricing indications from a transaction that occurred a significant period prior to a valuation date can be challenged—especially if evidence indicates changes in the subject company, industry, or economy between the transaction date and the valuation date.

▶ *Changes between transaction date and valuation date.* Unlike the guideline public company method, which develops pricing multiples based on stock prices at or very near the valuation date, the guideline transactions method relies on pricing evidence from acquisitions of control of firms at different points in the past. In many industries, transactions are limited and transactions several months or more from a valuation date may be the only transaction evidence available. Changes in the marketplace could result in differing risk and growth expectations requiring an adjustment to the pricing multiple.

EXAMPLE 6

Valuation Using Guideline Transactions Method

In addition to the income approach and the guideline public company method, the guideline transactions method was considered and applied. Duvall and his advisers noted:

▶ Pricing multiples from several recent acquisitions of private companies in the industry indicated a MVIC to EBITDA multiple of 6.0.

► Several of the acquisitions studied were viewed as similar to Able because of similar revenue bases and limited diversification. The overall risk and growth characteristics of the acquired companies and Able were viewed as similar.

1. Discuss differences between pricing multiples from the guideline transactions and guideline public company methods.
2. Explain the calculation of a pricing multiple using the guideline transactions method.
3. Calculate the pricing multiple appropriate for Able.
4. Calculate the value of Able using the guideline transactions method.

Solution to 1: The guideline transactions method considers market transactions involving the acquisition of the total equity of companies. As such, the pricing multiple more accurately reflects the value of total companies. Pricing multiples from guideline public companies typically reflect public trading in small blocks of stock. The multiples may not reflect the value of the total equity of the public companies.

Solution to 2: The pricing multiples from acquisitions are the basis for the pricing multiple. The risk and growth prospects of the acquired companies and the subject private company are assessed and an adjustment factor is applied. As the multiples reflect acquisitions of total equity, they reflect the value of total equity. No control premium adjustment is necessary.

Solution to 3: Calculation of the initial pricing multiple follows:

Able Manufacturing, Inc.
Development of Pricing Multiple
for Guideline Transactions Method

Initial MVIC to EBITDA from transactions		6.0
Relative risk and growth adjustment for Able	0%	0.0
Indicated multiple		6.0
Rounded to		6.0

Solution to 4: Valuation using the guideline transactions is similar to that from the guideline public company method except the control premium is already incorporated in the transaction multiple.

Able Manufacturing, Inc.
Guideline Transactions Method

EBITDA	$16,900,000
Pricing multiple	6.0
Indicated value of invested capital	101,400,000
Less: Debt capital	2,000,000
Indicated value of equity	$99,400,000

4.3.3 Prior Transaction Method

The prior transaction method (PTM) considers actual transactions in the stock of the subject company. Valuation can be based on either the actual price paid or the multiples implied from the transaction. The PTM is generally most relevant when considering the value of a minority equity interest in a company. For many private companies, there are no or very limited transactions in the stock.

If available and arm's length, the PTM would be expected to provide the most meaningful evidence of value. The PTM provides less reliable valuation evidence if transactions are infrequent. Transactions at different points in time may require significant adjustment, and the motivations of parties are uncertain.[36]

4.4 Asset-Based Approach to Private Company Valuation

The principle underlying the asset-based approach is that the value of ownership of an enterprise is equivalent to the fair value of its assets less the fair value of its liabilities. Of the three approaches to valuation, the asset-based approach (also referred to as the **cost approach** by many in the valuation profession) is generally considered to be the weakest from a conceptual standpoint for valuing an ongoing business enterprise.

The asset-based approach is rarely used for the valuation of going concerns. Reasons include the limited market data available to directly value intangible assets, difficulties in valuing certain tangible assets (such as special use plant and equipment), and the more readily available information to value operating companies as an integrated whole rather than on an asset-by-asset basis.

An operating company with nominal profits relative to the values of assets used and without prospects for doing better in the future might best be valued using an asset-based approach assuming the winding up of operations. In this case, its value as a going concern might be less than its value in liquidation (the value that could be realized through the liquidation of its assets) because the assets might be redeployed by buyers to higher valued uses. Resource and financial companies might also be valued based on an asset-based approach. Banks and finance companies largely consist of loan and securities portfolios that can be priced based on market variables. In such cases a summation of individual asset value estimates may give a lower-bound-type estimate of the overall value of the company. The asset-based approach may be appropriate for the valuation of holding (investment) companies, such as real estate investment trusts (REITs) and closed end investment companies (CEICs). For these entities, the underlying assets typically consist of real estate or securities that were valued using the market and/or income approaches. An asset-based approach may also be appropriate for very small businesses with limited intangible value or early stage companies.

For the valuation of an interest in a pooled investment vehicle, certain factors may suggest a value different from the net asset value per share. Manage-

---

[36] The PTM can provide insights on the value of development stage entities when revenues and cash flows are highly speculative. Many development stage companies fund development activities through several rounds of equity financing. As such, there may be a series of prior transactions providing valuation evidence. The equity financing often involves the sale of preferred stock with liquidation preferences and rights to convert to common stock. As development stage entities often have complex capital structures with different classes of equity securities with differing rights, significant adjustments are required. This process is complex and requires significant judgment. The AICPA Toolkit *Valuation of Privately-Held Equity Securities Issued as Compensation* provides further insights.

ment fees and carried interest may lead to an expectation of proceeds available to an investor and a value estimate that is less than the net asset value per share.[37] The relative growth and profit as a result of management expertise may also merit an upward or downward adjustment to the net asset value. Other factors, such as the possible effect of tax attributes (tax basis in the assets held by the entity) and diversification, and professional management benefits may also affect value.

Example 7 illustrates four definitions of values that a private business appraiser used to value the financial services subsidiary of a public company.

EXAMPLE 7

Valuation of a Financial Services Company

In a valuation of a financial services company, a business appraiser estimated four values for the company using four different approaches, which he characterized as follows:

1. *Discounted cash flow approach.* The appraiser estimated value as the present value of projected FCFE for the next 10 years to which was added the present value of the capitalized value of the 11th-year cash flow.

2. *Market approach.* The appraiser used the GPCM with price-to-cash flow, price-to-book, and price-to-earnings multiples, and made adjustments to reflect differences in risk and growth, applying the resulting multiples to the company's cash flow, book value, and earnings, respectively.

3. *Adjusted book value approach, going-concern basis.* The appraiser adjusted the book values of assets and liabilities to better reflect market values and obtained the adjusted book value of equity, which was the estimate of value based on this approach. The definition of market value used was: "Market value is...the most probable price that an asset should bring in a competitive and open market under all conditions requisite to a fair sale, the buyer and seller each acting prudently and knowledgeably, and assuming the price is not affected by undue stimulus."

4. *Adjusted book value approach, orderly liquidation basis.* The appraiser adjusted the book values of assets and liabilities to better reflect orderly liquidation values and obtained the liquidation book value of equity, which was the estimate of value based on this approach. The definition of orderly liquidation value used was: "Orderly liquidation value [is] the price [the asset] would bring if exposed for sale on the open market, with a reasonable time allowed to find

---

[37] **Carried interest** or "carry" represents a share of any profits that is paid to the general partner (manager) of an investment partnership, such as a private equity or hedge fund, as a form of compensation designed to be an incentive to the manager to maximize performance of the investment fund. A manager's carried interest allocation is in addition to any investment that the manager may have in the investment partnership. To receive a carried interest, the manager typically must first return all capital contributed by the investors and in certain cases the fund must also return a previously agreed on rate of return (the *hurdle rate*) to investors.

a purchaser, both buyer and seller having knowledge of the uses and purposes to which the asset is adapted and for which it is capable of being used, the seller being compelled to sell and the buyer being willing, but not compelled, to buy."

State and explain which of the above methods would be expected to produce the lowest value estimate.

Solution: Methods 1, 2, and 3 recognize a going-concern value for the company; method 4 does not, so the value estimates under 4 should be the lowest. In general, using individual assets in a coordinated way in the operation of a business as implicitly assumed in 1 and 2 should increase value. Between 3 and 4, the element of the seller being compelled to sell should result in 4 being the lowest estimate.

4.5 Valuation Discounts and Premiums

Control and/or marketability adjustments are often included in valuations of interests in private companies. This area is one of the primary differences in the valuation of interests in private companies. The following chart is adapted from Hitchner[38] and presents the relationship of these concepts and other concepts discussed in this reading. As the chart indicates, the inclusion of discounts depends, in part, on the starting point of a valuation.

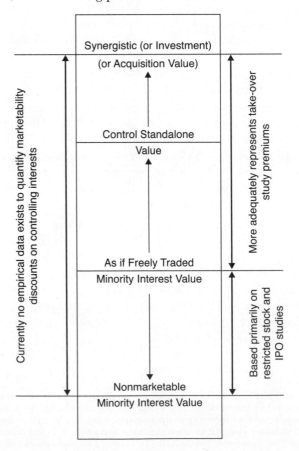

---

[38] Hitchner (2006).

Starting at the top of the chart, the highest possible value indication for an entity would be its investment value to the optimal synergistic buyer. This value reflects a controlling interest assumption, which also increases value. Below the control value of the enterprise to a strategic buyer is the value of the enterprise to a standalone (financial) buyer. In this case, specific synergies to the buyer are not available. The "As If Freely Traded/Minority Interest Value" represents the value of a noncontrolling equity interest that is readily marketable. This value would be equivalent to the price at which most publicly traded companies trade in the market. The lowest level of value is the "Nonmarketable/Minority Interest Value." This value reflects the reduction to value associated with the lack of control and ready marketability associated with small equity interests in private companies.

The application of control premiums and lack of control and marketability discounts is fact-specific and estimates may vary dramatically. Variations in estimated discounts and premiums may relate to the challenging comparability of the data used to quantify discounts. Discounts may also vary based on interpretation of the importance of the size of shareholding and distribution of shares, the relationship of parties, state law affecting minority shareholder rights, and other factors.

The timing of a potential liquidity event is one key consideration. An interest in a private company that is pursuing either an IPO or a strategic sale might be valued with relatively modest valuation discounts. An equity interest in a private company that has not paid dividends and has no prospect for a liquidity event would likely require much higher valuation discounts.

4.5.1 Lack of Control Discounts

A **discount for lack of control** (DLOC) is an amount or percentage deducted from the pro rata share of 100 percent of the value of an equity interest in a business to reflect the absence of some or all of the powers of control.[39]

Lack of control discounts may be necessary for valuing noncontrolling equity interests in private companies if the value of total equity was developed on a controlling interests basis. The lack of control may be disadvantageous to an investor because of the inability to select directors, officers, and management that control the operations of an entity. Without control, an investor is unable to distribute cash or other property, to buy and sell assets, to obtain financing, and to bring about other actions, which could affect the value of the investment, the timing of distributions, and the ultimate return to the investor.

Although an interest may lack control, the effect on value of the lack of control is uncertain. The U.S. SEC suggests that evidence of "disproportionate returns" is important in supporting the application of lack of control discounts. Disproportionate returns would result when control shareholders increase their returns through above-market compensation and other actions that reduce the returns available to minority shareholders. For private companies seeking a liquidity event through an IPO or strategic sale of the entity, the likelihood of actions by a control group that reduce the earnings of an entity is reduced.

Data available for estimating a lack of control discount are limited and interpretations can vary markedly. For interests in operating companies, control premium data from acquisitions of public companies had been used frequently in the past. The factors cited earlier in this reading on the calculation of a control premium should also be considered for estimating a lack of control discount.

---

[39] International Glossary of Business Valuation Terms.

Noting the uncertainties in demonstrating the adverse financial impact of the lack of control of an interest and finding appropriate data to measure the lack of control, the equation used frequently in the calculation of a lack of control discount is:

$$DLOC = 1 - [1/(1 + Control\ premium)].$$

For example, if a 20 percent control premium is assumed, the associated DLOC is $1 - (1/1.20) = 0.167$ or 16.7 percent.

The following sets forth the typical application of DLOC based on the different methods of valuation.

Method	Basis of Valuation	DLOC Expected?
GTM	Control	Yes
GPCM	Typically minority	No
CCM/FCF	Control or minority	Depends on cash flows

Valuation indications from the CCM and FCF methods of the income approach are generally agreed to be a controlling interest value if cash flows and the discount rate are estimated on a controlling interest basis. If control cash flows are not used and/or the discount rate does not reflect an optimal capital structure, the resulting value is generally believed to reflect a lack of control basis.

Some analysts believe trading in REITs and CEICs may provide a basis for the estimation of lack of control discounts as well. As individual REITs and CEICs may trade at premiums, discounts, or near their net asset value at different points in time, the use of this data to quantify the lack of control is challenging and outside the scope of this reading.

4.5.2 Lack of Marketability Discounts

A **discount for lack of marketability** (DLOM) is an amount or percentage deducted from the value of an ownership interest to reflect the relative absence of marketability.[40]

Lack of marketability discounts are frequently applied in the valuation of noncontrolling equity interests in private companies. Although a DLOM is different from a DLOC, the two discounts are often linked; that is, if a valuation is on a noncontrolling interest basis, a lack of marketability discount is typically appropriate. Key variables affecting marketability include prospects for liquidity, contractual arrangements affecting marketability, restrictions on transferability, pool of potential buyers, risk or volatility, size and timing of distributions (duration of asset), uncertainty of value, and concentration of ownership.[41] At a minimum, an interest that lacks marketability involves a potential opportunity cost associated with the inability to redeploy investment funds.

Restricted stock transactions and IPOs are two types of data typically used to quantify lack of marketability discounts. Although generally agreed by valuation

---

[40] International Glossary of Business Valuation Terms.

[41] As reported in paragraph 57 (page 24) of AICPA "Stock Practice Aid."

professionals as the best available data to support discounts, these sources are subject to significant differences in their interpretation.

In the United States, SEC Rule 144 provides certain restrictions on the resale of unregistered stock in public companies. Shares acquired prior to an IPO are an example of shares that might be subject to Rule 144 restrictions. These restrictions prevent resale of shares subject to the requirements of Rule 144 in an attempt to maintain an orderly trading market for the publicly traded shares. Restricted stock is essentially identical to freely traded stock of a public company except for the trading restrictions. Unlike interests in private companies, restricted stock transactions typically involve shares that will enjoy ready marketability in the near future.[42]

The relationship of stock sales prior to initial public offerings is another source of marketability discounts. In many companies (especially early stage or high growth companies) approaching an IPO, value may be increasing as levels of risk and uncertainty decline because the company is progressing in its development. Reduction in risk associated with realization of the predicted cash flows or a narrowing of the ranges of possible future cash flows would lead to a reduction in the discount rate.[43] Some studies have attempted to adjust for this factor.

Put options have also been used to quantify lack of marketability discounts. As the first step of this process, an at-the-money put option is priced. The value of the put option as a percentage of the value of the stock before any DLOM provides an estimate of the DLOM as a percentage. DLOM based on put options are used most often for equity interests in development stage companies. For these companies, liquidity in the short to intermediate term is frequently a key objective of investors.

The key assumptions are the expected term until a liquidity event and the level of volatility associated with the company. One advantage of the put option analysis is the ability to directly address perceived risk of the private company through the volatility estimate. The volatility estimate may better capture the risks of the stock compared with restricted stock or IPO transactions in which volatility may be one of many variables influencing the level of discount. An estimate of volatility can be developed at the valuation date based on either historical volatilities of public companies or the volatility estimates embedded in publicly traded options. Put options only provide price protection (the protection lasts for the life of the option). The put option, however, does not provide liquidity for the asset holding, raising a concern on the use of this form of estimate of the DLOM.

In addition to control and marketability discounts, a variety of other potential valuation discounts exist that may require consideration. These include key person discounts, portfolio discounts (discount for non-homogeneous assets), and possible discounts for nonvoting shares.

If both lack of control and lack of marketability discounts are appropriate, these discounts are applied in sequence and are essentially multiplicative rather than additive. The discounts are multiplicative as the valuation process involves discrete steps—first moving from a controlling to a noncontrolling basis and

---

[42] Some commentators have noted that the sale of blocks of restricted stock that significantly exceed public trading activity in the stock may be the most comparable data for quantifying a lack of marketability discount. If the block size significantly exceeds trading volumes, large blocks of restricted shares may still be illiquid when Rule 144 restrictions terminate. A private sale of this block may reflect a valuation discount related to the price risk associated with the holding.

[43] The AICPA "Stock Practice Aid" comments on risk reductions in pre-IPO and IPO companies as follows: "The cost of equity capital for a private enterprise prior to its IPO generally ranges from 20 to 35 percent," in paragraph 117; and in paragraph 119, "By contrast, the cost of equity capital for a newly public enterprise generally ranges from 15 to 25 percent."

then moving from a marketable to a nonmarketable basis. For an equity interest in which a 10 percent lack of control discount and a 20 percent lack of marketability discount are believed to be appropriate, the total discount is 28 percent $[1 - (1 - 10\%)(1 - 20\%)]$ rather than 30 percent $(10\% + 20\%)$.

EXAMPLE 8

Application of Valuation Discounts

Suppose that Jane Doe owns 10 percent of the stock of Able, and that the remaining 90 percent is held by CEO John Smith. Smith is interested in selling Able to a third party. Smith advised Doe that if Able isn't sold he has no reason to purchase Doe's 10 percent interest. Assume the following:

- Valuation discounts assuming imminent transaction:
  - Lack of control discount = 0 percent.
  - Lack of marketability discount = 5 percent.
- Valuation discounts assuming continued operation as a private company:
  - Lack of control discount: incorporated through use of reported earnings rather than normalized earnings.
  - Lack of marketability discount = 25 percent.
- Indicated value of equity in operations:
  - $96,000,000 in sale scenario.
  - $80,000,000 in "stay private scenario."[44]

1. Discuss the relevance of valuation discounts assuming an imminent sale of Able.
2. Explain which estimate of equity value should be used and calculate the value of Doe's equity interest in Able assuming a sale is likely.
3. Discuss the relevance of valuation discounts assuming Able continues as a private company.
4. Explain which estimate of equity value should be used and calculate the value of Doe's equity interest assuming Able continues as a private company.
5. Contrast the valuation conclusions and discuss factors that contribute to the difference in the concluded values.

---

[44] The treatment of nonoperating assets varies when a minority interest in the stock is appraised. Able holds nonoperating assets consisting of certain real estate. In the event of a sale, many buyers would not be interested in the nonoperating assets. The nonoperating assets could be distributed to the shareholders prior to the sale of the stock to a buyer. Alternatively, Able could sell the operating assets and liabilities to a buyer resulting in Able holding the real estate assets and cash from sale of the business operations. When liquidation of the entity is likely, inclusion of nonoperating assets values would seem appropriate. When continued operation as a private firm is expected, the benefit to minority shareholders from nonoperating assets is less certain. In this case, some appraisers would exclude these nonoperating assets from their equity valuation.

Solution to 1: The sale of Able can only be completed with Smith's concurrence given his 90 percent equity interest. If a sale of Able seems imminent, valuation discounts associated with Doe's 10 percent equity interest would be modest. The controlling shareholder, Smith, would maximize the sales proceeds to himself and any other shareholder(s). Hence, the lack of control associated with a small minority equity interest would not be a factor.[45] The pending transaction being driven by the controlling shareholder reduces the adverse impact of the limited marketability of an interest in a private company.

Solution to 2: If a sale is viewed as highly likely, the $96,000,000 equity value would be appropriate. This equity value uses normalized earnings and a discount rate based on an optimal capital structure in the calculation of the capitalization rate applied to earnings.

Able Manufacturing, Inc.
Valuation of Doe's 10 Percent Equity Interest
Sale of Company Viewed as Highly Likely

Indicated value of equity in operations	$96,000,000
Interest appraised	10%
Pro rata value of 10 percent equity interest	9,600,000
Less: Lack of control discount of 0 percent	0
Value assuming ready marketability	9,600,000
Less: Lack of marketability discount of 5 percent	480,000
Indicated value of Doe's 10 percent equity interest	$ 9,120,000

Solution to 3: If Smith has no intent to sell the company; the above-market expenses may continue. With the above-market expenses, the reported earnings would be lower than the normalized earnings. Use of reported earnings rather than normalized earnings is one possible means of capturing the adverse impact associated with the lack of control of a small minority equity interest.

Given the absence of any potential liquidity event and the above-market expenses, little market for the stock exists. A higher lack of marketability discount would be appropriate for the interest in this situation.

Solution to 4: If continuing as a private company is viewed as highly likely, the $80,000,000 equity value would be appropriate. This equity value uses reported earnings and a discount rate based on the actual capital structure (not optimal) in the calculation of the capitalization rate applied to earnings.

---

[45] When the controlling stockholder sells, he is not always obligated to offer the minority shareholders the same price. The analyst should investigate this fact. Factors to consider include 1) intent of the controlling stockholder, 2) articles of incorporation, and 3) legal statutes on corporate governance and shareholder rights.

> **Able Manufacturing, Inc.**
> **Valuation of Doe's 10 Percent Equity Interest**
> **Continued Operation as a Private Company Likely**
>
> | | |
> |---|---:|
> | Indicated value of equity in operations | $80,000,000 |
> | Interest appraised | 10% |
> | Pro rata value of 10% equity interest | 8,000,000 |
> | Less: Lack of control discount[46] | 0 |
> | Value assuming ready marketability | 8,000,000 |
> | Less: Lack of marketability discount of 25% | 2,000,000 |
> | Indicated value of Doe's 10% equity interest | $ 6,000,000 |
>
> **Solution to 5:** The value of Doe's 10 percent minority equity interest differs markedly in the two scenarios. The imminent sale scenario results in a higher value indication for Doe's equity interest as a result of the higher value of the company and the lower valuation discounts. The value of the company would be higher because of the use of normalized earnings rather than reported earnings. A lower pricing multiple might also be warranted. The discount rate might be lower in the event an optimal capital structure is used rather than the existing structure. The lack of control is less important in the event of an imminent liquidity event such as a sale. The lack of marketability of a small equity interest is also less important in this instance.

We have seen that in private company valuation, as in most types of valuation beyond the simplest, a range of approaches and estimates can be argued even apart from differences resulting from different forecasts or business assumptions. A perception also exists that there is excessive divergence in valuation practices and estimates of value and that valuation standards could benefit the consumers of valuations. The next section briefly surveys the state of standardization initiatives.

4.6 Business Valuation Standards and Practices

Prior to recent increases in the use of fair value estimates in financial reporting, many business appraisers focused primarily on tax, divorce, and commercial litigation related valuations. The impact on third parties was limited and concern regarding the quality of appraisals was modest. Appraisers were perceived by some as advocates for their clients. The U.S. savings and loan crisis of the late 1980s and early 1990s and the increasing role of fair value estimates in financial reporting under IFRS and U.S. GAAP demonstrate the potential effect of valua-

---

[46] As noted in the example, the impact on the value of the 10 percent equity interest was assumed to be captured in the use of reported rather than normalized earnings. The actual capital structure was also used rather than the optimal capital structure. A wide range of practice exists in the treatment of the lack of control for a minority equity interest in a private firm.

tion estimates on third parties. Increased third party reliance is contributing to a greater focus by a variety of parties on valuation estimates, practices, and standards.

The intent of valuation standards is to protect users of valuations and the community at large. Standards typically cover the development and reporting of the valuation. The Uniform Standards of Professional Appraisal Practice (USPAP) was instituted as a result of the failures of many savings and loan institutions in the United States (with a significant third party impact). Real estate appraisals that overvalued properties were perceived to have contributed to significant mortgage defaults that impaired the capital reserves and operating ability of many financial institutions.

USPAP was created by the Appraisal Foundation, a U.S. quasi-governmental entity. The Appraisal Foundation is the congressionally authorized source of appraisal standards and appraiser qualifications. USPAP includes standards pertaining to fixed asset, real estate, and business valuations.[47]

Although USPAP includes business valuation related standards, business appraisers are typically not required by law to adhere to these standards.[48] Although many appraisals used in connection with mortgage lending require a USPAP compliant appraisal, business valuations—including valuations used for financial reporting by public companies—do not involve mandatory compliance with USPAP or other professional standards.

The 8th edition of International Valuation Standards (IVS) issued by the International Valuation Standards Committee (IVSC) became effective on 31 July 2007. As of late 2008, these standards have been adopted by 53 countries and 59 valuation societies/institutes. Although the focus on business valuation has increased in recent years, these standards and the IVSC had previously primarily focused on real estate and tangible asset related issues.

The American Institute of Certified Public Accountants (AICPA) Consulting Services Executive Committee issued its Statement of Standards on Valuation Services (SSVS) that became effective on 1 January 2008. The AICPA requires that AICPA members and member companies comply with the SSVS. Nonmember appraisers, however, do not need to adhere to SVSS.

Other groups have also released valuation guidance. In October 2006, The International Private Equity and Venture Capital Valuation Board (IPEV Board) issued the International Private Equity and Venture Capital Valuation Guidelines. Members of the IPEV Board include French, British, and other European private equity and venture capital associations. The Private Equity Industry Guidelines Group (PEIGG) is a volunteer group of industry-wide representatives formed to debate and establish a set of reporting guidelines on valuations. In March 2007, the PEIGG released an update on U.S. private equity valuation guidelines.

Because buyers and users of valuations are often not aware of these standards, compliance is practically at the option of the individual appraiser. Certain appraisal organizations require their members to adhere to a particular set of standards. For example, in the United States, the American Society of Appraisers (ASA) requires member compliance with USPAP. The AICPA requires its members to comply with its standards. In addition, some states require all CPAs to

---

[47] USPAP standards 9 and 10 pertain to the valuation of interests in business enterprises or intangible assets. Standard 9 covers the development of a valuation estimate. Standard 10 covers the reporting of the results of an appraisal analysis.

[48] Compliance with USPAP is required in the United States for "federally related transactions." Federally related transactions include loans made by a financial institution that include involvement of a federal financial regulatory agency.

comply with the AICPA's standards. Given the confidentiality of valuation reports, it is not possible for these organizations to ensure that compliance requirements are being met.

For financial reporting, ensuring reasonable fair value estimates involves a number of parties. Independent valuation specialists are the first element of insuring accurate fair value estimates. As a part of the audit process, fair value estimates prepared by a third party or management are reviewed by auditors and/or their valuation specialist. This third party review plays a critical role in assessing the accuracy of fair value estimates that are included in audited financial statements. For companies registered with the U.S. SEC, fair value estimates may also be subject to comment by the staff of the SEC. In the United States, the quality of audits is assessed through the actions of the Public Company Accounting Oversight Board (PCAOB), peer review of accounting companies, and other actions.[49]

Valuation standards provide limited technical guidance as a result of the diverse and dynamic nature of valuations. Technical guidance has been released periodically, primarily for certain valuations used in a financial reporting context. In the late 1990s, the valuation of technology acquired in business combinations in the United States led to restatements of asset values in financial statements. Subsequently, the AICPA released the IPRD Practice Aid providing guidance on the valuation of technology assets. The Stock Practice Aid was released to provide technical guidance for the valuation of stock in the context of stock option grants and other share-based payments. The Appraisal Foundation is also involved in efforts to provide technical guidance to appraisers. A working group recently released a draft of a "best practices" document providing guidance in the area of intangible asset valuation. Other technical guidance documents are being prepared as well. The IVSC has also issued a discussion draft on the valuation of intangible assets.

Future developments regarding valuation standards are uncertain. Users of valuation services are becoming increasingly aware of the importance of obtaining competent valuation services. Accounting and regulatory bodies and educators recognize the importance of fair value estimates and are increasing efforts in this area.

Valuators of private companies and related assets take considerable care to understand the definition(s) of value that are appropriate in a particular assignment. The IPRD Practice Aid and SFAS No. 157 address the differences between investment value and fair value. The differing valuation assumptions depending on the definition of value can result in materially different conclusions of value. The use of investment value rather than fair value based assumptions led to the accounting restatements of certain overstatements of the value of acquired in-process technology. Concerns regarding appropriate assumptions to use in purchase price allocations are an area of current concern in which the definition of value is an important consideration. In some cases, accounting standards, regulations, or legal considerations may direct valuators to approach a valuation executed for a particular purpose using a specific definition of value. In other cases a valuator may estimate and report on value from multiple possible perspectives to show the range of value estimates that could be argued.

---

[49] The PCAOB is a private sector, not-for-profit corporation created by the Sarbanes–Oxley Act of 2002 to oversee the auditors of public companies. The PCAOB inspects the audit operations of accounting firms with SEC registered clients. Inspection reports from these examinations are posted on the PCAOB website at PCAOB.org. The inspection reports include comments on audit areas (including fair value estimates) where the need for additional audit procedures is noted.

SUMMARY

This reading provides an overview of key elements of private company valuation and contrasts public and private company valuations.

▶ Company- and stock-specific factors may influence the selection of appropriate valuation methods and assumptions for private company valuations. Stock-specific factors may result in a lower value for an equity interest in a private company relative to a public company.

▶ Company-specific factors in which private companies differ from public companies include:

- ▶ stage in lifecycle;
- ▶ size;
- ▶ overlap of shareholders and management;
- ▶ quality/depth of management;
- ▶ quality of financial and other information;
- ▶ pressure from short-term investors;
- ▶ tax concerns.

▶ Stock-specific factors that frequently affect the value of private companies include:

- ▶ liquidity of equity interests in business;
- ▶ concentration of control;
- ▶ potential agreements restricting liquidity.

▶ Private company valuations are typically performed for three different reasons: transactions, compliance (financial or tax reporting), or litigation. Acquisition related valuation issues and financial reporting valuation issues are of greatest importance in assessing public companies.

▶ Different definitions (standards) of value exist. The use of a valuation and key elements pertaining to the appraised company will help determine the appropriate definition. Key definitions of value include:

- ▶ fair market value;
- ▶ market value;
- ▶ fair value for financial reporting;
- ▶ fair value in a litigation context;
- ▶ investment value;
- ▶ intrinsic value.

▶ Private company valuations may require adjustments to the income statements to develop estimates of the normalized earnings of the company. Adjustments may be required for nonrecurring, non-economic, or other unusual items to eliminate anomalies and/or facilitate comparisons.

▶ Within the income approach, the free cash flow method is frequently used to value larger, mature private companies. For smaller companies or in special situations, the capitalized cash flow method and residual income method may also be used.

▶ Within the market approach, three methods are regularly used: the guideline public company method, guideline transactions method, and prior transactions method.

► An asset-based approach is infrequently used in the valuation of private companies. This approach may be appropriate for companies that are worth more in liquidation than as a going concern. This approach is also applied for asset holding companies, very small companies, or companies that were recently formed and have limited operating histories.

► Control and marketability issues are important and challenging elements in the valuation of private companies and equity interests therein.

► If publicly traded companies are used as the basis for pricing multiple(s), control premiums may be appropriate in measuring the value of the total equity of a private company. Control premiums have also been used to estimate lack of control discounts.

► Discounts for lack of control are used to convert a controlling interest value into a noncontrolling equity interest value. Evidence of the adverse impact of the lack of control is an important consideration in assessing this discount.

► Discounts for lack of marketability are often used in the valuation of noncontrolling equity interests in private companies. A DLOM may not be appropriate if there is a high likelihood of a liquidity event in the immediate future.

► Quantification of DLOM can be challenging because of limited data, differences in the interpretation of available data, and different interpretations of the impact of the lack of marketability on a private company.

► DLOM can be estimated based on 1) private sales of restricted stock in public companies relative to their freely traded share price, 2) private sales of stock in companies prior to a subsequent IPO, and 3) the pricing of put options.

► The intent of valuation standards is to protect users of valuations and the community at large. Standards typically cover the development and reporting of a valuation.

► A number of organizations have released valuation standards. No single set of valuation standards covers the valuation of private companies.

PRACTICE PROBLEMS FOR READING 43

1. Two companies are considering the acquisition of Target Company. Buyer A is a strategic buyer and Buyer B is a financial buyer. The following information pertains to Target Company:

> Sales = £28,000,000
> Reported EBITDA = £4,500,000
> Reported executive compensation = £1,000,000
> Normalized executive compensation = £500,000
> Reduced SG&A from eliminating duplicate general and administrative functions = £600,000

Calculate the pro forma EBITDA estimates that the strategic and financial buyers would each develop in an acquisitions analysis of Target Company.

2. Using the build-up method and assuming that no adjustment for industry risk is required, calculate an equity discount rate for a small company, given the following information:

> Equity risk premium = 5.0 percent
> Mid-cap equity risk premium = 3.5 percent
> Small stock risk premium = 4.2 percent
> Income return on long-term bonds = 5.1 percent
> Total return on intermediate-term bonds = 5.3 percent
> Company-specific risk premium = 3.0 percent
> 20-year Treasury bond yield as of the valuation date = 4.5 percent

3. Using the capitalized cash flow method (CCM), calculate the fair market value of 100 percent of the equity of a hypothetical company, given the following information:

> Current year's reported free cash flow to equity = $1,400,000
> Current year's normalized free cash flow to equity = $1,800,000
> Long-term interest bearing debt = $2,000,000
> Weighted average cost of capital = 15 percent
> Equity discount rate = 18 percent
> Long-term growth rate of FCFE = 5.5 percent

4. You have been asked to value Pacific Corporation, Inc., using an excess earnings method, given the following information:

> Working capital balance = $2,000,000
> Fair value of fixed assets = $5,500,000
> Book value of fixed assets = $4,000,000
> Normalized earnings of firm = $1,000,000
> Required return on working capital = 5.0 percent
> Required return on fixed assets = 8.0 percent
> Required return on intangible assets = 15.0 percent
> Weighted average cost of capital = 10.0 percent
> Long-term growth rate of residual income = 5.0 percent

Based on this information:

A. What is the value of Pacific's intangible assets?

B. What is the market value of invested capital?

5. An appraiser has been asked to determine the combined level of valuation discounts for a small equity interest in a private company. The appraiser concluded that an appropriate control premium is 15 percent. A discount for lack of marketability was estimated at 25 percent. Given these factors, what is the combined discount?

The following information relates to Questions 6–11

Alan Chin, the chief executive officer of Thunder Corporation, has asked his chief financial officer, Constance Ebinosa, to prepare a valuation of Thunder for the purpose of selling the company to a private investment partnership. Thunder is a profitable $200 million annual sales U.S. domiciled manufacturer of generic household products. Customers consist of several grocery store chains in the United States. Competitors include large companies such as Procter & Gamble, Clorox, and Unilever. Thunder has been in business for 15 years and is privately owned by the original shareholders, none of whom are employed by the company. The company's senior management has been in charge of the company's operations for most of the past 15 years and expects to remain in that capacity after any sale.

The partnership has expectations about Thunder similar to the current shareholders and management of Thunder. These investors expect to hold Thunder for an intermediate period of time and then bring the company public when market conditions are more favorable than currently.

Chin is concerned about what definition of value should be used when analyzing Thunder. He notes that the stock market has been very volatile recently. He also wonders whether fair market value can be realistically estimated when the most similar recent private market transactions may not have been at arm's length.

Chin asks Ebinosa whether there will be differences in the process of valuing a private company like Thunder compared with a public company. Ebinosa replies that differences do exist and mentions several factors an analyst must consider.

Ebinosa also explains that several approaches are available for valuing private companies. She mentions that one possibility is to use an asset-based approach because Thunder has a relatively large and efficient factory and warehouse for its products. A real estate appraiser can readily determine the value of these facilities. A second method would be the market approach and using an average of the price-to-earnings multiples for Procter & Gamble and Clorox. A third possibility is a discounted free cash flow approach. The latter would focus on a continuation of Thunder's trend of slow profitable growth during the past ten years.

The private investment partnership has mentioned that they are likely to use an income approach as one of their methods. Ebinosa decides to validate the estimates they make. She assumes for the next 12 months that Thunder's revenues increase by the long-term annual growth rate of 3 percent. She also makes the following assumptions to calculate the free cash flow to the firm for the next 12 months:

▶ Gross profit margin is 45 percent.

▶ Depreciation is 2 percent of revenues.

▶ Selling, general, and administrative expenses are 24 percent of revenues.

▶ Capital expenditures equal 125 percent of depreciation to support the current level of revenues.

▶ Additional capital expenditures of 15 percent of incremental revenues are needed to fund future growth.

▶ Working capital investment equals 8 percent of incremental revenues.

▶ Marginal tax rate on EBIT is 35 percent.

Chin knows that if an income approach is used then the choice of discount rate may have a large influence on the estimated value. He makes two statements regarding discount rate estimates:

1. If the CAPM method is used to estimate the discount rate with a beta estimate based on public companies with operations and revenues similar to Thunder, then a small stock premium should be added to the estimate.

2. The weighted average cost of capital of the private investment partnership should be used to value Thunder.

Ebinosa decides to calculate a value of Thunder's equity using the capitalized cash flow method (CCM) and decides to use the build-up method to estimate Thunder's required return on equity. She makes the following assumptions:

▶ Growth of FCFE is at a constant annual rate of 3 percent.

▶ Free cash flow to equity for the year ahead is $2.5 million.

▶ Risk free rate is 4.5 percent.

▶ Equity risk premium is 5.0 percent.

▶ Size premium is 2.0 percent.

6. Given Chin's concerns, the *most appropriate* definition of value for Thunder is:

   A. intrinsic value.

   B. investment value.

   C. fair market value.

7. The *least likely* factor that would be a source of differences in valuing Thunder compared with valuing a publicly traded company is:

   A. access to public debt markets.

   B. agency problems.

   C. the size of the company.

8. Ebinosa can *best* value Thunder using the:

   A. excess earnings approach.

   B. asset-based approach.

   C. discounted free cash flow approach.

9. The free cash flow to the firm is *closest* to:

   A. $23,031,000.

   B. $25,441,000.

   C. $36,091,000.

10. Regarding the two statements about discount rate estimates, Chin is:

   A. correct with respect to adding the small stock premium and correct with respect to the weighted average cost of capital.

   B. correct with respect to adding the small stock premium and incorrect with respect to the weighted average cost of capital.

   C. incorrect with respect to adding the small stock premium and incorrect with respect to the weighted average cost of capital.

11. The indicated value of Thunder's equity using the build-up method and the capitalized cash flow method (CCM) based on free cash flow to equity is *closest* to:

   A. $29.41 million.

   B. $38.46 million.

   C. $125.00 million.

The following information relates to Questions 12–17[1]

The Senior Vice President of Acquisitions for Northland Industries, Angela Lanton, and her head analyst, Michael Powell, are evaluating several potential investments. Northland is a diversified holding company for numerous businesses. One of Northland's divisions is a manufacturer of fine papers and that division has alerted Lanton about Oakstar Timber, a supplier that may be available for purchase. Oakstar's sole owner, Felix Tanteromo, has expressed interest in exchanging his ownership of Oakstar for a combination of cash and Northland Industries securities.

Oakstar's main asset is 10,000 hectares of timberland in the western part of Canada. The land is a combination of new and old growth Douglas fir trees. The value of this timberland has been steadily increasing since Oakstar acquired it. Oakstar manages the land on a sustained yield basis (i.e., so it continues to produce timber indefinitely) and contracts with outside forestry companies to evaluate, harvest, and sell the timber. Oakstar's income is in the form of royalties (fees paid to Oakstar based on the number of cubic meters harvested). Oakstar's balance sheet as of 31 December 2008 is as follows.

Oakstar Timber Balance Sheet
Year Ended 31 December 2008

Assets	
Cash	$ 500,000
Inventory	25,000
Accounts receivable	50,000
Plant and equipment (cost less depreciation)	750,000
Land	10,000,000
Total assets	$11,325,000

Liabilities and Equity	
Accounts payables	$ 75,000
Long-term bank loan	1,500,000
Common stock	9,750,000
Total liabilities and equity	$11,325,000

In addition to the balance sheet, Powell is gathering other data to assist in valuing Oakstar and has found information on recent sales of timberland in the western part of Canada. Douglas fir properties have averaged $6,178 per hectare for tracts that are not contiguous and do not have a developed road

---

[1]Currency in Canadian dollars.

system for harvesting the timber. For tracts with these features, as possessed by Oakstar, the average price is $8,750 per hectare. Properties near urban areas and having potential for residential and recreational second home development command up to $20,000 per hectare. Oakstar's land lacks this potential. Lanton believes these values would form the basis of an asset-based valuation for Oakstar, with the additional assumption that other assets and liabilities on the balance sheet are assumed to be worth their stated values.

The second company under evaluation, FAMCO, Inc., is a family-owned electronic manufacturing company with annual sales of $120 million. The family wants to monetize the value of their ownership in FAMCO with a view to later investing part of the proceeds in a diversified stock portfolio. Lanton has asked Powell to obtain data for both an income-based and market-based valuation. Powell has obtained the recent annual income statement and additional data needed to calculate normalized earnings as follows.

FAMCO, Inc.
Income Statement
Year Ending 31 December 2008

Revenues		$120,000,000
Gross profit		85,000,000
Selling, general, and administrative expenses		23,000,000
Pro forma EBITDA		$ 62,000,000
Depreciation and amortization		3,500,000
Pro forma earnings before interest and taxes		$ 58,500,000
Less: Interest		1,000,000
Earnings before taxes (EBT)		$ 57,500,000
Pro forma taxes on EBT	40%	23,000,000
Operating income after tax		$ 34,500,000

Additional data for FAMCO is provided in the following table. Included are estimates by Powell of the compensation paid to family members and the smaller amount of salary expense for replacement employees if Northland acquires the company (reflecting perceived above-market compensation of the family group executives). He believes the current debt of FAMCO can be replaced with a more optimal level of debt at a lower interest rate. These will be reflected in a normalized income statement.

FAMCO, Inc.

Current debt level	$10,000,000
Current interest rate	10%
Salaries of employed family members	$ 7,000,000
Salaries of replacement employees	$ 5,400,000
New debt level	$25,000,000
New interest rate	8%

Powell also recognizes that a value needs to be assigned to FAMCO's intangibles consisting of patents and other intangible assets. Powell prepares an additional estimate of excess earnings and intangibles value using the capitalized cash flow method. He projects the following data for 2009:

FAMCO, Inc—Intangibles Valuation Data

Working capital balance	$10,000,000
Fair value of fixed assets	$45,000,000
Normalized income to the company	$35,000,000
Required return on working capital	8%
Required return on fixed assets	12%
Required return on intangible assets	20%
Weighted average cost of capital	14.5%
Future growth rate	6%

Lanton asks Powell to also use the market approach to valuation with a focus on the guideline transactions method. Powell prepares a table showing relevant information regarding three recent guideline transactions and market conditions at the time of the transactions. Powell's assumptions about FAMCO include its expected fast growth and moderate level of risk.

Target Firm	Target's Risk	Target's Growth	Consideration	Market Conditions
Firm 1	High	Slow	Cash	Normal, rising trend
Firm 2	Moderate	Fast	Stock	Prices near peak
Firm 3	Moderate	Fast	Cash	Normal, rising trend

Although Northland is interested in acquiring all of the stock of FAMCO, the acquisition of a 15 percent equity interest in FAMCO is also an option. Lanton asks Powell about the valuation of small equity interests in private entities and notes that control and marketability are important factors that lead to adjustments in value estimates for small equity interests. Powell mentions that the control premium paid for the most similar guideline firm used in the analysis suggests a discount for lack of control of 20 percent. The discount for lack of marketability was estimated at 15 percent.

12. Which of the following statements concerning asset-based valuation as applied to Oakstar is *most* accurate? The approach is applicable:

   A. only when a guideline public company for the valuation is not available.

   B. because natural resources with determinable market values constitute the majority of Oakstar's total value.

   C. because as a passive collector of royalties, Oakstar has no meaningful capital expenditures and free cash flow is irrelevant.

13. Using an asset-based approach, the value (net of debt) of Oakstar is *closest* to:

   A. $62,250,000.

   B. $87,250,000.

   C. $199,750,000.

14. The normalized earnings after tax for FAMCO is *closest* to:

   A. $32,940,000.

   B. $34,260,000.

   C. $34,860,000.

15. Using the excess earnings method, the value of the intangibles is *closest* to:

   A. $144.0 million.

   B. $205.7 million.

   C. $338.8 million.

16. The guideline transaction that is *most likely* applicable to FAMCO is:

   A. Firm 1.

   B. Firm 2.

   C. Firm 3.

17. The total discount for both control and marketability is *closest* to:

   A. 15 percent.

   B. 32 percent.

   C. 35 percent.

SOLUTIONS FOR READING 43

1. A strategic buyer seeks to eliminate unnecessary expenses. The strategic buyer would adjust the reported EBITDA by the amount of the officers' excess compensation. A strategic buyer could also eliminate redundant manufacturing costs estimated at £600,000. The pro forma EBITDA a strategic buyer might use in its acquisition analysis is the reported EBITDA of £4,500,000 plus the nonmarket compensation expense of £500,000 plus the operating synergies (cost savings) of £600,000. The adjusted EBITDA for the strategic buyer is £4,500,000 + £500,000 + £600,000 = £5,600,000. The financial buyer would also make the adjustment to normalize officers' compensation but would not be able to eliminate redundant manufacturing expenses. Thus, adjusted EBITDA for the financial buyer would be £4,500,000 + £500,000 = £5,000,000.

2. The build-up method is substantially similar to the extended CAPM except that beta is excluded from the calculation. The equity return requirement is calculated as risk-free rate plus equity risk premium for large capitalization stocks plus small stock risk premium plus company-specific risk premium: 4.5 + 5.0 + 4.2 + 3.0 = 16.7 percent. Although practice may vary, in this case, there was no adjustment for industry risk.

3. There are FCFF and FCFE variations of the CCM. In this problem, the data permit the application of just the FCFE variation. According to that variation, the estimated value of equity equals the normalized free cash flow to equity estimate for next period divided by the capitalization rate for equity. The capitalization rate is the required rate of return for equity less the long-term growth rate in free cash flow to equity. Using the current $1.8 million of free cash flow to equity, the 18 percent equity discount rate, and the long-term growth rate of 5.5 percent yields a value indication of [($1.8 million)(1.055)]/(0.18 − 0.055) = $1.899 million/0.125 = $15.19 million.

4. The excess earnings consist of any remaining income after returns to working capital and fixed assets are considered. Fair value estimates and rate of return requirements for working capital and fixed assets are provided. The return required for working capital is $2,000,000 × 5.0 percent = $100,000 and the return required for fixed assets is $5,500,000 × 8.0 percent = $440,000, or $540,000 in total.

    A. The residual income for intangible assets is $460,000 (the normalized earnings of $1,000,000 less the $540,000 required return for working capital and intangible assets). The value of intangible assets can then be calculated using the capitalized cash flow method. The intangibles value is $4,830,000 based on $483,000 of year-ahead residual income available to the intangibles capitalized at 10.0 percent (15.0 percent discount rate for intangibles less 5.0 percent long-term growth rate of residual income).

    B. The market value of invested capital is the total of the values of working capital, fixed assets, and intangible assets. This value is $2,000,000 + $5,500,000 + $4,830,000 = $12,330,000.

5. The valuation of a small equity interest in a private company would typically be calculated on a basis that reflects the lack of control and lack of marketability of the interest. The control premium of 15 percent must first

be used to provide an indication of a discount for lack of control (DLOC). A lack of control discount can be calculated using the formula Lack of control discount = 1 − [1/ (1 + Control premium)]. In this case, a lack of control discount of approximately 13 percent is calculated as 1 − [1/(1 + 15%)]. The discount for lack of marketability (DLOM) was specified. Valuation discounts are applied sequentially and are not added. The formula is (Pro rata control value) × (1 − DLOC) × (1 − DLOM). A combined discount of approximately 35 percent is calculated as 1 − (1 − 13%) × (1 − 25%) = 0.348 or 34.8 percent.

6. A is correct. Both the current shareholders and the future shareholders (the private investment group) share the same expectations. It is most reasonable to assume that both are concerned with Thunder's intrinsic value, which market prices should reflect when the company is brought public under less volatile market conditions.

7. B is correct. The size of Thunder and its probable lack of access to public debt markets are potential factors affecting the valuation of Thunder compared with a public company. Given that the separation of ownership and control at Thunder is similar to that at public companies, however, agency problems are not a distinguishing factor in its valuation.

8. C is correct. The excess earnings method would rarely be applied to value the equity of a company particularly when it is not needed to value intangibles. The asset-based approach is less appropriate because it is infrequently used to estimate the business enterprise value of operating companies. By contrast, the free cash flow method is broadly applicable and readily applied in this case.

9. A is correct. Using Ebinosa's assumptions:

Revenues ($200,000,000 × 1.03 =)		$206,000,000
Gross profit	45%[a]	92,700,000
Selling, general, and administrative expenses	24%[a]	49,440,000
Pro forma EBITDA		43,260,000
Depreciation	2%[a]	4,120,000
Pro forma EBIT		39,140,000
Pro forma taxes on EBIT	35%[b]	13,699,000
Operating income after tax		$ 25,441,000
Plus: Depreciation		4,120,000
Less: Capital expenditures on current sales	125%[c]	5,150,000
Less: Capital expenditures to support future sales	15%[d]	900,000
Less: Working capital requirement	8%[d]	480,000
Free cash flow to the firm		$ 23,031,000

[a] Percent of revenues
[b] Percent of EBIT
[c] Percent of depreciation
[d] Percent of incremental revenues

10. C is correct. Both statements by Chin are incorrect. If the CAPM is used with public companies with similar operations and similar revenue size, as stated, then the calculation likely captures the small stock premium and should not be added to the estimate. Small stock premiums are associated with build-up models and the expanded CAPM, rather than the CAPM *per se*. The correct weighted average cost of capital should reflect the risk of Thunder's cash flows not the risk of the acquirer's cash flows.

11. A is correct. The return on equity is the sum of the risk free rate, equity risk premium, and the size premium for a total of $4.5 + 5.0 + 2.0 = 11.5$ percent. The value of the firm using the CCM is $V = FCFE_1/(r - g) = 2.5/(0.115 - 0.03) = \$29.41$ million.

12. B is correct. Oakstar's primary asset is timberland whose market value can be determined from comparable land sales.

13. B is correct. In the absence of market value data for assets and liabilities, the analyst usually must use book value data (the reading explicitly makes the assumption that book values accurately reflect market values as well). Except for timberland, market values for assets are not available. Thus, all other assets are assumed to be valued by their book values, which sum to $\$500,000 + \$25,000 + \$50,000 + \$750,000 = \$1,325,000$. The value of the land is determined by the value of $8,750 per hectare for properties comparable to Oakstar's. Thus, the value of Oakstar's land is $\$8,750 \times 10,000 = \$87,500,000$. Liabilities are assumed to be worth the sum of their book value or $1,575,000. Thus, Estimated value = Total assets − Liabilities = $\$1,325,000 + \$87,500,000 - \$1,575,000 = \$87,250,000$.

14. C is correct. The new interest level is $2,000,000 instead of $1,000,000. SG&A expenses are reduced by $1,600,000 (= \$5,400,000 - \$7,000,000$) to $21,400,000 by salary expense savings. Other than a calculation of a revised provision for taxes, no other changes to the income statement results in normalized earnings before tax of $58,100,000 and normalized earnings after tax of $34,860,000.

15. B is correct:

> Return on working capital = $0.08 \times \$10,000,000 = \$800,000$
> Return on fixed assets = $0.12 \times \$45,000,000 = \$5,400,000$
> Return on intangibles = $\$35,000,000 - \$800,000 - \$5,400,000 = \$28,800,000$

Value of intangibles using CCM = $\$28,800,000/(0.20 - 0.06) = \$205.71$ million.

16. C is correct. Firm 3 matches FAMCO in both risk and growth. Firm 1 fails on these factors. In addition, Firm 3 is a better match to FAMCO than Firm 2 because the offer for Firm 3 was a cash offer in normal market conditions whereas Firm 2 was a stock offer in a boom market and the value does not reflect risk and growth in the immediate future.

17. B is correct. Both discounts apply and they are multiplicative rather than additive:

> $1 - (1 - 0.20)(1 - 0.15) = 1 - 0.68 = 32$ percent.

A priori probability A probability based on logical analysis rather than on observation or personal judgment.

Abandonment option The ability to terminate a project at some future time if the financial results are disappointing.

Abnormal earnings See *Residual income*.

Absolute dispersion The amount of variability present without comparison to any reference point or benchmark.

Absolute frequency The number of observations in a given interval (for grouped data).

Absolute valuation model A model that specifies an asset's intrinsic value.

Accelerated methods of depreciation Depreciation methods that allocate a relatively large proportion of the cost of an asset to the early years of the asset's useful life.

Account With the accounting systems, a formal record of increases and decreases in a specific asset, liability, component of owners' equity, revenue, or expense.

Account format A method of presentation of accounting transactions in which effects on assets appear at the left and effects on liabilities and equity appear at the right of a central dividing line; also known as T-account format.

Accounting estimates Estimates of items such as the useful lives of assets, warranty costs, and the amount of uncollectible receivables.

Accounting profit (income before taxes or pretax income) Income as reported on the income statement, in accordance with prevailing accounting standards, before the provisions for income tax expense.

Accounting risk The risk associated with accounting standards that vary from country to country or with any uncertainty about how certain transactions should be recorded.

Accounts payable Amounts that a business owes to its vendors for goods and services that were purchased from them but which have not yet been paid.

Accounts receivable turnover Ratio of sales on credit to the average balance in accounts receivable.

Accrual basis Method of accounting in which the effect of transactions on financial condition and income are recorded when they occur, not when they are settled in cash.

Accrued expenses (accrued liabilities) Liabilities related to expenses that have been incurred but not yet paid as of the end of an accounting period—an example of an accrued expense is rent that has been incurred but not yet paid, resulting in a liability "rent payable."

Accrued interest Interest earned but not yet paid.

Accumulated benefit obligation Under U.S. GAAP, a measure used in estimating a defined-benefit pension plan's liabilities, defined as "the actuarial present value of benefits (whether vested or non-vested) attributed by the pension benefit formula to employee service rendered before a specified date and based on employee service and compensation (if applicable) prior to that date."

Accumulated depreciation An offset to property, plant, and equipment (PPE) reflecting the amount of the cost of PPE that has been allocated to current and previous accounting periods.

Acquiring company, or acquirer The company in a merger or acquisition that is acquiring the target.

Acquisition The purchase of some portion of one company by another; the purchase may be for assets, a definable segment of another entity, or the purchase of an entire company.

Acquisition method A method of accounting for a business combination where the acquirer is required to measure each identifiable asset and liability at fair value. This method was the result of a joint project of the IASB and FASB aiming at convergence in standards for the accounting of business combinations.

Active factor risk The contribution to active risk squared resulting from the portfolio's different-than-benchmark exposures relative to factors specified in the risk model.

Active investment managers Managers who hold portfolios that differ from their benchmark portfolio in an attempt to produce positive risk-adjusted returns.

Active portfolio In the context of the Treynor-Black model, the portfolio formed by mixing analyzed stocks of perceived nonzero alpha values. This portfolio is ultimately mixed with the passive market index portfolio.

Active return The return on a portfolio minus the return on the portfolio's benchmark.

Active risk The standard deviation of active returns.

Active risk squared The variance of active returns; active risk raised to the second power.

Active specific risk or **asset selection risk** The contribution to active risk squared resulting from the portfolio's active weights on individual assets as those weights interact with assets' residual risk.

Active strategy In reference to short-term cash management, an investment strategy characterized by monitoring and attempting to capitalize on market conditions to optimize the risk and return relationship of short-term investments.

Activity ratios (asset utilization or operating efficiency ratios) Ratios that measure how efficiently a company performs day-to-day tasks, such as the collection of receivables and management of inventory.

Addition rule for probabilities A principle stating that the probability that A or B occurs (both occur) equals the probability that A occurs, plus the probability that B occurs, minus the probability that both A and B occur.

Add-on interest A procedure for determining the interest on a bond or loan in which the interest is added onto the face value of a contract.

Adjusted beta Historical beta adjusted to reflect the tendency of beta to be mean reverting.

Adjusted present value (APV) As an approach to valuing a company, the sum of the value of the company, assuming no use of debt, and the net present value of any effects of debt on company value.

Adjusted R^2 A measure of goodness-of-fit of a regression that is adjusted for degrees of freedom and hence does not automatically increase when another independent variable is added to a regression.

After-tax cash flow (ATCF) Net operating income less debt service and less taxes payable on income from operations.

After-tax equity reversion (ATER) Sales price less disposition costs, amortized mortgage loan balance, and capital gains taxes.

Agency costs Costs associated with the conflict of interest present when a company is managed by non-owners. Agency costs result from the inherent conflicts of interest between managers and equity owners.

Agency costs of equity The smaller the stake that managers have in the company, the less is their share in bearing the cost of excessive perquisite consumption or not giving their best efforts in running the company.

Agency problem, or **principal-agent problem** A conflict of interest that arises when the agent in an agency relationship has goals and incentives that differ from the principal to whom the agent owes a fiduciary duty.

Agency relationships An arrangement whereby someone, an agent, acts on behalf of another person, the principal.

Aging schedule A breakdown of accounts into categories of days outstanding.

Allowance for bad debts An offset to accounts receivable for the amount of accounts receivable that are estimated to be uncollectible.

Alpha (or **abnormal return**) The return on an asset in excess of the asset's required rate of return; the risk-adjusted return.

Alternative hypothesis The hypothesis accepted when the null hypothesis is rejected.

American Depositary Receipt A negotiable certificate issued by a depositary bank that represents ownership in a non-U.S. company's deposited equity (i.e., equity held in custody by the depositary bank in the company's home market).

American option An option that can be exercised at any time until its expiration date.

Amortization The process of allocating the cost of intangible long-term assets having a finite useful life to accounting periods; the allocation of the amount of a bond premium or discount to the periods remaining until bond maturity.

Amortizing and accreting swaps A swap in which the notional principal changes according to a formula related to changes in the underlying.

Analysis of variance (ANOVA) The analysis of the total variability of a dataset (such as observations on the dependent variable in a regression) into components representing different sources of variation; with reference to regression, ANOVA provides the inputs for an *F*-test of the significance of the regression as a whole.

Annual percentage rate The cost of borrowing expressed as a yearly rate.

Annuity A finite set of level sequential cash flows.

Annuity due An annuity having a first cash flow that is paid immediately.

Anticipation stock Excess inventory that is held in anticipation of increased demand, often because of seasonal patterns of demand.

Antidilutive With reference to a transaction or a security, one that would increase earnings per share (EPS) or result in EPS higher than the company's basic EPS—antidilutive securities are not included in the calculation of diluted EPS.

Arbitrage 1) The simultaneous purchase of an undervalued asset or portfolio and sale of an overvalued but equivalent asset or portfolio, in order to obtain a riskless profit on the price differential. Taking advantage of a market inefficiency in a risk-free manner. 2) The condition in a financial market in which equivalent assets or combinations of assets sell for two different prices, creating an opportunity to profit at no risk with no commitment of money. In a well-functioning financial market, few arbitrage opportunities are possible. 3) A risk-free operation that earns an expected positive net profit but requires no net investment of money.

Arbitrage opportunity An opportunity to conduct an arbitrage; an opportunity to earn an expected positive net profit without risk and with no net investment of money.

Arbitrage portfolio The portfolio that exploits an arbitrage opportunity.

Arithmetic mean The sum of the observations divided by the number of observations.

Arrears swap A type of interest rate swap in which the floating payment is set at the end of the period and the interest is paid at that same time.

Asian call option A European-style option with a value at maturity equal to the difference between the stock price at maturity and the average stock price during the life of the option, or $0, whichever is greater.

Asset beta The unlevered beta; reflects the business risk of the assets; the asset's systematic risk.

Asset purchase An acquisition in which the acquirer purchases the target company's assets and payment is made directly to the target company.

Asset retirement obligations (AROs) The fair value of the estimated costs to be incurred at the end of a tangible asset's service life. The fair value of the liability is determined on the basis of discounted cash flows.

Assets Resources controlled by an enterprise as a result of past events and from which future economic benefits to the enterprise are expected to flow.

Asset-based approach Approach that values a private company based on the values of the underlying assets of the entity less the value of any related liabilities.

Asset-based loan A loan that is secured with company assets.

Asset-based valuation An approach to valuing natural resource companies that estimates company value on the basis of the market value of the natural resources the company controls.

Assignment of accounts receivable The use of accounts receivable as collateral for a loan.

Asymmetric information The differential of information between corporate insiders and outsiders regarding the company's performance and prospects. Managers typically have more information about the company's performance and prospects than owners and creditors.

At the money An option in which the underlying value equals the exercise price.

Autocorrelation The correlation of a time series with its own past values.

Automated Clearing House An electronic payment network available to businesses, individuals, and financial institutions in the United States, U.S. Territories, and Canada.

Autoregressive (AR) model A time series regressed on its own past values, in which the independent variable is a lagged value of the dependent variable.

Available-for-sale investments Debt and equity securities not classified as either held-to-maturity or held-for-trading securities. The investor is willing to sell but not actively planning to sell. In general, available-for-sale securities are reported at fair value on the balance sheet.

Backtesting With reference to portfolio strategies, the application of a strategy's portfolio selection rules to historical data to assess what would have been the strategy's historical performance.

Backward integration A merger involving the purchase of a target ahead of the acquirer in the value or production chain; for example, to acquire a supplier.

Backwardation A condition in the futures markets in which the benefits of holding an asset exceed the costs, leaving the futures price less than the spot price.

Balance of payments accounts A country's record of international trading, borrowing, and lending.

Balance sheet (statement of financial position or **statement of financial condition)** The financial statement that presents an entity's current financial position by disclosing resources the entity controls (its assets) and the claims on those resources (its liabilities and equity claims), as of a particular point in time (the date of the balance sheet).

Balance sheet ratios Financial ratios involving balance sheet items only.

Balance-sheet-based accruals ratio The difference between net operating assets at the end and the beginning of the period compared to the average net operating assets over the period.

Balance-sheet-based aggregate accruals The difference between net operating assets at the end and the beginning of the period.

Band-of-investment method A widely used approach to estimate an overall capitalization rate. It is based on the premise that debt and equity financing is typically involved in a real estate transaction.

Bank discount basis A quoting convention that annualizes, on a 360-day year, the discount as a percentage of face value.

Bargain purchase When a company is acquired and the purchase price is less than the fair value of the net assets. The current treatment of the excess of fair value over the purchase price is different under IFRS and U.S. GAAP. The excess is never accounted for as negative goodwill.

Basic earnings per share (EPS) Net earnings available to common shareholders (i.e., net income minus preferred dividends) divided by the weighted average number of common shares outstanding during the period.

Basis point value (BPV) Also called *present value of a basis point* or *price value of a basis point* (PVBP), the change in the bond price for a 1 basis point change in yield.

Basis swap 1) An interest rate swap involving two floating rates. 2) A swap in which both parties pay a floating rate.

Bayes' formula A method for updating probabilities based on new information.

Bear hug A tactic used by acquirers to circumvent target management's objections to a proposed merger by submitting the proposal directly to the target company's board of directors.

Bear spread An option strategy that involves selling a put with a lower exercise price and buying a put with a higher exercise price. It can also be executed with calls.

Before-tax cash flow A measure of the expected annual cash flow from the operation of a real estate investment after all expenses but before taxes.

Benchmark A comparison portfolio; a point of reference or comparison.

Benchmark value of the multiple In using the method of comparables, the value of a price multiple for the comparison asset; when we have comparison assets (a group), the mean or median value of the multiple for the group of assets.

Bernoulli random variable A random variable having the outcomes 0 and 1.

Bernoulli trial An experiment that can produce one of two outcomes.

Bill-and-hold basis Sales on a bill-and-hold basis involve selling products but not delivering those products until a later date.

Binomial model A model for pricing options in which the underlying price can move to only one of two possible new prices.

Binomial random variable The number of successes in n Bernoulli trials for which the probability of success is constant for all trials and the trials are independent.

Binomial tree The graphical representation of a model of asset price dynamics in which, at each period, the asset moves up with probability p or down with probability $(1 - p)$.

Block Orders to buy or sell that are too large for the liquidity ordinarily available in dealer networks or stock exchanges.

Blockage factor An illiquidity discount that occurs when an investor sells a large amount of stock relative to its trading volume (assuming it is not large enough to constitute a controlling ownership).

Bond equivalent yield A calculation of yield that is annualized using the ratio of 365 to the number of days to maturity. Bond equivalent yield allows for the restatement and comparison of securities with different compounding periods.

Bond indenture A legal contract specifying the terms of a bond issue.

Bond option An option in which the underlying is a bond; primarily traded in over-the-counter markets.

Bond yield plus risk premium approach An estimate of the cost of common equity that is produced by summing the before-tax cost of debt and a risk premium that captures the additional yield on a company's stock relative to its bonds. The additional yield is often estimated using historical spreads between bond yields and stock yields.

Bond-equivalent basis A basis for stating an annual yield that annualizes a semiannual yield by doubling it.

Bond-equivalent yield The yield to maturity on a basis that ignores compounding.

Bonding costs Costs borne by management to assure owners that they are working in the owners' best interest (e.g., implicit cost of non-compete agreements).

Book value equity per share The amount of book value (also called carrying value) of common equity per share of common stock, calculated by dividing the book value of shareholders' equity by the number of shares of common stock outstanding.

Book value of equity (or **book value**) Shareholders' equity (total assets minus total liabilities) minus the value of preferred stock; common shareholders' equity.

Bootstrapping earnings An increase in a company's earnings that results as a consequence of the idiosyncrasies of a merger transaction itself rather than because of resulting economic benefits of the combination.

Bottom-up analysis With reference to investment selection processes, an approach that involves selection from all securities within a specified investment universe, i.e., without prior narrowing of the universe on the basis of macroeconomic or overall market considerations.

Bottom-up forecasting approach A forecasting approach that involves aggregating the individual company forecasts of analysts into industry forecasts, and finally into macroeconomic forecasts.

Bottom-up investing An approach to investing that focuses on the individual characteristics of securities rather than on macroeconomic or overall market forecasts.

Box spread An option strategy that combines a bull spread and a bear spread having two different exercise prices, which produces a risk-free payoff of the difference in the exercise prices.

Break point In the context of the weighted average cost of capital (WACC), a break point is the amount of capital at which the cost of one or more of the sources of capital changes, leading to a change in the WACC.

Breakeven point The number of units produced and sold at which the company's net income is zero (revenues = total costs).

Breakup value or **private market value** The value derived using a sum-of-the-parts valuation.

Breusch–Pagan test   A test for conditional heteroskedasticity in the error term of a regression.

Broker   1) An agent who executes orders to buy or sell securities on behalf of a client in exchange for a commission. 2) *See* Futures commission merchants.

Brokerage   The business of acting as agents for buyers or sellers, usually in return for commissions.

Build-up method   A method for determining the required rate of return on equity as the sum of risk premiums, in which one or more of the risk premiums is typically subjective rather than grounded in a formal equilibrium model.

Built-up method   A method of identifying the basic elements of the overall capitalization rate.

Bull spread   An option strategy that involves buying a call with a lower exercise price and selling a call with a higher exercise price. It can also be executed with puts.

Bundling   Offering two or more products for sale as a set.

Business risk   The risk associated with operating earnings. Operating earnings are uncertain because total revenues and many of the expenditures contributed to produce those revenues are uncertain.

Butterfly spread   An option strategy that combines two bull or bear spreads and has three exercise prices.

Buy-side analysts   Analysts who work for investment management firms, trusts, and bank trust departments, and similar institutions.

Call   An option that gives the holder the right to buy an underlying asset from another party at a fixed price over a specific period of time.

Cannibalization   Cannibalization occurs when an investment takes customers and sales away from another part of the company.

Cap   1) A contract on an interest rate, whereby at periodic payment dates, the writer of the cap pays the difference between the market interest rate and a specified cap rate if, and only if, this difference is positive. This is equivalent to a stream of call options on the interest rate. 2) A combination of interest rate call options designed to hedge a borrower against rate increases on a floating-rate loan.

Capital account   A record of foreign investment in a country minus its investment abroad.

Capital allocation line (CAL)   A graph line that describes the combinations of expected return and standard deviation of return available to an investor from combining the optimal portfolio of risky assets with the risk-free asset.

Capital asset pricing model (CAPM)   An equation describing the expected return on any asset (or portfolio) as a linear function of its beta relative to the market portfolio.

Capital budgeting   The allocation of funds to relatively long-range projects or investments.

Capital charge   The company's total cost of capital in money terms.

Capital market line (CML)   The line with an intercept point equal to the risk-free rate that is tangent to the efficient frontier of risky assets; represents the efficient frontier when a risk-free asset is available for investment.

Capital rationing   A capital rationing environment assumes that the company has a fixed amount of funds to invest.

Capital structure   The mix of debt and equity that a company uses to finance its business; a company's specific mixture of long-term financing.

Capitalization rate   The divisor in the expression for the value of a perpetuity.

Capitalized cash flow model (method)   In the context of private company valuation, valuation model based on an assumption of a constant growth rate of free cash flow to the firm or a constant growth rate of free cash flow to equity.

Capitalized inventory costs   Costs of inventories including costs of purchase, costs of conversion, other costs to bring the inventories to their present location and condition, and the allocated portion of fixed production overhead costs.

Caplet   Each component call option in a cap.

Capped swap   A swap in which the floating payments have an upper limit.

Captive finance subsidiary   A wholly-owned subsidiary of a company that is established to provide financing of the sales of the parent company.

Capture hypothesis   A theory of regulatory behavior that predicts that regulators will eventually be captured by special interests of the industry being regulated.

Carried interest   A share of any profits that is paid to the general partner (manager) of an investment partnership, such as a private equity or hedge fund, as a form of compensation designed to be an incentive to the manager to maximize performance of the investment fund.

Carrying amount (book value)   The amount at which an asset or liability is valued according to accounting principles.

Cash   In accounting contexts, cash on hand (e.g., petty cash and cash not yet deposited to the bank) and demand deposits held in banks and similar accounts that can be used in payment of obligations.

Cash basis   Accounting method in which the only relevant transactions for the financial statements are those that involve cash.

Cash conversion cycle (net operating cycle)   A financial metric that measures the length of time required for a company to convert cash invested in its operations to cash received as a result of its operations; equal to days of inventory on hand + days of sales outstanding − number of days of payables.

Cash equivalents   Very liquid short-term investments, usually maturing in 90 days or less.

Cash flow additivity principle   The principle that dollar amounts indexed at the same point in time are additive.

Cash flow at risk (CFAR)   A variation of VAR that reflects the risk of a company's cash flow instead of its market value.

Cash flow from operations (cash flow from operating activities or operating cash flow)   The net amount of cash provided from operating activities.

Cash flow statement (statement of cash flows)   A financial statement that reconciles beginning-of-period and end-of-period balance sheet values of cash; consists of three parts: cash flows from operating activities, cash flows from investing activities, and cash flows from financing activities.

Cash offering   A merger or acquisition that is to be paid for with cash; the cash for the merger might come from the acquiring company's existing assets or from a debt issue.

Cash price or **spot price**   The price for immediate purchase of the underlying asset.

Cash ratio   A liquidity ratio calculated as (cash + short-term marketable investments) divided by current liabilities; measures a company's ability to meet its current obligations with just the cash and cash equivalents on hand.

Cash settlement   A procedure used in certain derivative transactions that specifies that the long and short parties engage in the equivalent cash value of a delivery transaction.

Cash-flow-statement-based accruals ratio   The difference between reported net income on an accrual basis and the cash flows from operating and investing activities compared to the average net operating assets over the period.

Cash-flow-statement-based aggregate accruals The difference between reported net income on an accrual basis and the cash flows from operating and investing activities.

Cash-generating unit The smallest identifiable group of assets that generates cash inflows that are largely independent of the cash inflows of other assets or groups of assets.

Catalyst An event or piece of information that causes the marketplace to re-evaluate the prospects of a company.

Central limit theorem A result in statistics that states that the sample mean computed from large samples of size n from a population with finite variance will follow an approximate normal distribution with a mean equal to the population mean and a variance equal to the population variance divided by n.

Centralized risk management or **companywide risk management** When a company has a single risk management group that monitors and controls all of the risk-taking activities of the organization. Centralization permits economies of scale and allows a company to use some of its risks to offset other risks. (See also *enterprise risk management*.)

Chain rule of forecasting A forecasting process in which the next period's value as predicted by the forecasting equation is substituted into the right-hand side of the equation to give a predicted value two periods ahead.

Chart of accounts A list of accounts used in an entity's accounting system.

Cheapest to deliver A bond in which the amount received for delivering the bond is largest compared with the amount paid in the market for the bond.

Cherry-picking When a bankrupt company is allowed to enforce contracts that are favorable to it while walking away from contracts that are unfavorable to it.

Classical growth theory A theory of economic growth based on the view that the growth of real GDP per person is temporary and that when it rises above subsistence level, a population explosion eventually brings it back to subsistence level.

Classified balance sheet A balance sheet organized so as to group together the various assets and liabilities into subcategories (e.g., current and noncurrent).

Clean surplus accounting Accounting that satisfies the condition that all changes in the book value of equity other than transactions with owners are reflected in income. The bottom-line income reflects all changes in shareholders' equity arising from other than owner transactions. In the absence of owner transactions, the change in shareholders' equity should equal net income. No adjustments such as translation adjustments bypass the income statement and go directly to shareholders equity.

Clean surplus relation The relationship between earnings, dividends, and book value in which ending book value is equal to the beginning book value plus earnings less dividends, apart from ownership transactions.

Clearinghouse An entity associated with a futures market that acts as middleman between the contracting parties and guarantees to each party the performance of the other.

Clientele effect The preference some investors have for shares that exhibit certain characteristics.

Closeout netting Netting the market values of *all* derivative contracts between two parties to determine one overall value owed by one party to another in the event of bankruptcy.

Coefficient of variation (CV) The ratio of a set of observations' standard deviation to the observations' mean value.

Cointegrated Describes two time series that have a long-term financial or economic relationship such that they do not diverge from each other without bound in the long run.

Collar An option strategy involving the purchase of a put and sale of a call in which the holder of an asset gains protection below a certain level, the exercise price of the put, and pays for it by giving up gains above a certain level, the exercise price of the call. Collars also can be used to provide protection against rising interest rates on a floating-rate loan by giving up gains from lower interest rates.

Combination A listing in which the order of the listed items does not matter.

Commercial paper Unsecured short-term corporate debt that is characterized by a single payment at maturity.

Committed lines of credit A bank commitment to extend credit up to a pre-specified amount; the commitment is considered a short-term liability and is usually in effect for 364 days (one day short of a full year).

Commodity forward A contract in which the underlying asset is oil, a precious metal, or some other commodity.

Commodity futures Futures contracts in which the underlying is a traditional agricultural, metal, or petroleum product.

Commodity option An option in which the asset underlying the futures is a commodity, such as oil, gold, wheat, or soybeans.

Commodity swap A swap in which the underlying is a commodity such as oil, gold, or an agricultural product.

Common size statements Financial statements in which all elements (accounts) are stated as a percentage of a key figure such as revenue for an income statement or total assets for a balance sheet.

Common-size analysis The restatement of financial statement items using a common denominator or reference item that allows one to identify trends and major differences; an example is an income statement in which all items are expressed as a percent of revenue.

Company fundamental factors Factors related to the company's internal performance, such as factors relating to earnings growth, earnings variability, earnings momentum, and financial leverage.

Company share-related factors Valuation measures and other factors related to share price or the trading characteristics of the shares, such as earnings yield, dividend yield, and book-to-market value.

Comparable company A company that has similar business risk; usually in the same industry and preferably with a single line of business.

Comparables (comps, guideline assets, guideline companies) Assets used as benchmarks when applying the method of comparables to value an asset.

Comparative advantage A person or country has a comparative advantage in an activity if that person or country can perform the activity at a lower opportunity cost than anyone else or any other country.

Compiled financial statements Financial statements that are not accompanied by an auditor's opinion letter.

Complement In probability, with reference to an event S, the event that S does not occur; in economics, a good that is used in conjunction with another good.

Completed contract A method of revenue recognition in which the company does not recognize any revenue until the contract is completed; used particularly in long-term construction contracts.

Component cost of capital The rate of return required by suppliers of capital for an individual source of a company's funding, such as debt or equity.

Compounding The process of accumulating interest on interest.

Comprehensive income   All changes in equity other than contributions by, and distributions to, owners; income under clean surplus accounting; includes all changes in equity during a period except those resulting from investments by owners and distributions to owners; comprehensive income equals net income plus other comprehensive income.

Conditional expected value   The expected value of a stated event given that another event has occurred.

Conditional heteroskedasticity   Heteroskedasticity in the error variance that is correlated with the values of the independent variable(s) in the regression.

Conditional probability   The probability of an event given (conditioned on) another event.

Conditional variances   The variance of one variable, given the outcome of another.

Confidence interval   A range that has a given probability that it will contain the population parameter it is intended to estimate.

Conglomerate discount   The discount possibly applied by the market to the stock of a company operating in multiple, unrelated businesses.

Conglomerate merger   A merger involving companies that are in unrelated businesses.

Consistent   With reference to estimators, describes an estimator for which the probability of estimates close to the value of the population parameter increases as sample size increases.

Consolidation   The combining of the results of operations of subsidiaries with the parent company to present financial statements as if they were a single economic unit. The assets, liabilities, revenues and expenses of the subsidiaries are combined with those of the parent company, eliminating intercompany transactions.

Constant dividend payout ratio policy   A policy in which a constant percentage of net income is paid out in dividends.

Constant maturity swap or **CMT swap**   A swap in which the floating rate is the rate on a security known as a constant maturity treasury or CMT security.

Constant maturity treasury or **CMT**   A hypothetical U.S. Treasury note with a constant maturity. A CMT exists for various years in the range of 2 to 10.

Contango   A situation in a futures market where the current futures price is greater than the current spot price for the underlying asset.

Contingent claims   Derivatives in which the payoffs occur if a specific event occurs; generally referred to as options.

Contingent consideration   Potential future payments to the seller that are contingent on the achievement of certain agreed on occurrences.

Continuing residual income   Residual income after the forecast horizon.

Continuous random variable   A random variable for which the range of possible outcomes is the real line (all real numbers between ($-\infty$ and $+\infty$) or some subset of the real line.

Continuous time   Time thought of as advancing in extremely small increments.

Continuously compounded return   The natural logarithm of 1 plus the holding period return, or equivalently, the natural logarithm of the ending price over the beginning price.

Contra account   An account that offsets another account.

Contribution margin   The amount available for fixed costs and profit after paying variable costs; revenue minus variable costs.

Control premium   An increment or premium to value associated with a controlling ownership interest in a company.

Controlling interest   An investment where the investor exerts control over the investee, typically by having a greater than 50 percent ownership in the investee.

Convenience yield   The nonmonetary return offered by an asset when the asset is in short supply, often associated with assets with seasonal production processes.

Conventional cash flow   A conventional cash flow pattern is one with an initial outflow followed by a series of inflows.

Conversion factor   An adjustment used to facilitate delivery on bond futures contracts in which any of a number of bonds with different characteristics are eligible for delivery.

Convertible debt   Debt with the added feature that the bondholder has the option to exchange the debt for equity at prespecified terms.

Corporate governance   The system of principles, policies, procedures, and clearly defined responsibilities and accountabilities used by stakeholders to overcome the conflicts of interest inherent in the corporate form.

Corporate raider   A person or organization seeking to profit by acquiring a company and reselling it, or seeking to profit from the takeover attempt itself (e.g., greenmail).

Corporation   A legal entity with rights similar to those of a person. The chief officers, executives, or top managers act as agents for the firm and are legally entitled to authorize corporate activities and to enter into contracts on behalf of the business.

Correlation   A number between -1 and $+1$ that measures the comovement (linear association) between two random variables.

Correlation analysis   The analysis of the strength of the linear relationship between two data series.

Cost approach to value   A method of valuing property based on site value plus current construction costs less accrued depreciation.

Cost averaging   The periodic investment of a fixed amount of money.

Cost leadership   The competitive strategy of being the lowest cost producer while offering products comparable to those of other firms, so that products can be priced at or near the industry average.

Cost of capital   The rate of return that suppliers of capital require as compensation for their contribution of capital.

Cost of carry   The cost associated with holding some asset, including financing, storage, and insurance costs. Any yield received on the asset is treated as a negative carrying cost.

Cost of carry model   A model for pricing futures contracts in which the futures price is determined by adding the cost of carry to the spot price.

Cost of debt   The cost of debt financing to a company, such as when it issues a bond or takes out a bank loan.

Cost of equity   The required rate of return on common stock.

Cost of goods sold   For a given period, equal to beginning inventory minus ending inventory plus the cost of goods acquired or produced during the period.

Cost of preferred stock   The cost to a company of issuing preferred stock; the dividend yield that a company must commit to pay preferred stockholders.

Cost recovery method   A method of revenue recognition in which the seller does not report any profit until the cash amounts paid by the buyer—including principal and interest on any financing from the seller—are greater than all the seller's costs for the merchandise sold.

Cost structure   The mix of a company's variable costs and fixed costs.

Cost-of-service regulation   Regulation that allows prices to reflect only the actual average cost of production and no monopoly profits.

Covariance A measure of the co-movement (linear association) between two random variables.

Covariance matrix A matrix or square array whose entries are covariances; also known as a variance–covariance matrix.

Covariance stationary Describes a time series when its expected value and variance are constant and finite in all periods and when its covariance with itself for a fixed number of periods in the past or future is constant and finite in all periods.

Covered call An option strategy involving the holding of an asset and sale of a call on the asset.

Covered interest arbitrage A transaction executed in the foreign exchange market in which a currency is purchased (sold) and a forward contract is sold (purchased) to lock in the exchange rate for future delivery of the currency. This transaction should earn the risk-free rate of the investor's home country.

Crawling peg A policy regime is one that selects a target path for the exchange rate with intervention in the foreign exchange market to achieve that path.

Creative response Behavior on the part of a firm that allows it to comply with the letter of the law but violate the spirit, significantly lessening the law's effects.

Credit With respect to double-entry accounting, a credit records increases in liability, owners' equity, and revenue accounts or decreases in asset accounts; with respect to borrowing, the willingness and ability of the borrower to make promised payments on the borrowing.

Credit analysis The evaluation of credit risk; the evaluation of the creditworthiness of a borrower or counterparty.

Credit derivatives A contract in which one party has the right to claim a payment from another party in the event that a specific credit event occurs over the life of the contract.

Credit risk or **default risk** The risk of loss caused by a counterparty's or debtor's failure to make a promised payment.

Credit scoring model A statistical model used to classify borrowers according to creditworthiness.

Credit spread option An option on the yield spread on a bond.

Credit swap A type of swap transaction used as a credit derivative in which one party makes periodic payments to the other and receives the promise of a payoff if a third party defaults.

Credit VAR, default VAR, or **credit at risk** A variation of VAR that reflects credit risk.

Credit-linked notes Fixed-income securities in which the holder of the security has the right to withhold payment of the full amount due at maturity if a credit event occurs.

Creditor nation A country that during its entire history has invested more in the rest of the world than other countries have invested in it.

Creditworthiness The perceived ability of the borrower to pay what is owed on the borrowing in a timely manner; it represents the ability of a company to withstand adverse impacts on its cash flows.

Cross-product netting Netting the market values of all contracts, not just derivatives, between parties.

Cross-sectional analysis Analysis that involves comparisons across individuals in a group over a given time period or at a given point in time.

Cross-sectional data Observations over individual units at a point in time, as opposed to time-series data.

Cumulative distribution function A function giving the probability that a random variable is less than or equal to a specified value.

Cumulative relative frequency For data grouped into intervals, the fraction of total observations that are less than the value of the upper limit of a stated interval.

Currency forward A forward contract in which the underlying is a foreign currency.

Currency option An option that allows the holder to buy (if a call) or sell (if a put) an underlying currency at a fixed exercise rate, expressed as an exchange rate.

Currency swap A swap in which each party makes interest payments to the other in different currencies.

Current account A record of receipts from exports of goods and services, payments for imports of goods and services, net income and net transfers received from the rest of the world.

Current assets, or **liquid assets** Assets that are expected to be consumed or converted into cash in the near future, typically one year or less.

Current cost With reference to assets, the amount of cash or cash equivalents that would have to be paid to buy the same or an equivalent asset today; with reference to liabilities, the undiscounted amount of cash or cash equivalents that would be required to settle the obligation today.

Current credit risk The risk associated with the possibility that a payment currently due will not be made.

Current exchange rate For accounting purposes, the spot exchange rate on the balance sheet date.

Current liabilities Short-term obligations, such as accounts payable, wages payable, or accrued liabilities, that are expected to be settled in the near future, typically one year or less.

Current rate method Approach to translating foreign currency financial statements for consolidation in which all assets and liabilities are translated at the current exchange rate. The current rate method is the prevalent method of translation.

Current ratio A liquidity ratio calculated as current assets divided by current liabilities.

Current taxes payable Tax expenses that have been recognized and recorded on a company's income statement but which have not yet been paid.

Cyclical businesses Businesses with high sensitivity to business- or industry-cycle influences.

Daily settlement See *Marking to market.*

Data mining The practice of determining a model by extensive searching through a dataset for statistically significant patterns.

Day trader A trader holding a position open somewhat longer than a scalper but closing all positions at the end of the day.

Days of inventory on hand (DOH) An activity ratio equal to the number of days in the period divided by inventory turnover over the period.

Days of sales outstanding (DSO) An activity ratio equal to the number of days in period divided by receivables turnover.

Dead-hand provision A poison pill provision that allows for the redemption or cancellation of a poison pill provision only by a vote of continuing directors (generally directors who were on the target company's board prior to the takeover attempt).

Dealing securities Securities held by banks or other financial intermediaries for trading purposes.

Debit With respect to double-entry accounting, a debit records increases of asset and expense accounts or decreases in liability and owners' equity accounts.

Debt covenants Agreements between the company as borrower and its creditors.

Debt incurrence test A financial covenant made in conjunction with existing debt that restricts a company's ability to incur additional debt at the same seniority based on one or more financial tests or conditions.

Debt rating approach A method for estimating a company's before-tax cost of debt based upon the yield on comparably rated bonds for maturities that closely match that of the company's existing debt.

Debt ratings An objective measure of the quality and safety of a company's debt based upon an analysis of the company's ability to pay the promised cash flows, as well as an analysis of any indentures.

Debt with warrants Debt issued with warrants that give the bondholder the right to purchase equity at prespecified terms.

Debtor nation A country that during its entire history has borrowed more in the rest of the world than other countries have lent in it.

Debt-to-assets ratio A solvency ratio calculated as total debt divided by total assets.

Debt-to-capital ratio A solvency ratio calculated as total debt divided by total debt plus total shareholders' equity.

Debt-to-equity ratio A solvency ratio calculated as total debt divided by total shareholders' equity.

Decentralized risk management A system that allows individual units within an organization to manage risk. Decentralization results in duplication of effort but has the advantage of having people closer to the risk be more directly involved in its management.

Deciles Quantiles that divide a distribution into 10 equal parts.

Decision rule With respect to hypothesis testing, the rule according to which the null hypothesis will be rejected or not rejected; involves the comparison of the test statistic to rejection point(s).

Declaration date The day that the corporation issues a statement declaring a specific dividend.

Deductible temporary differences Temporary differences that result in a reduction of or deduction from taxable income in a future period when the balance sheet item is recovered or settled.

Deep in the money Options that are far in-the-money.

Deep out of the money Options that are far out-of-the-money.

Default risk premium An extra return that compensates investors for the possibility that the borrower will fail to make a promised payment at the contracted time and in the contracted amount.

Defensive interval ratio A liquidity ratio that estimates the number of days that an entity could meet cash needs from liquid assets; calculated as (cash + short-term marketable investments + receivables) divided by daily cash expenditures.

Deferred tax assets A balance sheet asset that arises when an excess amount is paid for income taxes relative to accounting profit. The taxable income is higher than accounting profit and income tax payable exceeds tax expense. The company expects to recover the difference during the course of future operations when tax expense exceeds income tax payable.

Deferred tax liabilities A balance sheet liability that arises when a deficit amount is paid for income taxes relative to accounting profit. The taxable income is less than the accounting profit and income tax payable is less than tax expense. The company expects to eliminate the liability over the course of future operations when income tax payable exceeds tax expense.

Defined benefit obligation Under IFRS, the liability of a defined benefit pension.

Defined-benefit pension plans Plan in which the company promises to pay a certain annual amount (defined benefit) to the employee after retirement. The company bears the investment risk of the plan assets.

Defined-contribution pension plans Individual accounts to which an employee and typically the employer makes contributions, generally on a tax-advantaged basis. The amounts of contributions are defined at the outset, but the future value of the benefit is unknown. The employee bears the investment risk of the plan assets.

Definition of value (or **standard of value**) A specification of how "value" is to be understood in the context of a specific valuation.

Definitive merger agreement A contract signed by both parties to a merger that clarifies the details of the transaction, including the terms, warranties, conditions, termination details, and the rights of all parties.

Degree of confidence The probability that a confidence interval includes the unknown population parameter.

Degree of financial leverage (DFL) The ratio of the percentage change in net income to the percentage change in operating income; the sensitivity of the cash flows available to owners when operating income changes.

Degree of operating leverage (DOL) The ratio of the percentage change in operating income to the percentage change in units sold; the sensitivity of operating income to changes in units sold.

Degree of total leverage The ratio of the percentage change in net income to the percentage change in units sold; the sensitivity of the cash flows to owners to changes in the number of units produced and sold.

Degrees of freedom (df) The number of independent observations used.

Delivery A process used in a deliverable forward contract in which the long pays the agreed-upon price to the short, which in turn delivers the underlying asset to the long.

Delivery option The feature of a futures contract giving the short the right to make decisions about what, when, and where to deliver.

Delta The relationship between the option price and the underlying price, which reflects the sensitivity of the price of the option to changes in the price of the underlying.

Delta hedge An option strategy in which a position in an asset is converted to a risk-free position with a position in a specific number of options. The number of options per unit of the underlying changes through time, and the position must be revised to maintain the hedge.

Delta-normal method A measure of VAR equivalent to the analytical method but that refers to the use of delta to estimate the option's price sensitivity.

Dependent With reference to events, the property that the probability of one event occurring depends on (is related to) the occurrence of another event.

Dependent variable The variable whose variation about its mean is to be explained by the regression; the left-hand-side variable in a regression equation.

Depreciation The process of systematically allocating the cost of long-lived (tangible) assets to the periods during which the assets are expected to provide economic benefits.

Deregulation The elimination or phasing out of regulations on economic activity.

Derivative A financial instrument whose value depends on the value of some underlying asset or factor (e.g., a stock price, an interest rate, or exchange rate).

Derivatives dealers Commercial and investment banks that make markets in derivatives.

Descriptive statistics The study of how data can be summarized effectively.

Designated fair value instruments Financial instruments that an entity chooses to measure at fair value per IAS 39 or SFAS 159. Generally, the election to use the fair value option is irrevocable.

Diff swaps A swap in which the payments are based on the difference between interest rates in two countries but payments are made in only a single currency.

Differential expectations Expectations that differ from consensus expectations.

Differentiation The competitive strategy of offering unique products or services along some dimensions that are widely valued by buyers so that the firm can command premium prices.

Diffuse prior The assumption of equal prior probabilities.

Diluted earnings per share (diluted EPS) Net income, minus preferred dividends, divided by the number of common shares outstanding considering all dilutive securities (e.g., convertible debt and options); the EPS that would result if all dilutive securities were converted into common shares.

Diluted shares The number of shares that would be outstanding if all potentially dilutive claims on common shares (e.g., convertible debt, convertible preferred stock, and employee stock options) were exercised.

Dilution A reduction in proportional ownership interest as a result of the issuance of new shares.

Diminishing balance method An accelerated depreciation method, i.e., one that allocates a relatively large proportion of the cost of an asset to the early years of the asset's useful life.

Direct debit program An arrangement whereby a customer authorizes a debit to a demand account; typically used by companies to collect routine payments for services.

Direct financing lease A type of finance lease, from a lessor perspective, where the present value of the lease payments (lease receivable) equals the carrying value of the leased asset. The revenues earned by the lessor are financing in nature.

Direct format (direct method) With reference to the cash flow statement, a format for the presentation of the statement in which cash flow from operating activities is shown as operating cash receipts less operating cash disbursements.

Direct income capitalization approach Division of net operating income by an overall capitalization rate to arrive at market value.

Direct sales-comparison approach Method of valuing property based on recent sales prices of similar properties.

Direct write-off method An approach to recognizing credit losses on customer receivables in which the company waits until such time as a customer has defaulted and only then recognizes the loss.

Dirty surplus accounting Accounting in which some income items are reported as part of stockholders' equity rather than as gains and losses on the income statement; certain items of comprehensive income bypass the income statement and appear as direct adjustments to shareholders' equity.

Dirty surplus items Items that affect comprehensive income but which bypass the income statement.

Disbursement float The amount of time between check issuance and a check's clearing back against the company's account.

Discount To reduce the value of a future payment in allowance for how far away it is in time; to calculate the present value of some future amount. Also, the amount by which an instrument is priced below its face value.

Discount for lack of control An amount or percentage deducted from the pro rata share of 100 percent of the value of an equity interest in a business to reflect the absence of some or all of the powers of control.

Discount for lack of marketability An amount or percentage deducted from the value of an ownership interest to reflect the relative absence of marketability.

Discount interest A procedure for determining the interest on a loan or bond in which the interest is deducted from the face value in advance.

Discount rate Any rate used in finding the present value of a future cash flow.

Discounted cash flow analysis In the context of merger analysis, it is an estimate of a target company's value found by discounting the company's expected future free cash flows to the present.

Discrete random variable A random variable that can take on at most a countable number of possible values.

Discrete time Time thought of as advancing in distinct finite increments.

Discriminant analysis A multivariate classification technique used to discriminate between groups, such as companies that either will or will not become bankrupt during some time frame.

Dispersion The variability around the central tendency.

Divestiture The sale, liquidation, or spin-off of a division or subsidiary.

Dividend coverage ratio The ratio of net income to dividends.

Dividend discount model (DDM) A present value model of stock value that views the intrinsic value of a stock as present value of the stock's expected future dividends.

Dividend discount model based approach An approach for estimating a country's equity risk premium. The market rate of return is estimated as the sum of the dividend yield and the growth rate in dividends for a market index. Subtracting the risk-free rate of return from the estimated market return produces an estimate for the equity risk premium.

Dividend displacement of earnings The concept that dividends paid now displace earnings in all future periods.

Dividend imputation tax system A taxation system which effectively assures that corporate profits distributed as dividends are taxed just once, at the shareholder's tax rate.

Dividend policy The strategy a company follows with regard to the amount and timing of dividend payments.

Dividend payout ratio The ratio of cash dividends paid to earnings for a period.

Dividend rate The most recent quarterly dividend multiplied by four.

Dividends per share The dollar amount of cash dividends paid during a period per share of common stock.

Double declining balance depreciation An accelerated depreciation method that involves depreciating the asset at double the straight-line rate. This rate is multiplied by the book value of the asset at the beginning of the period (a declining balance) to calculate depreciation expense.

Double taxation system Corporate earnings are taxed twice when paid out as dividends. First, corporate earnings are taxed regardless of whether they will be distributed as dividends or retained at the G-13 corporate level, and second, dividends are taxed again at the individual shareholder level.

Double-entry accounting The accounting system of recording transactions in which every recorded transaction affects at least two accounts so as to keep the basic accounting equation (assets = liabilities + owners' equity) in balance.

Down transition probability The probability that an asset's value moves down in a model of asset price dynamics.

Downstream A transaction between two affiliates, an investor company and an associate company such that the investor company records a profit on its income statement. An example is a sale of inventory by the investor company to the associate.

Drag on liquidity When receipts lag, creating pressure from the decreased available funds.

Due diligence Investigation and analysis in support of a recommendation; the failure to exercise due diligence may sometimes result in liability according to various securities laws.

Dummy variable A type of qualitative variable that takes on a value of 1 if a particular condition is true and 0 if that condition is false.

Dumping The sale by a foreign firm of exports at a lower price than the cost of production.

DuPont analysis An approach to decomposing return on investment, e.g., return on equity, as the product of other financial ratios.

Duration A measure of an option-free bond's average maturity. Specifically, the weighted average maturity of all future cash flows paid by a security, in which the weights are the present value of these cash flows as a fraction of the bond's price. A measure of a bond's price sensitivity to interest rate movements.

Dutch Book theorem A result in probability theory stating that inconsistent probabilities create profit opportunities.

Dynamic hedging A strategy in which a position is hedged by making frequent adjustments to the quantity of the instrument used for hedging in relation to the instrument being hedged.

Earnings at risk (EAR) A variation of VAR that reflects the risk of a company's earnings instead of its market value.

Earnings expectation management Attempts by management to encourage analysts to forecast a slightly lower number for expected earnings than the analysts would otherwise forecast.

Earnings game Management's focus on reporting earnings that meet consensus estimates.

Earnings management activity Deliberate activity aimed at influencing reporting earnings numbers, often with the goal of placing management in a favorable light; the opportunistic use of accruals to manage earnings.

Earnings per share The amount of income earned during a period per share of common stock.

Earnings yield Earnings per share divided by price; the reciprocal of the P/E ratio.

Economic exposure The risk associated with changes in the relative attractiveness of products and services offered for sale, arising out of the competitive effects of changes in exchange rates.

Economic growth The expansion of production possibilities that results from capital accumulation and technological change.

Economic growth rate The annual percentage change in real GDP.

Economic order quantity–reorder point An approach to managing inventory based on expected demand and the predictability of demand; the ordering point for new inventory is determined based on the costs of ordering and carrying inventory, such that the total cost associated with inventory is minimized.

Economic profit See *Residual income.*

Economic sectors Large industry groupings.

Economic value added (EVA®) A commercial implementation of the residual income concept; the computation of EVA® is the net operating profit after taxes minus the cost of capital, where these inputs are adjusted for a number of items.

Economies of scale In reference to mergers, it is the savings achieved through the consolidation of operations and elimination of duplicate resources.

Effective annual rate The amount by which a unit of currency will grow in a year with interest on interest included.

Effective annual yield (EAY) An annualized return that accounts for the effect of interest on interest; EAY is computed by compounding 1 plus the holding period yield forward to one year, then subtracting 1.

Efficiency In statistics, a desirable property of estimators; an efficient estimator is the unbiased estimator with the smallest variance among unbiased estimators of the same parameter.

Efficient frontier The portion of the minimum-variance frontier beginning with the global minimum-variance portfolio and continuing above it; the graph of the set of portfolios offering the maximum expected return for their level of variance of return.

Efficient portfolio A portfolio offering the highest expected return for a given level of risk as measured by variance or standard deviation of return.

Elasticity A measure of sensitivity; the incremental change in one variable with respect to an incremental change in another variable.

Electronic funds transfer The use of computer networks to conduct financial transactions electronically.

Empirical probability The probability of an event estimated as a relative frequency of occurrence.

Enhanced derivatives products companies (EDPC) A type of subsidiary engaged in derivatives transactions that is separated from the parent company in order to have a higher credit rating than the parent company.

Enterprise risk management A form of *centralized risk management* that typically encompasses the management of a broad variety of risks, including insurance risk.

Enterprise value (EV) Total company value (the market value of debt, common equity, and preferred equity) minus the value of cash and investments.

Enterprise value multiple A valuation multiple that relates the total market value of all sources of a company's capital (net of cash) to a measure of fundamental value for the entire company (such as a pre-interest earnings measure).

Entry price The price paid to buy an asset.

Equilibrium The condition in which supply equals demand.

Equitizing cash A strategy used to replicate an index. It is also used to take a given amount of cash and turn it into an equity position while maintaining the liquidity provided by the cash.

Equity Assets less liabilities; the residual interest in the assets after subtracting the liabilities.

Equity carve-out A form of restructuring that involves the creation of a new legal entity and the sale of equity in it to outsiders.

Equity charge The estimated cost of equity capital in money terms.

Equity dividend rate Income rate that reflects the relationship between equity income and equity capital.

Equity forward A contract calling for the purchase of an individual stock, a stock portfolio, or a stock index at a later date at an agreed-upon price.

Equity method A basis for reporting investment income in which the investing entity recognizes a share of income as earned rather than as dividends when received. These transactions are typically reflected in Investments in Associates or Equity Method Investments.

Equity options Options on individual stocks; also known as stock options.

Equity risk premium The expected return on equities minus the risk-free rate; the premium that investors demand for investing in equities.

Equity swap A swap transaction in which at least one cash flow is tied to the return to an equity portfolio position, often an equity index.

Error autocorrelation The autocorrelation of the error term.

Error term The portion of the dependent variable that is not explained by the independent variable(s) in the regression.

Estimate The particular value calculated from sample observations using an estimator.

Estimated (or **fitted**) **parameters** With reference to regression analysis, the estimated values of the population intercept and population slope coefficient(s) in a regression.

Estimation With reference to statistical inference, the subdivision dealing with estimating the value of a population parameter.

Estimator An estimation formula; the formula used to compute the sample mean and other sample statistics are examples of estimators.

Eurodollar A dollar deposited outside the United States.

European option An option that can only be exercised on its expiration date.

Event Any outcome or specified set of outcomes of a random variable.

Excess kurtosis Degree of peakedness (fatness of tails) in excess of the peakedness of the normal distribution.

Exchange for physicals (EFP) A permissible delivery procedure used by futures market participants, in which the long and short arrange a delivery procedure other than the normal procedures stipulated by the futures exchange.

Exchange rate The value of the U.S. dollar in terms of other currencies in the foreign exchange market.

Exchange ratio The number of shares that target stockholders are to receive in exchange for each of their shares in the target company.

Ex-dividend Trading ex-dividend refers to shares that no longer carry the right to the next dividend payment.

Ex-dividend date The first date that a share trades without (i.e., "ex") the dividend.

Ex-dividend price The price at which a share first trades without (i.e., "ex") the right to receive an upcoming dividend.

Exercise or **exercising the option** The process of using an option to buy or sell the underlying.

Exercise date The day that employees actually exercise the options and convert them to stock.

Exercise price (strike price, striking price, or **strike)** The fixed price at which an option holder can buy or sell the underlying.

Exercise rate or **strike rate** The fixed rate at which the holder of an interest rate option can buy or sell the underlying.

Exhaustive Covering or containing all possible outcomes.

Exit price The price received to sell an asset or transfer a liability.

Expanded CAPM An adaptation of the CAPM that adds to the CAPM a premium for small size and company-specific risk.

Expectational arbitrage Investing on the basis of differential expectations.

Expected holding-period return The expected total return on an asset over a stated holding period; for stocks, the sum of the expected dividend yield and the expected price appreciation over the holding period.

Expected value The probability-weighted average of the possible outcomes of a random variable.

Expensed Taken as a deduction in arriving at net income.

Expenses Outflows of economic resources or increases in liabilities that result in decreases in equity (other than decreases because of distributions to owners); reductions in net assets associated with the creation of revenues.

Expiration date The date on which a derivative contract expires.

Exports The goods and services that we sell to people in other countries.

Exposure to foreign exchange risk The risk of a change in value of an asset or liability denominated in a foreign currency due to a change in exchange rates.

External growth Company growth in output or sales that is achieved by buying the necessary resources externally (i.e., achieved through mergers and acquisitions).

Externality The effect of an investment on other things besides the investment itself.

Face value (also **principal, par value, stated value,** or **maturity value**) The amount of cash payable by a company to the bondholders when the bonds mature; the promised payment at maturity separate from any coupon payment.

Factor A common or underlying element with which several variables are correlated.

Factor risk premium (or **factor price**) The expected return in excess of the risk-free rate for a portfolio with a sensitivity of 1 to one factor and a sensitivity of 0 to all other factors.

Factor sensitivity (also **factor betas** or **factor loadings**) An asset's sensitivity to a particular factor; a measure of the response of return to each unit of increase in a factor, holding all other factors constant.

Fair market value The market price of an asset or liability that trades regularly.

Fair value The amount at which an asset (or liability) could be bought (or incurred) or sold (or settled) in a current transaction between willing parties, that is, other than in a forced or liquidation sale; the price that would be received to sell an asset or paid to transfer a liability in an orderly transaction between market participants at the measurement date.

Fiduciary call A combination of a European call and a risk-free bond that matures on the option expiration day and has a face value equal to the exercise price of the call.

Finance lease (capital lease) Essentially, the purchase of some asset by the buyer (lessee) that is directly financed by the seller (lessor).

Financial analysis The process of selecting, evaluating, and interpreting financial data in order to formulate an assessment of a company's present and future financial condition and performance.

Financial distress Heightened uncertainty regarding a company's ability to meet its various obligations because of lower or negative earnings.

Financial flexibility The ability to react and adapt to financial adversities and opportunities.

Financial futures Futures contracts in which the underlying is a stock, bond, or currency.

Financial leverage The extent to which a company can effect, through the use of debt, a proportional change in the return on common equity that is greater than a given proportional change in operating income; also, short for the financial leverage ratio.

Financial leverage ratio A measure of financial leverage calculated as average total assets divided by average total equity.

Financial reporting quality The accuracy with which a company's reported financials reflect its operating performance and their usefulness for forecasting future cash flows.

Financial risk The risk that environmental, social, or governance risk factors will result in significant costs or other losses to a company and its shareholders; the risk arising from a company's obligation to meet required payments under its financing agreements.

Financial transaction A purchase involving a buyer having essentially no material synergies with the target (e.g., the purchase of a private company by a company in an unrelated industry or by a private equity firm would typically be a financial transaction).

Financing activities Activities related to obtaining or repaying capital to be used in the business (e.g., equity and long-term debt).

First-differencing A transformation that subtracts the value of the time series in period $t - 1$ from its value in period t.

First-in, first-out (FIFO) The first in, first out, method of accounting for inventory, which matches sales against the costs of items of inventory in the order in which they were placed in inventory.

First-order serial correlation Correlation between adjacent observations in a time series.

Fixed asset turnover An activity ratio calculated as total revenue divided by average net fixed assets.

Fixed charge coverage A solvency ratio measuring the number of times interest and lease payments are covered by operating income, calculated as (EBIT + lease payments) divided by (interest payments + lease payments).

Fixed costs Costs that remain at the same level regardless of a company's level of production and sales.

Fixed exchange rate An exchange rate pegged at a value decided by the government or central bank and that blocks the unregulated forces of demand and supply by direct intervention in the foreign exchange market.

Fixed-income forward A forward contract in which the underlying is a bond.

Fixed-rate perpetual preferred stock Nonconvertible, noncallable preferred stock with a specified dividend rate that has a claim on earnings senior to the claim of common stock, and no maturity date.

Flexible exchange rate An exchange rate is determined by demand and supply with no direct intervention in the foreign exchange market by the central bank.

Flip-in pill A poison pill takeover defense that dilutes an acquirer's ownership in a target by giving other existing target company shareholders the right to buy additional target company shares at a discount.

Flip-over pill A poison pill takeover defense that gives target company shareholders the right to purchase shares of the acquirer at a significant discount to the market price, which has the effect of causing dilution to all existing acquiring company shareholders.

Float In the context of customer receipts, the amount of money that is in transit between payments made by customers and the funds that are usable by the company.

Float factor An estimate of the average number of days it takes deposited checks to clear; average daily float divided by average daily deposit.

Floating-rate loan A loan in which the interest rate is reset at least once after the starting date.

Floor A combination of interest rate put options designed to hedge a lender against lower rates on a floating-rate loan.

Floor traders or **locals** Market makers that buy and sell by quoting a bid and an ask price. They are the primary providers of liquidity to the market.

Floored swap A swap in which the floating payments have a lower limit.

Floorlet Each component put option in a floor.

Flotation cost Fees charged to companies by investment bankers and other costs associated with raising new capital.

Focus The competitive strategy of seeking a competitive advantage within a target segment or segments of the industry, either on the basis of cost leadership (**cost focus**) or differentiation (**differentiation focus**).

Foreign currency The money of other countries regardless of whether that money is in the form of notes, coins, or bank deposits.

Foreign currency transactions Transactions that are denominated in a currency other than a company's functional currency.

Foreign exchange market The market in which the currency of one country is exchanged for the currency of another.

Forward contract An agreement between two parties in which one party, the buyer, agrees to buy from the other party, the seller, an underlying asset at a later date for a price established at the start of the contract.

Forward dividend yield A dividend yield based on the anticipated dividend during the next 12 months.

Forward integration A merger involving the purchase of a target that is farther along the value or production chain; for example, to acquire a distributor.

Forward P/E (also **leading P/E** or **prospective P/E**) A P/E calculated on the basis of a forecast of EPS; a stock's current price divided by next year's expected earnings.

Forward price or **forward rate** The fixed price or rate at which the transaction scheduled to occur at the expiration of a forward contract will take place. This price is agreed on at the initiation date of the contract.

Forward rate agreement (FRA) A forward contract calling for one party to make a fixed interest payment and the other to make an interest payment at a rate to be determined at the contract expiration.

Forward swap A forward contract to enter into a swap.

Franking credit A tax credit received by shareholders for the taxes that a corporation paid on its distributed earnings.

Free cash flow The actual cash that would be available to the company's investors after making all investments necessary to maintain the company as an ongoing enterprise (also referred to as free cash flow to the firm); the internally generated funds that can be distributed to the company's investors (e.g., shareholders and bondholders) without impairing the value of the company.

Free cash flow hypothesis The hypothesis that higher debt levels discipline managers by forcing them to make fixed debt service payments and by reducing the company's free cash flow.

Free cash flow method Income approach that values an asset based on estimates of future cash flows discounted to present value by using a discount rate reflective of the risks associated with the cash flows.

Free cash flow to equity The cash flow available to a company's common shareholders after all operating expenses, interest, and principal payments have been made, and necessary investments in working and fixed capital have been made.

Free cash flow to equity model A model of stock valuation that views a stock's intrinsic value as the present value of expected future free cash flows to equity.

Free cash flow to the firm The cash flow available to the company's suppliers of capital after all operating expenses (including taxes) have been paid and necessary investments in working and fixed capital have been made.

Free cash flow to the firm model A model of stock valuation that views the value of a firm as the present value of expected future free cash flows to the firm.

Frequency distribution A tabular display of data summarized into a relatively small number of intervals.

Frequency polygon A graph of a frequency distribution obtained by drawing straight lines joining successive points representing the class frequencies.

Friendly transaction A potential business combination that is endorsed by the managers of both companies.

Full price   The price of a security with accrued interest.

Functional currency   The currency of the primary economic environment in which an entity operates.

Fundamental beta   A beta that is based at least in part on fundamental data for a company.

Fundamental factor models   A multifactor model in which the factors are attributes of stocks or companies that are important in explaining cross-sectional differences in stock prices.

Fundamentals   Economic characteristics of a business such as profitability, financial strength, and risk.

Future value (FV)   The amount to which a payment or series of payments will grow by a stated future date.

Futures commission merchants (FCMs)   Individuals or companies that execute futures transactions for other parties off the exchange.

Futures contract   A variation of a forward contract that has essentially the same basic definition but with some additional features, such as a clearinghouse guarantee against credit losses, a daily settlement of gains and losses, and an organized electronic or floor trading facility.

Futures exchange   A legal corporate entity whose shareholders are its members. The members of the exchange have the privilege of executing transactions directly on the exchange.

Gains   Asset inflows not directly related to the ordinary activities of the business.

Gamma   A numerical measure of how sensitive an option's delta is to a change in the underlying.

General Agreement on Tariffs and Trade   An international agreement signed in 1947 to reduce tariffs on international trade.

Generalized least squares   A regression estimation technique that addresses heteroskedasticity of the error term.

Geometric mean   A measure of central tendency computed by taking the nth root of the product of n non-negative values.

Giro system   An electronic payment system used widely in Europe and Japan.

Going-concern assumption   The assumption that the business will maintain its business activities into the foreseeable future.

Going-concern value   A business's value under a going-concern assumption.

Goodwill   An intangible asset that represents the excess of the purchase price of an acquired company over the value of the net assets acquired.

Government sector surplus or **deficit**   An amount equal to net taxes minus government expenditure on goods and services.

Grant date   The day that options are granted to employees; usually the date that compensation expense is measured if both the number of shares and option price are known.

Greenmail   The purchase of the accumulated shares of a hostile investor by a company that is targeted for takeover by that investor, usually at a substantial premium over market price.

Gross domestic product   A money measure of the goods and services produced within a country's borders over a stated time period.

Gross income multiplier (GIM)   A ratio derived from the market; sales price divided by annual gross income equals GIM.

Gross profit (gross margin)   Sales minus the cost of sales (i.e., the cost of goods sold for a manufacturing company).

Gross profit margin   The ratio of gross profit to revenues.

Grouping by function   With reference to the presentation of expenses in an income statement, the grouping together of expenses serving the same function, e.g., all items that are costs of good sold.

Grouping by nature   With reference to the presentation of expenses in an income statement, the grouping together of expenses by similar nature, e.g., all depreciation expenses.

Growth accounting   A tool that calculates the contribution to real GDP growth of each of its sources.

Growth investors   With reference to equity investors, investors who seek to invest in high-earnings-growth companies.

Growth option or **expansion option**   The ability to make additional investments in a project at some future time if the financial results are strong.

Growth phase   A stage of growth in which a company typically enjoys rapidly expanding markets, high profit margins, and an abnormally high growth rate in earnings per share.

Guideline public companies   Public-company comparables for the company being valued.

Guideline public company method   A variation of the market approach; establishes a value estimate based on the observed multiples from trading activity in the shares of public companies viewed as reasonably comparable to the subject private company.

Guideline transactions method   A variation of the market approach; establishes a value estimate based on pricing multiples derived from the acquisition of control of entire public or private companies that were acquired.

Harmonic mean   A type of weighted mean computed by averaging the reciprocals of the observations, then taking the reciprocal of that average.

Hedge ratio   The relationship of the quantity of an asset being hedged to the quantity of the derivative used for hedging.

Hedging   A general strategy usually thought of as reducing, if not eliminating, risk.

Held-for-trading securities (trading securities)   Debt or equity financial assets bought with the intention to sell them in the near term, usually less than three months; securities that a company intends to trade.

Held-to-maturity investments   Debt (fixed-income) securities that a company intends to hold to maturity; these are presented at their original cost, updated for any amortization of discounts or premiums.

Herfindahl–Hirschman Index   A measure of market concentration that is calculated by summing the squared market shares for competing companies in an industry; high HHI readings or mergers that would result in large HHI increases are more likely to result in regulatory challenges.

Heteroskedastic   With reference to the error term of a regression, having a variance that differs across observations.

Heteroskedasticity   The property of having a nonconstant variance; refers to an error term with the property that its variance differs across observations.

Heteroskedasticity-consistent standard errors   Standard errors of the estimated parameters of a regression that correct for the presence of heteroskedasticity in the regression's error term.

Histogram   A bar chart of data that have been grouped into a frequency distribution.

Historical cost   In reference to assets, the amount paid to purchase an asset, including any costs of acquisition and/or preparation; with reference to liabilities, the amount of proceeds received in exchange in issuing the liability.

Historical equity risk premium approach   An estimate of a country's equity risk premium that is based upon the historical averages of the risk-free rate and the rate of return on the market portfolio.

Historical exchange rates   For accounting purposes, the exchange rates that existed when the assets and liabilities were initially recorded.

Historical method   A method of estimating VAR that uses data from the returns of the portfolio over a recent past period and compiles this data in the form of a histogram.

Historical simulation (or **back simulation**) Another term for the historical method of estimating VAR. This term is somewhat misleading in that the method involves not a *simulation* of the past but rather what *actually happened* in the past, sometimes adjusted to reflect the fact that a different portfolio may have existed in the past than is planned for the future.

Holder-of-record date The date that a shareholder listed on the corporation's books will be deemed to have ownership of the shares for purposes of receiving an upcoming dividend; two business days after the ex-dividend date.

Holding period return The return that an investor earns during a specified holding period; a synonym for total return.

Holding period yield (HPY) The return that an investor earns during a specified holding period; holding period return with reference to a fixed-income instrument.

Homogenization Creating a contract with standard and generally accepted terms, which makes it more acceptable to a broader group of participants.

Homoskedasticity The property of having a constant variance; refers to an error term that is constant across observations.

Horizontal analysis Common-size analysis that involves comparing a specific financial statement with that statement in prior or future time periods; also, cross-sectional analysis of one company with another.

Horizontal common-size analysis A form of common-size analysis in which the accounts in a given period are used as the benchmark or base period, and every account is restated in subsequent periods as a percentage of the base period's same account.

Horizontal merger A merger involving companies in the same line of business, usually as competitors.

Hostile transaction An attempt to acquire a company against the wishes of the target's managers.

Human capital The value of skills and knowledge possessed by the workforce.

Hurdle rate The rate of return that must be met for a project to be accepted.

Hypothesis With reference to statistical inference, a statement about one or more populations.

Hypothesis testing With reference to statistical inference, the subdivision dealing with the testing of hypotheses about one or more populations.

Identifiable intangible An intangible that can be acquired singly and is typically linked to specific rights or privileges having finite benefit periods (e.g., a patent or trademark).

If-converted method A method for accounting for the effect of convertible securities on earnings per share (EPS) that specifies what EPS would have been if the convertible securities had been converted at the beginning of the period, taking account of the effects of conversion on net income and the weighted average number of shares outstanding.

Illiquidity discount See *Liquidity discount.*

Impairment Diminishment in value as a result of carrying (book) value exceeding fair value and/or recoverable value.

Impairment of capital rule A legal restriction that dividends cannot exceed retained earnings.

Implied repo rate The rate of return from a cash-and-carry transaction implied by the futures price relative to the spot price.

Implied volatility The volatility that option traders use to price an option, implied by the price of the option and a particular option-pricing model.

Implied yield A measure of the yield on the underlying bond of a futures contract implied by pricing it as though the underlying will be delivered at the futures expiration.

Imports The goods and services that we buy from people in other countries.

Imputation In reference to corporate taxes, a system that imputes, or attributes, taxes at only one level of taxation. For countries using an imputation tax system, taxes on dividends are effectively levied only at the shareholder rate. Taxes are paid at the corporate level but they are *attributed* to the shareholder. Shareholders deduct from their tax bill their portion of taxes paid by the company.

Income Increases in economic benefits in the form of inflows or enhancements of assets, or decreases of liabilities that result in an increase in equity (other than increases resulting from contributions by owners).

Income approach Valuation approach that values an asset as the present discounted value of the income expected from it.

Income statement (**statement of operations** or **profit and loss statement**) A financial statement that provides information about a company's profitability over a stated period of time.

Income tax paid The actual amount paid for income taxes in the period; not a provision, but the actual cash outflow.

Income tax payable The income tax owed by the company on the basis of taxable income.

Income tax recoverable The income tax expected to be recovered, from the taxing authority, on the basis of taxable income. It is a recovery of previously remitted taxes or future taxes owed by the company.

Incremental cash flow The cash flow that is realized because of a decision; the changes or increments to cash flows resulting from a decision or action.

Indenture A written contract between a lender and borrower that specifies the terms of the loan, such as interest rate, interest payment schedule, maturity, etc.

Independent With reference to events, the property that the occurrence of one event does not affect the probability of another event occurring.

Independent and identically distributed (IID) With respect to random variables, the property of random variables that are independent of each other but follow the identical probability distribution.

Independent projects Independent projects are projects whose cash flows are independent of each other.

Independent variable A variable used to explain the dependent variable in a regression; a right-hand-side variable in a regression equation.

Index amortizing swap An interest rate swap in which the notional principal is indexed to the level of interest rates and declines with the level of interest rates according to a predefined schedule. This type of swap is frequently used to hedge securities that are prepaid as interest rates decline, such as mortgage-backed securities.

Index option An option in which the underlying is a stock index.

Indexing An investment strategy in which an investor constructs a portfolio to mirror the performance of a specified index.

Indirect format (indirect method) With reference to cash flow statements, a format for the presentation of the statement which, in the operating cash flow section, begins with net income then shows additions and subtractions to arrive at operating cash flow.

Industry structure An industry's underlying economic and technical characteristics.

Infant-industry argument The argument that it is necessary to protect a new industry to enable it to grow into a mature industry that can compete in world markets.

Inflation premium An extra return that compensates investors for expected inflation.

Information ratio (IR) Mean active return divided by active risk; or alpha divided by the standard deviation of diversifiable risk.

Initial margin requirement The margin requirement on the first day of a transaction as well as on any day in which additional margin funds must be deposited.

Initial public offering (IPO) The initial issuance of common stock registered for public trading by a formerly private corporation.

In-process research and development Research and development costs relating to projects that are not yet completed, such as have been incurred by a company that is being acquired.

In-sample forecast errors The residuals from a fitted time-series model within the sample period used to fit the model.

Instability in the minimum-variance frontier The characteristic of minimum-variance frontiers that they are sensitive to small changes in inputs.

Installment Said of a sale in which proceeds are to be paid in installments over an extended period of time.

Installment method (installment-sales method) With respect to revenue recognition, a method that specifies that the portion of the total profit of the sale that is recognized in each period is determined by the percentage of the total sales price for which the seller has received cash.

Intangible assets Assets lacking physical substance, such as patents and trademarks.

Interest coverage A solvency ratio calculated as EBIT divided by interest payments.

Interest rate A rate of return that reflects the relationship between differently dated cash flows; a discount rate.

Interest rate call An option in which the holder has the right to make a known interest payment and receive an unknown interest payment.

Interest rate cap or **cap** A series of call options on an interest rate, with each option expiring at the date on which the floating loan rate will be reset, and with each option having the same exercise rate. A cap in general can have an underlying other than an interest rate.

Interest rate collar A combination of a long cap and a short floor, or a short cap and a long floor. A collar in general can have an underlying other than an interest rate.

Interest rate floor or **floor** A series of put options on an interest rate, with each option expiring at the date on which the floating loan rate will be reset, and with each option having the same exercise rate. A floor in general can have an underlying other than the interest rate.

Interest rate forward See *Forward rate agreement*.

Interest rate option An option in which the underlying is an interest rate.

Interest rate parity A formula that expresses the equivalence or parity of spot and forward rates, after adjusting for differences in the interest rates.

Interest rate put An option in which the holder has the right to make an unknown interest payment and receive a known interest payment.

Interest rate swap A swap in which the underlying is an interest rate. Can be viewed as a currency swap in which both currencies are the same and can be created as a combination of currency swaps.

Intergenerational data mining A form of data mining that applies information developed by previous researchers using a dataset to guide current research using the same or a related dataset.

Internal rate of return (IRR) Rate of return that discounts future cash flows from an investment to the exact amount of the investment; the discount rate that makes the present value of an investment's costs (outflows) equal to the present value of the investment's benefits (inflows).

Interquartile range The difference between the third and first quartiles of a dataset.

Interval With reference to grouped data, a set of values within which an observation falls.

Interval scale A measurement scale that not only ranks data but also gives assurance that the differences between scale values are equal.

In-the-money Options that, if exercised, would result in the value received being worth more than the payment required to exercise.

Intrinsic value or **exercise value** The value of an asset given a hypothetically complete understanding of the asset's investment characteristics; the value obtained if an option is exercised based on current conditions.

Inventory The unsold units of product on hand.

Inventory blanket lien The use of inventory as collateral for a loan. Though the lender has claim to some or all of the company's inventory, the company may still sell or use the inventory in the ordinary course of business.

Inventory turnover An activity ratio calculated as cost of goods sold divided by average inventory.

Inverse floater A floating-rate note or bond in which the coupon is adjusted to move opposite to a benchmark interest rate.

Inverse price ratio The reciprocal of a price multiple, e.g., in the case of a P/E ratio, the "earnings yield" E/P (where P is share price and E is earnings per share).

Investing activities Activities which are associated with the acquisition and disposal of property, plant, and equipment; intangible assets; other long-term assets; and both long-term and short-term investments in the equity and debt (bonds and loans) issued by other companies.

Investment constraints Internal or external limitations on investments.

Investment objectives Desired investment outcomes; includes risk objectives and return objectives.

Investment opportunity schedule A graphical depiction of a company's investment opportunities ordered from highest to lowest expected return. A company's optimal capital budget is found where the investment opportunity schedule intersects with the company's marginal cost of capital.

Investment strategy An approach to investment analysis and security selection.

Investment value The value to a specific buyer, taking account of potential synergies based on the investor's requirements and expectations.

IRR rule An investment decision rule that accepts projects or investments for which the IRR is greater than the opportunity cost of capital.

Joint probability The probability of the joint occurrence of stated events.

Joint probability function A function giving the probability of joint occurrences of values of stated random variables.

Joint venture An entity (partnership, corporation, or other legal form) where control is shared by two or more entities called venturers.

Justified (fundamental) P/E The price-to-earnings ratio that is fair, warranted, or justified on the basis of forecasted fundamentals.

Justified price multiple (or **warranted price multiple** or **intrinsic price multiple**) The estimated fair value of the price multiple, usually based on forecasted fundamentals or comparables.

Just-in-time method Method of managing inventory that minimizes in-process inventory stocks.

kth order autocorrelation The correlation between observations in a time series separated by k periods.

Kurtosis The statistical measure that indicates the peakedness of a distribution.

Labor productivity The quantity of real GDP produced by an hour of labor.

Lack of marketability discount An extra return to investors to compensate for lack of a public market or lack of marketability.

Laddering strategy A form of active strategy which entails scheduling maturities on a systematic basis within the investment portfolio such that investments are spread out equally over the term of the ladder.

Last-in, first-out (LIFO) The last in, first out, method of accounting for inventory, which matches sales against the costs of items of inventory in the reverse order the items were placed in inventory (i.e., inventory produced or acquired last are assumed to be sold first).

Law of one price The condition in a financial market in which two equivalent financial instruments or combinations of financial instruments can sell for only one price. Equivalent to the principle that no arbitrage opportunities are possible.

Leading dividend yield Forecasted dividends per share over the next year divided by current stock price.

Leading P/E (or **forward P/E** or **prospective P/E**) A stock's current price divided by the next year's expected earnings.

Legal risk The risk that failures by company managers to effectively manage a company's environmental, social, and governance risk exposures will lead to lawsuits and other judicial remedies, resulting in potentially catastrophic losses for the company; the risk that the legal system will not enforce a contract in case of dispute or fraud.

Legislative and regulatory risk The risk that governmental laws and regulations directly or indirectly affecting a company's operations will change with potentially severe adverse effects on the company's continued profitability and even its long-term sustainability.

Lemons problem The potential for asymmetric information to bring about a general decline in product quality in an industry.

Leptokurtic Describes a distribution that is more peaked than a normal distribution.

Lessee The party obtaining the use of an asset through a lease.

Lessor The owner of an asset that grants the right to use the asset to another party.

Level of significance The probability of a Type I error in testing a hypothesis.

Leverage In the context of corporate finance, leverage refers to the use of fixed costs within a company's cost structure. Fixed costs that are operating costs (such as depreciation or rent) create operating leverage. Fixed costs that are financial costs (such as interest expense) create financial leverage.

Leveraged buyout (LBO) A transaction whereby the target company management team converts the target to a privately held company by using heavy borrowing to finance the purchase of the target company's outstanding shares.

Leveraged floating-rate note or **leveraged floater** A floating-rate note or bond in which the coupon is adjusted at a multiple of a benchmark interest rate.

Leveraged recapitalization A post-offer takeover defense mechanism that involves the assumption of a large amount of debt that is then used to finance share repurchases; the effect is to dramatically change the company's capital structure while attempting to deliver a value to target shareholders in excess of a hostile bid.

Liabilities Present obligations of an enterprise arising from past events, the settlement of which is expected to result in an outflow of resources embodying economic benefits; creditors' claims on the resources of a company.

LIFO layer liquidation (LIFO liquidation) With respect to the application of the LIFO inventory method, the liquidation of old, relatively low-priced inventory; happens when the volume of sales rises above the volume of recent purchases so that some sales are made from relatively old, low-priced inventory.

LIFO reserve The difference between inventory reported as FIFO and inventory reported as LIFO (FIFO inventory value less LIFO inventory value).

Likelihood The probability of an observation, given a particular set of conditions.

Limit down A limit move in the futures market in which the price at which a transaction would be made is at or below the lower limit.

Limit move A condition in the futures markets in which the price at which a transaction would be made is at or beyond the price limits.

Limit up A limit move in the futures market in which the price at which a transaction would be made is at or above the upper limit.

Linear association A straight-line relationship, as opposed to a relationship that cannot be graphed as a straight line.

Linear interpolation The estimation of an unknown value on the basis of two known values that bracket it, using a straight line between the two known values.

Linear regression Regression that models the straight-line relationship between the dependent and independent variable(s).

Linear trend A trend in which the dependent variable changes at a constant rate with time.

Liquidation To sell the assets of a company, division, or subsidiary piecemeal, typically because of bankruptcy; the form of bankruptcy that allows for the orderly satisfaction of creditors' claims after which the company ceases to exist.

Liquidation value The value of a company if the company were dissolved and its assets sold individually.

Liquidity A company's ability to satisfy its short-term obligations using assets that are most readily converted into cash; the ability to trade a futures contract, either selling a previously purchased contract or purchasing a previously sold contract.

Liquidity discount A reduction or discount to value that reflects the lack of depth of trading or liquidity in that asset's market.

Liquidity premium An extra return that compensates investors for the risk of loss relative to an investment's fair value if the investment needs to be converted to cash quickly.

Liquidity ratios Financial ratios measuring the company's ability to meet its short-term obligations.

Liquidity risk The risk that a financial instrument cannot be purchased or sold without a significant concession in price due to the size of the market.

Local currency The currency of the country where a company is located.

Lockbox system A payment system in which customer payments are mailed to a post office box and the banking institution retrieves and deposits these payments several times a day, enabling the company to have use of the fund sooner than in a centralized system in which customer payments are sent to the company.

Locked limit A condition in the futures markets in which a transaction cannot take place because the price would be beyond the limits.

Logit model   A qualitative-dependent-variable multiple regression model based on the logistic probability distribution.

Log-linear model   With reference to time-series models, a model in which the growth rate of the time series as a function of time is constant.

Log-log regression model   A regression that expresses the dependent and independent variables as natural logarithms.

London Interbank Offer Rate (LIBOR)   The Eurodollar rate at which London banks lend dollars to other London banks; considered to be the best representative rate on a dollar borrowed by a private, high-quality borrower.

Long   The buyer of a derivative contract. Also refers to the position of owning a derivative.

Longitudinal data   Observations on characteristic(s) of the same observational unit through time.

Long-lived assets (or **long-term assets**)   Assets that are expected to provide economic benefits over a future period of time, typically greater than one year.

Long-term contract   A contract that spans a number of accounting periods.

Long-term debt-to-assets ratio   The proportion of a company's assets that is financed with long-term debt.

Long-term equity anticipatory securities (LEAPS)   Options originally created with expirations of several years.

Long-term liability   An obligation that is expected to be settled, with the outflow of resources embodying economic benefits, over a future period generally greater than one year.

Look-ahead bias   A bias caused by using information that was not available on the test date.

Losses   Asset outflows not directly related to the ordinary activities of the business.

Lower bound   The lowest possible value of an option.

Macaulay duration   The duration without dividing by 1 plus the bond's yield to maturity. The term, named for one of the economists who first derived it, is used to distinguish the calculation from modified duration. (See also *modified duration*.)

Macroeconomic factor   A factor related to the economy, such as the inflation rate, industrial production, or economic sector membership.

Macroeconomic factor model   A multifactor model in which the factors are surprises in macroeconomic variables that significantly explain equity returns.

Maintenance margin requirement   The margin requirement on any day other than the first day of a transaction.

Management buyout (MBO)   A corporate transaction in which management repurchases all outstanding common stock, usually using the proceeds of debt issuance.

Managerialism theories   Theories that posit that corporate executives are motivated to engage in mergers to maximize the size of their company rather than shareholder value.

Manufacturing resource planning (MRP)   The incorporation of production planning into inventory management. A MRP analysis provides both a materials acquisition schedule and a production schedule.

Margin   The amount of money that a trader deposits in a margin account. The term is derived from the stock market practice in which an investor borrows a portion of the money required to purchase a certain amount of stock. In futures markets, there is no borrowing so the margin is more of a down payment or performance bond.

Marginal investor   An investor in a given share who is very likely to be part of the next trade in the share and who is therefore important in setting price.

Market approach   Valuation approach that values an asset based on pricing multiples from sales of assets viewed as similar to the subject asset.

Market efficiency   A finance perspective on capital markets that deals with the relationship of price to intrinsic value. The **traditional efficient markets formulation** asserts that an asset's price is the best available estimate of its intrinsic value. The **rational efficient markets formulation** asserts that investors should expect to be rewarded for the costs of information gathering and analysis by higher gross returns.

Market-extraction method   Method used to estimate the overall capitalization rate by dividing the sale price of a comparable income property into the net operating income.

Market price of risk   The slope of the capital market line, indicating the market risk premium for each unit of market risk.

Market rate   The rate demanded by purchasers of bonds, given the risks associated with future cash payment obligations of the particular bond issue.

Market risk   The risk associated with interest rates, exchange rates, and equity prices.

Market risk premium   The expected excess return on the market over the risk-free rate.

Market share test   The percentage of a market that a particular firm supplies; used as the primary measure of monopoly power.

Market timing   Asset allocation in which the investment in the market is increased if one forecasts that the market will outperform T-bills.

Market value of invested capital   The market value of debt and equity.

Marketability discount   A reduction or discount to value for shares that are not publicly traded.

Market-oriented investors   With reference to equity investors, investors whose investment disciplines cannot be clearly categorized as value or growth.

Marking to market   A procedure used primarily in futures markets in which the parties to a contract settle the amount owed daily. Also known as the *daily settlement*.

Markowitz decision rule   A decision rule for choosing between two investments based on their means and variances.

Mark-to-market   The revaluation of a financial asset or liability to its current market value or fair value.

Matching principle   The accounting principle that expenses should be recognized when the associated revenue is recognized.

Matching strategy   An active investment strategy that includes intentional matching of the timing of cash outflows with investment maturities.

Materiality   The condition of being of sufficient importance so that omission or misstatement of the item in a financial report could make a difference to users' decisions.

Matrix pricing   In the fixed income markets, to price a security on the basis of valuation-relevant characteristics (e.g., debt-rating approach).

Mature growth rate   The earnings growth rate in a company's mature phase; an earnings growth rate that can be sustained long term.

Mature phase   A stage of growth in which the company reaches an equilibrium in which investment opportunities on average just earn their opportunity cost of capital.

Maturity premium   An extra return that compensates investors for the increased sensitivity of the market value of debt to a change in market interest rates as maturity is extended.

Mean   The sum of all values in a distribution or dataset, divided by the number of values summed; a synonym of arithmetic mean.

Mean absolute deviation   With reference to a sample, the mean of the absolute values of deviations from the sample mean.

Mean excess return   The average rate of return in excess of the risk-free rate.

Mean reversion   The tendency of a time series to fall when its level is above its mean and rise when its level is below its mean; a mean-reverting time series tends to return to its long-term mean.

Mean–variance analysis   An approach to portfolio analysis using expected means, variances, and covariances of asset returns.

Measure of central tendency   A quantitative measure that specifies where data are centered.

Measure of location   A quantitative measure that describes the location or distribution of data; includes not only measures of central tendency but also other measures such as percentiles.

Measurement scales   A scheme of measuring differences. The four types of measurement scales are nominal, ordinal, interval, and ratio.

Median   The value of the middle item of a set of items that has been sorted into ascending or descending order; the 50th percentile.

Merger   The absorption of one company by another; two companies become one entity and one or both of the pre-merger companies ceases to exist as a separate entity.

Mesokurtic   Describes a distribution with kurtosis identical to that of the normal distribution.

Method based on forecasted fundamentals   An approach to using price multiples that relates a price multiple to forecasts of fundamentals through a discounted cash flow model.

Method of comparables   An approach to valuation that involves using a price multiple to evaluate whether an asset is relatively fairly valued, relatively undervalued, or relatively overvalued when compared to a benchmark value of the multiple.

Minimum-variance frontier   The graph of the set of portfolios that have minimum variance for their level of expected return.

Minimum-variance portfolio   The portfolio with the minimum variance for each given level of expected return.

Minority active investments   Investments in which investors exert significant influence, but not control, over the investee. Typically, the investor has 20 to 50% ownership in the investee.

Minority interest (noncontrolling interest)   The proportion of the ownership of a subsidiary not held by the parent (controlling) company.

Minority passive investments (passive investments)   Investments in which the investor has no significant influence or control over the operations of the investee.

Mismatching strategy   An active investment strategy whereby the timing of cash outflows is not matched with investment maturities.

Mispricing   Any departure of the market price of an asset from the asset's estimated intrinsic value.

Mixed factor models   Factor models that combine features of more than one type of factor model.

Mixed offering   A merger or acquisition that is to be paid for with cash, securities, or some combination of the two.

Modal interval   With reference to grouped data, the most frequently occurring interval.

Mode   The most frequently occurring value in a set of observations.

Model risk   The use of an inaccurate pricing model for a particular investment, or the improper use of the right model.

Model specification   With reference to regression, the set of variables included in the regression and the regression equation's functional form.

Modified duration   A measure of a bond's price sensitivity to interest rate movements. Equal to the Macaulay duration of a bond divided by one plus its yield to maturity.

Molodovsky effect   The observation that P/Es tend to be high on depressed EPS at the bottom of a business cycle, and tend to be low on unusually high EPS at the top of a business cycle.

Momentum indicators   Valuation indicators that relate either price or a fundamental (such as earnings) to the time series of their own past values (or in some cases to their expected value).

Monetary assets and liabilities   Assets and liabilities with value equal to the amount of currency contracted for, a fixed amount of currency. Examples are cash, accounts receivable, mortgages receivable, accounts payable, bonds payable, and mortgages payable. Inventory is not a monetary asset. Most liabilities are monetary.

Monetary/nonmonetary method   Approach to translating foreign currency financial statements for consolidation in which monetary assets and liabilities are translated at the current exchange rate. Nonmonetary assets and liabilities are translated at historical exchange rates (the exchange rates that existed when the assets and liabilities were acquired).

Money market   The market for short-term debt instruments (one-year maturity or less).

Money market yield (or CD equivalent yield)   A yield on a basis comparable to the quoted yield on an interest-bearing money market instrument that pays interest on a 360-day basis; the annualized holding period yield, assuming a 360-day year.

Moneyness   The relationship between the price of the underlying and an option's exercise price.

Money-weighted rate of return   The internal rate of return on a portfolio, taking account of all cash flows.

Monitoring costs   Costs borne by owners to monitor the management of the company (e.g., board of director expenses).

Monopolization   The possession of monopoly power in the relevant market and the willful acquisition or maintenance of that power, as distinguished from growth or development as a consequence of a superior product, business acumen, or historical accident.

Monte Carlo simulation method   An approach to estimating a probability distribution of outcomes to examine what might happen if particular risks are faced. This method is widely used in the sciences as well as in business to study a variety of problems.

Multicollinearity   A regression assumption violation that occurs when two or more independent variables (or combinations of independent variables) are highly but not perfectly correlated with each other.

Multiple linear regression   Linear regression involving two or more independent variables.

Multiple linear regression model   A linear regression model with two or more independent variables.

Multiple R   The correlation between the actual and forecasted values of the dependent variable in a regression.

Multiplication rule for probabilities   The rule that the joint probability of events A and B equals the probability of A given B times the probability of B.

Multi-step format   With respect to the format of the income statement, a format that presents a subtotal for gross profit (revenue minus cost of goods sold).

Multivariate distribution   A probability distribution that specifies the probabilities for a group of related random variables.

Multivariate normal distribution   A probability distribution for a group of random variables that is completely defined by the means and variances of the variables plus all the correlations between pairs of the variables.

Mutually exclusive events   Events such that only one can occur at a time.

Mutually exclusive projects Mutually exclusive projects compete directly with each other. For example, if Projects A and B are mutually exclusive, you can choose A or B, but you cannot choose both.

***n* Factorial** For a positive integer *n*, the product of the first *n* positive integers; 0 factorial equals 1 by definition. *n* factorial is written as *n*!.

Negative serial correlation Serial correlation in which a positive error for one observation increases the chance of a negative error for another observation, and vice versa.

Neoclassical growth theory A theory of economic growth that proposes that real GDP per person grows because technological change induces a level of saving and investment that makes capital per hour of labor grow.

Net asset balance sheet exposure When assets translated at the current exchange rate are greater in amount than liabilities translated at the current exchange rate. Assets exposed to translation gains or losses exceed the exposed liabilities.

Net book value The remaining (undepreciated) balance of an asset's purchase cost. For liabilities, the face value of a bond minus any unamortized discount, or plus any unamortized premium.

Net borrower A country that is borrowing more from the rest of the world than it is lending to it.

Net exports The value of exports of goods and services minus the value of imports of goods and services.

Net income (loss) The difference between revenue and expenses; what remains after subtracting all expenses (including depreciation, interest, and taxes) from revenue.

Net lender A country that is lending more to the rest of the world than it is borrowing from it.

Net liability balance sheet exposure When liabilities translated at the current exchange rate are greater than assets translated at the current exchange rate. Liabilities exposed to translation gains or losses exceed the exposed assets.

Net operating assets The difference between operating assets (total assets less cash) and operating liabilities (total liabilities less total debt).

Net operating cycle An estimate of the average time that elapses between paying suppliers for materials and collecting cash from the subsequent sale of goods produced.

Net operating profit less adjusted taxes, or NOPLAT A company's operating profit with adjustments to normalize the effects of capital structure.

Net present value (NPV) The present value of an investment's cash inflows (benefits) minus the present value of its cash outflows (costs).

Net profit margin (profit margin or return on sales) An indicator of profitability, calculated as net income divided by revenue; indicates how much of each dollar of revenues is left after all costs and expenses.

Net realisable value Estimated selling price in the ordinary course of business less the estimated costs necessary to make the sale.

Net revenue Revenue after adjustments (e.g., for estimated returns or for amounts unlikely to be collected).

Netting When parties agree to exchange only the net amount owed from one party to the other.

New growth theory A theory of economic growth based on the idea that real GDP per person grows because of the choices that people make in the pursuit of profit and that growth can persist indefinitely.

Node Each value on a binomial tree from which successive moves or outcomes branch.

No-growth company A company without positive expected net present value projects.

No-growth value per share The value per share of a no-growth company, equal to the expected level amount of earnings divided by the stock's required rate of return.

Nominal exchange rate The value of the U.S. dollar expressed in units of foreign currency per U.S. dollar.

Nominal rate A rate of interest based on the security's face value.

Nominal risk-free interest rate The sum of the real risk-free interest rate and the inflation premium.

Nominal scale A measurement scale that categorizes data but does not rank them.

Nonconventional cash flow In a nonconventional cash flow pattern, the initial outflow is not followed by inflows only, but the cash flows can flip from positive (inflows) to negative (outflows) again (or even change signs several times).

Noncurrent Not due to be consumed, converted into cash, or settled within one year after the balance sheet date.

Noncurrent assets Assets that are expected to benefit the company over an extended period of time (usually more than one year).

Nondeliverable forwards (NDFs) Cash-settled forward contracts, used predominately with respect to foreign exchange forwards.

Nonearning assets Cash and investments (specifically cash, cash equivalents, and short-term investments).

Nonlinear relation An association or relationship between variables that cannot be graphed as a straight line.

Nonmonetary assets and liabilities Assets and liabilities that are not monetary assets and liabilities. Nonmonetary assets include inventory, fixed assets, and intangibles, and nonmonetary liabilities include deferred revenue.

Nonparametric test A test that is not concerned with a parameter, or that makes minimal assumptions about the population from which a sample comes.

Nonstationarity With reference to a random variable, the property of having characteristics such as mean and variance that are not constant through time.

Nontariff barrier Any action other than a tariff that restricts international trade.

Normal backwardation The condition in futures markets in which futures prices are lower than expected spot prices.

Normal contango The condition in futures markets in which futures prices are higher than expected spot prices.

Normal distribution A continuous, symmetric probability distribution that is completely described by its mean and its variance.

Normalized earnings Earnings adjusted for nonrecurring, noneconomic, or other unusual items to eliminate anomalies and/or facilitate comparisons.

Normalized earnings per share (or normal earnings per share) The earnings per share that a business could achieve currently under mid-cyclical conditions.

Normalized P/E P/Es based on normalized EPS data.

North American Free Trade Agreement An agreement, which became effective on January 1, 1994, to eliminate all barriers to international trade between the United States, Canada, and Mexico after a 15-year phasing-in period.

Notes payable Amounts owed by a business to creditors as a result of borrowings that are evidenced by (short-term) loan agreements.

***n*-Period moving average** The average of the current and immediately prior *n* − 1 values of a time series.

NPV rule An investment decision rule that states that an investment should be undertaken if its NPV is positive but not undertaken if its NPV is negative.

NTM P/E   Next twelve months P/E: current market price divided by an estimated next twelve months EPS.

Null hypothesis   The hypothesis to be tested.

Number of days of inventory   An activity ratio equal to the number of days in a period divided by the inventory ratio for the period; an indication of the number of days a company ties up funds in inventory.

Number of days of payables   An activity ratio equal to the number of days in a period divided by the payables turnover ratio for the period; an estimate of the average number of days it takes a company to pay its suppliers.

Number of days of receivables   Estimate of the average number of days it takes to collect on credit accounts.

Objective probabilities   Probabilities that generally do not vary from person to person; includes a priori and objective probabilities.

Off-balance sheet financing   Arrangements that do not result in additional liabilities on the balance sheet but nonetheless create economic obligations.

Official settlements account   A record of the change in official reserves, which are the government's holdings of foreign currency.

Off-market FRA   A contract in which the initial value is intentionally set at a value other than zero and therefore requires a cash payment at the start from one party to the other.

Offsetting   A transaction in exchange-listed derivative markets in which a party re-enters the market to close out a position.

One third rule   The rule that, on the average, with no change in technology, a 1 percent increase in capital per hour of labor brings a 1/3 percent increase in labor productivity.

One-sided hypothesis test (or **one-tailed hypothesis test**)   A test in which the null hypothesis is rejected only if the evidence indicates that the population parameter is greater than (smaller than) θ_0. The alternative hypothesis also has one side.

Operating activities   Activities that are part of the day-to-day business functioning of an entity, such as selling inventory and providing services.

Operating breakeven   The number of units produced and sold at which the company's operating profit is zero (revenues = operating costs).

Operating cycle   A measure of the time needed to convert raw materials into cash from a sale; it consists of the number of days of inventory and the number of days of receivables.

Operating lease   An agreement allowing the lessee to use some asset for a period of time; essentially a rental.

Operating leverage   The use of fixed costs in operations.

Operating profit (operating income)   A company's profits on its usual business activities before deducting taxes.

Operating profit margin (operating margin)   A profitability ratio calculated as operating income (i.e., income before interest and taxes) divided by revenue.

Operating return on assets (operating ROA)   A profitability ratio calculated as operating income divided by average total assets.

Operating risk   The risk attributed to the operating cost structure, in particular the use of fixed costs in operations; the risk arising from the mix of fixed and variable costs; the risk that a company's operations may be severely affected by environmental, social, and governance risk factors.

Operations risk or **operational risk**   The risk of loss from failures in a company's systems and procedures (for example, due to computer failures or human failures) or events completely outside of the control of organizations (which would include "acts of God" and terrorist actions).

Opportunity cost   The value that investors forgo by choosing a particular course of action; the value of something in its best alternative use.

Opportunity set   The set of assets available for investment.

Optimal capital structure   The capital structure at which the value of the company is maximized.

Optimizer   A specialized computer program or a spreadsheet that solves for the portfolio weights that will result in the lowest risk for a specified level of expected return.

Option   A financial instrument that gives one party the right, but not the obligation, to buy or sell an underlying asset from or to another party at a fixed price over a specific period of time. Also referred to as contingent claims.

Option price, option premium, or **premium**   The amount of money a buyer pays and seller receives to engage in an option transaction.

Orderly liquidation value   The estimated gross amount of money that could be realized from the liquidation sale of an asset or assets, given a reasonable amount of time to find a purchaser or purchasers.

Ordinal scale   A measurement scale that sorts data into categories that are ordered (ranked) with respect to some characteristic.

Ordinary annuity   An annuity with a first cash flow that is paid one period from the present.

Ordinary least squares (OLS)   An estimation method based on the criterion of minimizing the sum of the squared residuals of a regression.

Ordinary shares (common stock or **common shares)**   Equity shares that are subordinate to all other types of equity (e.g., preferred equity).

Organic growth   Company growth in output or sales that is achieved by making investments internally (i.e., excludes growth achieved through mergers and acquisitions).

Orthogonal   Uncorrelated; at a right angle.

Other comprehensive income   Changes to equity that bypass (are not reported in) the income statement; the difference between comprehensive income and net income.

Other post-employment benefits   Promises by the company to pay benefits in the future, other than pension benefits, such as life insurance premiums and all or part of health care insurance for its retirees.

Other receivables   Amounts owed to the company from parties other than customers.

Outcome   A possible value of a random variable.

Outliers   Small numbers of observations at either extreme (small or large) of a sample.

Out-of-sample forecast errors   The differences between actual and predicted value of time series outside the sample period used to fit the model.

Out-of-sample test   A test of a strategy or model using a sample outside the time period on which the strategy or model was developed.

Out-of-the-money   Options that, if exercised, would require the payment of more money than the value received and therefore would not be currently exercised.

Overall capitalization rate   A ratio in property valuation; net operating income divided by sale price. Also known as the going-in rate.

Overnight index swap (OIS)   A swap in which the floating rate is the cumulative value of a single unit of currency invested at an overnight rate during the settlement period.

Owners' equity   The excess of assets over liabilities; the residual interest of shareholders in the assets of an entity after deducting the entity's liabilities.

Paired comparisons test   A statistical test for differences based on paired observations drawn from samples that are dependent on each other.

Paired observations   Observations that are dependent on each other.

Pairs arbitrage   A trade in two closely related stocks that involves buying the relatively undervalued stock and selling short the relatively overvalued stock.

Pairs arbitrage trade   A trade in two closely related stocks involving the short sale of one and the purchase of the other.

Pairs trading   An approach to trading that uses pairs of closely related stocks, buying the relatively undervalued stock and selling short the relatively overvalued stock.

Panel data   Observations through time on a single characteristic of multiple observational units.

Parameter   A descriptive measure computed from or used to describe a population of data, conventionally represented by Greek letters.

Parameter instability   The problem or issue of population regression parameters that have changed over time.

Parametric test   Any test (or procedure) concerned with parameters or whose validity depends on assumptions concerning the population generating the sample.

Partial regression coefficients or **partial slope coefficients**   The slope coefficients in a multiple regression.

Partnership   A business owned and operated by more than one individual.

Passive portfolio   A market index portfolio.

Passive strategy   In reference to short-term cash management, it is an investment strategy characterized by simple decision rules for making daily investments.

Payables turnover   An activity ratio calculated as purchases divided by average trade payables.

Payer swaption   A swaption that allows the holder to enter into a swap as the fixed-rate payer and floating-rate receiver.

Payment date   The day that the company actually mails out (or electronically transfers) a dividend payment.

Payment netting   A means of settling payments in which the amount owed by the first party to the second is netted with the amount owed by the second party to the first; only the net difference is paid.

Payoff   The value of an option at expiration.

Payout policy   The principles by which a company distributes cash to common shareholders by means of cash dividends and/or share repurchases.

Payout ratio   The percentage of total earnings paid out in dividends in any given year (in per-share terms, DPS/EPS).

Pecking order theory   The theory that managers take into account how their actions might be interpreted by outsiders and thus order their preferences for various forms of corporate financing. Forms of financing that are least visible to outsiders (e.g., internally generated funds) are most preferable to managers and those that are most visible (e.g., equity) are least preferable.

PEG   The P/E-to-growth ratio, calculated as the stock's P/E divided by the expected earnings growth rate.

PEG ratio   The ratio of P/E-to-growth, calculated as the stock's P/E divided by the expected earnings growth rate in percent.

Pension obligation   The present value of future benefits earned by employees for service provided to date. Under IFRS it is defined as "the present value, without deducting any plan assets, of expected future payments required to settle the obligation arising from employee service in the current and prior periods."

Per unit contribution margin   The amount that each unit sold contributes to covering fixed costs—that is, the difference between the price per unit and the variable cost per unit.

Percentage-of-completion   A method of revenue recognition in which, in each accounting period, the company estimates what percentage of the contract is complete and then reports that percentage of the total contract revenue in its income statement.

Percentiles   Quantiles that divide a distribution into 100 equal parts.

Perfect capital markets   Markets in which, by assumption, there are no taxes, transactions costs, or bankruptcy costs, and in which all investors have equal ("symmetric") information.

Perfect collinearity   The existence of an exact linear relation between two or more independent variables or combinations of independent variables.

Performance appraisal   The evaluation of risk-adjusted performance; the evaluation of investment skill.

Performance guarantee   A guarantee from the clearinghouse that if one party makes money on a transaction, the clearinghouse ensures it will be paid.

Performance measurement   The calculation of returns in a logical and consistent manner.

Period costs   Costs (e.g., executives' salaries) that cannot be directly matched with the timing of revenues and which are thus expensed immediately.

Periodic inventory system   An inventory accounting system in which inventory values and costs of sales are determined at the end of the accounting period.

Periodic rate   The quoted interest rate per period; the stated annual interest rate divided by the number of compounding periods per year.

Permanent differences   Differences between tax and financial reporting of revenue (expenses) that will not be reversed at some future date. These result in a difference between the company's effective tax rate and statutory tax rate and do not result in a deferred tax item.

Permutation   An ordered listing.

Perpetual inventory system   An inventory accounting system in which inventory values and costs of sales are continuously updated to reflect purchases and sales.

Perpetuity   A perpetual annuity, or a set of never-ending level sequential cash flows, with the first cash flow occurring one period from now.

Pet projects   Projects in which influential managers want the corporation to invest. Often, unfortunately, pet projects are selected without undergoing normal capital budgeting analysis.

Plain vanilla swap   An interest rate swap in which one party pays a fixed rate and the other pays a floating rate, with both sets of payments in the same currency.

Platykurtic   Describes a distribution that is less peaked than the normal distribution.

Point estimate   A single numerical estimate of an unknown quantity, such as a population parameter.

Point of sale   Systems that capture transaction data at the physical location in which the sale is made.

Poison pill   A pre-offer takeover defense mechanism that makes it prohibitively costly for an acquirer to take control of a target without the prior approval of the target's board of directors.

Poison puts   A pre-offer takeover defense mechanism that gives target company bondholders the right to sell their bonds back to the target at a pre-specified redemption price, typically at or above par value; this defense increases the need for cash and raises the cost of the acquisition.

Pooled estimate   An estimate of a parameter that involves combining (pooling) observations from two or more samples.

Pooling of interests accounting method   A method of accounting in which combined companies were portrayed as if they had always operated as a single economic entity. Called pooling of interests under U.S. GAAP and uniting of interests under IFRS. (No longer allowed under U.S. GAAP or IFRS.)

Population   All members of a specified group.

Population mean   The arithmetic mean value of a population; the arithmetic mean of all the observations or values in the population.

Population standard deviation   A measure of dispersion relating to a population in the same unit of measurement as the observations, calculated as the positive square root of the population variance.

Population variance   A measure of dispersion relating to a population, calculated as the mean of the squared deviations around the population mean.

Portfolio implementation problem   The part of the execution step of the portfolio management process that involves the implementation of portfolio decisions by trading desks.

Portfolio performance attribution   The analysis of portfolio performance in terms of the contributions from various sources of risk.

Portfolio possibilities curve   A graphical representation of the expected return and risk of all portfolios that can be formed using two assets.

Portfolio selection/composition problem   The part of the execution step of the portfolio management process in which investment strategies are integrated with expectations to select a portfolio of assets.

Position trader   A trader who typically holds positions open overnight.

Positive serial correlation   Serial correlation in which a positive error for one observation increases the chance of a positive error for another observation, and a negative error for one observation increases the chance of a negative error for another observation.

Posterior probability   An updated probability that reflects or comes after new information.

Potential credit risk   The risk associated with the possibility that a payment due at a later date will not be made.

Power of a test   The probability of correctly rejecting the null—that is, rejecting the null hypothesis when it is false.

Precautionary stocks   A level of inventory beyond anticipated needs that provides a cushion in the event that it takes longer to replenish inventory than expected or in the case of greater than expected demand.

Pre-investing   The strategy of using futures contracts to enter the market without an immediate outlay of cash.

Premise of value   The status of a company in the sense of whether it is assumed to be a going concern or not.

Prepaid expense   A normal operating expense that has been paid in advance of when it is due.

Present value (PV)   The present discounted value of future cash flows: For assets, the present discounted value of the future net cash inflows that the asset is expected to generate; for liabilities, the present discounted value of the future net cash outflows that are expected to be required to settle the liabilities.

Present (price) value of a basis point (PVBP)   The change in the bond price for a 1 basis point change in yield. Also called *basis point value* (BPV).

Present value of growth opportunities (or **value of growth**)   The difference between the actual value per share and the no-growth value per share.

Present value model or **discounted cash flow model**   A model of intrinsic value that views the value of an asset as the present value of the asset's expected future cash flows.

Presentation currency   The currency in which financial statement amounts are presented.

Pretax margin   A profitability ratio calculated as earnings before taxes divided by revenue.

Price discovery   A feature of futures markets in which futures prices provide valuable information about the price of the underlying asset.

Price limits   Limits imposed by a futures exchange on the price change that can occur from one day to the next.

Price momentum   A valuation indicator based on past price movement.

Price multiple   The ratio of a stock's market price to some measure of value per share.

Price relative   A ratio of an ending price over a beginning price; it is equal to 1 plus the holding period return on the asset.

Price to book value   A valuation ratio calculated as price per share divided by book value per share.

Price to cash flow   A valuation ratio calculated as price per share divided by cash flow per share.

Price to sales   A valuation ratio calculated as price per share divided by sales per share.

Priced risk   Risk for which investors demand compensation for bearing (e.g., equity risk, company-specific factors, macroeconomic factors).

Price-setting option   The operational flexibility to adjust prices when demand varies from forecast. For example, when demand exceeds capacity, the company could benefit from the excess demand by increasing prices.

Principal   The amount of funds originally invested in a project or instrument; the face value to be paid at maturity.

Prior probabilities   Probabilities reflecting beliefs prior to the arrival of new information.

Prior transaction method   A variation of the market approach; considers actual transactions in the stock of the subject private company.

Private sector surplus or **deficit**   An amount equal to saving minus investment.

Probability   A number between 0 and 1 describing the chance that a stated event will occur.

Probability density function   A function with non-negative values such that probability can be described by areas under the curve graphing the function.

Probability distribution   A distribution that specifies the probabilities of a random variable's possible outcomes.

Probability function   A function that specifies the probability that the random variable takes on a specific value.

Probit model   A qualitative-dependent-variable multiple regression model based on the normal distribution.

Production-flexibility   The operational flexibility to alter production when demand varies from forecast. For example, if demand is strong, a company may profit from employees working overtime or from adding additional shifts.

Profitability ratios   Ratios that measure a company's ability to generate profitable sales from its resources (assets).

Project sequencing   To defer the decision to invest in a future project until the outcome of some or all of a current project is known. Projects are sequenced through time, so that investing in a project creates the option to invest in future projects.

Proportionate consolidation   A method of accounting for joint ventures where the venturer's share of the assets, liabilities, income and expenses of the joint venture are combined on a line-by-line basis with similar items on the venturer's financial statements.

Protective put   An option strategy in which a long position in an asset is combined with a long position in a put.

Provision   In accounting, a liability of uncertain timing or amount.

Proxy fight　An attempt to take control of a company through a shareholder vote.

Proxy statement　A public document that provides the material facts concerning matters on which shareholders will vote.

Pseudo-random numbers　Numbers produced by random number generators.

Pull on liquidity　When disbursements are paid too quickly or trade credit availability is limited, requiring companies to expend funds before they receive funds from sales that could cover the liability.

Purchase method　A method of accounting for a business combination where the acquiring company allocates the purchase price to each asset acquired and liability assumed at fair value. If the purchase price exceeds the allocation, the excess is recorded as goodwill.

Purchased in-process research and development costs　Costs of research and development in progress at an acquired company; often, part of the purchase price of an acquired company is allocated to such costs.

Purchasing power gain　A gain in value caused by changes in price levels. Monetary liabilities experience purchasing power gains during periods of inflation.

Purchasing power loss　A loss in value caused by changes in price levels. Monetary assets experience purchasing power losses during periods of inflation.

Purchasing power parity　The equal value of different monies.

Pure discount instruments　Instruments that pay interest as the difference between the amount borrowed and the amount paid back.

Pure factor portfolio　A portfolio with sensitivity of 1 to the factor in question and a sensitivity of 0 to all other factors.

Pure-play method　A method for estimating the beta for a company or project; it requires using a comparable company's beta and adjusting it for financial leverage differences.

Put　An option that gives the holder the right to sell an underlying asset to another party at a fixed price over a specific period of time.

Put–call parity　An equation expressing the equivalence (parity) of a portfolio of a call and a bond with a portfolio of a put and the underlying, which leads to the relationship between put and call prices.

Put–call–forward parity　The relationship among puts, calls, and forward contracts.

***p*-Value**　The smallest level of significance at which the null hypothesis can be rejected; also called the marginal significance level.

Pyramiding　Controlling additional property through reinvestment, refinancing, and exchanging.

Qualifying special purpose entities　Under U.S. GAAP, a special purpose entity structured to avoid consolidation that must meet qualification criteria.

Qualitative dependent variables　Dummy variables used as dependent variables rather than as independent variables.

Quality of earnings analysis　The investigation of issues relating to the accuracy of reported accounting results as reflections of economic performance; quality of earnings analysis is broadly understood to include not only earnings management, but also balance sheet management.

Quantile (or fractile)　A value at or below which a stated fraction of the data lies.

Quartiles　Quantiles that divide a distribution into four equal parts.

Quick assets　Assets that can be most readily converted to cash (e.g., cash, short-term marketable investments, receivables).

Quick ratio, or **acid test ratio**　A stringent measure of liquidity that indicates a company's ability to satisfy current liabilities with its most liquid assets, calculated as (cash + short-term marketable investments + receivables) divided by current liabilities.

Quintiles　Quantiles that divide a distribution into five equal parts.

Quota　A quantitative restriction on the import of a particular good, which specifies the maximum amount that can be imported in a given time period.

Random number　An observation drawn from a uniform distribution.

Random number generator　An algorithm that produces uniformly distributed random numbers between 0 and 1.

Random variable　A quantity whose future outcomes are uncertain.

Random walk　A time series in which the value of the series in one period is the value of the series in the previous period plus an unpredictable random error.

Range　The difference between the maximum and minimum values in a dataset.

Rate of return　The proportional annual benefit that results from making an investment.

Rate-of-return regulation　Regulation that seeks to keep the rate of return in the industry at a competitive level by not allowing excessive prices to be charged.

Ratio scales　A measurement scale that has all the characteristics of interval measurement scales as well as a true zero point as the origin.

Ratio spread　An option strategy in which a long position in a certain number of options is offset by a short position in a certain number of other options on the same underlying, resulting in a risk-free position.

Rational efficient markets formulation　See *Market efficiency*.

Real exchange rate　The relative price of foreign-made goods and services to U.S.-made goods and services.

Real GDP per person　Real GDP divided by the population.

Real options　Options that relate to investment decisions such as the option to time the start of a project, the option to adjust its scale, or the option to abandon a project that has begun.

Real risk-free interest rate　The single-period interest rate for a completely risk-free security if no inflation were expected.

Realizable value (settlement value)　With reference to assets, the amount of cash or cash equivalents that could currently be obtained by selling the asset in an orderly disposal; with reference to liabilities, the undiscounted amount of cash or cash equivalents expected to be paid to satisfy the liabilities in the normal course of business.

Recapture premium　Provision for a return of investment, net of value appreciation.

Receivables turnover　An activity ratio equal to revenue divided by average receivables.

Receiver swaption　A swaption that allows the holder to enter into a swap as the fixed-rate receiver and floating-rate payer.

Reconciliation　Resolving differences in indications of value when estimating market value.

Regime　With reference to a time series, the underlying model generating the times series.

Regression coefficients　The intercept and slope coefficient(s) of a regression.

Regulatory risk　The risk associated with the uncertainty of how derivative transactions will be regulated or with changes in regulations.

Rejection point (or critical value)　A value against which a computed test statistic is compared to decide whether to reject or not reject the null hypothesis.

Relative dispersion　The amount of dispersion relative to a reference value or benchmark.

Relative frequency With reference to an interval of grouped data, the number of observations in the interval divided by the total number of observations in the sample.

Relative strength (RSTR) indicators Valuation indicators that compare a stock's performance during a period either to its own past performance or to the performance of some group of stocks.

Relative valuation models A model that specifies an asset's value relative to the value of another asset.

Rent seeking The pursuit of wealth by capturing economic rent—consumer surplus, producer surplus, or economic profit.

Reorganization Agreements made by a company in bankruptcy under which a company's capital structure is altered and/or alternative arrangements are made for debt repayment; U.S. Chapter 11 bankruptcy. The company emerges from bankruptcy as a going concern.

Replacement value The market value of a swap.

Report format With respect to the format of a balance sheet, a format in which assets, liabilities, and equity are listed in a single column.

Reporting unit An operating segment or one level below an operating segment (referred to as a component).

Reputational risk The risk that a company will suffer an extended diminution in market value relative to other companies in the same industry due to a demonstrated lack of concern for environmental, social, and governance risk factors.

Required rate of return The minimum rate of return required by an investor to invest in an asset, given the asset's riskiness.

Residual autocorrelations The sample autocorrelations of the residuals.

Residual claim The owners' remaining claim on the company's assets after the liabilities are deducted.

Residual dividend approach A dividend payout policy under which earnings in excess of the funds necessary to finance the equity portion of company's capital budget are paid out in dividends.

Residual dividend policy A policy in which dividends are paid from any internally generated funds remaining after such funds are used to finance positive NPV projects.

Residual income (or **economic profit** or **abnormal earnings**) Earnings for a given time period, minus a deduction for common shareholders' opportunity cost in generating the earnings.

Residual income method (or **excess earnings method**) Income approach that estimates the value of all intangible assets of the business by capitalizing future earnings in excess of the estimated return requirements associated with working capital and fixed assets.

Residual income model (RIM) (also **discounted abnormal earnings model** or **Edwards-Bell-Ohlson model**) A model of stock valuation that views intrinsic value of stock as the sum of book value per share plus the present value of the stock's expected future residual income per share.

Residual loss Agency costs that are incurred despite adequate monitoring and bonding of management.

Retail method An inventory accounting method in which the sales value of an item is reduced by the gross margin to calculate the item's cost.

Return on assets (ROA) A profitability ratio calculated as net income divided by average total assets; indicates a company's net profit generated per dollar invested in total assets.

Return on common equity (ROCE) A profitability ratio calculated as (net income − preferred dividends) divided by average common equity; equal to the return on equity ratio when no preferred equity is outstanding.

Return on equity (ROE) A profitability ratio calculated as net income divided by average shareholders' equity.

Return on invested capital (ROIC) The after-tax net operating profits as a percent of total assets or capital.

Return on total capital A profitability ratio calculated as EBIT divided by the sum of short- and long-term debt and equity.

Revaluation The process of valuing long-lived assets at fair value, rather than at cost less accumulated depreciation. Any resulting profit or loss is either reported on the income statement and/or through equity under revaluation surplus.

Revenue The amount charged for the delivery of goods or services in the ordinary activities of a business over a stated period; the inflows of economic resources to a company over a stated period.

Reverse stock split A reduction in the number of shares outstanding with a corresponding increase in share price, but no change to the company's underlying fundamentals.

Reviewed financial statements A type of non-audited financial statements; typically provide an opinion letter with representations and assurances by the reviewing accountant that are less than those in audited financial statements.

Revolving credit agreements The strongest form of short-term bank borrowing facilities; they are in effect for multiple years (e.g., 3–5 years) and may have optional medium-term loan features.

Rho The sensitivity of the option price to the risk-free rate.

Risk budgeting The establishment of objectives for individuals, groups, or divisions of an organization that takes into account the allocation of an acceptable level of risk.

Risk governance The setting of overall policies and standards in risk management.

Risk management The process of identifying the level of risk an entity wants, measuring the level of risk the entity currently has, taking actions that bring the actual level of risk to the desired level of risk, and monitoring the new actual level of risk so that it continues to be aligned with the desired level of risk.

Risk premium The expected return on an investment minus the risk-free rate.

Risk-neutral probabilities Weights that are used to compute a binomial option price. They are the probabilities that would apply if a risk-neutral investor valued an option.

Risk-neutral valuation The process by which options and other derivatives are priced by treating investors as though they were risk neutral.

Robust The quality of being relatively unaffected by a violation of assumptions.

Robust standard errors Standard errors of the estimated parameters of a regression that correct for the presence of heteroskedasticity in the regression's error term.

Root mean squared error (RMSE) The square root of the average squared forecast error; used to compare the out-of-sample forecasting performance of forecasting models.

Roy's safety first criterion A criterion asserting that the optimal portfolio is the one that minimizes the probability that portfolio return falls below a threshold level.

Rule of 70 A rule that states that the number of years it takes for the level of a variable to double is approximately 70 divided by the annual percentage growth rate of the variable.

Rule of 72 The principle that the approximate number of years necessary for an investment to double is 72 divided by the stated interest rate.

Safety stock A level of inventory beyond anticipated needs that provides a cushion in the event that it takes longer to replenish inventory than expected or in the case of greater than expected demand.

Safety-first rules Rules for portfolio selection that focus on the risk that portfolio value will fall below some minimum acceptable level over some time horizon.

Sales Generally, a synonym for revenue; "sales" is generally understood to refer to the sale of goods, whereas "revenue" is understood to include the sale of goods or services.

Sales returns and allowances An offset to revenue reflecting any cash refunds, credits on account, and discounts from sales prices given to customers who purchased defective or unsatisfactory items.

Sales risk Uncertainty with respect to the quantity of goods and services that a company is able to sell and the price it is able to achieve; the risk related to the uncertainty of revenues.

Sales-type lease A type of finance lease, from a lessor perspective, where the present value of the lease payments (lease receivable) exceeds the carrying value of the leased asset. The revenues earned by the lessor are operating (the profit on the sale) and financing (interest) in nature.

Salvage value The amount the company estimates that it can sell the asset for at the end of its useful life.

Sample A subset of a population.

Sample excess kurtosis A sample measure of the degree of a distribution's peakedness in excess of the normal distribution's peakedness.

Sample kurtosis A sample measure of the degree of a distribution's peakedness.

Sample mean The sum of the sample observations, divided by the sample size.

Sample selection bias Bias introduced by systematically excluding some members of the population according to a particular attribute—for example, the bias introduced when data availability leads to certain observations being excluded from the analysis.

Sample skewness A sample measure of degree of asymmetry of a distribution.

Sample standard deviation The positive square root of the sample variance.

Sample statistic or statistic A quantity computed from or used to describe a sample.

Sample variance A sample measure of the degree of dispersion of a distribution, calculated by dividing the sum of the squared deviations from the sample mean by the sample size minus 1.

Sampling The process of obtaining a sample.

Sampling distribution The distribution of all distinct possible values that a statistic can assume when computed from samples of the same size randomly drawn from the same population.

Sampling error The difference between the observed value of a statistic and the quantity it is intended to estimate.

Sampling plan The set of rules used to select a sample.

Sandwich spread An option strategy that is equivalent to a short butterfly spread.

Sarbanes–Oxley Act An act passed by the U.S. Congress in 2002 that created the Public Company Accounting Oversight Board (PCAOB) to oversee auditors.

Scaled earnings surprise Unexpected earnings divided by the standard deviation of analysts' earnings forecasts.

Scalper A trader who offers to buy or sell futures contracts, holding the position for only a brief period of time. Scalpers attempt to profit by buying at the bid price and selling at the higher ask price.

Scatter plot A two-dimensional plot of pairs of observations on two data series.

Scenario analysis Analysis that shows the changes in key financial quantities that result from given (economic) events, such as the loss of customers, the loss of a supply source, or a catastrophic event; a risk management technique involving examination of the performance of a portfolio under specified situations. Closely related to stress testing.

Screening The application of a set of criteria to reduce a set of potential investments to a smaller set having certain desired characteristics.

Seats Memberships in a derivatives exchange.

Sector neutral Said of a portfolio for which economic sectors are represented in the same proportions as in the benchmark, using market-value weights.

Sector neutralizing Measure of financial reporting quality by subtracting the mean or median ratio for a given sector group from a given company's ratio.

Sector rotation strategy A type of top-down investing approach that involves emphasizing different economic sectors based on considerations such as macroeconomic forecasts.

Securities Act of 1933 An act passed by the U.S. Congress in 1933 that specifies the financial and other significant information that investors must receive when securities are sold, prohibits misrepresentations, and requires initial registration of all public issuances of securities.

Securities Exchange Act of 1934 An act passed by the U.S. Congress in 1934 that created the Securities and Exchange Commission (SEC), gave the SEC authority over all aspects of the securities industry, and empowered the SEC to require periodic reporting by companies with publicly traded securities.

Securities offering A merger or acquisition in which target shareholders are to receive shares of the acquirer's common stock as compensation.

Security market line (SML) The graph of the capital asset pricing model.

Segment debt ratio Segment liabilities divided by segment assets.

Segment margin Segment profit (loss) divided by segment revenue.

Segment ROA Segment profit (loss) divided by segment assets.

Segment turnover Segment revenue divided by segment assets.

Sell-side analysts Analysts who work at brokerages.

Semideviation The positive square root of semivariance (sometimes called semistandard deviation).

Semilogarithmic Describes a scale constructed so that equal intervals on the vertical scale represent equal rates of change, and equal intervals on the horizontal scale represent equal amounts of change.

Semivariance The average squared deviation below the mean.

Sensitivity analysis Analysis that shows the range of possible outcomes as specific assumptions are changed.

Serially correlated With reference to regression errors, errors that are correlated across observations.

Service period The period benefited by the employee's service, usually the period between the grant date and the vesting date.

Settlement date or payment date The date on which the parties to a swap make payments.

Settlement period The time between settlement dates.

Settlement price The official price, designated by the clearinghouse, from which daily gains and losses will be determined and marked to market.

Settlement risk When settling a contract, the risk that one party could be in the process of paying the counterparty while the counterparty is declaring bankruptcy.

Share repurchase   A transaction in which a company buys back its own shares. Unlike stock dividends and stock splits, share repurchases use corporate cash.

Shareholders' equity   Total assets minus total liabilities.

Share-the-gains, share-the-pains theory   A theory of regulatory behavior that holds that regulators must take account of the demands of three groups: legislators, who established and oversee the regulatory agency; firms in the regulated industry; and consumers of the regulated industry's products.

Shark repellents   A pre-offer takeover defense mechanism involving the corporate charter (e.g., staggered boards of directors and supermajority provisions).

Sharpe ratio   The average return in excess of the risk-free rate divided by the standard deviation of return; a measure of the average excess return earned per unit of standard deviation of return.

Sharpe's measure   Reward-to-volatility ratio; ratio of portfolio excess return to standard deviation.

Short   The seller of a derivative contract. Also refers to the position of being short a derivative.

Shortfall risk   The risk that portfolio value will fall below some minimum acceptable level over some time horizon.

Simple interest   The interest earned each period on the original investment; interest calculated on the principal only.

Simple random sample   A subset of a larger population created in such a way that each element of the population has an equal probability of being selected to the subset.

Simple random sampling   The procedure of drawing a sample to satisfy the definition of a simple random sample.

Simulation   Computer-generated sensitivity or scenario analysis that is based on probability models for the factors that drive outcomes.

Simulation trial   A complete pass through the steps of a simulation.

Single-payment loan   A loan in which the borrower receives a sum of money at the start and pays back the entire amount with interest in a single payment at maturity.

Single-step format   With respect to the format of the income statement, a format that does not subtotal for gross profit (revenue minus cost of goods sold).

Sinking fund factor   Amount that must be set aside each period to have $1 at some future point in time.

Skewed   Not symmetrical.

Skewness   A quantitative measure of skew (lack of symmetry); a synonym of skew.

Sole proprietorship   A business owned and operated by a single person.

Solvency   With respect to financial statement analysis, the ability of a company to fulfill its long-term obligations.

Solvency ratios   Ratios that measure a company's ability to meet its long-term obligations.

Sovereign yield spread   An estimate of the country spread (country equity premium) for a developing nation that is based on a comparison of bonds yields in country being analyzed and a developed country. The sovereign yield spread is the difference between a government bond yield in the country being analyzed, denominated in the currency of the developed country, and the Treasury bond yield on a similar maturity bond in the developed country.

Spearman rank correlation coefficient   A measure of correlation applied to ranked data.

Special purpose entity (special purpose vehicle or variable interest entity)   A non-operating entity created to carry out a specified purpose, such as leasing assets or securitizing receivables; can be a corporation, partnership, trust, limited liability, or partnership formed to facilitate a specific type of business activity.

Specific identification method   An inventory accounting method that identifies which specific inventory items were sold and which remained in inventory to be carried over to later periods.

Spin-off   A form of restructuring in which shareholders of a parent company receive a proportional number of shares in a new, separate entity; shareholders end up owning stock in two different companies where there used to be one.

Split-off   A form of restructuring in which shareholders of the parent company are given shares in a newly created entity in exchange for their shares of the parent company.

Split-rate tax system   In reference to corporate taxes, a split-rate system taxes earnings to be distributed as dividends at a different rate than earnings to be retained. Corporate profits distributed as dividends are taxed at a lower rate than those retained in the business.

Spread   An option strategy involving the purchase of one option and sale of another option that is identical to the first in all respects except either exercise price or expiration.

Spreadsheet modeling   As used in this book, the use of a spreadsheet in executing a dividend discount model valuation, or other present value model valuation.

Spurious correlation   A correlation that misleadingly points towards associations between variables.

Stable dividend policy   A policy in which regular dividends are paid that reflect long-run expected earnings. In contrast to a constant dividend payout ratio policy, a stable dividend policy does not reflect short-term volatility in earnings.

Standard cost   With respect to inventory accounting, the planned or target unit cost of inventory items or services.

Standard deviation   The positive square root of the variance; a measure of dispersion in the same units as the original data.

Standard normal distribution (or **unit normal distribution**)   The normal density with mean equal to 0 and standard deviation (σ) equal to 1.

Standardized beta   With reference to fundamental factor models, the value of the attribute for an asset minus the average value of the attribute across all stocks, divided by the standard deviation of the attribute across all stocks.

Standardized unexpected earnings (SUE)   Unexpected earnings per share divided by the standard deviation of unexpected earnings per share over a specified prior time period.

Standardizing   A transformation that involves subtracting the mean and dividing the result by the standard deviation.

Stated annual interest rate or **quoted interest rate**   A quoted interest rate that does not account for compounding within the year.

Stated rate (nominal rate or **coupon rate)**   The rate at which periodic interest payments are calculated.

Statement of cash flows (cash flow statement)   A financial statement that reconciles beginning-of-period and end-of-period balance sheet values of cash; provides information about an entity's cash inflows and cash outflows as they pertain to operating, investing, and financing activities.

Statement of changes in shareholders' equity (statement of owners' equity)   A financial statement that reconciles the beginning-of-period and end-of-period balance sheet values of shareholders' equity; provides information about all factors affecting shareholders' equity.

Statement of retained earnings   A financial statement that reconciles beginning-of-period and end-of-period balance sheet values of retained income; shows the linkage between the balance sheet and income statement.

Static trade-off theory of capital structure A theory pertaining to a company's optimal capital structure; the optimal level of debt is found at the point where additional debt would cause the costs of financial distress to increase by a greater amount than the benefit of the additional tax shield.

Statistic A quantity computed from or used to describe a sample of data.

Statistical factor models A multifactor model in which statistical methods are applied to a set of historical returns to determine portfolios that best explain either historical return covariances or variances.

Statistical inference Making forecasts, estimates, or judgments about a larger group from a smaller group actually observed; using a sample statistic to infer the value of an unknown population parameter.

Statistically significant A result indicating that the null hypothesis can be rejected; with reference to an estimated regression coefficient, frequently understood to mean a result indicating that the corresponding population regression coefficient is different from 0.

Statistics The science of describing, analyzing, and drawing conclusions from data; also, a collection of numerical data.

Statutory merger A merger in which one company ceases to exist as an identifiable entity and all its assets and liabilities become part of a purchasing company.

Stock grants The granting of stock to employees as a form of compensation.

Stock options (stock option grants) The granting of stock options to employees as a form of compensation.

Stock purchase An acquisition in which the acquirer gives the target company's shareholders some combination of cash and securities in exchange for shares of the target company's stock.

Stock-out losses Profits lost from not having sufficient inventory on hand to satisfy demand.

Storage costs or **carrying costs** The costs of holding an asset, generally a function of the physical characteristics of the underlying asset.

Straddle An option strategy involving the purchase of a put and a call with the same exercise price. A straddle is based on the expectation of high volatility of the underlying.

Straight-line method A depreciation method that allocates evenly the cost of a long-lived asset less its estimated residual value over the estimated useful life of the asset.

Strangle A variation of a straddle in which the put and call have different exercise prices.

Strap An option strategy involving the purchase of two calls and one put.

Strategic transaction A purchase involving a buyer that would benefit from certain synergies associated with owning the target firm.

Stratified random sampling A procedure by which a population is divided into subpopulations (strata) based on one or more classification criteria. Simple random samples are then drawn from each stratum in sizes proportional to the relative size of each stratum in the population. These samples are then pooled.

Stress testing A set of techniques for estimating losses in extremely unfavorable combinations of events or scenarios.

Strip An option strategy involving the purchase of two puts and one call.

Structured note A variation of a floating-rate note that has some type of unusual characteristic such as a leverage factor or in which the rate moves opposite to interest rates.

Subjective probability A probability drawing on personal or subjective judgment.

Subsidiary merger A merger in which the company being purchased becomes a subsidiary of the purchaser.

Subsistence real wage rate The minimum real wage rate needed to maintain life.

Sum-of-the-parts valuation A valuation that sums the estimated values of each of a company's businesses as if each business were an independent going concern.

Sunk cost A cost that has already been incurred.

Supernormal growth Above average or abnormally high growth rate in earnings per share.

Surprise The actual value of a variable minus its predicted (or expected) value.

Survey approach An estimate of the equity risk premium that is based upon estimates provided by a panel of finance experts.

Survivorship bias Bias that may result when failed or defunct companies are excluded from membership in a group.

Sustainable growth rate The rate of dividend (and earnings) growth that can be sustained over time for a given level of return on equity, keeping the capital structure constant and without issuing additional common stock.

Swap An agreement between two parties to exchange a series of future cash flows.

Swap spread The difference between the fixed rate on an interest rate swap and the rate on a Treasury note with equivalent maturity; it reflects the general level of credit risk in the market.

Swaption An option to enter into a swap.

Synthetic call The combination of puts, the underlying, and risk-free bonds that replicates a call option.

Synthetic forward contract The combination of the underlying, puts, calls, and risk-free bonds that replicates a forward contract.

Synthetic index fund An index fund position created by combining risk-free bonds and futures on the desired index.

Synthetic lease A lease that is structured to provide a company with the tax benefits of ownership while not requiring the asset to be reflected on the company's financial statements.

Synthetic put The combination of calls, the underlying, and risk-free bonds that replicates a put option.

Systematic factors Factors that affect the average returns of a large number of different assets.

Systematic sampling A procedure of selecting every kth member until reaching a sample of the desired size. The sample that results from this procedure should be approximately random.

Takeover A merger; the term may be applied to any transaction, but is often used in reference to hostile transactions.

Takeover premium The amount by which the takeover price for each share of stock must exceed the current stock price in order to entice shareholders to relinquish control of the company to an acquirer.

Tangible assets Long-term assets with physical substance that are used in company operations, such as land (property), plant, and equipment.

Tangible book value per share Common shareholders' equity minus intangible assets from the balance sheet, divided by the number of shares outstanding.

Target balance A minimum level of cash to be held available—estimated in advance and adjusted for known funds transfers, seasonality, or other factors.

Target capital structure A company's chosen proportions of debt and equity.

Target company, or **target** The company in a merger or acquisition that is being acquired.

Target payout ratio A strategic corporate goal representing the long-term proportion of earnings that the company intends to distribute to shareholders as dividends.

Target semideviation The positive square root of target semivariance.

Target semivariance The average squared deviation below a target value.

Tariff A tax that is imposed by the importing country when an imported good crosses its international boundary.

Tax base (tax basis) The amount at which an asset or liability is valued for tax purposes.

Tax expense An aggregate of an entity's income tax payable (or recoverable in the case of a tax benefit) and any changes in deferred tax assets and liabilities. It is essentially the income tax payable or recoverable if these had been determined based on accounting profit rather than taxable income.

Tax loss carry forward A taxable loss in the current period that may be used to reduce future taxable income.

Tax risk The uncertainty associated with tax laws.

Taxable income The portion of an entity's income that is subject to income taxes under the tax laws of its jurisdiction.

Taxable temporary differences Temporary differences that result in a taxable amount in a future period when determining the taxable profit as the balance sheet item is recovered or settled.

t-Distribution A symmetrical distribution defined by a single parameter, degrees of freedom, that is largely used to make inferences concerning the mean of a normal distribution whose variance is unknown.

Technical indicators Momentum indicators based on price.

Temporal method A variation of the monetary/nonmonetary translation method that requires not only monetary assets and liabilities, but also nonmonetary assets and liabilities that are measured at their current value on the balance sheet date to be translated at the current exchange rate. Assets and liabilities are translated at rates consistent with the timing of their measurement value. This method is typically used when the functional currency is other than the local currency.

Tender offer A public offer whereby the acquirer invites target shareholders to submit ("tender") their shares in return for the proposed payment.

Tenor The original time to maturity on a swap.

Terminal price multiple The price multiple for a stock assumed to hold at a stated future time.

Terminal share price The share price at a particular point in the future.

Terminal value of the stock (or continuing value of the stock) The analyst's estimate of a stock's value at a particular point in the future.

Termination date The date of the final payment on a swap; also, the swap's expiration date.

Terms of trade The quantity of goods and services that a country exports to pay for its imports of goods and services.

Test statistic A quantity, calculated based on a sample, whose value is the basis for deciding whether or not to reject the null hypothesis.

Theory of contestable markets A hypothesis concerning pricing behavior that holds that even though there are only a few firms in an industry, they are forced to price their products more or less competitively because of the ease of entry by outsiders. The key aspect of a contestable market is relatively costless entry into and exit from the industry.

Theta The rate at which an option's time value decays.

Tie-in sales Purchases of one product that are permitted by the seller only if the consumer buys another good or service from the same firm.

Time series A set of observations on a variable's outcomes in different time periods.

Time to expiration The time remaining in the life of a derivative, typically expressed in years.

Time value decay The loss in the value of an option resulting from movement of the option price toward its payoff value as the expiration day approaches.

Time value of money The principles governing equivalence relationships between cash flows with different dates.

Time value or speculative value The difference between the market price of the option and its intrinsic value, determined by the uncertainty of the underlying over the remaining life of the option.

Time-period bias The possibility that when we use a time-series sample, our statistical conclusion may be sensitive to the starting and ending dates of the sample.

Time-series data Observations of a variable over time.

Time-weighted rate of return The compound rate of growth of one unit of currency invested in a portfolio during a stated measurement period; a measure of investment performance that is not sensitive to the timing and amount of withdrawals or additions to the portfolio.

Tobin's q The ratio of the market value of debt and equity to the replacement cost of total assets.

Top-down analysis With reference to investment selection processes, an approach that starts with macro selection (i.e., identifying attractive geographic segments and/or industry segments) and then addresses selection of the most attractive investments within those segments.

Top-down forecasting approach A forecasting approach that involves moving from international and national macroeconomic forecasts to industry forecasts and then to individual company and asset forecasts.

Top-down investing An approach to investing that typically begins with macroeconomic forecasts.

Total asset turnover An activity ratio calculated as revenue divided by average total assets.

Total invested capital The sum of market value of common equity, book value of preferred equity, and face value of debt.

Total probability rule A rule explaining the unconditional probability of an event in terms of probabilities of the event conditional on mutually exclusive and exhaustive scenarios.

Total probability rule for expected value A rule explaining the expected value of a random variable in terms of expected values of the random variable conditional on mutually exclusive and exhaustive scenarios.

Total return swap A swap in which one party agrees to pay the total return on a security. Often used as a credit derivative, in which the underlying is a bond.

Tracking portfolio A portfolio having factor sensitivities that are matched to those of a benchmark or other portfolio.

Tracking risk (tracking error) The standard deviation of the differences between a portfolio's returns and its benchmark's returns; a synonym of active risk.

Trade credit A spontaneous form of credit in which a purchaser of the goods or service is financing its purchase by delaying the date on which payment is made.

Trade receivables (commercial receivables or accounts receivable) Amounts customers owe the company for products that have been sold as well as amounts that may be due from suppliers (such as for returns of merchandise).

Trade-weighted index The average exchange rate, with individual currencies weighted by their importance in U.S. international trade.

Trading securities (held-for-trading securities)   Securities held by a company with the intent to trade them.

Traditional efficient markets formulation   See *Market efficiency*.

Trailing dividend yield   Current market price divided by the most recent quarterly per-share dividend multiplied by four.

Trailing P/E (or current P/E)   A stock's current market price divided by the most recent four quarters of earnings per share.

Transaction exposure   The risk of a change in value between the transaction date and the settlement date of an asset or liability denominated in a foreign currency.

Transactions motive   In the context of inventory management, the need for inventory as part of the routine production–sales cycle.

Transition phase   The stage of growth between the growth phase and the mature phase of a company in which earnings growth typically slows.

Translation exposure   The risk associated with the conversion of foreign financial statements into domestic currency.

Treasury shares   Shares that were issued and subsequently repurchased by the company.

Treasury stock method   A method for accounting for the effect of options (and warrants) on earnings per share (EPS) that specifies what EPS would have been if the options and warrants had been exercised and the company had used the proceeds to repurchase common stock.

Tree diagram   A diagram with branches emanating from nodes representing either mutually exclusive chance events or mutually exclusive decisions.

Trend   A long-term pattern of movement in a particular direction.

Trimmed mean   A mean computed after excluding a stated small percentage of the lowest and highest observations.

Trust receipt arrangement   The use of inventory as collateral for a loan. The inventory is segregated and held in trust, and the proceeds of any sale must be remitted to the lender immediately.

t-Test   A hypothesis test using a statistic (*t*-statistic) that follows a *t*-distribution.

Two-sided hypothesis test (or two-tailed hypothesis test)   A test in which the null hypothesis is rejected in favor of the alternative hypothesis if the evidence indicates that the population parameter is either smaller or larger than a hypothesized value.

Type I error   The error of rejecting a true null hypothesis.

Type II error   The error of not rejecting a false null hypothesis.

U.S. interest rate differential   The U.S. interest rate minus the foreign interest rate.

U.S. official reserves   The government's holding of foreign currency.

Unbiasedness   Lack of bias. A desirable property of estimators, an unbiased estimator is one whose expected value (the mean of its sampling distribution) equals the parameter it is intended to estimate.

Unbilled revenue (accrued revenue)   Revenue that has been earned but not yet billed to customers as of the end of an accounting period.

Unclassified balance sheet   A balance sheet that does not show subtotals for current assets and current liabilities.

Unconditional heteroskedasticity   Heteroskedasticity of the error term that is not correlated with the values of the independent variable(s) in the regression.

Unconditional probability (or marginal probability)   The probability of an event *not* conditioned on another event.

Underlying   An asset that trades in a market in which buyers and sellers meet, decide on a price, and the seller then delivers the asset to the buyer and receives payment. The underlying is the asset or other derivative on which a particular derivative is based. The market for the underlying is also referred to as the spot market.

Underlying earnings (or persistent earnings, continuing earnings, or core earnings)   Earnings excluding nonrecurring components.

Unearned fees   Unearned fees are recognized when a company receives cash payment for fees prior to earning them.

Unearned revenue (deferred revenue)   A liability account for money that has been collected for goods or services that have not yet been delivered; payment received in advance of providing a good or service.

Unexpected earnings (also earnings surprise)   The difference between reported earnings per share and expected earnings per share.

Unidentifiable intangible   An intangible that cannot be acquired singly and that typically possesses an indefinite benefit period; an example is accounting goodwill.

Unit root   A time series that is not covariance stationary is said to have a unit root.

Uniting of interests method   A method of accounting in which combined companies were portrayed as if they had always operated as a single economic entity. Called pooling of interests under U.S. GAAP and uniting of interests under IFRS. (No longer allowed under U.S. GAAP or IFRS.)

Units-of-production method   A depreciation method that allocates the cost of a long-lived asset based on actual usage during the period.

Univariate distribution   A distribution that specifies the probabilities for a single random variable.

Unlimited funds   An unlimited funds environment assumes that the company can raise the funds it wants for all profitable projects simply by paying the required rate of return.

Up transition probability   The probability that an asset's value moves up.

Upstream   A transaction between two affiliates, an investor company and an associate company such that the associate company records a profit on its income statement. An example is a sale of inventory by the associate to the investor company.

Valuation   The process of determining the value of an asset or service on the basis of variables perceived to be related to future investment returns, or on the basis of comparisons with closely similar assets.

Valuation allowance   A reserve created against deferred tax assets, based on the likelihood of realizing the deferred tax assets in future accounting periods.

Valuation ratios   Ratios that measure the quantity of an asset or flow (e.g., earnings) in relation to the price associated with a specified claim (e.g., a share or ownership of the enterprise).

Value   The amount for which one can sell something, or the amount one must pay to acquire something.

Value at risk (VAR)   A money measure of the minimum value of losses expected during a specified time period at a given level of probability.

Value investors   With reference to equity investors, investors who are focused on paying a relatively low share price in relation to earnings or assets per share.

Variable costs   Costs that fluctuate with the level of production and sales.

Variance   The expected value (the probability-weighted average) of squared deviations from a random variable's expected value.

Variation margin   Additional margin that must be deposited in an amount sufficient to bring the balance up to the initial margin requirement.

Vega The relationship between option price and volatility.

Venture capital investors Private equity investors in development-stage companies.

Venturers The owners of a joint venture. Each is active in the management and shares control of the joint venture.

Vertical analysis Common-size analysis using only one reporting period or one base financial statement; for example, an income statement in which all items are stated as percentages of sales.

Vertical common-size analysis The most common type of common-size analysis, in which the accounts in a given period are compared to a benchmark item in that same year.

Vertical merger A merger involving companies at different positions of the same production chain; for example, a supplier or a distributor.

Versioning Selling a product in slightly altered forms to different groups of consumers.

Vested benefit obligation Under U.S. GAAP, a measure used in estimating a defined-benefit pension plan's liabilities, defined as the "actuarial present value of vested benefits."

Vested benefits Future benefits promised to the employee regardless of continuing service. Benefits typically vest after a specified period of service or a specified period of service combined with age.

Vesting date The date that employees can first exercise stock options; vesting can be immediate or over a future period.

Visibility The extent to which a company's operations are predictable with substantial confidence.

Volatility As used in option pricing, the standard deviation of the continuously compounded returns on the underlying asset.

Voluntary export restraint An agreement between two governments in which the government of the exporting country agrees to restrain the volume of its own exports.

Warehouse receipt arrangement The use of inventory as collateral for a loan; similar to a trust receipt arrangement except there is a third party (i.e., a warehouse company) that supervises the inventory.

Weighted average cost An inventory accounting method that averages the total cost of available inventory items over the total units available for sale.

Weighted harmonic mean See *Harmonic mean*.

Weighted mean An average in which each observation is weighted by an index of its relative importance.

Weighted-average cost of capital (WACC) A weighted average of the after-tax required rates of return on a company's common stock, preferred stock, and long-term debt, where the weights are the fraction of each source of financing in the company's target capital structure.

White knight A third party that is sought out by the target company's board to purchase the target in lieu of a hostile bidder.

White squire A third party that is sought out by the target company's board to purchase a substantial minority stake in the target—enough to block a hostile takeover without selling the entire company.

White-corrected standard errors A synonym for robust standard errors.

Winner's curse The tendency for the winner in certain competitive bidding situations to overpay, whether because of overestimation of intrinsic value, emotion, or information asymmetries.

Winsorized mean A mean computed after assigning a stated percent of the lowest values equal to one specified low value, and a stated percent of the highest values equal to one specified high value.

Working capital The difference between current assets and current liabilities.

Working capital management The management of a company's short-term assets (such as inventory) and short-term liabilities (such as money owed to suppliers).

Working capital turnover A comparison of revenues with working capital to produce a measure that shows how efficiently working capital is employed.

World Trade Organization An international organization that places greater obligations on its member countries to observe the GATT rules.

Write-down A reduction in the value of an asset as stated in the balance sheet.

Yield The actual return on a debt security if it is held to maturity.

Yield beta A measure of the sensitivity of a bond's yield to a general measure of bond yields in the market that is used to refine the hedge ratio.

Yield spread The difference between the yield on a bond and the yield on a default-free security, usually a government note, of the same maturity. The yield spread is primarily determined by the market's perception of the credit risk on the bond.

Yield to maturity The annual return that an investor earns on a bond if the investor purchases the bond today and holds it until maturity.

Zero-cost collar A transaction in which a position in the underlying is protected by buying a put and selling a call with the premium from the sale of the call offsetting the premium from the purchase of the put. It can also be used to protect a floating-rate borrower against interest rate increases with the premium on a long cap offsetting the premium on a short floor.

INDEX